myPerspectives™

ENGLISH LANGUAGE ARTS

SAVVAS
LEARNING COMPANY

ISBN-13: 978-0-13-333872-0
ISBN-10:   0-13-333872-X

19 20

Welcome!

*my*Perspectives™ *English Language Arts* is a student-centered learning environment where you will analyze text, cite evidence, and respond critically about your learning. You will take ownership of your learning through goal-setting, reflection, independent text selection, and activities that allow you to collaborate with your peers.

Each unit of study includes selections of different genres—including multimedia—all related to a relevant and meaningful Essential Question. As you read, you will engage in activities that inspire thoughtful discussion and debate with your peers allowing you to formulate, and defend, your own perspectives.

*my*Perspectives *ELA* offers a variety of ways to interact directly with the text. You can annotate by writing in your print consumable, or you can annotate in your digital Student Edition. In addition, exciting technology allows you to access multimedia directly from your mobile device and communicate using an online discussion board!

We hope you enjoy using *my*Perspectives *ELA* as you develop the skills required to be successful throughout college and career.

Authors' Perspectives

*my*Perspectives is informed by a team of respected experts whose experiences working with students and study of instructional best practices have positively impacted education. From the evolving role of the teacher to how students learn in a digital age, our authors bring new ideas, innovations, and strategies that transform teaching and learning in today's competitive and interconnected world.

"The teaching of English needs to focus on engaging a new generation of learners. How do we get them excited about reading and writing? How do we help them to envision themselves as readers and writers? And, how can we make the teaching of English more culturally, socially, and technologically relevant? Throughout the curriculum, we've created spaces that enhance youth voice and participation and that connect the teaching of literature and writing to technological transformations of the digital age."

Ernest Morrell, Ph.D.

is the Macy professor of English Education at Teachers College, Columbia University, a class of 2014 Fellow of the American Educational Research Association, and the Past-President of the National Council of Teachers of English (NCTE). He is also the Director of Teachers College's Institute for Urban and Minority Education (IUME). He is an award-winning author and in his spare time he coaches youth sports and writes poems and plays. Dr. Morrell has influenced the development of *my*Perspectives in Assessment, Writing & Research, Student Engagement, and Collaborative Learning.

Elfrieda Hiebert, Ph.D.

is President and CEO of TextProject, a nonprofit that provides resources to support higher reading levels. She is also a research associate at the University of California, Santa Cruz. Dr. Hiebert has worked in the field of early reading acquisition for 45 years, first as a teacher's aide and teacher of primary-level students in California and, subsequently, as a teacher and researcher. Her research addresses how fluency, vocabulary, and knowledge can be fostered through appropriate texts. Dr. Hiebert has influenced the development of *my*Perspectives in Vocabulary, Text Complexity, and Assessment.

> " The signature of complex text is challenging vocabulary. In the systems of vocabulary, it's important to provide ways to show how concepts can be made more transparent to students. We provide lessons and activities that develop a strong vocabulary and concept foundation—a foundation that permits students to comprehend increasingly more complex text."

Kelly Gallagher, M.Ed.

teaches at Magnolia High School in Anaheim, California, where he is in his thirty-first year. He is the former co-director of the South Basin Writing Project at California State University, Long Beach. Mr. Gallagher has influenced the development of *my*Perspectives in Writing, Close Reading, and the Role of Teachers.

> " The *my*Perspectives classroom is dynamic. The teacher inspires, models, instructs, facilitates, and advises students as they evolve and grow. When teachers guide students through meaningful learning tasks and then pass them ownership of their own learning, students become engaged and work harder. This is how we make a difference in student achievement—by putting students at the center of their learning and giving them the opportunities to choose, explore, collaborate, and work independently."

> " It's critical to give students the opportunity to read a wide range of highly engaging texts and to immerse themselves in exploring powerful ideas and how these ideas are expressed. In *my*Perspectives, we focus on building up students' awareness of how academic language works, which is especially important for English language learners."

Jim Cummins, Ph.D.

is a Professor Emeritus in the Department of Curriculum, Teaching and Learning of the University of Toronto. His research focuses on literacy development in multilingual school contexts as well as on the potential roles of technology in promoting language and literacy development. In recent years, he has been working actively with teachers to identify ways of increasing the literacy engagement of learners in multilingual school contexts. Dr. Cummins has influenced the development of *my*Perspectives in English Language Learner and English Language Development support.

UNIT INTRODUCTION

WHOLE-CLASS LEARNING

PERFORMANCE TASK

SMALL-GROUP LEARNING

PERFORMANCE TASK

DIGITAL 🖰 PERSPECTIVES

🅑 SCAN FOR MULTIMEDIA

Use the BouncePage app whenever you see "Scan for Multimedia" to access:

- Unit Introduction Videos
- Media Selections
- Modeling Videos
- Selection Audio Recordings

Additional digital resources can be found in:

- Interactive Student Edition
- *my*Perspectives+

UNIT 2 Animal Allies

INDEPENDENT LEARNING

These selections can be accessed via the Interactive Student Edition.

PERFORMANCE-BASED ASSESSMENT PREP

PERFORMANCE-BASED ASSESSMENT

UNIT REFLECTION

DIGITAL PERSPECTIVES

SCAN FOR MULTIMEDIA

Use the BouncePage app whenever you see "Scan for Multimedia" to access:

- Unit Introduction Videos
- Media Selections
- Modeling Videos
- Selection Audio Recordings

Additional digital resources can be found in:

- Interactive Student Edition
- *my*Perspectives+

UNIT **3** Modern Technology

INDEPENDENT LEARNING

These selections can be accessed via the Interactive Student Edition.

PERFORMANCE-BASED ASSESSMENT PREP

PERFORMANCE-BASED ASSESSMENT

UNIT REFLECTION

DIGITAL PERSPECTIVES

SCAN FOR MULTIMEDIA

Use the BouncePage app whenever you see "Scan for Multimedia" to access:

- Unit Introduction Videos
- Media Selections
- Modeling Videos
- Selection Audio Recordings

Additional digital resources can be found in:

- Interactive Student Edition
- *my*Perspectives+

(👤) INDEPENDENT LEARNING

These selections can be accessed via the Interactive Student Edition.

(✓) PERFORMANCE-BASED ASSESSMENT

UNIT REFLECTION

DIGITAL ⌨ PERSPECTIVES

SCAN FOR MULTIMEDIA

Use the BouncePage app whenever you see "Scan for Multimedia" to access:

- Unit Introduction Videos
- Media Selections
- Modeling Videos
- Selection Audio Recordings

Additional digital resources can be found in:

- Interactive Student Edition
- *my*Perspectives+

UNIT **5** Exploration

(👤) INDEPENDENT LEARNING

These selections can be accessed via the Interactive Student Edition.

(✓) PERFORMANCE-BASED ASSESSMENT PREP

(✓) PERFORMANCE-BASED ASSESSMENT

UNIT REFLECTION

DIGITAL ⌖ PERSPECTIVES

SCAN FOR MULTIMEDIA Use the BouncePage app whenever you see "Scan for Multimedia" to access:

- Unit Introduction Videos
- Media Selections
- Modeling Videos
- Selection Audio Recordings

Additional digital resources can be found in:
- Interactive Student Edition
- *my*Perspectives+

Interactive Student Edition

*my*Perspectives is completely interactive because you can work directly in your digital or print Student Edition.

All activities that you complete in your Interactive Student Edition are saved automatically. You can access your notes quickly so that reviewing work to prepare for tests and projects is easy!

Enter answers to prompts right in your digital Notebook and "turn it in" to your teacher.

The in-line annotation tool allows you to practice close reading by highlighting and adding comments about the text.

Interactivities are available for you to complete and submit directly to your teacher.

8:31 PM   85%

◀ Back to Realize   MENU

Unit 1: Survival > Whole-Class Learning > The Seventh Man

The Seventh Man
Haruki Murakami
ANCHOR TEXT | SHORT STORY

▷ Background 👤 Author ☰ Standards

1 "A huge wave nearly swept me away," said the seventh man, almost whispering. "It happened one September afternoon when I was ten years old."

2 The man was the last one to tell his story that night. The hands of the clock had moved past ten. The small group that huddled in a circle could hear the wind tearing through the darkness outside, heading west. It shook the trees, set the windows to rattling, and moved past the house with one final whistle.

3 "It was the biggest wave I had ever seen in my life," he said. "A strange wave. An <u>absolute</u> giant."

4 He paused.

5 "It just barely missed me, but in my place it swallowed everything that mattered most to me and swept it off to another world. I took years to find it again to recover from the experience—precious years that can never be replaced."

6 The seventh man appeared to be in his mid-fifties. He was a thin man, tall, with a moustache, and next to his right eye he had a short but deep-looking scar that could have been made by the stab of a small blade. Stiff, bristly patches of white marked his short hair. His face had the look you see on people when they can't quite find the words they need. In his case, though, the expression seemed to have been there from long before, as though it were part of him. The man wore a simple blue shirt under a grey tweed coat, and every now and then he would bring his hand to his collar. None of those assembled there knew his name or what he did for a living.

   He cleared his throat, and for a moment or two his words were lost in the darkness. The others waited for him to go on.

7 "In my case, it was a wave," he said. "There's no way for me to tell, of course, what it will be for each of you. But in my case it just happened to take the form of a gigantic¹² wave. It presented itself to me all of a sudden one day, without warning. And it was devastating."

▾ MAKING MEANING

▾ Research

Research to Clarify Choose at least one unfamiliar detail from the text. Briefly research that detail. In what way does the information you learned shed light on an aspect of the story?

▣ Notebook

▸ Close Read the Text
▸ Analyze the Text
▸ Analyze Craft and Structure

▾ LANGUAGE DEVELOPMENT

▸ Concept Vocabulary

▾ Word Network

Add interesting survival words from the text to your Word Network

⤢ Open activity

SURVIVAL

danger
rescue
risky

🔧 Tool Kit: Word Network Model ›

▸ Word Study
▸ Conventions

As you read the selections in this Unit, **identify interesting words related to the idea of** survival and add them to your **Word Network.**

Type here   Type here
Type here   Type here
danger   Type here
rescue   SURVIVAL
risky   Type here
Type here   Type here
Type here   Type here
Type here   Type here
Type here Type here

the shops in town lowered their shutters in preparation for the storm. Starting early in the morning, my father and brother went around the house nailing shut all the storm-doors, while my mother spent the day in the kitchen cooking emergency provisions. We filled bottles and canteens with water, and packed our most important possessions in rucksacks[2] for possible evacuation. To the adults, typhoons were an annoyance and a threat they had to face almost annually, but to the kids, removed as we were from such practical concerns, it was just a great big circus, a wonderful source of excitement.

12   Just after noon the color of the sky began to change all of a sudden. There was something strange and unreal about it. I stayed outside on the porch, watching the sky, until the wind began to howl and the rain began to beat against the house with a weird dry sound, like handfuls of sand. Then we closed the last storm-door and gathered together in one room of the darkened house, listening to the radio. This particular storm did not have a great deal of rain, it said, but the winds were doing a lot of damage, blowing roofs off houses and capsizing ships. Many people had been killed or injured by flying debris. Over and over again, they warned people against leaving their homes. Every once in a while, the house would creak and shudder as if a huge hand were shaking it, and sometimes there would be a great crash of some heavy-sounding object against a storm-door. My father guessed that these were tiles blowing off the neighbors' houses. For lunch we ate the rice and omelettes my mother had cooked, waiting for the typhoon to blow past.

13   But the typhoon gave no sign of blowing past. The radio said it had lost momentum[3] almost as soon as it came ashore at S. Province, and now it was moving north-east at the pace of a slow runner. The wind kept up its savage howling as it tried ... stood on land.

14   Perhaps an hour had gone by with the ... when a hush fell over everything. All of a ... could hear a bird crying in the distance. M... door a crack and looked outside. The win... rain had ceased to fall. Thick, gray clouds ...
... showed here and ...

NOTES

This sentence is leading up to an exciting story.

CLOSE READ

ANNOTATE: In paragraph 12, annotate at least four vivid details about the storm. Underline those that compare one thing to another.

QUESTION: What is being compared? What picture does each detail create in the reader's mind?

CONCLUDE: How do these descriptions help you visualize the typhoon?

Typhoons are powerful, scary storms that can do a lot of damage.

Use the close-read prompts to guide you through an analysis of the text. You can highlight, circle, and underline the text right in your print Student Edition.

Respond to questions and activities directly in your book!

🔨 WORD NETWORK

Add interesting survival words from the text to your Word Network.

Ⓘ LANGUAGE DEVELOPMENT

THE SEVENTH MAN

Concept Vocabulary

desperate	hallucination	profound
entranced	premonition	meditative

Why These Words? These concept words help to reveal the emotional state of the seventh man. For example, when the wave approaches, the seventh man is *entranced*, waiting for it to attack. After the wave hits, the seventh man believes he sees his friend K. in the wave and claims that this experience was no *hallucination*. Notice that both words relate to experiences that occur only in the mind of the seventh man.

1. How does the concept vocabulary sharpen the reader's understanding of the mental or emotional state of the seventh man?
   These words are descriptive and precise.

2. What other words in the selection connect to this concept?
   ominous, overcome, nightmares

Practice

📓 **Notebook** The concept vocabulary words appear in "The Seventh Man."

1. Use each concept word in a sentence that demonstrates your understanding of the word's meaning.

2. Challenge yourself to replace the concept word with one or two synonyms. How does the word change affect the meaning of your sentence? For example, which sentence is stronger? Which has a more positive meaning?

Word Study

Latin suffix: -tion The Latin suffix *-tion* often indicates that a word is a noun. Sometimes this suffix is spelled *-ion* or *-ation*. These related suffixes mean "act, state, or condition of." In "The Seventh Man," the word *premonition* means "the state of being forewarned."

1. Record a definition of *hallucination* based on your understanding of its root word and the meaning of the suffix *-tion*.
   The condition of seeing something that is not real

2. Look back at paragraphs 37–40 and find two other words that use the suffix *-tion*. Identify the root word that was combined with the suffix. Record a definition for each word.
   cooperate + -tion—the state of working together
   direct + -tion—the state of being guided

Digital Resources

You can access digital resources from your print Student Edition, or from Savvas Realize™.

To watch videos or listen to audio from your print Student Edition, all you need is a device with a camera and Pearson's BouncePages app!

ANCHOR TEXT | SHORT STORY

The
Seventh Man

Haruki Murakami

BACKGROUND
Hurricanes that originate in the northwest Pacific Ocean are called typhoons. They can stretch up to 500 miles in diameter and produce high winds, heavy rains, enormous waves, and severe flooding. On average, Japan is hit by three severe typhoons each year due to its location and climatic conditions.

SCAN FOR
MULTIMEDIA

1   "**A** huge wave nearly swept me away," said the seventh man, almost whispering. "It happened one September afternoon when I was ten years old."

2   The man was the last one to tell his story that night. The hands of the clock had moved past ten. The small group that huddled in

NOTES

CLOSE READ
ANNOTATE: Mark details in paragraph 2 that

How to watch a video or listen to audio:

1. Download Pearson's BouncePages App from the Apple App or Google Play Store.

2. Open the app on your mobile device.

3. Aim your camera so the page from your Student Edition is viewable on your screen.

4. Tap the screen to scan the page.

5. Press the "Play" button on the page that appears on your device.

6. View the video or listen to the audio directly from your device!

Amazing Stories of Rescues and Survival in Nepal
122

Digital resources, including audio and video, can be accessed in the Interactive Student Edition. Your teacher might also assign activities for you to complete online.

Interactive Student Edition
ONLINE STUDENT EDITION

Unit 1: Immigrant Voices

Unit 2: Survival

Unit 3: The Literature of Civil Rights

Unit 4: Tragic Romances

Unit 5: Journeys of Transformation

SAVVAS eText 2.0 for Schools

Unit 2: Survival

UNIT 2
Survival

The quest for survival is powerful. It is primitive. What determines who lives and who dies?

UNIT INTRODUCTION

WHOLE-CLASS LEARNING

SMALL-GROUP LEARNING

INDEPENDENT LEARNING

PERFORMANCE-BASED ASSESSMENT

UNIT REFLECTION

You will also find digital novels, interactive lessons, and games!

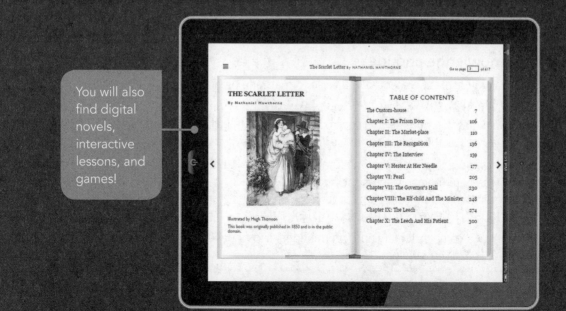

The Scarlet Letter by NATHANIEL HAWTHORNE   Go to page [3] of 617

THE SCARLET LETTER
By Nathaniel Hawthorne

Illustrated by Hugh Thomson
This book was originally published in 1850 and is in the public domain.

Standards Overview

English Language Arts will prepare you to succeed in college and your future career. The College and Career Readiness Anchor Standards define what you need to achieve by the end of high school, and the grade-specific Standards define what you need to know by the end of your current grade level.

The following provides an overview of the Standards.

Standards for Reading

College and Career Readiness Anchor Standards for Reading

Key Ideas and Details

1. Read closely to determine what the text says explicitly and to make logical inferences from it; cite specific textual evidence when writing or speaking to support conclusions drawn from the text.

2. Determine central ideas or themes of a text and analyze their development; summarize the key supporting details and ideas.

3. Analyze how and why individuals, events, and ideas develop and interact over the course of a text.

Craft and Structure

4. Interpret words and phrases as they are used in a text, including determining technical, connotative, and figurative meanings, and analyze how specific word choices shape meaning or tone.

5. Analyze the structure of texts, including how specific sentences, paragraphs, and larger portions of the text (e.g., a section, chapter, scene, or stanza) relate to each other and the whole.

6. Assess how point of view or purpose shapes the content and style of a text.

Integration of Knowledge and Ideas

7. Integrate and evaluate content presented in diverse formats and media, including visually and quantitatively, as well as in words.

8. Delineate and evaluate the argument and specific claims in a text, including the validity of the reasoning as well as the relevance and sufficiency of the evidence.

9. Analyze how two or more texts address similar themes or topics in order to build knowledge or to compare the approaches the authors take.

Range of Reading and Level of Text Complexity

10. Read and comprehend complex literary and informational texts independently and proficiently.

Grade 6 Reading Standards for Literature

Standard

Key Ideas and Details

Cite textual evidence to support analysis of what the text says explicitly as well as inferences drawn from the text.

Determine a theme or central idea of a text and how it is conveyed through particular details; provide a summary of the text distinct from personal opinions or judgments.

Describe how a particular story's or drama's plot unfolds in a series of episodes as well as how the characters respond or change as the plot moves toward a resolution.

Craft and Structure

Determine the meaning of words and phrases as they are used in a text, including figurative and connotative meanings; analyze the impact of a specific word choice on meaning and tone.

Analyze how a particular sentence, chapter, scene, or stanza fits into the overall structure of a text and contributes to the development of the theme, setting, or plot.

Explain how an author develops the point of view of the narrator or speaker in a text.

Integration of Knowledge and Ideas

Compare and contrast the experience of reading a story, drama, or poem to listening to or viewing an audio, video, or live version of the text, including contrasting what they "see" and "hear" when reading the text to what they perceive when they listen or watch.

Compare and contrast texts in different forms or genres (e.g., stories and poems; historical novels and fantasy stories) in terms of their approaches to similar themes and topics.

Range of Reading and Level of Text Complexity

By the end of the year, read and comprehend literature, including stories, dramas, and poems, in the grades 6–8 text complexity band proficiently, with scaffolding as needed at the high end of the range.

Standards Overview

Grade 6 Reading Standards for Informational Text

Standard

Key Ideas and Details

Cite textual evidence to support analysis of what the text says explicitly as well as inferences drawn from the text.

Determine a central idea of a text and how it is conveyed through particular details; provide a summary of the text distinct from personal opinions or judgments.

Analyze in detail how a key individual, event, or idea is introduced, illustrated, and elaborated in a text (e.g., through examples or anecdotes).

Craft and Structure

Determine the meaning of words and phrases as they are used in a text, including figurative, connotative, and technical meanings.

Analyze how a particular sentence, paragraph, chapter, or section fits into the overall structure of a text and contributes to the development of the ideas.

Determine an author's point of view or purpose in a text and explain how it is conveyed in the text.

Integration of Knowledge and Ideas

Integrate information presented in different media or formats (e.g., visually, quantitatively) as well as in words to develop a coherent understanding of a topic or issue.

Trace and evaluate the argument and specific claims in a text, distinguishing claims that are supported by reasons and evidence from claims that are not.

Compare and contrast one author's presentation of events with that of another (e.g., a memoir written by and a biography on the same person).

Range of Reading and Level of Text Complexity

By the end of the year, read and comprehend literary nonfiction in the grades 6–8 text complexity band proficiently, with scaffolding as needed at the high end of the range.

Standards for Writing

College and Career Readiness Anchor Standards for Writing

Text Types and Purposes

1. Write arguments to support claims in an analysis of substantive topics or texts, using valid reasoning and relevant and sufficient evidence.

2. Write informative/explanatory texts to examine and convey complex ideas and information clearly and accurately through the effective selection, organization, and analysis of content.

3. Write narratives to develop real or imagined experiences or events using effective technique, well-chosen details, and well-structured event sequences.

Production and Distribution of Writing

4. Produce clear and coherent writing in which the development, organization, and style are appropriate to task, purpose, and audience.

5. Develop and strengthen writing as needed by planning, revising, editing, rewriting, or trying a new approach.

6. Use technology, including the Internet, to produce and publish writing and to interact and collaborate with others.

Research to Build and Present Knowledge

7. Conduct short as well as more sustained research projects based on focused questions, demonstrating understanding of the subject under investigation.

8. Gather relevant information from multiple print and digital sources, assess the credibility and accuracy of each source, and integrate the information while avoiding plagiarism.

9. Draw evidence from literary or informational texts to support analysis, reflection, and research.

Range of Writing

10. Write routinely over extended time frames (time for research, reflection, and revision) and shorter time frames (a single sitting or a day or two) for a range of tasks, purposes, and audiences.

Grade 6 Writing Standards

Standard

Text Types and Purposes

Write arguments to support claims with clear reasons and relevant evidence.

Introduce claim(s) and organize the reasons and evidence clearly.

Standards Overview

Grade 6 Writing Standards

Standard

Text Types and Purposes (continued)

Use precise words and phrases, relevant descriptive details, and sensory language to capture the action and convey experiences and events.

Provide a conclusion that follows from and reflects on the narrated experiences or events.

Production and Distribution of Writing

Produce clear and coherent writing in which the development, organization, and style are appropriate to task, purpose, and audience. (Grade-specific expectations for writing types are defined in standards 1–3 above.)

With some guidance and support from peers and adults, develop and strengthen writing as needed by planning, revising, editing, rewriting, or trying a new approach. (Editing for conventions should demonstrate command of Language standards 1–3 up to and including grade 6.)

Use technology, including the Internet, to produce and publish writing as well as to interact and collaborate with others; demonstrate sufficient command of keyboarding skills to type a minimum of three pages in a single sitting.

Research to Build and Present Knowledge

Conduct short research projects to answer a question, drawing on several sources and refocusing the inquiry when appropriate.

Gather relevant information from multiple print and digital sources; assess the credibility of each source; and quote or paraphrase the data and conclusions of others while avoiding plagiarism and providing basic bibliographic information for sources.

Draw evidence from literary or informational texts to support analysis, reflection, and research.

Apply *grade 6 Reading standards* to literature (e.g., "Compare and contrast texts in different forms or genres [e.g., stories and poems; historical novels and fantasy stories] in terms of their approaches to similar themes and topics").

Apply *grade 6 Reading standards* to literary nonfiction (e.g., "Trace and evaluate the argument and specific claims in a text, distinguishing claims that are supported by reasons and evidence from claims that are not").

Range of Writing

Write routinely over extended time frames (time for research, reflection, and revision) and shorter time frames (a single sitting or a day or two) for a range of discipline-specific tasks, purposes, and audiences.

Standards Overview

Standards for Speaking and Listening

Comprehension and Collaboration

1. Prepare for and participate effectively in a range of conversations and collaborations with diverse partners, building on others' ideas and expressing their own clearly and persuasively.

2. Integrate and evaluate information presented in diverse media and formats, including visually, quantitatively, and orally.

3. Evaluate a speaker's point of view, reasoning, and use of evidence and rhetoric.

Presentation of Knowledge and Ideas

4. Present information, findings, and supporting evidence such that listeners can follow the line of reasoning and the organization, development, and style are appropriate to task, purpose, and audience.

5. Make strategic use of digital media and visual displays of data to express information and enhance understanding of presentations.

6. Adapt speech to a variety of contexts and communicative tasks, demonstrating command of formal English when indicated or appropriate.

Grade 6 Standards for Speaking and Listening

Standard

Comprehension and Collaboration

Engage effectively in a range of collaborative discussions (one-on-one, in groups, and teacher-led) with diverse partners on *grade 6 topics, texts, and issues,* building on others' ideas and expressing their own clearly.

Come to discussions prepared, having read or studied required material; explicitly draw on that preparation by referring to evidence on the topic, text, or issue to probe and reflect on ideas under discussion.

Follow rules for collegial discussions, set specific goals and deadlines, and define individual roles as needed.

Pose and respond to specific questions with elaboration and detail by making comments that contribute to the topic, text, or issue under discussion.

Review the key ideas expressed and demonstrate understanding of multiple perspectives through reflection and paraphrasing.

Interpret information presented in diverse media and formats (e.g., visually, quantitatively, orally) and explain how it contributes to a topic, text, or issue under study.

Delineate a speaker's argument and specific claims, distinguishing claims that are supported by reasons and evidence from claims that are not.

Presentation of Knowledge and Ideas

Present claims and findings, sequencing ideas logically and using pertinent descriptions, facts, and details and nonverbal elements to accentuate main ideas or themes; use appropriate eye contact, adequate volume, and clear pronunciation.

Include multimedia components (e.g., graphics, images, music, sound) and visual displays in presentations to clarify information.

Adapt speech to a variety of contexts and tasks, demonstrating command of formal English when indicated or appropriate. (See grade 6 Language standards 1 and 3 for specific expectations.)

Standards Overview

Standards for Language

College and Career Readiness Anchor Standards for Language

Conventions of Standard English

1. Demonstrate command of the conventions of standard English grammar and usage when writing or speaking.

2. Demonstrate command of the conventions of standard English capitalization, punctuation, and spelling when writing.

Knowledge of Language

3. Apply knowledge of language to understand how language functions in different contexts, to make effective choices for meaning or style, and to comprehend more fully when reading or listening.

Vocabulary Acquisition and Use

4. Determine or clarify the meaning of unknown and multiple-meaning words and phrases by using context clues, analyzing meaningful word parts, and consulting general and specialized reference materials, as appropriate.

5. Demonstrate understanding of figurative language, word relationships, and nuances in word meanings.

6. Acquire and use accurately a range of general academic and domain-specific words and phrases sufficient for reading, writing, speaking, and listening at the college and career-readiness level; demonstrate independence in gathering vocabulary knowledge when considering a word or phrase important to comprehension or expression.

Grade 6 Standards for Language

Standard

Conventions of Standard English

Demonstrate command of the conventions of standard English grammar and usage when writing or speaking.
Ensure that pronouns are in the proper case (subjective, objective, possessive).
Use intensive pronouns (e.g., *myself, ourselves*).
Recognize and correct inappropriate shifts in pronoun number and person.*
Recognize and correct vague pronouns (i.e., ones with unclear or ambiguous antecedents).*

Grade 6 Standards for Language

Standard

Conventions of Standard English (continued)

Recognize variations from standard English in their own and others' writing and speaking, and identify and use strategies to improve expression in conventional language.*

Demonstrate command of the conventions of standard English capitalization, punctuation, and spelling when writing.

Use punctuation (commas, parentheses, dashes) to set off nonrestrictive/parenthetical elements.*

Spell correctly.

Knowledge of Language

Use knowledge of language and its conventions when writing, speaking, reading, or listening.

Vary sentence patterns for meaning, reader/listener interest, and style.*

Maintain consistency in style and tone.

Vocabulary Acquisition and Use

Determine or clarify the meaning of unknown and multiple-meaning words and phrases based on *grade 6 reading and content*, choosing flexibly from a range of strategies.

Use context (e.g., the overall meaning of a sentence or paragraph; a word's position or function in a sentence) as a clue to the meaning of a word or phrase.

Use common, grade-appropriate Greek or Latin affixes and roots as clues to the meaning of a word (e.g., *audience, auditory, audible*).

Consult reference materials (e.g., dictionaries, glossaries, thesauruses), both print and digital, to find the pronunciation of a word or determine or clarify its precise meaning or its part of speech.

Verify the preliminary determination of the meaning of a word or phrase (e.g., by checking the inferred meaning in context or in a dictionary).

Demonstrate understanding of figurative language, word relationships, and nuances in word meanings.

Interpret figures of speech (e.g., personification) in context.

Use the relationship between particular words (e.g., cause/effect, part/whole, item/category) to better understand each of the words.

Distinguish among the connotations (associations) of words with similar denotations (definitions) (e.g., *stingy, scrimping, economical, unwasteful, thrifty*).

Acquire and use accurately grade-appropriate general academic and domain-specific words and phrases; gather vocabulary knowledge when considering a word or phrase important to comprehension or expression.

Childhood

You face challenges every day, but learning how to deal with them is part of growing up.

Best of the Bee

💬 **Discuss It** Do you think competition should be part of everyone's childhood?

Write your response before sharing your ideas.

SCAN FOR
MULTIMEDIA

UNIT 1

ESSENTIAL QUESTION:

What are some of the challenges and triumphs of growing up?

LAUNCH TEXT
NONFICTION
NARRATIVE MODEL
Wagon Train at Dusk

👤 WHOLE-CLASS LEARNING

ANCHOR TEXT: MEMOIR IN VERSE

from Brown Girl Dreaming
Jacqueline Woodson

MEDIA: COMIC STRIP

Gallery of *Calvin and Hobbes* Comics
Bill Watterson

👥 SMALL-GROUP LEARNING

PUBLIC DOCUMENT

Declaration of the Rights of the Child
The United Nations General Assembly

MAGAZINE ARTICLE

Michaela DePrince: The War Orphan Who Became a Ballerina
William Kremer

▶ MEDIA CONNECTION: Michaela DePrince— Ballet Dancer

COMPARE

MEMOIR

from Bad Boy
Walter Dean Myers

POETRY

I Was a Skinny Tomboy Kid
Alma Luz Villanueva

👤 INDEPENDENT LEARNING

NOVEL EXCERPT

from Peter Pan
J. M. Barrie

POETRY

Oranges
Gary Soto

ESSAY

The Boy Nobody Knew
Faith Ringgold

SHORT STORY

Raymond's Run
Toni Cade Bambara

SHORT STORY

Eleven
Sandra Cisneros

PERFORMANCE TASK

WRITING FOCUS:
Write a Nonfiction Narrative

PERFORMANCE TASK

SPEAKING AND LISTENING FOCUS:
Present a Retelling

PERFORMANCE-BASED ASSESSMENT PREP

Review Evidence for a Nonfiction Narrative

PERFORMANCE-BASED ASSESSMENT

Narration: Nonfiction Narrative and Oral Recitation

PROMPT:

When did a challenge lead to a triumph?

Unit Goals

Throughout this unit, you will deepen your understanding of the stage of life known as childhood through reading, writing, speaking, listening, and presenting. These goals will help you succeed on the Unit Performance-Based Assessment.

Rate how well you meet these goals right now. You will revisit your ratings later when you reflect on your growth during this unit.

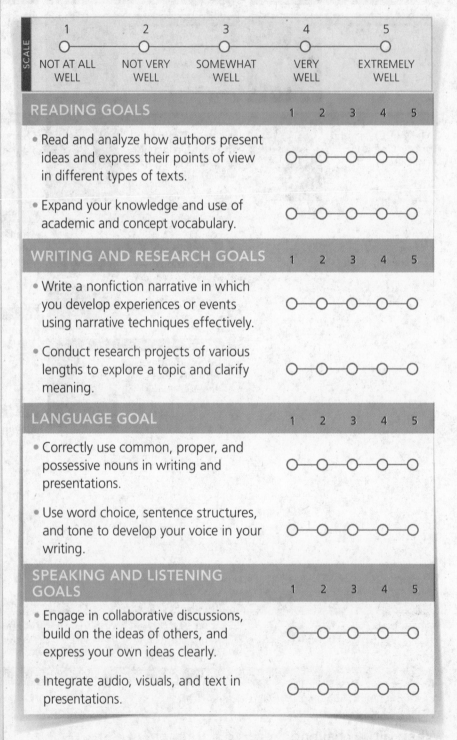

SCALE	1 NOT AT ALL WELL	2 NOT VERY WELL	3 SOMEWHAT WELL	4 VERY WELL	5 EXTREMELY WELL

READING GOALS	1	2	3	4	5
• Read and analyze how authors present ideas and express their points of view in different types of texts.					
• Expand your knowledge and use of academic and concept vocabulary.					

WRITING AND RESEARCH GOALS	1	2	3	4	5
• Write a nonfiction narrative in which you develop experiences or events using narrative techniques effectively.					
• Conduct research projects of various lengths to explore a topic and clarify meaning.					

LANGUAGE GOAL	1	2	3	4	5
• Correctly use common, proper, and possessive nouns in writing and presentations.					
• Use word choice, sentence structures, and tone to develop your voice in your writing.					

SPEAKING AND LISTENING GOALS	1	2	3	4	5
• Engage in collaborative discussions, build on the ideas of others, and express your own ideas clearly.					
• Integrate audio, visuals, and text in presentations.					

▤ STANDARDS

Language
Acquire and use accurately grade-appropriate general academic and domain-specific words and phrases; gather vocabulary knowledge when considering a word or phrase important to comprehension or expression.

SCAN FOR MULTIMEDIA

Academic Vocabulary: Nonfiction Narrative

Understanding and using academic terms can help you read, write, and speak with precision and clarity. Here are five academic words that will be useful to you in this unit as you analyze and write nonfiction narratives.

Complete the chart.

1. Review each word, its root, and the mentor sentences.

2. Use the information and your own knowledge to predict the meaning of each word.

3. For each word, list at least two related words.

4. Refer to the dictionary or other resources if needed.

TIP
FOLLOW THROUGH
Study the words in this chart, and mark them or their forms wherever they appear in the unit.

WORD	MENTOR SENTENCES	PREDICT MEANING	RELATED WORDS
reflect ROOT: **-flect-** "bend"	**1.** Nathan needs time to *reflect* on his actions before he apologizes. **2.** Sometimes it is better to stop and *reflect* on your thoughts before expressing your opinion.		reflection; reflective
notable ROOT: **-not-** "mark"	**1.** The museum features the famous paintings of many *notable* artists. **2.** The politician's win in her district was a *notable* success in her campaign for governor.		
contribute ROOT: **-trib-** "pay"; "give"	**1.** You can *contribute* to the discussion by voicing your thoughts on the subject. **2.** John was asked to *contribute* a short story to the literary magazine, to be published in the next issue.		
recognize ROOT: **-cogn-** "know"	**1.** Shay and Brooke did not *recognize* their cousin because he had grown so much since they last saw him. **2.** We *recognize* our veterans by honoring them with a parade.		
memorize ROOT: **-mem-** "mind"	**1.** It is difficult to *memorize* all of the different grammar rules for a foreign language. **2.** The actors must *memorize* their lines before the opening night of the play.		

This selection is an example of a **nonfiction narrative**, a type of writing in which an author tells a true story. This is the type of writing you will develop in the Performance-Based Assessment at the end of the unit.

As you read, look at the way the author describes events and experiences. Mark the text to help you answer this question: What descriptive details make this narrative realistic and memorable?

Wagon Train at Dusk

NOTES

1   "Sometimes you just have to laugh," I tell my daughter, who is having an especially bad day. She's lost her favorite bracelet, she turned in the wrong homework assignment, and she just found out she would be playing Marshmallow #2 in the class play.

2   "Oh, you wouldn't understand," Sarah says, sulkily.

3   I ask her if I've ever told her the story of the diorama.

4   "Yes, Dad. More than once," she says.

5   That doesn't stop me. "When I was in the sixth grade," I say in my storyteller's voice, "we had to make shoebox dioramas of a scene from American history. I decided to do a wagon train traveling across the Great Plains in the mid-1800s."

6   Sarah pretends she isn't rolling her eyes, but I keep going. "I wanted it to be great. A diorama to end all dioramas! I wanted to be famous. I wanted to be on the local news. But what I really wanted was to show up Jorge Nuñez," I say.

7   "Jorge and I had been in the same class since fourth grade. We were pretty evenly matched when it came to test scores and homework, but for hands-on projects, there was no one like Jorge. He always came up with these unique creations, beautifully conceived and executed. Jorge's mom and dad were architects, so maybe he had a leg up, but who knows."

8   Sarah shrugs in sympathy—which I take as permission to continue. "As soon as I heard Jorge announce that he was making a shoebox diorama of a log cabin, I decided to go one better. I'd

SCAN FOR
MULTIMEDIA

create a fleet of Conestoga wagons in a circle formation around a campfire at dusk, with miniature people and horses and dogs made of pipe cleaners, and children running around playing hoops. It would be a masterpiece. And that's just how it turned out: a masterpiece! I carried it upstairs to my room and that night I went to sleep with a smile on my face, imagining Jorge's reaction."

9   "Then," I go on, "in the middle of the night I was jolted awake by a ripping sound. My heart stopped. I felt sick. *I know that sound*, I thought. There was no mistaking what it was—Lucy was demolishing my masterpiece! You couldn't even tell what it was supposed to be! I lay there in a stupor of self-pity and the sense that nothing in the world would ever be right again. *The dog ate my diorama*, I thought, and I pictured myself saying this in class. I pictured the hoots and guffaws and hollers. I pictured my teacher's puzzled expression as she tried to work out if I was being serious." I make the expression myself, and Sarah smiles.

10   "Then I said it out loud: *The dog ate my diorama*. It was funny, actually. The more I said it, the funnier it got. I started laughing. I laughed until my sides hurt. I couldn't stop laughing."

11   "And then?" Sarah says, knowing what comes next.

12   "Well," I say, "I picked up all the pieces and put them in the box and took the whole thing to school. I called it 'Wagon Train After a Tornado.' The teacher loved it. Everyone enjoyed my story. I think Jorge was actually jealous."

13   Sarah gives a reluctant smile, like she's supposed to. "So," she says, remembering that there's a lesson in there somewhere, "you learned to laugh at bad things. Right?"

14   I shake my head. "Nope," I tell her. "I learned that some things aren't so bad." ❧

WORD NETWORK FOR CHILDHOOD

Vocabulary A Word Network is a collection of words related to a topic. As you read the selections in this unit, identify interesting words related to childhood, and add them to your Word Network. For example, you might begin by adding words from the Launch Text, such as *sulkily*, *diorama,* and *homework*. Continue to add words as you complete this unit.

sulkily

diorama

CHILDHOOD

homework

 Tool Kit
Word Network Model

Summary

Write a summary of "Wagon Train at Dusk." A **summary** is a concise, complete, and accurate overview of a text. It should not include a statement of your opinion or an analysis.

Launch Activity

Participate in a Group Discussion Consider this statement: **You need to overcome obstacles to learn new things.**

Prepare for the discussion by thinking about the topic:

- Have you ever faced a challenge that led to success? Do you know someone who has had this experience?
- Does learning new things have to be challenging?

Decide your position, and record a brief explanation.

☐ Strongly Agree ☐ Agree ☐ Disagree ☐ Strongly Disagree

Form a small group with other students. Then, discuss your responses to the prompt and the questions. When you have finished your conversation, write a summary of the main points you covered. Share your summary with the class.

QuickWrite

Consider class discussions, the video, and the Launch Text as you think about the prompt. Record your first thoughts here.

PROMPT: **When did a challenge lead to a triumph?**

EVIDENCE LOG FOR CHILDHOOD

Review your QuickWrite. Summarize your thoughts in one sentence to record in your Evidence Log. Then, record textual details or evidence from "Wagon Train at Dusk" that support your thinking.

Prepare for the Performance-Based Assessment at the end of the unit by completing the Evidence Log after each selection.

🔧 **Tool Kit**
Evidence Log Model

Title of Text: _____ Date: _____

CONNECTION TO PROMPT	TEXT EVIDENCE/DETAILS	ADDITIONAL NOTES/IDEAS

How does this text change or add to my thinking? Date: _____

SCAN FOR MULTIMEDIA

ESSENTIAL QUESTION:

What are some of the challenges and triumphs of growing up?

You deal with challenges every day. Some are big challenges, while others are small. Whatever the challenge is, you learn and grow from that experience. As you read, you will work with your whole class to explore the ways that people can learn from and triumph over childhood challenges.

Whole-Class Learning Strategies

Throughout your life, in school, in your community, and in your career, you will continue to learn and work in large-group environments.

Review these strategies and the actions you can take to practice them as you work with your whole class. Add ideas of your own for each strategy. Get ready to use these strategies during Whole-Class Learning.

STRATEGY	ACTION PLAN
Listen actively	• Eliminate distractions. For example, put your cellphone away. • Keep your eyes on the speaker. •
Clarify by asking questions	• If you're confused, other people probably are, too. Ask a question to help your whole class. • If you see that you are guessing, ask a question instead. •
Monitor understanding	• Notice what information you already know and be ready to build on it. • Ask for help if you are struggling. •
Interact and share ideas	• Share your ideas and answer questions, even if you are unsure. • Build on the ideas of others by adding details or making a connection. •

SCAN FOR
MULTIMEDIA

CONTENTS

About the Author

Jacqueline Woodson
(b. 1964) was born in Columbus, Ohio. She recalls being happiest as a child when she was writing: "I wrote on paper bags and my shoes and denim binders." A 2008 Newbery Honor winner, Woodson believes that writers need to be honest and to listen to the voices of young people.

🔧 **Tool Kit**
First-Read Guide and Model Annotation

from Brown Girl Dreaming

Concept Vocabulary

You will encounter the following words as you read the excerpt from *Brown Girl Dreaming*. Before reading, note how familiar you are with each word. Then, rank the words in order from most familiar (1) to least familiar (6).

WORD	YOUR RANKING
squish	
humming	
twist	
twirl	
shushes	
feathery	

After completing the first read, come back to the concept vocabulary and review your rankings. Mark changes to your original rankings as needed.

First Read MEMOIR IN VERSE

Apply these strategies as you conduct your first read. You will have an opportunity to complete the close-read notes after your first read.

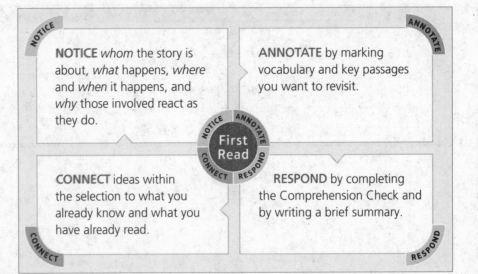

NOTICE *whom* the story is about, *what* happens, *where* and *when* it happens, and *why* those involved react as they do.

ANNOTATE by marking vocabulary and key passages you want to revisit.

CONNECT ideas within the selection to what you already know and what you have already read.

RESPOND by completing the Comprehension Check and by writing a brief summary.

First Read

from
Brown Girl Dreaming

Jacqueline Woodson

BACKGROUND

As a child in the 1960s, Jacqueline Woodson moved with her family from Greenville, South Carolina, to Brooklyn, in New York City. Her memoir *Brown Girl Dreaming* tells of her childhood experiences growing up in both places. In a memoir, an author recalls important events in his or her life. *Brown Girl Dreaming* is unique as a memoir because it is written in verse, or as poetry.

SCAN FOR
MULTIMEDIA

brooklyn rain

The rain here is different than the way
it rains in Greenville. No sweet smell of honeysuckle.
No soft **squish** of pine. No slip and slide through grass.
Just Mama saying, *Stay inside today. It's raining,*
5 and me at the window. Nothing to do but
watch
the gray sidewalk grow darker,
watch
the drops slide down the glass pane,
10 watch
people below me move fast, heads bent.

Already there are stories
in my head. Already color and sound and words.

NOTES

squish (skwihsh) *n.* spongy, cushioned feeling when walking on a flexible surface

humming (HUHM ihng) *v.*
singing with closed lips
and without words

Already I'm
15 drawing circles on the glass, **humming**
myself someplace far away from here.

Down south, there was always someplace else to go
you could step out into the rain and
Grandma would let you
20 lift your head and stick out your tongue
be happy.

Down south already feels like a long time ago
but the stories in my head
take me back there, set me down in Daddy's garden
25 where the sun is always shining.

* * *

another way

While our friends are watching TV or playing outside,
we are in our house, knowing that begging our mother
to turn the television on is useless, begging her for
ten minutes outside will only mean her saying,
5 *No.* Saying,
You can run wild with your friends anytime. Today
I want you to find another way to play.

And then one day my mother
comes home with two shopping bags
10 filled with board games—Monopoly, checkers, chess,
Ants in the Pants, Sorry, Trouble,
just about every game we've ever seen
in the commercials between
our Saturday morning cartoons.

15 So many games, we don't know
where to begin playing, so we let Roman choose.
And he chooses Trouble
because he likes the sound the die makes
when it pops inside
20 its plastic bubble. And for days and days,
it is Christmas in November,
games to play when our homework is done,
Monopoly money to count
and checkers to slam down on boards, ants to flip
25 into blue plastic pants,
chess pieces to practice moving until we understand
their power
and when we don't, Roman and I argue
that there's another way to play

30 called *Our Way*. But Hope and Dell tell us
    that we're too immature to even begin to understand
    then bend over the chessboard in silence, each becoming
    the next chess champ of the house, depending on the day
    and the way the game is played.

35 Sometimes, Roman and I leave Hope and Dell alone
    go to another corner of the room and become
    what the others call us—*the two youngest*,
    playing games we know the rules to
    tic-tac-toe and checkers,
40 hangman and connect the dots

    but mostly, we lean over their shoulders
    as quietly as we can, watching
    waiting
    wanting to understand
45 how to play another way.

* * *

gifted

Everyone knows my sister
is brilliant. The letters come home folded neatly
inside official-looking envelopes that my sister proudly
hands over to my mother.
5 Odella has achieved
Odella has excelled at
Odella has been recommended to
Odella's outstanding performance in

She is gifted
10 we are told.
And I imagine presents surrounding her.

I am not gifted. When I read, the words **twist**
twirl across the page.
When they settle, it is too late.
15 The class has already moved on.

I want to catch words one day. I want to hold them
then blow gently,
watch them float
right out of my hands.

CLOSE READ
ANNOTATE: In "gifted," mark the words that are repeated in lines 5–7.

QUESTION: Why has the poet chosen to repeat these words?

CONCLUDE: What effect does this repetition have on the reader?

twist (twihst) *v.* wind or spin around one another

twirl (twurl) *v.* turn around and around quickly

* * *

sometimes

There is only one other house on our block
where a father doesn't live. When somebody asks why,
the boy says, *He died.*
The girl looks off, down the block, her thumb
5   slowly rising to her mouth. The boy says,
I was a baby. Says, *She doesn't remember him*
and points to his silent sister.

Sometimes, I lie about my father.
He died, I say, *in a car wreck* or
10 *He fell off a roof* or maybe
He's coming soon.
Next week and
next week and
next week . . . but
15 if my sister's nearby
she shakes her head. Says,
She's making up stories again.
Says,
We don't have a father anymore.
20 Says,
Our grandfather's our father now.
Says,
Sometimes, that's the way things happen.

* * *

uncle robert

Uncle Robert has moved to New York City!

I hear him taking the stairs
two at a time and then
he is at our door, knocking loud until our mother
    opens it,
5   curlers in her hair, robe pulled closed, whispering,
It's almost midnight, don't you wake my children!

But we are already awake, all four of us, smiling
    and jumping around
my uncle: *What'd you bring me?*

Our mama **shushes** us, says,
10 *It's too late for presents and the like.*
But we want presents and the like.
And she, too, is smiling now, happy to see her
    baby brother who lives all the way over
in Far Rockaway where the ocean is right there
if you look out your window.

CLOSE READ

ANNOTATE: Mark words that indicate the exact words of Woodson and her sister in lines 9–23 of "sometimes."

QUESTION: What can you tell about Woodson from these lines? What can you tell about her sister?

CONCLUDE: How does this dialogue help you understand the differences between Woodson and her sister?

shushes (SHUHSH ihz) *v.* tells or signals someone to be quiet

15 Robert opens his hand to reveal a pair of silver earrings,
   says to my sister, *This is a gift for how smart you are.*
   I want
   to be smart like Dell, I want
   someone to hand me silver and gold
20 just because my brain clicks into thinking whenever
   it needs to but
   I am not smart like Dell so I watch her press
      the silver moons into her ears
   I say, *I know a girl ten times smarter than her. She gets*
      diamonds every time she gets a hundred on a test.
      And Robert looks at me, his dark eyes smiling, asks,
      Is that something you made up? Or something real?
   In my own head,
25 it's real as anything.

   In my head
   all kinds of people are doing all kinds of things.
   I want to tell him this, that
   the world we're living in right here in Brownsville isn't
30 the only place. But now my brothers are asking,

   What'd you bring me, and my uncle is pulling gifts
      from his pockets,
   from his leather briefcase, from inside his socks.
      He hands
   my mother a record, a small 45—James Brown,[1]
      who none of us
   like because he screams when he sings. But my mother
      puts it on the record player, turned way down low
      and then even us kids are dancing around—
      Robert showing us the steps he learned
      at the Far Rockaway parties. His feet are magic
35 and we all try to slide across the floor like he does,
   our own feet, again and again,
   betraying us.

   Teach us, Robert! we keep saying. *Teach us!*

                        ❄ ❄ ❄

   ----

   1. **James Brown** (1933–2006) American singer and dancer, and founding father of funk
      music. He is often referred to as the "Godfather of Soul."

NOTES

CLOSE READ
ANNOTATE: Mark details in lines 15–23 of "uncle robert" that show what the poet is thinking.

QUESTION: Why might the poet have included these details? *He must have thought that would give people emotion.*

CONCLUDE: What do these details suggest about the poet's character?

feathery (FEH<u>TH</u> uhr ee)
adj. light and airy, like the touch of a feather

CLOSE READ
ANNOTATE: Mark details in lines 4-8 of "wishes" that refer to things you can touch. Mark other words that refer to things you can feel or think, but cannot touch.

QUESTION: Why does the poet use these different kinds of details?

CONCLUDE: How do these details help the reader understand what the wishes mean to the children?

wishes

When he takes us to the park, Uncle Robert tells us,
If you catch a dandelion puff, you can make a wish.
Anything you want will come true, he says as
we chase the **feathery** wishes around swings,
5 beneath sliding boards,
until we can hold them in our hands,
close our eyes tight, whisper our dream
then set it floating out into the universe hoping
our uncle is telling the truth,
10 hoping each thing we wish for
will one day come true.

* * *

believing

The stories start like this—

Jack and Jill went up a hill, my uncle sings.
I went up a hill yesterday, I say.
What hill?
5 *In the park.*
What park?
Halsey Park.
Who was with you?
Nobody.
10 *But you're not allowed to go to the park without anyone.*
I just did.
Maybe you dreamed it, my uncle says.
No, I really went.

And my uncle likes the stories I'm making up.

15 *. . . Along came a spider and sat down beside her.*
I got bit by a spider, I say.
When?
The other day.
Where?
20 *Right on my foot.*
Show us.
It's gone now.

But my mother accuses me of lying.
If you lie, she says, *one day you'll steal.*

25 *I won't steal.*
It's hard to understand how one leads to the other,
how stories could ever
make us criminals.

It's hard to understand
30 the way my brain works—so different
from everybody around me.
How each new story
I'm told becomes a thing
that happens,
35 in some other way
to me . . . !

Keep making up stories, my uncle says.
You're lying, my mother says.

Maybe the truth is somewhere in between
40 all that I'm told
and memory.

"another way," "believing," "brooklyn rain," "gifted," "sometimes," "uncle robert," "wishes" and "believing" from *Brown Girl Dreaming* by Jacqueline Woodson, copyright © 2014 by Jacqueline Woodson. Used by permission of Nancy Paulsen Books, an imprint of Penguin Young Readers Group, a division of Penguin Random House LLC.

NOTES

CLOSE READ
ANNOTATE: In lines 23–38 of "believing," mark words that show how the poet's mother reacts to her stories. Then, mark words that show how her uncle reacts.

QUESTION: Why does the poet include these different reactions?

CONCLUDE: How does this contrast help the reader better understand the poet's struggle?

Comprehension Check

Complete the following items after you finish your first read.

1. In "brooklyn rain," what does Woodson's mother say?

2. In "gifted," what does the poet hope she will one day be able to do with words?

3. In "uncle robert," what do Woodson and her siblings want their uncle to teach them?

4. **Notebook** Write a mini-summary (one or two sentences) of each poem in the excerpt from *Brown Girl Dreaming*.

- -

RESEARCH

Research to Clarify Choose at least one unfamiliar detail from the excerpt. Briefly research that detail. In what way does the information you learned help you better understand an aspect of the memoir?

Close Read the Text

1. This model, from lines 1–6 of "brooklyn rain," shows two sample annotations, along with questions and conclusions. Close read the passage, and find another detail to annotate. Then, write a question and your conclusion.

> **ANNOTATE:** These phrases appeal to the senses of smell and touch.
>
> **QUESTION:** Why does Woodson use language that appeals to the senses?
>
> **CONCLUDE:** These phrases create images for readers of how Woodson experienced the rain in Greenville.

ANNOTATE: The word *No* repeats.

QUESTION: Why does Woodson repeat the word *No*?

CONCLUDE: The repetition emphasizes the ways in which Woodson's life in Brooklyn is different from her life in Greenville.

> The rain here is different than the way/it rains in Greenville. No sweet smell of honeysuckle./No soft squish of pine. No slip and slide through grass./Just mama saying, *Stay inside today. It's raining,*/and me at the window. Nothing to do but/watch . . .

2. For more practice, go back into the text, and complete the close-read notes.

3. Revisit a section of the text you found important during your first read. Read this section closely, and **annotate** what you notice. Ask yourself **questions** such as "Why did the author make this choice?" What can you **conclude**?

🔧 **Tool Kit**
Close-Read Guide and
Model Annotation

Analyze the Text

CITE TEXTUAL EVIDENCE to support your answers.

📓 **Notebook** Respond to these questions.

1. (a) List three details from the poems that connect to an aspect of Woodson's personality. (b) **Make Inferences** What do these details suggest about Woodson as a child?

2. Speculate Why do you think Woodson likes to make up stories so much?

3. Make a Judgment Woodson's mother worries that if Woodson lies, one day she will steal. Do you think this is a reasonable concern? Explain.

4. Essential Question: *What are some of the challenges and triumphs of growing up?* What have you learned about the challenges and triumphs of growing up from reading this selection?

▤ STANDARDS

Reading Literature
• Analyze how a particular sentence, chapter, scene, or stanza fits into the overall structure of a text and contributes to the development of the theme, setting, or plot.
• Explain how an author develops the point of view of the narrator or speaker in a text.

Reading Informational Text
• Analyze how a particular sentence, paragraph, chapter, or section fits into the overall structure of a text and contributes to the development of the ideas.
• Determine an author's point of view or purpose in a text and explain how it is conveyed in the text.

Analyze Craft and Structure

Memoir and Poetry In a **memoir,** an author tells a true story of an important time in his or her life. Most memoirs are written in **first-person point of view,** or from the author's perspective. The author tells what happened and what he or she thought and felt about it. Memoirs are usually written in **prose,** or complete sentences and paragraphs. Most also use dialogue to show how people speak and what they are like. In this memoir, Jacqueline Woodson takes a different approach. Instead of prose, she tells her story in a series of poems that include these elements:

- **stanzas,** or sections, rather than paragraphs

- complete sentences that are broken up into separate lines

- language that breaks certain rules— for example, Woodson sometimes uses sentence fragments and nonstandard capitalization (see the sentence fragment in lines 32–36 of "believing")

Woodson's choice to tell her story through poems affects how readers understand it. It allows Woodson to emphasize certain words, phrases, and ideas. She also uses storytelling elements, such as dialogue. This combination of poetry and storytelling helps Woodson immerse readers even more deeply into her childhood world.

Practice

CITE TEXTUAL EVIDENCE
to support your answers.

Notebook Respond to these questions.

1. (a) Identify one example of a private thought or feeling Woodson shares in her memoir. (b) Explain how the use of first-person point of view allows her to share this detail.

2. (a) Identify the sentence fragments in lines 2–3 of "brooklyn rain." (b) Explain how these fragments help to create a vivid picture of the rain in Greenville.

3. (a) In lines 4–11 of "brooklyn rain," what word appears on its own line three times? (b) Read the lines aloud. Why do you think Woodson chose to set this word apart in this way?

4. (a) In line 23 of "sometimes," Woodson's sister says "Sometimes, that's the way things happen." What does this tell you about her sister's feelings about life? (b) How might the stories of Woodson's childhood be different if they were told from her sister's point of view?

from BROWN GIRL DREAMING

Concept Vocabulary

squish	twist	shushes
humming	twirl	feathery

Why These Words? These concept words are all examples of **sensory language**, or words that appeal to the five senses: touch, sight, smell, hearing, and taste. In *Brown Girl Dreaming,* Woodson uses these sensory words to create **imagery**, or vivid word pictures. Imagery helps readers understand ideas in a deeper way than plain explanations might allow. For example, the words *twist* and *twirl* help the reader understand Woodson's difficulty with reading: "the words twist / twirl across the page."

1. How does the concept vocabulary sharpen the reader's understanding of Woodson's feelings?

2. What other words in the selection are examples of sensory language?

Practice

📓 **Notebook** The concept vocabulary words appear in *Brown Girl Dreaming.*

1. Find each concept vocabulary word in the text, and write down the sentence in which it appears. Then, rewrite each sentence without using any sensory language. Make sure the sentence has the same basic meaning. For example, "When I read, the words twist / twirl across the page" might become "When I read, I have trouble following the words."

2. How did your changes affect the meaning of the sentences? Did removing the sensory language improve your understanding of the concept vocabulary? If so, how?

Word Study

📓 **Notebook** **Onomatopoeia** The concept vocabulary words *squish*, *humming*, and *shushes* are examples of **onomatopoeia,** or words that imitate the sounds they mean. Animal sounds—such as *woof*, *moo*, and *meow*—are other examples of onomatopoeia.

1. Use each onomatopoeic concept vocabulary word in a sentence of your own.

2. Jot down other examples of onomatopoeia that you have come across in your own experience or in the selection.

⟐ WORD NETWORK

Add words related to childhood from the text to your Word Network.

☰ STANDARDS

Reading Literature
Determine the meaning of words and phrases as they are used in a text, including figurative and connotative meanings; analyze the impact of a specific word choice on meaning and tone.

Language
• Demonstrate command of the conventions of standard English capitalization, punctuation, and spelling when writing.
• Use knowledge of language and its conventions when writing, speaking, reading, or listening.
• Demonstrate understanding of figurative language, word relationships, and nuances in word meanings.

Conventions

Common, Proper, and Possessive Nouns A **noun** names a person, a place, a thing, or an idea. Here are several types of nouns:

- A **common noun** names any one of a class of people, places, things, or ideas. Common nouns are not capitalized.

- A **proper noun** names a specific person, place, thing, or idea. Proper nouns are capitalized. However, a poet may sometimes choose not to capitalize a proper noun, for effect or for style. For example, Jacqueline Woodson doesn't capitalize *brooklyn*, even though it is the name of a specific place.

- A **possessive noun** shows ownership. Possessive nouns function as adjectives by modifying a noun or pronoun in a sentence. Most singular possessive nouns end in an apostrophe and the letter *s* (*'s*). An example is *sister's*. Most plural possessive nouns end in the letter *s* and an apostrophe (*s'*). An example is *sisters'*.

The chart shows examples of common, proper, and possessive nouns from the excerpt from *Brown Girl Dreaming*.

COMMON NOUNS	PROPER NOUNS	POSSESSIVE NOUNS
And my uncle likes the stories I'm making up. ("believing," line 14)	*. . . Robert showing us the steps he learned / at the Far Rockaway parties.* ("uncle robert," lines 33–34)	*. . . stories in my head / take me back there, set me down in Daddy's garden. . . .* ("brooklyn rain," lines 23–24)

Read It

1. In each sentence, mark proper nouns that should be capitalized. Add an apostrophe to possessive nouns where needed.

   a. hopes home in south carolina is very different from ericas home in new york.

   b. jacquelines plans for the weekend include hiking in smith park and calling her grandmother in arizona.

   c. uncle roberts silly songs and dance lessons make us smile and laugh.

2. Reread "brooklyn rain." Then, mark at least one common noun, one proper noun, and one possessive noun in the poem.

Write It

🗐 **Notebook** Write a paragraph about the similarities and the differences between Woodson and her sister Odella. Include at least two proper nouns and one possessive noun. Label all common nouns.

from BROWN GIRL DREAMING

Writing to Sources

In *Brown Girl Dreaming,* Jacqueline Woodson tells stories in poem form about specific moments from her childhood. In each poem, she also shares her thoughts and feelings about the moment she describes. The separate poems work together to tell the story of Woodson's childhood.

Assignment

Write a brief **poem** in which you use Woodson's memoir as inspiration. Follow these steps:

- Choose a single moment on which to focus. It can be something small or seemingly unimportant. For example, you might write about what you see from your window in the morning, or about eating lunch at school. Then, write a regular prose paragraph in which you describe the moment. Include details that show what the moment looked and felt like.

- Change your paragraph into a poem by applying elements of poetry such as the ones Woodson uses. For example, break up sentences to make poetic lines. Consider repeating important words or setting them on their own lines. You may even play with incomplete sentences or fragments. Try to make the moment you described in your paragraph even more vivid as a poem.

- Once your poem is organized, consider adding dialogue or more descriptive details. Alternatively, you may need to cut some details. Work to make your poem capture the moment and make it fresh and alive for readers.

Vocabulary Connection Consider using several of the concept vocabulary words in your writing.

squish	twist	shushes
humming	twirl	feathery

Reflect on Your Writing

After you have written your poem, answer the following questions.

1. What was the most challenging part of the assignment?

2. What poetic and narrative techniques did you use in your writing? How did they help you bring your ideas to life?

3. Why These Words? The words you choose make a difference in your writing. Which words did you choose to create a vivid picture for your readers?

STANDARDS

Writing
- Write narratives to develop real or imagined experiences or events using effective technique, relevant descriptive details, and well-structured event sequences.
  b. Use narrative techniques, such as dialogue, pacing, and description, to develop experiences, events, and/or characters.
  d. Use precise words and phrases, relevant descriptive details, and sensory language to convey experiences and events.
- Draw evidence from literary or informational texts to support analysis, reflection, and research.
  a. Apply *grade 6 Reading standards* to literature.

Speaking and Listening

Assignment

In the last three lines of the excerpt, Woodson questions the differences between the ideas in her head and reality: *"Maybe the truth is somewhere in between / all that I'm told / and memory."* Woodson also discusses how her mother often says she is lying. In telling stories, do you think Woodson is lying or just using her imagination? Is there a point at which the use of imagination becomes a lie? Take a position on these questions, and participate in a brief **partner discussion** in which you express your views. Use examples from the text and from your own experience to support your ideas. After you and your partner talk, regroup with the class and share highlights of your discussion.

1. **Prepare for the Discussion** Decide whether you think Woodson's use of imagination as a child goes so far it could be considered lying. Then, determine why you feel this way. Note examples from the text and your own experience to support your reasons.

2. **Discuss With Your Partner** Use your notes as you and your partner talk about the issue. Consider the following questions:

   - Do you and your partner agree on your basic position?

   - If so, do you have similar or different reasons and examples that support your position?

   - If not, do the reasons and examples your partner offers change your opinion?

3. **Discuss With Your Class** Begin the class discussion by having each set of partners take turns offering a different idea about Woodson's use of imagination. Do not repeat an idea that was already introduced by your classmates; try to come up with a new idea even if it was not the one you had originally planned on sharing. Once each set of partners has contributed, discuss the ways in which your ideas are similar and different.

4. **Reflect on the Discussion** After both the partner and group discussions, consider how talking about ideas helped you better understand your own thinking. Did your initial position change as a result of the discussions? Why or why not?

EVIDENCE LOG

Before moving on to a new selection, go to your Evidence Log, and record what you learned from *Brown Girl Dreaming*.

STANDARDS

Speaking and Listening
Engage effectively in a range of collaborative discussions with diverse partners on *grade 6 topics, texts, and issues*, building on others' ideas and expressing their own clearly.

a. Come to discussions prepared, having read or studied required material; explicitly draw on that preparation by referring to evidence on the topic, text, or issue to probe and reflect on ideas under discussion.
b. Follow rules for collegial discussions, set specific goals and deadlines, and define individual roles as needed.
c. Pose and respond to specific questions with elaboration and detail by making comments that contribute to the topic, text, or issue under discussion.
d. Review the key ideas expressed and demonstrate understanding of multiple perspectives through reflection and paraphrasing.

About the Artist

The cartoonist **Bill Watterson** (b. 1958) is the creator of the popular *Calvin and Hobbes* comic strip and a two-time recipient of the Reuben Award for Outstanding Cartoonist of the Year. He graduated from Kenyon College in Ohio, and he had his first *Calvin and Hobbes* strip published at the age of twenty-seven. Watterson fought against the commercialization and merchandising of his comics.

Gallery of *Calvin and Hobbes* Comics

Media Vocabulary

The following words will be useful to you as you analyze, discuss, and write about the comic strips.

panel: individual frame of a comic, depicting a single moment	• Panels work together to tell a story. • Panels cannot show everything that happens, so readers must use their imaginations to fill in the blanks.
encapsulation: choice of important scenes to display in each panel	• The layout of the scenes influences the readers' interpretations. • Authors and cartoonists can use size and shape to give more or less weight, or importance, to scenes.
speech balloon: display of what a character is speaking or thinking	• The size, shape, and color of the speech balloon can show the emotion of the speaker. • Speech balloons can also show emotion or meaning through the use of punctuation marks.

First Review MEDIA: ART AND PHOTOGRAPHY

Apply these strategies as you conduct your first review. You will have an opportunity to complete a close review after your first review.

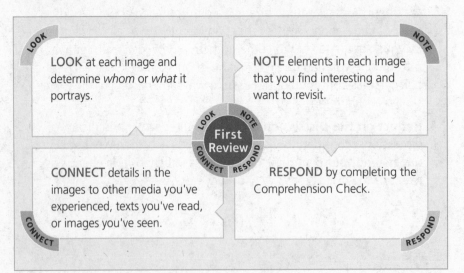

LOOK at each image and determine *whom* or *what* it portrays.

NOTE elements in each image that you find interesting and want to revisit.

CONNECT details in the images to other media you've experienced, texts you've read, or images you've seen.

RESPOND by completing the Comprehension Check.

Gallery of *Calvin and Hobbes* Comics

Bill Watterson

BACKGROUND

Calvin and Hobbes was a highly popular comic strip that ran from 1985 to 1995. It follows the adventures of Calvin, a clever six-year-old with a wild imagination, and his stuffed tiger and imaginary friend, Hobbes. *Calvin and Hobbes* has appeared in thousands of newspapers worldwide and has attracted fans of all ages.

SCAN FOR
MULTIMEDIA

NOTES

CARTOON 1: Ghosts

CARTOON 2: Do You Like Her?

CARTOON 3: Snowman Xing

NOTES

Comprehension Check

Complete the following items after you finish your first review.

1. In "Ghosts," where are Calvin and Hobbes?

2. In "Do You Like Her?" how does Calvin respond when Hobbes asks him whether he likes the new girl in his class?

3. In "Snowman Xing," why does Calvin's dad yell to Calvin that he's late for work?

4. 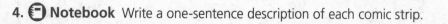 **Notebook** Write a one-sentence description of each comic strip.

GALLERY OF *CALVIN AND HOBBES* COMICS

Close Review

Revisit the comic strips and your first-review notes. Write down any new observations that seem important. What **questions** do you have? What can you **conclude**?

Analyze the Media

⊟ **Notebook** Respond to these questions.

1. **Make Inferences** An **inference** is a conclusion you draw about something that is not directly stated or shown. **(a)** In "Ghosts," what do you think happens between the third and fourth panels? **(b)** What details in the comic support your inference?

2. **Speculate** Why do you think Calvin refuses to answer Hobbes's questions about the new girl in class? Explain.

3. **Draw Conclusions** What can you tell about the relationship between Calvin and Hobbes ? Explain, citing details from the comics that you used to draw your conclusion.

4. **Essential Question: *What are some of the challenges and triumphs of growing up?*** What have you learned about the challenges and triumphs of growing up by reading these comic strips?

LANGUAGE DEVELOPMENT

Media Vocabulary

panel	encapsulation	speech balloon

Respond to these questions.

1. Why might Watterson have included only one panel in "Snowman Xing"?

2. In "Do You Like Her?" how does Watterson indicate that a character is speaking with emotion?

3. In "Ghosts," some of the panels include dialogue, whereas others do not. Why do you think Watterson chose to have panels without dialogue in this comic strip?

STANDARDS

Reading Literature
Cite textual evidence to support analysis of what the text says explicitly as well as inferences drawn from the text.

Writing
Conduct short research projects to answer a question, drawing on several sources and refocusing the inquiry when appropriate.

Speaking and Listening
• Engage effectively in a range of collaborative discussions with diverse partners on *grade 6 topics, texts, and issues,* building on others' ideas and expressing their own clearly.
  a. Come to discussions prepared, having read or studied required material; explicitly draw on that preparation by referring to evidence on the topic, text, or issue to probe and reflect on ideas under discussion.
  c. Pose and respond to specific questions with elaboration and detail by making comments that contribute to the topic, text, or issue under discussion.
  d. Review the key ideas expressed and demonstrate understanding of multiple perspectives through reflection and paraphrasing.
• Interpret information presented in diverse media and formats and explain how it contributes to a topic, text, or issue under study.

Research

> ## Assignment
>
> *Calvin and Hobbes* was a very popular comic strip, which appeared in newspapers for more than ten years. Conduct research in preparation for a **class discussion** about what made this comic strip so popular. In your research, look for examples of the comic strip from different years, information about Bill Watterson, and comments by fans in response to the comics.

Conduct Research To prepare for the class discussion, consider these questions, and perform research to answer them.

- What did fans like about the comic strip?
- Why did Watterson create *Calvin and Hobbes*? What were his influences?
- What qualities do you think made the comic strip successful for so long?
- Do you think the comic strip would still be popular today? Why or why not?

As you conduct your research, follow these guidelines.

- Consult multiple reliable sources of information—both print and digital. Ask yourself questions like the ones in the chart to make sure the sources you consult are reliable.

MAIN QUESTION	RELATED QUESTIONS
Does the source have a good reputation?	• Who is responsible for the information? Is it a person, a publisher, or another organization? • Do people generally agree that the source is trustworthy?
Does the source present solid facts?	• Does the source present mostly facts or mostly opinions? • If it expresses opinions, does it clearly say so?
Does the source avoid bias—prejudice or an unfair opinion?	• Does the source ignore any facts that are important? • Does the source twist the meaning of any facts?

- Jot down relevant details and examples to support your ideas during the class discussion.
- Write down any additional questions that your research raises and that you would like to discuss with the class.

Hold a Discussion As a class, discuss the findings of your research. Keep the following tips in mind:

- Support your ideas by citing specific details from the selection and your research.
- If you are unsure of what other classmates are trying to say, ask questions to help them expand on their ideas.
- Reflect on new ideas that other classmates express, and paraphrase their ideas to confirm your understanding of them. To paraphrase, restate their ideas in your own words.

✎ EVIDENCE LOG

Before moving on to a new selection, go to your Evidence Log, and record what you learned from the gallery of *Calvin and Hobbes* comics.

WRITING TO SOURCES

• *from* BROWN GIRL DREAMING

• GALLERY OF *CALVIN AND HOBBES* COMICS

🔧 **Tool Kit**
Student Model
of a Narrative

ACADEMIC
VOCABULARY

As you craft your
nonfiction narrative,
consider using some of the
academic vocabulary you
learned in the beginning
of the unit.

reflect
notable
contribute
recognize
memorize

⬛ STANDARDS
Writing
• Write narratives to develop
real or imagined experiences or
events using effective technique,
relevant descriptive details, and
well-structured event sequences
• Write routinely over extended time
frames and shorter time frames for
a range of discipline-specific tasks,
purposes, and audiences.

Write a Nonfiction Narrative

You have read selections in which people use their imaginations in different ways to shape their childhood worlds. In the *Calvin and Hobbes* comics, a young boy experiences life's ups and downs with his constant companion and imaginary friend. In the excerpt from *Brown Girl Dreaming,* Jacqueline Woodson describes how she used her imagination to navigate the challenges of growing up. Now, you will explore this idea by writing a personal narrative in which you tell a story about your own experience with imagination.

Assignment

In the poem "another day," Jacqueline Woodson's mother tells the children, "Today I want you to find another way to play." Write a **personal narrative** in response to the following prompt:

> **When did you have to use your imagination to find another way to do something?**

For example, perhaps you found another way to play, solve a problem, make a friend, or learn a new skill. In your narrative, tell the story of your experience and reflect on the ways in which using your imagination made things better.

Elements of a Nonfiction Narrative

A **nonfiction narrative** is a true story. A **personal narrative** is a true story about the writer's own life. In a personal narrative, the writer uses the first-person point of view to relate experiences and events.

A well-written nonfiction narrative contains the following elements:

• a conflict or problem
• people who play a role in the events described in the narrative
• a clear sequence of events with transitional words and phrases that show shifts in time or setting
• narrative techniques, such as dialogue, description, and pacing, that help to convey experiences and events in a memorable way
• precise words, descriptive details, and sensory language that show what settings and people are like
• a conclusion that follows from the experiences and events in the narrative

Model Nonfiction Narrative For a model of a well-crafted nonfiction narrative, see the Launch Text, "Wagon Train at Dusk."

Challenge yourself to find all of the elements of an effective nonfiction narrative in the text. You will have an opportunity to review these elements as you prepare to write your own nonfiction narrative.

Prewriting / Planning

Focus Your Topic Reread the assignment. Consider the experience you would like to describe in your narrative. Summarize what happens in your narrative by completing this sentence starter.

I used my imagination to find another way to do something when _____

_____ .

Explore Setting Vivid, specific descriptions of places in your story can help your readers better understand your experiences and insights. Use the chart to write down the places you want to describe. Then, note sensory details you can use to bring those places to life for readers.

PLACES	SENSORY DETAILS (sights, sounds, smells, tastes, sensations)

Gather Details About People and Events Now that you have thought about the setting of your narrative, gather details about the people and events. To do so, think about these questions:

- **Events:** *What events triggered the need for you to use your imagination? What events occurred as a result?*

- **People:** *Who are the main characters of your narrative? What specific words describe their personalities? How did they respond to the events you are describing?*

Study the Launch Text to identify ways in which the writer uses details to make the people, setting, and events come alive.

Identify the Conflict A successful narrative centers around a clear conflict. Narrow your focus by identifying a specific conflict you will explore in your nonfiction story. To do so, ask yourself these questions:

- What did I want? Why did I have to find another way to get it? Who or what was getting in the way?

- How did using my imagination help me overcome this obstacle?

STANDARDS

Writing
Write narratives to develop real or imagined experiences or events using effective technique, relevant descriptive details, and well-structured event sequences.
  b. Use narrative techniques, such as dialogue, pacing, and description, to develop experiences, events, and/or characters

  d. Use precise language and domain-specific vocabulary to inform about or explain the topic.

Drafting

Organize a Sequence of Events Narratives are often organized in **chronological order**, so that one event leads to the next in the order in which they actually happened. Use the organizer to list the events of your story in chronological order. Fill out the "First" line and the "Next" lines. Add more lines, if necessary.

CHRONOLOGICAL SEQUENCE OF EVENTS
1. First:
2. Next:
3. Next:
4. Next:
5. Next:

Signal Shifts Think about places in your story where the sequence of events might be more complicated. Consider these questions:

- Does the story start out in one setting and move to another?
- Does a new person enter the story?
- Does something happen either before or after the main events?

Time-order transitions, such a *first, then, next, earlier,* and *later* can help you establish a clear order of events. **Spatial-order transitions** such as *in front of, in the distance, beyond,* and *nearby* can help you make settings clearer. Determine which transition words to use, and where in your narrative to use them.

Write a First Draft Use your chronological list as a guide as you draft your story. Add an introduction in which you describe the setting and people involved. Add a conclusion in which you reflect on what the experiences you describe meant to you or what you learned from them.

Copyright © SAVVAS Learning Company LLC. All Rights Reserved.

STANDARDS

Writing

Write narratives to develop real or imagined experiences or events using effective technique, relevant descriptive details, and well-structured event sequences.

a. Engage and orient the reader by establishing a context and introducing a narrator and/or characters; organize an event sequence that unfolds naturally and logically.

c. Use a variety of transition words, phrases, and clauses to convey sequence and signal shifts from one time frame or setting to another.

e. Provide a conclusion that follow from the narrated experiences or events.

LANGUAGE DEVELOPMENT

Author's Style: Voice

Voice A writer's **voice** is the personality that comes through his or her language. It is the quality that makes your writing sound like you. These literary elements help to create a writer's voice:

- **Word Choice:** the words a writer chooses
- **Sentence Structure:** the way the writer constructs sentences
- **Tone:** the writer's attitude toward the subject

Read It

This chart identifies some of the elements that create the voice of the author of the Launch Text.

Vivid Words	*jolted awake by a ripping sound*
Short and Long Sentences	• *That doesn't stop me.* • *He always came up with these unique creations, beautifully conceived and executed.*
Casual Tone	*"Nope," I tell her.*

Write It

Ask yourself the following questions to help develop your voice.

- Am I using words with which I am comfortable, even as I try to stretch my vocabulary?
- Do my descriptions really show how I see things?
- Does my writing seem true and authentic?

Also, make sure to consider your readers by varying your sentence structures. For example, avoid beginning too many sentences with the word *I*. Instead, develop your voice by trying out different types of sentences. The chart shows some options.

ORIGINAL	HOW TO ADD VARIETY	REVISION
I was happy to see my father at the airport.	Start your sentence with a word that describes your emotion or mood.	Delighted, I watched my father emerge from behind the sliding glass door into the baggage claim area.
I excitedly waved to him as soon as he noticed me.	Move another part of the sentence to the beginning.	As soon as he noticed me, I excitedly waved to him.
He told me he had some good news to share with me.	Start with a direct quotation instead of writing that someone said something.	"Katie," he started, "I've been waiting all week to tell you this."

> **TIP**
>
> **STYLE**
> Use sensory language to make your descriptions come alive. Don't just tell readers that a noise was loud—use precise words to show them.

STANDARDS

Writing
Write narratives to develop real or imagined experiences or events using effective technique, relevant descriptive details, and well-structured event sequences.

  d. Use precise words and phrases, relevant descriptive details, and sensory language to convey experiences and events.

Language
Use knowledge of language and its conventions when writing, speaking, reading, or listening.

  a. Vary sentence patterns for meaning, reader/listener interest, and style.

Revising

Evaluating Your Draft

Use the following checklist to evaluate the effectiveness of your first draft. Then, use the checklist and the instruction on this page to guide your revision.

FOCUS AND ORGANIZATION	EVIDENCE AND ELABORATION	CONVENTIONS
☐ Provides an introduction that establishes the setting and introduces the people being described.	☐ Effectively uses narrative techniques, such as dialogue, pacing, and description.	☐ Is free of grammar and spelling errors.
☐ Presents a clear chronological sequence of events that are linked by a variety of transitions.	☐ Uses descriptive details, sensory language, and precise words and phrases.	☐ Uses a variety of sentence lengths and avoids beginning too many sentences with *I*.
☐ Provides a conclusion that follows from the events and experiences in the narrative.	☐ Establishes the writer's voice through word choice, sentence structure, and tone.	

Copyright © SAVVAS Learning Company LLC. All Rights Reserved.

WORD NETWORK

Include words from your Word Network in your narrative.

STANDARDS

Writing
Write narratives to develop real or imagined experiences or events using effective technique, relevant descriptive details, and well-structured event sequences.

b. Use narrative techniques, such as dialogue, pacing, and description, to develop experiences, events, and/or characters.

d. Use precise words and phrases, relevant descriptive details, and sensory language to convey experiences and events.

e. Provide a conclusion that follows from the narrated experiences or events.

Revising for Evidence and Elaboration

Add Narrative Techniques Scan your draft and note places where the story seems dull. Bring those sections to life by using dialogue or pacing.

- **Dialogue** refers to spoken conversations in a text. Find explanations in your narrative that would be more exciting as dialogue. Make sure your dialogue accurately reflects what people really said. Use quotation marks to set off dialogue from the rest of the text.

- **Pacing** is the sense of speed with which a story moves forward. Look for places where a series of short sentences would speed up the action. Use longer, descriptive sentences to show a person or setting.

Use Precise Language To write a lively narrative that holds your readers' interest, avoid vague words and phrases that leave the reader with questions such as *What kind? How? In what way? How often?* and *To what extent?* As you review and revise your work, replace vague words with precise words that convey your ideas more vividly and accurately. Here are some examples:

Instead of...

noun: stuff	*use*	toys, postcards, t-shirts
verb: said	*use*	exclaimed, shouted, asked
adjective: nice	*use*	friendly, generous, kind
adverb: slowly	*use*	lazily, casually, carefully

PEER REVIEW

Exchange narratives with a classmate. Use the checklist to evaluate your classmate's narrative and provide supportive feedback.

1. Are the setting and people developed using descriptive details?

☐ yes ☐ no   If no, suggest how the writer can revise to strengthen his or her descriptions.

2. Is there a clear sequence of events that is clarified by transitions?

☐ yes ☐ no   If no, explain what confused you.

3. Does the narrative end with a memorable conclusion that reflects on the experiences described in the narrative?

☐ yes ☐ no   If no, tell the writer what you think might be missing.

4. What is the strongest part of your classmate's narrative? Why?

_____

_____

Editing and Proofreading

Edit for Conventions Reread your draft, and correct errors in grammar and word usage. Be sure you have included a variety of sentence types.

Proofread for Accuracy As you proofread, make sure that any dialogue is enclosed in quotation marks. Refer to the Launch Text for examples of how to punctuate dialogue.

Publishing and Presenting

Create a final version of your narrative in a digital format. Use a class or school Web site, a class whiteboard, or email to share and comment on other classmates' narratives. As you comment, consider the ways in which your narratives are similar and different. Remember to be polite and respectful when commenting on the work of others.

Reflecting

Reflect on what you learned as you wrote your narrative. How did writing about a personal experience help you better understand its significance? What was the hardest part of this assignment? What did you learn from reviewing the work of others?

▤ STANDARDS

Writing
• Produce clear and coherent writing in which the development, organization, and style are appropriate to task, purpose, and audience.
• With some guidance and support from peers and adults, develop and strengthen writing as needed by planning, revising, editing, rewriting, or trying a new approach.
• Use technology, including the Internet, to produce and publish writing as well as to interact and collaborate with others; demonstrate sufficient command of keyboarding skills to type a minimum of three pages in a single sitting.

ESSENTIAL QUESTION:

What are some of the challenges and triumphs of growing up?

Growing up isn't always easy. Some challenges are difficult to overcome, but learning how to persevere through hardships is a triumph in itself. It is a triumph because every new experience is a lesson learned. You will work in a group to continue your exploration of some of these challenges and triumphs.

Small-Group Learning Strategies

Throughout your life, in school, in your community, and in your career, you will continue to learn and work with others.

Review these strategies and the actions you can take to practice them as you work in teams. Add ideas of your own for each step. Use these strategies during Small-Group Learning.

STRATEGY	ACTION PLAN
Prepare	• Complete your assignments so that you are prepared for group work. • Organize your thinking so you can contribute to your group's discussion. •
Participate fully	• Make eye contact to signal that you are listening and taking in what is being said. • Use text evidence when making a point. •
Support others	• Build on ideas from others in your group. • Invite others who have not yet spoken to do so. •
Clarify	• Paraphrase the ideas of others to ensure that your understanding is correct. • Ask follow-up questions. •

SCAN FOR
MULTIMEDIA

CONTENTS

PERFORMANCE TASK

SPEAKING AND LISTENING FOCUS

Present a Retelling

After reading the selections, your group will plan and deliver a retelling of the childhood experiences explored in one of the selections. You will enhance your retelling with multimedia.

Working as a Team

1. **Take a Position** In your group, discuss the following question:

   What ideas and experiences about growing up can young people share with one another?

   As you take turns sharing your ideas, be sure to provide reasons and examples. After all group members have shared, discuss the ideas and what they mean to you.

2. **List Your Rules** As a group, decide on the rules that you will follow as you work together. Two samples are provided. Add two more of your own. You may add or revise rules based on your experience together.

   - Everyone should participate in group discussions.
   - People should not interrupt.

   - _____

     _____

   - _____

     _____

3. **Apply the Rules** Share what you have learned about growing up. Make sure each person in the group contributes. Take notes and be prepared to share with the class one thing that you heard from another member of your group.

4. **Name Your Group** Choose a name that reflects the unit topic.

   Our group's name: _____

5. **Create a Communication Plan** Decide how you want to communicate with one another. For example, you might use online collaboration tools, email, or instant messaging.

   Our group's decision: _____

   _____

Making a Schedule

First, find out the due dates for the Small-Group activities. Then, preview the texts and activities with your group and make a schedule for completing the tasks.

SELECTION	ACTIVITIES	DUE DATE
Declaration of the Rights of the Child		
Michaela DePrince: The War Orphan Who Became a Ballerina		
from Bad Boy		
I Was a Skinny Tomboy Kid		

Working on Group Projects

Different projects require different roles. As your group works together, you'll find it more effective if each person has a specific role. Before beginning a project, discuss the necessary roles, and choose one for each group member. Here are some possible roles; add your own ideas.

Project Manager: monitors the schedule and keeps everyone on task

Researcher: organizes research activities

Recorder: takes notes during group meetings

_____

_____

_____

_____

_____

_____

_____

SCAN FOR
MULTIMEDIA

Declaration of the Rights of the Child

Concept Vocabulary

As you perform your first read, you will encounter these words.

entitled	enactment	compulsory

Base Words If these words are unfamiliar, look for base words you know. Use your knowledge of the "inside" word, along with context, to determine meaning. Here is an example of how to apply the strategy.

Unfamiliar Word: *complimentary*

Context: She made **complimentary** remarks about the <u>tasty</u> food.

Familiar "Inside" Word: *compliment*, meaning "something good to say about someone or something"

Conclusion: The food was tasty, which is a good thing. *Complimentary* may mean "expressing good comments."

Confirm: Use a dictionary to verify the meaning you infer.

Apply your knowledge of base words and other vocabulary strategies to determine the meanings of unfamiliar words you encounter during your first read.

First Read NONFICTION

Apply these strategies as you conduct your first read. You will have an opportunity to complete a close read after your first read.

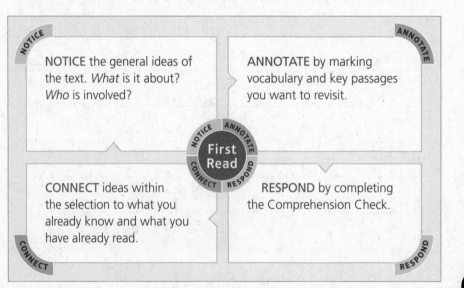

NOTICE the general ideas of the text. *What* is it about? *Who* is involved?

ANNOTATE by marking vocabulary and key passages you want to revisit.

CONNECT ideas within the selection to what you already know and what you have already read.

RESPOND by completing the Comprehension Check.

First Read

Copyright © SAVVAS Learning Company LLC. All Rights Reserved.

☰ STANDARDS

Reading Informational Text
By the end of the year, read and comprehend literary nonfiction in the grades 6–8 text complexity band proficiently, with scaffolding as needed at the high end of the range.

Language
Determine or clarify the meaning of unknown and multiple-meaning words and phrases based on *grade 6 reading and content*, choosing flexibly from a range of strategies.

Declaration of the Rights of the Child

The United Nations General Assembly

BACKGROUND

In the late nineteenth century, many countries began to officially recognize that children need special legal protection. The Declaration of the Rights of the Child, which was adopted by the United Nations in 1959, is the first major international agreement on children's rights. It was inspired by the original declaration written by Eglantyne Jebb, a British activist.

SCAN FOR MULTIMEDIA

1   THIS DECLARATION OF THE RIGHTS OF THE CHILD to the end that he may have a happy childhood and enjoy for his own good and for the good of society the rights and freedoms herein set forth, and calls upon parents, upon men and women as individuals, and upon voluntary organizations, local authorities and national governments to recognize these rights and strive for their observance by legislative and other measures progressively taken in accordance[1] with the following principles:

2   The child shall enjoy all the rights set forth in this Declaration. Every child, without any exception whatsoever, shall be **entitled** to these rights, without distinction or discrimination on account of race, color, sex, language, religion, political or other opinion, national or social origin, property, birth or other status, whether of himself or of his family.

NOTES

Mark base words or indicate another strategy you used that helped you determine meaning. Confirm the definition by consulting a dictionary.

entitled (ehn TY tuhld) *v.*

MEANING:

---

1. **accordance** (uh KAWRD uhns) *n.* agreement.

3   The child shall enjoy special protection, and shall be given opportunities and facilities,[2] by law and by other means, to enable him to develop physically, mentally, morally, spiritually and socially in a healthy and normal manner and in conditions of freedom and dignity. In the **enactment** of laws for this purpose, the best interests of the child shall be the paramount consideration.

4   The child shall be entitled from his birth to a name and a nationality.

5   The child shall enjoy the benefits of social security. He shall be entitled to grow and develop in health; to this end, special care and protection shall be provided both to him and to his mother, including adequate pre-natal and post-natal care.[3] The child shall have the right to adequate nutrition, housing, recreation and medical services.

6   The child who is physically, mentally or socially handicapped shall be given the special treatment, education and care required by his particular condition.

7   The child, for the full and harmonious development of his personality, needs love and understanding. He shall, wherever possible, grow up in the care and under the responsibility of his parents, and, in any case, in an atmosphere of affection and of moral and material security; a child of tender years shall not, save in exceptional circumstances, be separated from his mother. Society and the public authorities shall have the duty to extend particular care to children without a family and to those without adequate means of support. Payment of State and other assistance towards the maintenance of children of large families is desirable.

8   The child is entitled to receive education, which shall be free and **compulsory**, at least in the elementary stages. He shall be given an education which will promote his general culture and enable him, on a basis of equal opportunity, to develop his abilities, his individual judgment, and his sense of moral and social responsibility, and to become a useful member of society. The best interests of the child shall be the guiding principle of those responsible for his education and guidance; that responsibility lies in the first place with his parents. The child shall have full opportunity for play and recreation, which should be

---

2. **facilities** (fuh SIHL uh teez) *n*. buildings designed for a specific purpose.
3. **pre-natal and post-natal care** care given to women before and after the birth of a child.

directed to the same purposes as education; society and the public authorities shall endeavor to promote the enjoyment of this right.

9   The child shall in all circumstances be among the first to receive protection and relief.

10   The child shall be protected against all forms of neglect, cruelty and exploitation. He shall not be the subject of traffic, in any form. The child shall not be admitted to employment before an appropriate minimum age; he shall in no case be caused or permitted to engage in any occupation or employment which would prejudice his health or education, or interfere with his physical, mental or moral development.

11   The child shall be protected from practices which may foster racial, religious and any other form of discrimination. He shall be brought up in a spirit of understanding, tolerance, friendship among peoples, peace and universal brotherhood, and in full consciousness[4] that his energy and talents should be devoted to the service of his fellow men. ❧

_____

4. **consciousness** (KON shuhs nihs) *n.* awareness or understanding.

Comprehension Check

Complete the following items after you finish your first read. Review and clarify details with your group.

1. Which children are entitled to the rights this document sets forth?

2. Identify two rights defined or described in this document.

3. According to the document, what should children who are physically or mentally disabled be given?

RESEARCH

Research to Clarify Choose at least one unfamiliar detail from the text. Briefly research that detail. In what way does the information you learned shed light on an aspect of the Declaration?

DECLARATION OF THE RIGHTS
OF THE CHILD

GROUP DISCUSSION

When your group rereads paragraph 8, read it aloud, with each person taking turns to read one sentence. Doing so may give you a stronger sense of what the writers of the document had in mind.

WORD NETWORK

Add words related to childhood from the text to your Word Network.

STANDARDS

Reading Informational Text
• Analyze in detail how a key individual, event, or idea is introduced, illustrated, and elaborated in a text.
• Analyze how a particular sentence, paragraph, chapter, or section fits into the overall structure of a text and contributes to the development of the ideas.
Language
Determine or clarify the meaning of unknown and multiple-meaning words and phrases based on *grade 6 reading and content,* choosing flexibly from a range of strategies.
  b. Use common, grade-appropriate Greek or Latin affixes and roots as a clue to the meaning of a word or phrase.

Close Read the Text

With your group, revisit sections of the text you marked during your first read. **Annotate** details that you notice. What **questions** do you have? What can you **conclude**?

Analyze the Text

CITE TEXTUAL EVIDENCE
to support your answers.

Notebook Complete the activities.

1. **Review and Clarify** With your group, reread paragraph 8 of the Declaration. Discuss the kind of education to which all children are entitled, according to the document. What did the UN General Assembly hope education would accomplish for children?

2. **Present and Discuss** Now, work with your group to share passages from the selection that you found especially important. Take turns presenting your passages. Discuss what you noticed in the selection, what questions you asked, and what conclusions you reached.

3. **Essential Question:** *What are some of the challenges and triumphs of growing up?* What has this text taught you about childhood? Discuss with your group.

LANGUAGE DEVELOPMENT

Concept Vocabulary

entitled	enactment	compulsory

Why These Words? The concept vocabulary words from the text are related. With your group, determine what the words have in common. Write your ideas, and add another word that fits the category.

Practice

Notebook Check your understanding of the concept vocabulary words by using them in sentences. In each sentence, provide context clues that hint at the vocabulary word's meaning.

Word Study

Notebook **Latin Root: -*puls*-** The Declaration states that education for children should be free and compulsory. The word *compulsory* is formed from the Latin root -*puls*- (also spelled -*pel*-), which means "push," "drive," or "force." Write a definition of *compulsory* that shows how the root -*puls*- contributes to its meaning. Find another word formed from this root. Write the word and its meaning.

Analyze Craft and Structure

Development of Ideas: Structure The Declaration of the Rights of the Child expresses its ideas using a simple structure. Paragraph 1 explains the purpose and goal of the Declaration. Paragraph 2 explains the scope of the Declaration, or the people and rights that it covers. Paragraphs 3–11 list and describe specific rights.

CITE TEXTUAL EVIDENCE to support your answers.

Practice

Notebook Work together to answer the questions and complete the activities.

1. Reread paragraph 1. What are the purpose and goal of the Declaration?

2. Reread paragraph 2. Whose rights does the Declaration set forth?

3. Choose three paragraphs from paragraphs 3–11. In the chart, identify the paragraphs you have chosen. List the rights that each paragraph describes. Then, state whether you think the rights are described in a way that is confusing or clear. Explain why.

PARAGRAPH	RIGHTS LISTED	CLEAR OR CONFUSING? WHY?

4. As a group, discuss whether the text is organized effectively. Would the issues being presented have been clearer or more powerful if statistics, charts, or personal stories had been included? Why or why not?

5. Why do you think the United Nations General Assembly organized the information in this way? Discuss with your group. Come to an agreement about at least two reasons. Write them here.

DECLARATION OF THE RIGHTS
OF THE CHILD

Conventions

Pronoun Case Effective writing involves correct usage of pronouns. A **pronoun** is a word that takes the place of one or more nouns or other pronouns. **Pronoun case** is the form a pronoun takes to show whether it is being used as a subject, an object, or a possessive. Writers use pronouns to avoid repetition of nouns in their writing, and the case they use depends on the pronoun's function in a sentence.

There are three pronoun cases, as shown in the chart.

PRONOUN CASE	EXAMPLES
Nominative (or **Subjective**) **Case:** names the subject of a verb or is used in the predicate after a linking verb nominative pronouns: I, you, he, she, it, we, you, they	He likes the sound of the train on the tracks. They searched online for the article. The singers of the duet will be she and I.
Objective Case: names the direct object of a verb, the indirect object of a verb, or the object of a preposition objective pronous: me, you, him, her, it, us, you, them	Domingo sent it to Mel. Please give me the earrings. The cafeteria chefs had prepared a meal for us.
Possessive Case: shows ownership possessive pronouns: my, your, his, her, its, our, their, mine, yours, hers, ours, theirs	After an hour of running, my legs ached. Please stick out your tongue for the doctor. Theo works during his summer breaks.

Read It

1. Mark the pronouns in each sentence. Label the case of each pronoun.

   a. Children are not responsible for their own education.

   b. When a child is born, he or she will be entitled to special human rights.

   c. Children are important, and we protect them from discrimination.

   d. The child shall be entitled from his birth to a name and a nationality.

Write It

📓 **Notebook** Read the example. Notice that the underlined text has been replaced with a pronoun. Do the same for the sentences in items 1–3.

> **Original:** The writer of the first declaration is Eglantyne Jebb.
>
> **Revision:** The writer of the first declaration is **she.**

1. Eglantyne Jebb's goal was to help children.

2. As a result, Eglantyne Jebb founded an organization.

3. The name of the organization is Save the Children.

📋 **STANDARDS**

Language
Demonstrate command of the conventions of standard English grammar and usage when writing or speaking.
a. Ensure that pronouns are in the proper case.

Writing to Sources

Assignment

Choose one of the options and write a response. If necessary, conduct brief research to support or develop your ideas. Work with your group to discuss and plan, but do your own writing.

☐ **Option 1:** Write an **informational article** that describes the purposes for which the Declaration of the Rights of the Child was written. What do you think the writers wanted to achieve? Make sure readers understand the main ideas of the Declaration by including a summary.

☐ **Option 2:** Choose two of the rights listed in the Declaration that you feel are most important. Then, write a brief **essay** in which you explain the reasons for your choices. Why do these rights matter matter so much? Include details from the text as well as your own opinions and any examples you might find through research.

Project Plan Before you begin, meet as a group to discuss each student's choice of project and to share ideas. Go back to the Declaration and work together to clarify any sections that might be confusing. Then, work independently to write.

Finding Examples Choose passages from the Declaration that clearly support your ideas. Make sure you quote them accurately. Use a chart like this one to keep track of your examples. Remember to include appropriate citations.

EXAMPLE	IDEA IT SUPPORTS	CITATION INFORMATION

Present Organize a brief presentation in which you explain the different main ideas each member of your group expressed. Share your presentation with the class.

EVIDENCE LOG

Before moving on to a new selection, go to your Evidence Log and record what you learned from the Declaration of the Rights of the Child.

STANDARDS

Writing
Write informative/explanatory texts to examine a topic and convey ideas, concepts, and information through the selection, organization, and analysis of relevant content.

About the Author

William Kremer is a feature writer at the British Broadcasting Corporation (BBC), a major radio, television, and media company.

Michaela DePrince: The War Orphan Who Became a Ballerina

Concept Vocabulary

As you perform your first read of "Michaela DePrince: The War Orphan Who Became a Ballerina," you will encounter these words.

antagonism	refugee	distraught

Context Clues To find the meaning of an unfamiliar word, look for **context clues**—other words and phrases that appear nearby in the text. There are various types of context clues that can help you as you read.

> **Context:** Rather than wearing **leotards** during dance class, she covered herself with sweatshirts.
>
> **Conclusion:** The girl covers herself with sweatshirts instead of leotards during dance class. *Leotards* must be another type of clothing. Perhaps they are a type of clothing worn by dancers in particular.

Apply your knowledge of context clues and other vocabulary strategies to determine the meanings of unfamiliar words you encounter during your first read.

First Read NONFICTION

Apply these strategies as you conduct your first read. You will have an opportunity to complete a close read after your first read.

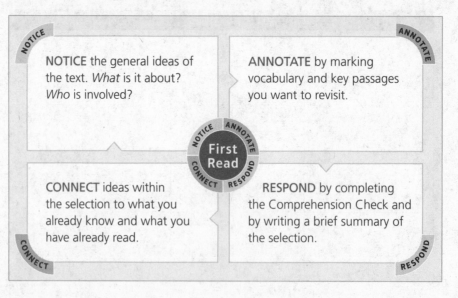

NOTICE the general ideas of the text. *What* is it about? *Who* is involved?

ANNOTATE by marking vocabulary and key passages you want to revisit.

CONNECT ideas within the selection to what you already know and what you have already read.

RESPOND by completing the Comprehension Check and by writing a brief summary of the selection.

First Read

NOTICE · ANNOTATE · CONNECT · RESPOND

:≡ STANDARDS

Reading Informational Text
By the end of the year, read and comprehend literary nonfiction in the grades 6–8 text complexity band proficiently, with scaffolding as needed at the high end of the range.

Language
Determine or clarify the meaning of unknown and multiple-meaning words and phrases based on *grade 6 reading and content*, choosing flexibly from a range of strategies.
  a. Use context as a clue to the meaning of a word or phrase.

Michaela DePrince:

The War Orphan Who Became a Ballerina

William Kremer

BACKGROUND

From 1991 to 2002, Sierra Leone went through a violent civil war. During this decade, life in Sierra Leone was extremely dangerous due to a near complete lack of law in the country. Tens of thousands of people lost their lives, and countless families were torn apart. Children who lost their parents during the war became known as "war orphans."

SCAN FOR
MULTIMEDIA

NOTES

1   A professional stage debut is a huge event in the life of any ballerina, but Michaela DePrince's recent tour of South Africa also marked the end of an extraordinary journey from her childhood as a war orphan in Sierra Leone.

2   "I got out of a terrible place," says DePrince. "I had no idea I would be here—I'm living my dream every single day."

3   She was born in Sierra Leone in 1995. Her parents named her Mabinty, but after they both died during the civil war, she was sent to an orphanage, where she became a number.

antagonism (an TAG uh nihz uhm) *n.*

MEANING:

4   "They named us from one to 27," she recalls. "One was the favorite child of the orphanage and 27 was the least favorite."

5   DePrince was number 27, because she suffers from vitiligo, a condition in which patches of skin lose pigmentation.[1] To the "Aunties" who ran the orphanage, it was evidence of the evil spirit within the three-year-old. She still recalls the fierce **antagonism** of the women.

6   "They thought of me as a devil's child. They told me every day how I wasn't going to get adopted, because nobody would want a devil's child," she says.

7   Although the other girls in the orphanage were encouraged not to play with her, DePrince formed a close friendship with child number 26, also called Mabinty, who was disliked by the Aunties because she was left-handed.

8   The pair shared a sleeping mat. At night, when Michaela had bad dreams, her "mat-mate" would soothe her with kind words and stories.

*   *   *

9   Her memories of early childhood are fragmentary—moments of piercing clarity which have been reassembled in date order. She believes it was soon after witnessing the killing of her teacher that she stumbled upon something that was to shape the rest of her life—a discarded magazine.

10   "There was a lady on it, she was on her tippy-toes, in this pink, beautiful tutu. I had never seen anything like this—a costume that stuck out with glitter on it, with just so much beauty. I could just see the beauty in that person and the hope and the love and just everything that I didn't have.

11   "And I just thought: 'Wow! This is what I want to be.'"

12   DePrince ripped the photograph out of the magazine and, for the lack of anywhere else to keep it, stuffed the treasured scrap in her underwear.

13   One day, the orphanage was warned it would be bombed and the children were marched to a distant **refugee** camp. Here DePrince learned that her beloved mat-mate was to be adopted.

14   An American woman, Elaine DePrince, had come to the camp to adopt child number 26, now called Mia. For a moment, Michaela was **distraught** because she believed that all the other children would be taken to new homes and she would be left behind.

refugee (rehf yoo JEE) *n.*

MEANING:

distraught (dihs TRAWT) *adj.*

MEANING:

---

1. **pigmentation** (pihg muhn TAY shuhn) *n.* natural coloring.

15 But abruptly there was a change of plan. When the Aunties told Elaine DePrince that Michaela was unlikely to find another home, she decided to adopt both girls.

16 Michaela remembers struggling to understand what was happening. She was intoxicated[2] by the American woman with her dazzling blonde hair, but there was something else on her mind too.

17 "I was looking at people's feet because I thought: 'Everyone has to have [ballet] pointe shoes, they have to have pointe shoes because these are people from the US!'"

18 Not only was Elaine not wearing any pointe shoes, but as Michaela found when she looked through her suitcase that night, she had none in her luggage either.

19 Her new mother quickly noticed Michaela's obsession with ballet.

20 "We found a *Nutcracker*[3] video and I watched it 150 times," Michaela says.

21 When they finally went to see a stage performance, she was able to point out to her mother the places where dancers had missed their steps.

22 Elaine enrolled five-year-old Michaela in the Rock School of Dance in Philadelphia, making the 45-minute drive from New Jersey every day.

23 But DePrince remained a shy girl, painfully self-conscious of her vitiligo. "That was all I would think about when I was on stage. I had trouble looking at myself in the mirror," she says.

24 Instead of glorying in the glittery tutus and bodices that had drawn her to ballet, she covered herself up whenever possible with turtleneck sweaters.

25 One day, DePrince asked one of her ballet teachers if she thought her skin condition might hold back her career. The teacher asked her what she was talking about. She hadn't even noticed the pale patches on her skin—she'd just been watching her steps. That was a significant moment for her.

26 But, she says, being a black ballet dancer is hard, even in the US. She thinks the problem is that in the corps de ballet—the group of ballerinas who are not soloists—girls are supposed to look the same.

---

2. **intoxicated** (ihn TOK sih kay tihd) *adj.* overwhelmed and excited.
3. **[The] Nutcracker** popular ballet with music by the famous Russian composer Peter Illyich Tchaikovsyk (1840–1893).

27 "It is a challenge," she says. "If you look at [ballet] companies you won't really see any black girls. You might see a mixed-race girl but there are only one or two black soloists in the whole U.S."

28 Now 17, DePrince recently completed a tour with the Dance Theater of Harlem, many of whose dancers are African American, or mixed-race.

29 "I have become more upbeat—I used to be very shy," she says.

30 "Now I've grown up and I'm so happy with the way things are turning out." ❧

MEDIA CONNECTION

Michaela DePrince—Ballet Dancer

◉ Discuss It How does viewing this video add to your understanding of the difficulties Michaela faced as a child?

Write your response before sharing your ideas.

SCAN FOR
MULTIMEDIA

Comprehension Check

Complete the following items after you finish your first read. Review and clarify details with your group.

1. Why did the Aunties at the orphanage dislike Michaela?

2. How did Michaela first learn about ballet and ballerinas?

3. How did Michaela finally leave the orphanage?

4. 📓 **Notebook** Confirm your understanding of the selection by writing a brief summary of what happened to Michaela after she left the orphanage.

RESEARCH

Research to Clarify Choose at least one unfamiliar detail from the text. Briefly research that detail. In what way does the information you learned shed light on an aspect of the article?

MICHAELA DEPRINCE:
THE WAR ORPHAN WHO
BECAME A BALLERINA

GROUP DISCUSSION

As you discuss the article, make sure everyone in your group has a chance to speak. Take turns expressing your ideas.

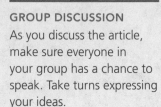 **WORD NETWORK**

Add words related to childhood from the text to your Word Network.

STANDARDS

Language
• Determine or clarify the meaning of unknown and multiple-meaning words and phrases based on *grade 6 reading and content,* choosing flexibly from a range of strategies.
  c. Consult reference materials, both print and digital, to find the pronunciation of a word or determine or clarify its precise meaning or its part of speech.
  d. Verify the preliminary determination of the meaning of a word or phrases.
• Demonstrate understanding of figurative language, word relationships, and nuances in word meanings.
  b. Use the relationship between particular words to better understand each of the words.

Close Read the Text

With your group, revisit sections of the text you marked during your first read. **Annotate** details that you notice. What **questions** do you have? What can you **conclude**?

Analyze the Text

CITE TEXTUAL EVIDENCE to support your answers.

📓 **Notebook** Complete the activities.

1. **Review and Clarify** With your group, reread paragraph 17 of the selection. Why do you think Michaela thought that everyone from the United States had to have pointe shoes? What does this tell you about Michaela and her ideas about the United States?

2. **Present and Discuss** Now, work with your group to share passages from the selection that you found especially important. Take turns presenting your passages. Discuss what you noticed in the selection, what questions you asked, and what conclusions you reached.

3. **Essential Question:** *What are some of the challenges and triumphs of growing up?* What has this article taught you about challenges that some children face and how they overcome them? Discuss with your group.

LANGUAGE DEVELOPMENT

Concept Vocabulary

antagonism	refugee	distraught

Why These Words? The concept vocabulary words from the text are related. With your group, determine what the words have in common. Write your ideas and add another word that fits the category.

Practice

📓 **Notebook** Check your understanding of the concept vocabulary words by using them in a paragraph. Include context clues that hint at each word's meaning. Share and discuss your paragraph with your group.

Word Study

📓 **Notebook Synonyms and Antonyms** One way to better understand a word is to find **synonyms**, or words that have a same or similar meaning, and **antonyms**, words that have an opposite meaning. For example, one synonym of *antagonism* is *hostility*. One antonym is *friendship*.

Using a dictionary, determine and verify the precise meaning of *antagonism*. Then, find two more synonyms and two more antonyms for *antagonism* in a thesaurus. Write a sentence for each word you find.

Analyze Craft and Structure

Biographical Writing When a nonfiction text tells a story, it is a work of **narrative nonfiction.** Biographical writing is one type of narrative nonfiction. In **biographical writing,** an author tells the story of another person's life. This type of writing has specific features:

- The subject is a real-life person. The work presents facts and actual events from the subject's life.
- The writer uses **direct quotations,** or the subject's exact words, to show his or her thoughts and feelings.
- The writer may describe other people's views of the subject. He or she may use quotations from people who know the subject well.

Authors of biographies use these elements to develop a portrait in words and to tell the story of the person about whom they are writing.

Practice

CITE TEXTUAL EVIDENCE to support your answers.

🔲 **Notebook** Work independently to answer the questions and complete the activity. Then, share and discuss your responses with your group.

1. (a) What information about Michaela DePrince does the writer include in paragraphs 1 and 2? (b) Why might this information interest readers in her story?

2. Use the chart to identify examples of each element of biographical writing used in paragraphs 2–8. Explain how the author uses each item to add to the reader's understanding of DePrince.

ELEMENT OF BIOGRAPHY	EXAMPLES	READER'S UNDERSTANDING
Facts		
Actual Events		
Direct Quotations		
Other People's Views		

3. (a) What turning point, or major change, does the author describe in paragraph 10? (b) Why is this moment so important to DePrince? (c) What other moment described in the biography is a turning point in DePrince's life? Explain your choice.

4. (a) Describe the struggles DePrince faced after she started studying ballet. (b) Cite specific examples of a fact, an actual event, and a direct quotation that help readers understand those struggles.

STANDARDS
Reading Informational Text
• Analyze in detail how a key individual, event, or idea is introduced, illustrated, and elaborated in a text.
• Analyze how a particular sentence, paragraph, chapter, or section fits into the overall structure of a text and contributes to the development of the ideas.

Michaela DePrince: The War Orphan Who Became a Ballerina **57**

MICHAELA DEPRINCE:
THE WAR ORPHAN WHO
BECAME A BALLERINA

Conventions

Reflexive and Intensive Pronouns A **pronoun** is a word that takes the place of one or more nouns or other pronouns. Reflexive pronouns and intensive pronouns are forms of pronouns that end with *-self* or *-selves*. These pronoun forms look the same, but they function differently within a sentence.

	SINGULAR	PLURAL
First Person	myself	ourselves
Second Person	yourself	yourselves
Third Person	himself, herself, itself	themselves

A **reflexive pronoun** reflects, or directs, the action of a verb back on its subject. It indicates that the person or thing performing the action of the verb is also receiving the action. A reflexive pronoun is essential to the meaning of its sentence.

An **intensive pronoun** simply emphasizes the noun or pronoun to which it refers. It usually appears very close to the noun or pronoun it emphasizes. An intensive pronoun can be removed from a sentence without changing its meaning. In the chart, subjects are underlined and pronouns are set in italics.

EXAMPLES OF REFLEXIVE PRONOUNS	EXAMPLES OF INTENSIVE PRONOUNS
I bought *myself* a new paintbrush.	I *myself* chose the paintbrush I wanted.
Luke made *himself* late for school.	Luke *himself* should have known better.
Emil and Maria were mad at *themselves* for losing the cat.	Emil and Maria *themselves* searched for the lost cat.

Read It

Mark the reflexive or intensive pronoun in each of these passages from "Michaela DePrince: The War Orphan Who Became a Ballerina." Then, write whether the pronoun is reflexive or intensive.

1. "That was all I would think about when I was on stage. I had trouble looking at myself in the mirror," she says.

2. Instead of glorying in the glittery tutus and bodices that had drawn her to ballet, she covered herself up whenever possible with turtleneck sweaters.

Write It

Write three sentences about Michaela DePrince's life using intensive pronouns. Use a different intensive pronoun in each sentence.

STANDARDS

Language
Demonstrate command of the conventions of standard English grammar and usage when writing or speaking.
  b. Use intensive pronouns.

Speaking and Listening

Assignment

With your group, write and deliver an **oral presentation**. Choose from the following options:

☐ **Option 1:** Michaela DePrince talks about the difficulties of being an African American ballerina. Conduct research on another African American dancer. Then, prepare and deliver a **personality profile** of the dancer you chose. Compare and contrast his or her experience with DePrince's. Include descriptive details and a logical sequence of ideas so that the points of comparison and contrast are clear to your audience.

☐ **Option 2:** Becoming a ballet dancer takes hard work and many years of training. Research to learn about the challenges aspiring dancers face. Then, write and deliver an **informative report** in which you talk about why DePrince's success is so impressive. Include facts, descriptive details, and ideas that are ordered in a way that will make sense to readers.

Make an Outline Creating an outline will help your group organize ideas in an order that makes sense. An outline is a list of the main ideas in your presentation. If your group is doing a personality profile, your ideas will be points of comparison and contrast between DePrince and another dancer. If your group is doing an informative report, your ideas will focus on the importance of DePrince's success.

Work with your group to create an outline by using the following structure. Write a sentence for each line of the outline.

I. Thesis Statement: _____

II. Body of Presentation

　A. First Idea: _____

　B. Second Idea: _____

　C. Third Idea: _____

III. Conclusion (Importance of Ideas): _____

Practice and Present Practice your presentation before you deliver it to the class. Use the following tips while delivering your presentation.

- Speak clearly and comfortably without rushing.
- Vary the tone and pitch of your voice to help your audience understand your points and to add interest. Avoid speaking flatly and without emotion.
- Use appropriate and varied body language. Maintain eye contact to keep your audience's attention.

TIP

GROUP DISCUSSION
If your group cannot agree on which project to complete, work together to resolve the issue so that most of the group is happy. Agree beforehand that everyone will go along with the decision.

✐ EVIDENCE LOG

Before moving on to a new selection, go to your Evidence Log and record what you've learned from "Michaela DePrince: The War Orphan Who Became a Ballerina."

☰ STANDARDS

Speaking and Listening
Present claims and findings, sequencing ideas logically and using pertinent descriptions, facts, and details to accentuate main ideas or themes; use appropriate eye contact, adequate volume, and clear pronunciation.

from BAD BOY

Comparing Texts

In this lesson, you will read a memoir excerpt and a poem expressing a similar theme. The work you do with your group on this memoir will prepare you to compare it with the poem.

I WAS A SKINNY
TOMBOY KID

About the Author

By the age of five, **Walter Dean Myers** (1937–2014) was reading daily newspapers. Despite this impressive start with words, Myers did not think writing would be his career. However, in his twenties, he won a writing contest and went on to find success as an author of young adult books. Myers often wrote about his African American heritage and his life growing up in Harlem, a part of New York City.

:::standards-icon::: STANDARDS

Reading Informational Text
By the end of the year, read and comprehend literary nonfiction in the grades 6–8 text complexity band proficiently, with scaffolding as needed at the high end of the range.

Language
Determine or clarify the meaning of unknown and multiple-meaning words and phrases based on *grade 6 reading and content,* choosing flexibly from a range of strategies.
   a. Use context as a clue to the meaning of a word or phrase.

from Bad Boy

Concept Vocabulary

As you perform your first read of the excerpt from *Bad Boy,* you will encounter these words.

> respected   desperate   disgusted

Context Clues To find the meaning of an unfamiliar word, look for **context clues**—other words and phrases that appear nearby in the text. There are various types of context clues that can help you as you read.

> **Context:** Marcus hid the **trove** of baseball cards he'd collected for many years under his bed.
>
> **Conclusion:** Marcus collected baseball cards for many years and hid them. Perhaps *trove* means "valuable, hidden collection."

Apply your knowledge of context clues and other vocabulary strategies to determine the meanings of unfamiliar words you encounter during your first read.

First Read NONFICTION

Apply these strategies as you conduct your first read. You will have an opportunity to complete a close read after your first read.

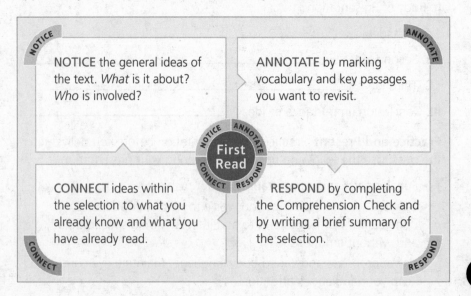

NOTICE the general ideas of the text. *What* is it about? *Who* is involved?

ANNOTATE by marking vocabulary and key passages you want to revisit.

CONNECT ideas within the selection to what you already know and what you have already read.

RESPOND by completing the Comprehension Check and by writing a brief summary of the selection.

from **Bad Boy**

Walter Dean Myers

BACKGROUND

In his memoir, Walter Dean Myers describes his childhood growing up in Harlem, New York, in the 1940s and 1950s. This excerpt takes place when Myers is in elementary school. Earlier in the chapter, his teacher, Mrs. Conway, lent him books to read after noticing his interest in reading.

SCAN FOR
MULTIMEDIA

NOTES

Mark context clues or indicate another strategy you used that helped you determine meaning.

respected (rih SPEHK tihd) *adj.*

MEANING:

1   There were two categories of friends in my life: those with whom I played ball and everyone else. Athletes were highly **respected** in the black community, and boys my age were encouraged to play some sport. I loved playing ball. I would play basketball in the mornings with the boys who were just reaching

their teens, and then stoop ball or punchball on the block with boys my age. Sometimes Eric and I would go down to the courts on Riverside Drive and play there. And I was a bad, bad loser. Most of my prayers, when they weren't for the Dodgers,[1] were quick ones in the middle of a game, asking God to let me win. I liked other sports as well and even followed the New York Rangers hockey team in the papers for a while until I found out that all the references to ice meant just that, that they were skating on ice. There wasn't any ice to skate on in Harlem, so I gave up hockey.

2   With school out and me not having access to Mrs. Conway's cache[2] of books, I rediscovered the George Bruce Branch of the public library on 125th Street. Sometimes on rainy days I would sit in the library and read. The librarians always suggested books that were too young for me, but I still went on a regular basis. I could never have afforded to buy the books and was pleased to have the library with its free supply.

3   Being a boy meant to me that I was not particularly like girls. Most of the girls I knew couldn't play ball, and that excluded them from most of what I wanted to do with my life. Dorothy Dodson, daughter of the Wicked Witch,[3] read books, and I knew she did, but she couldn't stand me and was more than happy to tell me so on a number of occasions. Sometimes I would see other children on the trolley with books under their arms and suspected that they were like me somehow. I felt a connection with these readers but didn't know what the connection was. I knew there were things going on in my head, a fantasy life, that somehow corresponded to the books I read. I also felt a kind of comfort with books that I did not experience when I was away from them. Away from books I was, at times, almost **desperate** to fill up the spaces of my life. Books filled those spaces for me.

4   As much as I enjoyed reading, in the world in which I was living it had to be a secret vice.[4] When I brought a book home from the library, I would sometimes run into older kids who would tease me about my reading. It was, they made it clear, not what boys did. And though by now I was fighting older boys and didn't mind that one bit, for some reason I didn't want to fight about books. Books were special and said something about me that I didn't want to reveal. I began taking a brown paper bag to the library to bring my books home in.

Mark context clues or indicate another strategy you used that helped you determine meaning.

desperate (DEHS puhr iht) *adj.*

MEANING:

---

1. **Dodgers** Brooklyn Dodgers, an American professional baseball team, which moved to Los Angeles, California, after the 1957 season.
2. **cache** (kash) *n.* hidden supply.
3. **Wicked Witch** Walter's nickname for Mrs. Dodson, a neighbor he dislikes.
4. **vice** (vys) *n.* bad habit.

5   That year I learned that being a boy meant that I was supposed to do certain things and act in a certain way. I was very comfortable being a boy, but there were times when the role was uncomfortable. We often played ball in the church gym, and one rainy day, along with my brother Mickey and some of "my guys," I went to the gym, only to find a bevy of girls exercising on one half of the court. We wanted to run a full-court game, so we directed a few nasty remarks to the other side of the small gym. Then we saw that the girls were doing some kind of dance, so we imitated them, cracking ourselves up.

6   When the girls had finished their dancing, they went through some stretching exercises. A teenager, Lorelle Henry, was leading the group, and she was pretty, so we sent a few *woo-woo*s her way.

7   "I bet you guys can't even do these stretching exercises," Lorelle challenged.

8   We scoffed, as expected.

9   "If you can do these exercises, we'll get off the court," Lorelle said. "If not, you go through the whole dance routine with us."

10   It was a way to get rid of the girls, and we went over to do the exercises. Not one of us was limber[5] enough to do the stretching exercises, and soon we were all trying to look as **disgusted** as we could while we hopped around the floor to the music.

11   They danced to music as a poem was being read. I liked the poem, which turned out to be "The Creation" by James Weldon Johnson. I liked dancing, too, but I had to pretend that I didn't like it. No big deal. I was already keeping reading and writing poems a secret; I would just add dancing. ❧

---

5. **limber** (LIHM buhr) *adj.* flexible.

NOTES

Mark context clues or indicate another strategy you used that helped you determine meaning.

disgusted (dihs GUHS tihd) *adj.*

MEANING:

Comprehension Check

Complete the following items after you finish your first read. Review and clarify details with your group.

1. What are the two categories of friends in young Myers's life?

2. Why does young Myers keep his love of reading books secret?

3. What two other secrets does young Myers have?

4. **Notebook** Confirm your understanding of the selection by writing a brief summary.

- -

RESEARCH

Research to Clarify Choose at least one unfamiliar detail from the text. Briefly research that detail. In what way does the information you learned shed light on an aspect of the memoir?

from BAD BOY

Close Read the Text

With your group, revisit sections of the text you marked during your first read. **Annotate** what you notice. What **questions** do you have? What can you **conclude**?

Analyze the Text

> **CITE TEXTUAL EVIDENCE**
> to support your answers.

📓 **Notebook** Complete the activities.

1. **Review and Clarify** With your group, reread paragraph 4 of the selection. Why do you think young Myers decides he doesn't want to fight about books? What does this tell you about Myers and what books mean to him?

2. **Present and Discuss** Now, work with your group to share passages from the selection that you found especially important. Take turns presenting your passages. Discuss what you noticed in the selection, what questions you asked, and what conclusions you reached.

3. **Essential Question: *What are some of the challenges and triumphs of growing up?*** What has this memoir taught you about childhood? Discuss with your group.

LANGUAGE DEVELOPMENT

Concept Vocabulary

respected	desperate	disgusted

Why These Words? The concept vocabulary words from the text are related. With your group, determine what the words have in common. Write your ideas, and add another word that fits the category.

Practice

📓 **Notebook** Check your understanding of these words from the text by using them in a brief paragraph. Make sure to include context clues that hint at each word's meaning.

Word Study

Latin Root: *-spec-* The word *respected* is formed from the Latin prefix *re-*, which means "back," and the Latin root *-spec-*, which means "look" or "see." With this information, you can make an inference about the meaning of the word.

Check the exact meaning of *respected* in a dictionary, and use the word in a sentence. Then, find two other words formed from the root *-spec-*. Explain how each word you found relates to looking or seeing.

> **TIP**
>
> **GROUP DISCUSSION**
> There may be times when you don't understand what your classmate is saying. If that happens, politely ask your classmate to clarify his or her idea. You can say something like, "I don't understand what you mean. Will you please explain that?"

🔗 **WORD NETWORK**

Add words related to childhood from the text to your Word Network.

≡ **STANDARDS**

Language
Determine or clarify the meaning of unknown and multiple-meaning words and phrases based on *grade 6 reading and content,* choosing flexibly from a range of strategies.
  b. Use common, grade-appropriate Greek or Latin affixes and roots as clues to the meaning of a word.
  c. Consult reference materials, both print and digital, to find the pronunciation of a word or determine or clarify its precise meaning or its part of speech.

from BAD BOY

Analyze Craft and Structure

Central Idea A **central idea** is the main message or idea expressed in a nonfiction text. A central idea is always related to the **author's purpose,** or the reason that an author writes a text. In most essays, the author states the central idea directly. However, in narrative nonfiction, such as memoirs, the author suggests the central detail through details. To identify the central idea, readers examine the details in a text and then decide what they think the central idea is.

In the excerpt from *Bad Boy,* the central idea is that society wrongly expects boys to act a certain way.

Practice

CITE TEXTUAL EVIDENCE
to support your answers.

Work with your group to complete the following activities.

1. Identify specific details from the excerpt from *Bad Boy* that help build the central idea. Use the chart to capture your notes.

CENTRAL IDEA: BOYS ARE SUPPOSED TO ACT A CERTAIN WAY	
DETAIL	HOW IT CONNECTS TO CENTRAL IDEA

2. Which detail do you think is most effective in supporting the central idea? Explain your choice.

3. If you were writing a text with the same central idea as *Bad Boy,* what examples or types of evidence would you use as support?

≣ STANDARDS

Reading Informational Text
• Cite textual evidence to support analysis of what the text says explicitly as well as inferences drawn from the text.
• Determine a central idea of a text and how it is conveyed through particular details; provide a summary of the text distinct from personal opinions or judgments.
• Analyze how a particular sentence, paragraph, chapter, or section fits into the overall structure of a text and contributes to the development of the ideas.

Conventions

Adjectives and Adverbs Writers use adjectives and adverbs to make their writing more precise and lively. An **adjective** is a word that describes a noun or pronoun. An adjective answers one of these questions: *What kind? Which one? How many?* or *How much?* This chart shows examples of adjectives and the questions they answer.

WHAT KIND?	WHICH ONE?	HOW MANY?	HOW MUCH?
<u>brick</u> house	<u>that</u> judge	<u>one</u> lion	<u>no</u> time
<u>white</u> paper	<u>each</u> answer	<u>several</u> roses	<u>enough</u> sugar
<u>American</u> cheese	<u>my</u> sister	<u>both</u> brothers	<u>some</u> milk

An **adverb** is a word that modifies a verb, an adjective, or another adverb. An adverb answers one of these questions: *Where? When? In what way?* or *To what extent?* This chart shows examples of adverbs and the questions they answer.

WHERE?	WHEN?	IN WHAT WAY?	TO WHAT EXTENT?
pushed <u>down</u>	will leave <u>soon</u>	works <u>carefully</u>	<u>nearly</u> won
stand <u>nearby</u>	went <u>yesterday</u>	smiled <u>happily</u>	<u>fully</u> agrees
will walk <u>there</u>	swims <u>often</u>	chewed <u>noisily</u>	<u>barely</u> ate

Read It

Read each of these sentences from the excerpt from *Bad Boy*. Working individually, label each underlined word as an adjective or an adverb. Then, discuss with your group what question each one is answering.

1. <u>Sometimes</u> on <u>rainy</u> days I would sit in the library and read.

2. The librarians <u>always</u> suggested books that were <u>too</u> <u>young</u> for me. . . .

3. We wanted to run a <u>full-court</u> game, so we directed a <u>few</u> <u>nasty</u> remarks to the <u>other</u> side of the <u>small</u> gym.

Write It

Write a paragraph about the excerpt from *Bad Boy*. Include at least four adjectives and four adverbs. Label each adjective or adverb. Then, mark the word it describes or modifies.

TIP

CLARIFICATION

Adverbs that answer the question *In what way?* are called adverbs of manner. Adverbs of manner are easy to recognize because they usually end with -ly. Refer to the Grammar Handbook to learn more about adjectives and adverbs.

 EVIDENCE LOG

Before moving on to a new selection, go to your Evidence Log and record what you learned from *Bad Boy*.

STANDARDS

Language
Demonstrate command of the conventions of standard English grammar and usage when writing or speaking.

Comparing Texts

Now, you will read the poem "I Was a Skinny Tomboy Kid." After reading, you will compare and contrast the theme of this poem with that of the excerpt from *Bad Boy*.

I WAS A SKINNY
TOMBOY KID

About the Poet

Alma Luz Villanueva
(b. 1944) was raised in the Mission District of San Francisco by her maternal grandmother, a Yaqui Indian healer. Although Villanueva now writes in English, the inspiration for her works is rooted in the Spanish language and in the Yaqui prayers her grandmother used to sing every morning.

I Was a Skinny Tomboy Kid

Concept Vocabulary

As you perform your first read of "I Was a Skinny Tomboy Kid," you will encounter these words.

> clenched   stubborn   tenseness

Context Clues If these words are unfamiliar to you, try using **context clues**—other words and phrases in nearby text—to help you determine their meanings.

> **Context:** Marta **deceptively** hid the winning card in her hand until the end, so that no one would suspect she had it.
>
> **Conclusion:** The word *hid* and the clause *so that no one would suspect she had it* tell you Marta is doing something in a secretive way to prevent others from guessing she has the card. *Deceptively* may mean "in a way meant to mislead others."

Apply your knowledge of context clues and other vocabulary strategies to determine the meanings of unfamiliar words you encounter during your first read.

First Read POETRY

Apply these strategies as you conduct your first read. You will have an opportunity to complete a close read after your first read.

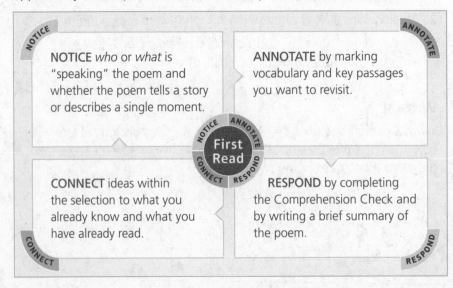

NOTICE who or what is "speaking" the poem and whether the poem tells a story or describes a single moment.

ANNOTATE by marking vocabulary and key passages you want to revisit.

CONNECT ideas within the selection to what you already know and what you have already read.

RESPOND by completing the Comprehension Check and by writing a brief summary of the poem.

First Read

Copyright © SAVVAS Learning Company LLC. All Rights Reserved.

I Was a Skinny Tomboy Kid

Alma Luz Villanueva

BACKGROUND

Although the word *tomboy* was originally defined as "a rude or noisy boy," it grew to be a label for a girl whose behavior and appearance were not considered to be traditionally feminine. In this poem, the speaker relates her experiences growing up in San Francisco, California, as a self-described tomboy.

I was a skinny tomboy kid
who walked down the streets
with my fists **clenched** into
         tight balls.

SCAN FOR
MULTIMEDIA

NOTES

Mark context clues or indicate another strategy you used that helped you determine meaning.

clenched (klehncht) *adj.*

MEANING:

5 I knew all the roofs
And back yard fences,
    I liked traveling that way
       sometimes
   not touching
10   the sidewalks
    for blocks and blocks
      it made
        me feel

     victorious
15   somehow
over the streets.
I liked to fly
   from roof
     to roof
20   the gravel
       falling
         away
beneath my feet,
   I liked
25   the edge
   of almost
not making it.
 and the freedom
   of riding
30   my bike
    to the ocean
and smelling it
   long before
I could see it,
35   and I traveled disguised
    as a boy
    (I thought)
    in an old army jacket
     carrying my
40   fishing tackle
    to the piers, and
     bumming[1] bait
   and a couple of cokes
and catching crabs
45   sometimes and
  selling them
to some chinese guys

1. **bumming** getting by asking.

and i'd give
           the fish away,
50 I didn't like fish
           I just liked to fish—
           and I vowed
                to never
                     grow up
55   to be a woman and
           be helpless like
                my mother,
     but then I didn't realize
     the kind of guts
60   it often took
           for her to just keep
                standing
     where she was.

     I grew like a thin, **stubborn** weed
65 watering myself whatever way I could
     believing in my own myth
           transforming my reality
                and creating a
                      legendary/self
70 every once in a while
           late at night
           in the deep
           darkness of my sleep
           I wake
75   with a **tenseness**
     in my arms
           and I follow
                it from my elbow to
                     my wrist
80 and realize
           my fists are tightly clenched
     and the streets come grinning
           and I forget who I'm protecting
     and I coil up
85   in a self/mothering fashion
           and tell myself
     it's o.k.

Mark context clues or indicate
another strategy you used that
helped you determine meaning.

stubborn (STUHB uhrn) *adj.*

MEANING:

Mark context clues or indicate
another strategy you used that
helped you determine meaning.

tenseness (TEHNS nihs) *n.*

MEANING:

Comprehension Check

Complete the following items after you finish your first read. Review and clarify details with your group.

1. What gives the speaker a sense of freedom?

2. What does the speaker not want to be when she grows up?

3. Why does the speaker give away the fish she catches?

4. 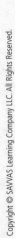 **Notebook** Confirm your understanding of the poem by writing a brief summary.

- -

RESEARCH

Research to Clarify Choose at least one unfamiliar detail from the text. Briefly research that detail. In what way does the information you learned shed light on an aspect of the poem?

Close Read the Text

With your group, revisit sections of the text you marked during your first read. **Annotate** details that you notice. What **questions** do you have? What can you **conclude**?

Close Read

ANNOTATE · QUESTION · CONCLUDE

I WAS A SKINNY TOMBOY KID

Analyze the Text

CITE TEXTUAL EVIDENCE to support your answers.

📓 **Notebook** Complete the activities.

1. **Review and Clarify** With your group, reread lines 52–63 of the poem. Why do you think the speaker says her mother had "guts"? What does this suggest about the speaker's family and her life?

2. **Present and Discuss** Now, work with your group to share passages from the selection that you found especially important. Take turns presenting your passages. Discuss what you noticed in the selection, what questions you asked, and what conclusions you reached.

3. **Essential Question:** *What are some of the challenges and triumphs of growing up?* What has this poem taught you about childhood? Discuss with your group.

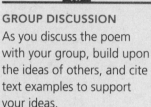

TIP

GROUP DISCUSSION
As you discuss the poem with your group, build upon the ideas of others, and cite text examples to support your ideas.

LANGUAGE DEVELOPMENT

Concept Vocabulary

clenched	stubborn	tenseness

Why These Words? The concept vocabulary words from the text are related. With your group, determine what the words have in common. Write your ideas, and add two more words that fit the category.

Practice

📓 **Notebook** Check your understanding of the concept vocabulary words by completing the following activities:
- Describe a situation in which someone might have *clenched* teeth.
- Describe what a person might do if he or she were *stubborn*.
- Describe what someone might do to relieve a feeling of *tenseness*.

Share your sentences with your group. Discuss whether each vocabulary word has been used correctly.

Word Study

📓 **Notebook** **Anglo-Saxon Suffix: -ness** The speaker of the poem describes waking up with a tenseness in her arms. The Anglo-Saxon suffix -*ness* means "the condition, state, or quality of being" and changes an adjective, such as *tense*, into a noun. Find two additional words that end with the suffix -*ness*. Write a sentence that contains each of those words.

WORD NETWORK

Add words related to childhood from the text to your Word Network.

STANDARDS

Language
Determine or clarify the meaning of unknown and multiple-meaning words and phrases based on *grade 6 reading and content*, choosing flexibly from a range of strategies.

I WAS A SKINNY TOMBOY KID

Analyze Craft and Structure

Theme The **theme** of a literary work is the insight or message about life that it expresses. Sometimes, the theme of a literary work is stated directly. More often, it is only implied, or hinted at.

When a theme is not stated directly, readers must use details in the text to draw their own conclusions. To determine an implied theme, group together details that seem connected. Then, try to figure out what message the writer is expressing with those details.

One possible theme of "I Was a Skinny Tomboy Kid," is that being different can be difficult. The poet does not state this theme directly. Instead, she suggests the theme through the thoughts, feelings, and actions of the speaker. She also suggests the theme through the way she organizes the lines of the poem to emphasize certain words and phrases.

Practice

CITE TEXTUAL EVIDENCE to support your answers.

📓 **Notebook** Work with your group to complete the following activities.

1. Use the chart to list details from the poem that imply the possible theme. Consider details that relate to the speaker's thoughts and feelings, appearance, and actions.

POSSIBLE THEME: BEING DIFFERENT CAN BE DIFFICULT
Speaker's Thoughts and Feelings:
Speaker's Appearance:
Speaker's Actions:

2. With your group, discuss the following questions, and then share your thoughts with the rest of the class.

   - What does this poem suggest about the "rules" that govern how a girl or boy should act?

   - Does the speaker challenge or break these rules? Explain.

STANDARDS

Reading Literature
• Cite textual evidence to support analysis of what the text says explicitly as well as inferences drawn from the text.
• Determine a theme or central idea of a text and how it is conveyed through particular details; provide a summary of the text distinct from personal opinions or judgments.
• Analyze how a particular sentence, chapter, scene, or stanza fits into the overall structure of a text and contributes to the development of the theme, setting, or plot.

Author's Style

Figurative Language Language that is not meant to be taken literally is called **figurative language.** Figurative language often takes the form of a comparison that represents a fresh, new way of looking at something. The chart shows three types of figurative language, along with examples: simile, metaphor, and personification.

TYPE OF FIGURATIVE LANGUAGE	EXAMPLE
A **simile** compares two unlike things using a word such as *like* or *as*.	He roared through the house <u>like a storm</u>.
A **metaphor** compares two unlike things without using a word such as *like* or *as*.	He <u>was a storm</u> roaring though the house.
Personification involves giving human qualities to nonhuman things.	The ocean waves <u>kissed the shores</u> of the sandy beach.

Read It

Reread lines 64–87 of "I Was a Skinny Tomboy Kid." In the middle column of the chart, identify one simile and one use of personification. In the right-hand column, write in your own words the literal meaning of each example you found.

TYPE OF FIGURATIVE LANGUAGE	EXAMPLE	MEANING
simile		
personification		

Write It

📓 **Notebook** Write a paragraph that tells a story. Include at least two examples of figurative language in your story—at least one simile and one use of personification. Then, label each example as either simile or personification.

▤ STANDARD

Language
Demonstrate understanding of figurative language, word relationships, and nuances in word meanings.
  a. Interpret figures of speech in context.

I Was a Skinny Tomboy Kid **75**

from BAD BOY

I WAS A SKINNY TOMBOY KID

STANDARDS

Reading Literature
Compare and contrast texts in different forms or genres in terms of their approaches to similar themes and topics.

Reading Informational Text
Compare and contrast one author's presentation of events with that of another.

Writing to Compare

The memoir *Bad Boy* and the poem "I Was a Skinny Tomboy Kid" share a central idea or theme: Being different can be difficult. Both texts share insights about being oneself and about fitting in.

Assignment

Write a **compare-and-contrast essay** in which you analyze the ways in which the memoir and the poem present ideas about how boys and girls are "supposed" to act. Also, discuss similarities and differences in how the form of each text allows those ideas to be presented. Work with your group to analyze the texts. Then, work independently to write your essay.

Prewriting

Analyze the Texts When you compare two texts, you note how they are alike. When you contrast them, you note how they are different. With your group, compare and contrast the memoir and poem, and make notes in the chart. As you work, consider the major parts of each text, such as structure, word choice, and use of figurative language. For example, you might use one row to compare and contrast word choice in each text and another row to compare and contrast figurative language.

from BAD BOY	I WAS A SKINNY TOMBOY KID

📓 **Notebook** Answer the questions.

1. What are the advantages of a memoir for expressing ideas?

2. What are the advantages of a poem for expressing ideas?

3. Which text do you think does a better job of expressing ideas about how boys and girls are "supposed" to act? Why?

Drafting

Create an Organizational Plan Now that you have analyzed the texts with your group, write your essay on your own. First, review the chart you filled in with your group, and choose the information you will use in your essay. Also, consider whether there is any additional material your group may have missed.

Next, think about how you will present your information. Will you write about each selection separately, and then compare and contrast them? Or will you compare and contrast the selections category by category, perhaps starting with word choice in both selections and then moving on to figurative language? Either plan is fine as long as you follow it consistently.

Provide Support Make sure you support your ideas with examples from both selections. Use quotation marks for examples that you copy word for word, even if they are just phrases. Review each example to make sure it is directly related to the idea you want to express.

Use Transitions Your essay will read more smoothly if you use transitional words and phrases to show connections among ideas. Some of the most common transitions are shown in the chart:

for example	therefore	on the other hand
for instance	as a result	however
specifically	similarly	in contrast

Review, Revise, and Edit

After writing your essay, review it and look for ways to improve it.

- Have you discussed how the selections present ideas about how boys and girls are "supposed to" act?
- Have you expressed your ideas clearly?
- Have you used transitions to connect your ideas?
- Have you supported your ideas with details from both selections?
- Did you check your grammar, punctuation, and spelling? Did you correct any errors you found?

✏ EVIDENCE LOG

Before moving on to a new selection, go to your Evidence Log and record what you've learned from the excerpt from *Bad Boy* and "I Was a Skinny Tomboy Kid."

☰ STANDARDS

Writing
- Write informative/expository texts to examine a topic and convey ideas, concepts, and information through the selection, organization, and analysis of relevant content.
  a. Introduce a topic; organize ideas, concepts, and information, using strategies such as definition, classification, comparison/contrast, and cause/effect; include formatting, graphics, and multimedia when useful to aiding comprehension.
  b. Develop the topic with relevant facts, definitions, concrete details, quotations, or other information and examples.
  c. Use appropriate transitions to clarify the relationships among ideas and concepts.

- Draw evidence from literary or informational texts to support analysis, reflection, and research.
  a. Apply *grade 6 Reading standards* to literature.
  b. Apply *grade 6 Reading standards* to literary nonfiction.

Language
Demonstrate command of the conventions of standard English capitalization, punctuation, and spelling when writing.
  b. Spell correctly.

Present a Retelling

Assignment

A retelling is a new version of a text that keeps the content recognizable but also changes it. A retelling may show a story from a different perspective or move it to a different setting. Deliver a **retelling** of the childhood challenges presented in either the magazine article, the memoir excerpt, or the poem from this section. In your retelling, you may wish to refer to one or more of the rights set forth in the Declaration of the Rights of the Child. Enhance your presentation with media.

Plan With Your Group

Analyze the Text With your group, review the texts you have read during Small-Group Learning. Consider the ways in which childhood challenges are presented in each text. Capture your ideas and observations in the chart.

SELECTION	CHILDHOOD CHALLENGES
Declaration of the Rights of the Child	
Michaela DePrince: The War Orphan Who Became a Ballerina	
from Bad Boy	
I Was a Skinny Tomboy Kid	

As a group, choose one text on which to focus. Then, divide the text into sections, and have each group member focus on a different section. As you plan your retelling, keep this idea in mind: A successful retelling is true to the ideas in the original text but presents them in way that is new or fresh.

Gather Evidence and Media Examples Reread the text to find the points you wish to emphasize and to figure out where adding media would have the biggest impact. Work as a group to locate video, audio, or images that will clarify your ideas and make your retelling come alive. For example, if you want to make clear for an audience how difficult it was for Michaela DePrince to become a ballerina, you might find a video that shows the sweat and hard work of a ballet class.

STANDARDS

Speaking and Listening
• Present claims and findings, sequencing ideas logically and using pertinent descriptions, facts, and details to accentuate main ideas or themes; use appropriate eye contact, adequate volume, and clear pronunciation.
• Include multimedia components and visual displays in presentations to clarify information.
• Adapt speech to a variety of contexts and tasks, demonstrating command of formal English when indicated or appropriate.

Organize Your Ideas With your group, brainstorm for ways to organize your presentation, including ways to integrate multimedia. Make sure that you think of your audience and organize materials in a way that will make sense to a first-time viewer.

Rehearse With Your Group

Practice With Your Group Before you present your retelling to the class, practice delivering it as a group. Make sure that each member uses a an appropriate tone. Also, work to make eye contact with viewers, and to speak clearly and loudly so that you can be heard and understood by everyone in the audience.

As you practice your presentation, use this checklist to evaluate the effectiveness of your group's first run-through. Then, use your evaluation and the instruction here to guide your revision.

CONTENT	USE OF MEDIA	PRESENTATION TECHNIQUES
☐ The retelling is true to the ideas expressed in the text the group has chosen.	☐ The media are relevant to the ideas expressed in the text the group has chosen.	☐ The media are visible and audible.
☐ The retelling expresses the ideas from the text in a way that is new or fresh.	☐ The media add interest and contribute new ideas to the spoken portion of the retelling.	☐ The transitions between speakers are smooth.
		☐ Each presenter speaks clearly.

Fine-Tune the Content Check to be sure you have emphasized key events in the original text. Also, review details that describe characters and situations. Add descriptive details as needed.

Improve Your Use of Media Make sure you are using media that add in meaningful ways to your ideas. Also, make sure that all media choices work well with the spoken portions of your presentation.

Brush Up on Your Presentation Techniques Avoid speaking in a flat, uninterested, or bored tone. Instead, vary your tone and speak with enthusiasm and liveliness.

Present and Evaluate

Remember that you are giving this presentation as a group. Everyone is equally important, and each person represents the entire group. Don't let your attention wander when other members of your group are giving their parts of the presentation. In addition, give other groups your full attention when they are giving their presentations.

ESSENTIAL QUESTION:

What are some of the challenges and triumphs of growing up?

Young people have different points of view about growing up. In this section, you will choose one additional selection about childhood for your final reading experience in this unit. Follow these steps to help you choose.

Look Back Think about the selections you have already read. What more do you want to know about the topic of childhood?

Look Ahead Preview the selections by reading the descriptions. Which one seems most interesting and appealing to you?

Look Inside Take a few minutes to scan through the text you chose. Make another selection if this text doesn't meet your needs.

Independent Learning Strategies

Throughout your life, in school, in your community, and in your career, you will need to rely on yourself to learn and work on your own. Review these strategies and the actions you can take to practice them during Independent Learning. Add ideas of your own for each category.

STRATEGY	ACTION PLAN
Create a schedule	• Understand your goals and deadlines. • Make a plan for what to do each day. •
Practice what you've learned	• Use First-Read and Close-Read Strategies to deepen your understanding. • Evaluate the usefulness of the evidence to help you understand the topic. • Consider the quality and reliability of the source. •
Take notes	• Record important ideas and information. • Review your notes before preparing to share with a group. •

SCAN FOR
MULTIMEDIA

Choose one selection. Selections are available online only.

 SCAN FOR MULTIMEDIA

First-Read Guide

Use this page to record your first-read ideas.

🔧 **Tool Kit**
First-Read Guide and
Model Annotation

Selection Title: _____

NOTICE

NOTICE new information or ideas you learn about the unit topic as you first read this text.

ANNOTATE

ANNOTATE by marking vocabulary and key passages you want to revisit.

CONNECT

CONNECT ideas within the selection to other knowledge and the selections you have read.

RESPOND

RESPOND by writing a brief summary of the selection.

▤ STANDARD

Reading Read and comprehend complex literary and informational texts independently and proficiently.

Close-Read Guide

Use this page to record your close-read ideas.

Selection Title: _____

Close Read the Text

Revisit sections of the text you marked during your first read. Read these sections closely and **annotate** what you notice. Ask yourself **questions** about the text. What can you **conclude**? Write down your ideas.

Analyze the Text

Think about the author's choices of patterns, structure, techniques, and ideas included in the text. Select one and record your thoughts about what this choice conveys.

QuickWrite

Pick a paragraph from the text that grabbed your interest. Explain the power of this passage.

_____
_____
_____
_____
_____
_____
_____
_____

☷ STANDARD

Reading Read and comprehend complex literary and informational texts independently and proficiently.

Share Your Independent Learning

Prepare to Share

What are some of the challenges and triumphs of growing up?

Even when you read or learn something independently, you can continue to grow when you share what you have learned with others. Reflect on the text you explored independently, and write notes about its connection to the unit. In your notes, consider why this text belongs in this unit.

Learn From Your Classmates

💬 Discuss It Share your ideas about the text you explored on your own. As you talk with others in your class, jot down a few ideas that you learned from them.

Reflect

Review your notes, and mark the most important insight you gained from these writing and discussion activities. Explain how this idea adds to your understanding of childhood challenges and triumphs.

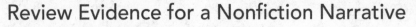

Review Evidence for a Nonfiction Narrative

At the beginning of this unit, you wrote your first thoughts about a life experience that might answer the following question:

When did a challenge lead to a triumph?

EVIDENCE LOG

Review your Evidence Log and your QuickWrite from the beginning of the unit. Did you learn anything new?

NOTES

Identify at least three pieces of evidence that interested you about the challenges and triumphs of growing up.

1.

2.

3.

Identify a real-life experience that illustrates one of your ideas about childhood challenges and triumphs.

_____

Develop your thoughts into a topic sentence for a nonfiction narrative. Complete this sentence starter:
Although it was challenging when _____

_____,

the end result was a triumph in that _____

_____.

Evaluate the Strength of Your Details Do you have enough details to write a well-developed and engaging narrative about real-life events? If not, make a plan.

☐ Brainstorm for details to add   ☐ Talk with my classmates

☐ Reread a selection   ☐ Ask an expert

☐ Other: _____

_____

STANDARDS

Writing
Write narratives to develop real or imagined experiences or events using effective technique, relevant descriptive details, and well-structured event sequences.
  a. Engage and orient the reader by establishing a context and introducing a narrator and/or characters; organize an event sequence that unfolds naturally and logically.

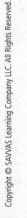

SOURCES

- WHOLE-CLASS SELECTIONS
- SMALL-GROUP SELECTIONS
- INDEPENDENT-LEARNING SELECTION

PART 1
Writing to Sources: Nonfiction Narrative

In this unit, you have read about different challenges and triumphs of growing up. Some of the selections described hardships and confusing changes, whereas other selections described the joys of discovery.

Assignment

Write a **nonfiction narrative** in which you tell about a real-life experience that answers this question:

When did a challenge lead to a triumph?

The experience may be yours, or it may be that of someone you know. Begin by giving your reader background about the experience. Then, present a natural, logical series of events that shows how a challenge led to a triumph. Conclude by reflecting on the importance of the experience.

⊹ WORD NETWORK

As you write and revise your nonfiction narrative, use your Word Network to help vary your word choices.

Reread the Assignment Review the assignment to be sure you fully understand it. The task may reference some of the academic words presented at the beginning of the unit. Be sure you understand each of the words here in order to complete the assignment correctly.

Academic Vocabulary

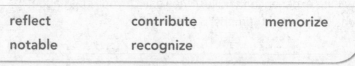

reflect	contribute	memorize
notable	recognize	

Review the Elements of Nonfiction Narrative Before you begin writing, read the Nonfiction Narrative Rubric. Once you have completed your first draft, check it against the rubric. If one or more of the elements are missing or not as strong as they could be, revise your narrative to add or strengthen those components.

⊟ STANDARDS

Writing
Write narratives to develop real or imagined experiences or events using effective technique, relevant descriptive details, and well-structured event sequences.

86 UNIT 1 • CHILDHOOD

Nonfiction Narrative Rubric

	Focus and Organization	Evidence and Elaboration	Conventions
4	The introduction is engaging and introduces the characters and situation in a way that appeals to readers. Events in the narrative progress in logical order and are linked by clear transitions. The conclusion effectively follows from the narrated experiences or events.	The narrative effectively includes techniques such as dialogue and description to add interest and to develop the characters and events. The narrative effectively includes precise words and phrases, relevant descriptive details, and sensory language to convey experiences and events. The narrative effectively establishes voice through word choice, sentence structure, and tone.	The narrative consistently uses standard English conventions of usage and mechanics. The narrative effectively varies sentence patterns for meaning, reader interest, and style.
3	The introduction is somewhat engaging and clearly introduces the characters and situation. Events in the narrative progress logically and are often linked by transition words. The conclusion mostly follows from the narrated experiences or events.	The narrative mostly includes dialogue and description to add interest and develop experiences and events. The narrative mostly includes precise words and sensory language to convey experiences and events. The narrative mostly establishes voice through word choice, sentence structure, and tone.	The narrative mostly demonstrates accuracy in standard English conventions of usage and mechanics. The narrative mostly varies sentence patterns for meaning, reader interest, and style.
2	The introduction occasionally introduces characters. Events in the narrative progress somewhat logically and are sometimes linked by transition words. The conclusion adds very little to the narrated experiences or events.	The narrative includes some dialogue and descriptions. The words in the narrative vary between vague and precise, and some sensory language is included. The narrative occasionally establishes voice through word choice, sentence structure, and tone.	The narrative demonstrates some accuracy in standard English conventions of usage and mechanics. The narrative occasionally varies sentence patterns for meaning, reader interest, and style.
1	The introduction does not introduce characters and an experience, or there is no clear introduction. The events in the narrative do not progress logically. The ideas seem disconnected and the sentences are not linked by transitional words and phrases. The conclusion does not connect to the narrative or there is no conclusion.	Dialogue and descriptions are not included in the narrative. The narrative does not incorporate sensory language or precise words to convey experiences and to develop characters. The narrative does not establish voice through word choice, sentence structure, and tone.	The narrative contains mistakes in standard English conventions of usage and mechanics. The narrative does not vary sentence patterns for meaning, reader interest, and style.

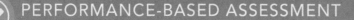

PART 2
Speaking and Listening: Recitation

Assignment
After completing the final draft of your nonfiction narrative, plan and present a **recitation,** in which you tell the story to classmates.

Do not simply read your narrative aloud. Examine what you have written, and adapt it for a listening audience. Follow these steps to make your recitation lively and engaging.

- Go back to your narrative, and annotate key events or descriptions that you want to emphasize.
- Mark places in the narrative where you intend to slow down or speed up.
- Add transitions as needed, to help a listening audience follow along.
- Use appropriate eye contact. Make sure to speak loudly enough for people to hear you, and pronounce words clearly.

Review the Rubric The criteria by which your recitation will be evaluated appear in the rubric below. Review these criteria before presenting to ensure that you are prepared.

STANDARDS
Speaking and Listening
Adapt speech to a variety of contexts and tasks, demonstrating command of formal English when indicated or appropriate.

	Content	Presentation Techniques
3	The presentation has an engaging introduction, a logical sequence of events, and a meaningful conclusion.	The speaker maintains effective eye contact and speaks clearly and with adequate volume.
	The presentation effectively includes narrative techniques and a variety of transitions for clarity.	The speaker varies tone and volume to create an engaging presentation.
	The presentation effectively includes descriptive details relevant to the story.	
2	The presentation has an introduction, a somewhat logical sequence of events, and a conclusion.	The speaker sometimes maintains effective eye contact and speaks somewhat clearly and with adequate volume.
	The presentation includes some narrative techniques and some transitions for clarity.	The speaker sometimes varies tone and emphasis to create an engaging presentation.
	The presentation includes some descriptive details.	
1	The presentation does not have a logical sequence of events, and lacks an introduction or conclusion.	The speaker does not maintain effective eye contact or speak clearly with adequate volume.
	The presentation does not include narrative techniques and transitions.	The speaker does not vary tone and emphasis to create an engaging presentation.
	The presentation does not include descriptive details.	

Reflect on the Unit

Now that you've completed the unit, take a few moments to reflect on your learning.

Reflect on the Unit Goals

Look back at the goals at the beginning of the unit. Use a different-colored pen to rate yourself again. Think about readings and activities that contributed the most to the growth of your understanding. Record your thoughts.

Reflect on the Learning Strategies

Discuss It Write a reflection on whether you were able to improve your learning based on your Action Plans. Think about what worked, what didn't, and what you might do to keep working on these strategies. Record your ideas before a class discussion.

Reflect on the Text

Choose a selection that you found challenging, and explain what made it difficult.

Explain something that surprised you about a text in the unit. Which activity taught you the most about childhood? What did you learn?

SCAN FOR
MULTIMEDIA

Animal Allies

Animals and people can form unique relationships. How can these relationships affect both the animal and the person?

People of the Horse:
Special Bond

💬 Discuss It Is the relationship between animals and people truly a special bond?

Write your response before sharing your ideas.

SCAN FOR
MULTIMEDIA

UNIT 2

ESSENTIAL QUESTION:

How can people and animals relate to each other?

LAUNCH TEXT
INFORMATIVE/
EXPLANATORY MODEL
Reading Buddies

WHOLE-CLASS LEARNING

ANCHOR TEXT: MEMOIR

from My Life With the Chimpanzees
Jane Goodall

ANCHOR TEXT: HISTORICAL FICTION

Hachiko: The True Story of a Loyal Dog
Pamela S. Turner

▸ MEDIA CONNECTION:
The Secret Life of the Dog

SMALL-GROUP LEARNING

COMPARE

POETRY

A Blessing
James Wright

POETRY

Predators
Linda Hogan

ESSAY

Monkey Master
Waldemar Januszczak

SHORT STORY

Black Cowboy, Wild Horses
Julius Lester

INDEPENDENT LEARNING

NOVEL EXCERPT

from The Wind in the Willows
Kenneth Grahame

FABLE

How the Camel Got His Hump
from Just So Stories
Rudyard Kipling

NEWS ARTICLE

The Girl Who Gets Gifts From Birds
Katy Sewall

NEWS ARTICLE

Pet Therapy: How Animals and Humans Heal Each Other
Julie Rovner

PERFORMANCE TASK

WRITING FOCUS:
Write an Explanatory Essay

PERFORMANCE TASK

SPEAKING AND LISTENING FOCUS:
Deliver an Informative Presentation

PERFORMANCE-BASED ASSESSMENT PREP

Review Evidence for an Explanatory Essay

PERFORMANCE-BASED ASSESSMENT

Explanatory Text: Essay and Informative Presentation

PROMPT:

How can animals and people help one another?

Unit Goals

Throughout this unit, you will deepen your understanding of the ways that people and animals can relate to each other by reading, writing, speaking, listening, and presenting. These goals will help you succeed on the Unit Performance-Based Assessment.

Rate how well you meet these goals right now. You will revisit your ratings later when you reflect on your growth during this unit.

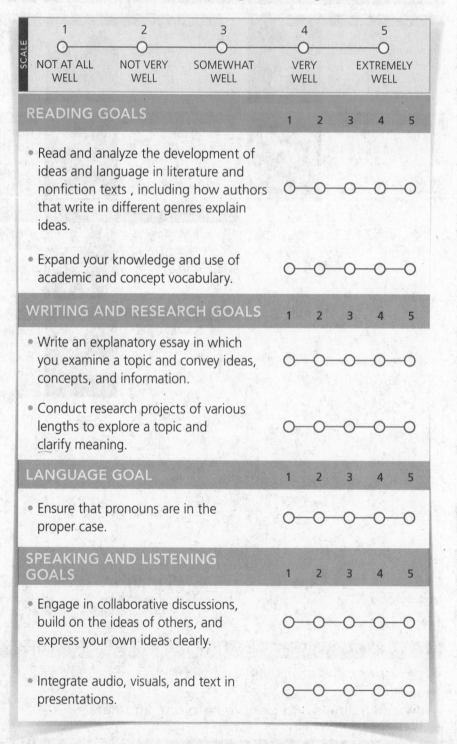

SCALE	1	2	3	4	5
	NOT AT ALL WELL	NOT VERY WELL	SOMEWHAT WELL	VERY WELL	EXTREMELY WELL

READING GOALS   1   2   3   4   5

- Read and analyze the development of ideas and language in literature and nonfiction texts , including how authors that write in different genres explain ideas.

- Expand your knowledge and use of academic and concept vocabulary.

WRITING AND RESEARCH GOALS   1   2   3   4   5

- Write an explanatory essay in which you examine a topic and convey ideas, concepts, and information.

- Conduct research projects of various lengths to explore a topic and clarify meaning.

LANGUAGE GOAL   1   2   3   4   5

- Ensure that pronouns are in the proper case.

SPEAKING AND LISTENING GOALS   1   2   3   4   5

- Engage in collaborative discussions, build on the ideas of others, and express your own ideas clearly.

- Integrate audio, visuals, and text in presentations.

:≡ STANDARDS

Language
Acquire and use accurately grade-appropriate general academic and domain-specific words and phrases; gather vocabulary knowledge when considering a word or phrase important to comprehension or expression.

SCAN FOR MULTIMEDIA

Academic Vocabulary: Informative/ Explanatory Text

FOLLOW THROUGH
Study the words in this chart, and mark them or their forms wherever they appear in the unit.

Understanding and using academic terms can help you read, write, and speak with precision and clarity. Here are five academic words that will be useful to you in this unit as you analyze and write informative and explanatory texts.

Complete the chart.

1. Review each word, its root, and mentor sentences.

2. Use the information and your own knowledge to predict the meaning of each word.

3. For each word, list at least two related words.

4. Refer to the dictionary or other resources if needed.

WORD	MENTOR SENTENCES	PREDICT MEANING	RELATED WORDS
exclude ROOT: **-clud-** "shut"	1. He prefers to invite his entire class to his birthday party rather than *exclude* anyone. 2. To *exclude* people from the club based on their age would be unfair.		include; conclusive
illustrate ROOT: **-lus-** "shine"	1. Can you give me an example to *illustrate* that idea? I'm confused. 2. I gathered pictures of my family to *illustrate* my autobiographical narrative.		
community ROOT: **-commun-** "common"	1. *Community* leaders regularly meet to discuss the town's issues. 2. The business *community* is important to the growth of the town.		
elaborate ROOT: **-lab-** "work"	1. Because Sara's instructions were hard to understand, Frank asked her to *elaborate* in detail. 2. You may first create an outline to list the key points, but then you must support and *elaborate* on your ideas with examples.		
objective ROOT: **-ject-** "throw"	1. The *objective* in a soccer game is to score goals by putting the ball in the other team's net. 2. When Mike drafted his resume, he made sure to state his *objective* for career success.		

LAUNCH TEXT | INFORMATIVE/EXPLANATORY MODEL

This selection is an example of an informative/explanatory text, a type of writing in which an author presents facts and details in a way that allows readers to understand a topic or process. This is the type of writing you will develop in the Performance-Based Assessment at the end of the unit.

As you read, look at the way the ideas are introduced and explained. Mark the text to help you determine key ideas and details.

Reading Buddies

NOTES

1   In a school library across town, a third-grade boy is reading his favorite book to a dog named Theo. The boy is petting the dog as he reads, and the dog has its paw on the boy's foot. Both seem relaxed and happy, but what is a dog doing in a school library?

2   Theo, a five-year-old border collie, is one of more than 2,300 dogs around the country that have been trained to listen to people read aloud. He is part of a program that began in Utah in 1999. Through this program, teams of dogs and their handlers were sent out to schools and libraries to serve as reading companions for kids who were having trouble reading. Since then, similar reading programs have popped up in every region of the United States. They have helped thousands of kids improve not only their reading skills but also their attitudes about reading.

3   There are many reasons kids can have trouble reading. Some have learning disabilities. Some think it's boring. Some are new to English. Others just haven't found a book they like.

4   Whatever the cause, struggling readers have one thing in common: They lack confidence. Learning to read is often less about reading skills than it is about confidence. To a struggling reader, an animal listener can produce less anxiety than a human listener.

SCAN FOR
MULTIMEDIA

NOTES

5   Dogs are the ideal reading companions. They aren't in a hurry, so you can read at your own pace. They won't stop you when you've pronounced something wrong. They won't laugh at you or make you feel self-conscious. When you read to a dog, you are not as likely to feel judged. You get a chance to focus on the book you're reading rather than your performance.

6   "I never finished a whole book before," said a 10-year-old girl who participated in the program. She had been reading at a first-grade level and hardly ever practiced, because she was too shy to read aloud. But after a few weeks of reading to a dog companion, she finished the book. She was proud of herself for having overcome such a major hurdle!

7   Reading is like any other skill—the more you practice, the better you get. But it's hard to find someone who has the time to sit down and listen. Readers can also feel nervous about making mistakes. "But if you're practicing with a dog," said one reading specialist, "you don't mind making the mistake. In fact, you'll probably correct it."

8   More and more libraries and schools are using dogs to help kids improve their reading skills and confidence level. Sometimes, when people read to dogs, it's the *dogs* that benefit. For example, the Arizona Animal Welfare League & Society for Prevention of Cruelty to Animals is using reading as a tool to help shelter animals become happier, more well-adjusted pets. Program volunteers spend time reading to dogs and cats who are waiting to be adopted. Reading calms the animals down and makes them more comfortable around people.

9   Through the experience of reading, humans and animals are helping each other develop the skills they need to take on life's challenges—whatever those challenges happen to be. ❧

🔧 WORD NETWORK FOR ANIMAL ALLIES

Vocabulary A Word Network is a collection of words related to a topic. As you read the selections in this unit, identify interesting words related to the relationships between animals and people, and add them to your Word Network. For example, you might begin by adding words from the Launch Text, such as *participated*, *handlers*, and *well-adjusted*. Continue to add words as you complete this unit.

participated

handlers

ANIMAL/HUMAN RELATIONSHIPS

well-adjusted

🔧 **Tool Kit** Word Network Model

Summary

Write a summary of "Reading Buddies." A **summary** is a concise, complete, and accurate overview of a text. It should not include a statement of your opinion or an analysis.

Launch Activity

Conduct a Discussion Consider this question: **Is using animal reading buddies a good way to improve reading skills?**

- Record your position on the statement and explain your thinking.

  ☐ Strongly Agree   ☐ Agree   ☐ Disagree   ☐ Strongly Disagree

  _____

  _____

- Form small groups to share your opinions. Give examples from stories you have heard or read, including the Launch Text.

- Listen respectfully and carefully to the ideas expressed, and reflect on each other's perspectives thoughtfully.

- Finally, write a short paragraph stating whether the discussion changed your opinion. Explain the reasons your opinion either changed or stayed the same.

QuickWrite

Consider class discussions, the video, and the Launch Text as you think about the prompt. Record your first thoughts here.

PROMPT: **How can animals and people help one another?**

✐ EVIDENCE LOG FOR ANIMAL ALLIES

Review your QuickWrite. Summarize your thoughts in one sentence to record in your Evidence Log. Then, record evidence from "Reading Buddies" that supports your thinking.

Prepare for the Perfomance-Based Assessment at the end of the unit by completing the Evidence Log after each selection.

🔧 Tool Kit
Evidence Log Model

Title of Text: _____   Date: _____

CONNECTION TO PROMPT	TEXT EVIDENCE/DETAILS	ADDITIONAL NOTES/IDEAS

How does this text change or add to my thinking?   Date: _____

SCAN FOR
MULTIMEDIA

ESSENTIAL QUESTION:

How can people and animals relate to each other?

Over thousands of years humans and animals have formed important relationships. For example, humans rely on some animals to help with farmwork, rescue, or transportation; some animals rely on humans for protection, shelter, and food. The selections you are going to read present insights into the bonds that exist between people and animals.

Whole-Class Learning Strategies

Throughout your life, in school, in your community, and in your career, you will continue to learn and work in large-group environments.

Review these strategies and the actions you can take to practice them as you work with your whole class. Add ideas of your own for each strategy. Get ready to use these strategies during Whole-Class Learning.

STRATEGY	ACTION PLAN
Listen actively	• Eliminate distractions. For example, put your cellphone away. • Keep your eyes on the speaker. •
Clarify by asking questions	• If you're confused, other people probably are, too. Ask a question to help your whole class. • If you see that you are guessing, ask a question instead. •
Monitor understanding	• Notice what information you already know and be ready to build on it. • Ask for help if you are struggling. •
Interact and share ideas	• Share your ideas and answer questions, even if you are unsure. • Build on the ideas of others by adding details or making a connection. •

SCAN FOR
MULTIMEDIA

CONTENTS

PERFORMANCE TASK

WRITING FOCUS

Write an Explanatory Essay
The Whole-Class readings present animals as intelligent creatures with unique personalities. After reading, you will write an explanatory essay in which you explain the traits these authors believe people and animals share.

About the Author

Dame **Jane Goodall** (b. 1934) is the most celebrated primatologist, or researcher of primates (which includes apes, chimpanzees, and monkeys), of the twentieth century. She spent extended periods living with and observing chimpanzees in the wild. Dr. Goodall did most of her research in Tanzania at the Gombe Stream Game Reserve (now a national park), where she lived from 1960 to 1975. In 1977, she co-founded the Jane Goodall Institute for Wildlife Research, Education, and Conservation.

🔧 Tool Kit
First-Read Guide and Model Annotation

STANDARDS

Reading Informational Text
By the end of the year, read and comprehend literary nonfiction in the grades 6–8 text complexity band proficiently, with scaffolding as needed at the high end of the range.

from My Life With the Chimpanzees

Concept Vocabulary

You will encounter the following words as you read this excerpt from *My Life With the Chimpanzees*. Before reading, note how familiar you are with each word. Then, rank the words in order from most familiar (1) to least familiar (6).

WORD	YOUR RANKING
vanished	
miserable	
irritable	
threateningly	
impetuous	
dominate	

After completing the first read, come back to the concept vocabulary and review your rankings. Mark changes to your original rankings as needed.

First Read NONFICTION

Apply these strategies as you conduct your first read. You will have an opportunity to complete the close-read notes after your first read.

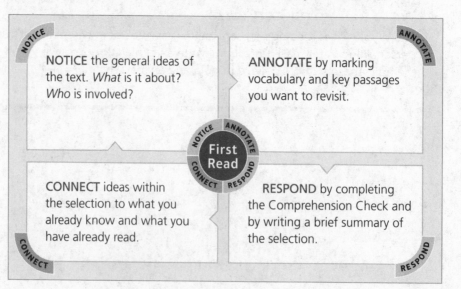

NOTICE the general ideas of the text. *What* is it about? *Who* is involved?

ANNOTATE by marking vocabulary and key passages you want to revisit.

First Read

CONNECT ideas within the selection to what you already know and what you have already read.

RESPOND by completing the Comprehension Check and by writing a brief summary of the selection.

from
My Life With the **Chimpanzees**

Jane Goodall

BACKGROUND
Gombe Stream National Park in Tanzania, Africa, is best known as the site of Jane Goodall's groundbreaking chimpanzee research. The park covers only about 20 square miles, but is home to a great variety of animals. Dr. Goodall's research in Gombe was supported by the famous paleontologist Louis Leakey. In this account, Dr. Goodall occasionally refers to Dr. Leakey by his first name only.

SCAN FOR MULTIMEDIA

NOTES

1   July 16, 1960, was a day I shall remember all my life. It was when I first set foot on the shingle and sand beach of Chimpanzee Land—that is, Gombe National Park. I was twenty-six years old.

2   Mum and I were greeted by the two African game scouts who were responsible for protecting the thirty square miles of the park. They helped us to find a place where we could put up our old ex-army tent.

3   We chose a lovely spot under some shady trees near the small, fast-flowing Kakombe Stream. In Kigoma (before setting out), we had found a cook, Dominic. He put up his little tent some distance from ours and quite near the lake.

4   When camp was ready I set off to explore. It was already late afternoon, so I could not go far. There had been a grass fire not long before, so all the vegetation of the more open ridges and peaks had burned away. This made it quite easy to move around, except that the slopes above the valley were very steep in places, and I slipped several times on the loose, gravelly soil.

5　I shall never forget the thrill of that first exploration. Soon after leaving camp I met a troop of baboons. They were afraid of the strange, white-skinned creature (that was I) and gave their barking alarm call, "Waa-hoo! Waa-hoo!" again and again. I left them, hoping that they would become used to me soon—otherwise, I thought, all the creatures of Gombe would be frightened. As I crossed a narrow ravine crowded with low trees and bushes I got very close to a beautiful red-gold bushbuck—a forest antelope about the size of a long-legged goat. I knew it was female because she had no horns. When she scented me she kept quite still for a moment and stared toward me with her big dark eyes. Then, with a loud barking call, she turned and bounded away.

6　When I got to one of the high ridges I looked down into the valley. There the forest was dark and thick. That was where I planned to go the next day to look for chimpanzees.

7　When I got back to camp it was dusk. Dominic had made a fire and was cooking our supper. That evening, and for the next four days, we had fresh food from Kigoma, but after that we ate out of cans. Louis had not managed to find very much money for our expedition, so our possessions were few and simple—a knife, fork, and spoon each, a couple of tin plates and tin mugs. But that was all we needed. After supper, Mum and I talked around our campfire, then snuggled into our two cots in the tent.

8　Early the next morning I set out to search for chimpanzees. I had been told by the British game ranger in charge of Gombe not to travel about the mountains by myself—except near camp. Otherwise, I had to take one of the game scouts with me. So I set off with Adolf. That first day we saw two chimps feeding in a tall tree. As soon as they saw us they leapt down and **vanished**. The next day we saw no chimps at all. Nor the day after. Nor the day after that.

9　A whole week went by before we found a very big tree full of tiny round red fruits that Adolf told me were called *msulula*. From the other side of the valley we could watch chimps arriving at the tree, feeding, then climbing down and vanishing into the forest. I decided to camp in the best viewing site so that I could see them first thing in the morning. I spent three days in that valley and I saw a lot of chimps. But they were too far away and the foliage of the tree was too thick. It was disappointing and frustrating, and I didn't have much to tell Mum when I got back.

10　There was another problem that I had to cope with—Adolf was very lazy. He was almost always late in the morning. I decided to try another man, Rashidi. He was far better and helped me a lot, showing me the trails through the forests and the best ways to move from one valley to the next. He had sharp eyes and spotted chimps from far away.

CLOSE READ

ANNOTATE: In paragraph 8, mark the repetition of words that describe Dr. Goodall's experience with the chimps after the first day.

QUESTION: Why do you think Dr. Goodall has chosen to repeat these words?

CONCLUDE: How does this repetition help communicate Goodall's experience to the reader?

vanished (VAN ihsht) *v.* disappeared

11   But even after several months, the chimps had not become used to us. They ran off if we got anywhere near to them. I begged the game ranger to let me move about the forests by myself. I promised that I would always tell Rashidi in which direction I was going, so that he would know where to look for me if I failed to turn up in the evening. The game ranger finally gave in. At last I could make friends with the chimpanzees in my own way.

12   Every morning I got up when I heard the alarm clock at 5:30 A.M. I ate a couple of slices of bread and had a cup of coffee from the Thermos flask. Then I set off, climbing to where I thought the chimps might be.

13   Most often, I went to the Peak. I discovered that from this high place I had a splendid view in all directions. I could see chimps moving in the trees and I could hear if they called. At first I watched from afar, through my binoculars, and never tried to get close. I knew that if I did, the chimps would run silently away.

14   Gradually I began to learn about the chimps' home and how they lived. I discovered that, most of the time, the chimps wandered about in small groups of six or less, not in a big troop like the baboons. Often a little group was made up of a mother with her children, or two or three adult males by themselves. Sometimes many groups joined together, especially when there was delicious ripe fruit on one big tree. When the chimps got together like that, they were very excited, made a lot of noise, and were easy to find.

15   Eventually I realized that the chimps I watched from the Peak were all part of one group—a community. There were about fifty chimps belonging to this community. They made use of three of the valleys to the north of the Kakombe Valley (where our tent was) and two valleys to the south. These valleys have lovely sounding names: Kasakela, Linda, and Rutanga in the north, Mkenke and Nyasanga in the south.

16   From the Peak I noted which trees the chimps were feeding in and then, when they had gone, I scrambled down and collected some of the leaves, flowers, or fruits so they could be identified later. I found that the chimps eat mostly fruits but also a good many kinds of leaves, blossoms, seeds, and stems. Later I would discover that they eat a variety of insects and sometimes hunt and kill prey animals to feed on meat.

17   During those months of gradual discovery, the chimps very slowly began to realize that I was not so frightening after all. Even so, it was almost a year before I could approach to within one hundred yards, and that is not really very close. The baboons got used to me much more quickly. Indeed, they became a nuisance around our camp by grabbing any food that we accidentally left lying on the table.

NOTES

CLOSE READ

ANNOTATE: In paragraph 17, mark details that show how the chimps behave. Mark other details that show how the baboons behave.

QUESTION: Why does Goodall contrast the chimps' and baboons' behavior?

CONCLUDE: What does this contrast reveal about the chimps?

18   I began to learn more about the other creatures that shared the forests with the chimpanzees. There were four kinds of monkeys in addition to the baboons, and many smaller animals such as squirrels and mongooses. There was also a whole variety of nocturnal (nighttime) creatures: porcupines and civets (creatures looking rather like raccoons) and all manners of rats and mice. Only a very few animals in the forests at Gombe were potentially dangerous—mainly buffalo and leopards. Bush pigs can be dangerous too, but only if you threaten them or their young. And, of course, there are poisonous snakes—seven different kinds.

19   Once, as I arrived on the Peak in the early morning before it was properly light, I saw the dark shape of a large animal looming in front of me. I stood quite still. My heart began to beat fast, for I realized it was a buffalo. Many hunters fear buffalo more than lions or elephants.

20   By a lucky chance the wind was blowing from him to me, so he couldn't smell me. He was peacefully gazing in the opposite direction and chewing his cud. He hadn't heard my approach—always I try to move as quietly as I can in the bush. So, though I was only ten yards from him, he had no idea I was there. Very slowly I retreated.

21   Another time, as I was sitting on the Peak, I heard a strange mewing sound. I looked around and there, about fifteen yards away, a leopard was approaching. I could just see the black and white tip of its tail above the tall grass. It was walking along the little trail that led directly to where I sat.

22   Leopards are not usually dangerous unless they have been wounded. But I was frightened of them in those days—probably as a result of my experience with the leopard and the wolfhound[1] two years before. And so, very silently, I moved away and looked for chimps in another valley.

23   Later I went back to the Peak. I found that, just like any cat, that leopard had been very curious. There, in the exact place where I had been sitting, he had left his mark—his droppings.

24   Most of the time, though, nothing more alarming than insects disturbed my vigils on the Peak. It began to feel like home. I carried a little tin trunk up there. In it I kept a kettle, some sugar and coffee, and a tin mug. Then, when I got tired from a long trek to another valley, I could make a drink in the middle of the day. I kept a blanket up there, too, and when the chimps slept near the Peak, I slept there, so that I could be close by in the morning. I loved to be up there at night, especially when there was a moon. If I heard the coughing grunt of a leopard, I just prayed and pulled the blanket over my head!

---

1. **leopard and the wolfhound** Previously, Goodall saw a leopard kill a large hunting dog.

25   Chimps sleep all night, just as we do. From the Peak I often watched how they made their nests, or beds. First the chimp bent a branch down over some solid foundation, such as a fork or two parallel branches. Holding it in place with his feet, he then bent another over it. Then he folded the end of the first branch back over the second. And so on. He often ended up by picking lots of small, soft, leafy twigs to make a pillow. Chimps like their comfort! I've learned over the years that infants sleep in their nest with their mothers until they are about five years old or until the next baby is born and the older child has to make its own bed.

26   I never returned to camp before sunset. But even when I slept on the Peak, I first went down to have supper with Mum and tell her what I had seen that day. And she would tell me what she had been doing.

27   Mum set up a clinic. She handed out medicine to any of the local Africans, mostly fishermen, who were sick. Once she cured an old man who was very ill indeed. Word about this cure spread far and wide, and sometimes patients would walk for miles to get treatment from the wonderful white woman-doctor.

28   Her clinic was very good for me. It meant that the local people realized we wanted to help. When Mum had to go back to England after four months to manage things at home, the Africans wanted, in turn, to help me.

29   Of course, Mum worried about leaving me on my own. Domi... s a wonderful cook and great company. He was not really n... Louis Leakey asked Hassan to come all the way from Lak... to help with the boat and engine. It was lovely to see his ... smiling face again, and his arrival relieved Mum's min...

30   Of course, I ... her after she'd gone, but I didn't have time to be lonely. The ... s so much to do.

31   Soon after she... I got back one evening and was greeted by an excited Dominic... e told me that a big male chimp had spent an hour feeding on t... fruit of one of the oil-nut palms growing in the camp clearing. Afte... ward he had climbed down, gone over to my tent, and taken the bananas that had just been put there for my supper.

32   This was fantastic news. For months the chimps had been running off when they saw me—now one had actually visited my camp! Perhaps he would come again.

33   The next day I waited, in case he did. What a luxury to lie in until 7:00 A.M. As the hours went by I began to fear that the chimp wouldn't come. But finally, at about four in the afternoon, I heard a rustling in the undergrowth opposite my tent, and a black shape appeared on the other side of the clearing.

CLOSE READ

ANNOTATE: In paragraph 32, mark the punctuation that Dr. Goodall uses to describe her reaction to the news about the chimpanzee visit.

QUESTION: Why might she have chosen to use this punctuation?

CONCLUDE: What does the punctuation reveal about her reaction?

Dr. Goodall was the first person to observe chimps like this one using grass and sticks to "fish" for termites.

NOTES

34　　I recognized him at once. It was the handsome male with the dense white beard. I had already named him David Greybeard. Quite calmly he climbed into the palm and feasted on its nuts. And then he helped himself to the bananas I had set out for him.

35　　There were ripe palm nuts on that tree for another five days, and David Greybeard visited three more times and got lots of bananas.

36　　A month later, when another palm tree in camp bore ripe fruit, David again visited us. And on one of those occasions he actually took a banana from my hand. I could hardly believe it.

37　　From that time on things got easier for me. Sometimes when I met David Greybeard out in the forest, he would come up to see if I had a banana hidden in my pocket. The other chimps stared with amazement. Obviously I wasn't as dangerous as they had thought. Gradually they allowed me closer and closer.

38　　It was David Greybeard who provided me with my most exciting observation. One morning, near the Peak, I came upon him squatting on a termite mound. As I watched, he picked a blade of grass, poked it into a tunnel in the mound, and then withdrew it. The grass was covered with termites all clinging on with their jaws. He picked them off with his lips and scrunched them up. Then he fished for more. When his piece of grass got bent, he dropped it, picked up a little twig, stripped the leaves off it, and used that.

39　　I was really thrilled. David had used objects as tools! He had also changed a twig into something more suitable for fishing termites. He had actually *made* a tool. Before this observation, scientists had thought that only humans could make tools. Later I would learn that chimpanzees use more objects as tools than any creature except for us. This finding excited Louis Leakey more than any other.

40　　In October the dry season ended and it began to rain. Soon the golden mountain slopes were covered with lush green grass. Flowers appeared, and the air smelled lovely. Most days it rained just a little. Sometimes there was a downpour. I loved being out in the forest in the rain. And I loved the cool evenings when I could lace the tent shut and make it cozy inside with a storm lantern. The only trouble was that everything got damp and grew mold.

Scorpions and giant poisonous centipedes sometimes appeared in the tent—even, a few times, a snake. But I was lucky—I never got stung or bitten.

41 The chimpanzees often seemed **miserable** in the rain. They looked cold, and they shivered. Since they were clever enough to use tools, I was surprised that they had not learned to make shelters. Many of them got coughs and colds. Often, during heavy rain, they seemed **irritable** and bad tempered.

42 Once, as I walked through thick forest in a downpour, I suddenly saw a chimp hunched in front of me. Quickly I stopped. Then I heard a sound from above. I looked up and there was a big chimp there, too. When he saw me he gave a loud, clear wailing *wraaaah*—a spine-chilling call that is used to threaten a dangerous animal. To my right I saw a large black hand shaking a branch and bright eyes glaring **threateningly** through the foliage. Then came another savage *wraaaah* from behind. Up above, the big male began to sway the vegetation. I was surrounded. I crouched down, trying to appear as nonthreatening as possible.

43 Suddenly a chimp charged straight toward me. His hair bristled with rage. At the last minute he swerved and ran off. I stayed still. Two more chimps charged nearby. Then, suddenly, I realized I was alone again. All the chimps had gone.

44 Only then did I realize how frightened I had been. When I stood up my legs were trembling! Male chimps, although they are only four feet tall when upright, are at least three times stronger than a grown man. And I weighed only about ninety pounds. I had become very thin with so much climbing in the mountains and only one meal a day. That incident took place soon after the chimps had lost their initial terror of me but before they had learned to accept me calmly as part of their forest world. If David Greybeard had been among them, they probably would not have behaved like that, I thought.

45 After my long days in the forests I looked forward to supper. Dominic always had it ready for me when I got back in the evenings. Once a month he went into Kigoma with Hassan. They came back with new supplies, including fresh vegetables and fruit and eggs. And they brought my mail—that was something I really looked forward to.

46 After supper I would get out the little notebook in which I had scribbled everything I had seen while watching the chimps during the day. I would settle down to write it all legibly into my journal. It was very important to do that every evening, while it was all fresh in my mind. Even on days when I climbed back to sleep near the chimps, I always wrote up my journal first.

47 Gradually, as the weeks went by, I began to recognize more and more chimpanzees as individuals. Some, like Goliath, William,

miserable (MIHZ uhr uh buhl) *adj.* extremely unhappy or uncomfortable

irritable (IHR uh tuh buhl) *adj.* easily annoyed or angered

threateningly (THREHT uhn ihng lee) *adv.* in a frightening or alarming way

NOTES

CLOSE READ

ANNOTATE: In paragraphs 48–49, mark the words that describe how the chimps look and behave.

QUESTION: Why do you think Dr. Goodall chose to include these descriptions of the chimps and their behavior?

CONCLUDE: How do these descriptions help the reader better understand the chimps?

impetuous (ihm PEHCH yoo uhs) *adj.* acting suddenly with little thought

and old Flo, I got to know well, because David Greybeard sometimes brought them with him when he visited camp. I always had a supply of bananas ready in case the chimps arrived.

48   Once you have been close to chimps for a while they are as easy to tell apart as your classmates. Their faces look different, and they have different characters. David Greybeard, for example, was a calm chimp who liked to keep out of trouble. But he was also very determined to get his own way. If he arrived in camp and couldn't find any bananas, he would walk into my tent and search. Afterward, all was chaos. It looked as though some burglar had raided the place! Goliath had a much more excitable, **impetuous** temperament. William, with his long-shaped face, was shy and timid.

49   Old Flo was easy to identify. She had a bulbous nose and ragged ears. She came to camp with her infant daughter, whom I named Fifi, and her juvenile son, Figan. Sometimes adolescent Faben came, too. It was from Flo that I first learned that in the wild, female chimps have only one baby every five or six years. The older offspring, even after they have become independent, still spend a lot of time with their mothers, and all the different family members help one another.

50   Flo also taught me that female chimps do not have just one mate. One day she came to my camp with a pink swelling on her rump. This was a sign that she was ready for mating. She was followed by a long line of suitors. Many of them had never visited my camp before, and they were scared. But they were so attracted to Flo that they overcame their fear in order to keep close to her. She allowed them all to mate with her at different times.

51   Soon after the chimps had begun to visit my camp, the National Geographic Society, which was giving Louis money for my research, sent a photographer to Gombe to make a film. Hugo van Lawick was a Dutch baron. He loved and respected animals just as I did, and he made a wonderful movie. One year later, in England, we got married.

52   By then I had left Gombe for a while, to start my own studies at Cambridge University. I hated to leave, but I knew I would soon be back. I had promised Louis that I would work hard and get my Ph.D. degree.

53   After I got the degree, Hugo and I went back to Gombe together. It was a very exciting time, as Flo had just had a baby, little Flint. That was the first wild chimpanzee infant that I ever saw close up, nearly four years after I had begun my research.

54   Flo came very often to camp looking for bananas. Fifi, now six years old, and Figan, five years older, were still always with her. Fifi loved her new baby brother. When he was four months old

she was allowed to play with and groom him. Sometimes Flo let her carry him when they moved through the forest. During that time, Fifi learned a lot about how to be a good mother.

55   Flint learned to walk and climb when he was six months old. And he learned to ride on his mother's back during travel, instead of always clinging on underneath. He gradually spent more time playing with his two older brothers. They were always very gentle with him. So were other youngsters of the community. They had to be, for if Flo thought any other chimps were too rough, she would charge over and threaten or even attack them.

> Gradually, as the weeks went by, I began to recognize more and more chimpanzees as individuals.

56   I watched how Flint gradually learned to use more and more of the different calls and gestures that chimpanzees use to communicate with each other. Some of these gestures are just like ours—holding hands, embracing, kissing, patting one another on the back. They mean about the same, too. And although they do not make up a language the way human words do, all the different calls do help the chimpanzees know what is happening, even if they are far away when they hear the sounds. Each call (there are at least thirty, perhaps more) means something different.

57   Flo was the top-ranked female of her community and could **dominate** all the others. But she could not boss any of the males. In chimpanzee society, males are the dominant sex. Among the males themselves, there is a social order, and one male at the top is the boss.

dominate (DOM uh nayt) *v.* rule or control

58   The first top-ranking male I knew was Goliath. Then, in 1964, Mike took over. He did this by using his brain. He would gather up one or two empty kerosene cans from my camp and hit and kick them ahead of him as he charged toward a group of adult males. It was a spectacular performance and made a lot of noise. The other chimps fled. So Mike didn't need to fight to get to the top—which was just as well, as he was a very small chimp. He was top male for six years.

59   The adult males spend a lot of time in each other's company. They often patrol the boundaries of their territory and may attack chimpanzees of different communities if they meet. These conflicts are very brutal, and the victim may die. Only young females can move from one community to another without being hurt. In fact, the big males sometimes go out looking for such females and try to take them back into their own territory.

This photo from 1965 shows Dr. Goodall in her Gombe Stream camp with the chimp she named David Greybeard.

NOTES

60   As the months went by, I learned more and more. I recorded more and more details when I watched the chimpanzees. Instead of writing the information in notebooks, I started to use a little tape recorder. Then I could keep my eyes on the chimps all the time. By the end of each day there was so much typing to be done that I found I couldn't do it all myself. I needed an assistant to help. Soon, with even more chimps coming to camp, I needed other people to help with the observations.

61   There were always more fascinating things to watch and record, more people to help write everything down. What had started as a little camp for Mum and me ended up, six years later, as a research center, where students could come and collect information for their degrees. I was the director. ✒

Reprinted with the permission of Simon & Schuster Books for Young Readers, an imprint of Simon & Schuster Children's Publishing Division from *My Life With the Chimpanzees* by Jane Goodall. Copyright 1988, 1996 Byron Preiss Visual Publications, Inc. Text copyright © 1998, 1996 Jane Goodall.

Comprehension Check

Complete the following items after you finish your first read.

1. Why have Jane Goodall and her mother come to Gombe National Park?

2. At first, how do the chimpanzees react to Goodall?

3. What type of service does Goodall's mother set up for the local people?

4. Why does Goodall leave Gombe?

5. How does Goodall's camp become a research center?

📔 **Notebook** Write a brief summary of the excerpt from *My Life With the Chimpanzees* to demonstrate your understanding.

- -

RESEARCH

Research to Clarify Choose at least one unfamiliar detail from the text. Briefly research that detail. In what way does the information you learned shed light on an aspect of the memoir?

Research to Explore Choose something that interested you from the text, and formulate a research question.

from MY LIFE WITH THE
CHIMPANZEES

Close Read the Text

1. This model, from paragraph 42 of the text, shows two sample annotations, along with questions and conclusions. Close read the passage, and find another detail to annotate. Then, write a question and conclusion.

Close
Read

ANNOTATE: The writer has included a series of words that describe her actions.

QUESTION: What effect is created by this word choice?

CONCLUDE: The words help to create a feeling of suspense.

ANNOTATE: This passage contains a lot of descriptive details.

QUESTION: What effect does this use of language create?

CONCLUDE: The word choice, including the onomatopoeic *wraaaah*, brings to life a scary incident.

> Once, as I walked through thick forest in a downpour, I suddenly saw a chimp hunched in front of me. Quickly I stopped. Then I heard a sound from above. I looked up and there was a big chimp there, too. When he saw me he gave a loud, clear wailing *wraaaah*—a spine-chilling call that is used to threaten a dangerous animal.

🔧 **Tool Kit**
Close-Read Guide and
Model Annotation

2. For more practice, go back into text and complete the close-read notes.

3. Revisit a section of the text you found important during your first read. Read this section closely and **annotate** what you notice. Ask yourself **questions** such as "Why did the author make this choice?" What can you **conclude**?

Analyze the Text

CITE TEXTUAL EVIDENCE
to support your answers.

📓 Notebook **Respond to these questions.**

1. Make Inferences What do David Greybeard's visits to Dr. Goodall's camp show about the chimpanzees' changing response to her presence?

2. Speculate How might understanding the chimpanzees' system of gestures and calls change the way people think about the animals?

3. Essential Question: *How can people and animals relate to each other?* What have you learned from this memoir about how people and animals interact?

📋 STANDARDS

Reading Informational Text
• Cite textual evidence to support analysis of what the text says explicitly as well as inferences drawn from the text.

• Determine an author's point of view or purpose in a text and explain how it is conveyed in the text.

Analyze Craft and Structure

Author's Purpose *My Life With the Chimpanzees* is a **memoir,** a type of nonfiction in which an author tells about a memorable time in his or her own life. A memoir, then, is a type of true story.

Like all narratives, authors of memoir have a purpose for writing. An **author's purpose** is his or her main reason for writing. For example, an author's purpose may be to inform, persuade, entertain, describe, or express feelings. In many cases, an author has more than one purpose. For example an author may write about the impacts of an oil spill to both inform readers as well as to persuade them to take action. To determine an **author's purpose,** make inferences, or educated guesses, based on the details he or she includes in the text.

Practice

📓 **Notebook** Complete the following activity, and then respond to the questions.

1. Reread the passages from the memoir shown in the chart, and mark important details in each. Then, explain what each passage shows about Goodall's experiences.

PASSAGE FROM TEXT	WHAT IT SHOWS
I shall never forget the thrill of that first exploration. Soon after leaving camp I met a troop of baboons. They were afraid of the strange, white-skinned creature (that was I) and gave their barking alarm call, "Waa-hoo! Waa-hoo!" again and again. I left them, hoping that they would become used to me soon—otherwise, I thought, all the creatures of Gombe would be frightened. (paragraph 5)	
Only a very few animals in the forests at Gombe were potentially dangerous—mainly buffalo and leopards. Bush pigs can be dangerous too, but only if you threaten them or their young. And, of course, there are poisonous snakes—seven different kinds. (paragraph 18)	
There were always more fascinating things to watch and record, more people to help write everything down. What had started as a little camp for Mum and me ended up, six years later, as a research center, where students could come and collect information for their degrees. I was the director. (paragraph 61)	

2. Review the notes you entered into the chart. What might be Goodall's overall purpose for writing?

3. (a) Does the title of this memoir, *My Life With the Chimpanzees,* help to indicate the writer's main purpose? (b) If not, what might be a better title?

from MY LIFE WITH THE CHIMPANZEES

Concept Vocabulary

vanished	irritable	impetuous
miserable	threateningly	dominate

Why These Words? The six concept words describe different aspects of the chimpanzees' behavior. For example, the chimpanzees appear *miserable* and *irritable* in the rain. Notice that both words describe what the chimpanzees seem to be feeling.

1. How does the concept vocabulary sharpen the reader's understanding of chimpanzees' behavior?

2. What other words in the selection connect to this concept?

Practice

Notebook The words listed above appear in *My Life With the Chimpanzees.* Use each concept vocabulary word in a sentence that shows the word's meaning. Then, find at least one **synonym,** or word with a similar meaning, and one **antonym,** or word with an opposite meaning, for each word.

Word Study

Latin Suffix: -able The Latin suffix *-able* means "capable of, given to, or tending to," and it usually indicates that a word is an adjective. In *My Life With the Chimpanzees,* the word *irritable* means "tending to be irritated," or "tending to be easily annoyed." Knowing the **base word,** or "inside" word, along with the suffix can help you determine the meaning of an unfamiliar word. For example, in the word *irritable,* the base word is *irritate.*

1. How does the definition of the suffix *-able* help you understand the meaning of the vocabulary word *miserable*?

2. Review paragraph 48 and find a word with the suffix *-able*. Identify the base word. Then, write a definition for the word.

Conventions

Commas, Parentheses, and Dashes Punctuation marks help writers organize their thoughts and divide sentences into meaningful parts.

A **comma** signals readers to pause. It is used to separate words or groups of words in a list or series.

EXAMPLE: *The chimps ate bananas, seeds, flowers, stems, and meat.*

Commas are also used to set off nonessential elements in a sentence, such as phrases or clauses. A **nonessential,** or **nonrestrictive, element** is one that is not needed to convey the main idea of a sentence. It can be deleted without affecting the sentence's basic meaning.

TIP

CLARIFICATION
Refer to the Grammar Handbook to learn more about these terms.

SET OFF NONESSENTIAL APPOSITIVE PHRASE	SET OFF NONESSENTIAL PARTICIPIAL PHRASE	SET OFF NONESSENTIAL RELATIVE CLAUSE
David Greybeard, <u>the boldest chimp</u>, was the first she met.	The chimps, <u>hidden in the treetops</u>, watched her every move.	The chimps, <u>whom Goodall named</u>, have unique personalities.

Like commas, **parentheses** also set apart nonessential elements from the rest of a sentence. However, parentheses suggest the information they contain is even less important than information set off by commas.

EXAMPLE: *The chimps made tools <u>(twigs or grass blades)</u> to gather food.*

Dashes are another type of punctuation mark used to set apart nonessential elements. They have the added effect of indicating a sudden or strong interruption in thought.

EXAMPLE: *Jane Goodall was young<u>—surprisingly so—</u>when she first went to Africa to study chimpanzees.*

Read It

1. Each of the following sentences should contain one or more commas, parentheses, or dashes. Add the indicated punctuation correctly.
   a. The many supplies Jane and her mother brought included food medicines writing materials blankets and pillows. (commas)
   b. Chimpanzees eat mostly fruits bananas especially but also plants, stems, seeds, blossoms, and leaves. (parentheses)
   c. Jane discovered that chimps enjoy sleeping in comfort just as people do. (dash)
2. Reread paragraph 15. Mark one example each of a comma, parentheses, and a dash. Then, explain the purpose of each mark.

Write It

📓 **Notebook** Punctuate this paragraph correctly.

Jane Goodall first began her work in the 1950s and despite the years that have gone by remains well-known for her study of chimpanzees. She was first to learn that chimpanzees are not strictly vegetarians they eat meat, too. She was also one of the first scientists to give names to the chimpanzees she studied usually the chimps were numbered.

from MY LIFE WITH THE CHIMPANZEES

Writing to Sources

A **how-to essay** is a type of explanatory essay that provides step-by-step instructions for how to do or make something.

Assignment

Dr. Goodall describes the process, or steps, by which she earned the chimpanzees' trust. Review the text, and record concrete details and other information related to the process Goodall used to gain the chimpanzees' friendship. Then, write a brief **how-to essay** that describes the process.

- State and explain each step clearly, and support your explanation with details from the text.
- Use formatting, such as boldface headings, to distinguish each step in the process. Describe each step in complete sentences.
- Use transitions, such as *first, next, then,* and *finally,* to clarify the position of each step in the process.
- Use precise language to explain exactly what Dr. Goodall did in each step.

Vocabulary and Conventions Connection Try to include several of the concept vocabulary words in your essay. Also, remember to use commas, parentheses or dashes to set off nonessential sentence elements.

vanished	irritable	impetuous
miserable	threateningly	dominate

Reflect on Your Writing

Notebook After you have written your explanatory essay, answer the following questions.

1. How did explaining the steps in Dr. Goodall's process help you to understand her research?

2. Which details from the excerpt did you include in your writing? How did they help to convey the steps of the process?

3. **Why These Words?** The words you choose make a difference in your writing. Which words did you specifically choose to explain the steps in the process clearly?

STANDARDS

Writing
Write informative/explanatory texts to examine a topic and convey ideas, concepts, and information through the selection, organization, and analysis of relevant content.

a. Introduce a topic; organize ideas, concepts, and information using strategies such as definition, classification, comparison/contrast, and cause/effect; include formatting, graphics, and multimedia when useful to aiding comprehension.
b. Develop the topic with relevant facts, definitions, concrete details, quotations, or other information and examples.
c. Use appropriate transitions to clarify the relationships among ideas and concepts.
d. Use precise language and domain-specific vocabulary to inform about or explain the topic.

Speaking and Listening

Assignment

Dr. Goodall describes several chimpanzee behaviors that are similar to human behaviors. Participate in a **class discussion** in which you compare and contrast these behaviors.

1. **Explore the Topic** Think about details from the text as you explore the topic. Cite passages from the memoir as evidence. Also, include relevant examples from your own experience. To prepare for the discussion, consider the following questions.

   • What chimpanzee behaviors does Dr. Goodall describe that are similar to human behaviors?

   • What makes the chimpanzee behavior seem like that of humans?

   • Do these similarities help you better understand chimpanzees? Why, or why not?

2. **Conduct the Discussion** As your classmates contribute their ideas about the topic, give your full attention to each speaker. If you disagree with a statement, express your reasons respectfully and politely. Do not interrupt other classmates when they are speaking. When it is your turn to contribute, speak clearly and loudly enough to be heard by the entire class.

3. **Evaluate the Discussion** During the discussion, listen closely as your classmates share their ideas. Use a guide like the one shown to evaluate the group discussion.

EVALUATION GUIDE

Rate each statement on a scale of 1 (not demonstrated) to 5 (demonstrated).

☐ Each class member had the opportunity to contribute his or her ideas.

☐ Class members listened closely as each person spoke and did not interrupt one other.

☐ Class members expressed disagreements respectfully.

Reflect Write a few sentences in which you reflect on what you have learned from the discussion. In what ways has this knowledge increased your understanding of the relationship between humans and animals?

✐ EVIDENCE LOG

Before moving on to a new selection, go to your Evidence Log, and record what you learned from *My Life With the Chimpanzees.*

☷ STANDARDS

Speaking and Listening
Engage effectively in a range of collaborative discussions with diverse partners on *grade 6 topics, texts, and issues,* building on others' ideas and expressing their own clearly.
a. Come to discussions prepared, having read or studied required material; explicitly draw on that preparation by referring to evidence on the topic, text, or issue to probe and reflect on ideas under discussion.
b. Follow rules for collegial discussions, set specific goals and deadlines, and define individual roles as needed.
c. Pose and respond to specific questions with elaboration and detail by making comments that contribute to the topic, text, or issue under discussion.
d. Review the key ideas expressed and demonstrate understanding of multiple perspectives through reflection and paraphrasing.

About the Author

Pamela S. Turner (b. 1957) grew up in Southern California. She has always been interested in writing, and has said that the very first thing she remembers wanting to be was a children's author. Turner has lived all over the world. While living in Japan, she heard the story of Hachiko. When she returned to the United States, she wrote her first book, *Hachiko: The True Story of a Loyal Dog*. Since then, she has written many other books for children, and has won numerous awards for her writing.

 **Tool Kit** First-Read Guide and Model Annotation

STANDARDS

Reading Literature
By the end of the year, read and comprehend literature, including stories, dramas, and poems, in the grades 6–8 text complexity band proficiently, with scaffolding as needed at the high end of the range.

Hachiko: The True Story of a Loyal Dog

Concept Vocabulary

You will encounter the following words as you read this work of historical fiction. Before reading, note how familiar you are with each word. Then, rank the words in order from most familiar (1) to least familiar (5).

WORD	YOUR RANKING
timidly	
anxiously	
patiently	
thoughtfully	
silently	

After completing the first read, come back to the concept vocabulary and review your rankings. Mark changes to your original rankings as needed.

First Read FICTION

Apply these strategies as you conduct your first read. You will have an opportunity to complete the close-read notes after your first read.

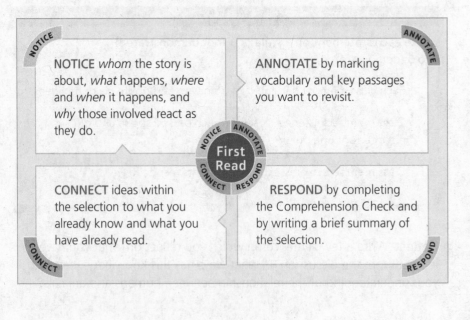

NOTICE *whom* the story is about, *what* happens, *where* and *when* it happens, and *why* those involved react as they do.

ANNOTATE by marking vocabulary and key passages you want to revisit.

CONNECT ideas within the selection to what you already know and what you have already read.

RESPOND by completing the Comprehension Check and by writing a brief summary of the selection.

Hachiko:
The True Story of a Loyal Dog

Pamela S. Turner

SCAN FOR MULTIMEDIA

NOTES

1 When I was six years old, my family moved to a little house in Tokyo near the Shibuya train station. At first the trains frightened me. But after a while, I grew to enjoy their power and the furious noises they made. One day I begged Mama to take me to meet Papa as he came home on the afternoon train. She laughed and said, "Kentaro, you have become big and brave, just like a samurai!" Together we walked to the station. Mama and I had stopped near the station entrance when I noticed the dog.

2 He was sitting quietly, all alone, by a newspaper stand. He had thick, cream-colored fur, small pointed ears, and a broad, bushy tail that curved up over his back. I wondered if the dog was a stray, but he was wearing a nice leather harness and looked healthy and strong.

3 His brown eyes were fixed on the station entrance.

4 Just then, Papa appeared. He was chatting with an older man. The dog bounded over to the man, his entire body wiggling and quivering with delight. His eyes shone, and his mouth curled up into something that looked, to me, just like a smile.

5 "Ah, Kentaro! You see, Dr. Ueno, you are not the only one who has someone to welcome him," said Papa. He introduced us to the older man. "Dr. Ueno works with me at Tokyo Imperial University."

6 "What is your dog's name?" I asked **timidly**. The dog was beautiful, but his sharp face reminded me of a wolf's. I grabbed Mama's kimono and stepped behind her, just in case.

7 "Don't be afraid," said Dr. Ueno kindly. "This is Hachiko. He is big, but still a puppy. He walks me to the station every morning and waits for me to come home every afternoon. I think Hachiko stores up all his joy, all day long, and then lets it all out at once!"

8 Hachiko stood wagging his tail next to Dr. Ueno. I reached to touch him, and he bounced forward and sniffed my face. I yelped and jumped back behind Mama.

9 They all laughed. "Oh, Kentaro, don't worry—he just wants to get to know you," said Dr. Ueno. "Dogs can tell a lot about people just by smelling them. Why, Hachiko probably knows what you ate for lunch!"

10 From that day on, I went to the train station almost every afternoon. But I no longer went to see the trains. I went to see

timidly (TIHM ihd lee) *adv.* in a shy or fearful way; cautiously

CLOSE READ
ANNOTATE: In paragraphs 4 and 5, mark details that indicate Dr. Ueno's age. Mark details in paragraph 7 that indicate Hachiko's age.

QUESTION: Why does the author include these details?

CONCLUDE: How do these details help set up the situation that occurs in the story?

Hachiko. He was always there, waiting near the newspaper stand. I often saved a morsel from my lunch and hid it in one of my pockets.

11 Hachiko would sniff me all over, wagging his tail, until he found a sticky bit of fish or soybean cake. Then he would nudge me with his nose, as if to say, "Give me my prize!" When it was cold, I would bury my face in the thick ruff of creamy fur around his neck.

12 One day in May, I was waiting at the station with Hachiko. The moment I saw Papa, I knew something was wrong. He was alone, and he walked hunched over, staring sadly at the gray pavement under his feet.

anxiously (ANGK shuhs lee)
adv. in a worried, uneasy manner; nervously

13 "What's the matter, Papa?" I asked him **anxiously**, standing with one hand on Hachiko's broad head. He sighed. "Kentaro, let's go home." Hachiko's bright brown eyes followed us as we walked away, but he stayed behind, waiting for Dr. Ueno.

14 When we got home, Papa told us that Dr. Ueno had died that morning at the university. I was stunned. "But what will happen to Hachiko?" I asked, blinking hard to keep the tears back. "What will he do?"

15 The next day, I went back to check on Hachiko, but he was not there. Papa told me that Hachiko had been taken several miles away to live with some of Dr. Ueno's relatives. "But I'll never see him again!" I cried. "Why can't he live with us?"

16 "We don't have room for a dog," protested Papa. "And Hachiko really belongs to Dr. Ueno's relatives, now that Dr. Ueno is dead. Hachiko is better off having a home than sitting in a train station."

17 But Hachiko had other ideas. A few days later he was back at Shibuya Station, **patiently** waiting, his brown eyes fixed on the entrance. Hachiko had run back to his old home, and from there to Shibuya Station.

patiently (PAY shuhnt lee)
adv. bearing annoyance, hardship, or pain calmly and without complaint or anger

18 Mama and Papa let me take food and water to Hachiko every day. Other people at the station took an interest in Hachiko. Men and women who rode Papa and Dr. Ueno's train stopped by to scratch his ears and say a few kind words. One day I saw an old man filling Hachiko's water bowl as Hachiko licked his hand. The old man's hair was streaked with gray, and he was stooped, as if he had spent most of his life bent over the ground. But his eyes were as sharp and bright as Hachiko's.

19 "Are you young Kentaro?" the old man asked. I nodded. "I am Mr. Kobayashi. I was Dr. Ueno's gardener.

20 "Dr. Ueno told me that you and Hachiko often wait for the afternoon train together."

21 "Do you still take care of the house where Dr. Ueno lived?" I asked.

22 "Yes," said Mr. Kobayashi. "Hachiko comes back to the house every night to sleep on the porch. But in the morning, he walks to the station just like he did with Dr. Ueno. When the last train leaves the station, he returns home."

23   We were both silent. Then I asked, "Do you think Hachiko knows that Dr. Ueno died?"

24   Mr. Kobayashi said **thoughtfully**, "I don't know, Kentaro. Perhaps he still hopes that Dr. Ueno will return someday. Or perhaps he knows Dr. Ueno is dead, but he waits at the station to honor his master's memory."

25   As the years passed and Hachiko got older, he became very stiff and could barely walk to Shibuya Station. But still he went, every day. People began collecting money to build a statue of Hachiko at the station. Papa, Mama, and I all gave money, and we were very happy when the statue was placed next to the spot where Hachiko had waited for so many years.

26   One chilly morning I woke to the sound of Mama crying. "What's wrong?" I asked as I stumbled into the kitchen. Papa sat **silently** at the table, and Mama turned her tear-stained face to me. "Hachiko died last night at Shibuya Station," she choked. "Still waiting for Dr. Ueno."

27   Later that day we all went to the station. To our great surprise, Hachiko's spot near the newspaper stand was covered in flowers placed there by his many friends.

28   Old Mr. Kobayashi was there. He shuffled over to me and put a hand on my shoulder.

29   "Hachiko didn't come back to the house last night," he said quietly. "I walked to the station and found him. I think his spirit is with Dr. Ueno's, don't you?"

30   "Yes," I whispered.

31   The big bronze statue of Hachiko is a very famous meeting place. Shibuya Station is enormous now, and hundreds of thousands of people travel through it every day. People always say to each other, "Let's meet at Hachiko." Today Hachiko is a place where friends and family long separated come together again. 🐾

MEDIA CONNECTION

The Secret Life of the Dog

Discuss It How does viewing this video add to your understanding of the relationship between dogs and people? Write your response before sharing your ideas.

Comprehension Check

Complete the following items after you finish your first read.

1. How does Kentaro first meet Hachiko?

2. According to the story, what do people say today when they want to meet at Shibuya Station?

3. **Notebook** Write a three-sentence summary of the selection.

RESEARCH
Research to Clarify
Formulate a research question that you might use to find out more about the real-life Hachiko.

HACHIKO: THE TRUE STORY OF
A LOYAL DOG

Close Read the Text

1. This model, from paragraph 4, shows two sample annotations, along with questions and conclusions. Close read the passage, and find another detail to annotate. Then, write a question and conclusion.

ANNOTATE: The author uses vivid language to describe Hachiko's movements.

QUESTION: Why does the author choose these words to describe Hachiko's movements?

CONCLUDE: These vivid words create a word picture of Hachiko's joy.

ANNOTATE: Thie idea of a dog smiling is interesting.

QUESTION: Why does the author describe Hachiko in this way?

CONCLUDE: This description makes Hachiko's feelings seem like strong human emotions.

> Just then, Papa appeared. He was chatting with an older man. The dog bounded over to the man, his entire body wiggling and quivering with delight. His eyes shone, and his mouth curled up into something that looked, to me, just like a smile.

🔧 Tool Kit
Close-Read Guide and
Model Annotation

2. For more practice, go back into the text and complete the close-read note.

3. Revisit a section of the text you found important during your first read. Read this section closely and **annotate** what you notice. Ask yourself **questions** such as "Why did the author make this choice?" What can you **conclude**?

⠿ STANDARDS

Reading Literature
• Determine a theme or central idea of a text and how it is conveyed through particular details; provide a summary of the text distinct from personal opinions or judgments.

• Describe how a particular story's or drama's plot unfolds in a series of episodes as well as how the characters respond or change as the plot moves toward a resolution.

• Analyze how a particular sentence, chapter, scene, or stanza fits into the overall structure of a text and contributes to the development of the theme, setting, or plot.

Analyze the Text

CITE TEXTUAL EVIDENCE
to support your answers.

📄 Notebook Respond to these questions.

1. Interpret What does the statue of Hachiko **symbolize,** or represent, to the people of Japan?

2. Compare and Contrast How does Kentaro's loyalty to Hachiko compare with Hachiko's loyalty to Dr. Ueno?

3. Essential Question: *How can people and animals relate to each other?* What have you learned about the connection between people and animals from reading this selection?

Analyze Craft and Structure

Historical Fiction When writers base fictional stories on real events from the past, it is called **historical fiction.** Historical fiction uses facts, but blends them with elements from the author's imagination. Historical fiction shows what the past *might* have been like. Certain literary elements are especially important in this type of fiction:

- **Setting** is the time and place in which a story occurs. In historical fiction, the setting must accurately show real places. In addition, made-up places have to be believable.

- **Conflict** is the struggle or problem characters face. A story shows how a conflict begins, increases, and ends. In historical fiction, the conflict may show how a situation or character (such as a dog) became famous or important.

- **Theme** is a message about life or human nature that a story reveals. Historical fiction combines real and imaginative elements to express a theme.

In this story, Hachiko and Dr. Ueno are real. They lived in Tokyo, Japan, in the early twentieth-century. Shibuya Station is also a real place. Dr. Ueno's death and Hachiko's actions really happened. However, Kentaro and his parents are fictional. Their actions are also fictional, although they are likely based on things real people felt and did.

Practice

 Notebook Respond to these questions.

1. How does the setting at the beginning of the story compare with the description of Shibuya Station at the end? Explain how this change shows the importance of Hachiko's story to the people of Tokyo.

2. (a) In the chart, record details that show the loyalty shown between Hachiko and other characters in the story. (b) What possible theme do these details suggest?

	LOYALTY TO HACHIKO	LOYALTY FROM HACHIKO
Dr. Ueno		
Kentaro		
Mr. Kobayashi		
others		
THEME		

3. Both Hachiko and Kentaro face conflicts following Dr. Ueno's death. (a) How do they deal with these conflicts? (b) What results from their efforts? Explain.

4. Focus on paragraphs 18–24, in which Kentaro meets Mr. Kobayashi. How does this scene relate to the story as a whole?

HACHIKO: THE TRUE STORY OF
A LOYAL DOG

Concept Vocabulary

timidly	anxiously	patiently
thoughtfully	silently	

Why These Words? The five concept vocabulary words all show how people act and react to one another. For example, when Kentaro first meets Hachiko, he asks the dog's name *timidly*, with shyness and caution.

1. How does the concept vocabulary convey the characters' emotional responses to important events in the story?

2. What other words in the selection relate to this concept?

Practice

 Notebook The concept vocabulary words appear in the selection. Use a thesaurus to find at least one **synonym,** or word with a similar meaning, and one **antonym,** or word with an opposite meaning, for each concept vocabulary word. Then, use a dictionary to determine the precise meaning of each synonym and antonym.

Word Study

Anglo-Saxon Suffix: -ly Each of the concept vocabulary words ends with -*ly*. The Anglo-Saxon suffix -*ly* can be added to an adjective to form an adverb that modifies a verb. An adverb ending in -*ly* is called an **adverb of manner** because it describes the manner or way in which an action takes place.

1. Review each concept vocabulary word as Turner uses it in the selection. Identify the verb each concept word modifies by showing the way in which it takes place.

2. Scan paragraphs 2 and 7, and find two more words with the suffix -*ly*. Then, write a definition for each word that shows your understanding of the suffix -*ly*.

ⵗ WORD NETWORK

Add words related to people and animals from the text to your Word Network.

☰ STANDARDS

Language
• Demonstrate command of the conventions of standard English capitalization, punctuation, and spelling when writing.
  b. Spell correctly.
• Determine or clarify the meaning of unknown and multiple-meaning words and phrases based on *grade 6 reading and content,* choosing flexibly from a range of strategies.
  d. Verify the preliminary determination of the meaning of a word or phrase.
• Demonstrate understanding of figurative language, word relationships, and nuances in word meanings.
  b. Use the relationship between particular words to better understand each of the words.

Conventions

Spelling and Capitalization Most nouns follow straightforward spelling rules when changing from singular to plural. For example, you simply add *-s* or *-es* to the end of the singular word. The nouns *train, watch,* and *hero* are singular. The plural forms are *trains, watches,* and *heroes.* Other nouns need additional spelling changes to go from singular to plural. For these **irregular plurals,** follow these rules.

SPELLING OF SINGULAR NOUN	RULE	EXAMPLES
Ends with a consonant plus *-y*	Change the *y* to *i* and add *-es*	*story, stories* *memory, memories*
Ends in *-f* or *-fe*	Change the *f* to *v* and add *-es* or *-s*	*life, lives* *yourself, yourselves*

It is also important to follow rules for correct capitalization. Here are some capitalization rules to use:

CAPITALIZE	EXAMPLE
the first word in a sentence	*Just* then, Papa appeared.
the first word in a line of dialogue	"*But* what will happen to Hachiko?" I asked.
the pronoun *I*	*I* went to see Hachiko.
a proper noun or adjective	*Shibuya Station* is enormous now.
a person's title if used as part of the name	*Dr. Ueno* said, "His name is Hachiko."

Read It

1. Correct the capitalization in each of the following sentences. Explain the reasons for your corrections.

   a. hachiko was born in japan in november of 1923.

   b. the loyal dog walked from his home to shibuya station each day.

   c. "are you kentaro?" the old man asked. "i am mr. kobayashi."

2. Reread paragraph 5 of "Hachiko: The True Story of a Loyal Dog." Mark the proper nouns.

Write It

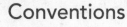 **Notebook** Write a paragraph about Hachiko. Spell plural nouns correctly, and observe the rules of capitalization.

HACHIKO: THE TRUE STORY OF
A LOYAL DOG

Writing to Sources

"Hachiko: The True Story of a Loyal Dog" tells the story of a boy and a dog. This story is narrated by Kentaro, a character in the story. Readers get to learn about Hachiko through Kentaro's eyes.

Assignment

Write your own version, or **story adaptation,** of "Hachiko: The True Story of a Loyal Dog." In your adaptation, change the narrator, and tell the story through Hachiko's eyes. Follow these steps:

- Reread the story, and identify main plot events.
- Take careful note of Hachiko's actions. Also, note his relationships with Dr. Ueno, Mr. Kobayashi, and other human beings in the story.
- Then, relate the story from Hachiko's point of view. As Hachiko tells the story, use details that show what he saw, smelled, heard, and felt as he lived through his experiences.

Vocabulary and Conventions Connection Consider including several of the concept vocabulary words. Also, remember to follow spelling and capitalization rules when writing.

timidly	anxiously	patiently
thoughtfully	silently	

Reflect on Your Writing

After you have written your story adaptation, answer the following questions.

1. What was the most challenging part of the assignment?

2. How might you revise your story to improve it?

3. Why These Words? The words you choose make a difference in your writing. Which words did you specifically choose to bring your narrator to life?

STANDARDS

Writing
• Write narratives to convey real or imagined experiences or events using effective technique, relevant descriptive details, and well-structured event sequences.
a. Engage and orient the reader by establishing a context and introducing a narrator and/or characters; organize an event sequence that unfolds naturally and logically.

• Draw evidence from literary or informational texts to support analysis, reflection, and research.
a. Apply *grade 6 Reading standards* to literature.

Speaking and Listening
• Engage effectively in a range of collaborative discussions with diverse partners on *grade 6 topics, texts, and issues,* building on others' ideas and expressing their own clearly.
a. Come to discussions prepared, having read or studied required material; explicitly draw on that preparation by referring to evidence on the topic, text, or issue to probe and reflect on ideas under discussion.
b. Follow rules for collegial discussions, set specific goals and deadlines, and define individual roles as needed.

• Present claims and findings, sequencing ideas logically and using pertinent descriptions, facts, and details to accentuate main ideas or themes; use appropriate eye contact, adequate volume, and clear pronunciation

Speaking and Listening

The unique relationship between dogs and people is important in many stories you may have heard or read.

> ### Assignment
>
> Briefly research a real-life account of a dog who performed a heroic act. Then, hold a **partner discussion** with a classmate. During the discussion, share the story you researched, and discuss similarities and differences between the dog heroes you learned about and Hachiko.
>
> Follow these steps as a guide.

1. **Perform Research** Locate a story of a heroic dog that you enjoy. If you are researching online, choose specific keywords to narrow your search. For example, you might use the keywords "dog" and "hero." When you find a story you like, make a copy of it.

2. **Read Your Stories Aloud** Choose a partner, and take turns reading your stories aloud to each other. Read clearly, and vary your tone to give expression to the reading.

3. **Listen Closely** Listen attentively as your partner reads aloud. Take notes as you listen to use in your discussion.

4. **Discuss Your Observations** Once you have finished reading your stories aloud, talk about the similarities and differences you see between the dogs you researched and Hachiko.

5. **Evaluate** Use an evaluation guide like the one shown to evaluate your partner discussion.

DISCUSSION EVALUATION GUIDE

Rate each statement on a scale of 1 (not demonstrated) to 5 (demonstrated).

☐ Each partner was prepared to share stories, information, and observations.

☐ Each partner presented a story and related ideas in a focused way.

☐ Each partner listened closely and provided feedback and comments.

☐ Partners took turns speaking, and built on each other's ideas.

✎ EVIDENCE LOG

Before moving on to a new selection, go to your Evidence Log and record what you learned from "Hachiko: The True Story of a Loyal Dog."

WRITING TO SOURCES

• *from* MY LIFE WITH THE CHIMPANZEES

• HACHIKO: THE TRUE STORY OF A LOYAL DOG

Write an Explanatory Essay

You have read an excerpt from a memoir and a work of historical fiction that demonstrate ways in which people and animals interact. In the excerpt from *My Life With the Chimpanzees,* Dr. Jane Goodall describes what she learned about chimpanzees, including how intelligent they are and how they behave in a group. In "Hachiko: The True Story of a Loyal Dog," Pamela S. Turner tells the story of a dog's loyalty to his owner.

Assignment

Use your knowledge of the excerpt from *My Life With the Chimpanzees* and "Hachiko: The True Story of a Loyal Dog" to consider qualities that human beings and animals seem to share. Write an **explanatory essay** that answers the question:

> ### What qualities do Goodall and Turner believe people and animals share?

Think about the experiences Goodall has with the chimpanzees and the way Turner describes Dr. Ueno and Hachiko. Identify feelings and ways of behaving that the two authors suggest animals and people have in common.

🔧 **Tool Kit**
Student Model of an Explanatory Essay

ACADEMIC VOCABULARY

As you craft your explanatory essay, consider using some of the academic vocabulary you learned in the beginning of the unit.

exclude
illustrate
community
elaborate
objective

📋 **STANDARDS**

Writing
• Write informative/explanatory texts to examine a topic and convey ideas, concepts, and information through the selection, organization, and analysis of relevant content.
• Write routinely over extended time frames and shorter time frames for a range of discipline-specific tasks, purposes, and audiences.

Elements of an Explanatory Essay

An **explanatory essay** uses facts, examples, and other information to explain a subject or topic. The purpose of an explanatory essay is to help readers better understand a topic.

A successful explanatory essay contains these elements:

- an introduction that states a clear central idea, or thesis
- a logical organization that helps readers follow the explanation
- concrete details, quotations, and examples that support the explanation
- transitions that connect ideas and show the relationships among them
- precise language and vocabulary to explain a topic
- a formal style
- a concluding statement that completes the explanation given in the essay

Model Informative/Explanatory Text For a model of a well-crafted informative/explanatory text, see the Launch Text, "Reading Buddies."

Challenge yourself to find all of the elements of an explanatory essay in the text. You will have an opportunity to review these elements as you prepare to write your own essay.

LAUNCH TEXT

Reading Buddies

Prewriting / Planning

Write a Working Thesis Now that you have read and thought about the selections, write a sentence in which you state your **thesis**, or central idea. As you continue to write your essay, you may revise your thesis or even change it entirely. For now, it will help guide you in developing ideas and choosing supporting details from the selections.

Working Thesis: _____

_____.

Gather Evidence From Sources After you have crafted a working thesis, look for evidence from the two texts to support it. Take notes on the following types of evidence you may want to use:

- **facts:** information that can be proved true

- **examples:** descriptions of specific people, things, or situations that support a general idea

Connect Across Texts The excerpt from *My Life With the Chimpanzees* includes facts about many different chimpanzees. In contrast, "Hachiko: The True Story of a Loyal Dog" focuses on one dog and his relationships with the people who care for him. The two texts offer different kinds of evidence, but they are both valuable. As you write, work to include details from both texts. Incorporate that evidence in different ways; for example, consider using both paraphrases and direction quotations.

- **Direct quotations** are an author's exact words. Use direct quotations when the precise words an author uses are especially interesting or important.

- If the author's ideas are valuable, but the specific words are not as important, **paraphrase** the information by restating it in your own words. Be careful to choose precise language and vocabulary when you paraphrase to be sure you accurately communicate the author's ideas.

Incorporating evidence in different ways will help you to express and support your ideas about the topic with accuracy and precision.

✐ EVIDENCE LOG

Review your Evidence Log and identify key details you may want to cite in your essay.

☷ STANDARDS

Writing
Write informative/explanatory texts to examine a topic and convey ideas, concepts, and information through the selection, organization, and analysis of relevant content.
b. Develop the topic with relevant facts, definitions, concrete details, quotations, or other information and examples.
d. Use precise language and domain-specific vocabulary to inform about or explain the topic.

STANDARDS

Writing

Write informative/explanatory texts to examine a topic and convey ideas, concepts, and information through the selection, organization, and analysis of relevant content.

a. Introduce a topic; organize ideas, concepts, and information, using strategies such as definition, classification, comparison/ contrast, and cause/effect; include formatting, graphics, and multimedia when useful to aiding comprehension.

f. Provide a concluding statement or section that follows from the information or explanation presented.

Drafting

Organize Your Essay As you write your essay, organize your ideas and evidence into three main sections:

- the **introduction** in which you introduce your topic and your thesis, and identify the main points you will make in the essay
- the **body** in which you explain the main points in more detail
- the **conclusion** in which you circle back to your thesis and restate it in a new way

Each paragraph in the body of your essay should have a clear main idea that relates to your thesis. State the main idea in a **topic sentence**. Then, explain the main idea and use details from the text to show how it is accurate or correct. The outline shows how the Launch Text is organized. Notice how each body paragraph includes a main idea that supports the thesis of the essay. Use it as a model to create an outline for your essay.

LAUNCH TEXT

Model: "Reading Buddies" Outline

INTRODUCTION

Paragraph 1 introduces the topic. Paragraph 2 introduces the thesis: *Reading programs that team up dogs and children help kids improve their reading skills.*

BODY

Paragraphs 3 and 4 provide background information: *There are many reasons kids struggle with reading.*

Paragraph 5 supports the thesis: *Dogs are the ideal reading companions for many reasons.*

Paragraph 6 provides an example to support the point made in paragraph 5: *One girl finished reading a whole book to a dog.*

Paragraph 7 supports the thesis: *Dogs enable kids to practice their reading skills in a nonthreatening way.*

Paragraph 8 supports the thesis: *Visiting schools and libraries helps dogs become more well-adjusted.*

CONCLUSION

Paragraph 9 restates the thesis: *The reading program helps both children and dogs.*

Explanatory Essay Outline

INTRODUCTION

_____

BODY

_____

CONCLUSION

Write a First Draft Use your outline to write your first draft. Remember to state your thesis in your introduction and to provide a strong conclusion. Cite details and examples from the texts to support your thesis.

LANGUAGE DEVELOPMENT: CONVENTIONS

Revising for Correct Pronoun Case

A **pronoun** is a word that takes the place of a noun or another pronoun. English has three cases, or forms, of pronouns. **Nominative, or subjective, case** is used for the subjects of verbs and for subject predicates. **Objective case** is used for direct and indirect objects and for objects of prepositions. **Possessive case** is used to show ownership.

Read It

This chart shows personal pronouns grouped by case.

CASE	PRONOUNS	FUNCTION IN A SENTENCE	EXAMPLE
Nominative/ Subjective	I, we, you, he, she, it, they	Subject of a verb	*She* told a story.
		Subject predicate	The storyteller was *she*.
Objective	me, us, you, him, her, it, them	Direct object	Amy told *it* to Anthony.
		Indirect object	Amy told *him* the story.
		Object of a preposition	Amy told the story to *him*.
Possessive	my, mine, our, ours, your, yours, his, her hers, its, their, theirs,	To show ownership	Amy told *her* story to Anthony.

Write It

Pronoun case can be confusing when you use compound subjects or objects. To make sure you have chosen the correct case, try using the pronoun alone with the verb. If it sounds wrong, it probably is.

1. **Compound Subject / Example Sentence:** The <u>dog and *me*</u> wait by the station.
   Pronoun Used Alone: *Me* wait by the station.
   Conclusion: The objective case sounds wrong. The nominative case is needed. The sentence should read: The <u>dog and *I*</u> wait by the station.

2. **Compound Object / Example Sentence:** The chimps play with <u>Jane and *I*</u>.
   Pronoun Used Alone: The chimps play with *I*.
   Conclusion: The nominative case sounds wrong. The objective case is needed. The sentence should read: The chimps play with <u>Jane and *me*.</u>

▦ STANDARDS

Language
Demonstrate command of the conventions of standard English grammar and usage when writing or speaking.
  a. Ensure that pronouns are in the proper case.
  e. Recognize variations from standard English in their own and others' writing and speaking, and identify and use strategies to improve expression in conventional language.

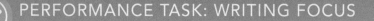

Revising

Evaluating Your Draft

Use the following checklist to evaluate the effectiveness of your first draft. Then, use your evaluation and the instruction on this page to guide your revision.

FOCUS AND ORGANIZATION	EVIDENCE AND ELABORATION	CONVENTIONS
☐ Provides an introduction that includes a thesis statement.	☐ Develops main ideas with strong facts and relevant details from the texts.	☐ Uses correct pronoun case.
☐ Establishes a logical organization that is easy for readers to follow.	☐ Provides examples for each major point.	☐ Establishes and maintains a formal style.
☐ Provides a conclusion that follows from the ideas presented earlier in the essay.	☐ Uses precise language to express and support ideas.	
☐ Uses transitions that show clear relationships among ideas.		

Copyright © SAVVAS Learning Company LLC. All Rights Reserved.

Revising for Focus and Organization

Use Transitions Reread your draft, paying careful attention to the organization of your ideas. Note any places where the relationship of one idea to the next is not clear. Consider using transitions to improve the flow of your ideas.

TO SHOW . . .	TRANSITIONS
Similarities	*equally important, moreover, as well as, similarly, in addition*
Differences	*however, on the other hand, although, despite, in contrast, yet*
Examples	*for instance, including, for example, especially, in other words*

Revising for Evidence and Elaboration

Use a Formal Style An explanatory essay uses facts and examples to support a central idea. It should not include informal statements of your opinion. As you revise your essay, review your word choices. Avoid the following types of words or statements:

- words that suggest a bias, such as *excellent* or *awful,* unless supported by factual evidence
- superlative adjectives, such as *most, least, best,* and *worst,* unless supported by factual evidence

---

⬡ WORD NETWORK

Include words from your Word Network in your explanatory essay.

⬛ STANDARDS

Writing
Write informative/explanatory texts to examine a topic and convey ideas, concepts, and information through the selection, organization, and analysis of relevant content.
c. Use appropriate transitions to clarify the relationships among ideas and concepts.
e. Establish and maintain a formal style.

PEER REVIEW

Exchange essays with a classmate. Use the checklist to evaluate your classmate's essay and provide supportive feedback.

1. Is the thesis clear?

☐ yes ☐ no   If no, explain what confused you.

2. Are ideas clearly stated and supported by facts and examples?

☐ yes ☐ no   If no, point out which points need more support.

3. Does the conclusion logically wrap up the essay?

☐ yes ☐ no   If no, suggest information that you feel is missing.

4. What is the strongest part of your classmate's essay?

Editing and Proofreading

Edit for Conventions Reread your draft for accuracy and consistency. Correct errors in grammar and word usage. Review your essay to be sure the pronouns you use are in the proper case. Refer to the strategies given in the Language Development section to identify and correct errors in pronoun case.

Proofread for Accuracy Read your draft carefully, correcting errors in spelling and punctuation. Remember to check the selection texts for the correct spelling of proper names.

Publishing and Presenting

Create a final version of your essay. Then, using the information from your essay and computer software, develop, design, and present an **informative booklet** about human and animal interaction. Choose a font or style that is easy to read and creates an attractive text. Then, exchange booklets with your classmates and give one another feedback. Take turns noting which booklets contained information that was similar to the information in yours, and which suggested very different ideas. Contribute in positive, supportive ways to the discussion, and listen closely when it is someone else's turn to speak.

Reflecting

Think about what you learned by writing your essay and what you learned from reading the essays and booklets of your classmates. What could you do differently the next time you need to write an explanatory essay that might make it stronger?

STANDARDS

Writing
• Produce clear and coherent writing in which the development, organization, and style are appropriate to task, purpose, and audience.

• With some guidance and support from peers and adults, develop and strengthen writing as needed by planning, revising, editing, rewriting, or trying a new approach.

• Use technology, including the Internet, to produce and publish writing as well as to interact and collaborate with others; demonstrate sufficient command of keyboarding skills to type a minimum of three pages in a single sitting.

ESSENTIAL QUESTION:

How can people and animals relate to each other?

Sometimes animals communicate with other kinds of animals. Other times, they communicate with people. How is the relationship between animal species similar to and different from the relationship between animals and people? You will work in a group to continue your exploration of these relationships.

Small-Group Learning Strategies

Throughout your life, in school, in your community, and in your career, you will continue to learn and work with others.

Review these strategies and the actions you can take to practice them as you work in teams. Add ideas of your own for each step. Use these strategies during Small-Group Learning.

STRATEGY	ACTION PLAN
Prepare	• Complete your assignments so that you are prepared for group work. • Organize your thinking so you can contribute to your group's discussion. •
Participate fully	• Make eye contact to signal that you are listening and taking in what is being said. • Use text evidence when making a point. •
Support others	• Build on ideas from others in your group. • Invite others who have not yet spoken to join the discussion. •
Clarify	• Paraphrase the ideas of others to ensure that your understanding is correct. • Ask follow-up questions. •

SCAN FOR
MULTIMEDIA

CONTENTS

PERFORMANCE TASK
SPEAKING AND LISTENING FOCUS
Deliver an Informative Presentation
The Small-Group readings explore ways in which people and animals relate to or communicate with one another. After reading, your group will create an informative multimedia presentation about the ideas presented in these texts.

Working as a Team

1. **Take a Position** In your group, discuss the following question:

   What are some ways that animals can communicate with each other and with other animal species?

   As you take turns sharing your ideas, be sure to provide examples that illustrate them. After all group members have shared, discuss the ways in which animal communication is similar to and different from human communication.

2. **List Your Rules** As a group, decide on the rules that you will follow as you work together. Two examples are provided. Add two more of your own. You may add or revise rules based on your experience together.

   • Everyone should participate in group discussions.

   • People should not interrupt.

   • _____

   _____

   • _____

   _____

3. **Apply the Rules** Practice working as a group. Share what you have learned about the ways in people and animals relate to one another. Make sure each person in the group contributes. Take notes and be prepared to share with the class one thing that you heard from another member of your group.

4. **Name Your Group** Choose a name that reflects the unit topic.

   Our group's name: _____

5. **Create a Communication Plan** Decide how you want to share information with one another. For example, you might use online collaboration tools, email, or instant messaging.

   Our group's decision: _____

   _____

Making a Schedule

First, find out the due dates for the Small-Group activities. Then, preview the texts and activities with your group and make a schedule for completing the tasks.

SELECTION	ACTIVITIES	DUE DATE
A Blessing		
Predators		
Monkey Master		
Black Cowboy, Wild Horses		

Working on Group Projects

As your group works together, you'll find it more effective if each person has a specific role. Different projects require different roles. Before beginning a project, discuss the necessary roles, and choose one for each group member. Here are some possible roles; add your own ideas.

Project Manager: monitors the schedule and keeps everyone on task

Researcher: organizes research activities

Recorder: takes notes during group meetings

_____

_____

_____

_____

 SCAN FOR MULTIMEDIA

A BLESSING

Comparing Texts

In this lesson, you will read and compare two poems. First, you will complete the first-read and close-read activities for "A Blessing." The work you do with your group on this title will help prepare you for the comparing task.

PREDATORS

About the Author

James Wright (1927–1980) was a Pulitzer Prize–winning American poet born in Martins Ferry, Ohio. He was known as a master of a variety of writing styles, and for the beauty and emotional quality of his work. His early poems often focused on isolation and loneliness. However, his later poetry often praised the joy and comfort that could be found in the natural world.

A Blessing

Concept Vocabulary

As you perform your first read of "A Blessing" you will encounter these words.

shyly	loneliness	blossom

Context Clues To find the meaning of unfamiliar words, look for clues in the context, which is made up of words and punctuation that surround the unknown word. There are various types of context clues that may help you as you read. Here are two examples:

> **Synonyms:** The horses <u>searched</u> and **foraged** for grass on the sandy field with little success.
>
> **Contrast of Ideas:** Petra is **shrewd,** but her twin sister is very <u>foolish</u>.

Apply your knowledge of context clues and other vocabulary strategies to determine the meanings of unfamiliar words you encounter during your first read.

First Read POETRY

Apply these strategies as you conduct your first read. You will have an opportunity to complete a close read after your first read.

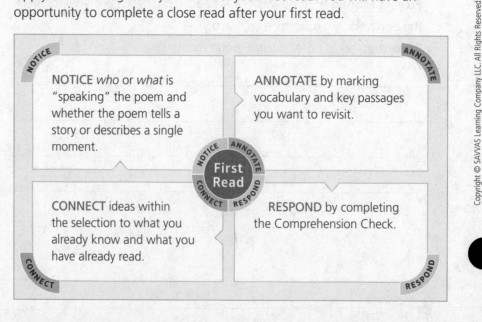

NOTICE *who* or *what* is "speaking" the poem and whether the poem tells a story or describes a single moment.

ANNOTATE by marking vocabulary and key passages you want to revisit.

First Read

CONNECT ideas within the selection to what you already know and what you have already read.

RESPOND by completing the Comprehension Check.

☰ STANDARDS

Reading Literature
By the end of the year, read and comprehend literature, including stories, dramas, and poems, in the grades 6–8 text complexity band proficiently, with scaffolding as needed at the high end of the range.

Language
Determine or clarify the meaning of unknown and multiple-meaning words and phrases based on *grade 6 reading and content*, choosing flexibly from a range of strategies.
    a. Use context as a clue to the meaning of a word or phrase.

A Blessing

James Wright

BACKGROUND

For thousands of years, people have relied on horses to carry their belongings, plow fields, and to take them farther and faster than they could go on their own two feet. But the relationship with horses is not only about work—we can share a deep emotional connection with these graceful animals.

SCAN FOR MULTIMEDIA

Just off the highway to Rochester, Minnesota,
Twilight bounds softly forth on the grass.
And the eyes of those two Indian ponies
Darken with kindness.
5 They have come gladly out of the willows
To welcome my friend and me.
We step over the barbed wire into the pasture
Where they have been grazing all day, alone.
They ripple tensely, they can hardly contain their happiness
10 That we have come.
They bow **shyly** as wet swans. They love each other.
There is no **loneliness** like theirs.

At home once more,
They begin munching the young tufts[1] of spring in the darkness.
15 I would like to hold the slenderer one in my arms,
For she has walked over to me
And nuzzled my left hand.
She is black and white,
Her mane falls wild on her forehead,
20 And the light breeze moves me to caress her long ear
That is delicate as the skin over a girl's wrist.
Suddenly I realize
That if I stepped out of my body I would break
Into **blossom**.

---

1. **tufts** (tuhfts) *n.* bunches of soft material, such as grass.

Mark context clues or indicate another strategy you used that helped you determine meaning.

blossom (BLOS uhm) *n.*

MEANING:

Comprehension Check

Complete the following items after you finish your first read. Review and clarify details with your group.

1. Where does the poem take place?

2. Who greets the speaker and the speaker's friend?

3. What does the "slenderer one" do that moves the speaker?

RESEARCH

Research to Clarify Choose at least one unfamiliar detail from the poem. Briefly research that detail. In what way does the information you learned shed light on an aspect of the poem?

Close Read the Text

With your group, revisit sections of the text you marked during your first read. **Annotate** details that you notice. What **questions** do you have? What can you **conclude**?

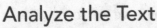

Analyze the Text

CITE TEXTUAL EVIDENCE to support your answers.

📓 **Notebook** Complete the activities.

1. **Review and Clarify** With your group, reread "A Blessing." What are some words or phrases that help you visualize, or picture in your mind, the setting of the poem?

2. **Present and Discuss** Now, work with your group to share lines from the poem that you found especially important. Take turns presenting the lines you chose. Discuss what you noticed in the poem, what questions you asked, and what conclusions you reached.

3. **Essential Question:** *How can people and animals relate to each other?* What has this poem taught you about the ways people and animals can relate to each other? Discuss with your group.

> **TIP**
>
> **GROUP DISCUSSION**
> Your group members might have different opinions of the poem. When you discuss your opinions, be supportive of other members' views. Remember to cite evidence from the poem to support your opinions.

LANGUAGE DEVELOPMENT

Concept Vocabulary

shyly	loneliness	blossom

Why These Words? The three concept vocabulary words from the poem are related. With your group, determine what the words have in common. How do these word choices enhance the impact of the text?

Practice

📓 **Notebook** The concept vocabulary words appear in "A Blessing." For each word, write a sentence in which you use the word correctly.

Word Study

Multiple-Meaning Words Many words in English have multiple meanings, or more than one definition. For example, the word *blossom*, which appears in the poem "A Blessing," has several meanings, and can be a verb or a noun. With your group, write a definition of *blossom* as it is used in the poem. Then, use a dictionary to find another definition for *blossom*. Finally, find two more multiple-meaning words in the poem. Record the words and two definitions for each word.

> 🔲 **WORD NETWORK**
>
> Add words related to people and animals from the text to your Word Network.

> ▤ **STANDARDS**
>
> **Language**
> Determine or clarify the meaning of unknown and multiple-meaning words and phrases based on grade 6 reading and content, choosing flexibly from a range of strategies.
>   c. Consult reference materials, both print and digital, to find the pronunciation of a word or determine or clarify its precise meaning or its part of speech.

A BLESSING

Analyze Craft and Structure

Elements of Poetry "A Blessing" is a **lyric poem,** which is a short work about a moment in time or a single insight. Most lyric poems use literary devices to add meaning and beauty. For example, a poet may use **sound devices,** or groups of words that create sound patterns. These are two types of sound devices:

- **Repetition:** the use of any part of language more than once—it could be a letter, a word, a phrase, or a sentence.
- **Alliteration:** repetition of the same consonant sound at the beginning of words that are close together—in this line, the "l" sound creates alliteration: "leave me a little love."

Sound devices may make a line of poetry sound like flowing water, banging drums, or anything in between.

Poets also use **figurative language,** which are imaginative descriptions. One common type of figurative language is the simile. A **simile** is a comparison of two unlike things that uses a comparing word, such as "like" or "as." This line is a simile: *papers fill the room like hay in a barn.*

A poem's subject and language combine to create a certain **tone,** or attitude. You can describe tone with the same words you use to name emotions, such as *sad, peaceful,* or *loving.*

Practice

CITE TEXTUAL EVIDENCE to support your answers.

Notebook Read the poem or individual lines aloud to help you hear the poet's use of literary devices. Then, work with your group to answer the questions.

1. What sound device appears in line 9? Explain.

2. **(a)** What sound device appears in lines 23–24? **(b)** How does this sound device add to the poem's effect? For example, how does it help emphasize important words?

3. **(a)** What comparing word is used to create a simile in line 11? **(b)** What two unlike things are compared? **(c)** Why do you think the poet uses this simile? What quality does it give to the two ponies?

4. Explain the simile that appears in lines 20–21: **(a)** What two unlike things are compared? **(b)** What quality does this simile give to the pony it describes?

5. How would you describe the tone of this poem? Identify specific words that help create that tone.

STANDARDS
Reading Literature
Determine the meaning of words and phrases as they are used in a text, including figurative and connotative meanings; analyze the impact of a specific word choice on meaning and tone.

142 UNIT 2 • ANIMAL ALLIES

Conventions

Verbs and Verb Tenses A **verb** expresses an action or a state of being. Every complete sentence includes at least one verb. There are two main types of verbs: action verbs and linking verbs.

- An **action verb** refers to physical or mental activity. *Jump* and *run* are action verbs. *Guess* and *wish* are also action verbs even though they refer to ways of thinking or feeling rather than physical activities.

- A **linking verb** connects a noun or a pronoun to a word that identifies, renames, or describes it. Linking verbs include all forms of the verb *be* (such as *am, is, were,* or *will be*), and certain other verbs such as *seem* and *become.*

  Examples:

  They *were* hungry.
  She *became* interested.

When a verb is used in a sentence, it has a **tense.** A verb tense shows when the action takes place. The three simple tenses are **present tense, past tense,** and **future tense.** To form the past tense of regular verbs—such as *march, bake,* and *talk*—add *-ed* or *-d.* Some verbs, such as *go,* are irregular. Their forms in different tenses do not follow a set pattern. For irregular verbs, you need to memorize the tense changes.

TENSE	REGULAR VERB: *bake*	IRREGULAR VERB: *be*
Present	I bake	He is
Past	I baked	He was
Future	I will bake	He will be

Read It

1. Identify the verb in each line from the poem. State whether it is an action verb or a linking verb. Then, identify its tense.

   a. They bow shyly as wet swans.

   b. And nuzzled my left hand.

   c. There is no loneliness like theirs.

2. Reread lines 18–21 from the poem. Mark each verb. State whether it is an action verb or a linking verb. Then, identify its tense.

Write It

Notebook Rewrite each line. Change the tense of the verb to the one indicated in parentheses.

1. And the eyes of those two Indian ponies darken with kindness. (future tense)

2. Twilight bounds softly forth on the grass. (past tense)

3. And nuzzled my left hand (present tense)

EVIDENCE LOG

Before moving on to a new selection, go to your Evidence Log and record what you learned from "A Blessing."

STANDARDS

Language
Demonstrate command of the conventions of standard English grammar and usage when writing or speaking.

A Blessing **143**

Comparing Texts

Complete the first-read and close-read activities for "Predators." Then, compare this poem with "A Blessing."

A BLESSING

PREDATORS

About the Author

Linda Hogan (b. 1947) is an award-winning Chickasaw novelist, essayist, environmentalist, and poet. Her writing often addresses topics such as the environment and Native American history. An activist and educator, Hogan has been a featured speaker at numerous international conferences and events on the environment and literature. She lives in the Colorado mountains and is currently the Chickasaw Nation's writer-in-residence.

Predators

Concept Vocabulary

As you perform your first read of "Predators," you will encounter these words.

cultivate	wild	domesticated

Context Clues To find the meaning of unfamiliar words, look for clues in the context, which is made up of the words and punctuation that surround the unknown word in a text. There are different types of context clues that may help you as you read. Here are two examples:

> **Synonym:** The dogs **gazed**, or watched, as the foxes walked into the woods.
>
> **Elaborating Details:** The faded colors and **indistinct** shapes show that the artist was losing his sight.

Apply your knowledge of context clues and other vocabulary strategies to determine the meanings of unfamiliar words you encounter during your first read.

First Read POETRY

Apply these strategies as you conduct your first read. You will have an opportunity to complete a close read after your first read.

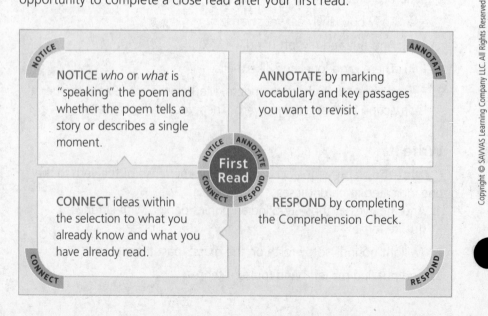

NOTICE who or what is "speaking" the poem and whether the poem tells a story or describes a single moment.

ANNOTATE by marking vocabulary and key passages you want to revisit.

CONNECT ideas within the selection to what you already know and what you have already read.

RESPOND by completing the Comprehension Check.

First Read

Predators

Linda Hogan

BACKGROUND

Habitat loss is a major threat to wildlife in the United States. As people use more land and alter natural environments, wild animals are forced to move into places where people and domestic animals live. Foxes are one type of wild animal that has been seen in residential neighborhoods in increasing numbers. The female fox is called a "vixen."

SCAN FOR
MULTIMEDIA

NOTES

I cannot smell the scent of the cat
who slept on this sweater, but do know
how the garden swells with old
and pungent* herb art. In sun the fox

---

pungent (PUHN juhnt) *adj.* strong-smelling

NOTES

Mark context clues or indicate another strategy you used that helped you determine meaning.

cultivate (KUHL tuh vayt) *v.*

MEANING:

wild (wyld) *adj.*

MEANING:

domesticated (duh MEHS tuh kay tihd) *adj.*

MEANING:

5 bows to my feline and her good
dog friends who rule this land. I hoe
and **cultivate**, find my dead aim
in the trust that many tales spun

this tract long before I came.
10 The dogs do not understand **wild** nature.
I also was **domesticated**.
Oh, give me strength to watch their sorry
looks as a bevy of vixen

feed on a much smaller body
15 not the cat's . . . But it could be.

Comprehension Check

Complete the following items after you finish your first read. Review and clarify details with your group.

1. What is the setting of the poem?

2. According to the speaker, how does the fox react to the cat and dogs?

3. What are the vixens doing at the end of the poem?

- -

RESEARCH

Research to Clarify Choose at least one unfamiliar detail from the poem. Briefly research that detail. In what way does the information you learned shed light on an aspect of the poem?

Research to Explore Choose something from the text that interests you, and formulate a research question.

Close Read the Text

With your group, revisit sections of the text you marked during your first read. **Annotate** details that you notice. What **questions** do you have? What can you **conclude**?

ANNOTATE · QUESTION · Close Read · CONCLUDE

Analyze the Text

CITE TEXTUAL EVIDENCE to support your answers.

 Notebook Complete the activities.

1. **Review and Clarify** With your group, reread "Predators." Why might the speaker say dogs do not understand wild nature?

2. **Present and Discuss** Now, work with your group to share lines from the poem that you found especially important. Take turns presenting the lines you chose. Discuss what you noticed in the text, what questions you asked, and what conclusions you reached.

3. **Essential Question: How can people and animals relate to each other?** What has this poem taught you about the ways people and animals can relate to each other? Discuss with your group.

> **TIP**
>
> **GROUP DISCUSSION**
> Be sure to identify specific lines or words from the poem so your group members can follow your thinking.

LANGUAGE DEVELOPMENT

Concept Vocabulary

> cultivate   wild   domesticated

Why These words? The three concept vocabulary words from the text are related. With your group, determine what the words have in common. How do these word choices enhance the impact of the text?

Practice

 Notebook The concept vocabulary words appear in "Predators." Work together as a group to write a sentence for each word.

Word Study

Latin Root: -dom- The speaker in "Predators" describes both herself and dogs as domesticated. The word *domesticated* is formed from the Latin root *-dom-*, which may mean "house" or "home," but which may also mean "lord" or "master."

Write a definition of *domesticated* that shows how the root *-dom-* contributes to its meaning. Then, find three other words formed from the same root. Write the words and their meanings.

> ⊞ **WORD NETWORK**
>
> Add words related to people and animals from the text to your Word Network.

> **STANDARDS**
> Language
> Determine or clarify the meaning of unknown and multiple-meaning words and phrases based on *grade 6 reading and content,* choosing flexibly from a range of strategies.
>   b. Use common, grade-appropriate Greek or Latin affixes and roots as clues to the meaning of a word.

PREDATORS

Analyze Craft and Structure

Poetic Structures Poetry features certain structures, or ways of being organized, that are different from prose. These structures include lines and stanzas.

- A **line** is a group of words arranged into a row. The point at which a line ends, or breaks, is important. It is a choice the poet makes for specific reasons. For example, the poet may want a line to include a certain number of syllables or have a certain rhythm. In some cases, a line break happens at the end of a sentence or in a place where a reader would naturally pause. In other cases, the line ends but the sentence continues onto the next line.

- A **stanza** is a group of lines. Like paragraphs in prose, each stanza in a poem may focus on a single main idea. **Stanza structure** refers to the way a poet organizes the stanzas. A poet may make all the stanzas in a poem the same length or different lengths. Stanzas are named by the number of lines they contain:

two lines: *couplet* **four lines:** *quatrain*
six lines: *sestet* **eight lines:** *octave*

All of the choices a poet makes about line lengths, line breaks, and stanzas add to the effect and meaning of a poem. They are tools that help the poet emphasize certain words or phrases, give a poem a particular shape and order, and add to its emotional impact on readers.

Practice

CITE TEXTUAL EVIDENCE to support your answers.

🔲 **Notebook** Work with your group to answer the questions.

1. The poem includes four stanzas. What type of stanza is used in stanzas 1 and 2? Explain.

2. **(a)** How many lines make up the poem's final stanza? **(b)** What is the name for this type of stanza?

3. Complete the chart to analyze the line breaks in this poem. Identify lines by number.

Which lines in the poem break at the end of a sentence?	
Where does the sentence that begins in the middle of line 4 end?	
Where does the sentence that begins at the end of line 6 end?	
Where does the sentence that begins on line 12 end?	

4. Use the analysis you did in question three to answer these questions: **(a)** In lines 10 and 11, the speaker simply states an observation. How does the structure of each line add to the statement-like quality? **(b)** How does the poet use line breaks to create a flow from stanza to stanza? Explain.

Copyright © SAVVAS Learning Company LLC. All Rights Reserved.

:::: **STANDARDS**

Reading Literature
Analyze how a particular sentence, chapter, scene, or stanza fits into the overall structure of a text and contributes to the development of the theme, setting, or plot.

Author's Style

Word Choice and Tone Word choice, or **diction,** is an important part of a poet's style. A poet's diction may have many different qualities. For example, it might be simple, old-fashioned, modern, formal, or informal. Often, a poet will use different types of diction, even within a single poem.

When making specific word choices, a poet will consider the word's meaning and the emotional qualities it conveys. These two elements of word meaning are called denotation and connotation:

- **Denotation** is a word's definition. You will find a word's denotation in a dictionary.
- **Connotations** are a word's emotional associations. Even if words are synonyms that share denotations, their connotations may be very different. For example, the word *car* has no connotation—it is a neutral word. *Junker* is a synonym for *car,* but it suggests a broken-down vehicle. *Classic* is also a synonym for *car* but it suggests a vehicle worthy of showing in a parade.

Read It

In her poem "Predators," Linda Hogan uses simple words that may be familiar to even young children. She also mixes in sophisticated words that may be unfamiliar to many readers. Complete the chart by adding words from "Predators" that fit the two categories. Work independently. Then, share and discuss your responses with your group. Two words have been done for you.

SIMPLE DICTION	SOPHISTICATED DICTION
Cat	Pungent

Write It

🖥 **Notebook** Choose one of the words from the "sophisticated" column of the chart. Use a dictionary to identify the word's meaning. Then, use a thesaurus to find a synonym. Rewrite the line from Hogan's poem, replacing it with a synonym. Explain how this revision changes the meaning or emotional quality of the line.

:: STANDARDS

Reading Literature
Determine the meaning of words and phrases as they are used in a text, including figurative and connotative meanings; analyze the impact of a specific word choice on meaning and tone.

Language
Demonstrate understanding of of figurative language, word relationships, and nuances in word meanings.
  c. Distinguish among the connotations of words with similar denotations.

A BLESSING

PREDATORS

Writing to Compare

In "A Blessing" and "Predators," two different poets describe encounters with or observations of animals. Deepen your understanding of the poems by comparing them. Then, share your insights in writing.

Assignment

Write a **comparison-and-contrast essay** in which you discuss similarities and differences in how the two poems present people and animals. In your essay, discuss the following questions:

- The animals: Are the animals wild, tame, or both?
- The speakers' feelings: Does the speaker feel peaceful, troubled, or both? Why?
- The title: What do the titles suggest about the speakers' attitudes?
- The conclusions: What new understanding does each speaker gain?

Work together as a group to analyze the poems. Then, work independently to write your essay.

Planning and Prewriting

Analyze the Texts With your group, discuss the questions as they relate to each poem on its own. Use the chart to write your notes and to identify relevant details from the poems.

	A BLESSING	PREDATORS
What animals are presented? Are they wild, tame, or both?		
How does the speaker feel in the presence of the animals?		
What does the title suggest about the speaker's attitude?		
At the end of the poem, what does the speaker learn or understand?		

 Notebook Respond to these questions.

1. Which poem is more positive about the role of animals in the world? Explain.

2. Which poem conveys a stronger sense about what the animals' experience is like? Explain.

Drafting

Determine Your Central Idea In one sentence state the central idea or thesis that you will explain in your essay:

Central Idea/Thesis: _____

_____

As you write, your ideas may change. After you write each paragraph, revisit your thesis to make sure it expresses your ideas.

Choose a Structure Decide how you want to organize your essay. Will you discuss one poem in full before moving on to the second poem? Or will you discuss one important idea at a time, drawing examples from both poems?

Decide on the main idea you will develop in each paragraph of your essay. Consider stating that idea clearly in a topic sentence at the beginning of each paragraph. Double check that the main idea of each paragraph supports the central idea of the essay as a whole as stated in your thesis. Include at least two pieces of evidence from the texts to support each main idea. Make sure the quotations you choose from the poems strongly support your thesis and main ideas.

Reviewing and Revising

Review the Criteria Once you are done drafting, share your essay with your group. As you review one another's work, look for the following elements:

☐ stays on subject and addresses both poems effectively

☐ identifies clear similarities and differences between the two poems

☐ includes details and quotations from the poems that clearly relate to the thesis and main ideas.

☐ ends with a strong conclusion that refers back to the thesis

☐ is clearly written and uses correct punctuation, capitalization, spelling, and grammar

Give Feedback Each member of your group may have different strengths and weaknesses in their writing. For example, one person may need to clarify the thesis, another might need help with organization, and still another may need to choose details more effectively. Provide suggestions to one another in a positive way, but make sure each person finds his or her own solutions.

🖉 **EVIDENCE LOG**

Before moving on to a new selection, go to your Evidence Log and record what you've learned from "Predators."

▤ **STANDARDS**

Writing

• Write informative/explanatory texts to examine a topic and convey ideas, concepts, and information through the selection, organization, and analysis of relevant content.
  a. Introduce a topic; organize ideas, concepts, and information, using strategies such as definition, classification, comparison/contrast, and cause/effect; include formatting, graphics, and multimedia when useful to aiding comprehension.
  b. Develop the topic with relevant facts, definitions, concrete details, quotations, or other information and examples.
  f. Provide a concluding statement or section that follows from the information or explanation presented.

• With some guidance and support from peers and adults, develop and strengthen writing as needed by planning, revising, editing, rewriting, or trying a new approach.

• Draw evidence from literary or informational texts to support analysis, reflection, and research.
  a. Apply *grade 6 Reading standards* to literature.

About the Author
Waldemar Januszczak
(b. 1954) is the longest-serving art critic in the British national press. The son of Polish immigrants, Januszczak studied the History of Art at Manchester University and in 1977 published his first piece of art criticism. From 1979 to 1987, he served as the chief art critic for the *Guardian,* a British newspaper. In 1993, he became the art critic for another British newspaper called the *Sunday Times,* a position he still holds today. He has also made numerous movies about art.

Monkey Master
Concept Vocabulary

As you perform your first read of "Monkey Master," you will encounter these words.

purist	aesthetic	abstract

Using a Specialized Dictionary Some words have multiple meanings, especially when they are used in different fields of study. Consider the word *composition*:

Customary Meanings: the way in which something is made up of different parts or elements; the act of combining parts or elements to form a whole

Specialized Meaning: the way in which artistic elements, including color, lines, shapes, and space, are arranged in a work of art

To find the precise meanings of such terms, consult a specialized dictionary. A **specialized dictionary** is a reference source that provides information about words as they are used in a particular field of study, such as art or geography. As you read "Monkey Master," use a print or online art dictionary to determine the meanings of unfamiliar art terms you encounter.

First Read NONFICTION

Apply these strategies as you conduct your first read. You will have an opportunity to complete a close read after your first read.

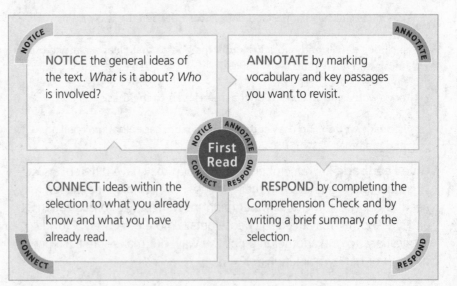

NOTICE the general ideas of the text. *What* is it about? *Who* is involved?

ANNOTATE by marking vocabulary and key passages you want to revisit.

First Read

CONNECT ideas within the selection to what you already know and what you have already read.

RESPOND by completing the Comprehension Check and by writing a brief summary of the selection.

STANDARDS

Reading Informational Text
By the end of the year, read and comprehend literary nonfiction in the grades 6–8 text complexity band proficiently, with scaffolding as needed at the high end of the range.

Language
Determine or clarify the meaning of unknown and multiple-meaning words and phrases based on *grade 6 reading and content,* choosing flexibly from a range of strategies.
  c. Consult reference materials, both print and digital, to find the pronunciation of a word or determine or clarify its precise meaning or its part of speech.

Monkey Master

Waldemar Januszczak

SCAN FOR
MULTIMEDIA

BACKGROUND

In this essay, the author describes and analyzes paintings created by a chimpanzee-artist named Congo during the 1950s. The author draws parallels between Congo's paintings and the works of some famous modern artists, such as Pablo Picasso and Wassily Kandinsky. These artists were considered pioneers of abstract art, which does not portray subjects as they appear in real life. Instead, abstract artists emphasize the process of making art as well as the formal elements of color and shape separate from realistic portrayals. They often work to express emotions and ideas in ways that challenge viewers' perceptions.

1   Can a monkey paint a good picture? It's a question that has come up a few times during my tenure as an art critic, as a result of various modern art jokes, scams, cons, and the like.

2   Normally, I would waste no time on the issue. It is, or was, my firmly held view that, in the field of art, monkeys do whatever they do by accident or coercion. Monkeys cannot paint.

3   Then along comes a fascinating and slightly worrying exhibition at London's Mayor Gallery, Ape Artists of the 1950s, and I am no longer so certain. In particular, along comes the artistic work of a talented chimpanzee named Congo.

NOTES

4   Having carefully examined Congo's paintings, all of which might best be described as examples of lyrical abstract expressionism,[1] I find myself assailed by doubts. I like Congo's paintings. A couple of them I love.

5   I am less sure of the output of the show's gorilla. And not much taken with the orangutan's pictures, either. But in all their cases, something of interest is undoubtedly being attempted, and for the whole show the feeling persists that the lessons being taught here pertain not only to monkeys, but also to us.

6   Congo was born in 1954 and produced about 400 paintings from the age of two to four. He died of tuberculosis in 1964. He appeared on television in the late 1950s, the star turn on *Zootime*, an animal magazine show presented live from London Zoo by animal behavioralist[2] and *The Naked Ape* author Desmond Morris.

7   Apparently, the experiments with Congo began by accident. One day, he picked up a pencil and drew a line. Then he drew more, until it was clear to Morris that the chimp's actions were deliberate.

8   After a short drawing phase, it was decided to move him on to painting. Morris had a baby's highchair and tray adapted to create a seating arrangement at which Congo could work.

9   There are photographs of Congo in action, in which particular attention is drawn to the grip with which he held the brush. It's similar to the way you or I might hold a pen, and was absolutely Congo's invention, apparently. If so, that is already a remarkable development.

10   Congo would be given a piece of paper and, in conditions of considerable concentration, would begin painting. The choice of colors was his, red being a particular favorite, blue being a color he disliked.

11   Fascinatingly, if you tried to take a picture away from Congo before he had finished with it, he would scream and throw fits. However, if he considered the picture done, no amount of cajoling would persuade him to continue. The master's work was complete. That was that.

12   The results have been placed in functional wooden frames and hung in a line in the no-frills exhibition box of the Mayor Gallery. The exhibition comes on the heels of a recent auction of some of Congo's works in London, at which an American collector paid $25,000 for one painting, 20 times the expected price.

13   But not even the Mayor Gallery's charmless presentation can dim the disquieting beauty of Congo's best pictures. They shine off the walls like stained glass.

---

1. **abstract expressionism** post–World War II American art movement in which artists reinvented abstract art to create a distinctly American style; characterized by rich expressions of emotion with an emphasis on the unplanned nature of the creative act or process.
2. **animal behavioralist** person who studies the behavior of animals to understand its causes, functions, and development; also called an animal behaviorist.

 In this photograph, Congo is at work on one of his many paintings. Notice how he holds his brush.

NOTES

^ The paintings that illustrate this essay are examples of Congo's artwork. Here is one of Congo's many paintings called simply *Composition*.

14   There's a cracker[3] called *Composition on White Card*, painted on August 17, 1958, which is dramatically, even shockingly, sparse.

15   An audacious pink splodge at the center plays a delicate game of tag across the paper with a couple of different blues. That's it. And it really works. For Congo to have finished this picture as he finished it—for a monkey to be this minimal—is deeply disconcerting.

_____
3. **cracker** British slang term for a thing or person that is especially good or exciting.

∧ This painting is another example of Congo's artwork. Notice that the brush strokes are deliberate.

NOTES

16   *Composition on Buff Paper*, painted on October 31, 1957, is perhaps Congo's masterpiece. Built compositionally around a central expanse of Congo's beloved crimson, it features an array of blacks and pale greens soaring around the red like vultures around a mountain. The mood is pure Kandinsky, the achievement profound. Not all of Congo's paintings get it as right. His range of painting gestures is narrow: The brush has a tendency to go round and round. He is as guilty as any monkey might be of overdoing things, and most of the paintings lack the specific character of the ones I have described. But the display never stops being remarkable.

17   What is really spooky is the care Congo always brings to working within the paper. Only rarely does the brush stray over the edge. And he clearly understands the notion of balance, too. If a pink has a blue on one side of it, and needs another blue on the other side, he will add one. The absence of muddiness, of colors mixed to sludge through mindless scrubbing, is also spectacular. When it comes to pigments, Congo is a **purist**.

18   So much so that there is some small room for doubt about the role played by Morris. It seems that although the paintings were made for *Zootime*, Congo was not often filmed painting them, because the studio activity put him off. Morris's experiments were mostly conducted off camera, which is a shame.

Use a specialized dictionary or indicate another strategy you used that helped you determine meaning.

purist (PYOOR ihst) *n.*

MEANING:

∧ In this painting, you can see Congo's use of clear colors that the author discusses in paragraph 17.

19   Not for a moment do I question the authenticity of the images, or the methods used to produce them, but it would have been interesting to see the extent of Morris's involvement in important **aesthetic** matters such as the choice of colored paper for Congo to work on. This use of red, orange, green paper has a considerable decorative impact on the final image. Congo may have selected the colors, but who came up with the original wheeze[4] of using impactful colored paper? How much guidance was Congo receiving?

20   I ask only because this intriguing show could profitably have been bigger, fuller, packed with more information.

21   I read, too, that Pablo Picasso was a collector of Congo's work. This does not surprise me. The notion of a painting monkey would have appealed to the devil in him. What's more, Congo, as an ape, could not reasonably have mounted any sort of challenge to the ultra-competitive Picasso's self-esteem.

22   Morris tells an excellent story of a journalist asking Picasso his opinion of Congo's work. Picasso left the room and returned, his arms swinging like an ape's and clutching his Congo painting, then jumped on the journalist and bit him. Artists and monkeys are brothers in arms, seemed to be the message.

23   On a similar tack, Salvador Dali is said to have quipped: "The hand of the chimpanzee is quasi-human; the hand of Jackson Pollock is totally animal."

24   Apart from Congo, there are works on show by Betsy, another chimpanzee, a gorilla named Sophie, and Alexander the

Use a specialized dictionary or indicate another strategy you used that helped you determine meaning.

aesthetic (ehs THEHT ihk) *adj.*

MEANING:

---

4. **wheeze** British slang term for a trick, idea, or plan.

^ In this composition, Congo has painted on a different-colored background.

Use a specialized dictionary or indicate another strategy you used that helped you determine meaning.

abstract (AB strakt) *adj*.

MEANING:

orangutan. With so few examples included, it is difficult to come to any worthwhile conclusions about these other simian maestros, though certainly it is surprising to see how fragile and even nervous are the touches of the huge gorilla.

25   Morris has attempted to give the display a truly gigantic story line by insisting on the importance of ape art to our general understanding of the aesthetic impulse. "It is the work of these apes, not that of prehistoric cave artists," he writes, "that can truly be said to represent the birth of art."

26   If that were so, then this would count as one of the most important exhibitions anyone has put on. I am moved to see it the other way round, from the point of view of the visitor, not the creator: Confronted by a pleasing assortment of **abstract** shapes, we humans have a wondrous ability to find meaning in them and to gain pleasure from them. Art, after all, is only as important as its audience. ❧

Comprehension Check

Complete the following items after you finish your first read. Review and clarify details with your group.

1. What is the name of the exhibition that the author discusses in the essay?

2. What does the author think of the paintings done by the gorilla and the orangutan?

3. Who is Desmond Morris?

4. According to the author, what color does Congo like? What color does he dislike?

5. According to the author, how much did an American art collector pay for one of Congo's paintings?

6. **Notebook** Confirm your understanding of the text by writing a brief summary.

RESEARCH

Research to Clarify Choose at least one unfamiliar detail from the text. Briefly research that detail. In what way does the information you learned shed light on an aspect of the essay?

MONKEY MASTER

Close Read the Text

With your group, revisit sections of the text you marked during your first read. **Annotate** details that you notice. What **questions** do you have? What can you **conclude**?

Analyze the Text

> **CITE TEXTUAL EVIDENCE**
> to support your answers.

Complete the activities.

1. **Review and Clarify** Review the essay with your group. According to the author, before attending the exhibition, how did he view art created by apes or other animals? In what ways have his thoughts on the topic changed?

2. **Present and Discuss** Now, work with your group to share the passages from the text that you found especially important. Take turns presenting your passages. Discuss what you noticed in the text, what questions you asked, and what conclusions you reached.

3. 📓 Notebook **Essential Question: *How can people and animals relate to each other?*** What have you learned from this essay about the interactions between people and animals? Discuss with your group.

LANGUAGE DEVELOPMENT

Concept Vocabulary

| purist | aesthetic | abstract |

Why These Words? The three concept vocabulary words from the text are related. With your group, determine what the words have in common. Record your ideas, and identify at least one more word that fits the category.

Practice

📓 Notebook Confirm your understanding of the concept vocabulary words by using each word in a sentence that shows your understanding of the word's meaning.

Word Study

📓 Notebook **Greek Suffix: *-ist*** The Greek suffix *-ist* means "person who does, makes, practices, is skilled in, or believes in." In the essay, the author says that Congo is a *purist* because he prefers the colors in his paintings to be clear and distinct. Use your knowledge of the suffix *-ist* to write a definition for *purist,* as well as for each of these words: *humorist, naturalist, realist.* Then, use a dictionary to confirm your understanding of the meaning of each word.

STANDARDS

Reading Informational Text
Integrate information presented in different media or formats as well as in words to develop a coherent understanding of a topic or issue.

Writing
• Conduct short research projects to answer a question, drawing on several sources and refocusing the inquiry when appropriate.
• Gather relevant information from multiple print and digital sources; assess the credibility of each source; and quote or paraphrase the data and conclusions of others while avoiding plagiarism and providing basic bibliographic information for sources.

Speaking and Listening
Engage effectively in a range of collaborative discussions with diverse partners on *grade 6 topics, texts, and issues*, building on others' ideas and expressing their own clearly.
  c. Pose and respond to specific questions with elaboration and detail by making comments that contribute to the topic, text, or issue under discussion.

Language
Determine or clarify the meaning of unknown and multiple-meaning words and phrases based on *grade 6 reading and content*, choosing flexibly from a range of strategies.
  b. Use common, grade-appropriate Greek or Latin affixes and roots as clues to the meaning of a word.
  d. Verify the preliminary determination of the meaning of a word or phrase.

Research and Discuss

Assignment

Conduct research, and then participate in a **group discussion** on one of the following topics:

☐ members of other animal species that create art

☐ Congo's life and why he was unique

Research and Take Notes First, decide as a group which topic you will research. Then, prepare for your discussion by following these steps.

- Use a variety of reliable print and online sources. Websites that end in *.gov* or *.edu* tend to be most reliable, but websites that end with *.org* or *.com* may also have useful information.

- Take notes on each source. First, write down information about the source, such as its title, its author, and how you found it.

- Then, write down relevant facts and ideas that you find in each source. For each fact or idea you write, note its exact location so that you can easily find it again.

- As you research, also look for relevant visuals, such as photographs or videos, that will be interesting to share with your group. Copy, print, or save any visuals that you like, and write down information about them. Look for information about your visuals in captions and in nearby text.

Use this chart to record notes from your research sources.

SOURCE INFORMATION	NOTES

Present and Discuss Share your findings with your group. When it is your turn to speak, consult the notes in your chart, and cite examples from your sources. Also share any visuals you found that are interesting and support your ideas. Respond to questions with details from your research. Listen closely as other group members speak, and ask questions that help other group members elaborate on their ideas about the topic.

 EVIDENCE LOG

Before moving on to a new selection, go to your Evidence Log, and record what you learned from "Monkey Master."

About the Author

Julius Lester (b. 1939), a native of St. Louis, Missouri, has been a folk singer, a civil rights photographer, a writer, and a professor of African American Studies and Judaic Studies. His works include novels, stories, poetry, nonfiction, and a memoir.

Black Cowboy, Wild Horses

Concept Vocabulary

As you perform your first read of "Black Cowboy, Wild Horses," you will encounter these words.

milled	skittered	quivering

Context Clues If these words are unfamiliar to you, try using **context clues**—other words and phrases that appear nearby in a text—to help you determine their meanings. There are various types of context clues that may help you as you read. Here are some examples:

> **Synonyms:** The passengers **griped** and <u>complained</u> when the bus got stuck in traffic.
>
> **Elaboration of Ideas:** Her music was an **amalgam** of genres, <u>mixing jazz, rock, and hip-hop</u>.
>
> **Contrast of Ideas:** <u>Instead of</u> **balking** at the challenge, we <u>bravely accepted</u> it.

Apply your knowledge of base words and other vocabulary strategies to determine the meanings of unfamiliar words you encounter during your first read.

First Read FICTION

Apply these strategies as you conduct your first read. You will have an opportunity to complete a close read after your first read.

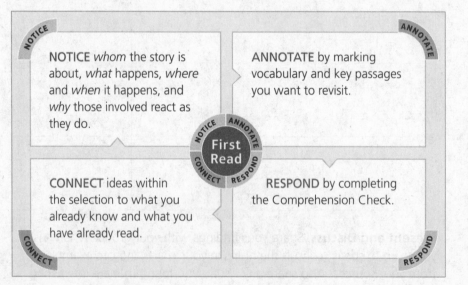

NOTICE *whom* the story is about, *what* happens, *where* and *when* it happens, and *why* those involved react as they do.

ANNOTATE by marking vocabulary and key passages you want to revisit.

CONNECT ideas within the selection to what you already know and what you have already read.

RESPOND by completing the Comprehension Check.

STANDARDS

Reading Literature
By the end of the year, read and comprehend literature, including stories, dramas, and poems, in the grades 6–8 text complexity band proficiently, with scaffolding as needed at the high end of the range.

Language
Determine or clarify the meaning of unknown and multiple-meaning words and phrases based on *grade 6 reading and content*, choosing flexibly from a range of strategies.
  a. Use context as a clue to the meaning of a word or phrase.

Black Cowboy, Wild Horses

Julius Lester

BACKGROUND

When Spanish explorers came to the Americas, they brought domesticated horses with them. Over time, some of these horses escaped into the wild, where they formed untamed herds and eventually spread west across the Great Plains. These wild horses became known as mustangs.

SCAN FOR
MULTIMEDIA

NOTES

1   First Light. Bob Lemmons rode his horse slowly up the rise. When he reached the top, he stopped at the edge of the bluff.[1] He looked down at the corral[2] where the other cowboys were beginning the morning chores, then turned away and stared at the land stretching as wide as love in every direction. The sky was curved as if it were a lap on which the earth lay napping like a curled cat. High above, a hawk was suspended on cold threads of unseen winds. Far, far away, at what looked to be the edge of the world, land and sky kissed.

2   He guided Warrior, his black stallion, slowly down the bluff. When they reached the bottom, the horse reared, eager to run across the vastness of the plains until he reached forever. Bob smiled and patted him gently on the neck. "Easy. Easy," he whispered. "We'll have time for that. But not yet."

---

1. **bluff** *n.* cliff.
2. **corral** (kuh RAL) *n.* fenced area for horses and cattle.

3   He let the horse trot for a while, then slowed him and began peering intently at the ground as if looking for the answer to a question he scarcely understood.

4   It was late afternoon when he saw them—the hoofprints of mustangs, the wild horses that lived on the plains. He stopped, dismounted, and walked around carefully until he had seen all the prints. Then he got down on his hands and knees to examine them more closely.

5   Some people learned from books. Bob had been a slave and never learned to read words. But he could look at the ground and read what animals had walked on it, their size and weight, when they had passed by, and where they were going. No one he knew could bring in mustangs by themselves, but Bob could make horses think he was one of them—because he was.

6   He stood, reached into his saddlebag, took out an apple, and gave it to Warrior, who chewed with noisy enthusiasm. It was a herd of eight mares, a colt, and a stallion. They had passed there two days ago. He would see them soon. But he needed to smell of sun, moon, stars, and wind before the mustangs would accept him.

7   The sun went down and the chilly night air came quickly. Bob took the saddle, saddlebag, and blanket off Warrior. He was cold, but could not make a fire. The mustangs would smell the smoke in his clothes from miles away. He draped a thick blanket around himself, then took the cotton sack of dried fruit, beef jerky, and nuts from his saddlebag and ate. When he was done, he lay his head on his saddle and was quickly asleep. Warrior grazed in the tall, sweet grasses.

8   As soon as the sun's round shoulders came over the horizon, Bob awoke. He ate, filled his canteen, and saddling Warrior, rode away. All day he followed the tracks without hurrying.

9   Near dusk, clouds appeared, piled atop each other like mountains made of fear. Lightning flickered from within them like candle flames shivering in a breeze. Bob heard the faint but distinct rumbling of thunder. Suddenly lightning vaulted from cloud to cloud across the curved heavens.

10   Warrior reared, his front hooves pawing as if trying to knock the white streaks of fire from the night sky. Bob raced Warrior to a nearby ravine[3] as the sky exploded sheets of light. And there, in the distance, beneath the ghostly light, Bob saw the herd of mustangs. As if sensing their presence, Warrior rose into the air once again, this time not challenging the heavens but almost in greeting. Bob thought he saw the mustang stallion rise in response as the earth shuddered from the sound of thunder.

11   Then the rain came as hard and stinging as remorse. Quickly Bob put on his poncho, and turning Warrior away from the wind

---

3. **ravine** (ruh VEEN) *n.* narrow canyon with steep sides.

and the rain, waited. The storm would pass soon. Or it wouldn't. There was nothing to do but wait.

12   Finally the rain slowed and then stopped. The clouds thinned, and there, high in the sky, the moon appeared as white as grief. Bob slept in the saddle while Warrior grazed on the wet grasses.

13   The sun rose into a clear sky and Bob was awake immediately. The storm would have washed away the tracks, but they had been going toward the big river. He would go there and wait.

14   By mid-afternoon he could see the ribbon of river shining in the distance. He stopped, needing only to be close enough to see the horses when they came to drink. Toward evening he saw a trail of rolling, dusty clouds.

15   In front was the mustang herd. As it reached the water, the stallion slowed and stopped. He looked around, his head raised, nostrils flared, smelling the air. He turned in Bob's direction and sniffed the air again.

16   Bob tensed. Had he come too close too soon? If the stallion smelled anything new, he and the herd would be gone and Bob would never find them again. The stallion seemed to be looking directly at him. Bob was too far away to be seen, but he did not even blink his eyes, afraid the stallion would hear the sound. Finally the stallion began drinking and the other horses followed. Bob let his breath out slowly. He had been accepted.

17   The next morning he crossed the river and picked up the herd's trail. He moved Warrior slowly, without sound, without dust. Soon he saw them grazing. He stopped. The horses did not notice him. After a while he moved forward, slowly, quietly. The stallion raised his head. Bob stopped.

18   When the stallion went back to grazing, Bob moved forward again. All day Bob watched the herd, moving only when it moved but always coming closer. The mustangs sensed his presence. They thought he was a horse.

19   So did he.

20   The following morning Bob and Warrior walked into the herd. The stallion eyed them for a moment. Then, as if to test this newcomer, he led the herd off in a gallop. Bob lay flat across Warrior's back and moved with the herd. If anyone had been watching, they would not have noticed a man among the horses.

21   When the herd set out early the next day, it was moving slowly. If the horses had been going faster, it would not have happened.

22   The colt fell to the ground as if she had stepped into a hole and broken her leg. Bob and the horses heard the chilling sound of the rattles. Rattlesnakes didn't always give a warning before they struck. Sometimes, when someone or something came too close, they bit with the fury of fear.

milled (mihld) *v.*

MEANING:

skittered (SKIHT uhrd) *v.*

MEANING:

23   The horses whinnied and pranced nervously, smelling the snake and death among them. Bob saw the rattler, as beautiful as a necklace, sliding silently through the tall grasses. He made no move to kill it. Everything in nature had the right to protect itself, especially when it was afraid.

24   The stallion galloped to the colt. He pushed at her. The colt struggled to get up, but fell to her side, shivering and kicking feebly with her thin legs. Quickly she was dead.

25   Already vultures circled high in the sky. The mustangs **milled** aimlessly. The colt's mother whinnied, refusing to leave the side of her colt. The stallion wanted to move the herd from there, and pushed the mare with his head. She refused to budge, and he nipped her on the rump. She **skittered** away. Before she could return to the colt, the stallion bit her again, this time harder. She ran toward the herd. He bit her a third time, and the herd was off. As they galloped away, Bob looked back. The vultures were descending from the sky as gracefully as dusk.

26   It was time to take over the herd. The stallion would not have the heart to fight fiercely so soon after the death of the colt. Bob galloped Warrior to the front and wheeled around, forcing the stallion to stop quickly. The herd, confused, slowed and stopped also.

27   Bob raised Warrior to stand high on his back legs, fetlocks pawing and kicking the air. The stallion's eyes widened. He snorted and pawed the ground, surprised and uncertain. Bob charged at the stallion.

28   Both horses rose on hind legs, teeth bared as they kicked at each other. When they came down, Bob charged Warrior at the stallion again, pushing him backward. Bob rushed yet again.

29   The stallion neighed loudly, and nipped Warrior on the neck. Warrior snorted angrily, reared, and kicked out with his forelegs, striking the stallion on the nose. Still maintaining his balance, Warrior struck again and again. The mustang stallion cried out in pain. Warrior pushed hard against the stallion. The stallion lost his footing and fell to the earth. Warrior rose, neighing triumphantly, his front legs pawing as if seeking for the rungs on which he could climb a ladder into the sky.

30   The mustang scrambled to his feet, beaten. He snorted weakly. When Warrior made as if to attack again, the stallion turned, whinnied weakly, and trotted away.

31   Bob was now the herd's leader, but would they follow him? He rode slowly at first, then faster and faster. The mustangs followed as if being led on ropes.

32   Throughout that day and the next he rode with the horses. For Bob there was only the bulging of the horses' dark eyes, the **quivering** of their flesh, the rippling of muscles and bending of

quivering (KWIHV uhr ihng) *n.*

MEANING:

bones in their bodies. He was now sky and plains and grass and river and horse.

33   When his food was almost gone. Bob led the horses on one last ride, a dark surge of flesh flashing across the plains like black lightning. Toward evening he led the herd up the steep hillside, onto the bluff, and down the slope toward the big corral. The cowboys heard him coming and opened the corral gate. Bob led the herd, but at the last moment he swerved Warrior aside, and the mustangs flowed into the fenced enclosure. The cowboys leaped and shouted as they quickly closed the gate.

34   Bob rode away from them and back up to the bluff. He stopped and stared out onto the plains. Warrior reared and whinnied loudly.

35   "I know," Bob whispered. "I know. Maybe someday."

36   Maybe someday they would ride with the mustangs, ride to that forever place where land and sky kissed, and then ride on. Maybe someday. ❧

NOTES

Comprehension Check

Complete the following items after you finish your first read. Review and clarify details with your group.

1. Who is Warrior?

2. What do Bob and Warrior dream of doing someday?

3. 📓 **Notebook** Confirm your understanding of the text by making a set of sketches, or quick drawings, of the story's most important events.

- -

RESEARCH

Research to Clarify Choose at least one unfamiliar detail from the text. Briefly research that detail. In what way does the information you learned shed light on an aspect of the story?

BLACK COWBOY, WILD HORSES

Close Read the Text

With your group, revisit sections of the text you marked during your first read. **Annotate** details that you notice. What **questions** do you have? What can you **conclude**?

Analyze the Text

CITE TEXTUAL EVIDENCE to support your answers.

📓 **Notebook** Complete the activities.

1. **Review and Clarify** With your group, reread paragraph 5 of the selection. What can Bob "read"? Having read the entire selection, why do you think the author describes Bob as one of the horses?

2. **Present and Discuss** Now, work with your group to share the passages from the text that you found especially important. Take turns presenting your passages. Discuss what you noticed in the text, what questions you asked, and what conclusions you reached.

3. **Essential Question:** *How can people and animals relate to each other?* What has this story taught you about how people and animals can relate to each other? Discuss with your group.

Concept Vocabulary

milled	skittered	quivering

Why These Words? The three concept vocabulary words from the text are related. With your group, determine what the words have in common. How do these word choices enhance the impact of the text?

Practice

📓 **Notebook** Confirm your understanding of these words by using them in sentences. Be sure to include context clues that hint at each word's meaning. If necessary, look up the precise meanings of the vocabulary words in a dictionary.

Word Study

Multiple-Meaning Words Some words have more than one meaning. For instance, the word *mill* has many different meanings and is used as several different parts of speech. Use a dictionary to look up two meanings for the noun *mill* and two meanings for the verb *mill*. Record your findings.

GROUP DISCUSSION

When you work in your group to answer the Analyze the Text questions, be sure to support your opinions and ideas with evidence from the text.

🔗 **WORD NETWORK**

Add words related to people and animals from the text to your Word Network.

☰ **STANDARDS**

Reading Literature
Describe how a particular story's or drama's plot unfolds in a series of episodes as well as how the characters respond or change as the plot moves toward a resolution.

Language
Determine or clarify the meaning of unknown and multiple-meaning words and phrases based on *grade 6 reading and content*, choosing flexibly from a range of strategies.

Analyze Craft and Structure

Story Structure: Plot A **plot** is the sequence of related events in a story. All plots center on a **conflict,** which is a struggle or problem the characters face. In some stories, the conflict comes from an outside force, such as nature or another character. In other stories, the conflict comes from within a character, who may have a desire or a goal that is difficult to achieve. Every plot follows a set of steps, or stages, in which the conflict is introduced, developed, and finally resolved.

- **Exposition:** The characters, setting, and basic situation are introduced.
- **Rising Action:** The conflict begins and starts to get more intense.
- **Climax:** The conflict reaches its point of greatest drama or tension.
- **Falling Action:** The eventual outcome of the story becomes clear. The tension in the story decreases.
- **Resolution:** The conflict comes to an end, and any loose ends are tied up.

Practice

CITE TEXTUAL EVIDENCE
to support your answers.

📓 **Notebook** Work independently to answer the questions. Then, share your responses with your group and discuss any differences.

1. (a) In this story, what does Bob Lemmons want to achieve? (b) Identify at least two problems Bob solves in order to achieve his goal. Explain your choices.

2. (a) What information about the setting, Bob Lemmons, and Warrior appears in the first two paragraphs? (b) To which stage of the story's plot do these paragraphs belong? Explain.

3. (a) What important information appears in paragraph 4? (b) Why is this information important? (c) To which stage of the story's plot do you think this paragraph belongs? Explain your thinking.

4. At what point do you think the story reaches its climax, or point of greatest tension? Explain your choice.

5. (a) At the end of the story, what unfulfilled longing does Bob express? (b) Why do you think the author ends with this open issue, rather than with Bob's successful achievement of his goal? Explain your thinking.

BLACK COWBOY, WILD HORSES

Conventions

Perfect Tenses of Verbs The three **perfect tenses** of a verb are used to tell when an action or condition was or will be completed.

- The **present perfect tense** shows an action or condition that began in the past and has consequences that continue into the present.
- The **past perfect tense** shows a past action or condition that ended before another past action began.
- The **future perfect tense** shows a future action or condition that will have ended before another begins.

To form one of the perfect tenses, combine a form of the helping verb *have* with the past participle of the main verb. This chart shows how to form the three perfect tenses.

PRESENT PERFECT TENSE	PAST PERFECT TENSE	FUTURE PERFECT TENSE
have, has + past participle	*had* + past participle	*will have* + past participle
She *has voted* in every election.	She *had voted* by the time we arrived.	I *will have voted* by the time the polls close tomorrow.

Read It

1. In these sentences from "Black Cowboy, Wild Horses," mark all of the verbs in the past perfect tense.

   a. Bob had been a slave and never learned to read words.

   b. But he could look at the ground and read what animals had walked on it, their size and weight, when they had passed by, and where they were going.

2. "Black Cowboy, Wild Horses" has several examples of verbs in the past perfect tense. However, there are no verbs in the present perfect tense or the future perfect tense. Discuss with your group why this is so. If needed, review the definitions of the three perfect tenses.

Write It

📓 **Notebook** Write three sentences for each of the following verbs: *talk, read*. Use the past perfect tense once, the present perfect tense once, and the future perfect tense once.

⌸ STANDARDS

Language
Demonstrate command of the conventions of standard English grammar and usage when writing or speaking.

Research

Assignment

Work with your group to research and create an **informative multimedia presentation** on one of the following topics:

☐ the real-life Bob Lemmons, including his life and work as a "mustanger" and cowboy

☐ another legendary cowboy, including his or her life and the reasons he or she became a famous figure

Incorporate text and a variety of multimedia to highlight the main ideas in your presentation. Conclude your presentation by comparing your topic to Julius Lester's portrayal of the legendary figure of Bob Lemmons in "Black Cowboy, Wild Horses."

Conduct Research Work with your group to decide on a topic, and determine a research assignment for each group member. For example, have some group members find text sources and others look for multimedia. As you conduct research, use notecards like the one shown to record important bibliographic information about your sources, both print and digital:

☐ Print   ☐ Digital   ☐ Text   ☐ Media

Title: _____

Author/Publisher: _____

Date of Access/Copyright Date: _____

URL/Other Location Information: _____

Organize Your Presentation After you have finished your research, work with your group to organize your presentation so that multimedia elements highlight the main points of your presentation. Rehearse with your group, and rearrange the elements of your presentation as necessary so that text and media are integrated and flow smoothly.

Include a Works-Cited List Plagiarism is the act of presenting someone else's ideas or research as your own—the equivalent of academic stealing, or fraud. Even if you restate the ideas in your own words, you still must credit the source that provides them. To avoid plagiarism, you must cite all your sources accurately. Use the notecards from your research to create a **Works-Cited list,** or **bibliography,** in which you credit all your sources according to the citation style your teacher prefers. Your Works-Cited list should appear at the end of your presentation.

✎ EVIDENCE LOG

Before moving on to a new selection, go to your Evidence Log, and record what you learned from "Black Cowboy, Wild Horses."

≣ STANDARDS

Writing
• Conduct short research projects to answer a question, drawing on several sources and refocusing the inquiry when appropriate.
• Gather relevant information from multiple print and digital sources; assess the credibility of each source; and quote or paraphrase the data and conclusions of others while avoiding plagiarism and providing basic bibliographic information for sources.

Speaking and Listening
• Engage effectively in a range of collaborative discussions with diverse partners on *grade 6 topics, texts, and issues,* building on others' ideas and expressing their own clearly.
  b. Follow rules for collegial discussions, set specific goals and deadlines, and define individual roles as needed.

• Include multimedia components and visual displays in presentations to clarify information.

Deliver an Informative Presentation

Assignment

You have read poems, an essay, and a short story that explore relationships between animals and people. With your group, plan and deliver an **informative multimedia presentation** that examines this topic:

> How can the bonds between people and animals be surprising?

Use images or other media to illustrate, emphasize, and clarify key points in your presentation. End with a brief question-and-answer session.

Plan With Your Group

Analyze the Text With your group, review the selections in Small-Group learning. Discuss how the people and animals relate to one another. In what ways are those relationships unexpected or surprising? Use the chart to list your ideas. Try to come to an agreement on the most important points in each selection.

TITLE	SURPRISING ASPECTS
A Blessing	
Predators	
Monkey Master	
Black Cowboy, Wild Horses	

Gather Evidence and Media Examples Go back over the selections to record specific examples that support your group's ideas about surprising connections between people and animals. Then, brainstorm for types of media you can use to illustrate each example. Consider photographs, illustrations, music, and video clips. Allow each group member to make suggestions.

STANDARDS

Speaking and Listening
• Present claims and findings, sequencing ideas logically and using pertinent descriptions, facts, and details to accentuate main ideas or themes; use appropriate eye contact, adequate volume, and clear pronunciation.
• Include multimedia components and visual displays in presentations to clarify information.

Organize Your Presentation As a group, work together to plan of your presentation. Organize everyone's work into a logical sequence. Then, make choices about your delivery. For example, decide who will introduce the presentation, who will read or present the text, who will handle the visuals or other media, who will present a conclusion, and who will be in charge of taking questions from the audience.

Rehearse With Your Group

Practice With Your Group Before delivering your presentation for the class, practice it as a group. Use this checklist to evaluate the effectiveness of your first run-through. Then, use your evaluation and these instructions to apply changes that will improve your content, use of media, and delivery techniques.

CONTENT	USE OF MEDIA	PRESENTATION TECHNIQUES
☐ The presentation clearly addresses the prompt. ☐ Ideas and information are organized in a logical sequence.	☐ Images and other media clearly illustrate the ideas and information. ☐ Images and other media are well-chosen and add interest to the presentation.	☐ Presenters make eye contact and speak clearly with adequate volume. ☐ Presenters use formal English.

Fine-Tune the Content If your presentation does not adequately address the prompt, work as a group to focus the content. Delete or revise any ideas or information that do not clearly connect to the topic.

Improve Your Use of Media Make sure you have enough media, but not too much. If you have long stretches without any media, consider adding some. Remove or replace any media that is not that interesting or relevant.

Brush Up on Your Presentation Techniques Practice a few times until your group is comfortable. Make sure everyone uses formal English and clearly pronounces words so that listeners can understand them.

Present and Evaluate

When you present as a group, be sure that each member has taken into account each of the checklist items. As you watch other groups' presentations, think about their content, media, and presentation techniques and how well they meet the criteria of the checklist. Listen attentively and politely. Did other presentations provide you with another way to view the topic?

■ STANDARDS

Speaking and Listening
Adapt speech to a variety of contexts and tasks, demonstrating command of formal English when indicated or appropriate.

ESSENTIAL QUESTION:

How can people and animals relate to each other?

Animals and people learn from each other in different ways. In this section, you will complete your study of the relationship between people and animals by exploring an additional selection related to the topic. You'll then share what you learn with classmates. To choose a text, follow these steps.

Look Back Think about the selections you have already studied. What more do you want to know about the relationships between people and animals?

Look Ahead Preview the texts by reading the descriptions. Which one seems most interesting and appealing to you?

Look Inside Take a few minutes to scan the text you chose. Choose a different one if this text doesn't meet your needs.

Independent Learning Strategies

Throughout your life, in school, in your community, and in your career, you will need to rely on yourself to learn and work on your own. Review these strategies and the actions you can take to practice them during Independent Learning. Add ideas of your own for each category.

STRATEGY	ACTION PLAN
Create a schedule	• Understand your goals and deadlines. • Make a plan for what to do each day. •
Practice what you have learned	• Use first-read and close-read strategies to deepen your understanding. • After you read, evaluate the usefulness of the evidence to help you understand the topic. • Consider the quality and reliability of the source. •
Take notes	• Record important ideas and information. • Review notes before preparing to share with a group. •

SCAN FOR
MULTIMEDIA

CONTENTS

Choose one selection. Selections are available online only.

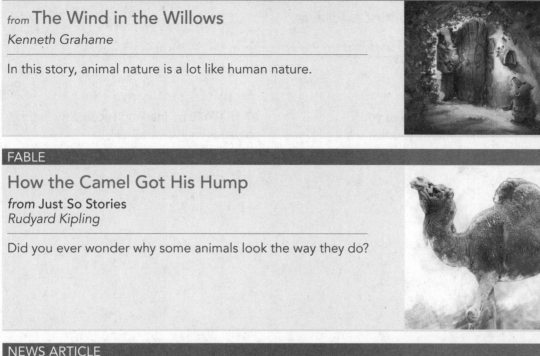

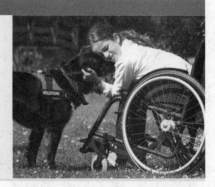
 SCAN FOR MULTIMEDIA

First-Read Guide

Use this page to record your first-read ideas.

Selection Title: _____

🔧 **Tool Kit**
First-Read Guide and
Model Annotation

NOTICE

NOTICE new information or ideas you learn about the unit topic as you first read this text.

ANNOTATE

ANNOTATE by marking vocabulary and key passages you want to revisit.

First Read

NOTICE · ANNOTATE · CONNECT · RESPOND

CONNECT

CONNECT ideas within the selection to other knowledge and the selections you have read.

RESPOND

RESPOND by writing a brief summary of the selection.

STANDARD

Reading Read and comprehend complex literary and informational texts independently and proficiently.

Close-Read Guide

Use this page to record your close-read ideas.

Selection Title: _____

Close Read the Text

Revisit sections of the text you marked during your first read. Read these sections closely and **annotate** what you notice. Ask yourself **questions** about the text. What can you **conclude**? Write down your ideas.

Analyze the Text

Think about the author's choices of patterns, structure, techniques, and ideas included in the text. Select one, and record your thoughts about what this choice conveys.

QuickWrite

Pick a paragraph from the text that grabbed your interest. Explain the power of this passage.

_____

_____

_____

_____

_____

_____

_____

STANDARD

Reading Read and comprehend complex literary and informational texts independently and proficiently.

Share Your Independent Learning

Prepare to Share

How can people and animals relate to each other?

Even when you read something independently, your understanding continues to grow when you share what you have learned with others. Reflect on the text you explored independently and write notes about its connection to the unit. In your notes, consider why this text belongs in this unit.

Learn From Your Classmates

Discuss It Share your ideas about the text you explored on your own. As you talk with others in your class, jot down a few ideas that you learn from them.

Reflect

Mark the most important insight you gained from these writing and discussion activities. Explain how this idea adds to your understanding of the relationship between people and animals.

☷ STANDARDS

Speaking and Listening
Engage effectively in a range of collaborative discussions with diverse partners on *grade 6 topics, texts, and issues,* building on others' ideas and expressing their own clearly.

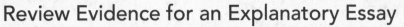

Review Evidence for an Explanatory Essay

At the beginning of this unit, you expressed an idea about the following statement:

How can animals and people help one another?

✏ EVIDENCE LOG

Review your Evidence Log and your QuickWrite from the beginning of the unit. Did you learn anything new?

NOTES

Identify three pieces of evidence from the texts you have read that show the unique relationships between people and animals.

1. _____

2. _____

3. _____

Identify a real-life example that illustrates one of your ideas about the relationship between people and animals:

_____

_____

Develop your thoughts into a starter sentence for an explanatory essay. Complete this sentence starter: *I learned that one of the ways that people and animals can relate to each other is*

_____

_____

Evaluate the Strength of Your Evidence Consider your central ideas. Do you have enough evidence to support your central ideas? If not, make a plan.

☐ Do more research   ☐ Talk with my classmates

☐ Reread a selection   ☐ Ask an expert

☐ Other: _____

⚏ STANDARDS
Writing
Write informative/explanatory texts to examine a topic and convey ideas, concepts, and information through the selection, organization, and analysis of relevant content.
  b. Develop the topic with relevant facts, definitions, concrete details, quotations, or other information and examples.

SOURCES

• WHOLE-CLASS SELECTIONS

• SMALL-GROUP SELECTIONS

• INDEPENDENT-LEARNING SELECTION

PART 1
Writing to Sources: Explanatory Essay

In this unit, you read about the different relationships between animals and people. In some cases, animals revealed a new way of looking at the world. In others, people and animals educated each other.

> **Assignment**
>
> Write an **explanatory essay** in which you answer the following question:
>
> ### How can animals and people help one another?
>
> Use evidence from the selections in this unit to elaborate on your explanation. Explain your ideas thoughtfully, and use transitions to make connections among them. Make sure that you use a formal style, and organize your essay in a logical way so that it is easy for readers to follow.

Reread the Assignment Review the assignment to be sure you fully understand it. The assignment may reference some of the academic words presented at the beginning of the unit. Be sure you understand each of the words given below in order to complete the assignment correctly.

Academic Vocabulary

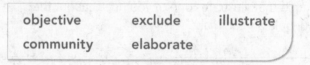

objective	exclude	illustrate
community	elaborate	

Review the Elements of Effective Explanatory Essays Before you begin writing, read the Explanatory Essay Rubric. Once you have completed your first draft, check it against the rubric. If one or more of the elements is missing or not as strong as it could be, revise your essay to add or strengthen that component.

⊹ WORD NETWORK

As you write and revise your explanatory essay, use your Word Network to help vary your word choices.

≣ STANDARDS

Writing
• Write informative/explanatory texts to examine a topic and convey ideas, concepts, and information through the selection, organization, and analysis of relevant content
• Write routinely over extended time frames and shorter time frames for a range of discipline-specific tasks, purposes, and audiences.

Explanatory Essay Rubric

	Focus and Organization	Evidence and Elaboration	Language Conventions
4	The introduction is clear, engaging, and establishes the topic in a compelling way. Ideas are well organized and progress logically. A variety of transitions are included to create cohesion and show the relationships among ideas. The conclusion follows from and supports the information presented in the essay.	The topic is developed with relevant facts, definitions, details, quotations, and other examples. The style of the essay is formal. The vocabulary is precise and relevant to the topic, audience, and purpose.	The essay always uses standard English conventions of usage and mechanics and has no errors.
3	The introduction is clear and engaging. Ideas are well organized. Transitions are included to show the relationships among ideas. The conclusion mostly follows from the information provided in the essay.	The topic is developed with some relevant facts, definitions, details, quotations, and other examples. The style of the essay is mostly formal. The vocabulary is generally appropriate for the topic, audience, and purpose.	The essay mostly uses standard English conventions of usage and mechanics and has few errors.
2	The introduction establishes the topic. Ideas are somewhat organized. A few transitions are included that show the relationships among ideas. The conclusion is related to the topic of the essay.	The topic is developed with a few facts, details, and examples. The style of the essay is sometimes formal and sometimes informal. The vocabulary is somewhat appropriate for the topic, audience, and purpose.	The essay often uses standard English conventions of usage and mechanics but also has many errors.
1	The topic is not clearly stated. Ideas are disorganized, and do not follow a logical sequence. Transitions are not included. The conclusion is not related to the essay topic or is nonexistent.	The topic is not developed with relevant evidence. The style is informal. The vocabulary is not appropriate for the topic, audience, and purpose.	The essay does not use standard English conventions of usage and mechanics.

PART 2
Speaking and Listening: Informative Presentation

Assignment
After completing the final draft of your essay, use it as the foundation for a brief **informative presentation.**

Do not simply read your essay aloud. Instead, take the following steps to make your presentation lively and engaging.

- Go back to your essay and annotate the most important ideas and supporting details from your introduction, body paragraphs, and conclusion.
- Refer to your annotated essay to guide your presentation and keep it focused.
- Speak clearly and make eye contact with your audience.

Review the Rubric Before you deliver your presentation, check your plans against the criteria listed in this rubric. If one or more of the elements is missing or not as strong as it could be, revise your presentation to meet all the criteria of the rubric.

STANDARDS
Speaking and Listening
Present claims and findings, sequencing ideas logically and using pertinent descriptions, facts, and details to accentuate main ideas or themes; use appropriate eye contact, adequate volume, and clear pronunciation.

	Content	Organization	Presentation
3	The introduction is engaging and clearly establishes the topic in a compelling way. The speaker points to key details and evidence to support his or her ideas. The conclusion is clear and reflects the information presented.	The presentation uses time effectively, devoting the right amount of time to each idea. Ideas progress logically, and transitions are used to connect ideas. Listeners can follow the presentation.	The speaker presents clearly and loudly enough for the audience to hear. The speaker maintains effective eye contact.
2	The introduction clearly establishes the topic. The speaker uses some evidence to support his or her ideas. The conclusion reflects the information presented.	The presentation mostly uses time effectively, but may spend too much or too little time on one part. Ideas progress somewhat logically, and a few transitions are used to connect ideas. Listeners can mostly follow the presentation.	The speaker presents clearly most of the time. The speaker makes some eye contact.
1	The introduction does not establish the topic. The speaker does not support his or her ideas with evidence. The conclusion is not related to the topic.	The presentation does not use time effectively. Ideas do not progress logically, and transitions are not used. Listeners have difficulty in following presentation.	The speaker presents too quickly or too slowly or not clearly. The speaker does not make eye contact with the audience.

Reflect on the Unit

Now that you have completed the unit, take a few moments to reflect on your learning.

Reflect on the Unit Goals

Look back at the goals at the beginning of the unit. Use a different colored pen to rate yourself again. Then, think about readings and activities that contributed the most to the growth of your understanding. Record your thoughts.

Reflect on the Learning Strategies

Discuss It Write a reflection on whether you were able to improve your learning based on your Action Plans. Think about what worked, what didn't, and what you might do to keep working on these strategies. Record your ideas before joining a class discussion.

Reflect on the Text

Choose a selection that you found challenging, and explain what made it difficult.

Describe something that surprised you about a text in the unit.

Which activity taught you the most about the relationships between people and animals? What did you learn?

SCAN FOR MULTIMEDIA

Modern Technology

Technology has become an important part of our lives, creating solutions but also new problems.

Dog Receives Prosthetic Legs Made by 3-D Printer

💬 **Discuss It** How does modern technology help us solve problems in new ways?

Write your response before sharing your ideas.

SCAN FOR MULTIMEDIA

UNIT 3

UNIT INTRODUCTION

ESSENTIAL QUESTION:

How is modern technology helpful and harmful to society?

LAUNCH TEXT
ARGUMENT MODEL
That's Not Progress!

WHOLE-CLASS LEARNING

ANCHOR TEXT: SHORT STORY

Feathered Friend
Arthur C. Clarke

ANCHOR TEXT: BLOG POST

Teens and Technology Share a Future
Stefan Etienne

ANCHOR TEXT: BLOG POST

The Black Hole of Technology
Leena Khan

COMPARE

MEDIA: VIDEO

The Internet of Things
IBM Social Media

SMALL-GROUP LEARNING

SHORT STORY

The Fun They Had
Isaac Asimov

BLOG POST

Is Our Gain Also Our Loss?
Cailin Loesch

MEDIA: PODCAST

Bored . . . and Brilliant? A Challenge to Disconnect From Your Phone
NPR

INDEPENDENT LEARNING

NEWS ARTICLE

7-Year-Old Girl Gets New Hand From 3-D Printer
John Rogers

NEWS ARTICLE

Screen Time Can Mess With the Body's "Clock"
Andrew Bridges

POETRY COLLECTION

All Watched Over by Machines of Loving Grace
Richard Brautigan

Sonnet, without Salmon
Sherman Alexie

NEWS ARTICLE

Teen Researchers Defend Media Multitasking
Sumathi Reddy

PERFORMANCE TASK

WRITING FOCUS:
Write an Argument

PERFORMANCE TASK

SPEAKING AND LISTENING FOCUS:
Deliver a Multimedia Presentation

PERFORMANCE-BASED ASSESSMENT PREP

Review Evidence for an Argument

PERFORMANCE-BASED ASSESSMENT

Argument: Essay and Oral Presentation

PROMPT:

Do we rely on technology too much?

Unit Goals

Throughout this unit, you will deepen your understanding of the impact of modern technology on society by reading, writing, speaking, listening, and presenting. These goals will help you succeed on the Unit Performance-Based Assessment.

Rate how well you meet these goals right now. You will revisit your ratings later when you reflect on your growth during this unit.

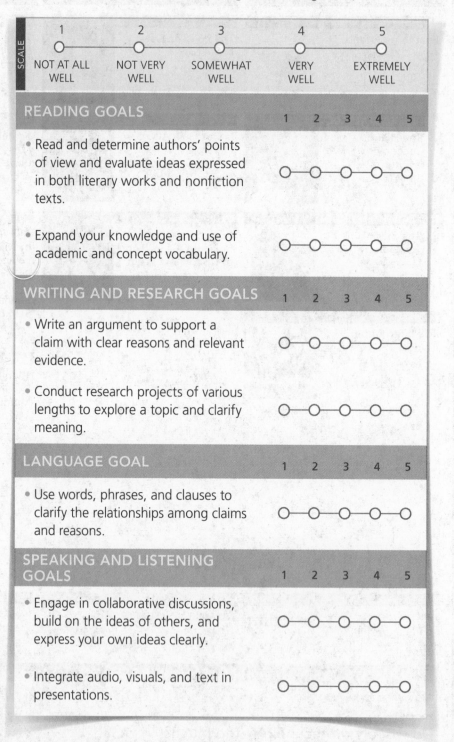

SCALE	1	2	3	4	5
	NOT AT ALL WELL	NOT VERY WELL	SOMEWHAT WELL	VERY WELL	EXTREMELY WELL

READING GOALS

	1	2	3	4	5
• Read and determine authors' points of view and evaluate ideas expressed in both literary works and nonfiction texts.					
• Expand your knowledge and use of academic and concept vocabulary.					

WRITING AND RESEARCH GOALS

	1	2	3	4	5
• Write an argument to support a claim with clear reasons and relevant evidence.					
• Conduct research projects of various lengths to explore a topic and clarify meaning.					

LANGUAGE GOAL

	1	2	3	4	5
• Use words, phrases, and clauses to clarify the relationships among claims and reasons.					

SPEAKING AND LISTENING GOALS

	1	2	3	4	5
• Engage in collaborative discussions, build on the ideas of others, and express your own ideas clearly.					
• Integrate audio, visuals, and text in presentations.					

☷ STANDARDS

Language
Acquire and use accurately grade-appropriate general academic and domain-specific words and phrases; gather vocabulary knowledge when considering a word or phrase important to comprehension or expression.

SCAN FOR
MULTIMEDIA

Academic Vocabulary: Argument

Understanding and using academic terms can help you read, write, and speak with precision and clarity. Here are five academic words that will be useful in this unit as you analyze and write argumentative texts.

Complete the chart.

1. Review each word, its root, and the mentor sentences.

2. Use the information and your own knowledge to predict the meaning of each word.

3. For each word, list at least two related words.

4. Refer to the dictionary or other resources if needed.

FOLLOW THROUGH
Study the words on this chart, and mark them or their forms wherever they appear in the unit.

WORD	MENTOR SENTENCES	PREDICT MEANING	RELATED WORDS
convince ROOT: **-vict-/-vinc-** "conquer"	1. To *convince* the jury, the lawyer presented evidence of the woman's innocence. 2. I will try to *convince* my mother that I need new clothes, even though she bought me a new shirt last week.		convincingly; unconvincing
certain ROOT: **-cert-** "sure"	1. The band became famous for having a *certain* jangly sound in their music. 2. I will be *certain* to study before the next test.		
sufficient ROOT: **-fic-/-fac-** "make"; "do"	1. We brought a *sufficient* amount of food and water for a week's worth of camping. 2. Studying an hour a day during the week before the test is *sufficient* to do well.		
declare ROOT: **-clar-** "clear"	1. Many officials will *declare* their support of the mayor's campaign by speaking at the press conference. 2. Ruthie was about to *declare* her innocence, but the chocolate stain on her face and the empty cookie jar told the truth.		
various ROOT: **-var-** "different"	1. There are *various* tips for effective public speaking, including speaking clearly and making eye contact. 2. We discussed *various* places to host the event—many of which were close to home.		

Unit Introduction **187**

This selection is an example of an **argument**, a type of writing in which the author states and supports a position or claim. This is the type of writing you will develop in the Performance-Based Assessment at the end of the unit.

As you read, notice the way that the writer builds an argument. Mark the text to help answer this question: What is the author's position and how does the author support it?

That's Not Progress!

1   Social networking has become a big part of our lives, and its negative effects can be overlooked. But mental health experts are starting to notice—and what they are finding is disturbing.

2   As the popularity of social media skyrockets, so do reports of "Facebook depression." Like other kinds of depression, its common signs are anxiety, low self-confidence, and loneliness.

3   This form of depression hits those who worry too much about what others think. It largely affects young people because they tend to worry most about others' opinions. The constant need to see how they're "measuring up" can cause people to feel huge amounts of stress.

4   Studies have found that people who get their sense of self-worth from others are more likely to keep checking their status. They want to monitor their updates, wall posts, and photos to see how well or how poorly they're measuring up. The feeling that they're missing out on something makes it hard to take a break. And they don't have to—smartphones have made it possible to log in from any place at any time. The result is more stress.

5   Social networking can cause serious emotional problems. Everyone knows the effects of online bullying. There are other ways to damage a person's self-confidence. "When 'friends'

SCAN FOR
MULTIMEDIA

NOTES

upload unflattering photos and post mean comments, it can seriously damage a person's self-image," says one mental health expert. In addition, getting no response to a post or not being "friended" can also be very painful.

6   The effects can be physical, too. Frequent users of social media often suffer from pain in their fingers and wrists. Blood vessels in their eyes and necks can narrow. Their backs can ache from being hunched over phones and computers for hours at a time.

7   Texting is another problem created by technology. Half the nation's youth send 50 or more text messages a day. One study found that young people send an average of 34 texts a night after they get into bed! This loss of sleep can affect the ability to concentrate, problem-solve, and learn.

8   Not all experts agree with this analysis. Some point to the benefits of social media. Dr. Megan Moreno is an assistant professor of pediatrics and adolescent medicine. She believes that social networking helps develop a young person's sense of community. She also believes that it can be used to identify youth who are most at risk for depression. "Our studies have found that adolescents often share feelings of depression on Facebook," she says. "Social media is a tool; it cannot in and of itself cause mental illness," says Dr. Moreno. She insists that young people had problems before computers came into being.

9   Maybe so. In the past, however, young people found ways to escape from their problems. Now, smartphones and other high-tech devices have made escape impossible. Is that progress?

10   Technology should simplify life, not complicate it. The danger of social media is that young users can eventually lose their ability to focus on what is most important in life—no matter what path they choose to follow. 🍃

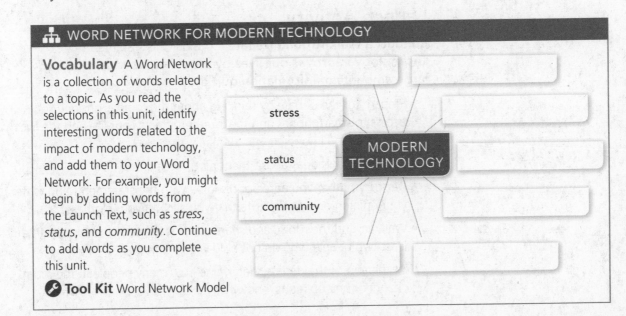

WORD NETWORK FOR MODERN TECHNOLOGY

Vocabulary A Word Network is a collection of words related to a topic. As you read the selections in this unit, identify interesting words related to the impact of modern technology, and add them to your Word Network. For example, you might begin by adding words from the Launch Text, such as *stress*, *status*, and *community*. Continue to add words as you complete this unit.

Tool Kit Word Network Model

stress

status

community

MODERN TECHNOLOGY

Summary

Write a summary of "That's Not Progress!" A **summary** is a concise, complete, and accurate overview of a text. It should not include a statement of your opinion or an analysis.

Launch Activity

Conduct a Walk-Around Debate Consider this statement: Technology improves our lives by providing us with access to large amounts of information quickly.

- Prepare for the debate by thinking about the topic. Consider how access to smartphones and the Internet affects your life and the lives of people you know.

- Jot down your ideas about the topic.

- Decide whether you agree or disagree with the statement, and write your opinion on a sticky note that you stick to your clothes.

- Walk around the room, and share your ideas about the topic with at least two people who do not hold your opinion.

- At the end of the debate, determine how many people in the room changed their opinions, and why.

QuickWrite

Consider class discussions, the video, and the Launch Text as you think about the prompt. Record your first thoughts here.

PROMPT: **Do we rely on technology too much?**

✐ EVIDENCE LOG FOR MODERN TECHNOLOGY

Review your QuickWrite. Summarize your point of view in one sentence to record in your Evidence Log. Then, record evidence from "That's Not Progress!" that supports your point of view.

After each selection, you will continue to use your Evidence Log to record the evidence you gather and the connections you make. This graphic shows what your Evidence Log looks like.

Title of Text: _____ Date: _____

CONNECTION TO PROMPT	TEXT EVIDENCE/DETAILS	ADDITIONAL NOTES/IDEAS

How does this text change or add to my thinking? Date: _____

🔧 Tool Kit
Evidence Log Model

SCAN FOR MULTIMEDIA

ESSENTIAL QUESTION:

How is modern technology helpful and harmful to society?

Technology and social media have become central parts of today's world—but are they truly improving our lives? You will work with your whole class to explore the impact of modern technology on society. The selections you will read present insights into its positive and negative effects.

Whole-Class Learning Strategies

Throughout your life, in school, in your community, and in your career, you will continue to learn and work in large-group environments.

Review these strategies and the actions you can take to practice them as you work with your whole class. Add ideas of your own for each step. Get ready to use these strategies during Whole-Class Learning.

STRATEGY	ACTION PLAN
Listen actively	• Eliminate distractions. For example, put your cellphone away. • Keep your eyes on the speaker. •
Clarify by asking questions	• If you're confused, other people probably are, too. Ask a question to help your whole class. • If you see that you are guessing, ask a question instead. •
Monitor understanding	• Notice what information you already know and be ready to build on it. • Ask for help if you are struggling. •
Interact and share ideas	• Share your ideas and answer questions, even if you are unsure. • Build on the ideas of others by adding details or making a connection. •

SCAN FOR
MULTIMEDIA

CONTENTS

PERFORMANCE TASK

WRITING FOCUS

Write an Argument
The Whole-Class selections illustrate ways in which technology has affected our everyday lives. After reading the texts and watching the video, you will write an argument in the form of an editorial about the impact of modern technology.

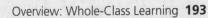

About the Author

With more than one hundred million copies of his books in print worldwide, **Arthur C. Clarke** (1917–2008) may have been the most successful science-fiction writer of all time. He is known for combining his knowledge of technology and science with touches of poetry. Clarke once said, "The only way of finding the limits of the possible is by going beyond them into the impossible."

🔧 Tool Kit

First-Read Guide and Model Annotation

Feathered Friend

Concept Vocabulary

You will encounter the following words as you read "Feathered Friend." Before reading, note how familiar you are with each word. Then, rank the words in order from most familiar (1) to least familiar (5).

WORD	YOUR RANKING
pathetically	
distressed	
mournfully	
apologetically	
lamented	

After completing the first read, come back to the concept vocabulary and review your rankings. Mark changes to your original rankings as needed.

First Read FICTION

Apply these strategies as you conduct your first read. You will have an opportunity to complete the close-read notes after your first read.

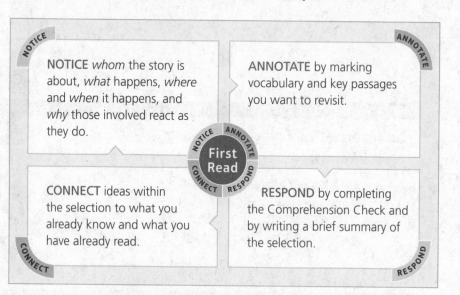

NOTICE whom the story is about, what happens, where and when it happens, and why those involved react as they do.

ANNOTATE by marking vocabulary and key passages you want to revisit.

CONNECT ideas within the selection to what you already know and what you have already read.

RESPOND by completing the Comprehension Check and by writing a brief summary of the selection.

First Read

≔ STANDARDS

Reading Literature
By the end of the year, read and comprehend literature, including stories, dramas, and poems, in the grades 6–8 text complexity band proficiently, with scaffolding as needed at the high end of the range.

Feathered Friend
Arthur C. Clarke

BACKGROUND
This story was written during the 1950s, a time of growth and technological advancement in the United States. The possibility of space exploration created a feeling of immense potential. This optimism about the future influenced all areas of the arts, especially popular literature, in what is now called the Golden Age of Science Fiction.

SCAN FOR
MULTIMEDIA

NOTES

1   To the best of my knowledge, there's never been a regulation that forbids one to keep pets in a space station. No one ever thought it was necessary—and even had such a rule existed, I am quite certain that Sven Olsen would have ignored it.

2   With a name like that, you will picture Sven at once as a six-foot-six Nordic giant, built like a bull and with a voice to match. Had this been so, his chances of getting a job in space would have been very slim. Actually he was a wiry little fellow, like most of the early spacers, and managed to qualify easily for the 150-pound bonus that kept so many of us on a reducing diet.

3   Sven was one of our best construction men, and excelled at the tricky and specialized work of collecting assorted girders as they floated around in free fall, making them do the slow-motion, three-dimensional ballet that would get them into their right positions, and fusing the pieces together when they were precisely dovetailed into the intended pattern: It was a skilled and difficult job, for a spacesuit is not the most convenient of garbs in which to work. However, Sven's team had one great advantage over the construction gangs you see putting up skyscrapers down on

Earth. They could step back and admire their handiwork without being abruptly parted from it by gravity. . . .

4 Don't ask me why Sven wanted a pet, or why he chose the one he did. I'm not a psychologist, but I must admit that his selection was very sensible. Claribel weighed practically nothing, her food requirements were tiny—and she was not worried, as most animals would have been, by the absence of gravity.

5 I first became aware that Claribel was aboard when I was sitting in the little cubbyhole laughingly called my office, checking through my lists of technical stores to decide what items we'd be running out of next. When I heard the musical whistle beside my ear, I assumed that it had come over the station intercom, and waited for an announcement to follow. It didn't; instead, there was a long and involved pattern of melody that made me look up with such a start that I forgot all about the angle beam just behind my head. When the stars had ceased to explode before my eyes, I had my first view of Claribel.

6 She was a small yellow canary, hanging in the air as motionless as a hummingbird—and with much less effort, for her wings were quietly folded along her sides. We stared at each other for a minute; then, before I had quite recovered my wits, she did a curious kind of backward loop I'm sure no earthbound canary had ever managed, and departed with a few leisurely flicks. It was quite obvious that she'd already learned how to operate in the absence of gravity, and did not believe in doing unnecessary work.

7 Sven didn't confess to her ownership for several days, and by that time it no longer mattered, because Claribel was a general pet. He had smuggled her up on the last ferry from Earth, when he came back from leave—partly, he claimed, out of sheer scientific curiosity. He wanted to see just how a bird would operate when it had no weight but could still use its wings.

8 Claribel thrived and grew fat. On the whole, we had little trouble concealing our guest when VIPs from Earth came visiting. A space station has more hiding places than you can count; the only problem was that Claribel got rather noisy when she was upset, and we sometimes had to think fast to explain the curious peeps and whistles that came from ventilating shafts and storage bulkheads. There were a couple of narrow escapes—but then who would dream of looking for a canary in a space station?

9 We were now on twelve-hour watches, which was not as bad as it sounds, since you need little sleep in space. Though of course there is no "day" and "night" when you are floating in permanent sunlight, it was still convenient to stick to the terms. Certainly when I woke that "morning" it felt like 6:00 A.M. on Earth. I had

a nagging headache, and vague memories of fitful, disturbed dreams. It took me ages to undo my bunk straps, and I was still only half awake when I joined the remainder of the duty crew in the mess. Breakfast was unusually quiet, and there was one seat vacant.

10   "Where's Sven?" I asked, not very much caring.

11   "He's looking for Claribel," someone answered. "Says he can't find her anywhere. She usually wakes him up."

12   Before I could retort that she usually woke me up, too, Sven came in through the doorway, and we could see at once that something was wrong. He slowly opened his hand, and there lay a tiny bundle of yellow feathers, with two clenched claws sticking **pathetically** up into the air.

13   "What happened?" we asked, all equally **distressed**.

14   "I don't know," said Sven **mournfully**. "I just found her like this."

15   "Let's have a look at her," said Jock Duncan, our cook-doctor-dietitian. We all waited in hushed silence while he held Claribel against his ear in an attempt to detect any heartbeat.

16   Presently he shook his head. "I can't hear anything, but that doesn't prove she's dead. I've never listened to a canary's heart," he added rather **apologetically**.

17   "Give her a shot of oxygen," suggested somebody, pointing to the green-banded emergency cylinder in its recess beside the door. Everyone agreed that this was an excellent idea, and Claribel was tucked snugly into a face mask that was large enough to serve as a complete oxygen tent for her.

18   To our delighted surprise, she revived at once. Beaming broadly, Sven removed the mask, and she hopped onto his finger. She gave her series of "Come to the cookhouse, boys" trills—then promptly keeled over again.

19   "I don't get it," **lamented** Sven. "What's wrong with her? She's never done this before."

20   For the last few minutes, something had been tugging at my memory. My mind seemed to be very sluggish that morning, as if I was still unable to cast off the burden of sleep. I felt that I could do with some of that oxygen—but before I could reach the mask, understanding exploded in my brain. I whirled on the duty engineer and said urgently:

21   "Jim! There's something wrong with the air! That's why Claribel's passed out. I've just remembered that miners used to carry canaries down to warn them of gas."

22   "Nonsense!" said Jim. "The alarms would have gone off. We've got duplicate circuits, operating independently."

NOTES

pathetically (puh THEHT ihk lee) *adv.* in a way that causes someone to feel pity

distressed (dih STREHST) *adj.* troubled; upset

mournfully (MAWRN fuh lee) *adv.* in a way that expresses grief or sadness

apologetically (uh pol uh JEHT ihk lee) *adv.* in a way that shows someone is sorry for having done or said something; regretfully

lamented (luh MEHN tihd) *v.* said in a way that showed sadness or sorrow

23   "Er—the second alarm circuit isn't connected up yet." His assistant reminded him. That shook Jim; he left without a word, while we stood arguing and passing the oxygen bottle around like a pipe of peace.

24   He came back ten minutes later with a sheepish expression. It was one of those accidents that couldn't possibly happen; we'd had one of our rare eclipses by Earth's shadow that night: Part of the air purifier had frozen up, and the single alarm in the circuit had failed to go off. Half a million dollars' worth of chemical and electronic engineering had let us down completely. Without Claribel, we should soon have been slightly dead.

25   So now, if you visit any space station, don't be surprised if you hear an inexplicable snatch of birdsong. There's no need to be alarmed; on the contrary, in fact. It will mean that you're being doubly safeguarded, at practically no extra expense. ❧

Comprehension Check

Complete the following items after you complete your first read.

1. Where does the story take place?

2. How does the narrator discover Claribel's presence?

3. Why does Sven bring Claribel onboard?

4. What causes Claribel to pass out?

5. **Notebook** Confirm your understanding of the story by writing a summary.

RESEARCH

Research to Clarify Choose at least one unfamiliar detail from the text. Briefly research that detail. In what way does the information you learned shed light on an aspect of the story?

Research to Explore Choose something from the text that interests you, and formulate a research question. For example, you may want to learn more about canaries or space stations.

Close Read the Text

1. This model, from paragraph 3 of the story, shows two sample annotations, along with questions and conclusions. Close read the passage, and find another detail to annotate. Then, write a question and your conclusion.

Close Read

ANNOTATE · QUESTION · CONCLUDE

> **ANNOTATE:** Some of these details are very technical, but others are very poetic.
>
> **QUESTION:** Why does Clarke use different types of language to describe Sven's movements?
>
> **CONCLUDE:** These details suggest that working in space is both freeing and beautiful, and exacting and scientific.

Sven was one of our best construction men, and excelled at the tricky and specialized work of collecting assorted girders as they floated around in free fall, making them do the slow-motion, three-dimensional ballet that would get them into their right positions, and fusing the pieces together when they were precisely dovetailed into the intended pattern. . . .

> **ANNOTATE:** The author combines familiar details of construction work with unfamiliar details of zero gravity.
>
> **QUESTION:** Why does the author make this choice?
>
> **CONCLUDE:** The combination of Earth-like details and space-related details creates a startling setting.

🔧 Tool Kit

Close-Read Guide and
Model Annotation

2. For more practice, go back into the story, and complete the close-read notes.

3. Revisit a section of the text you found important during your first read. Read this section closely, and **annotate** what you notice. Ask yourself **questions** such as "Why did the author make this choice?" "What can you **conclude**?"

Analyze the Text

CITE TEXTUAL EVIDENCE
to support your answers.

📓 **Notebook** Respond to these questions.

1. (a) **Infer** How do the crew members feel about Claribel? (b) **Draw Conclusions** What is the benefit of having a pet in the space station?

2. (a) **Synthesize** What events or factors help the narrator figure out that something is wrong with the air? (b) **Make a Judgment** Who is responsible for saving the crew's lives: Claribel or the narrator? Explain.

3. (a) What causes the failure of the alarm that was intended to warn about air quality? (b) **Speculate** What are some potential problems with using a canary instead of an electronic alarm system?
(c) **Evaluate** Which is a more reliable form of alarm? Explain.

⊟ STANDARDS

Reading Literature
• Cite textual evidence to support analysis of what the text says explicitly as well as inferences drawn from the text.

• Determine a theme or central idea of a text and how it is conveyed through particular details; provide a summary of the text distinct from personal opinions or judgments.

• Analyze how a particular sentence, chapter, scene, or stanza fits into the overall structure of a text and contributes to the development of the theme, setting, or plot.

Analyze Craft and Structure

Determine Theme The **theme** of a short story is the message or insight about life that it expresses. Sometimes, the narrator states the theme directly. More often, the theme is implied, or suggested by details in the text. To figure out the **implied theme** of a story, look closely at details, think about how they fit together, and consider what larger meaning they convey. To determine the theme of "Feathered Friend," focus on the following elements:

- the story's title
- the characters' thoughts and feelings
- the **setting** of the story, or when and where the story takes place
- the knowledge and insights that characters gain in the course of the story
- the outcome of the conflict and the effect the outcome has on the characters

Readers may interpret a story's theme in different ways. In order for an interpretation to be valid, it must take into account all of the story's important details.

Practice

CITE TEXTUAL EVIDENCE
to support your answers.

 Notebook Respond to these questions.

1. This diagram lists key details from "Feathered Friend" that suggest a theme. Consider the details. Then, write the theme they suggest.

> KEY DETAIL: *The station has advanced systems to protect the air quality.*

+

> KEY DETAIL: *One of the space-station workers smuggles aboard a canary.*

+

> KEY DETAIL: *The canary alerts the men when the air quality gets dangerously bad.*

=

> THEME:

2. Here is another possible theme expressed in "Feathered Friend": *Advanced technology leaves a void that people try to fill with companionship.* What details from the text connect to support this theme? Explain.

3. (a) What is the setting of "Feathered Friend"? (b) How does the setting contribute to the themes you explored in questions 1 and 2?

FEATHERED FRIEND

Concept Vocabulary

pathetically	mournfully	lamented
distressed	apologetically	

Why These Words? These concept vocabulary words all relate to feelings of sadness, suffering, or regret. For example, when something is wrong with Claribel, the crew members are *distressed,* and her owner speaks *mournfully*.

1. How does the concept vocabulary help readers appreciate Claribel's importance to the crew?

2. What other words do you know that connect to this concept?

Practice

🔲 **Notebook** Indicate whether the concept vocabulary word is used correctly in each sentence. Explain your answers.

1. The frightened cat hid in the corner and mewed *pathetically*.

2. We *lamented* the loss of our favorite teacher when she moved to another state.

3. The baby was so *distressed* by the attention that she grinned widely and clapped her hands.

4. The dog was old and sick, but I still cried *mournfully* when she died.

5. "I'm so happy that I won!" Kara cheered *apologetically*.

Word Study

Greek Root: -path- The Greek root -path- means "feeling" or "suffering." In "Feathered Friend," when Claribel is unwell, her claws stick up *pathetically* in the air. Claribel's claws are sticking up in a way that causes the crew members to feel sadness for her suffering.

1. Write a definition of the word *sympathy* that shows your understanding of the Greek root -path-. Then, use the word *sympathy* correctly in a sentence.

2. Use a dictionary to find the meaning of the word *empathy*. Write the definition. Then, explain how the definition connects to the meaning of the Greek root.

🗂 WORD NETWORK

Add words related to modern technology from the text to your Word Network.

☰ STANDARDS

Language

• Demonstrate command of the conventions of standard English grammar and usage when writing or speaking.

• Determine or clarify the meaning of unknown and multiple-meaning words and phrases based on *grade 6 reading and content,* choosing flexibly from a range of strategies.
  b. Use common, grade-appropriate Greek or Latin affixes and roots as clues to the meaning of a word.

• Demonstrate understanding of figurative language, word relationships, and nuances in word meanings.

Conventions

Compound Words "Feathered Friend" contains a wide assortment of **compound words,** words that are made up of two or more other words. They sometimes appear in closed form as a single word, as in *heartbeat*. In other cases, they are hyphenated, as in *three-dimensional*. Some compound words appear in open form as two separate words, as in *free fall*.

Compound words can function as various parts of speech, depending on how they are being used. Here are some examples:

PART OF SPEECH	EXAMPLES
noun	The **space station** was running low on supplies. **Skyscrapers** were visible from far away.
verb	The engineer **dovetailed** the girders. Alarms **safeguarded** the crew from danger.
adjective	**Earthbound** passengers boarded the shuttle. The technicians worked in **twelve-hour** shifts.
adverb	The bird jumped **sideways** when startled.

Read It

1. Reread paragraph 3 of "Feathered Friend," and mark the compound words you see. List the words.

2. Read each passage from "Feathered Friend," and mark the compound word or words. Then, identify each compound word's part of speech.

PASSAGE	PART OF SPEECH
1. . . . you will picture Sven at once as a six-foot-six Nordic giant, built like a bull and with a voice to match.	
2. She was a small yellow canary, hanging in the air as motionless as a hummingbird. . . .	
3. So now, . . . don't be surprised if you hear an inexplicable snatch of birdsong.	

Write It

three-dimensional	bulkhead	spacesuit
breakfast	headache	doorway

Notebook Write three sentences in which you use compound words. You may use the words in the chart, which appear in "Feathered Friend," or come up with words of your own.

FEATHERED FRIEND

Writing to Sources

An argument is a form of writing in which a writer states a claim, develops it with reasons, and supports it with evidence. The purpose of an argument is to convince readers to agree with the claim.

Assignment

One theme of "Feathered Friend" is that it is risky for people to become dependent on technology. Write a brief **argumentative essay** in which you take a position on that theme. Do you think the story expresses valid concerns about the risks of technology? Use details from the story, as well as your own observations and insights, to support your claim and craft a convincing argument.

Your essay should include:

- a claim, or clear statement of your position

- a logical organization, with words and phrases that show how your claim, reasons, and evidence connect

- relevant details from the story that support your claim

- a concluding statement that emphasizes the strength of your claim

Vocabulary and Conventions Connection In your argument, consider using several of the concept vocabulary words. If you use any compound words, look them up in a dictionary to see whether they should be hyphenated.

pathetically	mournfully	lamented
distressed	apologetically	

- -

Reflect on Your Writing

After you have written your argument, answer the following questions.

1. How did writing your argument strengthen your understanding of the story's theme?

2. Is your argument clear and easy to follow? If not, how might you improve the organization and support?

3. Why These Words? The words you choose make a difference in your writing. Which words did you specifically choose to make your argument persuasive, or convincing?

STANDARDS

Writing
- Write arguments to support claims with clear reasons and relevant evidence.
  - a. Introduce claim(s) and organize the reasons and evidence clearly.
  - b. Support claim(s) with clear reasons and relevant evidence, using credible sources and demonstrating an understanding of the topic or text.
  - c. Use words, phrases, and clauses to clarify the relationship among claim(s) and reasons.
  - e. Provide a concluding statement or section that follows from the argument presented.
- Conduct short research projects to answer a question, drawing on several sources and refocusing the inquiry when appropriate.

Speaking and Listening
- Present claims and findings, sequencing ideas logically and using pertinent descriptions, facts, and details to accentuate main ideas or themes; use appropriate eye contact, adequate volume, and clear pronunciation.
- Include multimedia components and visual displays in presentations to clarify information.

Speaking and Listening

Canaries were used in coal mines as a low-tech way to detect deadly gases, before the invention of high-tech devices. In "Feathered Friend," Arthur C. Clarke shows the benefits of high-tech and low-tech methods working together.

Assignment

Work with a partner to create a **multimedia presentation**. In your presentation, explain another way in which high-tech and low-tech methods can work well together. Conclude your presentation by reflecting on whether your research has changed your opinions about modern technology.

1. **Research the Topic** Research ways in which high-tech and low-tech methods can work together. Then, identify one example to be the focus of your presentation.

2. **Organize Your Multimedia** Your presentation should explain how high-tech and low-tech methods work together in the example you present. Make sure you present your multimedia components in the order that makes the most sense. They should help clarify the information you present.

3. **Consider Your Conclusion** Consider the new knowledge you have gained from your research. What have you learned? Have your opinions about modern technology changed? Share your thoughts with the class at the end of your presentation.

4. **Prepare Your Delivery** Practice delivering your presentation with your partner. Remember to do the following:
   - maintain eye contact with your audience
   - speak with enough volume that everyone can hear you
   - speak with clear pronunciation

5. **Evaluate Multimedia Presentations** Listen closely as your classmates deliver their presentations. Use an evaluation guide like the one shown to rate their deliveries.

EVALUATION GUIDE

Rate each statement on a scale of 1 (not demonstrated) to 5 (well demonstrated).

☐ The information and media were placed in a logical order.

☐ The presentation clearly addressed both high- and low-tech methods.

☐ The presentation ended with a strong conclusion.

☐ The speakers maintained eye contact and spoke clearly and with enough volume.

☑ EVIDENCE LOG

Before moving on to a new selection, go to your Evidence Log and record what you learned from "Feathered Friend."

TEENS AND TECHNOLOGY
SHARE A FUTURE

Comparing Texts

In this lesson, you will read and compare two arguments, in the form of blog posts, about the impact of modern technology. First, you will complete the first-read and close-read activities for "Teens and Technology Share a Future."

THE BLACK HOLE OF
TECHNOLOGY

About the Author

Stefan Etienne (b. 1997) was born in Miami and now lives in New York City. At age twelve, he founded a technology blog called LaptopMemo.com. Etienne blogs about consumer technology.

Teens and Technology Share a Future

Technical Vocabulary

You will encounter the following words as you read "Teens and Technology Share a Future." Before reading, rate how familiar you are with each word. Rank the words in order from most familiar (1) to least familiar (3).

WORD	YOUR RANKING
microchips	
trigonometry	
pixels	

After completing the first read, come back to the technical vocabulary and review your rankings. Mark changes to your original rankings as needed.

First Read NONFICTION

Apply these strategies as you conduct your first read. You will have an opportunity to complete the close-read notes after your first read.

🔧 **Tool Kit**
First-Read Guide and Model Annotation

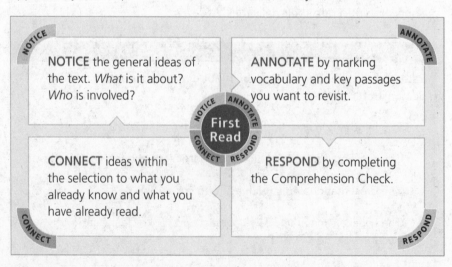

NOTICE the general ideas of the text. *What* is it about? *Who* is involved?

ANNOTATE by marking vocabulary and key passages you want to revisit.

CONNECT ideas within the selection to what you already know and what you have already read.

RESPOND by completing the Comprehension Check.

First Read

STANDARDS
Reading Informational Text
By the end of the year, read and comprehend literary nonfiction in the grades 6–8 text complexity band proficiently, with scaffolding as needed at the high end of the range.

Teens and Technology Share a Future

Stefan Etienne

BACKGROUND

The Internet puts an enormous amount of information at your fingertips. However, it only became widely available in the 1990s. It was first developed by the United States Defense Department as a communication tool in the 1970s. By the 2000s, about 360 million people, or 6% of the world's population, were connected to the Internet. This blog post discusses the impact of those changes.

SCAN FOR MULTIMEDIA

1   Perhaps it is the years of experience I've had in front of a computer, a laptop, or some sort of device with a screen. Talking about technology, attending press events in NYC,[1] and meeting the industry's most interesting people—all older than me, but all with the same childish hunger to see what comes next.

2   With its **microchips**, input methods, operating systems,[2] and everything in between, technology of the twenty-first century is a window into a new world for all of humanity, but especially for teenagers. Are you curious about something no one you know has even heard of? Then, search for it online—and maybe even come across the wrong answer, initially.

3   You do more research and eventually uncover the truth. Inside, you feel a little like Indiana Jones,[3] finding information that you believe will make you a more complete human being. In the grand scheme of things, you've done us all a great service: You've turned over a small stone of information, one in a river of millions. With every stone turned, our picture of the world becomes clearer.

NOTES

microchips (MY kroh chihps) *n.* small pieces of computer technology that have integrated circuits

CLOSE READ

ANNOTATE: In paragraph 3, mark the two comparisons the author makes.

QUESTION: Why does the author use these comparisons?

CONCLUDE: How do these comparisons help readers understand the writer's ideas?

---

1. **NYC** New York City.
2. **operating systems** basic software that allow devices to run applications.
3. **Indiana Jones** classic movie character, known for being an explorer and archaeologist.

NOTES

trigonometry (trihg uh NOM uh tree) *n.* field of math that deals with the relationships between the sides and angles of triangles

4   It's similar to my experience with the polar vortex[4] that has been plaguing New York for more than a month: Only when the sun breaks out for a moment do I realize how beautiful the snow can be. That's what computer technology can do—like sunshine breaking through the cold, it changes how we see things. When you filter out the useless Facebook messages, out-of-context tweets, and all the GIFs from Reddit,[5] you see that you—yes, you—are in control of your own information network. Best of all, you can do *anything* you want to do with it. There's no excuse to be confused by that math problem in **trigonometry**, or lack a source to cite in an essay. It's all on you now.

5   Of course, right off the bat, you may be thinking: "Here comes a geek, obsessed with technology, preaching about its effectiveness and adaptability, and how it's great for everyone who is currently a teenager."

6   You're absolutely right. But even if you are not as much of a geek as I am, you are still immersed in technology. How else would you be reading this blog? How else would you understand what "LOL" means, or be able to send a text message without even thinking about it?

7   The world is facing many problems, but young people—using the power of technology—have the opportunity to solve them. Technology connects us in ways no one has ever been connected before. As Henry David Thoreau[6] put it in an age before the Internet, "Could a greater miracle take place than for us to look through each other's eyes, for just an instant?" If only Thoreau had known that we would be able to look into another person's eyes—even if they are actually just **pixels** on a screen—thousands of miles away! What superpower could one possibly want when we have technology that lets us meet new people, invent new things, and help others?

8   Today's teenagers (as of 2014) have the potential to be the most influential and informed generation of human beings ever seen. But that will only happen if we step up to the challenge, wake up, and be prepared to take charge in an informed, responsible, and powerful way. (Hopefully, we will not make our problems worse.)

9   What is better than a will to do great things? The actual actions that will make those great things happen. ❧

pixels (PIHK suhlz) *n.* smallest elements of an image that can be individually processed in a video display system

---

4. **polar vortex** extremely cold wind near the North or South Pole. When this blog post was written, the cold air from the north polar vortex was affecting New York.
5. **GIFs . . . Reddit** animated digital images from an entertainment- and news-based social-networking website.
6. **Henry David Thoreau** nineteenth-century writer, known for his love of nature and living simply.

Comprehension Check

Complete the following items after you finish your first read.

1. According to the author, how is technology a "window into a new world"?

2. What does the author suggest people need to do to be in control of their own information network?

3. According to the author, in what way is technology like a superpower?

4. According to the author, what must this generation do to fulfill the potential it has to influence the world in a positive way?

5. What does the author say is better than wanting to do great things?

6. ⊟ **Notebook** List three important ideas from the selection to show your understanding.

- -

RESEARCH

Research to Clarify Choose at least one unfamiliar detail from the text. Briefly research that detail. In what way does the information you learned shed light on an aspect of the blog post?

Research to Explore Choose something that interested you from the text, and formulate a research question.

TEENS AND TECHNOLOGY
SHARE A FUTURE

Close Read the Text

1. This model, from paragraph 4 of the text, shows two sample annotations, along with questions and conclusions. Close read the passage, and find another detail to annotate. Then, write a question and your conclusion.

ANNOTATE: These are all very specific examples of different kinds of information we get from computer technology.

QUESTION: Why does the author mention such specific items?

CONCLUDE: Using specific terms helps make a connection to readers—they may recognize their own use of technology in these examples.

Close
Read

ANNOTATE: The author repeats the word *you.*

QUESTION: Why does the author put so much emphasis on *you*?

CONCLUDE: He is stressing the idea that we are all personally responsible for our uses of technology.

> When you filter out the useless Facebook messages, out-of-context tweets, and all the GIFs from Reddit, you see that you—yes, you—are in control of your own information network. Best of all, you can do *anything* you want to do with it.

Tool Kit
Close-Read Guide and
Model Annotation

2. For more practice, go back into the text, and complete the close-read notes.

3. Revisit a section of the text you found important during your first read. Read this section closely, and **annotate** what you notice. Ask yourself **questions** such as "Why did the blogger make this choice?" What can you **conclude**?

STANDARDS
Reading Informational Text
• Cite textual evidence to support analysis of what the text says explicitly as well as inferences drawn from the text.
• Analyze how a particular sentence, paragraph, chapter, or section fits into the overall structure of a text and contributes to the development of the ideas.
• Determine an author's point of view or purpose in a text and explain how it is conveyed in the text.
• Trace and evaluate the argument and specific claims in a text, distinguishing claims that are supported by reasons and evidence from claims that are not.

Analyze the Text

CITE TEXTUAL EVIDENCE
to support your answers.

Notebook Respond to these questions.

1. (a) **Paraphrase** Explain the blogger's comparison of technology to the polar vortex. (b) **Evaluate** Is his comparison effective? Explain.

2. **Speculate** Why do you think he specifically addresses teens?

3. **Interpret** What does the blogger mean when he says that teens must "take charge in an informed, responsible, and powerful way"?

4. **Essential Question: *How is modern technology helpful and harmful to society?*** What have you learned about the ways that technology can help or harm society from reading this blog post?

Analyze Craft and Structure

Author's Perspective: Argument This blog post is an example of an **argument**, a type of writing in which an author tries to persuade readers to think or do something specific. All persuasive writing presents a main **claim**, which is the author's position or opinion. The writer may include other claims that relate to the main one. Most writers use different types of details to support their claims. These supporting details are called *evidence*, and they may be any of the following types:

- logical reasons
- facts, or statements that can be proved true
- quotations from experts
- examples that help illustrate ideas

The author's claim reflects his or her **perspective**, or viewpoint. An author's perspective relates to his or her attitudes and experiences. For example, this blogger enjoys technology. His claim shows that perspective.

Practice

CITE TEXTUAL EVIDENCE
to support your answers.

📓 **Notebook** **Answer the following questions.**

1. (a) What is Etienne's main claim? (b) Identify two reasons he offers to support his claim.

2. (a) Identify a quotation from another author that Etienne uses to support his claim. (b) How does the quotation help strengthen his argument?

3. (a) Note two points at which Etienne says that technology can cause harm. (b) Why does he admit something that goes against his claim? (c) How does this actually strengthen his argument?

4. Etienne compares computer technology to a variety of different things. Use the chart to analyze whether each comparison makes his ideas clearer or has another effect.

COMPARISON	EFFECT
windows into a new world	
stones in a river	
superpowers	

TEENS AND TECHNOLOGY
SHARE A FUTURE

Technical Vocabulary

| microchips | trigonometry | pixels |

Why These Words? Like other fields, the technology industry has its own specialized vocabulary. These three technical vocabulary words are part of this specialized vocabulary.

1. How does the technical vocabulary sharpen the reader's understanding of the blogger's opinion about technology?

2. What other words in the blog post connect to this concept?

Practice

⊟ **Notebook** The technical vocabulary words appear in "Teens and Technology Share a Future."

1. Use each technical word in a sentence that demonstrates your understanding of the word's meaning.

2. With a partner, take turns listing as many words related to the technical vocabulary words as you can.

Word Study

Greek Suffix: -metry The Greek suffix -metry means "process of measuring." Trigonometry is a type of mathematics that uses the properties of triangles to determine unknown angles and lengths. Knowing the meaning of -metry can help you determine the meanings of other words.

1. The Greek root -hor- means "time." What kind of tool or device might someone use in the field of horometry?

2. The Greek root -opt- means "eye" or "sight." Why might someone visit a person who practices optometry?

☰ STANDARDS

Reading Informational Text
Determine the meaning of words and phrases as they are used in a text, including figurative, connotative, and technical meanings.

Language
• Demonstrate command of the conventions of standard English grammar and usage when writing or speaking.
• Demonstrate command of the conventions of standard English capitalization, punctuation, and spelling when writing.
  a. Use punctuation to set off nonrestrictive/parenthetical elements.
• Determine or clarify the meaning of unknown and multiple-meaning words and phrases based on grade 6 reading and content, choosing flexibly from a range of strategies.
  b. Use common, grade-appropriate Greek or Latin affixes and roots as clues to the meaning of a word.

Conventions

Appositives and Appositive Phrases Writers use appositives to add information that helps the reader understand certain nouns. An **appositive** is a noun or pronoun that identifies, renames, or explains another noun or pronoun next to it. An **appositive phrase** includes an appositive and its modifiers.

- If the information in an appositive or appositive phrase is restrictive, which means that it is essential to understanding the sentence, *do not* set it off with commas or dashes.

- If the information in the appositive or appositive phrase is nonrestrictive, or nonessential, *do* set it off with commas or dashes.

APPOSITIVE	APPOSITIVE PHRASE
My friend _Marcos_ is great at using technology. (essential)	I bought clothes from the website, _an online shop_. (nonessential)

Read It

1. Read these sentences. Mark each example of an appositive or an appositive phrase. Label each as essential or nonessential.

a. Examples of texting symbols include emoticons, picture portrayals of the writer's mood.

b. We replay GIFs—funny images of cats, usually—and laugh every single time.

c. The reference book _Oxford English Dictionary_ added new words in September 2015.

2. Read this passage from the selection. Mark the appositive or appositive phrase, and label it as essential or nonessential.

You've turned over a small stone of information, one in a river of millions.

Write It

🔲 **Notebook** Write a paragraph explaining when and how you usually use the Internet. Use at least two appositives or appositive phrases.

TIP

CLARIFICATION
Refer to the Grammar Handbook to learn more about these terms.

✏️ EVIDENCE LOG

Before moving on to a new selection, go to your Evidence Log and record what you've learned from "Teens and Technology Share a Future."

TEENS AND TECHNOLOGY SHARE A FUTURE

Comparing Texts

Read this blog post and complete the first-read and close-read activities. Then, compare the blogger's argument to the one expressed in "Teens and Technology Share a Future."

THE BLACK HOLE OF TECHNOLOGY

About the Author

Leena Khan (b. 2001) is an aspiring author. Khan lives in Saudi Arabia.

The Black Hole of Technology

Concept Vocabulary

You will encounter the following words as you read "The Black Hole of Technology." Before reading, rate how familiar you are with each word. Rank the words in order from most familiar (1) to least familiar (5).

WORD	YOUR RANKING
devouring	
absorbing	
process	
consumed	
digesting	

After completing the first read, come back to the concept vocabulary and review your rankings. Mark changes to your original rankings as needed.

First Read NONFICTION

Apply these strategies as you conduct your first read. You will have an opportunity to complete the close-read notes after your first read.

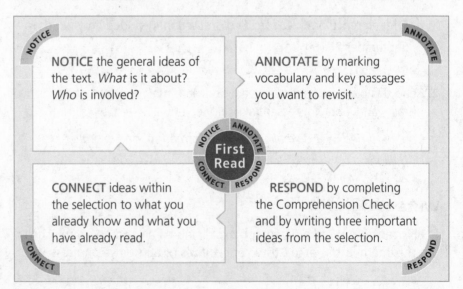

NOTICE the general ideas of the text. *What* is it about? *Who* is involved?

ANNOTATE by marking vocabulary and key passages you want to revisit.

First Read

CONNECT ideas within the selection to what you already know and what you have already read.

RESPOND by completing the Comprehension Check and by writing three important ideas from the selection.

STANDARDS

Reading Informational Text
By the end of the year, read and comprehend literary nonfiction in the grades 6–8 text complexity band proficiently, with scaffolding as needed at the high end of the range.

The Black Hole of Technology

Leena Khan

SCAN FOR
MULTIMEDIA

BACKGROUND

The first smartphone was introduced in 1993. Since then, smartphones have become the fastest-selling devices in history. By 2013, 22% of the world's total population owned a smartphone. Although many people also own personal computers, the smartphone is a portable device that allows people to stay connected wherever they go.

1   The black hole of endless, unimportant streams of technology-enabled information is **devouring** everyone living in the twenty-first century. No matter how much people may look at information, it does not mean they are **absorbing** it. Equating quality with speed and volume, people may read thousands of news headlines broadcasted across the world daily, yet they will forget them in a couple of hours. No one stops to **process** information anymore to determine its significance or importance. No one appreciates the value of personal interaction or nature. Everything is go, go, go. Not once do we stop. Before being introduced to my phone and computer, I had been more appreciative of the world around me. Now, I'm always **consumed** by my "tech," and I never stop to take a break.

2   "Did you guys see what Miley Cyrus[1] posted?" My friend Fouly only peeled her eyes away from her iPhone screen to ask us that question. I glanced around at my friends, and they all quickly checked Instagram[2] in the hopes that they hadn't missed Miley's latest update. I, on the other hand, glanced out the window separating us from the beautiful weather outside. We were 15 friends sitting inside under artificial lighting and with our hands

NOTES

devouring (dih VOW rihng)
v. taking in greedily

absorbing (ab ZAWR bihng)
v. learning; fully taking in

process (PROS ehs) *v.* gain an understanding of

consumed (kuhn SOOMD)
adj. absorbed; occupied

---

1. **Miley Cyrus** celebrity who has achieved fame as an actress and a singer.
2. **Instagram** online social-media platform.

digesting (dih JEH stihng) *v.* thinking over; mentally taking in

glued to our phones on a Friday, when the enticing warmth of the sun and delicate breeze were begging us to run around outside. Of course, our ears were deaf to nature's pleas, just like any other teenager nowadays. I put my phone down to shut the curtains, then I continued to mindlessly scroll through Miley's Instagram page.

3   I found myself longing for that Instagram page a week later, in an entirely different country. The scorching sun baked the back of my neck as my family and I walked along the wide, crowded dirt path on our way to visit yet another Cambodian temple. I slipped my phone out of my bag to check for a signal, but before I could even unlock it, it was snatched out of my hands.

4   "Leena, you're heading toward one of the most well preserved ancient wonders in the world. It would do you well to appreciate your surroundings!" my dad scolded.

5   My phone was wailing at me from the tight grip his hands had on it, but I had no choice but to ignore it, like I had been forced to do for the entire fall break. Huffing, I looked up and drank in our surroundings. There were tents perched on the sides of the sandy roads, and a couple of half-naked boys were jumping into a murky lake nearby. A toddler was laughing her head off, playing with an old man who I assumed was her grandfather. I missed all of this liveliness, the beauty of a community, because I was trapped in the black hole of technology. Everyone around me was smiling, despite having to live their lives in poverty. Then I noticed something I hadn't before: no one had a cellphone on them. There were no TVs, no radios, and their music came from live instruments instead of mp3 players and iPods. These people had nothing. Some of them were even walking around without shoes! How could they look so happy? Then I thought . . . Maybe it's because they don't have all that modern technology. They aren't subjected to the black hole of endless information.

6   I carried my insightful observations all the way to the temple, and my breath caught in my throat when we got there. It was stunning. When the guide started a long speech about the origin of the temple, I turned to face him. Then I realized I was inside of the black hole again. I was paying attention to the information the guide was throwing at me instead of also recognizing this once-in-a-lifetime experience. When would I be able to visit one of the seven wonders of the world again? The answer was pretty clear, so keeping one ear with the guide, and turning the rest of myself to the temple, I soaked in the extraordinary sight before me. For once, I wasn't **digesting** useless information. I wasn't typing into my phone, or watching any screen at all. In a life of go, go, go I had finally stopped.

7   It was then that I vowed that the next time my friends and I are absorbed in our phones on a sunny day, I won't close the curtains. Next time I'm walking along any road, I'll value my surroundings instead of texting on a device. From now on, I will make sure that the endless information flying my way won't go in one ear and out the other. I will find the significance in things and recognize it, because that's something many people fail to do—by falling into the technology trap. Escape the black hole of technology, because when you do . . . you feel free. ❧

Comprehension Check

Complete the following items after you finish your first read.

1. What does the author do when a friend points out a new Miley Cyrus post?

2. Where do the author and her family go on vacation?

3. Why does the author's father take away her cellphone?

4. 🖹 **Notebook** Write three important ideas from the selection.

- -

RESEARCH

Research to Clarify Choose at least one unfamiliar detail from the text. Briefly research that detail. In what way does the information you learned shed light on an aspect of the blog post?

THE BLACK HOLE OF TECHNOLOGY

Close Read the Text

1. This model, from paragraph 5 of the text, shows two sample annotations, along with questions and conclusions. Close read the passage, and find another detail to annotate. Then, write a question and your conclusion.

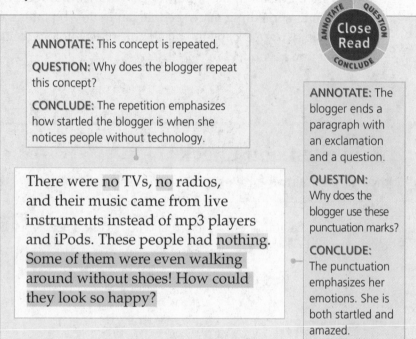

ANNOTATE: This concept is repeated.

QUESTION: Why does the blogger repeat this concept?

CONCLUDE: The repetition emphasizes how startled the blogger is when she notices people without technology.

ANNOTATE: The blogger ends a paragraph with an exclamation and a question.

QUESTION: Why does the blogger use these punctuation marks?

CONCLUDE: The punctuation emphasizes her emotions. She is both startled and amazed.

> There were no TVs, no radios, and their music came from live instruments instead of mp3 players and iPods. These people had nothing. Some of them were even walking around without shoes! How could they look so happy?

2. For more practice, go back into the text, and complete the close-read notes.

3. Revisit a section of the text you found important during your first read. Read this section closely, and **annotate** what you notice. Ask yourself **questions** such as "Why did the blogger make this choice?" What can you **conclude**?

🔧 **Tool Kit**
Close-Read Guide and Model Annotation

Analyze the Text

CITE TEXTUAL EVIDENCE to support your answers.

📓 **Notebook** Respond to these questions.

1. **Analyze** Why does Leena Khan feel the urge to check her cellphone for a signal when she is walking toward a temple in Cambodia?

2. (a) **Analyze** Why does she draw a connection between listening to the guide and accessing data on her cellphone? (b) **Evaluate** Do you agree that the two things are similar? Why or why not?

3. **Speculate** Leena Khan vows to "find the significance in things." Explain whether you think this will be easy to do once she returns home.

4. **Essential Question:** *How is modern technology helpful and harmful to society?* What have you learned about the ways that technology can harm society from reading this blog post?

📋 **STANDARDS**

Reading Informational Text
• Determine the meaning of words and phrases as they are used in a text, including figurative, connotative, and technical meanings.
• Determine an author's point of view or purpose in a text and explain how it is conveyed in the text.
• Trace and evaluate the argument and specific claims in a text, distinguishing claims that are supported by reasons and evidence from claims that are not.

Language
Interpret figures of speech in context.

Analyze Craft and Structure

Persuasive Techniques In a persuasive text, a writer attempts to convince readers to see a topic in a new way. The writer states a position, or **claim,** and then includes facts and other evidence to support it. Persuasive writers also use a variety of techniques to make their ideas more convincing. Here are some of those techniques:

- **Repetition:** *Repeating a word or phrase*—this emphasizes the word or idea and makes it more memorable.

- **Appeal to Emotion:** *Words, phrases, or stories that make readers feel something*—readers can be influenced by words that create positive feelings for the author's position and ones that create negative feelings for an opposing position.

- **Appeal to Reason:** *Facts and reasons that are organized in a clear way*—readers can follow a writer's thought process and be convinced by strong, well-connected logic.

Each of these techniques has strengths and weaknesses, so writers often use them in combination. Also, some techniques may be more effective for certain types of ideas or readers than others.

Practice

CITE TEXTUAL EVIDENCE to support your answers.

📓 **Notebook** Respond to these questions.

1. **(a)** What does Leena Khan want readers to do or think? **(b)** What position, or claim, does she express?

2. **(a)** Give three examples of words or phrases from the blog post that have positive associations. Explain your choices. **(b)** Note three examples of words or phrases that have negative associations. Explain your choices. **(c)** How do these word choices help Khan make her argument?

3. Besides emotional appeals, what other types of techniques from the list above are present in the blog post? Provide examples, and explain each choice.

4. **(a)** In your opinion, how well does Khan support her claim? Use details from the text to support your answer. **(b)** Do you think her argument would work as well for adults as it does for teenagers? Why or why not?

THE BLACK HOLE OF TECHNOLOGY

Concept Vocabulary

devouring	process	digesting
absorbing	consumed	

Why These Words? These concept words all relate to eating and taking in nutrients, but also apply to the way we take in information. For example, the same person who is *devouring* a plate of scrambled eggs in the morning could be later *devouring* an article about why people should limit the number of eggs they eat each week.

1. How does the concept vocabulary sharpen the reader's understanding of the blogger's attitude toward technology?

2. What other words in the selection connect to this concept?

Practice

⊟ **Notebook** The concept vocabulary words appear in "The Black Hole of Technology."

1. Use as many concept words as you can in a paragraph about the blog to demonstrate your understanding of each word's meaning.

2. Use a thesaurus to find two synonyms for each word.

Word Study

Multiple-Meaning Words A multiple-meaning word has more than one definition. In this text, Leena Khan uses the word *process*, which has more than one meaning. She describes how "no one stops to *process* information anymore," meaning "understand" or "make sense of." You most likely determined which meaning she intended by using context clues. You could also verify a word's meaning by using a dictionary.

1. Using the dictionary, find two more meanings of *process*. Then, use the word in two sentences that reflect the two meanings.

2. *Assimilate* is another multiple-meaning word that relates to the other concept vocabulary words. Use a dictionary to identify two meanings of *assimilate*. Then, write two sentences that use the word and reflect its distinct meanings.

⊡ WORD NETWORK

Add words related to modern technology from the text to your Word Network.

☷ STANDARDS

Reading Informational Text
Determine the meaning of words and phrases as they are used in a text, including figurative, connotative, and technical meanings.

Language
• Demonstrate command of the conventions of standard English grammar and usage when writing or speaking.
• Demonstrate command of the conventions of standard English capitalization, punctuation, and spelling when writing.
  a. Use punctuation to set off nonrestrictive/parenthetical elements.
• Determine or clarify the meaning of unknown and multiple-meaning words and phrases based on *grade 6 reading and content*, choosing flexibly from a range of strategies.
  a. Use context as a clue to the meaning of a word or phrase.
  d. Verify the preliminary determination of the meaning of a word or phrase.

Conventions

Independent and Dependent Clauses Understanding clauses is key to well-structured writing because clauses are used to build sentences. A **clause** is a group of words with its own subject and verb. The two major types of clauses are independent clauses and dependent clauses. An **independent clause** expresses a complete thought and can stand alone as a sentence. A **dependent clause**—also known as a **subordinate clause**—cannot stand alone as a complete sentence.

Many dependent clauses begin with subordinating conjunctions, such as *when* and *if*. A **relative clause** is one kind of dependent clause and begins with a relative pronoun, such as *who* or *that*.

TIP

CLARIFICATION
Refer to the Grammar Handbook to learn more about these terms.

KEY WORDS	EXAMPLES OF CLAUSES
Subordinating Conjunctions *after, although, because, before, if, since, unless, until, when, whether*	after we got home since I bought my new phone
Relative Pronouns *that, which, who, whom, whose*	whom I met at the airport that we often ignore

Place a comma after a dependent clause that opens a sentence. If the dependent clause is **nonrestrictive**, or not necessary to understand the main idea of the sentence, set it off with commas, dashes, or parentheses.

EXAMPLE: <u>When I have time</u>, I'll check her social media for any updates.

EXAMPLE: She wrote an opinion piece, <u>which was posted online</u>.

Read It

📓 **Notebook** Mark the dependent, or subordinate, clause in each sentence. Label the ones that are relative clauses.

1. I will find the significance in things, because many other people will fail to do so.
2. I was digesting information that was completely useless.
3. When the guide started a long speech on the origin of the temple, I turned to face him.

Write It

📓 **Notebook** Write a paragraph about the selection using subordinate clauses, including one or more relative clauses. Remember to set off nonrestrictive clauses with commas, dashes, or parentheses.

TEENS AND TECHNOLOGY
SHARE A FUTURE

THE BLACK HOLE OF TECHNOLOGY

TIP

Your classmates might have a different opinion about which point of view was more persuasive. Your goal is not to convince each other, but to examine the effectiveness of each argument.

Writing to Compare

You have read two blog posts that express different views of technology. Consider the arguments conveyed in "Teens and Technology Share a Future" and "The Black Hole of Technology." Which one presents a stronger case?

Assignment

Write an **argumentative essay** in which you compare and contrast the two blog posts and decide which one is more convincing. It does not need to be the blog you agree with personally, but the one you believe presents a stronger case. Consider the following questions:

- Which blogger presents stronger supporting evidence?
- Which blogger makes better use of persuasive techniques, including repetition and appeals to emotion and reason?
- Which blogger makes a stronger connection with the reader?
- Which blogger does a better job dealing with opposing opinions?

Prewriting

Analyze Arguments With a partner, take notes on each blogger's perspective, and discuss what you notice. Use the chart to capture your observations.

	TEENS AND TECHNOLOGY SHARE A FUTURE	THE BLACK HOLE OF TECHNOLOGY
strongest reasons		
persuasive techniques used		
opposing opinions addressed		
weaknesses		

Drafting

Organization After you have finished your discussion, decide on a position statement, or thesis, stating which blog post you found to be more effective. Then, plan how you will present your judgment. When you are writing about two subjects, block and point-by-point are two effective ways to organize your ideas.

Block Organization

I. Topic: "Teens and Technology Share a Future"

    A. Blogger's perspective and the reasons and examples used to support it

    B. Strengths and weaknesses of the argument

II. Topic: "The Black Hole of Technology"

    A. Blogger's perspective and the reasons and examples used to support it

    B. Strengths and weaknesses of the argument

III. Topic: Judgment

    A. Which blog is more effective

    B. Reasons for your judgment

Point-by-Point Organization

I. Topic: Points of View

    A. Blogger's point of view in "Teens and Technology Share a Future" and the reasons and examples used to support it

    B. Blogger's point of view in "The Black Hole of Technology" and the reasons and examples used to support it

II. Topic: Strengths and Weaknesses

    A. Strengths and weaknesses of "Teens and Technology Share a Future"

    B. Strengths and weaknesses of "The Black Hole of Technology"

III. Topic: Judgment

    A. Which blog is more effective

    B. Reasons for your judgment

Review, Revise, and Edit

Once you have finished writing, review and revise your essay. Refer back to your thesis. Make sure you have supported your thesis with solid reasons. Also, make sure you have included details from the blogs to support your reasons. If you see any weaknesses in your reasons or supporting evidence, go back and clarify your ideas or add more convincing details. Once you have finished, reread your essay to make sure you have spelled words correctly and used proper grammar.

✒ EVIDENCE LOG

Before moving on to a new selection, go to your Evidence Log and record what you learned from "The Black Hole of Technology."

☰ STANDARDS

Reading Informational Text

• Trace and evaluate the argument and specific claims in a text, distinguishing claims that are supported by reasons and evidence from claims that are not.

• Compare and contrast one author's presentation of events with that of another.

Writing

• Write arguments to support claims with clear reasons and relevant evidence.
  a. Introduce claim(s) and organize the reasons and evidence clearly.
  b. Support claim(s) with clear reasons and relevant evidence, using credible sources and demonstrating an understanding of the topic or text.
  e. Provide a concluding statement or section that follows from the argument presented.

• Draw evidence from literary or informational texts to support analysis, reflection, and research.
  b. Apply *grade 6 Reading standards* to literary nonfiction.

About IBM

International Business Machines Corporation (IBM) is one of the world's largest companies, employing nearly half a million people. In 1953, the company introduced its first computer, and in 1981 it introduced its version of the personal computer, a landmark event in the era of desktop computing.

The Internet of Things

Media Vocabulary

These words will be useful to you as you analyze, discuss, and write about videos.

images or graphics: representations of a person or thing	• Images or graphics, such as a map of a country, show a visual representation of what people, objects, or ideas look like.
animation: process of making films or cartoons from drawings, computer graphics, or photos	• Animation can make certain scenes more lively or help an audience understand a process.
audio: recorded sound	• Listening to audio in a video or on a website allows listeners to hear actual sound effects or voices.
voiceover: voice commenting on the action or narrating a film off-camera	• Voiceovers may provide additional background information for viewers or listeners.
narrator: person who tells a story	• In an informational video, the narrator reads or relates descriptions or explanations.

First Review MEDIA: VIDEO

Apply these strategies as you watch the video.

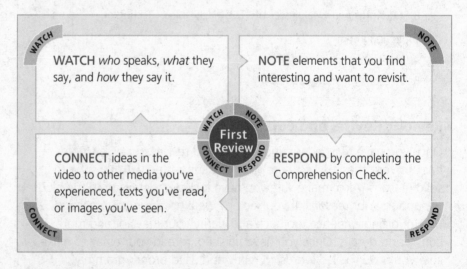

WATCH *who* speaks, *what* they say, and *how* they say it.

NOTE elements that you find interesting and want to revisit.

CONNECT ideas in the video to other media you've experienced, texts you've read, or images you've seen.

RESPOND by completing the Comprehension Check.

First Review

STANDARDS

Reading Informational Text
By the end of the year, read and comprehend literary nonfiction in the grades 6–8 text complexity band proficiently, with scaffolding as needed at the high end of the range.
Language
Acquire and use accurately grade-appropriate general academic and domain-specific words and phrases; gather vocabulary knowledge when considering a word or phrase important to comprehension or expression.

Notebook As you watch, write down your observations and questions, making sure to note time codes so you can easily revisit sections later.

The Internet of Things

IBM Social Media

BACKGROUND

The IBM "Smarter Planet" program promotes and discusses how global leaders can use new technologies and types of data to create a "smarter planet"—a world in which the smart use of information can matter as much as any other natural resource. This video was produced as part of their "Smarter Planet" series.

SCAN FOR
MULTIMEDIA

NOTES

Comprehension Check

Complete the following items after you finish your first review.

1. What enables us to capture data from natural and human systems?

2. According to the pyramid graphic, what is the ultimate goal of the data we get from the many sensors that stream information?

3. Where are some of the sensors that we might find in a city?

4. According to the video, how can connectivity, or "The Internet of Things," help create a smarter planet?

Close Review

Watch the video or parts of it again. Write any new observations that seem important. What **questions** do you have? What can you **conclude**?

Analyze the Media

📓 **Notebook** Respond to these questions.

1. **Evaluate** Do the narrators explain the concept of "The Internet of Things" clearly? Explain your position.

2. (a) **Analyze** Revisit the scene that shows the world map made up of devices. What does this scene add to the video? (b) **Evaluate** In your opinion, which images are most effective in helping the viewer understand the important ideas? Explain.

3. **Interpret** The narrator explains that the planet has "grown a central nervous system." What does this statement mean?

4. **Essential Question:** *How is modern technology helpful and harmful to society?* What have you learned about how technology helps or hurts society from watching this video?

Writing to Sources

Writing a summary can help you identify the most important points in an informational video.

THE INTERNET OF THINGS

> ### Assignment
>
> Write a brief **objective summary** of the video. An objective summary is a retelling of the most important ideas in an unbiased way.

To write an objective summary, follow these steps:

1. Watch the video, and take notes on the most important ideas.

2. Put the ideas in the correct order, and restate them in your own words.

3. Include important details from the video that help explain each main idea.

4. Use an objective tone in your writing. *Objective* means that you do not include your opinion.

Speaking and Listening

The video is a brief description of the concept of "The Internet of Things" and shows how being electronically interconnected benefits society.

> ### Assignment
>
> Prepare and deliver an **oral report** about the video.
>
> To prepare your oral report, take notes on the following:
>
> • Identify the source of the video. *Who* is delivering the information, and *what* is the purpose of the message?
>
> • Determine whether the information presented in the video is supported by facts or opinions. A **fact** is something that can be proved. An **opinion** can be supported, but not proved.
>
> • Consider the message the video conveys: What do the video makers want viewers to think or do? Is this message convincing?

Once you have taken notes, organize your information into **talking points**—a list of brief statements you can refer to while sharing your findings. Then, practice delivering your talking points. To do so, glance at your talking points, but then make eye contact with your audience. In addition, speak expressively, pausing to emphasize key words.

✐ EVIDENCE LOG

Before moving on to a new selection, go to your Evidence Log and record what you learned from the video.

▤ STANDARDS

Writing
Write informative/explanatory texts to examine a topic and convey ideas, concepts, and information through the selection, organization, and analysis of relevant content.

Speaking and Listening
• Interpret information presented in diverse media and formats and explain how it contributes to a topic, text, or issue under study.
• Present claims and findings, sequencing ideas logically and using pertinent descriptions, facts, and details to accentuate main ideas or themes; use appropriate eye contact, adequate volume, and clear pronunciation.

Write an Argument

In this section, you have examined four perspectives on technology. "Feathered Friend" shows the advantages of both high-tech and low-tech safety measures. In "Teens and Technology Share a Future," blogger Stefan Etienne argues that technology improves our lives. In "The Black Hole of Technology," blogger Leena Khan argues the opposite. "The Internet of Things" examines the complex systems that have resulted from improvements in technology.

🔧 Tool Kit

Student Model of an Argument

Assignment

Write a brief argument, in the form of an **editorial**, in which you state and support your position on this question:

> **Do electronic devices and online access really improve our lives?**

Draw evidence from the texts in this section to support your ideas.

Elements of an Editorial

An **editorial** is a kind of argument that is published in a print or digital newspaper or magazine. In an editorial, an author offers an opinion about an issue. A well-written editorial uses valid reasons and evidence to convince readers to agree with the author's position.

An effective editorial contains these elements:

- a precise claim, or position
- clear reasons and evidence that support the claim
- a logical organization that makes clear connections among claims, reasons, and evidence
- a concluding statement or section that logically completes the argument
- a formal and objective language and tone
- use of transitions to show the relationships between ideas

ACADEMIC VOCABULARY

As you craft your argument, consider using some of the academic vocabulary you learned in the beginning of the unit.

convince
certain
sufficient
declare
various

Model Argument For a model of a well-crafted argument, see the Launch Text, "That's Not Progress!"

Challenge yourself to find all of the elements of an effective argument in the text. You will have an opportunity to review these elements as you prepare to write your own editorial.

LAUNCH TEXT

That's Not Progress!

⧉ STANDARDS

Writing
- Write arguments to support claims with clear reasons and relevant evidence.
- Write routinely over extended time frames and shorter time frames for a range of discipline-specific tasks, purposes, and audiences.

Prewriting / Planning

Write a Claim After you have reviewed the selections, write a thesis statement—one sentence in which you state your claim. As you continue to write, you may revise your claim or even change it. For now, it will help you choose reasons and supporting evidence.

Claim: _____

_____ .

Plan Your Argument An effective argument successfully addresses counterclaims, or opposing positions. Plan to include evidence to show why those counterclaims are not strong enough to change your position. Complete these sentences to address a counterclaim.

An opposing view is _____ .

The evidence that supports this is _____ .

The reason I don't find the opposing view convincing is _____ .

Gather Evidence From Sources You can use different types of evidence to support your argument:

- **facts:** statements that can be proved true
- **statistics:** facts presented in the form of numbers
- **anecdotes:** brief stories that illustrate a point
- **quotations from experts:** statements from people with special knowledge of a subject
- **examples:** facts, ideas, or events that illustrate a general idea

A variety of evidence can make your argument stronger. For example, in the Launch Text, the writer uses facts and statistics:

Half the nation's youth send 50 or more text messages a day. One study found that young people send an average of 34 texts a night after they get into bed! This loss of sleep can affect the ability to concentrate, problem-solve, and learn.
—from "That's Not Progress!"

Take notes on the sources of your information. You will need to give credit to any words or ideas that are not your own.

EVIDENCE LOG

Review your Evidence Log and identify key details you may want to cite in your argument.

STANDARDS

Writing
Write arguments to support claims with clear reasons and relevant evidence.
  a. Introduce claim(s) and organize the reasons and evidence clearly.
  b. Support claim(s) with clear reasons and relevant evidence, using credible sources and demonstrating an understanding of the topic or text.

STANDARDS

Writing
• Write arguments to support claims with clear reasons and relevant evidence.
   e. Provide a concluding statement or section that follows from the argument presented.

• Draw evidence from literary or informational texts to support analysis, reflection, and research.
   a. Apply *grade 6 Reading standards* to literature.
   b. Apply *grade 6 Reading standards* to literary nonfiction.

Drafting

Organize Your Editorial To keep your organization simple and easy to follow, your editorial should include three parts:

- **the introduction,** in which you state your claim
- **the body,** in which you provide analysis, reasons, and evidence
- **the conclusion,** in which you summarize or restate your claim

Each part of your editorial should build on the part that came before, and every point should connect directly to your main claim. This outline shows the key sections of the Launch Text. Notice how the author traces the argument from its introduction through its conclusion. Note specific claims and evidence that support the argument. Create your outline.

LAUNCH TEXT

Model: "That's Not Progress!" Outline

INTRODUCTION
Paragraphs 1 and 2 introduce topic and state claim: *Social networking can lead to anxiety, low self-confidence, and loneliness in teens.*

BODY
Paragraphs 3–6 present support for claim: *Social networking affects mostly teens because they tend to worry about what others think. It also causes stress and lack of confidence.*

Paragraphs 7 and 8 present additional information: *Frequent users of social media may experience aches in areas such as fingers and eyes, as well as loss of sleep.*

Paragraphs 9 and 10 present a counterargument: *Social media can help prevent and identify depression.*

Paragraph 11 refutes, or disproves, counterargument: *Before social media, teens found ways to escape from their problems.*

CONCLUSION
Paragraph 12 restates claim: *Social media has negative effects for teenagers.*

Argument Outline

INTRODUCTION

BODY

CONCLUSION

Write a First Draft Use your outline to help organize your first draft. Include a precise claim in your introduction and offer evidence and support in the body of the editorial. Provide a strong conclusion that follows from your claim. As you write, make sure to keep your readers in mind. Define words they may not know. Also, explain situations or summarize texts so that your readers have the information they need to understand your ideas.

LANGUAGE DEVELOPMENT: STYLE

Transitions

Transitions are words and phrases that show how ideas relate to one another. Transitional words and phrases perform an essential function in an editorial because they help guide readers through the writer's thinking.

Read It

These sentences about the Launch Text use transitional expressions to show specific connections among ideas.

- *Also, she believes that it can be used to identify youth who are most at risk for depression.* **(shows addition)**

- *Facebook depression, however, has its own features.* **(shows contrast)**

- *For one thing, it hits those who worry too much about what others think; for another, it mostly affects young people.* **(illustrates or shows)**

Write It

As you draft your argument, choose transitional words and phrases that accurately show specific relationships among your ideas. Transitions are especially important when connecting one paragraph to the next.

If you want to . . .	consider using one of these transitions
list or add ideas	*first, finally, next, lastly, also, in addition*
show similarity	*similarly, likewise*
show contrast	*however, in contrast, although, on the other hand*
emphasize	*indeed, in fact, of course*
show effect	*therefore, consequently, thus, as a result*
illustrate or show	*for example, for instance, specifically*

PUNCTUATION

Punctuate transitions correctly.

- Use a comma after most transitions at the beginning of a sentence.

- Use a comma before and after a transition in the middle of a sentence unless the transition follows a semicolon. In that case, add a comma only *after* the transition.

☰ STANDARDS

Writing
Write arguments to support claims with clear reasons and relevant evidence.
  c. Use words, phrases, and clauses to clarify the relationships among claim(s) and reasons.

Revising

Evaluating Your Draft

Use the following checklist to evaluate the effectiveness of your first draft. Then, use your evaluation and the instruction on this page to guide your revision.

FOCUS AND ORGANIZATION	EVIDENCE AND ELABORATION	CONVENTIONS
☐ Provides an introduction that leads to the argument.	☐ Cites facts from credible and reliable sources to support the argument.	☐ Attends to the norms and conventions of the discipline, especially the correct use and punctuation of transitions.
☐ Introduces a precise claim.	☐ Demonstrates an understanding of the topic by providing adequate examples for each central idea.	
☐ Supports the claim with clear reasons and relevant evidence.		
☐ Provides a conclusion that follows from the argument.	☐ Uses vocabulary that is appropriate for the audience and purpose.	
☐ Establishes a logical organization and develops a progression throughout the argument.	☐ Establishes and maintains a formal style and an objective tone.	
☐ Uses transitional words and phrases to clarify the relationships between and among ideas.		

Copyright © SAVVAS Learning Company LLC. All Rights Reserved.

WORD NETWORK

Include interesting words from your Word Network in your editorial.

STANDARDS

Writing
Write arguments to support claims with clear reasons and relevant evidence.
b. Support claim(s) with clear reasons and relevant evidence, using credible sources and demonstrating an understanding of the topic or text.
c. Use words, phrases, and clauses to clarify the relationships among claim(s) and reasons.
d. Establish and maintain a formal style.

Revising for Focus and Organization

Identify and Support Claim Reread your editorial, and make sure your claim is clear and specific. Ask yourself: *What do I want to convince readers to do or think?* If necessary, rewrite your claim to make it clearer. Then, make sure all your reasons and evidence relate directly to your claim and support it. If you see any ideas or evidence that do not have strong, clear connections to your main claim, rewrite or delete them.

Revising for Evidence and Elaboration

Clarify Relationships If any of the connections between your ideas are vague, add or replace transitional words or expressions to make them clearer. Consider using these transitional phrases: *in addition, on the other hand, as a result,* or *in fact.*

Use Formal Style Editorials are more persuasive when they are written in a formal style. When presenting evidence and examples, mix in longer sentences and harder words. Avoid slang or informal language that will take away from the force of your argument.

Informal language: Technology is really messing up our lives.

Formal language: Technology is having a negative impact on our lives.

PEER REVIEW

Exchange editorials with a classmate. Use the checklist to evaluate your classmate's editorial and provide supportive feedback.

1. Is the claim clear?

☐ yes ☐ no   If no, explain what confused you.

2. Is the claim supported with clear reasons and relevant evidence?

☐ yes ☐ no   If no, point out what is missing.

3. Does the conclusion logically follow from the claim?

☐ yes ☐ no   If no, suggest how the writer might improve it.

4. What is the strongest part of your classmate's editorial?

_____

_____

Editing and Proofreading

Edit for Conventions Reread your draft for accuracy and consistency. Correct errors in grammar and word usage. Be sure that you have included transitional words and phrases that clarify the relationships among the claims and reasons in your editorial.

Proofread for Accuracy Read your draft carefully, looking for errors in spelling and punctuation. If you have any short sentences with related ideas, consider combining them with coordinating conjunctions such as *and, so, but,* and *or*.

Publishing and Presenting

Create a final version of your essay. Share it with your class so that your classmates can read it and make comments. In turn, review and comment on your classmates' work. Consider other students' editorials and the claims they express. Think about how theirs are similar to and different from your own. Remember to maintain a polite and respectful tone when commenting.

Reflecting

Think about what you learned by writing your editorial. What could you do differently the next time you need to write an editorial to make it easier and to make your argument stronger?

STANDARDS

Writing
• With some guidance and support from peers and adults, develop and strengthen writing as needed by planning, revising, editing, rewriting, or trying a new approach.
• Use technology, including the Internet, to produce and publish writing as well as to interact and collaborate with others; demonstrate sufficient command of keyboarding skills to type a minimum of three pages in a single sitting.

ESSENTIAL QUESTION:

How is modern technology helpful and harmful to society?

Modern technology has made our lives easier in many ways. It has also raised our expectations about how quickly tasks can be completed. You will read selections that examine the presence of modern technology and social media in our daily lives. You will work in a group to continue your exploration of living in a world that is increasingly dependent on technology.

Small-Group Learning Strategies

Throughout your life, in school, in your community, and in your career, you will continue to learn and work with others.

Review these strategies and the actions you can take to practice them as you work in teams. Add ideas of your own for each step. Use these strategies during Small-Group Learning.

STRATEGY	ACTION PLAN
Prepare	• Complete your assignments so that you are prepared for group work. • Organize your thinking so you can contribute to your group's discussion. •
Participate fully	• Make eye contact to signal that you are listening and taking in what is being said. • Use text evidence when making a point. •
Support others	• Build on ideas from others in your group. • Invite others who have not yet spoken to join the conversation •
Clarify	• Paraphrase the ideas of others to ensure that your understanding is correct. • Ask follow-up questions. •

SCAN FOR
MULTIMEDIA

CONTENTS

Working as a Team

1. **Take a Position** In your group, discuss the following question:

   Does having instant access to information always make our lives easier?

   As you take turns sharing your positions, be sure to provide examples or other support for your ideas. After all group members have shared, discuss the the ways in which instant access to information changes people's expectations.

2. **List Your Rules** As a group, decide on the rules that you will follow as you work together. Two samples are provided. Add two more of your own. You may add or revise rules based on your experience together.

   - Everyone should participate in group discussions.
   - People should not interrupt.

   - _____

     _____

   - _____

     _____

3. **Apply the Rules** Share what you have learned about technology. Make sure each person in the group contributes. Take notes and be prepared to share with the class one thing that you heard from another member of your group.

4. **Name Your Group** Choose a name that reflects the unit topic.

   Our group's name: _____

5. **Create a Communication Plan** Decide how you want to communicate with one another. For example, you might use online collaboration tools, email, or instant messaging.

   Our group's decision: _____

   _____

Making a Schedule

First, find out the due dates for the small-group activities. Then, preview the texts and activities with your group, and make a schedule for completing the tasks.

SELECTION	ACTIVITIES	DUE DATE
The Fun They Had		
Is Our Gain Also Our Loss?		
Bored . . . and Brilliant? A Challenge to Disconnect From Your Phone		

Working on Group Projects

As your group works together, you'll find it more effective if each person has a specific role. Different projects require different roles. Before beginning a project, discuss the necessary roles, and choose one for each group member. Here are some possible roles; add your own ideas.

Project Manager: monitors the schedule and keeps everyone on task

Researcher: organizes research activities

Recorder: takes notes during group meetings

_____

_____

_____

_____

_____

SCAN FOR
MULTIMEDIA

About the Author

Isaac Asimov (1920–1992) became a science-fiction fan after reading fantastic stories in magazines. Asimov's father discouraged his son's early interest, and described the magazines he loved as "junk." Still, Asimov's interest in science fiction continued, and he started writing his own stories at age eleven. At first, his stories were rejected, but Asimov developed into a visionary writer and became one of the most influential science-fiction authors of the twentieth century.

:::icon::: **STANDARDS**

Reading Literature
By the end of the year, read and comprehend literature, including stories, dramas, and poems, in the grades 6–8 text complexity band proficiently, with scaffolding as needed at the high end of the range.

Language
Determine or clarify the meaning of unknown and multiple-meaning words and phrases based on *grade 6 reading and content,* choosing flexibly from a range of strategies.

  a. Use context clues as a clue to the meaning of a word or phrase.

The Fun They Had

Concept Vocabulary

As you perform your first read of "The Fun They Had," you will encounter these words.

> sorrowfully   loftily   nonchalantly

Context Clues To find the meanings of unfamiliar words, look for clues in the context, which is made up of other words and phrases that surround the unknown word. There are different types of context clues that may help you as you read. Consider these examples:

> **Synonyms:** The director <u>blamed</u> and **criticized** Andre and Gaby for missing band rehearsal.
>
> **Elaborating Details:** Terry could be **arrogant**—<u>he really thought he was superior</u>—when he had the right answer.

Apply your knowledge of context clues and other vocabulary strategies to determine the meanings of unfamiliar words you encounter during your first read.

First Read FICTION

Apply these strategies as you conduct your first read. You will have an opportunity to complete a close read after your first read.

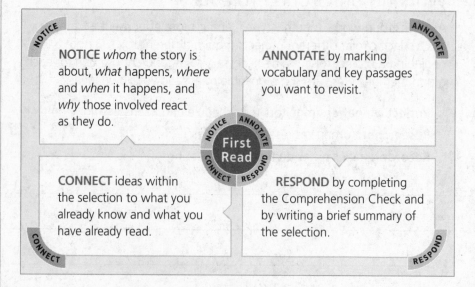

NOTICE *whom* the story is about, *what* happens, *where* and *when* it happens, and *why* those involved react as they do.

ANNOTATE by marking vocabulary and key passages you want to revisit.

CONNECT ideas within the selection to what you already know and what you have already read.

RESPOND by completing the Comprehension Check and by writing a brief summary of the selection.

First Read

The Fun They Had

Isaac Asimov

BACKGROUND

New methods of learning have been influenced by changes in technology. During ancient times, the Romans wrote on wax tablets. Children in the 1700s read and practiced writing on slates, or blackboards. In the 1900s, educational radio programs were introduced. In today's society, online education has become popular.

SCAN FOR MULTIMEDIA

1   Margie even wrote about it that night in her diary. On the page headed May 17, 2155, she wrote, "Today Tommy found a real book."

2   It was a very old book. Margie's grandfather once said that when he was a little boy, his grandfather told him that there was a time when all stories were printed on paper.

3   They turned the pages, which were yellow and crinkly, and it was awfully funny to read words that stood still instead of moving the way they were supposed to—on a screen, you know. And then, when they turned back to the page before, it had the same words on it that it had had when they read it the first time.

NOTES

4   "Gee," said Tommy, "what a waste. When you're through with the book, you just throw it away, I guess. Our television screen must have had a million books on it and it's good for plenty more. I wouldn't throw it away."

5   "Same with mine," said Margie. She was eleven and hadn't seen as many telebooks as Tommy had. He was thirteen.

6   She said, "Where did you find it?"

7   "In my house." He pointed without looking, because he was busy reading. "In the attic."

8   "What's it about?"

9   "School."

10   Margie was scornful. "School? What's there to write about school? I hate school." Margie always hated school, but now she hated it more than ever. The mechanical teacher had been giving her test after test in geography, and she had been doing worse and worse until her mother had shaken her head **sorrowfully** and sent for the county inspector.

Mark context clues or indicate another strategy you used that helped you determine meaning.

sorrowfully (SAWR oh fuhl ee) *adv.*

MEANING:

11   He was a round little man with a red face and a whole box of tools with dials and wires. He smiled at her and gave her an apple, then took the teacher apart. Margie had hoped he wouldn't know how to put it together again, but he knew how all right and, after an hour or so, there it was again, large and ugly, with a big screen on which all the lessons were shown and the questions were asked. That wasn't so bad. The part she hated most was the slot where she had to put homework and test papers. She always had to write them out in a punch code[1] they made her learn when she was six years old, and the mechanical teacher calculated the mark in no time.

> ## Why would anyone write about school?

12   The inspector had smiled after he was finished and patted her head. He said to her mother, "It's not the little girl's fault, Mrs. Jones. I think the geography sector was geared a little too quick. Those things happen sometimes. I've slowed it up to an average ten-year level. Actually, the overall pattern of her progress is quite satisfactory." And he patted Margie's head again.

13   Margie was disappointed. She had been hoping they would take the teacher away altogether. They had once taken Tommy's teacher away for nearly a month because the history sector had blanked out completely.

14   So she said to Tommy, "Why would anyone write about school?"

15   Tommy looked at her with very superior eyes. "Because it's not our kind of school, stupid. This is the old kind of school that

---

1. **punch code** card containing data that was used to program computers during the 1940s, when this story was written.

they had hundreds and hundreds of years ago." He added **loftily,** pronouncing the word carefully, "*Centuries* ago.".

16   Margie was hurt. "Well, I don't know what kind of school they had all that time ago." She read the book over his shoulder for a while, then said, "Anyway, they had a teacher."

17   "Sure they had a teacher, but it wasn't a *regular* teacher. It was a man."

18   "A man? How could a man be a teacher?"

19   "Well, he just told the boys and girls things and gave them homework and asked them questions."

20   "A man isn't smart enough."

21   "Sure he is. My father knows as much as my teacher."

22   "He can't. A man can't know as much as a teacher."

23   "He knows almost as much I betcha."

24   Margie wasn't prepared to dispute that. She said, "I wouldn't want a strange man in my house to teach me."

25   Tommy screamed with laughter, "You don't know much, Margie. The teachers didn't live in the house. They had a special building and all the kids went there."

26   "And all the kids learned the same thing?"

27   "Sure, if they were the same age."

28   "But my mother says a teacher has to be adjusted to fit the mind of each boy and girl it teaches and that each kid has to be taught differently."

29   "Just the same, they didn't do it that way then. If you don't like it, you don't have to read the book."

30   "I didn't say I didn't like it," Margie said quickly. She wanted to read about those funny schools.

31   They weren't even half finished when Margie's mother called, "Margie! School!"

32   Margie looked up. "Not yet, Mamma."

33   "Now," said Mrs. Jones. "And it's probably time for Tommy, too."

34   Margie said to Tommy, "Can I read the book some more with you after school?"

35   "Maybe," he said, **nonchalantly**. He walked away whistling, the dusty old book tucked beneath his arm.

36   Margie went into the schoolroom. It was right next to her bedroom, and the mechanical teacher was on and waiting for her. It was always on at the same time every day except Saturday and Sunday, because her mother said little girls learned better if they learned at regular hours.

37   The screen was lit up, and it said: "Today's arithmetic lesson is on the addition of proper fractions. Please insert yesterday's homework in the proper slot."

NOTES

Mark context clues or indicate another strategy you used that helped you determine meaning.

loftily (LAWF tih lee) *adv.*

MEANING:

Mark context clues or indicate another strategy you used that helped you determine meaning.

nonchalantly (non shuh LONT lee) *adv.*

MEANING:

38   Margie did so with a sigh. She was thinking about the old schools they had when her grandfather's grandfather was a little boy. All the kids from the whole neighborhood came, laughing and shouting in the schoolyard, sitting together in the schoolroom, going home together at the end of the day. They learned the same things so they could help one another on the homework and talk about it.

39   And the teachers were people. . . .

40   The mechanical teacher was flashing on the screen: "When we add the fractions ½ and ¼ . . . "

41   Margie was thinking about how the kids must have loved it in the old days. She was thinking about the fun they had. ❧

Comprehension Check

Complete the following items after you finish your first read. Review and clarify details with your group.

1. What does Tommy find in the attic?

2. Why does Margie hate school now more than ever?

3. Why does Margie's mother send for the county inspector?

4. What surprises Margie about teachers of the past?

5. 📓 **Notebook** Write three to five sentences to summarize the story.

- -

RESEARCH

Research to Clarify Choose at least one unfamiliar detail from the text. Briefly research that detail. In what way does the information you learned shed light on an aspect of the story?

Research to Explore Choose something that interested you from the text, and formulate a research question that you might use to find out more about the topic.

THE FUN THEY HAD

Close Read the Text

With your group, revisit sections of the text you marked during your first read. **Annotate** details that you notice. What **questions** do you have? What can you **conclude**?

Analyze the Text

CITE TEXTUAL EVIDENCE
to support your answers.

📑 Complete the activities.

1. **Review and Clarify** With your group, review the selection. How is Margie's school different from schools of the past?

2. **Present and Discuss** Share with your group the passages from the selection that you found especially important. Take turns presenting your passages. Discuss what you noticed in the selection, what questions you asked, and what conclusions you reached.

3. **Essential Question:** *How is modern technology helpful and harmful to society?* What has this article taught you about the impact of modern technology on society? Discuss with your group.

LANGUAGE DEVELOPMENT

Concept Vocabulary

sorrowfully	loftily	nonchalantly

Why These Words? The three concept vocabulary words from the text are related. With your group, determine what the words have in common. How do these word choices add to the impact of the text?

Practice

📓 **Notebook** Write a paragraph using the three concept vocabulary words. Your paragraph can be based on Asimov's characters and setting or it can be completely new.

Word Study

Anglo-Saxon Suffix: -ful The suffix *-ful* means "full of" or "having the qualities of." When added to a noun that names an emotion, the suffix creates an adjective that describes someone who feels that emotion. Use your knowledge of the suffix *-ful* to complete these activities.

1. When the suffix *-ly* is removed from the adverb *sorrowfully*, it becomes the adjective *sorrowful*. Define *sorrowful*.

2. Write three other words that end in *-ful* or *-fully*. Write their meanings.

Analyze Craft and Structure

Science-Fiction Writing Science fiction is a form, or genre, of fiction that imagines the technology and science of the future. Science-fiction stories balance technological and scientific ideas with realistic elements—characters, events, and situations that are true to life. These realistic details help readers relate to a story that may take place in very unfamiliar places. Most science fiction includes these types of elements:

- scientific ideas
- imaginary beings, such as futuristic robots or aliens from distant planets
- settings that are different from Earth or from Earth right now—These may be non-Earthly places, such as spaceships, other planets, or alternate universes. Or, they may be Earth, but in the future.
- plots that reflect issues in society today, such as the impact of technology or even political ideas—Science-fiction writers often place familiar issues into unfamiliar settings in order to explore their complexities and understand them better.

Like all other types of literature, science fiction conveys **themes,** or insights into life. These themes may relate to science and technology, or they may simply relate to human nature and society.

Practice

CITE TEXTUAL EVIDENCE
to support your answers.

1. Use the chart to identify passages from "The Fun They Had" that reflect each element of science fiction. Work individually, and then share your responses with your group.

THE FUN THEY HAD	
SCIENCE-FICTION ELEMENT	EXAMPLE FROM STORY
Scientific Ideas	
Imaginary Beings	
Alternate Setting	
Comment on Issues in Society Today	

📓 **Notebook** Answer the questions.

2. Consider this possible theme for the story: *Nothing, not even great technology, can replace human interaction.* Which story details support this theme? Explain.

3. In what ways might this story be considered a warning about the future? Explain your response.

THE FUN THEY HAD

Conventions

Action Verbs and Linking Verbs Verbs are an essential element of all sentences and clauses. A **verb** expresses action or indicates a state or condition.

An **action verb** can express a physical action, such as *shake* or *laugh*, or a mental action, such as *hope* or *learn*.

A **linking verb** connects a subject to a word in the predicate that renames, identifies, or describes it. The most common linking verb is *be*, with forms such as *are, was, were, is being,* and *have been*. Other common linking verbs include *appear, become, feel, look,* and *seem*.

ACTION VERBS	LINKING VERBS
Her mother *had shaken* her head. (The action is *shaking*.)	Tommy and Margie *are* students. (*Are* links *Tommy and Margie* to *students*. *Students* renames *Tommy and Margie*.)
All the kids *laughed* in the schoolyard. (The action is *laughing*.)	The girl *became* curious about the old book. (*Became* links *girl* to *curious*. *Curious* describes the *girl*.)

Read It

Identify the verb(s) in each sentence from the selection. Then, label each verb as an action verb or a linking verb.

1. Margie even wrote about it that night in her diary.

2. He was a round little man with a red face and a whole box of tools with dials and wires.

3. ". . . Actually, the overall pattern of her progress is quite satisfactory."

4. "Please insert yesterday's homework in the proper slot."

Write It

🗒 **Notebook** Imagine that you are Margie's friend in the year 2155. Write a journal entry describing your feelings about your mechanical teacher. Use at least three action verbs and two linking verbs in your writing.

▤ STANDARDS

Language
Demonstrate command of the conventions of standard English grammar and usage when writing or speaking.

Writing to Sources

Dialogue is the conversations that take place among characters in literary works. Authors use dialogue to move the plot forward, as well as to provide insights into characters' personalities and the ways they change.

Assignment

With your group, write a **scene with dialogue** in which Margie describes finding the old book to one of her friends. Choose one of the following options:

☐ Write the scene in dramatic form with characters' names appearing at the beginning of each new line of dialogue. Place in brackets any descriptions or lines not spoken by the characters.

☐ Write the scene in short-story form. All descriptions will appear in paragraphs. Indicate who is speaking, and set lines of dialogue in quotation marks.

Project Plan First, discuss Margie's character and what one of Margie's friends would be like. Then, describe how other aspects of this future time might be different from today and how to pull these ideas into the scene. Brainstorm for a few sample lines of dialogue that feel true to Margie's character and how you think her friend would react. Take notes during the discussion.

Then, use your discussion notes and the story as background to develop the scene. Decide on a logical sequence of events. Use narrative techniques, such as *pacing*. Pacing is similar to rhythm. You can either slow down the action of the scene or speed it up. Slow down action by adding more description and longer sentences. Speed up action by using short sentences that make things seem to happen quickly. When writing your scene, use precise words, vivid details, and descriptive language to show the setting and action.

Revise and Edit Work together to revise and edit the scene. Keep the following elements in mind:

- Are the events arranged in a logical order?
- Are the word choices descriptive, and do they capture the futuristic setting in which the conversation takes place?
- Does the dialogue contribute to the reader's understanding of the characters and plot?
- Do you use appropriate pacing to point out an important idea or to build suspense?

Present and Discuss Present your group's scene to the class and answer any questions your classmates may have.

✐ EVIDENCE LOG

Before moving on to a new selection, go to your Evidence Log and record what you learned from "The Fun They Had."

▦ STANDARDS

Writing
Write narratives to develop real or imagined experiences or events using effective technique, relevant descriptive details, and well-structured event sequences.

a. Engage and orient the reader by establishing a context and introducing a narrator and/or characters; organize an event sequence that unfolds naturally and logically.

b. Use narrative techniques, such as dialogue, pacing, and description, to develop experiences, events, and/or characters.

d. Use precise words and phrases, relevant descriptive details, and sensory language to convey experiences and events.

The Fun They Had **247**

About the Author

Cailin Loesch (b. 1997) is a web correspondent for *Teen Kids News*, which is an Emmy Award–winning television series.

Is Our Gain Also Our Loss?

Concept Vocabulary

As you perform your first read of "Is Our Gain Also Our Loss?" you will encounter these words.

gradually	nostalgic	continuation

Base Words If these words are unfamiliar to you, analyze each one to see whether it contains a base word you know. Then, use your knowledge of the base, or "inside," word, along with the context, to determine the meaning of the word. Here is an example of how to apply the strategy.

> **Unfamiliar Word:** *considerate*
>
> **Familiar "Inside" Word:** *consider*, with meanings including "think"
>
> **Context:** When we were too late to catch the bus, our neighbor was kind and **considerate** enough to drive us to the meeting.
>
> **Conclusion:** The neighbor is described in a positive way, and the word *considerate* is paired with the word *kind*. *Considerate* might mean "thinking about the needs or feelings of others."

Apply your knowledge of base words and other vocabulary strategies to determine the meanings of other unfamiliar words you encounter during your first read.

First Read NONFICTION

Apply these strategies as you conduct your first read. You will have an opportunity to complete a close read after your first read.

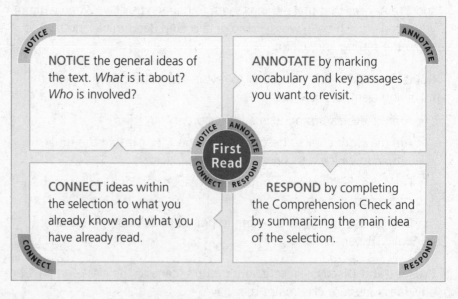

NOTICE the general ideas of the text. *What* is it about? *Who* is involved?

ANNOTATE by marking vocabulary and key passages you want to revisit.

CONNECT ideas within the selection to what you already know and what you have already read.

RESPOND by completing the Comprehension Check and by summarizing the main idea of the selection.

:: STANDARDS

Reading Informational Text
By the end of the year, read and comprehend literary nonfiction in the grades 6–8 text complexity band proficiently, with scaffolding as needed at the high end of the range.

Language
Determine or clarify the meaning of unknown and multiple-meaning words and phrases based on *grade 6 reading and content*, choosing flexibly from a range of strategies.

Is Our Gain Also Our Loss?

Cailin Loesch

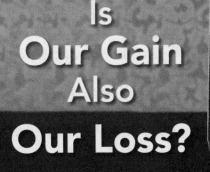

BACKGROUND

New technology changes our daily world with ever-increasing speed, often causing things to become obsolete, or out-of-date. These changes can leave older people longing for what they feel was the simpler, less complicated world of their youth. Is every generation destined to long for the past?

SCAN FOR MULTIMEDIA

NOTES

1   "When I was your age, I had to wait for the hourly report on TV in order to get the information that you have right at your fingertips. That's the problem with the world today."

2   It was the summer of 2012, and I was standing in the kitchen with my dad and sister—holding my iPhone—a towel and bathing suit thrown over my shoulder. I had just finished reading aloud the full-day weather report, and, until my dad spoke, had nothing on my mind but the gleaming pool water that seemed to be calling my name. I waited a moment for his comment to process, then looked down at my phone, analyzing it in a way that I had never before: feeling the cold, hard metal in my palm, and the smooth, sleek screen underneath my thumb.

3   I asked Dad to elaborate on his comment.

4   "When I was a young boy, we had a pool in our backyard. My brothers and I weren't allowed to go swimming until the temperature reached 75 degrees—not one degree less. And so we boys spent our summer mornings waiting by the TV for the hourly report that read the temperature, praying that it would say the number we wanted it to so that we could dive in. I have vivid memories of those mornings."

5   Suddenly, life in the 1970s seemed distant, and people detached. It occurred to me that my dad has experienced life like I will never know it, and that I have experienced life like my children will never know. I even started to think about how things have changed in the years that I've been alive. It's not just technology that's changing, either: It's our way of living. I've seen it with my own eyes, and it's only becoming clearer as the years go by.

gradually (GRAJ oo uhl ee) *adv.*

MEANING:

6   **Gradually,** evenings spent doing homework at lamp-lit desks covered in pencils, paper, and textbooks are turning into late nights under bedsheets and blankets, a Google Docs page pulled up, fingers typing aggressively on a keyboard that can barely be seen in the dark. It seems as though I am part of the last generation that will know the satisfied feeling of stapling together a completed research paper, pages still warm from the printer. People of the next generation will never go on a family trip to the local Blockbuster[1] in search of candy and a comedy for movie night. They might miss out on handwritten letters from their grandparents, available to read and reread for years. Do we even realize what we're all leaving behind?

7   This morning, I was sitting at the breakfast table eating cereal when my dad came in to say goodbye before he left for work. When he saw that I was eating Life cereal, a huge smile immediately crept across his face, and he started excitedly reciting a commercial that he remembered from his childhood. He called me into his office, where he threw himself down in front of his desktop computer to search for the ad on YouTube,[2] eager to take me back in time with him.

8   Watching the commercial, my modernly-adjusted ears picked up on a faint hum in the background of the actor's voices. There were no snappy graphics or fast-paced cuts. In fact, the colors were a bit faded and the actors' faces were only highlighted in dim lighting. Then I turned to my dad, who was still beaming, as if all the happy memories from his childhood were flashing before his eyes. Judging by his enthusiastic clapping at the end, he sure didn't seem to miss modern technology during those 30 seconds.

9   In a world of iPhones and missions to Mars, is it even possible that my childhood will ever be looked at in the way that I look at my dad's? By then, will our TV shows be even crisper? Will it be unimaginable that we needed long, easily tangled wires in our ears in order to listen to music? Will my kids marvel at the idea of us old-fashioned teenagers having to wait by wall outlets for our phones to get out of the dreaded red battery zone before heading out for the night? Will they laugh at us for using pieces of green paper to buy things?

10   The thing that has really stayed with me, though, is my dad's comment about how all these new technologies are a "problem." One day, will we late-millennials[3] feel **nostalgic** as we look back on our simpler days, where we sometimes got a 10-minute homework break when our laptops lost battery life, giving us an excuse to sit in peace in front of a warm fire while

nostalgic (nos TAL jihk) *adj.*

MEANING:

1. **Blockbuster** chain of stores where people rented movies in the form of physical DVDs or VHS tapes.
2. **YouTube** video-sharing website.
3. **late-millennials** people born between the early 1990s and the early 2000s.

we waited for them to charge? Will a lack of instant-charging mechanisms become the new lack of a weather.com app? Will we pull out our old Nintendo 3DS XLs to smile at what was once the hottest new piece of technology, recalling memories of online play with friends, in the same way that my dad smiled at an old commercial? Will we wish that things had never changed? They say that you should never try to fix what's not broken. Does the charm of the way things are now trump the need for things that are fresher, newer, and more advanced? Will we ever reach a point where there is no possible way to make any more "improvements"? And does this possibly inevitable peak signal impending doom or the **continuation** of tradition?

11   In my last-period sociology[4] class the other day, the teacher ended a class discussion about the impact of changing technology on society with a statement that summarized my thoughts on the matter and left me with something to think about:

12   "I don't know how new technology will affect future generations, and I don't know if it will do more good or bad."

13   I couldn't have said it better myself. ❧

NOTES

Mark base words or indicate another strategy you used that helped you determine meaning.

continuation (kuhn tihn yoo AY shuhn) *n.*

MEANING:

---

4. **sociology** (soh see OL uh jee) *n.* study of social behavior.

Comprehension Check

Complete these items after you finish your first read. Review and clarify details with your group.

1. Why were television weather reports significant to the author's father as a child?

2. 🗐 **Notebook** Summarize the main idea of the selection.

- -

RESEARCH

Research to Clarify Choose at least one unfamiliar detail from the text. Briefly research that detail. In what way does the information you learned shed light on an aspect of the selection?

IS OUR GAIN ALSO OUR LOSS?

Close Read the Text

With your group, revisit sections of the text you marked during your first read. **Annotate** details that you notice. What **questions** do you have? What can you **conclude**?

Analyze the Text

CITE TEXTUAL EVIDENCE
to support your answers.

Complete the activities.

1. **Review and Clarify** With your group, reread paragraphs 6–9 of the selection. Discuss how the author's conversations with her father changed her perspective on technology. Has reading this selection changed your own perspective on technology?

2. **Present and Discuss** Share with your group the passages from the selection that you found especially important. Take turns presenting your passages. Discuss what you noticed in the selection, what questions you asked, and what conclusions you reached.

3. **Essential Question:** *How is modern technology helpful and harmful to society?* What has this article taught you about the impact of modern technology on society? Discuss with your group.

TIP

GROUP DISCUSSION

Try not to interrupt other speakers. If you must interrupt (for instance, if someone is dominating the discussion), do so politely. For example, ask, "May I please add something?"

⚑ WORD NETWORK

Add words related to modern technology from the text to your Word Network.

⊞ STANDARDS

Reading Informational Text
• Cite textual evidence to support analysis of what the text says explicitly as well as inferences drawn from the text.
• Analyze in detail how a key individual, event, or idea is introduced, illustrated, and elaborated in a text.
• Analyze how a particular sentence, paragraph, chapter, or section fits into the overall structure of a text and contributes to the development of the ideas.
Language
• Determine or clarify the meaning of unknown and multiple-meaning words and phrases based on *grade 6 reading and content*, choosing flexibly from a range of strategies.
b. Use common, grade-appropriate Greek or Latin affixes and roots as clues to the meaning of a word.

LANGUAGE DEVELOPMENT

Concept Vocabulary

| gradually | nostalgic | continuation |

Why These Words? The concept vocabulary words from the text are related. With your group, determine what the words have in common. Write your ideas, and add another word that fits the category.

Practice

📄 **Notebook** Confirm your understanding of these words by using them in sentences. Give context clues that hint at the word's meaning.

Word Study

Latin Suffix: -ation The Latin suffix -*ation* means "the condition or process of." Adding this suffix changes a verb to a noun. In this text, the blogger refers to the "continuation of tradition." Using your knowledge, make an inference about what that phrase means. With your group, brainstorm for other verbs that can be turned into nouns with the suffix -*ation*. Then, find another example of a noun with the suffix -*ation* in the text.

Analyze Craft and Structure

Development of Ideas: Reflective Writing A **reflective essay** is a brief prose work in which an author presents his or her thoughts and feelings—or reflections—about an experience or an idea. Most reflective writing includes the following elements:

- descriptions of a specific event, time period, or person that leads to new ways of seeing something

- dialogue and other storytelling elements that convey experiences in vivid ways

- informal language with a thoughtful quality

- discussion of the insights gained from the experience

In "Is Our Gain Also Our Loss?" Cailin Loesch thinks deeply about her father's experiences growing up at a time when technology was not as advanced. She compares and contrasts her father's experiences and attitude toward his childhood with her own feelings about growing up in a world increasingly dependent on technology.

Practice

CITE TEXTUAL EVIDENCE to support your answers.

Using this chart, list the ways in which Loesch's observations of her father influence her own perspective. Work individually. Then, share your responses with your group.

IS OUR GAIN ALSO OUR LOSS?	
What memories of technology does Loesch's father have from his youth?	
How do her father's memories contrast with Loesch's experiences during her own childhood?	
What thoughts about the future do these contrasts inspire in Loesch?	

📝 **Notebook** Write a one-paragraph response to Loesch's thoughts at the end of the blog. Consider these questions:

- Do you think people will continue to look back fondly on the technology of their youth?
- Will they view current technology as a "problem," as Cailin's father does?

Share your responses with the group.

IS OUR GAIN ALSO OUR LOSS?

Conventions

Comparative and Superlative Degrees An **adjective** describes a person, a place, a thing, or an idea. An **adverb** describes a verb, an adjective, or another adverb. Adjectives and adverbs can be used to compare two or more items or actions. There are two degrees of comparison: **comparative degree** and **superlative degree**.

DEGREE OF COMPARISON	DEFINITION	ADJECTIVE EXAMPLES	ADVERB EXAMPLES
Comparative	compares two items or actions	*smaller, more frightened*	*more quickly, more easily*
Superlative	compares three or more items or actions	*smallest, most frightened*	*most quickly, most easily*

If an adjective has only one or two syllables, you can often add the suffixes -*er* and -*est* to form the comparative and superlative degrees. If the adjective is a longer word, use the words *more* and *most*. For most adverbs, use *more* and *most*. Do not use both forms (a suffix and the word *more* or *most*) at the same time.

Incorrect: We saw the *most largest* whale model at our local museum.

Correct: We saw the *largest* whale model at our local museum.

Read It

In each item from the text, identify the adjective or adverb used to make a comparison. Label each word as an adverb or an adjective. Then, write whether it is comparative or superlative.

1. Will we pull out our old Nintendo 3DS XLs to smile at what was once the hottest new piece of technology. . . .

2. By then, will our TV shows be even crisper?

Write It

⊟ **Notebook** Rewrite each sentence to include the type of modifier indicated in parentheses.

1. Suddenly, life in the 1970s seemed (distant), and people (detached). **(comparative adjectives)**

2. . . . late nights under bedsheets and blankets, a Google Docs page pulled up, fingers typing (aggressively) on a keyboard that can barely be seen in the dark. **(comparative adverb)**

▤ STANDARDS
Language
Demonstrate command of the conventions of standard English grammar and usage when writing or speaking.

Speaking and Listening

At the end of "Is Our Gain Also Our Loss?" Cailin Loesch asks several questions about whether the technology of her own youth will become outdated. Follow up on this question in a group activity.

Assignment

Take part in a **group discussion** about changing technology. Think of an example of an invention or a device you once thought was wonderful, but now think is outdated—like the video-game platform that Loesch mentions at the end of her blog. With your group, compare and contrast your feelings about this example of "progress" with examples offered by other members of the group and with Loesch's blog post.

Discussion Preparation Use the chart to organize your thoughts and plan what you will say during the group discussion.

CHANGING VIEWS TOWARD TECHNOLOGY	
What example of outdated technology will you discuss?	
When was it popular? What purpose did it serve?	
How did you feel when you first heard about it and saw it?	
How do you feel about it now?	
Why have your feelings about it changed?	
Do you feel the technology left a lasting impact on you or on society? Why or why not?	

Assign Tasks Before beginning the discussion, take a moment to assign jobs to individual group members. This could include a moderator to ensure everyone stays on topic and speaks in turn, a timekeeper to ensure the discussion doesn't dwell on a single topic for too long, and a recorder to take notes.

EVIDENCE LOG

Before moving on to a new selection, go to your Evidence Log and record what you learned from "Is Our Gain Also Our Loss?"

STANDARDS

Speaking and Listening
Engage effectively in a range of collaborative discussions with diverse partners on *grade 6 topics, texts, and issues*, building on others' ideas and expressing their own clearly.

a. Come to discussions prepared, having read or studied required material; explicitly draw on that preparation by referring to evidence on the topic, text, or issue to probe and reflect on ideas under discussion.
b. Follow rules for collegial discussions, set specific goals and deadlines, and define individual roles as needed.

About the Podcast

All Things Considered
began airing in 1971 and was the first news program on National Public Radio (NPR). It has since won numerous awards for excellence. The daily radio show mixes news stories with interviews, analysis, and commentaries on the arts and culture. In 2005, NPR first started making its programs available in the form of podcasts.

Bored . . . and Brilliant?
A Challenge to Disconnect From Your Phone

Media Vocabulary

These words will be useful to you as you analyze, discuss, and write about podcasts.

podcast: digital audio or video file or recording, usually part of a series, that can be downloaded from the Internet	• Many podcasts invite listeners to leave comments or share their thoughts about the shows. • Some podcasts are accompanied by a transcript, or the text of the spoken words.
host: someone who introduces and talks to the guests on a television or radio program	• Most hosts prepare for a program by learning about the background of the guests.
interview: recorded conversation in which someone is asked questions about his or her life, experiences, or opinions	• An interesting interview usually reveals new information about the person being interviewed. • The person conducting an interview typically creates a list of questions prior to the interview, but asks unplanned follow-up questions based on the interviewee's responses.

First Review MEDIA: AUDIO

Apply these strategies as you listen to the podcast.

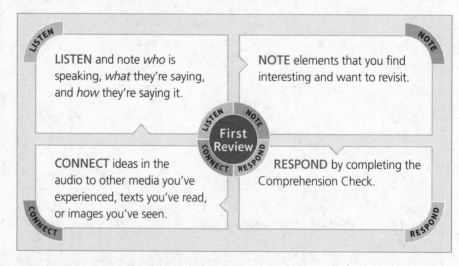

LISTEN and note *who* is speaking, *what* they're saying, and *how* they're saying it.

NOTE elements that you find interesting and want to revisit.

CONNECT ideas in the audio to other media you've experienced, texts you've read, or images you've seen.

RESPOND by completing the Comprehension Check.

Listening Strategy: Take Notes

📓 **Notebook** As you listen, write down your observations and questions, making sure to note time codes so you can easily visit sections later.

STANDARDS

Reading Informational Text
By the end of the year, read and comprehend literary nonfiction in the grades 6–8 text complexity band proficiently, with scaffolding as needed at the high end of the range.

Language
Acquire and use accurately grade-appropriate general academic and domain-specific words and phrases; gather vocabulary knowledge when considering a word or phrase important to comprehension or expression.

Bored . . . and Brilliant?
A Challenge to Disconnect From Your Phone

BACKGROUND

According to a survey by the research group Flurry, which is cited in this podcast, smartphones have taken over television as the most-watched kind of screen in the United States. In 2014, the average American spent almost three hours a day on his or her phone, just a little more than the average American spent watching television.

SCAN FOR
MULTIMEDIA

NOTES

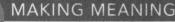

Comprehension Check

Complete the following items after you finish your first review. Review and clarify details with your group.

1. On average, about how long do cellphone users spend on their phones each day?

2. What are we really doing "when we think we're doing nothing"?

3. What did Dr. Sandi Mann research? What did she find out?

MEDIA VOCABULARY

Use these words as you discuss and write about the podcast.

podcast
host
interview

Close Review

With your group, listen to the podcast again. Write any new observations that seem important. What **questions** do you have? What can you **conclude**?

- -

Analyze the Media

CITE TEXTUAL EVIDENCE to support your answers.

📑 **Notebook** Respond to these questions.

1. Present and Discuss Choose a quote from the podcast that you found interesting or powerful. Explain what you notice, what questions it raises for you, and what conclusions you reached about it.

2. Review and Synthesize Do you agree that there is value in being bored? Should we use our cellphones less? Explain.

3. Essential Question: *How is modern technology helpful and harmful to society?* What has this podcast taught you about the impact of modern technology on society? Discuss with your group.

🔳 WORD NETWORK

Add words related to modern technology from the text to your Word Network.

Research

BORED . . . AND BRILLIANT?
A CHALLENGE TO DISCONNECT
FROM YOUR PHONE

Assignment

At the end of the podcast, Manoush Zomorodi issues listeners a challenge: "Start observing your own phone behavior, and get ready to rethink it." With your group, choose from these two options:

☐ Create a **multimedia slide show** to showcase interesting findings of the Bored and Brilliant challenge.

☐ Create a **brochure** to promote implementing the Bored and Brilliant challenge in your classroom.

Plan the Project To prepare your slide show or brochure, consider the following:

- Consult at least three credible online or print sources. To find online sources you can trust, consider looking for information published on educational or government sites—those with ".edu" or ".gov" at the end of their Web addresses.

- Conduct research to find relevant information, such as statistics and quotations from experts. Take notes on the sources of your information. You need to give credit to any words or ideas that are not your own.

- Assign everyone in your group a specific job, such as researching, writing, editing, presenting, or organizing multimedia.

Internet Research A search engine is a useful tool for finding information on the Internet. However, with millions of websites available, you can get overwhelmed by long lists of results. Use these tips to narrow down your searches. Note that they may not work for all search engines.

- **Minus Operator (–)** Add a minus sign before a term to indicate that you don't want results that include it. For example, typing "Bat -baseball" will give you information about the flying mammals, but not baseball bats. "NOT" may also be used instead of a minus sign.

- **Exact Phrases** If you want to search for an exact phrase, put it in quotation marks. Searching for "judge a book by its cover" will give you results that have those exact words, but will leave out other sites.

Present and Discuss Share your multimedia slide show or brochure with the rest of the class. Give your classmates an opportunity to ask questions, and support your answers with evidence from both your research and the podcast.

🖉 EVIDENCE LOG

Before moving on to a new selection, go to your Evidence Log and record what you learned from "Bored . . . and Brilliant? A Challenge to Disconnect From Your Phone."

≣ STANDARDS

Writing
- Write informative/explanatory texts to examine a topic and convey ideas, concepts, and information through the selection, organization, and analysis of relevant content.
- Gather relevant information from multiple print and digital sources; assess the credibility of each source; and quote or paraphrase the data and conclusions of others while avoiding plagiarism and providing basic bibliographic information for sources.

Speaking and Listening
Include multimedia components and visual displays in presentations to clarify information.

Deliver a Multimedia Presentation

Assignment

You have read about the effects of technology in the selections in this section. Work with your group to develop a **multimedia presentation** that addresses this question:

> Do the benefits of technology outweigh its disadvantages?

Plan With Your Group

Analyze the Text With your group, discuss the selections you have read. Take notes on the effects of technology presented in each selection. Then, determine what each selection suggests about the effects of technology on society: Does technology have mostly positive effects? Or, do the disadvantages outweigh the benefits? Record your ideas in a chart like the one shown.

TITLE	BENEFITS OF TECHNOLOGY	DRAWBACKS OF TECHNOLOGY
The Fun They Had		
Is Our Gain Also Our Loss?		
Bored . . . and Brilliant? A Challenge to Disconnect From Your Phone		

≡≡ STANDARDS

Writing
• Write arguments to support claims with clear reasons and relevant evidence.
   a. Introduce claim(s) and organize the reasons and evidence clearly.
   b. Support claim(s) with clear reasons and relevant evidence, using credible sources and demonstrating an understanding of the topic or text.
• Conduct short research projects to answer a question, drawing on several sources and refocusing the inquiry when appropriate.

Gather Evidence and Media Examples Scan the selections to record specific examples that support your group's claim. Use reliable print and online source materials to find evidence, such as statistics or quotations from experts, that supports your argument. Then, brainstorm for types of media you can use to illustrate and elaborate on each example. Consider including relevant photographs, illustrations, music, charts, graphs, and video clips. Allow each group member to make suggestions.

Organize Your Ideas To organize your presentation, first, rank your arguments from least important to most important. Once you have a sense of the arguments you want to make, write an introduction that will capture your audience's attention. Clearly state your position in the introduction. Then, explain the reasons for your position, providing at least two pieces of evidence for each reason. Finally, end with a strong restatement of your position. After you have organized your argument, decide the most effective way to incorporate multimedia components into your presentation.

Rehearse With Your Group

Practice With Your Group Rehearse your presentation with your group, and use this checklist to evaluate the effectiveness of your group's first rehearsal. Then, use the evaluation and these instructions to guide revisions to your presentation.

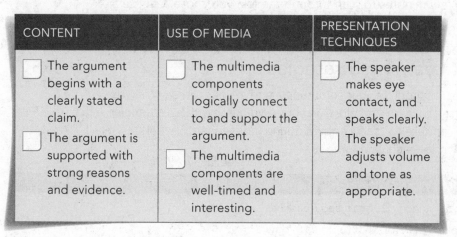

CONTENT	USE OF MEDIA	PRESENTATION TECHNIQUES
☐ The argument begins with a clearly stated claim. ☐ The argument is supported with strong reasons and evidence.	☐ The multimedia components logically connect to and support the argument. ☐ The multimedia components are well-timed and interesting.	☐ The speaker makes eye contact, and speaks clearly. ☐ The speaker adjusts volume and tone as appropriate.

Fine-Tune the Content If your argument does not begin with a clearly stated claim, revise to make your position clear.

Improve Your Use of Media For each piece of multimedia, ask yourself: *What aspect of the argument does this multimedia component support?*

Brush Up on Your Presentation Techniques Practice delivering your portion of the presentation. Then, practice delivering the entire presentation as a group and use feedback to tighten the presentation so that it has a good pace and rhythm.

Present and Evaluate

When it is your group's turn to present, be prepared to respond to questions and comments from your classmates. As you watch the other groups, consider the strength of their reasons and evidence, as well as their use of multimedia.

⊞ STANDARDS
Speaking and Listening
• Delineate a speaker's argument and specific claims, distinguishing claims that are supported by reasons and evidence from claims that are not.
• Present claims and findings, sequencing ideas logically and using pertinent descriptions, facts, and details to accentuate main ideas or themes; use appropriate eye contact, adequate volume, and clear pronunciation.
• Include multimedia components and visual displays in presentations to clarify information.

ESSENTIAL QUESTION:

How is modern technology helpful and harmful to society?

People use and rely on technological devices every day in different ways. In this section, you will complete your study of the impact of modern technology by exploring an additional selection related to the topic. You'll then share what you learn with classmates. To choose a text, follow these steps.

Look Back Think about the selections you have already studied. What more do you want to know about the topic of modern technology?

Look Ahead Preview the texts by reading the descriptions. Which one seems most interesting and appealing to you?

Look Inside Take a few minutes to scan through the text you chose. Choose a different one if this text doesn't meet your needs.

Independent Learning Strategies

Throughout your life, in school, in your community, and in your career, you will need to rely on yourself to learn and work on your own. Review these strategies and the actions you can take to practice them during Independent Learning. Add ideas of your own for each category.

STRATEGY	ACTION PLAN
Create a schedule	• Understand your goals and deadlines • Make a plan for what to do each day. •
Practice what you've learned	• Use first-read and close-read strategies to deepen your understanding. • After you read, evaluate the usefulness of the evidence to help you understand the topic. • Consider the quality and reliability of the source. •
Take notes	• Record important ideas and information. • Review your notes before preparing to share with a group. •

SCAN FOR
MULTIMEDIA

Choose one selection. Selections are available online only.

PERFORMANCE-BASED ASSESSMENT PREP

Review Evidence for an Argument

Complete your Evidence Log for the unit by evaluating what you've learned and synthesizing the information you've recorded.

SCAN FOR
MULTIMEDIA

First-Read Guide

Use this page to record your first-read ideas.

Tool Kit
First-Read Guide and
Model Annotation

Selection Title: _____

NOTICE

NOTICE new information or ideas you learn about the unit topic as you first read this text.

ANNOTATE

ANNOTATE by marking vocabulary and key passages you want to revisit.

NOTICE ANNOTATE
First Read
CONNECT RESPOND

CONNECT

CONNECT ideas within the selection to other knowledge and the selections you have read.

RESPOND

RESPOND by writing a brief summary of the selection.

STANDARD
Reading Read and comprehend complex literary and informational texts independently and proficiently.

Close-Read Guide

Use this page to record your first-read ideas.

Selection Title: _____

Close Read the Text

Revisit sections of the text you marked during your first read. Read these sections closely and **annotate** what you notice. Ask yourself **questions** about the text. What can you **conclude**? Write down your ideas.

Analyze the Text

Think about the author's choices of patterns, structure, techniques, and ideas included in the text. Select one and record your thoughts about what this choice conveys.

QuickWrite

Pick a paragraph from the text that grabbed your interest. Explain the power of this passage.

_____

_____

_____

_____

_____

_____

_____

_____

_____

_____

▤ STANDARD

Reading Read and comprehend complex literary and informational texts independently and proficiently.

📝 EVIDENCE LOG

Go to your Evidence Log and record what you learned from the text you read.

Share Your Independent Learning

Prepare to Share

How is modern technology helpful or harmful to society?

Even if you read something independently, your understanding continues to grow when you share what you have learned with others. Reflect on the text you explored independently, and write notes about its connection to the unit. In your notes, consider why this text belongs in this unit.

Learn From Your Classmates

💬 **Discuss It** Share your ideas about the text that you explored on your own. As you talk with your classmates, jot down ideas that you learn from them.

Reflect

Review your notes, and mark the most important insight you gained from these writing and discussion activities. Explain how this idea adds to your understanding of the impact of modern technology.

Review Evidence for an Argument

At the beginning of this unit you discussed the following statement with your classmates:

Do we rely on technology too much?

✐ EVIDENCE LOG

Review your Evidence Log and your QuickWrite from the beginning of the unit, and use your own knowledge. Has your position changed?

☐ YES	☐ NO
Identify at least three pieces of evidence that convinced you to change your mind.	Identify at least three pieces of evidence that supported your initial position.
1.	1.
2.	2.
3.	3.

State your position now: _____

_____

_____

Identify a possible counterargument: _____

_____

_____

Evaluate the Strength of Your Evidence Consider your argument. Do you have enough evidence to support your claim? Do you have enough evidence to address a counterargument? If not, make a plan.

☐ Do more research   ☐ Talk with my classmates

☐ Reread a selection   ☐ Ask an expert

▤ STANDARDS
Writing
Write arguments to support claims with clear reasons and relevant evidence.
  a. Introduce claim(s) and organize the reasons and evidence clearly.

SOURCES

- WHOLE-CLASS SELECTIONS
- SMALL-GROUP SELECTIONS
- INDEPENDENT-LEARNING SELECTION

PART 1

Writing to Sources: Argument

In this unit, you read, watched, and listened to selections about modern technology. These texts acknowledged the benefits of technology, but they also address the dangers of being dependent on and consumed by technology.

Assignment

Write an **argumentative essay** in which you state and defend a claim in response to the following question:

Do we rely on technology too much?

Use convincing evidence from at least three of the selections that you read in this unit to support your claim. Support your ideas with strong reasons and relevant evidence. Organize your ideas effectively so that your argument is easy to follow. Establish and maintain a formal tone. Include a conclusion that clearly relates to the main idea you expressed.

⊹ WORD NETWORK

As you write and revise your essay, use your Word Network to help vary your word choices.

Reread the Assignment Review the assignment to be sure you fully understand it. The assignment may refer to some of the academic words presented at the beginning of the unit. Be sure you understand each of the words given here to complete the assignment correctly.

---

convince	certain	sufficient
declare	various	

Review the Elements of Effective Argument Before you begin writing, read the Argument Rubric. Once you have completed your first draft, check it against the rubric. If one or more of the elements is missing or not as strong as it could be, revise your essay to add or strengthen that part.

☰ STANDARDS

Writing
- Write arguments to support claims with clear reasons and relevant evidence.
- Draw evidence from literary or informational texts to support analysis, reflection, and research.
  a. Apply *grade 6 Reading standards* to literature.
  b. Apply *grade 6 Reading standards* to literary nonfiction.
- Write routinely over extended time frames and shorter time frames for a range of discipline-specific tasks, purposes, and audiences.

Argument Rubric

	Focus and Organization	Evidence and Elaboration	Conventions
4	The introduction is engaging and states the claim in a compelling way. The claim is supported by clear reasons and relevant evidence, and opposing claims are addressed. Reasons and evidence are logically organized so that the argument is easy to follow. The conclusion clearly follows from the argument presented.	Sources are credible and accurate. The argument demonstrates an understanding of the topic. The tone of the argument is formal and objective.	The argument correctly uses standard English conventions of usage and mechanics.
3	The introduction is somewhat engaging and states the claim clearly. The claim is supported by reasons and evidence and opposing claims are acknowledged. Reasons and evidence are organized so that the argument can be followed. The conclusion mostly follows from the argument presented.	Sources are mostly credible and accurate. The argument mostly demonstrates an understanding of the topic. The tone of the argument is mostly formal and objective.	The argument mostly demonstrates accuracy in standard English conventions of usage and mechanics.
2	The introduction states the claim. The claim is supported by some reasons and evidence, and opposing claims may be briefly acknowledged. Reasons and evidence are organized somewhat logically. The conclusion somewhat follows from the argument presented.	Some sources are credible. The argument somewhat demonstrates an understanding of the topic. The tone of the argument is occasionally formal and objective.	The argument demonstrates some accuracy in standard English conventions of usage and mechanics.
1	The claim is not clearly stated. The claim is not supported by reasons and evidence, and opposing claims are not addressed. Reasons and evidence are disorganized and the argument is difficult to follow. The conclusion does not follow from the argument presented.	There is little or no credible evidence. The argument does not demonstrate an understanding of the topic. The tone of the argument is informal.	The argument contains mistakes in standard English conventions of usage and mechanics.

PART 2
Speaking and Listening: Oral Presentation

Assignment
After completing the final draft of your argument, use it as the foundation for a brief **oral presentation.**

Do not simply read your argument aloud. Take the following steps to make your presentation lively and engaging.

- Reread your argument and mark the claims and reasons from your introduction, body paragraphs, and conclusion. Refer to the annotations to guide your presentation.

- Use appropriate eye contact. Make sure to speak loudly enough for people to hear you and pronounce words clearly.

- Deliver your argument with confidence.

Review the Rubric Before you deliver your presentation, check your plans against this rubric. If one or more of the elements is missing or not as strong as it could be, revise your presentation.

STANDARDS
Speaking and Listening
• Present claims and findings, sequencing ideas logically and using pertinent descriptions, facts, and details to accentuate main ideas or themes; use appropriate eye contact, adequate volume, and clear pronunciation.
• Include multimedia components and visual displays in presentations to clarify information.

	Content	Organization	Presentation Techniques
3	The introduction is engaging and establishes the claim in a convincing way.	The speaker uses time effectively, spending the right amount on each part.	The speaker maintains appropriate eye contact and speaks clearly and with adequate volume.
	The presentation includes clear reasons and relevant evidence to support the claim.	Ideas progress logically, with clear transitions so that the argument is easy to follow.	The speaker presents the argument with energy and strong conviction.
	The conclusion follows from and restates the claim.		
2	The introduction partially establishes a claim.	The speaker uses time somewhat effectively, spending the right amount of time on most parts.	The speaker sometimes maintains appropriate eye contact and speaks somewhat clearly and with adequate volume.
	The presentation includes some clear reasons and relevant to support the claim.	Ideas progress logically, with some transitions between ideas. Listeners can mostly follow the speaker's argument.	The speaker presents with some energy and confidence.
	The conclusion restates some important information about the claim.		
1	The introduction does not clearly state a claim.	The speaker does not use time effectively and focuses too much time on some parts and too little on others.	The speaker does not maintain appropriate eye contact or speak clearly with adequate volume.
	The presentation does not include reasons or evidence to support a claim.	Ideas do not progress logically. Listeners have trouble following the argument.	The speaker's argument lacks energy or confidence.
	The conclusion does not restate important information about a claim.		

Reflect on the Unit

Now that you've completed the unit, take a few moments to reflect on your learning.

Reflect on the Unit Goals

Look back at the goals at the beginning of the unit. Use a different colored pen to rate yourself again. Think about readings and activities that contributed the most to the growth of your understanding. Record your thoughts.

Reflect on the Learning Strategies

 Discuss It Write a reflection on whether you were able to improve your learning based on your Action Plans. Think about what worked, what didn't, and what you might do to keep working on these strategies. Record your ideas before a class discussion.

Reflect on the Text

Choose a selection that you found challenging, and explain what made it difficult.

Describe something that surprised you about a text in the unit.

Which activity taught you the most about the impacts of modern technology on society? What did you learn?

Imagination

What kinds of adventures
can you experience when
you use your imagination?

Yo Ho Ho and a Rubber Ducky

Discuss It Do you think children experience
imaginative daydreams more than adults do?

Write your response before sharing your ideas.

UNIT INTRODUCTION

ESSENTIAL QUESTION:

Where can imagination lead?

LAUNCH TEXT FICTIONAL NARRATIVE MODEL
The Great Universal Undo

👤 WHOLE-CLASS LEARNING

COMPARE

ANCHOR TEXT: DRAMA

The Phantom Tollbooth, Act I
play by Susan Nanus, based on the book by Norton Juster

ANCHOR TEXT: DRAMA

The Phantom Tollbooth, Act II
play by Susan Nanus, based on the book by Norton Juster

MULTIMEDIA

from **The Phantom Tollbooth**

👥 SMALL-GROUP LEARNING

NOVEL EXCERPT

from **Alice's Adventures in Wonderland**
Lewis Carroll

POETRY

Jabberwocky
from Through the Looking-Glass
Lewis Carroll

▶ MEDIA CONNECTION:
Alice in Wonderland (1983)—Jabberwocky

REFLECTIVE ESSAY

The Importance of Imagination
Esha Chhabra

👤 INDEPENDENT LEARNING

NOVEL EXCERPT

from **The Wonderful Wizard of Oz**
L. Frank Baum

POETRY COLLECTION

Our Wreath of Rose Buds
Corrinne

Fantasy
Gwendolyn Bennett

NOVEL EXCERPT

The Shah of Blah
from Haroun and the Sea of Stories
Salman Rushdie

SHORT STORY

Prince Francis
Roddy Doyle

PERFORMANCE TASK

WRITING FOCUS:
Write a Short Story

PERFORMANCE TASK

SPEAKING AND LISTENING FOCUS:
Perform a Fictional Narrative

PERFORMANCE-BASED ASSESSMENT PREP

Review Notes for a Fictional Narrative

PERFORMANCE-BASED ASSESSMENT

Fictional Narrative: Short Story and Storytelling

PROMPT:

What might happen if a fictional character were to come into the real world?

Unit Goals

Throughout this unit, you will deepen your understanding of imagination by reading, writing, speaking, listening, and presenting. These goals will help you succeed on the Unit Performance-Based Assessment.

Rate how well you meet these goals right now. You will revisit your ratings later when you reflect on your growth during this unit.

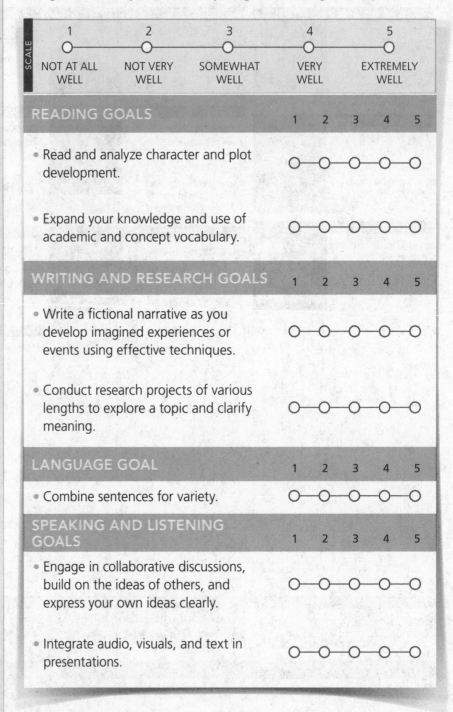

SCALE

1	2	3	4	5
NOT AT ALL WELL	NOT VERY WELL	SOMEWHAT WELL	VERY WELL	EXTREMELY WELL

READING GOALS 1 2 3 4 5

• Read and analyze character and plot development.

• Expand your knowledge and use of academic and concept vocabulary.

WRITING AND RESEARCH GOALS 1 2 3 4 5

• Write a fictional narrative as you develop imagined experiences or events using effective techniques.

• Conduct research projects of various lengths to explore a topic and clarify meaning.

LANGUAGE GOAL 1 2 3 4 5

• Combine sentences for variety.

SPEAKING AND LISTENING GOALS 1 2 3 4 5

• Engage in collaborative discussions, build on the ideas of others, and express your own ideas clearly.

• Integrate audio, visuals, and text in presentations.

≡ STANDARDS

Language
Acquire and use accurately grade-appropriate general academic and domain-specific words and phrases; gather vocabulary knowledge when considering a word or phrase important to comprehension or expression.

SCAN FOR MULTIMEDIA

Academic Vocabulary: Fictional Narrative

Understanding and using academic terms can help you read, write, and speak with precision and clarity. Here are five academic words that will be useful in this unit as you analyze and write fictional narratives.

Complete the chart.

1. Review each word, its root, and the mentor sentences.

2. Use the information and your own knowledge to predict the meaning of each word.

3. For each word, list at least two related words.

4. Refer to the dictionary or other resources if needed.

TIP

FOLLOW THROUGH
Study the words in this chart, and mark them or their forms wherever they appear in the unit.

WORD	MENTOR SENTENCES	PREDICT MEANING	RELATED WORDS
perspective ROOT: *-spec-* "see"	**1.** When she faces a problem, Lily tries to maintain a positive *perspective*. **2.** Sal gained a better *perspective* on the situation by learning more about it.		suspect; inspect
transform ROOT: *-form-* "shape"	**1.** The clay was soft and easy to *transform* from a lump into the shape of a vase. **2.** The caterpillar will *transform* into a butterfly.		
novelty ROOT: *-nov-* "new"	**1.** Having grown up in the city, riding a horse was a *novelty* for Ben. **2.** The shop was full of *novelty* items that tourists would buy.		
consequently ROOT: *-sequ-* "follow"	**1.** The pothole in the road was fixed, and *consequently* it was much easier to drive. **2.** Kayla missed the bus and *consequently* was late for practice.		
inspire ROOT: *-spir-* "breath"	**1.** The chef tried to *inspire* the students to try out different types of food. **2.** I think a day at the museum will *inspire* me to paint again.		

LAUNCH TEXT | FICTIONAL NARRATIVE

This selection is an example of a **fictional narrative**, a type of writing in which the author tells a story about made-up characters and events. This is the type of writing you will develop in the Performance-Based Assessment at the end of the unit.

As you read, consider how the author makes the characters and situation interesting. Mark the text to help answer this question: How does the author keep the reader interested and make the flow of events clear?

The Great Universal Undo

NOTES

1   If Alexander Dillahunt wasn't the world's worst typist, he was close. But that was okay. Fixing mistakes on a computer was a snap—especially if you caught them right away. That was the beauty of the Undo, Alexander thought: a tiny backwards arrow at the top of the screen that performed magic, allowing the user to go back to a more perfect, mistake-free moment in time.

2   That's how Alexander Dillahunt got it into his head to create the Universal Undo. The Universal Undo would do nothing short of "taking back" the last thing a person did.

3   Making a working model was simple. All Alexander needed to do was figure out how to take something in 2-D and make it 4-D (skipping over 3-D completely) and then get the whole thing to fit inside his smartphone. Finally, after a few weeks of trial and error, the Universal Undo was ready for a test run.

4   Alexander went into the kitchen and stood in front of the refrigerator. From there he walked to the cupboard. He waited a few seconds, then hit Universal Undo on his smartphone. Presto! Alexander was back at the refrigerator. He walked to the stove. He waited, hit Universal Undo—and there he was, back at the refrigerator again. Action undone!

5   Alexander took his new invention outside. By the traffic lights, he ran into Mrs. Bieberman, who was carrying a bag of groceries and holding the hand of her 3-year-old son Tommy.

SCAN FOR MULTIMEDIA

6   "Hello Mrs. Bieberman! Hi Tommy!" Alexander called out. He smiled. "That's a really silly hat you're wearing, Mrs. Bieberman!" Then he tapped his smartphone. If everything worked, his last comment would be Undone.

7   "Hello yourself, Alexander!" exclaimed Mrs. Bieberman.

8   *Good!* thought Alexander. *She hadn't heard it!* Flushed with excitement, he continued. "You know, your little boy looks like a toad." He paused, waiting for a response.

9   "I do *not* not look like a toe!" Tommy wailed and, still blubbering, started to play his video game. Had Alexander tapped Undo—or just imagined it? He couldn't remember.

10 "He can't go long without his game," Mrs. Bieberman said, sighing. "And only three years old." Alexander hadn't started playing video games until he was nine.

11 "I want a cookie!" said Tommy suddenly, tugging at the hem of his mother's skirt. Mrs. Bieberman reached into a bag of cookies and pulled one out. "I'll give you just one, Tommy." Tommy grabbed it and stuffed it in his mouth.

12 "How's your mother?" asked Mrs. Bieberman. "I should call her."

13 Alexander was aware of a *tap tapping* sound.

14 Mrs. Bieberman reached into a bag of cookies and pulled one out. "I'll give you just one, Tommy."

15 Alexander froze. *How could he have missed it?* He'd read all about multiple discovery—the idea that most inventions are made by a number of different people in different places at the same time. *How could he have thought he was the only one?*

16 "'Bye Mrs. Bieberman, Tommy" said Alexander in a shaky voice.

17 Tommy, his mouth crammed with cookie, looked into Alexander's eyes and hit a button on his video game. *Tap, tap-tap.*

18 Mrs. Bieberman reached into a bag of cookies and pulled one out. "I'll give you just one, Tommy." ❧

NOTES

⬡ WORD NETWORK FOR IMAGINATION

Vocabulary A Word Network is a collection of words related to a topic. As you read the selections in this unit, identify interesting words related to the idea of imagination and add them to your Word Network. For example, you might begin by adding words from the Launch Text, such as *invention*, *excitement*, and *discovery*. Continue to add words as you complete this unit.

invention

excitement

discovery

IMAGINATION

🔧 **Tool Kit**
Word Network Model

Summary

Write a summary of "The Great Universal Undo." A **summary** is a concise, complete, and accurate overview of a text. It should not include a statement of your opinion or an analysis.

Launch Activity

Participate in a Group Discussion Consider this statement: Imagination is more important than knowledge.

Prepare for the discussion by thinking about the topic.

- What has imagination led people to achieve?
- Do we need imagination to learn about the world?

Decide your position and write down a brief explanation.

☐ Strongly Agree ☐ Agree ☐ Disagree ☐ Strongly Disagree

Form a small group with other students. Then, discuss your responses to the prompt and the questions. When you have finished your conversation, write a summary of the main points you covered. Share your summary with the class.

QuickWrite

Consider class discussions, the video, and the Launch Text as you think about the prompt. Record your first thoughts here.

PROMPT: **What might happen if a fictional character were to come into the real world?**

✐ EVIDENCE LOG FOR IMAGINATION

Review your QuickWrite. Summarize your initial position in one sentence to record in your Evidence Log. Then, record evidence from "The Great Universal Undo" that supports your position.

After each selection, you will continue to use your Evidence Log to record the evidence you gather and the connections you make.

🔑 **Tool Kit**
Evidence Log Model

Title of Text: _____ Date: _____

CONNECTION TO PROMPT	TEXT EVIDENCE/DETAILS	ADDITIONAL NOTES/IDEAS

How does this text change or add to my thinking?   Date: _____

ESSENTIAL QUESTION:

Where can imagination lead?

When you use your imagination, the possibilities are endless. You might explore an unusual place or daydream about an exciting activity. But what lessons about yourself and your world did you learn from your imagined experience? You will work with your whole class to explore the concept of imagination. The selections you read will present insights into how people use their sense of imagination.

Whole-Class Learning Strategies

Throughout your life, in school, in your community, and in your career, you will continue to learn and work in large-group environments.

Review these strategies and the actions you can take to practice them as you work with your whole class. Add ideas of your own for each step. Get ready to use these strategies during Whole-Class Learning.

STRATEGY	ACTION PLAN
Listen actively	• Eliminate distractions. For example, put your cellphone away. • Keep your eyes on the speaker. •
Clarify by asking questions	• If you're confused, other people probably are, too. Ask a question to help your whole class. • If you see that you are guessing, ask a question instead. •
Monitor understanding	• Notice what information you already know and be ready to build on it. • Ask for help if you are struggling. •
Interact and share ideas	• Share your ideas and answer questions, even if you are unsure. • Build on the ideas of others by adding details or making a connection. •

SCAN FOR
MULTIMEDIA

COMPARE

PERFORMANCE TASK

WRITING FOCUS

Write a Fictional Narrative

The Whole-Class readings focus on one boy's fantastical adventures. After reading the drama and listening to the audio, you will write a short story about fantastical events and characters from your own imagination.

About the Playwright
Susan Nanus has written plays, television scripts, and movie screenplays. Like other dramatists, she sometimes bases her plays or screenplays on novels or other existing works. Her script for *The Phantom Tollbooth* was based on the novel by Norton Juster.

For a biography of Norton Juster, see Act II.

The Phantom Tollbooth, Act I

Concept Vocabulary

You will encounter the following words as you read *The Phantom Tollbooth*, Act I. Before reading, note how familiar you are with each word. Then, rank the words in order from most familiar (1) to least familiar (6).

WORD	YOUR RANKING
ignorance	
surmise	
presume	
speculate	
consideration	
misapprehension	

After completing the first read, come back to the concept vocabulary and review your rankings. Mark changes to your original rankings as needed.

First Read DRAMA

Apply these strategies as you conduct your first read. You will have an opportunity to complete the close-read notes after your first read.

Tool Kit
First-Read Guide and Model Annotation

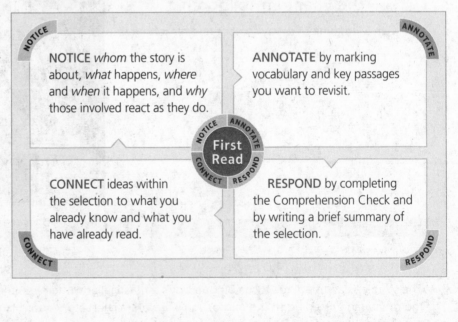

NOTICE whom the story is about, *what* happens, *where* and *when* it happens, and *why* those involved react as they do.

ANNOTATE by marking vocabulary and key passages you want to revisit.

First Read

CONNECT ideas within the selection to what you already know and what you have already read.

RESPOND by completing the Comprehension Check and by writing a brief summary of the selection.

STANDARDS
Reading Literature
By the end of the year, read and comprehend literature, including stories, dramas, and poems, in the grades 6–8 text complexity band proficiently, with scaffolding as needed at the high end of the range.

The Phantom Tollbooth Act I

Susan Nanus • Based on the book by Norton Juster

BACKGROUND

The writer of a drama is called a *playwright* or a *dramatist.* Playwright Susan Nanus adapted Norton Juster's novel *The Phantom Tollbooth* into a drama with two acts, or main sections. You will read Act I in this lesson.

SCAN FOR MULTIMEDIA

Cast (In order of appearance)

- The Clock
- Milo, A Boy
- The Whether Man
- Six Lethargarians
- Tock, The Watchdog (same as the Clock)
- Azaz the Unabridged, King of Dictionopolis
- The Mathemagician, King of Digitopolis
- Princess Sweet Rhyme
- Princess Pure Reason
- Gatekeeper of Dictionopolis
- Three Word Merchants
- The Letterman (fourth Word Merchant)
- Spelling Bee
- The Humbug

- The Duke of Definition
- The Minister of Meaning
- The Earl of Essence
- The Count of Connotation
- The Undersecretary of Understanding
- A Page
- Kakafonous A. Dischord, Doctor of Dissonance
- The Awful Dynne
- The Dodecahedron
- Miners of the Numbers Mine
- The Everpresent Wordsnatcher
- The Terrible Trivium
- The Demon of Insincerity
- Senses Taker

The Sets

1. MILO'S BEDROOM—with shelves, pennants, pictures on the wall, as well as suggestions of the characters of the Land of Wisdom.

2. THE ROAD TO THE LAND OF WISDOM—a forest, from which the Whether Man and the Lethargarians emerge.

3. DICTIONOPOLIS—a marketplace full of open air stalls as well as little shops. Letters and signs should abound.

4. DIGITOPOLIS—a dark, glittering place without trees or greenery, but full of shining rocks and cliffs, with hundreds of numbers shining everywhere.

5. THE LAND OF IGNORANCE—a gray, gloomy place full of cliffs and caves, with frightening faces. Different levels and heights should be suggested through one or two platforms or risers, with a set of stairs that lead to the castle in the air.

⌘ ⌘ ⌘

ignorance (IHG nuhr uhns) *n.* state of lacking knowledge, learning, or information

Act I

Scene i

1 [*The stage is completely dark and silent. Suddenly the sound of someone winding an alarm clock is heard, and after that, the sound of loud ticking is heard.*]

2 [*LIGHTS UP on the* Clock, *a huge alarm clock. The* Clock *reads 4:00. The lighting should make it appear that the* Clock *is suspended in mid-air (if possible). The* Clock *ticks for 30 seconds.*]

3 **Clock.** See that! Half a minute gone by. Seems like a long time when you're waiting for something to happen, doesn't it? Funny thing is, time can pass very slowly or very fast, and sometimes even both at once. The time now? Oh, a little after four, but what that means should depend on you. Too often, we do something simply because time tells us to. Time for school, time for bed, whoops, 12:00, time to be hungry. It can get a little silly, don't you think? Time is important, but it's what you do with it that makes it so. So my advice to you is

to use it. Keep your eyes open and your ears perked. Otherwise it will pass before you know it, and you'll certainly have missed something!

4 Things have a habit of doing that, you know. Being here one minute and gone the next.

5 In the twinkling of an eye.

6 In a jiffy.

7 In a flash!

8 I know a girl who yawned and missed a whole summer vacation. And what about that caveman who took a nap one afternoon, and woke up to find himself completely alone. You see, while he was sleeping, someone had invented the wheel and everyone had moved to the suburbs. And then of course, there is Milo. [*LIGHTS UP to reveal* Milo's *Bedroom. The* Clock *appears to be on a shelf in the room of a young boy—a room filled with books, toys, games, maps, papers, pencils, a bed, a desk. There is a dartboard with numbers and the face of the* Mathemagician, *a bedspread made from* King Azaz's *cloak, a kite looking like the* Spelling Bee, *a punching bag with the* Humbug's *face, as well as records, a television, a toy car, and a large box that is wrapped and has an envelope taped to the top. The sound of* FOOTSTEPS *is heard, and then enter* Milo *dejectedly. He throws down his books and coat, flops into a chair, and sighs loudly.*] Who never knows what to do with himself—not just sometimes, but always. When he's in school, he wants to be out, and when he's out he wants to be in. [*During the following speech,* Milo *examines the various toys, tools, and other possessions in the room, trying them out and rejecting them.*] Wherever he is, he wants to be somewhere else—and when he gets there, so what. Everything is too much trouble or a waste of time. Books—he's already read them. Games—boring. T.V.—dumb. So what's left? Another long, boring afternoon. Unless he bothers to notice a very large package that happened to arrive today.

9 **Milo.** [*Suddenly notices the package. He drags himself over to it, and disinterestedly reads the label.*] "For Milo, who has plenty of time." Well, that's true. [*Sighs and looks at it.*] No. [*Walks away.*] Well . . . [*Comes back. Rips open envelope and reads.*]

10 **A Voice.** "One genuine turnpike tollbooth,[1] easily assembled at home for use by those who have never traveled in lands beyond."

1. **turnpike tollbooth** A turnpike is a road that people pay a fee, or toll, to use. A tollbooth is the booth or gate at which tolls are collected.

2. precautionary (prih KAW shuh nehr ee) *adj.* done or made to prevent harm or danger.

11 **Milo.** Beyond what? [*Continues reading.*]

12 **A Voice.** "This package contains the following items:" [Milo *pulls the items out of the box and sets them up as they are mentioned.*] "One (1) genuine turnpike tollbooth to be erected according to directions. Three (3) precautionary[2] signs to be used in a precautionary fashion. Assorted coins for paying tolls. One (1) map, strictly up to date, showing how to get from here to there. One (1) book of rules and traffic regulations which may not be bent or broken. Warning! Results are not guaranteed. If not perfectly satisfied, your wasted time will be refunded."

13 **Milo.** [*Skeptically.*] Come off it, who do you think you're kidding? [*Walks around and examines tollbooth.*] What am I supposed to do with this? [*The ticking of the* Clock *grows loud and impatient.*] Well . . . what else do I have to do. [Milo *gets into his toy car and drives up to the first sign.*]

14 **Voice.** "HAVE YOUR DESTINATION IN MIND."

15 **Milo.** [*Pulls out the map.*] Now, let's see. That's funny. I never heard of any of these places. Well, it doesn't matter anyway. Dictionopolis. That's a weird name. I might as well go there. [*Begins to move, following map. Drives off.*]

16 **Clock.** See what I mean? You never know how things are going to get started. But when you're bored, what you need more than anything is a rude awakening.

17 [*The ALARM goes off very loudly as the stage darkens. The sound of the alarm is transformed into the honking of a car horn, and is then joined by the blasts, bleeps, roars and growls of heavy traffic. When the lights come up, Milo's bedroom is gone and we see a lonely road in the middle of nowhere.*]

Scene ii • The Road to Dictionopolis

1 [*Enter* Milo *in his car.*]

2 **Milo.** This is weird! I don't recognize any of this scenery at all. [*A SIGN is held up before* Milo, *startling him.*] Huh? [*Reads.*] WELCOME TO EXPECTATIONS. INFORMATION, PREDICTIONS AND ADVICE CHEERFULLY OFFERED. PARK HERE AND BLOW HORN. [Milo *blows horn.*]

3   **Whether Man.** [*A little man wearing a long coat and carrying an umbrella pops up from behind the sign he was holding. He speaks very fast and excitedly.*] My, my, my, my, my, welcome, welcome, welcome, welcome to the Land of Expectations, Expectations, Expectations! We don't get many travelers these days; we certainly don't get many travelers. Now what can I do for you? I'm the Whether Man.

4   **Milo.** [*Referring to the map.*] Uh . . . is this the right road to Dictionopolis?

5   **Whether Man.** Well now, well now, well now, I don't know of any wrong road to Dictionopolis, so if this road goes to Dictionopolis at all, it must be the right road, and if it doesn't, it must be the right road to somewhere else, because there are no wrong roads to anywhere. Do you think it will rain?

6   **Milo.** I thought you were the Weather Man.

7   **Whether Man.** Oh, no, I'm the Whether Man, not the weather man. [*Pulls out a SIGN or opens a FLAP of his coat, which reads: "WHETHER."*] After all, it's more important to know whether there will be weather than what the weather will be.

8   **Milo.** What kind of place is Expectations?

9   **Whether Man.** Good question, good question! Expectations is the place you must always go to before you get to where you are going. Of course, some people never go beyond Expectations, but my job is to hurry them along whether they like it or not. Now what else can I do for you? [*Opens his umbrella.*]

10 **Milo.** I think I can find my own way.

11 **Whether Man.** Splendid, splendid, splendid! Whether or not you find your own way, you're bound to find some way. If you happen to find my way, please return it. I lost it years ago. I imagine by now it must be quite rusty. You did say it was going to rain, didn't you? [*Escorts* Milo *to the car under the open umbrella.*] I'm glad you made your own decision. I do so hate to make up my mind about anything, whether it's good or bad, up or down, rain or shine. Expect everything, I always say, and the unexpected never happens. Goodbye, goodbye, goodbye, good . . .

NOTES

CLOSE READ

ANNOTATE: In paragraph 9, mark the **pun**, or play on words, that Whether Man makes about Expectations.

QUESTION: Why does the playwright include this pun?

CONCLUDE: What double meaning does the pun have? How does the double meaning add to the scene?

CLOSE READ
ANNOTATE: In paragraphs 14 and 15, mark the punctuation that separates characters' words.

QUESTION: Why does the author include ellipses in the Lethargarians' dialogue?

CONCLUDE: What does this punctuation show about how the Lethargarians speak?

12 [*A loud CLAP OF THUNDER is heard.*] Oh dear! [*He looks up at the sky, puts out his hand to feel for rain, and RUNS AWAY.* Milo *watches puzzledly and drives on.*]

13 **Milo.** I'd better get out of Expectations, but fast. Talking to a guy like that all day would get me nowhere for sure. [*He tries to speed up, but finds instead that he is moving slower and slower.*] Oh, oh, now what? [*He can barely move. Behind* Milo, *the* LETHARGARIANS *begin to enter from all parts of the stage. They are dressed to blend in with the scenery and carry small pillows that look like rocks. Whenever they fall asleep, they rest on the pillows.*] Now I really am getting nowhere. I hope I didn't take a wrong turn. [*The car stops. He tries to start it. It won't move. He gets out and begins to tinker with it.*] I wonder where I am.

14 **Lethargarian 1.** You're . . . in . . . the . . . Dol . . . drums . . . [Milo *looks around.*]

15 **Lethargarian 2.** Yes . . . the . . . Dol . . . drums . . . [*A YAWN is heard.*]

16 Milo. [*Yelling.*] WHAT ARE THE DOLDRUMS?

17 Lethargarian 3. The Doldrums, my friend, are where nothing ever happens and nothing ever changes. [*Parts of the Scenery stand up or Six People come out of the scenery colored in the same colors of the trees or the road. They move very slowly and as soon as they move, they stop to rest again.*] Allow me to introduce all of us. We are the Lethargarians at your service.

18 Milo. [*Uncertainly.*] Very pleased to meet you. I think I'm lost. Can you help me?

19 Lethargarian 4. Don't say think. [*He yawns.*] It's against the law.

20 Lethargarian 1. No one's allowed to think in the Doldrums. [*He falls asleep.*]

21 Lethargarian 2. Don't you have a rule book? It's local ordinance 175389-J. [*He falls asleep.*]

22 Milo. [*Pulls out rule book and reads.*] Ordinance 175389-J: "It shall be unlawful, illegal and unethical to think, think of thinking, **surmise**, **presume**, reason, meditate, or **speculate** while in the Doldrums. Anyone breaking this law shall be severely punished." That's a ridiculous law! Everybody thinks.

23 All The Lethargarians. We don't!

24 Lethargarian 2. And most of the time, you don't, that's why you're here. You weren't thinking and you weren't paying attention either. People who don't pay attention often get stuck in the Doldrums. Face it, most of the time, you're just like us. [*Falls, snoring, to the ground. Milo laughs.*]

25 Lethargarian 5. Stop that at once. Laughing is against the law. Don't you have a rule book? It's local ordinance 574381-W.

26 Milo. [*Opens rule book and reads.*] "In the Doldrums, laughter is frowned upon and smiling is permitted only on alternate Thursdays." Well, if you can't laugh or think, what can you do?

27 Lethargarian 6. Anything as long as it's nothing, and everything as long as it isn't anything. There's lots to do. We have a very busy schedule . . .

28 Lethargarian 1. At 8:00 we get up and then we spend from 8 to 9 daydreaming.

surmise (suhr MYZ) *v.* guess, using only intuition or imagination

presume (prih ZOOM) *v.* take for granted; assume something to be the case

speculate (SPEHK yuh layt) *v.* guess, using information that is uncertain or incomplete

29 **Lethargarian 2.** From 9:00 to 9:30 we take our early mid-morning nap . . .

30 **Lethargarian 3.** From 9:30 to 10:30 we dawdle and delay . . .

31 **Lethargarian 4.** From 10:30 to 11:30 we take our late early morning nap . . .

32 **Lethargarian 5.** From 11:30 to 12:00 we bide our time and then we eat our lunch.

33 **Lethargarian 6.** From 1:00 to 2:00 we linger and loiter . . .

34 **Lethargarian 1.** From 2:00 to 2:30 we take our early afternoon nap . . .

35 **Lethargarian 2.** From 2:30 to 3:30 we put off for tomorrow what we could have done today . . .

36 **Lethargarian 3.** From 3:30 to 4:00 we take our early late afternoon nap . . .

37 **Lethargarian 4.** From 4:00 to 5:00 we loaf and lounge until dinner . . .

38 **Lethargarian 5.** From 6:00 to 7:00 we dilly-dally . . .

39 **Lethargarian 6.** From 7:00 to 8:00 we take our early evening nap and then for an hour before we go to bed, we waste time.

40 **Lethargarian 1.** [*Yawning.*] You see, it's really quite strenuous doing nothing all day long, and so once a week, we take a holiday and go nowhere.

41 **Lethargarian 5.** Which is just where we were going when you came along. Would you care to join us?

42 **Milo.** [*Yawning.*] That's where I seem to be going, anyway. [*Stretching.*] Tell me, does everyone here do nothing?

43 **Lethargarian 3.** Everyone but the terrible Watchdog. He's always sniffing around to see that nobody wastes time. A most unpleasant character.

44 **Milo.** The Watchdog?

45 **Lethargarian 6.** THE WATCHDOG!

46 **All The Lethargarians.** [*Yelling at once.*] RUN! WAKE UP! RUN! HERE HE COMES! THE WATCHDOG! [*They all run off and ENTER a large dog with the head, feet, and tail of a dog, and the body of a clock, having the same face as the character the Clock.*]

47 **Watchdog.** What are you doing here?

48 **Milo.** Nothing much. Just killing time. You see . . .

49 **Watchdog.** KILLING TIME! [*His ALARM RINGS in fury.*] It's bad enough wasting time without killing it. What are you doing in the Doldrums, anyway? Don't you have anywhere to go?

50 **Milo.** I think I was on my way to Dictionopolis when I got stuck here. Can you help me?

51 **Watchdog.** Help you! You've got to help yourself. I suppose you know why you got stuck.

52 **Milo.** I guess I just wasn't thinking.

53 **Watchdog.** Precisely. Now you're on your way.

54 **Milo.** I am?

55 **Watchdog.** Of course. Since you got here by not thinking, it seems reasonable that in order to get out, you must start thinking. Do you mind if I get in? I love automobile rides. [*He gets in. They wait.*] Well?

56 **Milo.** All right. I'll try. [*Screws up his face and thinks.*] Are we moving?

57 **Watchdog.** Not yet. Think harder.

58 **Milo.** I'm thinking as hard as I can.

59 **Watchdog.** Well, think just a little harder than that. Come on, you can do it.

60 **Milo.** All right, all right . . . I'm thinking of all the planets in the solar system, and why water expands when it turns to ice, and all the words that begin with "q," and . . . [*The wheels begin to move.*] We're moving! We're moving!

61 **Watchdog.** Keep thinking.

62 **Milo.** [*Thinking.*] How a steam engine works and how to bake a pie and the difference between Fahrenheit and Centigrade . . .

63 **Watchdog.** Dictionopolis, here we come.

64 **Milo.** Hey, Watchdog, are you coming along?

65 **Tock.** You can call me Tock, and keep your eyes on the road.

66 **Milo.** What kind of place is Dictionopolis anyway?

67 **Tock.** It's where all the words in the world come from. It used to be a marvelous place, but ever since Rhyme and Reason left, it hasn't been the same.

68 **Milo.** Rhyme and Reason?

69 **Tock.** The two princesses. They used to settle all the arguments between their two brothers who rule over the Land of Wisdom. You see, Azaz is the king of Dictionopolis and the Mathemagician is the king of Digitopolis and they almost never see eye to eye on anything. It was the job of the Princesses Sweet Rhyme and Pure Reason to solve the differences between the two kings, and they always did so well that both sides usually went home feeling very satisfied. But then, one day, the kings had an argument to end all arguments . . .

70 [*The LIGHTS DIM on* Tock *and* Milo, *and come up on* King Azaz *of Dictionopolis on another part of the stage.* Azaz *has a great stomach, a grey beard reaching to his waist, a small crown, and a long robe with the letters of the alphabet written all over it.*]

71 **Azaz.** Of course, I'll abide by the decision of Rhyme and Reason, though I have no doubt as to what it will be. They will choose *words,* of course. Everyone knows that words are more important than numbers any day of the week.

72 [*The* Mathemagician *appears opposite* Azaz. *The* Mathemagician *wears a long flowing robe covered entirely with complex mathematical equations, and a tall pointed hat. He carries a long staff with a pencil point at one end and a large rubber eraser at the other.*]

73 **Mathemagician.** That's what you think, Azaz. People wouldn't even know what day of the week it is without *numbers.* Haven't you ever looked at a calendar? Face it, Azaz. It's numbers that count.

74 **Azaz.** Don't be ridiculous. [*To audience, as if leading a cheer.*] Let's hear it for WORDS!

75 **Mathemagician.** [*To audience, in the same manner.*] Cast your vote for NUMBERS!

76 **Azaz.** A, B, C's!

77 **Mathemagician.** 1, 2, 3's! [*A FANFARE is heard.*]

78 **Azaz and Mathemagician.** [*To each other.*] Quiet! Rhyme and Reason are about to announce their decision.

79 [Rhyme *and* Reason *appear.*]

CLOSE READ

ANNOTATE: In paragraphs 74–78, mark details that show to whom the characters are speaking.

QUESTION: Why does the playwright include this information?

CONCLUDE: How might these details affect how actors deliver their lines, and how an audience might respond?

80 **Rhyme.** Ladies and gentlemen, letters and numerals, fractions and punctuation marks—may we have your attention, please. After careful **consideration** of the problem set before us by King Azaz of Dictionopolis [Azaz *bows.*] and the Mathemagician of Digitopolis [Mathemagician *raises his hands in a victory salute.*] we have come to the following conclusion:

81 **Reason.** Words and numbers are of equal value, for in the cloak of knowledge, one is the warp and the other is the woof.

82 **Rhyme.** It is no more important to count the sands than it is to name the stars.

83 **Rhyme and Reason.** Therefore, let both kingdoms, Dictionopolis and Digitopolis, live in peace.

84 [*The sound of* CHEERING *is heard.*]

85 **Azaz.** Boo! is what I say. Boo and Bah and Hiss!

86 **Mathemagician.** What good are these girls if they can't even settle an argument in anyone's favor? I think I have come to a decision of my own.

87 **Azaz.** So have I.

88 **Azaz and Mathemagician.** [*To the* Princesses.] You are hereby banished from this land to the Castle-in-the-Air. [*To each other.*] And as for you, KEEP OUT OF MY WAY! [*They stalk off in opposite directions.*]

89 [*During this time, the set has been changed to the Market Square of Dictionopolis. LIGHTS come UP on the deserted square.*]

90 **Tock.** And ever since then, there has been neither Rhyme nor Reason in this kingdom. Words are misused and numbers are mismanaged. The argument between the two kings has divided everyone and the real value of both words and numbers has been forgotten. What a waste!

91 **Milo.** Why doesn't somebody rescue the Princesses and set everything straight again?

92 **Tock.** That is easier said than done. The Castle-in-the-Air is very far from here, and the one path which leads to it is guarded by ferocious demons. But hold on, here we are. [*A Man appears, carrying a Gate and a small Tollbooth.*]

93 **Gatekeeper.** AHHHHREMMMM! This is Dictionopolis, a happy kingdom, advantageously located in the foothills of

Confusion and caressed by gentle breezes from the Sea of Knowledge. Today, by royal proclamation, is Market Day. Have you come to buy or sell?

94 **Milo.** I beg your pardon?

95 **Gatekeeper.** Buy or sell, buy or sell. Which is it? You must have come here for a reason.

96 **Milo.** Well, I . . .

97 **Gatekeeper.** Come now, if you don't have a reason, you must at least have an explanation or certainly an excuse.

98 **Milo.** [*Meekly.*] Uh . . . no.

99 **Gatekeeper.** [*Shaking his head.*] Very serious. You can't get in without a reason. [*Thoughtfully*] Wait a minute. Maybe I have an old one you can use. [*Pulls out on old suitcase from the tollbooth and rummages through it.*] No . . . no . . . no . . . this won't do . . . hmmm . . .

100 **Milo.** [*To* Tock.] What's he looking for? [Tock *shrugs.*]

101 **Gatekeeper.** Ah! This is fine. [*Pulls out a Medallion on a chain. Engraved in the Medallion is: "WHY NOT?"*] Why not. That's a good reason for almost anything . . . a bit used, perhaps, but still quite serviceable. There you are, sir. Now I can truly say: Welcome to Dictionopolis.

102 [*He opens the Gate and walks off.* Citizens *and* Merchants *appear on all levels of the stage, and* Milo *and* Tock *find themselves in the middle of a noisy marketplace. As some people buy and sell their wares, others hang a large banner which reads: WELCOME TO THE WORD MARKET.*]

103 **Milo.** Tock! Look!

104 **Merchant 1.** Hey-ya, hey-ya, hey-ya, step right up and take your pick. Juicy tempting words for sale. Get your fresh-picked "ifs," "ands," and "buts"! Just take a look at these nice ripe "wheres" and "whens."

105 **Merchant 2.** Step right up, step right up, fancy, best-quality words here for sale. Enrich your vocabulary and expand your speech with such elegant items as "quagmire," "flabbergast," or "upholstery."

106 **Merchant 3.** Words by the bag, buy them over here. Words by the bag for the more talkative customer. A pound of "happys" at a very reasonable price. . . . very useful for

"Happy Birthday," "Happy New Year," "happy days," or "happy-go-lucky." Or how about a package of "goods," always handy for "good morning," "good afternoon," "good evening," and "goodbye."

107 **Milo.** I can't believe it. Did you ever see so many words?

108 **Tock.** They're fine if you have something to say. [*They come to a Do-It-Yourself Bin.*]

109 **Milo.** [*To* Merchant 4 *at the bin.*] Excuse me, but what are these?

110 **Merchant 4.** These are for people who like to make up their own words. You can pick any assortment you like or buy a special box complete with all the letters and a book of instructions. Here, taste an "A." They're very good. [*He pops one into* Milo's *mouth.*]

111 **Milo.** [*Tastes it hesitantly.*] It's sweet! [*He eats it.*]

NOTES

112 **Merchant 4.** I knew you'd like it. "A" is one of our bestsellers. All of them aren't that good, you know. The "Z," for instance—very dry and sawdusty. And the "X"? Tastes like a trunkful of stale air. But most of the others aren't bad at all. Here, try the "I."

113 **Milo.** [*Tasting.*] Cool! It tastes icy.

114 **Merchant 4.** [*To* Tock] How about the "C" for you? It's as crunchy as a bone. Most people are just too lazy to make their own words, but take it from me, not only is it more fun, but it's also *de*-lightful. [*Holds up a "D."*] *e*-lating. [*Holds up an "E."*] and extremely useful! [*Holds up a "U."*]

115 **Milo.** But isn't it difficult? I'm not very good at making words.

116 [*The* Spelling Bee, *a large colorful bee, comes up from behind.*]

117 **Spelling Bee.** Perhaps I can be of some assistance . . . a-s-s-i-s-t-a-n-c-e. [*The Three turn around and see him.*] Don't be alarmed . . . a-l-a-r-m-e-d. I am the Spelling Bee. I can spell anything. Anything. A-n-y-t-h-i-n-g. Try me. Try me.

118 **Milo.** [*Backing off*, Tock *on his guard.*] Can you spell goodbye?

119 **Spelling Bee.** Perhaps you are under the **misapprehension** . . . m-i-s-a-p-p-r-e-h-e-n-s-i-o-n that I am dangerous. Let me assure you that I am quite peaceful. Now, think of the most difficult word you can, and I'll spell it.

120 **Milo.** Uh . . . o.k. [*At this point*, Milo *may turn to the audience and ask them to help him choose a word or he may think of one on his own.*] How about . . . "Curiosity"?

121 **Spelling Bee.** [*Winking.*] Let's see now . . . uh . . . how much time do I have?

122 **Milo.** Just ten seconds. Count them off, Tock.

123 **Spelling Bee.** [*As* Tock *counts.*] Oh dear, oh dear. [*Just at the last moment, quickly.*] C-u-r-i-o-s-i-t-y.

124 **Merchant 4.** Correct! [ALL *Cheer.*]

125 **Milo.** Can you spell anything?

126 **Spelling Bee.** [*Proudly.*] Just about. You see, years ago, I was an ordinary bee minding my own business, smelling flowers all day, occasionally picking up part-time work in people's bonnets. Then one day, I realized that I'd never amount to anything without an education, so I decided that . . .

CLOSE READ

ANNOTATE: In paragraph 117, mark the words that contain hyphens between the letters.

QUESTION: Why does the playwright present the words in this way?

CONCLUDE: What does the punctuation tell you about what Spelling Bee is doing?

misapprehension (mihs ap ree HEHN shuhn) *n.* incorrect understanding; wrong idea

127 **Humbug.** [*Coming up in a booming voice.*] BALDERDASH! [*He wears a lavish coat, striped pants, checked vest, spats and a derby hat.*] Let me repeat . . . BALDERDASH! [*Swings his cane and clicks his heels in the air.*] Well, well, what have we here? Isn't someone going to introduce me to the little boy?

128 **Spelling Bee.** [*Disdainfully.*] This is the Humbug. You can't trust a word he says.

129 **Humbug.** NONSENSE! Everyone can trust a Humbug. As I was saying to the king just the other day . . .

130 **Spelling Bee.** You've never met the king. [*To Milo.*] Don't believe a thing he tells you.

131 **Humbug.** Bosh, my boy, pure bosh. The Humbugs are an old and noble family, honorable to the core. Why, we fought in the Crusades with Richard the Lionhearted, crossed the Atlantic with Columbus, blazed trails with the pioneers. History is full of Humbugs.

132 **Spelling Bee.** A very pretty speech . . . s-p-e-e-c-h. Now, why don't you go away? I was just advising the lad of the importance of proper spelling.

133 **Humbug.** BAH! As soon as you learn to spell one word, they ask you to spell another. You can never catch up, so why bother? [*Puts his arm around* Milo.] Take my advice, boy, and forget about it. As my great-great-great-grandfather George Washington Humbug used to say . . .

134 **Spelling Bee.** You, sir, are an impostor i-m-p-o-s-t-o-r who can't even spell his own name!

135 **Humbug.** What? You dare to doubt my word? The word of a Humbug? The word of a Humbug who has direct access to the ear of a King? And the king shall hear of this. I promise you . . .

136 **Voice 1.** Did someone call for the King?

137 **Voice 2.** Did you mention the monarch?

138 **Voice 3.** Speak of the sovereign?

139 **Voice 4.** Entreat the Emperor?

140 **Voice 5.** Hail his highness?

141 [*Five tall, thin gentlemen regally dressed in silks and satins, plumed hats, and buckled shoes appear as they speak.*]

142 Milo. Who are they?

143 Spelling Bee. The King's advisors. Or in more formal terms, his cabinet.

144 Minister 1. Greetings!

145 Minister 2. Salutations!

146 Minister 3. Welcome!

147 Minister 4. Good Afternoon!

148 Minister 5. Hello!

149 Milo. Uh . . . Hi.

150 [*All the* Ministers, *from here on called by their numbers, unfold their scrolls and read in order.*]

3. unabridged (uhn uh BRIHJD) *adj.* complete; not shortened.

151 Minister 1. By the order of Azaz the Unabridged . . .[3]

152 Minister 2. King of Dictionopolis . . .

153 Minister 3. Monarch of letters . . .

154 Minister 4. Emperor of phrases, sentences, and miscellaneous figures of speech . . .

155 Minister 5. We offer you the hospitality of our kingdom . . .

156 Minister 1. Country.

157 Minister 2. Nation.

158 Minister 3. State.

159 Minister 4. Commonwealth.

160 Minister 5. Realm.

161 Minister 1. Empire.

162 Minister 2. Palatinate.

163 Minister 3. Principality.

164 Milo. Do all those words mean the same thing?

165 Minister 1. Of course.

166 Minister 2. Certainly.

167 Minister 3. Precisely.

168 Minister 4. Exactly.

169 **Minister 5.** Yes.

170 **Milo.** Then why don't you use just one? Wouldn't that make a lot more sense?

171 **Minister 1.** Nonsense!

172 **Minister 2.** Ridiculous!

173 **Minister 3.** Fantastic!

174 **Minister 4.** Absurd!

175 **Minister 5.** Bosh!

176 **Minister 1.** We're not interested in making sense. It's not our job.

177 **Minister 2.** Besides, one word is as good as another, so why not use them all?

178 **Minister 3.** Then you don't have to choose which one is right.

179 **Minister 4.** Besides, if one is right, then ten are ten times as right.

180 **Minister 5.** Obviously, you don't know who we are.

181 [*Each presents himself and* Milo *acknowledges the introduction.*]

182 **Minister 1.** The Duke of Definition.

183 **Minister 2.** The Minister of Meaning.

184 **Minister 3.** The Earl of Essence.

185 **Minister 4.** The Count of Connotation.

186 **Minister 5.** The Undersecretary of Understanding.

187 **All Five.** And we have come to invite you to the Royal Banquet.

188 **Spelling Bee.** The banquet! That's quite an honor, my boy. A real h-o-n-o-r.

189 **Humbug.** DON'T BE RIDICULOUS! Everybody goes to the Royal Banquet these days.

190 **Spelling Bee.** [*To the* Humbug] True, everybody does go. But some people are invited and others simply push their way in where they aren't wanted.

191 **Humbug.** HOW DARE YOU? You buzzing little upstart, I'll show you who's not wanted . . . [*Raises his cane threateningly.*]

CLOSE READ

ANNOTATE: In paragraphs 182–186, mark the letters that start the two main words of each character's title.

QUESTION: Why do both main words of each character's title begin with the same letters?

CONCLUDE: What effect do these repeated sounds create?

192 **Spelling Bee.** You just watch it! I'm warning w-a-r-n-i-n-g you! [*At that moment, an ear-shattering blast of* TRUMPETS, *entirely* off-key, *is heard, and* a page *appears.*]

193 **Page.** King Azaz the Unabridged is about to begin the Royal banquet. All guests who do not appear promptly at the table will automatically lose their place. [*A huge Table is carried out with King Azaz sitting in a large chair, carried out at the head of the table.*]

194 **Azaz.** Places. Everyone take your places. [*All the characters, including the* Humbug *and the* Spelling Bee, *who forget their quarrel, rush to take their places at the table.* Milo *and* Tock *sit near the king.* Azaz *looks at* Milo.] And just who is this?

195 **Milo.** Your Highness, my name is Milo and this is Tock. Thank you very much for inviting us to your banquet, and I think your palace is beautiful!

196 **Minister 1.** Exquisite.

197 **Minister 2.** Lovely.

198 **Minister 3.** Handsome.

199 **Minister 4.** Pretty.

200 **Minister 5.** Charming.

201 **Azaz.** SILENCE! Now tell me, young man, what can you do to entertain us? Sing songs? Tell stories? Juggle plates? Do tumbling tricks? Which is it?

202 **Milo.** I can't do any of those things.

203 **Azaz.** What an ordinary little boy. Can't you do anything at all?

204 **Milo.** Well . . . I can count to a thousand.

205 **Azaz.** AARGH, numbers! Never mention numbers here. Only use them when we absolutely have to. Now, why don't we change the subject and have some dinner? Since you are the guest of honor, you may pick the menu.

206 **Milo.** Me? Well, uh . . . I'm not very hungry. Can we just have a light snack?

207 **Azaz.** A light snack it shall be!

NOTES

208 [*Azaz claps his hands. Waiters rush in with covered trays. When they are uncovered, Shafts of Light pour out. The light may be created through the use of battery-operated flashlights which are secured in the trays and covered with a false bottom. The Guests help themselves.*]

209 **Humbug.** Not a very substantial meal. Maybe you can suggest something a little more filling.

210 **Milo.** Well, in that case, I think we ought to have a square meal . . .

211 **Azaz.** [*Claps his hands.*] A square meal it is! [*Waiters serve trays of Colored Squares of all sizes. People serve themselves.*]

212 **Spelling Bee.** These are awful. [Humbug *coughs and all the Guests do not care for the food.*]

213 **Azaz.** [*Claps his hands and the trays are removed.*] Time for speeches. [*To Milo.*] You first.

214 **Milo.** [*Hesitantly.*] Your Majesty, ladies and gentlemen, I would like to take this opportunity to say that . . .

215 **Azaz.** That's quite enough. Mustn't talk all day.

216 **Milo.** But I just started to . . .

217 **Azaz.** NEXT!

218 **Humbug.** [*Quickly*] Roast turkey, mashed potatoes, vanilla ice cream.

219 **Spelling Bee.** Hamburgers, corn on the cob, chocolate pudding p-u-d-d-i-n-g. [*Each Guest names two dishes and a dessert.*]

220 **Azaz.** [*The last.*] Pâté de foie gras, soupe à l'oignon, salade endives, fromage et fruits et demi-tasse. [*He claps his hands. Waiters serve each Guest his Words.*] Dig in. [*To Milo.*] Though I can't say I think much of your choice.

221 **Milo.** I didn't know I was going to have to eat my words.

222 **Azaz.** Of course, of course, everybody here does. Your speech should have been in better taste.

223 **Minister 1.** Here, try some somersault. It improves the flavor.

224 **Minister 2.** Have a rigamarole. [*Offers breadbasket.*]

225 **Minister 3.** Or a ragamuffin.

226 **Minister 4.** Perhaps you'd care for a synonym bun.

CLOSE READ

ANNOTATE: In paragraphs 223–226, mark the words that sound like but are not actually a seasoning or food.

QUESTION: Why does the playwright use this wordplay?

CONCLUDE: What is the effect of these and other examples of wordplay throughout this scene?

227 **Minister 5.** Why not wait for your just desserts?

228 **Azaz.** Ah yes, the dessert. We're having a special treat today . . . freshly made at the half-bakery.

229 **Milo.** The half-bakery?

230 **Azaz.** Of course, the half-bakery! Where do you think half-baked ideas come from? Now, please don't interrupt. By royal command, the pastry chefs have . . .

231 **Milo.** What's a half-baked idea?

232 [Azaz *gives up the idea of speaking as a cart is wheeled in and the Guests help themselves.*]

233 **Humbug.** They're very tasty, but they don't always agree with you. Here's a good one. [Humbug *hands one to* Milo.]

234 **Milo.** [*Reads.*] "The earth is flat."

235 **Spelling Bee.** People swallowed that one for years. [*Picks up one and reads.*] "The moon is made of green cheese." Now, there's a half-baked idea.

236 [*Everyone chooses one and eats. They include: "It Never Rains But Pours, "Night Air Is Bad Air," "Everything Happens for the Best," "Coffee Stunts Your Growth."*]

237 **Azaz.** And now for a few closing words. Attention! Let me have your attention! [*Everyone leaps up and Exits, except for* Milo, Tock, *and the* Humbug.] Loyal subjects and friends, once again on this gala occasion, we have . . .

238 **Milo.** Excuse me, but everybody left.

239 **Azaz.** [*Sadly.*] I was hoping no one would notice. It happens every time.

240 **Humbug.** They're gone to dinner, and as soon as I finish this last bite, I shall join them.

241 **Milo.** That's ridiculous. How can they eat dinner right after a banquet?

242 **Azaz.** SCANDALOUS! We'll put a stop to it at once. From now on, by royal command, everyone must eat dinner before the banquet.

243 **Milo.** But that's just as bad.

244 **Humbug.** Or just as good. Things which are equally bad are also equally good. Try to look at the bright side of things.

245 **Milo.** I don't know which side of anything to look at. Everything is so confusing, and all your words only make things worse.

246 **Azaz.** How true. There must be something we can do about it.

247 **Humbug.** Pass a law.

248 **Azaz.** We have almost as many laws as words.

249 **Humbug.** Offer a reward. [Azaz *shakes his head and looks madder at each suggestion.*] Send for help? Drive a bargain? Pull the switch? Lower the boom? Toe the line?

250 [*As Azaz* continues to scowl, *the* Humbug *loses confidence and finally gives up.*]

251 **Milo.** Maybe you should let Rhyme and Reason return.

252 **Azaz.** How nice that would be. Even if they were a bother at times, things always went so well when they were here. But I'm afraid it can't be done.

253 **Humbug.** Certainly not. Can't be done.

254 **Milo.** Why not?

255 **Humbug.** [*Now siding with* Milo.] Why not, indeed?

256 **Azaz.** Much too difficult.

257 **Humbug.** Of course, much too difficult.

258 **Milo.** You could, if you really wanted to.

259 **Humbug.** By all means, if you really wanted to, you could.

260 **Azaz.** [*To* Humbug.] How?

261 **Milo.** [*Also to* Humbug.] Yeah, how?

262 **Humbug.** Why . . . uh, it's a simple task for a brave boy with a stout heart, a steadfast dog and a serviceable small automobile.

263 **Azaz.** Go on.

264 **Humbug.** Well, all that he would have to do is cross the dangerous, unknown countryside between here and Digitopolis, where he would have to persuade the Mathemagician to release the Princesses, which we know to

be impossible because the Mathemagician will never agree with Azaz about anything. Once achieving that, it's a simple matter of entering the Mountains of Ignorance from where no one has ever returned alive, an effortless climb up a two thousand foot stairway without railings in a high wind at night to the Castle-in-the-Air. After a pleasant chat with the Princesses, all that remains is a leisurely ride back through those chaotic crags where the frightening fiends have sworn to tear any intruder limb from limb and devour him down to his belt buckle. And finally after doing all that, a triumphal parade! If, of course, there is anything left to parade . . . followed by hot chocolate and cookies for everyone.

265 **Azaz.** I never realized it would be so simple.

266 **Milo.** It sounds dangerous to me.

267 **Tock.** And just who is supposed to make that journey?

268 **Azaz.** A very good question. But there is one far more serious problem.

269 **Milo.** What's that?

270 **Azaz.** I'm afraid I can't tell you that until you return.

271 **Milo.** But wait a minute, I didn't . . .

272 **Azaz.** Dictionopolis will always be grateful to you, my boy, and your dog. [Azaz *pats* Tock *and* Milo.]

273 **Tock.** Now, just one moment, sire . . .

274 **Azaz.** You will face many dangers on your journey, but fear not, for I can give you something for your protection. [Azaz *gives* Milo *a box*.] In this box are the letters of the alphabet. With them you can form all the words you will ever need to help you overcome the obstacles that may stand in your path. All you must do is use them well and in the right places.

275 **Milo.** [*Miserably.*] Thanks a lot.

276 **Azaz.** You will need a guide, of course, and since he knows the obstacles so well, the Humbug has cheerfully volunteered to accompany you.

277 **Humbug.** Now, see here . . . !

278 **Azaz.** You will find him dependable, brave, resourceful, and loyal.

279 **Humbug.** [*Flattered.*] Oh, your Majesty.

280 **Milo.** I'm sure he'll be a great help. [*They approach the car.*]

281 **Tock.** I hope so. It looks like we're going to need it.

282 [*The lights darken and the king fades from view.*]

283 **Azaz.** Good luck! Drive carefully! [*The three get into the car and begin to move. Suddenly a thunderously loud NOISE is heard. They slow down the car.*]

284 **Milo.** What was that?

285 **Tock.** It came from up ahead.

286 **Humbug.** It's something terrible, I just know it. Oh, no. Something dreadful is going to happen to us. I can feel it in my bones. [*The NOISE is repeated. They all look at each other fearfully as the lights fade.*] ❧

Comprehension Check

Complete the following items after you finish your first read.

1. What is in the package that Milo receives?

2. Who is Tock and what does he look like?

3. What do the merchants in the marketplace of Dictionopolis sell?

4. What does Azaz send Milo, Tock, and Humbug to do?

5. What does Azaz give Milo?

6. 🗐 **Notebook** Write a short summary of Act I to show your understanding.

RESEARCH

Research to Clarify Choose at least one unfamiliar detail from the text. Briefly research that detail. In what way does the information you learned shed light on an aspect of the play?

Research to Explore Choose something that interested you from the text and formulate a research question. Write your question here.

THE PHANTOM TOLLBOOTH,
ACT I

Close Read the Text

1. This model—from Act I, scene ii—shows two sample annotations, along with questions and conclusions. Close read the passage, and find another detail to annotate. Then, write a question and a conclusion.

ANNOTATE: These words suggest something easy and stress-free.

QUESTION: Why does the playwright use words that make the job sound so easy?

CONCLUDE: The contrast shows that Humbug is trying to play down the dangers. It also makes the passage funny.

ANNOTATE: These prepositional phrases add scary details.

QUESTION: Why does the playwright add the dangerous details in subordinate phrases?

CONCLUDE: The sentence structure shows that Humbug is telling the truth, but also trying to hide it.

> . . . it's a simple matter of entering the Mountains of Ignorance from where no one has ever returned alive, an effortless climb up a two thousand foot stairway without railings in a high wind at night to the Castle-in-the-Air. After a pleasant chat with the Princesses, all that remains is a leisurely ride back through those chaotic crags. . . .

🔧 **Tool Kit**
Close-Read Guide and Model Annotation

2. For more practice, go back into the text and complete the close-read notes.

3. Revisit a section of the text you found important during your first read. Read this section closely and **annotate** what you notice. Ask yourself **questions** such as "Why did the author make this choice?" What can you **conclude**?

STANDARDS

Reading Literature
• Describe how a particular story's or drama's plot unfolds in a series of episodes as well as how the characters respond or change as the plot moves toward a resolution.

• Analyze how a particular sentence, chapter, scene, or stanza fits into the overall structure of a text and contributes to the development of the theme, setting, or plot.

• Explain how an author develops the point of view of the narrator or speaker in a text.

Analyze the Text

CITE TEXTUAL EVIDENCE to support your answers.

📓 **Notebook** Respond to these questions.

1. **Interpret** The Clock says, ". . . when you're bored, what you need more than anything is a rude awakening." Explain what this means.

2. (a) What does the clock on Tock's body represent? (b) **Speculate** If Tock hadn't come along, would Milo still be in the Doldrums? Explain.

3. **Draw Conclusions** At the end of Act I, is Milo still bored? Explain.

4. **Make Inferences** Milo's bedroom contains images of characters from the Land of Wisdom. What might this mean about Milo's adventure?

5. **Essential Question:** *Where can imagination lead?* What have you learned about imagination from reading Act I of the play?

Analyze Craft and Structure

Dramatic Structures A **drama,** or play, is a story that is written to be performed in front of an audience. Dramas are divided into shorter sections called **acts.** Each act may contain several scenes. A **scene** is like a little play by itself. It presents action in a specific situation.

Like a novel or a short story, a drama has characters, settings, and a plot that revolves around conflict. However, in a drama, information about these elements is developed through the actors' words, or **dialogue.** In a **script,** or written form of a play, each character's name appears before his or her dialogue, as in this example:

Milo. I think I was on my way to Dictionopolis when I got stuck here. Can you help me?

Watchdog. Help you! You've got to help yourself. I suppose you know why you got stuck.

When reading a play, think about how each character's **point of view,** or personality and beliefs, is shown through dialogue. Also, notice how the drama provides most of the information about the conflict and moves the story forward.

Practice

CITE TEXTUAL EVIDENCE
to support your answers.

📝 **Notebook** **Respond to these questions.**

1. Complete this chart to explain what each passage of dialogue tells you about a character, the setting, and an action. An example has been provided.

DIALOGUE	WHAT IT TELLS YOU
Milo. I've never heard of any of these places. Well, it doesn't matter anyway. Dictionopolis. That's a weird name. I might as well go there.	Not caring about where he goes shows that Milo is not fully convinced about the value of this journey. It shows that a change in setting is about to happen. It also moves the action along by having Milo travel to a new place.
Gatekeeper. This is Dictionopolis, a happy kingdom, advantageously located in the foothills of Confusion and caressed by gentle breezes from the Sea of Knowledge.	
Watchdog. KILLING TIME!... It's bad enough wasting time without killing it. What are you doing in the Doldrums, anyway? Don't you have anywhere to go?	

2. Reread paragraphs 247–274 of Scene ii. How do these lines of dialogue help move the plot forward?

THE PHANTOM TOLLBOOTH,
ACT I

Concept Vocabulary

ignorance	presume	misapprehension
surmise	speculate	consideration

Why These Words? These concept words relate to people's level of knowledge and how they use their minds. For example, if you are *ignorant,* you lack knowledge. If you hold a *misapprehension,* you are confused about something.

1. How does the concept vocabulary sharpen the reader's understanding of some of the key ideas being explored in *The Phantom Tollbooth,* Act I?

2. What other words in the selection connect to this concept?

Practice

📓 **Notebook** The six concept vocabulary words appear in the play. Note whether the concept vocabulary word is used correctly in each sentence. Explain your reasoning.

1. Refusing to think about the problem, Monroe gave it all his *consideration.*

2. Rather than *speculate,* let's just wait to see if we made the squad.

3. My *misapprehension* led me to make a lot of mistakes on the test.

4. I *surmise* that it's raining since your coat is soaking wet.

5. Leena was eager to demonstrate her *ignorance* and skill.

6. You should not *presume* where I want to go; you should ask me.

Word Study

Denotation and Nuance The **denotation** of a word is its literal definition, which you would find in a dictionary. Two words that have the same denotation may have different **nuances,** or slight shades of difference in their meanings. For example, the concept vocabulary words *surmise* and *speculate* both mean "guess." However, *surmise* implies that the guessing is based on a hunch, or feeling. In contrast, *speculate* implies that the guessing is based on incomplete information.

Use a dictionary to look up these three words that have the same denotation: *stingy, economical, thrifty.* First, write down the denotation that they share. Then, explain the nuances in their exact meanings.

🔧 WORD NETWORK

Add words related to imagination from the text to your Word Network.

☰ STANDARDS

Language
• Demonstrate command of the conventions of standard English grammar and usage when writing or speaking.

• Demonstrate understanding of figurative language, word relationships, and nuances in word meanings.
  c. Distinguish among the connotations of words with similar denotations.

Conventions

Sentence Parts and Types Good writers know how to use sentence parts and sentence variation to make their writing more interesting. A **sentence** consists of a subject and a predicate, and it expresses a complete thought. It always begins with a capital letter.

TIP

CLARIFICATION
Refer to the Grammar Handbook to learn more about these terms.

- A **simple subject** is the single person, place, or thing about which the sentence is written.
- A **complete subject** includes the simple subject and any related words.
- A **simple predicate** is the verb that expresses the sentence's action.
- A **complete predicate** includes the simple predicate and related words, such as adverbs, objects, and prepositional phrases.
- A **compound subject** is made up of two or more nouns that share the same verb and are joined by conjunctions such as *and* or *or*.

Sentences can be classified according to the following functions:

TYPE OF SENTENCE	FUNCTION	END PUNCTUATION	SAMPLE SENTENCE
Declarative	States an idea	Period	We don't like this music.
Interrogative	Asks a question	Question mark	May I play football now?
Imperative	Gives an order or direction	Period or exclamation mark	Put this dish away.
Exclamatory	Expresses strong emotion	Exclamation mark	What a fun game this is!

Read It

Notebook Read these sentences from the play. Mark the complete subject and complete predicate in each sentence.

1. This package contains the following items.

2. I can count to a thousand.

3. All guests who do not appear promptly at the table will automatically lose their place.

Write It

Notebook Rewrite each sentence to change it into the type indicated.

1. You can't get in without a reason. (exclamatory)

2. Count them off. (interrogative)

3. May we have a light snack? (imperative)

4. How can they eat dinner right after a banquet? (declarative)

EVIDENCE LOG

Before moving on to a new selection, go to your Evidence Log and record what you learned from *The Phantom Tollbooth*, Act I.

About the Author

Norton Juster (b. 1929) designed buildings and other structures during his career as an architect. He took up creative writing in his spare time "as a relaxation" from architecture. When he began writing *The Phantom Tollbooth*, he thought it was just a short story for his own pleasure. Yet before long, Juster says, "it had created its own life, and I was hooked." *The Phantom Tollbooth* has been translated into many languages and adapted for film and audio. You will listen to an audio clip in the next lesson.

Tool Kit
First-Read Guide and Model Annotation

STANDARDS

Reading Literature
By the end of the year, read and comprehend literature, including stories, dramas, and poems, in the grades 6–8 text complexity band proficiently, with scaffolding as needed at the high end of the range.

The Phantom Tollbooth, Act II

Concept Vocabulary

You will encounter the following words as you read *The Phantom Tollbooth*, Act II. Before reading, note how familiar you are with each word. Then, rank the words in order from most familiar (1) to least familiar (6).

WORD	YOUR RANKING
suspiciously	
obstacle	
pessimistic	
malicious	
insincerity	
compromise	

After completing the first read, come back to the concept vocabulary and review your rankings. Mark changes to your original rankings as needed.

First Read DRAMA

Apply these strategies as you conduct your first read. You will have an opportunity to complete the close-read notes after your first read.

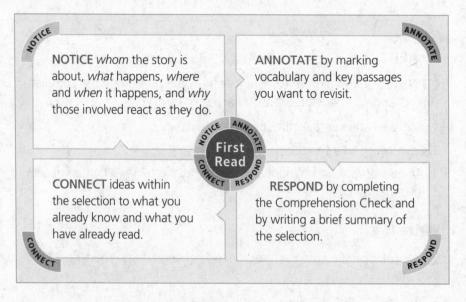

NOTICE *whom* the story is about, *what* happens, *where* and *when* it happens, and *why* those involved react as they do.

ANNOTATE by marking vocabulary and key passages you want to revisit.

CONNECT ideas within the selection to what you already know and what you have already read.

RESPOND by completing the Comprehension Check and by writing a brief summary of the selection.

First Read

The Phantom Tollbooth Act II

Susan Nanus

Based on the book by Norton Juster

REVIEW AND ANTICIPATE

In Act I, Milo is lifted from his boredom into a strange kingdom that is in conflict over the importance of letters and numbers. After traveling through Dictionopolis, he agrees to rescue Princesses Rhyme and Reason, who can settle the conflict. As Act II opens, Milo, Tock, and the Humbug arrive in the city of Digitopolis on their quest to rescue the princesses.

SCAN FOR
MULTIMEDIA

Act II

Scene i

1   *The set of Digitopolis glitters in the background, while Upstage Right near the road, a small colorful Wagon sits, looking quite deserted. On its side in large letters, a sign reads: "KAKAFONOUS A. DISCHORD Doctor of Dissonance."[1] Enter* Milo, Tock, *and* Humbug, *fearfully. They look at the wagon.*

NOTES

1. dissonance (DIHS uh nuhns) *n.* harsh or unpleasant combination of sounds.

2 **Tock.** There's no doubt about it. That's where the noise was coming from.

3 **Humbug.** [*To* Milo.] Well, go on.

4 **Milo.** Go on what?

5 **Humbug.** Go on and see who's making all that noise in there. We can't just ignore a creature like that.

6 **Milo.** Creature? What kind of creature? Do you think he's dangerous?

7 **Humbug.** Go on, Milo. Knock on the door. We'll be right behind you.

8 **Milo.** O.K. Maybe he can tell us how much further it is to Digitopolis.

9 [Milo *tiptoes up to the wagon and KNOCKS timidly. The moment he knocks, a terrible CRASH is heard inside the wagon, and Milo and the others jump back in fright. At the same time, the Door Flies Open, and from the dark interior, a Hoarse* Voice *inquires.*]

10 **Voice.** Have you ever heard a whole set of dishes dropped from the ceiling onto a hard stone floor? [*The Others are speechless with fright.* Milo *shakes his head.* Voice *happily.*] Have you ever heard an ant wearing fur slippers walk across a thick wool carpet? [Milo *shakes his head again.*] Have you ever heard a blindfolded octopus unwrap a cellophane-covered bathtub? [Milo *shakes his head a third time.*] Ha! I knew it. [*He hops out, a little man, wearing a white coat, with a stethoscope around his neck, and a small mirror attached to his forehead, and with very huge ears, and a mortar and pestle in his hands. He stares at Milo,* Tock *and Humbug.*] None of you looks well at all! Tsk, tsk, not at all. [*He opens the top or side of his Wagon, revealing a dusty interior resembling an old apothecary shop, with shelves lined with jars and boxes, a table, books, test tubes, and bottles and measuring spoons.*]

11 **Milo.** [*Timidly.*] Are you a doctor?

12 **Dischord.** [Voice.] I am KAKAFONOUS A. DISCHORD. DOCTOR OF DISSONANCE! [*Several small explosions and a grinding crash are heard.*]

13 **Humbug.** [*Stuttering with fear.*] What does the "A" stand for?

14 **Dischord.** AS LOUD AS POSSIBLE! [*Two screeches and a bump are heard.*] Now, step a little closer and stick out your tongues. [Dischord *examines them.*] Just as I expected. [*He opens a large dusty book and thumbs through the pages.*] You're all suffering from a severe lack of noise. [Dischord *begins running around, collecting bottles, reading the labels to himself as he goes along.*] "Loud Cries." "Soft Cries." "Bangs, Bongs, Swishes,

Swooshes." "Snaps and Crackles." "Whistles and Gongs." "Squeaks, Squawks, and Miscellaneous Uproar." [*As he reads them off, he pours a little of each into a large glass beaker and stirs the mixture with a wooden spoon. The concoction smokes and bubbles.*] Be ready in just a moment.

15 **Milo.** [*Suspiciously.*] Just what kind of doctor are you?

16 **Dischord.** Well, you might say, I'm a specialist. I specialize in noises, from the loudest to the softest, and from the slightly annoying to the terribly unpleasant. For instance, have you ever heard a square-wheeled steamroller ride over a street full of hard-boiled eggs? [*Very loud CRUNCHING SOUNDS are heard.*]

17 **Milo.** [*Holding his ears.*] But who would want all those terrible noises?

18 **Dischord.** [*Surprised at the question.*] Everybody does. Why, I'm so busy I can hardly fill all the orders for noise pills, racket lotion, clamor salve, and hubbub tonic. That's all people seem to want these days. Years ago, everyone wanted pleasant sounds and business was terrible. But then the cities were built and there was a great need for honking horns, screeching trains, clanging bells, and all the rest of those wonderfully unpleasant sounds we use so much today. I've been working overtime ever since and my medicine here is in great demand. All you have to do is take one spoonful every day, and you'll never have to hear another beautiful sound again. Here, try some.

19 **Humbug.** [*Backing away.*] If it's all the same to you, I'd rather not.

20 **Milo.** I don't want to be cured of beautiful sounds.

21 **Tock.** Besides, there's no such sickness as a lack of noise.

22 **Dischord.** How true. That's what makes it so difficult to cure. [*Takes a large glass bottle from the shelf.*] Very well, if you want to go all through life suffering from a noise deficiency,[2] I'll just give this to Dynne for his lunch. [*Uncorks the bottle and pours the liquid into it. There is a rumbling and then a loud explosion accompanied by smoke, out of which* Dynne, *a smog-like creature with yellow eyes and a frowning mouth, appears.*]

23 **Dynne.** [*Smacking his lips.*] Ahhh, that was good, Master. I thought you'd never let me out. It was really cramped in there.

24 **Dischord.** This is my assistant, the awful Dynne. You must forgive his appearance, for he really doesn't have any.

25 **Milo.** What is a Dynne?

suspiciously (suh SPIHSH uhs lee) *adv.* based on a lack of trust or belief; disbelievingly; cautiously

2. **deficiency** (dih FIHSH uhn see) *n.* shortage or lack.

CLOSE READ
ANNOTATE: In paragraphs 22–24, mark details that show what Dynne looks like and how he behaves.

QUESTION: Why does the playwright include these details?

CONCLUDE: What is the effect of these details, especially when added to Dischord's statement that Dynne "doesn't have" an appearance?

26 **Dischord.** You mean you've never heard of the awful Dynne? When you're playing in your room and making a great amount or noise, what do they tell you to stop?

27 **Milo.** That awful din.

28 **Dischord.** When the neighbors are playing their radio too loud late at night, what do you wish they'd turn down?

29 **Tock.** That awful din.

30 **Dischord.** And when the street on your block is being repaired and the drills are working all day, what does everyone complain of?

31 **Humbug.** [*Brightly.*] The dreadful row.

32 **Dynne.** The Dreadful Rauw was my grandfather. He perished in the great silence epidemic of 1712. I certainly can't understand why you don't like noise. Why, I heard an explosion last week that was so lovely, I groaned with appreciation for two days. [*He gives a loud groan at the memory.*]

33 **Dischord.** He's right, you know! Noise is the most valuable thing in the world.

34 **Milo.** King Azaz says words are.

35 **Dischord.** NONSENSE! Why, when a baby wants food, how does he ask?

36 **Dynne.** [*Happily.*] He screams!

37 **Dischord.** And when a racing car wants gas?

38 **Dynne.** [*Jumping for Joy.*] It chokes!

39 **Dischord.** And what happens to the dawn when a new day begins?

40 **Dynne.** [*Delighted.*] It breaks!

41 **Dischord.** You see how simple it is? [*To Dynne.*] Isn't it time for us to go?

42 **Milo.** Where to? Maybe we're going the same way.

43 **Dynne.** I doubt it. [*Picking up empty sacks from the table.*] We're going on our collection rounds. Once a day, I travel throughout the kingdom and collect all the wonderfully horrible and beautifully unpleasant sounds I can find and bring them back to the doctor to use in his medicine.

44 **Dischord.** Where are you going?

45 **Milo.** To Digitopolis.

46 **Dischord.** Oh, there are a number of ways to get to Digitopolis, if you know how to follow directions. Just take a look at the sign at the fork in the road. Though why you'd ever want to go there, I'll never know.

47 **Milo.** We want to talk to the Mathemagician.

48 **Humbug.** About the release of the Princesses Rhyme and Reason.

49 **Dischord.** Rhyme and Reason? I remember them. Very nice girls, but a little too quiet for my taste. In fact, I've been meaning to send them something that Dynne brought home by mistake and which I have absolutely no use for. [*He rummages through the wagon.*] Ah, here it is . . . or maybe you'd like it for yourself. [*Hands* Milo *a* package.]

50 **Milo.** What is it?

51 **Dischord.** The sounds of laughter. They're so unpleasant to hear, it's almost unbearable. All those giggles and snickers and happy shouts of joy. I don't know what Dynne was thinking of when he collected them. Here, take them to the Princesses or keep them for yourselves, I don't care. Well, time to move on. Goodbye now and good luck! [*He has shut the wagon by now and gets in. LOUD NOISES begin to erupt as* Dynne *pulls the wagon offstage.*]

52 **Milo.** [*Calling after them.*] But wait! The fork in the road . . . you didn't tell us where it is . . .

53 **Tock.** It's too late. He can't hear a thing.

54 **Humbug.** I could use a fork of my own, at the moment. And a knife and a spoon to go with it. All of a sudden, I feel very hungry.

55 **Milo.** So do I, but it's no use thinking about it. There won't be anything to eat until we reach Digitopolis. [*They get into the car.*]

56 **Humbug.** [*Rubbing his stomach.*] Well, the sooner the better is what I say. [*A SIGN suddenly appears.*]

57 **Voice.** [*A strange voice from nowhere.*] But which way will get you there sooner? That is the question.

58 **Tock.** Did you hear something?

59 **Milo.** Look! The fork in the road and a signpost to Digitopolis! [*They read the Sign.*]

60 **Humbug.** Let's travel by miles, it's shorter.

61 **Milo.** Let's travel by half inches. It's quicker.

CLOSE READ

ANNOTATE: In paragraph 51, mark terms that identify different kinds of laughter.

QUESTION: Why does the playwright include these details?

CONCLUDE: What is the effect of these details, especially in helping to portray Dischord?

62 **Tock.** But which road should we take? It must make a difference.

63 **Milo.** Do you think so?

64 **Tock.** Well, I'm not sure, but . . .

65 **Humbug.** He could be right. On the other hand, he could also be wrong. Does it make a difference or not?

66 **Voice.** Yes, indeed, indeed it does, certainly, my yes, it does make a difference.

67 [*The Dodecahedron appears, a 12-sided figure with a different face on each side, and with all the edges labeled with a small letter and all the angles labeled with a large letter. He wears a beret and peers at the others with a serious face. He doffs his cap and recites:*]

68 **Dodecahedron.** *My angles are many.*
My sides are not few.
I'm the Dodecahedron.
Who are you?

69　**Milo.** What's a Dodecahedron?

70　**Dodecahedron.** [*Turning around slowly.*] See for yourself. A Dodecahedron is a mathematical shape with 12 faces. [*All his faces appear as he turns, each face with a different expression. He points to them.*] I usually use one at a time. It saves wear and tear. What are you called?

71　**Milo.** Milo.

72　**Dodecahedron.** That's an odd name. [*Changing his smiling face to a frowning one.*] And you have only one face.

73　**Milo.** [*Making sure it is still there.*] Is that bad?

74　**Dodecahedron.** You'll soon wear it out using it for everything. Is everyone with one face called Milo?

75　**Milo.** Oh, no. Some are called Billy or Jeffery or Sally or Lisa or lots of other things.

76　**Dodecahedron.** How confusing. Here everything is called exactly what it is. The triangles are called triangles, the circles are called circles, and even the same numbers have the same name. Can you imagine what would happen if we named all the twos Billy or Jeffery or Sally or Lisa or lots of other things? You'd have to say Robert plus John equals four, and if the fours were named Albert, things would be hopeless.

.77　**Milo.** I never thought of it that way.

78　**Dodecahedron.** [*With an admonishing face.*] Then I suggest you begin at once, for in Digitopolis, everything is quite precise.

79　**Milo.** Then perhaps you can help us decide which road we should take.

80　**Dodecahedron.** [*Happily.*] By all means. There's nothing to it. [*As he talks, the three others try to solve the problem on a Large Blackboard that is wheeled onstage for the occasion.*] Now, if a small car carrying three people at 30 miles an hour for 10 minutes along a road 5 miles long at 11:35 in the morning starts at the same time as 3 people who have been traveling in a little automobile at 20 miles an hour for 15 minutes on another road exactly twice as long as half the distance of the other, while a dog, a bug, and a boy travel an equal distance in the same time or the same distance in an equal time along a third road in mid-October, then which one arrives first and which is the best way to go?

81　**Humbug.** Seventeen!

82　**Milo.** [*Still figuring frantically.*] I'm not sure, but . . .

83 **Dodecahedron.** You'll have to do better than that.

84 **Milo.** I'm not very good at problems.

85 **Dodecahedron.** What a shame. They're so very useful. Why, did you know that if a beaver 2 feet long with a tail a foot and a half long can build a dam 12 feet high and 6 feet wide in 2 days, all you would need to build Boulder Dam is a beaver 68 feet long with a 51 foot tail?

86 **Humbug.** [*Grumbling as his pencil snaps.*] Where would you find a beaver that big?

87 **Dodecahedron.** I don't know, but if you did, you'd certainly know what to do with him.

88 **Milo.** That's crazy.

89 **Dodecahedron.** That may be true, but it's completely accurate, and as long as the answer is right, who cares if the question is wrong?

90 **Tock.** [*Who has been patiently doing the first problem.*] All three roads arrive at the same place at the same time.

91 **Dodecahedron.** Correct! And I'll take you there myself. [*The blackboard rolls off, and all four get into the car and drive off.*] Now you see how important problems are. If you hadn't done this one properly, you might have gone the wrong way.

92 **Milo.** But if all the roads arrive at the same place at the same time, then aren't they all the right road?

93 **Dodecahedron.** [*Glaring from his upset face.*] Certainly not! They're all the wrong way! Just because you have a choice, it doesn't mean that any of them has to be right. [*Pointing in another direction.*] That's the way to Digitopolis and we'll be there any moment. [*Suddenly the lighting grows dimmer.*] In fact, we're here. Welcome to the Land of Numbers.

94 **Humbug.** [*Looking around at the barren landscape.*] It doesn't look very inviting.

95 **Milo.** Is this the place where numbers are made?

96 **Dodecahedron.** They're not made. You have to dig for them. Don't you know anything at all about numbers?

97 **Milo.** Well, I never really thought they were very important.

98 **Dodecahedron.** NOT IMPORTANT! Could you have tea for two without the 2? Or three blind mice without the 3? And how would you sail the seven seas without the 7?

99 **Milo.** All I meant was . . .

100 **Dodecahedron.** [*Continues shouting angrily.*] If you had high hopes, how would you know how high they were? And did you know that narrow escapes come in different widths? Would you travel the whole world wide without ever knowing how wide it was? And how could you do anything at long last without knowing how long the last was? Why, numbers are the most beautiful and valuable things in the world. Just follow me and I'll show you. [*He motions to them and pantomimes walking through rocky terrain with the others in tow. A Doorway similar to the Tollbooth appears and the Dodecahedron opens it and motions the others to follow him through.*] Come along, come along. I can't wait for you all day. [*They enter the doorway and the lights are dimmed very low, as to simulate the interior of a cave. The SOUNDS of scraping and tapping, scuffling and digging are heard around them. He hands them Helmets with flashlights attached.*] Put these on.

101 **Milo.** [*Whispering.*] Where are we going?

102 **Dodecahedron.** We're here. This is the numbers mine. [*LIGHTS UP A LITTLE, revealing Little Men digging and chopping, shoveling, and scraping.*] Right this way and watch your step. [*His voice echoes and reverberates. Iridescent*[3] *and glittery numbers seem to sparkle from everywhere.*]

103 **Milo.** [*Awed.*] Whose mine is it?

104 **Voice of Mathemagician.** By the four million eight hundred and twenty-seven thousand six hundred and fifty-nine hairs on my head, it's mine, of course! [*ENTER the Mathemagician, carrying his long staff which looks like a giant pencil.*]

105 **Humbug.** [*Already intimidated.*] It's a lovely mine, really it is.

106 **Mathemagician.** [*Proudly.*] The biggest number mine in the kingdom.

107 **Milo.** [*Excitedly.*] Are there any precious stones in it?

108 **Mathemagician.** Precious stones! [*Then softly.*] By the eight million two hundred and forty-seven thousand three hundred and twelve threads in my robe, I'll say there are. Look here. [*Reaches in a cart, pulls out a small object, polishes it vigorously, and holds it up to the light, where it sparkles.*]

109 **Milo.** But that's a five.

110 **Mathemagician.** Exactly. As valuable a jewel as you'll find anywhere. Look at some of the others. [*Scoops up others and pours them into Milo's arms. They include all numbers from 1 to 9 and an assortment of zeros.*]

NOTES

3. **iridescent** (ihr uh DEHS uhnt) *adj.* showing different colors when seen from different angles.

CLOSE READ

ANNOTATE: In paragraph 104 and again in paragraph 108, mark the items the Mathemagician counts.

QUESTION: Why does the playwright indicate that he counts items that are so small and plentiful?

CONCLUDE: What is the effect of these details?

111 **Dodecahedron.** We dig them and polish them right here, and then send them all over the world. Marvelous, aren't they?

112 **Tock.** They are beautiful. [*He holds them up to compare them to the numbers on his clock body.*]

113 **Milo.** So that's where they come from. [*Looks at them and carefully hands them back, but drops a few which smash and break in half.*] Oh. I'm sorry!

114 **Mathemagician.** [*Scooping them up.*] Oh, don't worry about that. We use the broken ones for fractions. How about some lunch? [*Takes out a little whistle and blows it. Two miners rush in carrying an immense cauldron which is bubbling and steaming. The workers put down their tools and gather around to eat.*]

115 **Humbug.** That looks delicious! [*Tock and Milo also look hungrily at the pot.*]

116 **Mathemagician.** Perhaps you'd care for something to eat?

117 **Milo.** Oh, yes, sir!

118 **Tock.** Thank you.

119 **Humbug.** [*Already eating.*] Ummm . . . delicious! [*All finish their bowls immediately.*]

120 **Mathemagician.** Please have another portion. [*They eat and finish.* Mathemagician *serves them again.*] Don't stop now. [*They finish.*] Come on, no need to be bashful. [*Serves them again.*]

121 **Milo.** [*To Tock and Humbug as he finishes again.*] Do you want to hear something strange? Each one I eat makes me a little hungrier than before.

122 **Mathemagician.** Do have some more. [*He serves them again. They eat frantically, until the* Mathemagician *blows his whistle again and the pot is removed.*]

123 **Humbug.** [*Holding his stomach.*] Uggghhh! I think I'm starving.

124 **Milo.** Me, too, and I ate so much.

125 **Dodecahedron.** [*Wiping the gravy from several of his mouths.*] Yes, it was delicious, wasn't it? It's the specialty of the kingdom . . . subtraction stew.

126 **Tock.** [*Weak from hunger.*] I have more of an appetite than when I began.

127 **Mathemagician.** Certainly, what did you expect? The more you eat, the hungrier you get, everyone knows that.

128 **Milo.** They do? Then how do you get enough?

129 **Mathemagician.** Enough? Here in Digitopolis, we have our meals when we're full and eat until we're hungry. That way, when you don't have anything at all, you have more than enough. It's a very economical system. You must have been stuffed to have eaten so much.

130 **Dodecahedron.** It's completely logical. The more you want, the less you get, and the less you get, the more you have. Simple arithmetic, that's all. [Tock, Milo *and* Humbug *look at him blankly.*] Now, look, suppose you had something and added nothing to it. What would you have?

131 **Milo.** The same.

132 **Dodecahedron.** Splendid! And suppose you had something and added less than nothing to it? What would you have then?

133 **Humbug.** Starvation! Oh, I'm so hungry.

134 **Dodecahedron.** Now, now, it's not as bad as all that. In a few hours, you'll be nice and full again . . . just in time for dinner.

135 **Milo.** But I only eat when I'm hungry.

136 **Mathemagician.** [*Waving the eraser of his staff.*] What a curious idea. The next thing you'll have us believe is that you only sleep when you're tired.

137 [*The mine has disappeared as well as the Miners.*]

138 **Humbug.** Where did everyone go?

139 **Mathemagician.** Oh, they're still in the mine. I often find that the best way to get from one place to another is to erase everything and start again. Please make yourself at home.

140 [*They find themselves in a unique room, in which all the walls, tables, chairs, desks, cabinets, and blackboards are labeled to show their heights, widths, depths, and distances to and from each other. To one side is a gigantic notepad on an artist's easel, and from hooks and strings hang a collection of rulers, measures, weights and tapes, and all other measuring devices.*]

141 **Milo.** Do you always travel that way? [*He looks around in wonder.*]

142 **Mathemagician.** No, indeed! [*He pulls a plumb line from a hook and walks.*] Most of the time I take the shortest distance between any two points. And of course, when I have to be in several places at once . . . [*He writes $3 \times 1 = 3$ on the notepad with his staff.*] I simply multiply. [Three Figures *looking like the* Mathemagician *appear on a platform above.*]

143 **Milo.** How did you do that?

144 **Mathemagician** and **The Three.** There's nothing to it, if you have a magic staff. [The Three Figures *cancel themselves out and disappear*.]

145 **Humbug.** That's nothing but a big pencil.

146 **Mathemagician.** True enough, but once you learn to use it, there's no end to what you can do.

147 **Milo.** Can you make things disappear?

148 **Mathemagician.** Just step a little closer and watch this. [*Shows them that there is nothing up his sleeve or in his hat. He writes:*]

$$4 + 9 - 2 \times 16 + 1 = 3 \times 6 - 67 + 8 \times 2 - 3 + 26 - 1 - 34 + 3 - 7 + 2 - 5 = $$ [*He looks up expectantly.*]

149 **Humbug.** Seventeen?

150 **Milo.** It all comes to zero.

CLOSE READ

ANNOTATE: In paragraphs 151 and 158, mark the directions that suggest the characters speak directly to the audience.

QUESTION: Why does the playwright include these directions?

CONCLUDE: If the actors were to follow these directions, how might they affect the audience's response?

151 **Mathemagician.** Precisely. [*Makes a theatrical bow and rips off paper from notepad.*] Now, is there anything else you'd like to see? [*At this point, an appeal to the audience to see if anyone would like a problem solved.*]

152 **Milo.** Well . . . can you show me the biggest number there is?

153 **Mathemagician.** Why, I'd be delighted. [*Opening a closet door.*] We keep it right here. It took four miners to dig it out. [*He shows them a huge "3" twice as high as the* Mathemagician.]

154 **Milo.** No, that's not what I mean. Can you show me the longest number there is?

155 **Mathemagician.** Sure. [*Opens another door.*] Here it is. It took three carts to carry it here. [*Door reveals an "8" that is as wide as the "3" was high.*]

156 **Milo.** No, no, that's not what I meant either. [*Looks helplessly at* Tock.]

157 **Tock.** I think what you would like to see is the number of the greatest possible magnitude.

158 **Mathemagician.** Well, why didn't you say so? [*He busily measures them and all other things as he speaks, and marks it down.*] What's the greatest number you can think of? [*Here, an appeal can also be made to the audience or* Milo *may think of his own answers.*]

159 **Milo.** Uh . . . nine trillion, nine hundred and ninety-nine billion, nine hundred ninety-nine million, nine hundred ninety-nine thousand, nine hundred and ninety-nine. [*He puffs.*]

160 **Mathemagician.** [*Writes that on the pad.*] Very good. Now add one to it. [*Milo or audience does.*] Now add one again. [*Milo or audience does so.*] Now add one again. Now add one again. Now add . . .

161 **Milo.** But when can I stop?

162 **Mathemagician.** Never. Because the number you want is always at least one more than the number you have, and it's so large that if you started saying it yesterday, you wouldn't finish tomorrow.

163 **Humbug.** Where could you ever find a number so big?

164 **Mathemagician.** In the same place they have the smallest number there is, and you know where that is?

165 **Milo.** The smallest number . . . let's see . . . one one-millionth?

166 **Mathemagician.** Almost. Now all you have to do is divide that in half and then divide that in half and then divide that in half and then divide that . . .

167 **Milo.** Doesn't that ever stop either?

168 **Mathemagician.** How can it when you can always take half of what you have and divide it in half again? Look. [*Pointing offstage.*] You see that line?

169 **Milo.** You mean that long one out there?

170 **Mathemagician.** That's it. Now, if you just follow that line forever, and when you reach the end, turn left, you will find the Land of Infinity. That's where the tallest, the shortest, the biggest, the smallest, and the most and the least of everything are kept.

171 **Milo.** But how can you follow anything forever? You know, I get the feeling that everything in Digitopolis is very difficult.

172 **Mathemagician.** But on the other hand, I think you'll find that the only thing you can do easily is be wrong, and that's hardly worth the effort.

173 **Milo.** But . . . what bothers me is . . . well, why is it that even when things are correct, they don't really seem to be right?

174 **Mathemagician.** [*Grows sad and quiet.*] How true. It's been that way ever since Rhyme and Reason were banished. [*Sadness turns to fury.*] And all because of that stubborn wretch Azaz! It's all his fault.

175 **Milo.** Maybe if you discussed it with him . . .

CLOSE READ
ANNOTATE: In paragraph 173, mark the ellipses, or punctuation that looks like three periods in a row.

QUESTION: Why does the author use ellipses here?

CONCLUDE: How might this punctuation affect the way in which an actor delivers this line?

176 **Mathemagician.** He's just too unreasonable! Why just last month, I sent him a very friendly letter, which he never had the courtesy to answer. See for yourself. [*Puts the letter on the easel. The letter reads:*]

177 4738 1919,

667 394107 5841 62589 85371 14

39588 7190434 203 27689 57131 481206.

5864 98053,

62179875073

178 **Milo.** But maybe he doesn't understand numbers.

179 **Mathemagician.** Nonsense! Everybody understands numbers. No matter what language you speak, they always mean the same thing. A seven is a seven everywhere in the world.

180 **Milo.** [*To* Tock *and* Humbug.] Everyone is so sensitive about what he knows best.

181 **Tock.** With your permission, sir, we'd like to rescue Rhyme and Reason.

182 **Mathemagician.** Has Azaz agreed to it?

183 **Tock.** Yes, sir.

184 **Mathemagician.** THEN I DON'T! Ever since they've been banished, we've never agreed on anything, and we never will.

185 **Milo.** Never?

186 **Mathemagician.** NEVER! And if you can prove otherwise, you have my permission to go.

187 **Milo.** Well then, with whatever Azaz agrees, you disagree.

188 **Mathemagician.** Correct.

189 **Milo.** And with whatever Azaz disagrees, you agree.

190 **Mathemagician.** [*Yawning, cleaning his nails.*] Also correct.

191 **Milo.** Then, each of you agrees that he will disagree with whatever each of you agrees with, and if you both disagree with the same thing, aren't you really in agreement?

192 **Mathemagician.** I'VE BEEN TRICKED! [*Figures it over, but comes up with the same answer.*]

193 **Tock.** And now may we go?

194 Mathemagician. [*Nods weakly.*] It's a long and dangerous journey. Long before you find them, the demons will know you're there. Watch out for them, because if you ever come face to face, it will be too late. But there is one other **obstacle** even more serious than that.

195 Milo. [*Terrified.*] What is it?

196 Mathemagician. I'm afraid I can't tell you until you return. But maybe I can give you something to help you out. [*Claps hands. ENTER the* Dodecahedron, *carrying something on a pillow. The* Mathemagician *takes it.*] Here is your own magic staff. Use it well and there is nothing it can't do for you. [*Puts a small, gleaming pencil in* Milo's *breast pocket.*]

197 Humbug. Are you sure you can't tell about that serious obstacle?

198 Mathemagician. Only when you return. And now the Dodecahedron will escort you to the road that leads to the Castle-in-the-Air. Farewell, my friends, and good luck to you. [*They shake hands, say goodbye, and the* Dodecahedron *leads them off.*] Good luck to you! [*To himself.*] Because you're sure going to need it. [*He watches them through a telescope and marks down the calculations.*]

199 Dodecahedron. [*He re-enters.*] Well, they're on their way.

200 Mathemagician. So I see . . . [Dodecahedron *stands waiting.*] Well, what is it?

201 Dodecahedron. I was just wondering myself, your Numbership. What actually is the serious obstacle you were talking about?

202 Mathemagician. [*Looks at him in surprise.*] You mean you really don't know?

203 BLACKOUT

obstacle (OB stuh kuhl) *n.* something that stands in the way or stops progress

CLOSE READ
ANNOTATE: Mark the stage direction after paragraph 202 that tells what happens after the Dodecahedron asks about the obstacle.

QUESTION: Why does the playwright include this stage direction?

CONCLUDE: How might this stage direction, if followed, affect a viewing audience?

Scene ii • The Land of Ignorance

1 *LIGHTS UP on* Rhyme *and* Reason, *in their castle, looking out two windows.*

2 **Rhyme.** *I'm worried sick I must confess*

    I wonder if they'll have success

     All others tried in vain,

     And were never seen or heard again.

3 **Reason.** Now, Rhyme, there's no need to be so **pessimistic**. Milo, Tock, and Humbug have just as much chance of succeeding as they do of failing.

4 **Rhyme.** *But the demons are so deadly smart*

    They'll stuff your brain and fill your heart

    With petty thoughts and selfish dreams

    And trap you with their nasty schemes.

5 **Reason.** Now, Rhyme, be reasonable, won't you? And calm down, you always talk in couplets when you get nervous. Milo has learned a lot from his journey. I think he's a match for the demons and that he might soon be knocking at our door. Now, come on, cheer up, won't you?

6 **Rhyme.** I'll try.

7 [*LIGHTS FADE on the* Princesses *and COME UP on the little Car, traveling slowly.*]

8 **Milo.** So this is the Land of Ignorance. It's so dark. I can hardly see a thing. Maybe we should wait until morning.

9 **Voice.** They'll be mourning for you soon enough. [*They look up and see a large, soiled, ugly bird with a dangerous beak and a* **malicious** *expression.*]

10 **Milo.** I don't think you understand. We're looking for a place to spend the night.

11 **Bird.** [*Shrieking.*] It's not yours to spend!

12 **Milo.** That doesn't make any sense, you see . . .

13 **Bird.** Dollars or cents. It's still not yours to spend.

14 **Milo.** But I don't mean . . .

15 **Bird.** Of course you're mean. Anybody who'd spend a night that doesn't belong to him is very mean.

16 **Tock.** Must you interrupt like that?

17 **Bird.** Naturally, it's my job. I take the words right out of your mouth. Haven't we met before? I'm the Everpresent Wordsnatcher.

pessimistic (pehs uh MIHS tihk) *adj.* expecting the worst, focused on the bad aspects of a situation

malicious (muh LIHSH uhs) *adj.* having or showing bad intentions

18 **Milo.** Are you a demon?

19 **Bird.** I'm afraid not. I've tried, but the best I can manage to be is a nuisance. [*Suddenly gets nervous as he looks beyond the three.*] And I don't have time to waste with you. [*Starts to leave.*]

20 **Tock.** What is it? What's the matter?

21 **Milo.** Hey, don't leave. I wanted to ask you some questions . . . Wait!

22 **Bird.** Weight? Twenty-seven pounds. Bye-bye. [*Disappears.*]

23 **Milo.** Well, he was no help.

24 **Man.** Perhaps I can be of some assistance to you? [*There appears a beautifully dressed man, very polished and clean.*] Hello, little boy. [*Shakes* Milo's *hand.*] And how's the faithful dog? [*Pats* Tock.] And who is this handsome creature? [*Tips his hat to* Humbug.]

25 **Humbug.** [*To others.*] What a pleasant surprise to meet someone so nice in a place like this.

26 **Man.** But before I help you out, I wonder if first you could spare me a little of your time, and help me with a few small jobs?

27 **Humbug.** Why, certainly.

28 **Tock.** Gladly.

29 **Milo.** Sure, we'd be happy to.

30 **Man.** Splendid, for there are just three tasks. First, I would like to move this pile of sand from here to there. [*Indicates through pantomime a large pile of sand.*] But I'm afraid that all I have is this tiny tweezers. [*Hands it to* Milo, *who begins moving the sand one grain at a time.*] Second, I would like to empty this well and fill that other, but I have no bucket, so you'll have to use this eyedropper. [*Hands it to* Tock, *who begins to work.*] And finally, I must have a hole in this cliff, and here is a needle to dig it. [Humbug *eagerly begins. The man leans against a tree and stares vacantly off into space. The LIGHTS indicate the passage of time.*]

31 **Milo.** You know something? I've been working steadily for a long time now, and I don't feel the least bit tired or hungry. I could go right on the same way forever.

32 **Man.** Maybe you will. [*He yawns.*]

33 **Milo.** [*Whispers to* Tock.] Well, I wish I knew how long it was going to take.

34 **Tock.** Why don't you use your magic staff and find out?

35 Milo. [*Takes out pencil and calculates. To* Man.] Pardon me, sir, but it's going to take 837 years to finish these jobs.

36 Man. Is that so? What a shame. Well then you'd better get on with them.

37 Milo. But . . . it hardly seems worthwhile.

38 Man. WORTHWHILE! Of course they're not worthwhile. I wouldn't ask you to do anything that was worthwhile.

39 Tock. Then why bother?

40 Man. Because, my friends, what could be more important than doing unimportant things? If you stop to do enough of them, you'll never get where you are going. [*Laughs villainously.*]

41 Milo. [*Gasps.*] Oh, no, you must be . . .

42 Man. Quite correct! I am the Terrible Trivium, demon of petty tasks and worthless jobs, ogre of wasted effort and monster of habit. [*They start to back away from him.*] Don't try to leave, there's so much to do, and you still have 837 years to go on the first job.

43 Milo. But why do unimportant things?

44 Man. Think of all the trouble it saves. If you spend all your time doing only the easy and useless jobs, you'll never have time to worry about the important ones which are so difficult. [*Walks toward them whispering.*] Now do come and stay with me. We'll have such fun together. There are things to fill and things to empty, things to take away and things to bring back, things to pick up and things to put down . . . [*They are transfixed⁴ by his soothing voice. He is about to embrace them when a* Voice *screams.*]

45 Voice. Run! Run! [*They all wake up and run with the Trivium behind. As the voice continues to call out directions, they follow until they lose the Trivium.*] RUN! RUN! This way! This way! Over here! Over here! Up here! Down there! Quick, hurry up!

46 Tock. [*Panting.*] I think we lost him.

47 Voice. Keep going straight! Keep going straight! Now step up! Now step up!

48 Milo. Look out! [*They all fall into a Trap.*] But he said "up"!

49 Voice. Well, I hope you didn't expect to get anywhere by listening to me.

50 Humbug. We're in a deep pit! We'll never get out of here.

51 Voice. That is quite an accurate evaluation of the situation.

52 Milo. [*Shouting angrily.*] Then why did you help us at all?

4. transfixed *v.* made motionless by horror or fascination.

53 **Voice.** Oh, I'd do as much for anybody. Bad advice is my specialty. [*A Little Furry Creature appears.*] I'm the demon of Insincerity. I don't mean what I say; I don't mean what I do; and I don't mean what I am.

54 **Milo.** Then why don't you go away and leave us alone!

55 **Insincerity.** (VOICE) Now, there's no need to get angry. You're a very clever boy and I have complete confidence in you. You can certainly climb out of that pit . . . come on, try . . .

56 **Milo.** I'm not listening to one word you say! You're just telling me what you think I'd like to hear, and not what is important.

57 **Insincerity.** Well, if that's the way you feel about it . . .

58 **Milo.** That's the way I feel about it. We will manage by ourselves without any unnecessary advice from you.

59 **Insincerity.** [*Stamping his foot.*] Well, all right for you! Most people listen to what I say, but if that's the way you feel, then I'll just go home. [*Exits in a huff.*]

60 **Humbug.** [*Who has been quivering with fright.*] And don't you ever come back! Well, I guess we showed him, didn't we?

61 **Milo.** You know something? This place is a lot more dangerous than I ever imagined.

62 **Tock.** [*Who's been surveying the situation.*] I think I figured a way to get out. Here, hop on my back. [Milo *does so.*] Now, you, Humbug, on top of Milo. [*He does so.*] Now hook your umbrella onto that tree and hold on. [*They climb over* Humbug, *then pull him up.*]

63 **Humbug.** [*As they climb.*] Watch it! Watch it, now. Ow, be careful of my back! My back! Easy, easy . . . oh, this is so difficult. Aren't you finished yet?

64 **Tock.** [*As he pulls up* Humbug.] There. Now, I'll lead for a while. Follow me, and we'll stay out of trouble. [*They walk and climb higher and higher.*]

65 **Humbug.** Can't we slow down a little?

66 **Tock.** Something tells me we better reach the Castle-in-the-Air as soon as possible, and not stop to rest for a single moment. [*They speed up.*]

67 **Milo.** What is it, Tock? Did you see something?

68 **Tock.** Just keep walking and don't look back.

69 **Milo.** You *did* see something!

70 **Humbug.** What is it? Another demon?

71 **Tock.** Not just one, I'm afraid. If you want to see what I'm talking about, then turn around. [*They turn around. The stage darkens and hundreds of Yellow Gleaming Eyes can be seen.*]

72 **Humbug.** Good grief! Do you see how many there are? Hundreds! The Overbearing Know-it-all, the Gross Exaggeration, the Horrible Hopping Hindsight . . . and look over there! The Triple Demons of **Compromise**! Let's get out of here! [*Starts to scurry.*] Hurry up, you two! Must you be so slow about everything?

73 **Milo.** Look! There it is, up ahead! The Castle-in-the-Air! [*They all run.*]

74 **Humbug.** They're gaining!

75 **Milo.** But there it is!

76 **Humbug.** I see it! I see it!

77 [*They reach the first step and are stopped by a little man in a frock coat, sleeping on a worn ledger. He has a long quill pen and a bottle of ink at his side. He is covered with ink stains over his clothes and wears spectacles.*]

78 **Tock.** Shh! Be very careful. [*They try to step over him, but he wakes up.*]

79 **Senses Taker.** [*From sleeping position.*] Names? [*He sits up.*]

80 **Humbug.** Well, I . . .

81 **Senses Taker.** *NAMES?* [*He opens book and begins to write, splattering himself with ink.*]

82 **Humbug.** Uh . . . Humbug, Tock, and this is Milo.

83 **Senses Taker.** Splendid, splendid. I haven't had an "M" in ages.

84 **Milo.** What do you want our names for? We're sort of in a hurry.

85 **Senses Taker.** Oh, this won't take long. I'm the official Senses Taker and I must have some information before I can take your sense. Now if you'll just tell me: [*Handing them a form to fill. Speaking slowly and deliberately.*] When you were born, where you were born, why you were born, how old you are now, how old you were then, how old you'll be in a little while . . .

86 **Milo.** I wish he'd hurry up. At this rate, the demons will be here before we know it!

compromise (KOM pruh myz) *n.* settlement of a disagreement in which each side gives up part of what it wanted

87 **Senses Taker.** . . . Your mother's name, your father's name, where you live, how long you've lived there, the schools you've attended, the schools you haven't attended . . .

88 **Humbug.** I'm getting writer's cramp.

89 **Tock.** I smell something very evil and it's getting stronger every second. [*To Senses Taker.*] May we go now?

90 **Senses Taker.** Just as soon as you tell me your height, your weight, the number of books you've read this year . . .

91 **Milo.** We have to go!

92 **Senses Taker.** All right, all right. I'll give you the short form. [*Pulls out a small piece of paper.*] Destination?

93 **Milo.** But we have to . . .

94 **Senses Taker.** *DESTINATION?*

95 **Milo, Tock** and **Humbug.** The Castle-in-the-Air! [*They throw down their papers and run past him up the first few stairs.*]

96 **Senses Taker.** Stop! I'm sure you'd rather see what I have to show you. [*Snaps his fingers; they freeze.*] A circus of your very own. [*CIRCUS MUSIC is heard.* Milo *seems to go into a trance.*] And wouldn't you enjoy this most wonderful smell? [*Tock sniffs and goes into a trance.*] And here's something I know you'll enjoy hearing . . . [*To* Humbug. *The sound of CHEERS and APPLAUSE for* Humbug *is heard, and he goes into a trance.*] There we are. And now, I'll just sit back and let the demons catch up with you.

97 [Milo *accidentally drops his package of gifts. The Package of Laughter from* Dr. Dischord *opens and the Sounds of Laughter are heard. After a moment,* Milo, Tock, *and* Humbug *join in laughing and the spells are broken.*]

98 **Milo.** There was no circus.

99 **Tock.** There were no smells.

100 **Humbug.** The applause is gone.

101 **Senses Taker.** I warned you I was the Senses Taker. I'll steal your sense of Purpose, your sense of Duty, destroy your sense of Proportion—and but for one thing, you'd be helpless yet.

102 **Milo.** What's that?

103 **Senses Taker.** As long as you have the sound of laughter, I cannot take your sense of Humor. Agh! That horrible sense of humor.

104 **Humbug.** HERE THEY COME! LET'S GET OUT OF HERE!

CLOSE READ

ANNOTATE: In paragraph 96, mark the stage directions that describe the Senses Taker's actions and their results.

QUESTION: Why does the playwright include these stage directions?

CONCLUDE: What is the effect of these directions? Would the playwright have been able to communicate the action without them?

105 [*The demons appear in nasty slithering hordes, running through the audience and up onto the stage, trying to attack* Tock, Milo, *and* Humbug. *The three heroes run past the* Senses Taker *up the stairs toward the Castle-in-the-Air with the demons snarling behind them.*]

106 **Milo.** Don't look back! Just keep going! [*They reach the castle. The two princesses appear in the windows.*]

107 **Princesses.** Hurry! Hurry! We've been expecting you.

108 **Milo.** You must be the Princesses. We've come to rescue you.

109 **Humbug.** And the demons are close behind!

110 **Tock.** We should leave right away.

111 **Princesses.** We're ready anytime you are.

112 **Milo.** Good, now if you'll just come out. But wait a minute—there's no door! How can we rescue you from the Castle-in-the-Air if there's no way to get in or out?

113 **Humbug.** Hurry, Milo! They're gaining on us.

114 **Reason.** Take your time, Milo, and think about it.

115 **Milo.** Ummm, all right . . . just give me a second or two. [*He thinks hard.*]

116 **Humbug.** I think I feel sick.

117 **Milo.** I've got it! Where's that package of presents? [*Opens the package of letters.*] Ah, here it is. [*Takes out the letters and sticks them on the door, spelling:*] E-N-T-R-A-N-C-E. Entrance. Now, let's see. [*Rummages through and spells in smaller letters:*] P-u-s-h. Push. [*He pushes and a door opens. The* Princesses *come out of the castle. Slowly, the demons ascend the stairway.*]

118 **Humbug.** Oh, it's too late. They're coming up and there's no other way down!

119 **Milo.** Unless . . . [*Looks at* Tock.] Well . . . Time flies, doesn't it?

120 **Tock.** Quite often. Hold on, everyone, and I'll take you down.

121 **Humbug.** Can you carry us all?

122 **Tock.** We'll soon find out. Ready or not, here we go! [*His alarm begins to ring. They jump off the platform and disappear. The demons, howling with rage, reach the top and find no one there. They see the* Princesses *and the heroes running across the stage and bound down the stairs after them and into the audience. There is a mad chase scene until they reach the stage again.*]

123 **Humbug.** I'm exhausted! I can't run another step.

124 **Milo.** We can't stop now . . .

CLOSE READ

ANNOTATE: In the stage directions in paragraph 105, mark the word the playwright uses to refer to Milo, Tock, and Humbug.

QUESTION: Why does the playwright use this term at this point in the play?

CONCLUDE: What does this word suggest about ways in which the three characters have changed?

125 **Tock.** Milo! Look out there! [*The armies of Azaz and Mathemagician appear at the back of the theater, with the Kings at their heads.*]

126 **Azaz.** [*As they march toward the stage.*] Don't worry, Milo, we'll take over now.

127 **Mathemagician.** Those demons may not know it, but their days are numbered!

128 **Spelling Bee.** Charge! C-H-A-R-G-E! Charge! [*They rush at the demons and battle until the demons run off howling. Everyone cheers. The* Five Ministers of Azaz *appear and shake Milo's hand.*]

129 **Minister 1.** Well done.

130 **Minister 2.** Fine job.

131 **Minister 3.** Good work!

132 **Minister 4.** Congratulations!

133 **Minister 5.** CHEERS! [*Everyone cheers again. A fanfare interrupts. A* Page *steps forward and reads from a large scroll:*]

134 **Page.** *Henceforth, and forthwith,*

    Let it be known by one and all.

    That Rhyme and Reason

    Reign once more in Wisdom.

135 [*The* Princesses *bow gracefully and kiss their brothers, the* Kings.]

136   *And furthermore,*

    The boy named Milo,

    The dog known as Tock,

    And the insect hereinafter referred to as the Humbug

    Are hereby declared to be Heroes of the Realm.

137 [*All bow and salute the heroes.*]

138 **Milo.** But we never could have done it without a lot of help.

139 **Reason.** That may be true, but you had the courage to try, and what you can do is often a matter of what you *will* do.

140 **Azaz.** That's why there was one very important thing about your quest we couldn't discuss until you returned.

141 **Milo.** I remember. What was it?

142 **Azaz.** Very simple. It was impossible!

143 **Mathemagician.** *Completely* impossible!

144 **Humbug.** Do you mean . . . ? [*Feeling faint.*] Oh . . . I think I need to sit down.

145 **Azaz.** Yes, indeed, but if we'd told you then, you might not have gone.

146 **Mathemagician.** And, as you discovered, many things are possible just as long as you don't know they're impossible.

147 **Milo.** I think I understand.

148 **Rhyme.** I'm afraid it's time to go now.

149 **Reason.** And you must say goodbye.

150 **Milo.** To everyone? [*Looks around at the crowd. To* Tock *and* Humbug.] Can't you two come with me?

151 **Humbug.** I'm afraid not, old man. I'd like to, but I've arranged for a lecture tour which will keep me occupied for years.

152 **Tock.** And they do need a watchdog here.

153 **Milo.** Well, O.K., then. [Milo *hugs the* Humbug.]

154 **Humbug.** [*Sadly.*] Oh, bah.

155 **Milo.** [*He hugs* Tock, *and then faces everyone.*] Well, goodbye. We all spent so much time together, I know I'm going to miss you. [*To the* Princesses.] I guess we would have reached you a lot sooner if I hadn't made so many mistakes.

156 **Reason.** You must never feel badly about making mistakes, Milo, as long as you take the trouble to learn from them. Very often you learn more by being wrong for the right reasons than you do by being right for the wrong ones.

157 **Milo.** But there's so much to learn.

158 **Rhyme.** That's true, but it's not just learning that's important. It's learning what to do with what you learn and learning why you learn things that matters.

159 **Milo.** I think I know what you mean, Princess. At least, I hope I do. [*The car is rolled forward and* Milo *climbs in.*] Goodbye! Goodbye! I'll be back someday! I will! Anyway, I'll try. [*As* Milo *drives the set of the Land of Ignorance move offstage.*]

160 **Azaz.** Goodbye! Always remember. Words! Words! Words!

161 **Mathemagician.** And numbers!

162 **Azaz.** Now, don't tell me you think numbers are as important as words?

163 **Mathemagician.** Is that so? Why I'll have you know . . . [*The set disappears, and* Milo's *Room is seen onstage.*]

164 **Milo.** [*As he drives on.*] Oh, oh. I hope they don't start all over again. Because I don't think I'll have much time in the near future to help them out. [*The sound of loud ticking is heard.* Milo *finds himself in his room. He gets out of the car and looks around.*]

165 **The Clock.** Did someone mention time?

166 **Milo.** Boy, I must have been gone for an awful long time. I wonder what time it is. [*Looks at the clock.*] Five o'clock. I wonder what day it is. [*Looks at calendar.*] It's still today! I've only been gone for an hour! [*He continues to look at his calendar, and then begins to look at his books and toys and maps and chemistry set with great interest.*]

167 **Clock.** An hour. Sixty minutes. How long it really lasts depends on what you do with it. For some people, an hour seems to last forever. For others, just a moment, and so full of things to do.

168 **Milo.** [*Looks at clock.*] Six o'clock already?

169 **Clock.** In an instant. In a trice. Before you have time to blink. [*The stage goes black in less than no time at all.*] ❧

Comprehension Check

Complete the following items after you finish your first read.

1. What gift does Dischord give Milo?

2. What does Dodecahedron look like?

3. What does Mathemagican give Milo before he goes to the Land of Ignorance?

4. What chases Milo, Tock, and Humbug up the stairway to the Castle-in-the-Air?

5. How does Tock help get everyone down from the Castle-in-the-Air?

6. ⊟ **Notebook** Write a summary of Act II to show your understanding.

RESEARCH

Research to Clarify Choose at least one unfamiliar detail from the text. Briefly research that detail. In what way does the information you learned shed light on an aspect of the play?

Research to Explore Choose something that interested you from the text, and formulate a research question.

THE PHANTOM TOLLBOOTH,
ACT II

Close Read the Text

1. This model—from paragraph 100 of Act II, scene i—shows two sample annotations, along with questions and conclusions. Close read the passage, and find another detail to annotate. Then, write a question and your conclusion.

Close Read
ANNOTATE · QUESTION · CONCLUDE

> **ANNOTATE:** All of these expressions use words related to size or shape but refer to types of feelings or experiences.
>
> **QUESTION:** Why does Dodecahedron refer to feelings or experiences—abstract ideas—as though they can be measured?
>
> **CONCLUDE:** In the world of the play, abstract ideas are concrete and "real."

> **ANNOTATE:** Dodecahedron repeats the words *know* and *knowing.*
>
> **QUESTION:** Why does the playwright have the character repeat these words?
>
> **CONCLUDE:** The repetition emphasizes the importance of knowledge to Dodecahedron.

> **Dodecahedron.** [*Continues shouting angrily.*] If you had high hopes, how would you know how high they were? And did you know that narrow escapes come in different widths? Would you travel the whole world wide without ever knowing how wide it was? And how could you do anything at long last without knowing how long the last was?

🔧 **Tool Kit**
Close-Read Guide and Model Annotation

2. For more practice, go back into the text, and complete the close-read notes.

3. Revisit a section of the text you found important during your first read. Read this section closely, and **annotate** what you notice. Ask yourself **questions** such as "Why did the author make this choice?" What can you **conclude?**

- - - - - - - - - -

Analyze the Text

CITE TEXTUAL EVIDENCE
to support your answers.

📓 Notebook Respond to these questions.

1. **Analyze** How does Dischord end up helping Milo on his quest?

2. **Deduce** How do Milo's solutions for getting the princesses out of the Castle-in-the-Air show his growth since the beginning of the play?

3. **Paraphrase** In your own words, restate Rhyme and Reason's advice to Milo at the end of Act II.

4. **Essential Question:** *Where can imagination lead?* What have you learned about where imagination can lead from reading this play?

≣ STANDARDS
Reading Literature
Analyze how a particular sentence, chapter, scene, or stanza fits into the overall structure of a text and contributes to the development of the theme, setting, or plot.

Analyze Craft and Structure

Dramatic Structures: Stage Directions The script of a play includes both dialogue and stage directions. Lines of dialogue tell readers what the characters say. **Stage directions** are the words in the script that the characters do not say. These directions tell the performers how and where to move and how to speak. They also provide information about scenery, lighting, and sound. Stage directions are usually printed in italics and set in brackets, as in this example.

> **Dodecahedron.** [*Glaring from his upset face.*] Certainly not! They're all the wrong way! Just because you have a choice, it doesn't mean that any of them has to be right. [*Pointing in another direction.*] …

Notice how the stage directions help readers visualize, or picture, the action. They also reveal important information about how characters feel, respond, and behave.

Practice

CITE TEXTUAL EVIDENCE
to support your answers.

📓 **Notebook** **Respond to these questions.**

1. Read the stage directions from Act II that appear in the chart. Explain the information about the characters or action each stage direction provides.

STAGE DIRECTION	INFORMATION PROVIDED
Mathemagician. Sure. [*Opens another door.*] Here it is. It took three carts to carry it here. [*Door reveals an "8" that is as wide as the "3" was high.*]	
Tock. [*Who's been surveying the situation.*] I think I figured a way to get out. Here, hop on my back. [*Milo does so.*] Now, you, Humbug, on top of Milo. [*He does so.*] Now hook your umbrella onto that tree and hold on. [*They climb over Humbug, then pull him up.*]	
Bird. I'm afraid not. I've tried, but the best I can manage to be is a nuisance. [*Suddenly gets nervous as he looks beyond the three.*] And I don't have time to waste with you. [*Starts to leave.*]	

2. **(a)** Identify and mark a point in Act II in which the stage directions are necessary to help you understand what characters are feeling or doing, or what is happening around them. **(b)** Find one place in the play that has no stage directions. Write your own stage directions for that section of the play. Explain how your stage directions make the action more clear.

THE PHANTOM TOLLBOOTH,
ACT II

Concept Vocabulary

suspiciously	pessimistic	insincerity
obstacle	malicious	compromise

Why These Words? The six concept vocabulary words relate to conflict, lack of trust, and feelings of doubt. For example, Milo *suspiciously* asks Dischord to describe the type of doctor he is. Princess Reason tells Rhyme not to be so *pessimistic*. Notice that both words relate to the characters' concerns about another character's honesty or intentions.

1. How does the concept vocabulary sharpen the reader's understanding of the conflict in the play?

2. What other words in the selection connect to this concept?

⚏ **WORD NETWORK**

Add words related to imagination from the text to your Word Network.

Practice

⬡ **Notebook** The concept vocabulary words appear in Act II.

1. With a partner, list as many related words for each concept vocabulary word as you can. For example, for *suspiciously* you might list *suspicious*.

2. For each concept vocabulary word, write a sentence in which you use the word correctly. Include context clues that hint at the meaning of the word.

Word Study

Latin Suffix: *-ity* The Latin suffix *-ity* indicates that a word is a noun. It means "the state or quality of." The word *insincerity,* which appears in Act II of the play, means "the state of being insincere."

1. Use your understanding of the suffix *-ity* to write a definition for the following words: *conformity* and *flexibility*.

2. Identify two other words that end with the suffix *-ity*. For each word, write a definition that demonstrates the meaning of the suffix. Then, consult a dictionary to check your work.

▤ STANDARDS
Language
• Demonstrate command of the conventions of standard English grammar and usage when writing or speaking.
• Use knowledge of language and its conventions when writing, speaking, reading, or listening.
   a. Vary sentence patterns for meaning, reader/listener interest, and style.
• Determine or clarify the meaning of unknown and multiple-meaning words and phrases based on *grade 6 reading and content,* choosing flexibly from a range of strategies.
   b. Use common, grade-appropriate Greek or Latin affixes and roots as clues to the meaning of a word.

Conventions

Sentence Structure Sentences can be classified according to the number and kinds of their clauses. A **clause** is a group of words with its own subject and verb.

An **independent,** or **main, clause** can stand alone as a sentence because it expresses a complete thought. A **dependent,** or **subordinate, clause** cannot stand alone—it depends on the main clause. A dependent clause usually begins with a relative pronoun, such as *who, which,* or *that,* or a subordinating conjunction, such as *because, if,* or *when.* The following chart shows how clauses are used to create three types of sentence structures and gives examples of each from *The Phantom Tollbooth,* Act II.

TIP

CLARIFICATION
Refer to the Grammar Handbook to learn more about these terms.

SIMPLE SENTENCE	COMPOUND SENTENCE	COMPLEX SENTENCE
Definition: a single independent clause	Definition: two or more independent clauses joined by a coordinating conjunction (such as *and, but, or*) or a semicolon	Definition: one independent clause and one or more dependent clauses (In the example, the dependent clauses are underlined.)
EXAMPLE: We want to talk to the Mathemagician.	EXAMPLE: I've been working steadily for a long time now, and I don't feel the least bit tired or hungry.	EXAMPLE: Here in Digitopolis, we have our meals <u>when we're full</u> and eat <u>until we're hungry.</u>

Read It

Mark the independent and dependent clauses. Then, label each sentence as simple, compound, or complex.

1. There are a number of ways to get to Digitopolis, if you follow the directions correctly.
2. All three roads arrive at the same place at the same time.
3. You'll take one spoonful every day, and you'll never hear another beautiful sound again.

Write It

🔲 **Notebook** Read the following example of a simple sentence. Notice that it has been rewritten twice. First, an independent clause was added to make a compound sentence. Then, a dependent clause was added to make a complex sentence. Do the same for sentences 1 and 2.

> **Simple:** Milo fixed the clock.
> **Compound:** Milo fixed the clock, *and he fixed the toy.*
> **Complex:** Milo fixed the clock *because it was broken.*

1. The Mathemagician mines numbers.
2. Rhyme and Reason are prisoners in the Land of Ignorance.

THE PHANTOM TOLLBOOTH,
ACT II

Writing to Sources

Although *The Phantom Tollbooth* is a play, readers see events from Milo's perspective. Rewriting a scene from another character's perspective can help you understand the play in a deeper way.

Assignment

Choose a scene from *The Phantom Tollbooth,* and write a **narrative retelling** from Tock's perspective.

- Reread a scene you found memorable or interesting. Note important details that reveal Tock's personality and reasons for his actions. Use these details to help develop Tock's perspective.

- Present a clear sequence of events for your scene. Remember, however, that you are not writing a script with stage directions. You are retelling the scene as a story.

- Write as if you were Tock. Include dialogue and description to show how Tock feels about other characters and the events taking place.

Vocabulary and Conventions Connection Consider including several of the concept vocabulary words. Also, remember to use a variety of sentence types in your writing.

suspiciously	pessimistic	insincerity
obstacle	malicious	compromise

Reflect on Your Writing

After you have written your retelling, answer the following questions.

1. How did writing from Tock's perspective help you better understand both Tock and Milo?

2. What did you find most difficult about rewriting the scene from Tock's perspective?

3. Why These Words? The words you choose make a difference in your writing. Which words did you specifically choose to add power to your narrative?

STANDARDS

Writing
Write narratives to develop real or imagined experiences or events using effective technique, relevant descriptive details, and well-structured event sequences.
  a. Engage and orient the reader by establishing a context and introducing a narrator and/or characters; organize an event sequence that unfolds naturally and logically.
  b. Use narrative techniques, such as dialogue, pacing, and description, to develop experiences, events, and/or characters.

Speaking and Listening

A dramatic reading of a play is a performance without costumes, scenery, or movement around the stage. The presenters use their voices and gestures to act out the roles and suggest the action.

Assignment

With your class, conduct a **dramatic reading** of a scene from *The Phantom Tollbooth*.

---

1. **Choose a Scene** As a class, decide whether you will all work on the same scene, or whether will have two groups work on two different scenes. Make sure everyone agrees that the scene or scenes you choose are interesting and exciting.

2. **Assign Roles** Decide who will play what roles. If necessary, one person can play more than one role, or you can divide a single role among several people. So, for example, one person might play the role of Milo for a while, and then another student might take over. Also, decide who will read the stage directions.

3. **Review the Scene** Reread the scene carefully to understand the characters' feelings and thoughts and the events taking place. Try out different ways of saying the lines to see which ones work best or create an interesting effect.

4. **Deliver the Dramatic Reading** Act out your role, reading the exact words in the script clearly. Make eye contact with the actor your character is talking to, and use gestures to reflect information in the stage directions. Vary the tone and volume of your voice to express the feelings behind the character's words. If you are reading the stage directions, speak clearly and loudly. Read as a storyteller would, with liveliness and emotion.

5. **Evaluate the Reading** Use an evaluation guide like the one shown to review your class's dramatic readings.

EVALUATION GUIDE

Rate each statement on a scale of 1 (not demonstrated) to 5 (demonstrated).

☐ The performers maintained appropriate eye contact.

☐ The performers delivered their lines clearly and expressively.

☐ The performers used gestures that reflected their characters and the stage directions.

☐ The performers adjusted speaking tone and volume to match their lines.

✎ EVIDENCE LOG

Before moving on to a new selection, go to your Evidence Log and record what you learned from *The Phantom Tollbooth*, Act II.

▦ STANDARDS

Speaking and Listening
Adapt speech to a variety of contexts and tasks, demonstrating command of formal English when indicated or appropriate.

THE PHANTOM
TOLLBOOTH (drama)

Comparing Text to Media

In this lesson, you will look at an image from an animated movie of *The Phantom Tollbooth* and listen to part of an audio performance of the play. You will then compare the image and audio with the text.

from THE PHANTOM
TOLLBOOTH (multimedia)

from The Phantom Tollbooth

Media Vocabulary

The first two concepts will be useful as you listen to the audio. The third will be useful as you evaluate the image from the movie.

stage directions (in audio): important information that is provided by the playwright about the setting, characters, and action	• In an audio-only performance, the stage directions are spoken aloud. • The actor reads the stage directions with expression, just as a storyteller would.
dialogue (in audio): spoken conversation between or among characters	• Most plays are made up mostly of dialogue. • Because actors in an audio performance cannot be seen by listeners, they must use their voices and other clues to make their roles and the story's action clear.
light and shadow (in images): drawing techniques that add depth to an image	• Light and shadow show which parts of an image are in front or behind. • Light and shadow create a mood, or overall feeling, in an image.

First Review MEDIA: MULTIMEDIA

Apply these strategies as you conduct your first review.

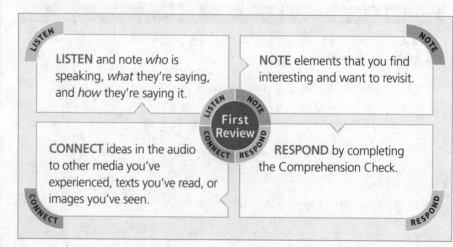

LISTEN and note *who* is speaking, *what* they're saying, and *how* they're saying it.

NOTE elements that you find interesting and want to revisit.

CONNECT ideas in the audio to other media you've experienced, texts you've read, or images you've seen.

RESPOND by completing the Comprehension Check.

First Review

STANDARDS

Reading Literature
By the end of the year, read and comprehend literature, including stories, dramas, and poems, in the grades 6–8 text complexity band proficiently, with scaffolding as needed at the high end of the range.

Language
Acquire and use accurately grade-appropriate general academic and domain-specific words and phrases; gather vocabulary knowledge when considering a word or phrase important to comprehension or expression.

from The Phantom Tollbooth

BACKGROUND
As you study the image and listen to the audio, consider how the experience of reading the play is similar to and different from the experience of viewing and listening to the multimedia.

SCAN FOR
MULTIMEDIA

Comprehension Check

Complete the following items after you finish your first review.

1. Who are the main characters in this scene?

2. Where are the characters going?

3. Whom do the characters meet?

4. What is the setting?

5. 🗐 **Notebook** Write a list of the characters and events featured in the audio performance.

RESEARCH

Research to Explore Choose something that interests you about the audio performance or the movie image, and briefly research it. For example, you might research how an audio production or animated film is made.

THE PHANTOM TOLLBOOTH
(multimedia)

Close Review

Study the image and listen to the audio again. Write any new observations that seem important. What **questions** do you have? What can you **conclude**?

Analyze the Media

Notebook Respond to these questions.

1. (a) Describe the characters shown in the image and the expressions on their faces. (b) **Analyze** What part of the story might this image be showing? Explain your reasoning.

2. **Interpret** In the audio performance, what do Dischord's actions and the tone of his voice show about his personality? Explain.

3. **Essential Question:** *Where can imagination lead?* What have you learned about imagination by watching the video?

LANGUAGE DEVELOPMENT

Media Vocabulary

stage directions	light and shadow
dialogue	

Use these words in your responses to the questions.

1. How would actors recording an audio version of *The Phantom Tollbooth* find stage directions helpful?

2. How does dialogue play an important role in this scene from *The Phantom Tollbooth?*

3. What do you notice about light and shadow in the image from the movie version of *The Phantom Tollbooth*? How would you describe the mood, or feeling, in this image?

WORD NETWORK

Add words related to imagination from the video to your Word Network.

STANDARDS

Speaking and Listening
Interpret information presented in diverse media and formats and explain how it contributes to a topic, text, or issue under study.

Language
Acquire and use accurately grade-appropriate general academic and domain-specific words and phrases; gather vocabulary knowledge when considering a word or phrase important to comprehension or expression.

THE PHANTOM TOLLBOOTH (drama)

from THE PHANTOM TOLLBOOTH
(multimedia)

Writing to Compare

You have read and analyzed *The Phantom Tollbooth*. You have also listened to an excerpt from an audio performance of the play. Now, deepen your understanding of the play by comparing the experience of reading it and listening to it.

Assignment

Write a **comparison-and-contrast essay** in which you talk about what you "see" and "hear" in your mind when you read *The Phantom Tollbooth*. Discuss how reading the play is like or unlike the experience of listening to the audio. Use examples from Act II of the text and the audio excerpt to support your ideas. End by explaining whether you prefer the play or audio performance, and which you think tells the story better.

Prewriting

Analyze the Texts A performance of a play shows how the actors and director interpret the characters and events. As you read the text, you may have imagined the story differently than they did. Use the chart to note similarities and differences between your own imagination and the audio performance.

	SIMILARITIES	DIFFERENCES
my imagination of characters vs. actors' portrayals		
my imagination of settings vs. presentation in the audio		
my imagination of sounds vs. sound effects and music		

📝 **Notebook** Respond to these questions.

1. Did listening to the audio help you picture the action? Or were you better able to imagine events by reading about them?

2. Were the actors' portrayals weak or strong? Why?

Drafting

Review Your Notes Look back at the notes you took during Prewriting. Then, write a statement that summarizes your analysis of the similarities and differences between reading and listening. This statement can serve as your thesis, or main idea.

General Statement/Thesis: _____

_____

Choose a Structure Decide how best to organize your essay. Point-by-point organization and block organization are two commonly used structures. Choose the approach that will help you explain your ideas thoroughly and clearly.

Point-by-Point Organization

I. Main Topic: Characters

   A. How I imagined characters as I read

   B. How characters were portrayed in the audio

II. Main Topic: Settings and Events

   A. How I imagined settings and events as I read

   B. How settings and events were portrayed in the audio

III. Evaluation: Which one I enjoyed more

Block Organization

I. Main Topic: How I imagined the story as I read

   A. Characters

   B. Settings and Events

II. Main Topic: How the audio performance presented the story

   A. Characters

   B. Settings and Events

III. Evaluation: Which one I enjoyed more

Review, Revise, and Edit

Use the following checklist to review, revise, and edit your draft.

☐ Did you include details and examples from the text and media?

☐ Did you organize your essay effectively?

☐ Did you review your essay and fix any grammar or spelling errors?

✎ EVIDENCE LOG

Before moving on to a new selection, go to your Evidence Log and record what you learned from the image and audio performance of *The Phantom Tollbooth*.

☰ STANDARDS

Reading Literature
Compare and contrast the experience of reading a story, drama, or poem to listening to or viewing an audio, video, or live version of the text, including contrasting what they "see" and "hear" when reading the text to what they perceive when they listen or watch.

Writing
Write informative/explanatory texts to examine a topic and convey ideas, concepts, and information through the selection, organization, and analysis of relevant content.
  a. Introduce a topic; organize ideas, concepts, and information, using strategies such as definition, classification, comparison/contrast, and cause/effect; include formatting, graphics, and multimedia when useful to aiding comprehension.

Speaking and Listening
Interpret information presented in diverse media and formats and explain how it contributes to a topic, text, or issue under study.

WRITING TO SOURCES

- THE PHANTOM TOLLBOOTH (drama)

- *from* THE PHANTOM TOLLBOOTH (multimedia)

🔧 **Tool Kit**
Student Model of a
Fictional Narrative

ACADEMIC VOCABULARY

As you craft your argument, consider using some of the academic vocabulary you learned in the beginning of the unit.

perspective

transform

novelty

consequently

inspire

≡ **STANDARDS**

Writing
- Write narratives to develop real or imagined experiences or events using effective technique, relevant descriptive details, and well-structured event sequences.
- Write routinely over extended time frames and shorter time frames for a range of discipline-specific tasks, purposes, and audiences.

Write a Fictional Narrative

You have read the play *The Phantom Tollbooth* and viewed media versions of the same story. In this imaginary land, Milo encounters all sorts of strange and magical creatures. After dodging demons and rescuing princesses, the boy learns that to find adventure, he simply has to notice his surroundings—and use his imagination.

Assignment

Think about the characters whose adventures unfold in *The Phantom Tollbooth*. Then, use your own imagination to write a new **short story** about one or more of those characters. Use this sentence opener to start your new tale:

> One day in the Kingdom of Wisdom, . . .

Your story should describe an imaginary setting, include interesting characters, and tell events in a clear order.

Elements of a Fictional Narrative

A **fictional narrative** is a story based on characters and events from the writer's imagination. Fictional narratives entertain, explore ideas, or send a message about life.

An effective fictional narrative includes these elements:

- a plot, or sequence of events, that make up the action of the story
- chronological order, or the order in which events occur in time
- a central conflict, or problem, that is introduced, developed, and resolved by the end of the story
- one main character, or *protagonist*, who faces and learns from a conflict
- a few minor characters who add interest to the story and help move the action along
- dialogue, or conversations between characters
- a clear setting, or the time and place in which the story occurs
- a clear point of view or perspective from which the story is told

Because a fictional narrative is brief, writers choose precise, or specific, words, and craft each element carefully.

Model Fictional Narrative For a model of a well-crafted fictional narrative, see the Launch Text, "The Great Universal Undo."

Challenge yourself to find all of the elements of an effective fictional narrative in the text. You will have an opportunity to review these elements as you prepare to write your own fictional narrative.

LAUNCH TEXT

The Great Universal Undo

Prewriting/Planning

Create a Story Map Reread the assignment. Brainstorm for ideas for characters, setting, and conflict. Remember that your narrative should feature an imaginative setting and interesting characters. Record your ideas in this chart.

CHARACTERS	SETTING	CONFLICT
Who the main character is and what the character is like:	Where the story takes place:	What the main problem is in the story:
Who the minor characters are and their role in the story:	When the story takes place:	How it is resolved:

Gather Details As you plan your story, gather important details that help your readers picture and understand how your characters look and act, where the characters are, and what they say and do. Include the following:

- **precise words:** specific words and phrases establish a clear description of characters and events
- **dialogue:** characters' conversations help move the action along. Dialogue also shows readers how the characters think, feel, and get along
- **sensory details:** words that describe how things look, sound, feel, taste, and smell help readers picture the setting and characters in the story

EVIDENCE LOG

Review your Evidence Log and identify key details you may want to cite in your fictional narrative.

STANDARDS

Writing
Write narratives to develop real or imagined experiences or events using effective technique, relevant descriptive details, and well-structured event sequences.
  b. Use narrative techniques, such as dialogue, pacing, and description, to develop experiences, events, and/or characters.
  d. Use precise words and phrases, relevant descriptive details, and sensory language to convey experiences and events.

Drafting

Develop Your Plot Use a plot diagram like the one shown to organize the sequence of events in your fictional narrative. Make sure the events follow a clear chronological, or time, order that moves smoothly from one event to the next. The plot diagram here shows key events in the Launch Text. The story follows this common plot pattern:

- The exposition introduces the characters and the conflict.
- The conflict develops during the rising action.
- The rising action leads to the climax, or point of greatest tension.
- In the falling action, events and emotions should slow down.
- In the resolution, the conflict is resolved, and loose ends are tied up.

Climax: Mrs. Bieberman explains that her son Tommy likes to play video games. She gives Tommy a cookie after he demands one.

Rising Action: Alexander tries the invention again, but something goes wrong.

Falling Action: Alexander is aware of a *tap tapping* sound as the scene with Tommy and the cookie is repeated.

Rising Action: Alexander tests his invention on Mrs. Bieberman and finds that it works.

Falling Action: Alexander realizes that Tommy has also invented the Undo.

Exposition: Alexander and his invention, the Undo, are described.

Resolution: Alexander's hunch is confirmed when Tommy looks at him and taps the screen to get another cookie.

STANDARDS

Writing
Write narratives to develop real or imagined experiences or events using effective technique, relevant descriptive details, and well-structured event sequences.
  a. Engage and orient the reader by establishing a context and introducing a narrator and/or characters; organize an event sequence that unfolds naturally and logically.
  e. Provide a conclusion that follows from the narrated experiences or events.

Write a First Draft Use your plot diagram to write your first draft. Review the elements of fictional narrative writing, as well as the story map you developed in the Prewriting/Planning section As you draft the plot events, be sure each event builds on the one before it and moves the plot toward the resolution of the conflict. The **conclusion** of your narrative should logically follow the events in the plot.

Establish Point of View Tell your story from a single point of view. Choose one of the following:

- In **first-person point of view,** your character is the one telling the story. Use first-person pronouns, such as *I, me, we,* and *us.*
- In **third-person point of view,** the story is told by a narrator who is not in the story. Use pronouns such as *he, she, they*, and *them.*

LANGUAGE DEVELOPMENT

Conventions: Combining Sentences for Variety

To add variety to your sentences and to avoid unnecessary repetition, include prepositional phrases, appositive phrases, participial phrases, and gerund phrases.

PHRASE	USE	EXAMPLE
prepositional phrase	as an adjective or as an adverb	The girl in the blue pants is my cousin. (adjective) I walked around the barrier to cross the street. (adverb)
appositive phrase	as a noun phrase	Winnie, the volleyball player, hugged him.
participial phrase	as an adjective	Skipping happily we laughed.
gerund phrase	as a noun	Washing clothes is necessary.

Read It

These sentences from the Launch Text reflect a variety of sentence patterns.

- **Making a working model** *was simple.* (gerund phrase)
- *That's how Alexander Dillahunt got it* **into his head** *to create the Universal Undo.* (prepositional phrase)
- *He paused,* **waiting for a response.** (participial phrase)
- *He'd read all about multiple discovery—***the idea that most inventions are made by a number of different people in different places at the same time.** (appositive phrase)

Write It

As you draft your fictional narrative, use a variety of sentence patterns. This chart provides ways to combine your sentences for variety.

ORIGINAL	ADD VARIETY	REVISION
They ate dinner. They went to bed.	Use a participial phrase.	Having eaten dinner, they went to bed.
The leaves fell. The ground was frozen.	Use a prepositional phrase.	The leaves fell onto the frozen ground.
The boy was a skilled soccer player. He was five years old.	Use an appositive phrase.	The boy, a skilled soccer player, was five years old.
We'd have to work all night. It seemed inevitable.	Use a gerund phrase.	Working all night seemed inevitable.

::: STANDARDS

Language
- Demonstrate command of the conventions of standard English grammar and usage when writing or speaking.
- Use knowledge of language and its conventions when writing, speaking, reading, or listening.
  a. Vary sentence patterns for meaning, reader/listener interest, and style.

Revising

Evaluating Your Draft

Use the following checklist to evaluate the effectiveness of your first draft. Then, use your evaluation and the instruction on this page to guide your revision.

FOCUS AND ORGANIZATION	EVIDENCE AND ELABORATION	CONVENTIONS
☐ Provides an introduction that establishes a setting and a clear point of view.	☐ Effectively uses pacing to create interest and tension in the story.	☐ Uses complete sentences and correct grammar and spelling.
☐ Presents a clear plot in chronological order.	☐ Uses sensory details and precise, descriptive language.	☐ Uses different sentence patterns for variety.
☐ Develops an interesting conflict.	☐ Uses dialogue to advance the plot and develop characters.	
☐ Provides a conclusion that follows from the narrative and resolves or wraps up the conflict.	☐ Uses transition words to signal shifts from one time frame or setting to another.	

🖧 WORD NETWORK

Include interesting words from your Word Network in your fictional narrative.

📇 STANDARDS

Writing
Write narratives to develop real or imagined experiences or events using effective technique, relevant descriptive details, and well-structured event sequences.
a. Engage and orient the reader by establishing a context and introducing a narrator and/or characters; organize an event sequence that unfolds naturally and logically.
b. Use narrative techniques, such as dialogue, pacing, and description, to develop experiences, events, and/or characters.
c. Use a variety of transition words, phrases, and clauses to convey sequence and signal shifts from one time frame or setting to another.

Revising for Focus and Organization

Evaluate Point of View and Character Development Check that the point of view you chose remains the same throughout the narrative. Have you written from a single point of view—either from a participant (first-person point of view) or an observer (third-person point of view)? How specific are your descriptions of your characters' appearances and personalities? Have you used dialogue to give your readers a strong sense of the characters and to move the plot forward?

Revising for Evidence and Elaboration

Make Logical Connections Between Events Review your narrative. Are the major events in your narrative clearly connected? If you cannot think of a clear connection between events, delete or revise one of the events. Use transitional words, phrases, and clauses, such as *meanwhile, back in Digitopolis*, and *while they were away*, to help show a shift in time or setting.

Adjust the Pacing Check the pacing, or the speed at which the action happens. Writers use pacing to keep readers engaged and create a desired effect. For example, speed up the pacing to build suspense. To create mystery, slow down the action.

PEER REVIEW

Exchange stories with a classmate. Use the checklist to evaluate your classmate's short story and provide supportive feedback.

1. Are the point of view and setting clear, and are the characters well developed through dialogue?

☐ yes ☐ no   If no, suggest how the writer might improve them.

2. Do the events in the plot unfold naturally and in chronological, or time, order?

☐ yes ☐ no   If no, explain what confused you.

3. Does the story's ending flow naturally from the events that came earlier?

☐ yes ☐ no   If no, tell what you think might be missing.

4. What is the strongest part of your classmate's short story? Why?

_____

_____

_____

Editing and Proofreading

Edit for Conventions Reread your draft for accuracy and consistency. Correct errors in grammar and word usage. Make sure to include a variety of sentence patterns to convey ideas clearly and keep readers engaged in your narrative.

Proofread for Accuracy Read your draft carefully, looking for errors in spelling and punctuation. Make sure that the dialogue is properly enclosed by quotation marks and that end punctuation is inside the closing quotation mark. Also, check that the speaker tag, which tells who is saying the quotation, is separated from the quotation by a comma.

Publishing and Presenting

Create a final version of your short story. Share it with your class. As you and your classmates exchange stories read each other's writing and make polite and respectful comments. Consider how each writer developed his or her plot and used techniques such as pacing, description, and dialogue. Think about how each writer introduced and resolved the main conflict, and compare it to your story.

Reflecting

Think about what you learned by writing your short story. What could you do differently the next time you write a short story to make it clearer and more interesting? What was the most difficult part of writing your short story?

⠿ STANDARDS
Writing
With some guidance and support from peers and adults, develop and strengthen writing as needed by planning, revising, editing, rewriting, or trying a new approach.

ESSENTIAL QUESTION:

Where can imagination lead?

Imagination can lead to new hobbies and new interests—even new adventures. You will read selections that examine how fictional characters and real-life people use their imaginations to face challenges and explore new worlds. You will work in a group to continue your exploration of the concept of imagination.

Small-Group Learning Strategies

Throughout your life, in school, in your community, and in your career, you will continue to learn and work with others.

Look at these strategies and the actions you can take to practice them as you work in teams. Add ideas of your own for each step. Use these strategies during Small-Group Learning.

STRATEGY	ACTION PLAN
Prepare	• Complete your assignments so that you are prepared for group work. • Organize your thinking so you can contribute to your group's discussion. •
Participate fully	• Make eye contact to signal that you are listening and taking in what is being said. • Use text evidence when making a point. •
Support others	• Build on ideas from others in your group. • Invite others who have not yet spoken to do so. •
Clarify	• Paraphrase the ideas of others to ensure that your understanding is correct. • Ask follow-up questions. •

SCAN FOR
MULTIMEDIA

CONTENTS

PERFORMANCE TASK

SPEAKING AND LISTENING FOCUS
Perform a Fictional Narrative
The Small-Group readings focus on the role imagination plays in both fictional
stories and real life situations. After reading, your group will write and perform a
fictional narrative in which you use your imagination to create a new adventure for a
familiar character.

Working as a Team

1. **Take a Position** In your group, discuss the following question:

   Can imaginary adventures be as important as real adventures?

   As you take turns sharing your positions, be sure to provide reasons for your choice. After all group members have shared, discuss some specific examples of real and imaginary adventures that support each position.

2. **List Your Rules** As a group, decide on the rules that you will follow as you work together. Two examples are provided; add two more rules of your own. You may add or revise rules based on your experience together.

   • Everyone should participate in group discussions.

   • People should not interrupt.

   • _____

     _____

   • _____

     _____

3. **Apply the Rules** Practice working as a group. Share what you have learned about imagination. Make sure each person in the group contributes. Take notes, and be prepared to share with the class one thing that you heard from another member of your group.

4. **Name Your Group** Choose a name that reflects the unit topic.

   Our group's name: _____

5. **Create a Communication Plan** Decide how you want to communicate with one another. For example, you might use online collaboration tools, email, or instant messaging.

   Our group's decision: _____

   _____

Making a Schedule

First, find out the due dates for the Small-Group activities. Then, preview the texts and activities with your group, and make a schedule for completing the tasks.

SELECTION	ACTIVITIES	DUE DATE
from Alice's Adventures in Wonderland		
Jabberwocky		
The Importance of Imagination		

Working on Group Projects

As your group works together, you'll find it more effective if each person has a specific role. Different projects require different roles. Before beginning a project, discuss the necessary roles and choose one for each group member. Here are some possible roles; add your own ideas.

Project Manager: monitors the schedule and keeps everyone on task

Researcher: organizes research activities

Recorder: takes notes during group meetings

_____

_____

_____

_____

_____

SCAN FOR
MULTIMEDIA

About the Author

Lewis Carroll (1832–1898) Charles Lutwidge Dodgson was a professor of mathematics and a talented photographer. Today, he is best remembered for two children's books he wrote under the pen name Lewis Carroll: *Alice's Adventures in Wonderland* (1865) and its sequel, *Through the Looking-Glass* (1871). Huge bestsellers almost from the moment they appeared, the Alice books have been the basis of numerous stage plays and films.

from Alice's Adventures in Wonderland

Concept Vocabulary

As you perform your first read of this excerpt from *Alice's Adventures in Wonderland*, you will encounter these words.

> peeped   wondered   curiosity

Context Clues To find the meaning of an unfamiliar word, look for clues in the context, which is made up of the words and phrases that surround the unknown word in a text. Here are two examples of how to use context clues to determine meaning:

> **Synonyms:** He **stumbled**, or tripped, over a toy that had been left on the floor.
>
> **Restatement of an Idea:** Tasha was **unaccompanied** in the empty room and felt lonely sitting by herself.

Apply your knowledge of context clues and other vocabulary strategies to determine the meanings of unfamiliar words you encounter during your first read.

First Read FICTION

Apply these strategies as you conduct your first read. You will have an opportunity to complete a close read after your first read.

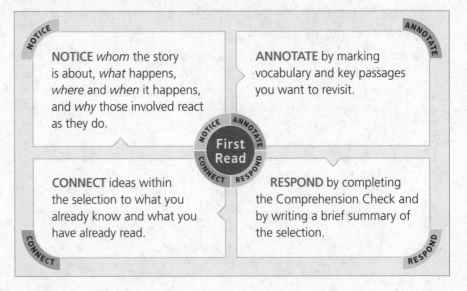

NOTICE *whom* the story is about, *what* happens, *where* and *when* it happens, and *why* those involved react as they do.

ANNOTATE by marking vocabulary and key passages you want to revisit.

CONNECT ideas within the selection to what you already know and what you have already read.

RESPOND by completing the Comprehension Check and by writing a brief summary of the selection.

:≡ STANDARDS

Reading Literature
By the end of the year, read and comprehend literature, including stories, dramas, and poems, in the grades 6–8 text complexity band proficiently, with scaffolding as needed at the high end of the range.

Language
Determine or clarify the meaning of unknown and multiple-meaning words and phrases based *on grade 6 reading and content,* choosing flexibly from a range of strategies.
  a. Use context as a clue to the meaning of a word or phrase.

from
Alice's Adventures in Wonderland

Lewis Carroll

BACKGROUND

In 1862, a shy English mathematician entertained his colleague's three young daughters by taking them on a boat trip. As they rowed down the River Thames, he decided to tell them a story, making it up as he went along. Afterwards, one of them, a 10-year-old girl named Alice Liddell, loved his story so much that she begged him to write it down. This "golden afternoon," as Lewis Carroll called it, was the inspiration for his novel *Alice's Adventures in Wonderland*.

SCAN FOR MULTIMEDIA

Chapter 1. Down the Rabbit-Hole

1   Alice was beginning to get very tired of sitting by her sister on the bank, and of having nothing to do: once or twice she had **peeped** into the book her sister was reading, but it had no pictures or conversations in it, "and what is the use of a book," thought Alice, "without pictures or conversation?"

x

NOTES

Mark context clues or indicate another strategy you used to help you determine meaning.

peeped (peept) *v.*

MEANING:

wondered (WUHN uhrd) *v.*

MEANING:

curiosity (kyoo ree OS uh tee) *n.*

MEANING:

2   So she was considering in her own mind (as well as she could, for the hot day made her feel very sleepy and stupid), whether the pleasure of making a daisy-chain\would be worth the trouble of getting up and picking the daisies, when suddenly a White Rabbit with pink eyes ran close by her.

3   There was nothing so *very* remarkable in that; nor did Alice think it so very much out of the way to hear the Rabbit say to itself, "Oh dear! Oh dear! I shall be late!" (when she thought it over afterwards, it occurred to her that she ought to have **wondered** at this, but at the time it all seemed quite natural); but when the Rabbit actually *took a watch out of its waistcoat-pocket,* and looked at it, and then hurried on, Alice started to her feet, for it flashed across her mind that she had never before seen a rabbit with either a waistcoat-pocket, or a watch to take out of it, and burning with **curiosity,** she ran across the field after it, and fortunately was just in time to see it pop down a large rabbit-hole under the hedge.

4   In another moment down went Alice after it, never once considering how in the world she was to get out again.

5   The rabbit-hole went straight on like a tunnel for some way, and then dipped suddenly down, so suddenly that Alice had not a moment to think about stopping herself before she found herself falling down a very deep well.

6   Either the well was very deep, or she fell very slowly, for she had plenty of time as she went down to look about her and to wonder what was going to happen next. First, she tried to look down and make out what she was coming to, but it was too dark to see anything; then she looked at the sides of the well, and noticed that they were filled with cupboards and book-shelves; here and there she saw maps and pictures hung upon pegs. She took down a jar from one of the shelves as she passed; it was labeled "ORANGE MARMALADE," but to her great disappointment it was empty: she did not like to drop the jar for fear of killing somebody, so managed to put it into one of the cupboards as she fell past it.

7   "Well!" thought Alice to herself, "after such a fall as this, I shall think nothing of tumbling down stairs! How brave they'll all think me at home! Why, I wouldn't say anything about it, even if I fell off the top of the house!" (Which was very likely true.)

8   Down, down, down. Would the fall *never* come to an end! "I wonder how many miles I've fallen by this time?" she said aloud. "I must be getting somewhere near the center of the earth. Let me see: that would be four thousand miles down, I think—" (for, you see, Alice had learned several things of this sort in her

lessons in the schoolroom, and though this was not a very good opportunity for showing off her knowledge, as there was no one to listen to her, still it was good practice to say it over) "—yes, that's about the right distance—but then I wonder what Latitude or Longitude I've got to?" (Alice had no idea what Latitude was, or Longitude either, but thought they were nice grand words to say.)

9   Presently she began again. "I wonder if I shall fall right *through* the earth! How funny it'll seem to come out among the people that walk with their heads downward! The Antipathies,[1] I think—" (she was rather glad there *was* no one listening, this time, as it didn't sound at all the right word)"—but I shall have to ask them what the name of the country is, you know. Please, Ma'am, is this New Zealand or Australia?" (and she tried to curtsey as she spoke—fancy *curtseying* as you're falling through the air! Do you think you could manage it?) "And what an ignorant little girl she'll think me for asking! No, it'll never do to ask: perhaps I shall see it written up somewhere."

10   Down, down, down. There was nothing else to do, so Alice soon began talking again. "Dinah'll miss me very much tonight, I should think!" (Dinah was the cat.) "'I hope they'll remember her saucer of milk at tea time. Dinah my dear! I wish you were down here with me! There are no mice in the air, I'm afraid, but you might catch a bat, and that's very like a mouse, you know. But do cats eat bats, I wonder?" And here Alice began to get rather sleepy, and went on saying to herself, in a dreamy sort of way, "Do cats eat bats? Do cats eat bats?" and sometimes, "Do bats eat cats?" for, you see, as she couldn't answer either question, it didn't much matter which way she put it. She felt that she was dozing off, and had just begun to dream that she was walking hand in hand with Dinah, and saying to her very earnestly, "Now, Dinah, tell me the truth: did you ever eat a bat?" when suddenly, thump! thump! down she came upon a heap of sticks and dry leaves, and the fall was over.

11   Alice was not a bit hurt, and she jumped up on to her feet in a moment: she looked up, but it was all dark overhead; before her was another long passage, and the White Rabbit was still in sight, hurrying down it. There was not a moment to be lost: away went Alice like the wind, and was just in time to hear it say, as it turned a corner, "Oh my ears and whiskers, how late it's getting!" She was close behind it when she turned the corner, but the Rabbit was no longer to be seen: she found herself in a long, low hall, which was lit up by a row of lamps hanging from the roof.

---

1. **The Antipathies** (an TIHP uh theez) Alice is trying to think of the word *Antipodes* (an TIHP uh deez), a name used by people in the northern hemisphere to refer to New Zealand and Australia.

12   There were doors all round the hall, but they were all locked; and when Alice had been all the way down one side and up the other, trying every door, she walked sadly down the middle, wondering how she was ever to get out again.

13   Suddenly she came upon a little three-legged table, all made of solid glass; there was nothing on it except a tiny golden key, and Alice's first thought was that it might belong to one of the doors of the hall; but, alas! either the locks were too large, or the key was too small, but at any rate it would not open any of them.

14   However, on the second time round, she came upon a low curtain she had not noticed before, and behind it was a little door about fifteen inches high: she tried the little golden key in the lock, and to her great delight it fitted!

15   Alice opened the door and found that it led into a small passage, not much larger than a rat-hole: she knelt down and looked along the passage into the loveliest garden you ever saw. How she longed to get out of that dark hall, and wander about among those beds of bright flowers and those cool fountains, but she could not even get her head though the doorway; "and even if my head would go through," thought poor Alice, "it would be of very little use without my shoulders. Oh, how I wish I could shut up like a telescope! I think I could, if I only know how to begin." For, you see, so many out-of-the-way things had happened lately, that Alice had begun to think that very few things indeed were really impossible. ❧

Comprehension Check

Complete the following items after you finish your first read. Review and clarify details with your group.

1. Why does Alice decide to follow the Rabbit?

2. What does Alice see in the well?

3. What is at the bottom of the well?

4. What is the purpose of the tiny golden key?

5. Why does Alice wish she was able to "shut up like a telescope"?

6. **⊟ Notebook** Write a summary of the excerpt from *Alice's Adventures in Wonderland* to confirm your understanding of the selection.

- -

RESEARCH

Research to Clarify Choose at least one unfamiliar detail from the text. Briefly research that detail. In what way does the information you learned shed light on an aspect of the story? Share your findings with your group.

Research to Explore Choose something that interested you from the text, and formulate a research question you might use to find out more about it.

from ALICE'S ADVENTURES IN
WONDERLAND

Close Read the Text

With your group, revisit sections of the text you marked
during your first read. **Annotate** details that you notice.
What **questions** do you have? What can you **conclude**?

- -

Analyze the Text

CITE TEXTUAL EVIDENCE
to support your answers.

📓 **Notebook** Complete the activities.

1. **Review and Clarify** With your group, reread paragraphs 6–10 of the
   excerpt. How do the details about what Alice is seeing and thinking
   help you to picture her experience as she falls?

2. **Present and Discuss** Discuss what you noticed in the selection, what
   questions you asked, and what conclusions you reached.

3. **Essential Question:** *Where can imagination lead?* What has this
   excerpt taught you about imagination? Discuss with your group.

WORD NETWORK

Add words related to
imagination from the text
to your Word Network.

LANGUAGE DEVELOPMENT

Concept Vocabulary

peeped   wondered   curiosity

Why These Words? The three concept vocabulary words from the
text are related. With your group, determine what the words have in
common. Write your ideas down, and add another word that relates to
this concept.

Practice

📓 **Notebook** Confirm your understanding of the words from the text
by using them in a paragraph about Alice's imagination. Be sure to use
context clues that hint at each word's meaning.

Word Study

Word Relationships Understanding the relationship between two
words can help you better understand each of the words. For example,
the three concept vocabulary words have a cause-and-effect relationship.
A person's *curiosity* may have caused him or her to have *wondered* about
something and then *peeped* to learn more.

Work with your group to determine the relationship in each of these
pairs of words: *elephant/vertebrate, state/republic, quench/thirst.* Consult
a dictionary if you are unsure of a word's meaning.

Analyze Craft and Structure

Characterization Authors develop characters and reveal their personalities, or character traits, through the process of **characterization.** There are two types of characterization: **direct characterization** and **indirect characterization.**

	DEFINITION	EXAMPLE
Direct Characterization	The author directly states or describes what a character is like.	Fernando is friendly.
Indirect Characterization	The author reveals a character's personality through his or her words and actions and through the thoughts, words, and actions of others.	Fernando smiled warmly and asked the new girl, "Do you want to join my friends and me for lunch?"

When an author uses indirect characterization, readers must **make inferences,** or educated guesses, about the characters based on details in the text. To make an inference, analyze the details the author provides about a character and decide what the details suggest about the character's personality.

Practice

CITE TEXTUAL EVIDENCE
to support your answers.

Work individually to analyze the passages from the excerpt identified in the chart. Use the chart to record your notes. First, decide whether the passage is an example of direct characterization or indirect characterization. Then, determine what the passage reveals about the character. Gather your notes and share them with your group.

SELECTION PASSAGE	TYPE OF CHARACTERIZATION	WHAT YOU LEARN ABOUT THE CHARACTER
Alice was beginning to get very tired of sitting by her sister on the bank, and of having nothing to do . . . (paragraph 1)		
In another moment down went Alice after it, never once considering how in the world she was to get out again. (paragraph 4)		
. . . [Alice] did not like to drop the jar for fear of killing somebody, so managed to put it into one of the cupboards as she fell past it. (paragraph 6)		

from ALICE'S ADVENTURES IN WONDERLAND

Conventions

Conjunctions and Interjections Writers improve the flow of their writing by using **conjunctions** to connect sentence parts and show the relationships between or among those parts. **Coordinating conjunctions** are used to connect sentence parts that are of equal importance. Here are some examples.

COORDINATING CONJUNCTIONS	EXAMPLE SENTENCE
and, or, but, nor, for, yet, so	The show was sold out, **yet** there were dozens of people waiting in line.

Notice that in the example sentence, the conjunction *yet* is preceded by a comma. A conjunction that joins two independent clauses is always preceded by a comma.

Any word, phrase, or sound that expresses a sudden feeling is called an **interjection.** Writers use interjections to add liveliness and a sense of realism to their work. Here are some examples:

EXAMPLES OF INTERJECTIONS	EXAMPLE SENTENCES
ah, aha, whoa, hey, oh no, oops, shh, well, wow, whew	**Oops**, I dropped the plate! **Oh no!** I forgot my homework.

In some cases, an interjection is followed by an exclamation mark. In other cases, an interjection may be followed by a comma, and an exclamation mark may appear at the end of the sentence.

Read It

Work individually to correctly label the coordinating conjunctions or interjections in each sentence from *Alice's Adventures in Wonderland*.

1. Oh, how I wish I could shut up like a telescope!

2. There was nothing else to do, so Alice soon began talking again.

3. "Well!" thought Alice to herself, "after such a fall as this, I shall think nothing of tumbling down stairs!"

Write It

Notebook Write a brief paragraph about an imaginary adventure. Use at least two coordinating conjunctions and two interjections in your paragraph. Then, exchange paragraphs with a group member, and label the conjunctions and interjections in your classmate's paragraph.

STANDARDS

Language
• Demonstrate command of the conventions of standard English grammar and usage when writing or speaking.
• Demonstrate command of the conventions of standard English capitalization, punctuation, and spelling when writing.

Research

> ## Assignment
>
> Since its publication in 1865, the characters from *Alice's Adventures in Wonderland* have been reimagined in various ways through illustrations as well as in movies. Work with your group to write a **research report** on one of the following topics:
>
> ☐ how Alice is portrayed in illustrated and animated versions of *Alice's Adventures in Wonderland,* including how these portrayals have changed over the years
>
> ☐ how Alice is portrayed in live-action movie versions of *Alice's Adventures in Wonderland,* including how these portrayals have changed over the years

Conduct Research As a group, choose your topic. Conduct research to find both textual information as well as illustrations, image stills, and other visuals to include in your report. Be sure to consult several credible print and digital sources, and record the bibliographic information for each source you use. Bibliographic information includes the title, author, and date of publication; if you are using an Internet source, you should also note the Web site address and date you accessed the information. Use this chart to keep track of your sources and the information you found in each.

SOURCE (INCLUDING BIBLIOGRAPHIC INFORMATION)	INFORMATION OR IMAGE OBTAINED FROM SOURCE

Write Your Report Work with your group to organize the information and images from your research into a report. Try different ways of sequencing the images in your report so that they highlight your main points. Each image should help readers to better understand the information you communicate in writing.

Cite Your Sources When you credit a source, you tell readers where you found your information and give them the bibliographic details necessary for locating the source themselves. Presenting someone else's ideas, research, or opinion as your own, even if you use different words, is **plagiarism**—the equivalent of academic stealing. To avoid plagiarism, review your report to be sure you have properly cited your sources, both within the text of your report and with a Works Cited list at the end. There are many different formats for citing sources; ask your teacher which one you should use in your report.

✍ EVIDENCE LOG

Before moving on to a new selection, go to your Evidence Log, and record what you learned from *Alice's Adventures in Wonderland.*

≣ STANDARDS

Writing
- Write informative/explanatory texts to examine a topic and convey ideas, concepts, and information through the selection, organization, and analysis of relevant content.
  a. Introduce a topic; organize ideas, concepts, and information, using strategies such as definition, classification, comparison/contrast, and cause/effect; include formatting, graphics, and multimedia when useful to aiding comprehension.
- Conduct short research projects to answer a question, drawing on several sources and refocusing the inquiry when appropriate.
- Gather relevant information from multiple print and digital sources; assess the credibility of each source; and quote or paraphrase the data and conclusions of others while avoiding plagiarism and providing basic bibliographic information for sources.

About the Poet

Lewis Carroll (1832–1898) is the pen name of Charles Lutwidge Dodgson, who was a British mathematics professor at Oxford University. Under his pen name, Dodgson wrote *Alice's Adventures in Wonderland* and *Through the Looking-Glass*. Like these classic novels, his poems are noted for their clever wordplay and delightfully zany word choices.

Jabberwocky

Concept Vocabulary

As you perform your first read of "Jabberwocky," you will encounter these words.

beware	foe	slain

Context Clues If these words are unfamiliar to you, try using context clues to help you determine their meanings. **Context clues** are other words and phrases that appear in nearby text. Even if you cannot figure out a word's exact definition, you can usually determine its part of speech—whether it is a noun, a verb, an adjective, or an adverb. Here is an example of how to apply this strategy.

> **Context:** The captain countermanded the directive of the officer.
>
> **Analysis:** It is difficult to tell exactly what the underlined words mean. However, the word *countermanded* ends in *-ed* and follows the subject of the sentence, *captain*. *Countermanded* must be a verb. Similarly, the word *directive* is in between the article *the* and the preposition *of*. *Directive* must be a noun.

In the poem you are about to read, you will encounter a number of invented words. These are words that the poet made up, so you will not find them in a dictionary. You may not be able to determine exactly what they mean, but you can use context clues to figure out their parts of speech.

First Read POETRY

Apply these strategies as you conduct your first read. You will have an opportunity to complete a close read after your first read.

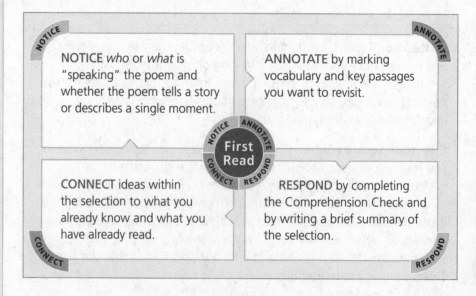

NOTICE *who* or *what* is "speaking" the poem and whether the poem tells a story or describes a single moment.

ANNOTATE by marking vocabulary and key passages you want to revisit.

First Read

CONNECT ideas within the selection to what you already know and what you have already read.

RESPOND by completing the Comprehension Check and by writing a brief summary of the selection.

⬛ STANDARDS

Reading Literature
By the end of the year, read and comprehend literature, including stories, dramas, and poems, in the grades 6–8 text complexity band proficiently, with scaffolding as needed at the high end of the range.
Language
Determine or clarify the meaning of unknown and multiple-meaning words and phrases based on *grade 6 reading and content*, choosing flexibly from a range of strategies.
    a. Use context as a clue to the meaning of a word or phrase.

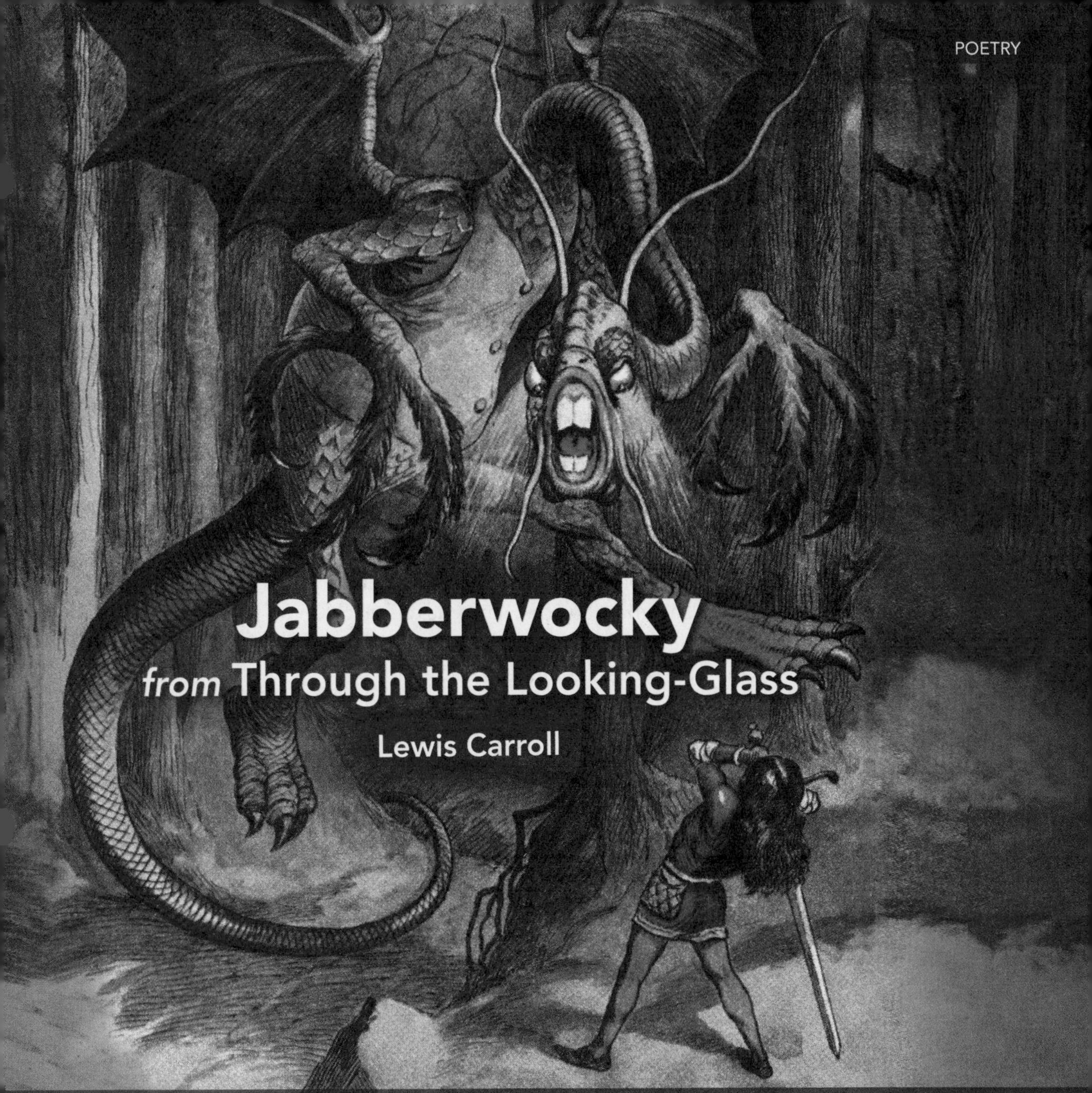

Jabberwocky
from Through the Looking-Glass

Lewis Carroll

SCAN FOR
MULTIMEDIA

BACKGROUND

In the first chapter of *Through the Looking-Glass*, the sequel to *Alice's Adventures in Wonderland*, Alice encounters a creature called a Jabberwock. Many of the invented words in Carroll's imaginative poem are made up of two different words. For example, *brillig* is a combination of *brilliant* and *broiling*.

NOTES

'Twas brillig, and the slithy toves
   Did gyre and gimble in the wabe;
All mimsy were the borogoves,
   And the mome raths outgrabe.

NOTES

Mark context clues or indicate another strategy you used to help you determine meaning.

beware (bee WAIR) *v.*

MEANING:

foe (foh) *n.*

MEANING:

slain (slayn) *v.*

MEANING:

5 "**Beware** the Jabberwock, my son!
    The jaws that bite, the claws that catch!
Beware the Jubjub bird, and shun
    The frumious Bandersnatch!"

He took his vorpal sword in hand;
10   Long time the manxome **foe** he sought—
So rested he by the Tumtum tree
    And stood awhile in thought.

And, as in uffish thought he stood,
    The Jabberwock, with eyes of flame,
15 Came whiffling through the tulgey wood,
    And burbled as it came!

One, two! One, two! And through and through
    The vorpal blade went snicker-snack!
He left it dead, and with its head
20   He went galumphing back.

"And hast thou **slain** the Jabberwock?
    Come to my arms, my beamish boy!
O frabjous day! Callooh! Callay!"
    He chortled in his joy.

25 'Twas brillig, and the slithy toves
    Did gyre and gimble in the wabe;
All mimsy were the borogoves,
    And the mome raths outgrabe.

MEDIA CONNECTION

Alice in Wonderland (1983)—Jabberwocky

💬 **Discuss It** How does listening to Alice read "Jabberwocky" in the video help you to better understand the poem?

Write your response before sharing your ideas.

SCAN FOR MULTIMEDIA

Comprehension Check

Complete the following items after you finish your first read. Review and clarify details with your group.

1. What does the speaker say to beware of? Who is the speaker addressing?

2. What three things does the speaker warn about in lines 5–8?

3. What happens to the Jabberwock at the end of the poem?

4. ⊖ **Notebook** Write 3 or 4 sentences in which you summarize what happens in the poem.

RESEARCH

Research to Clarify Choose at least one unfamiliar detail from the text. Briefly research that detail. In what way does the information you learned shed light on an aspect of the poem? Share your findings with your group.

Research to Explore Choose something that interested you from the text, and formulate a research question that you might use to find out more about it.

Close Read the Text

With your group, revisit sections of the text you marked during your first read. **Annotate** details that you notice. What **questions** do you have? What can you **conclude**?

Analyze the Text

CITE TEXTUAL EVIDENCE to support your answers.

Complete the activities.

1. **Review and Clarify** With your group, reread lines 17–20 and underline words that are repeated. Why do you think the poet repeats these words? How does this repetition help you to better understand what is happening at this point in the poem?

2. **Present and Discuss** Discuss what you noticed in the selection, what questions you asked, and what conclusions you reached.

3. **Essential Question:** *Where can imagination lead?* What has this poem taught you about imagination? Discuss with your group.

TIP

GROUP DISCUSSION
As you discuss "Jabberwocky" with your group, keep an open mind by considering all members' ideas about what the invented words might mean.

LANGUAGE DEVELOPMENT

Concept Vocabulary

beware	foe	slain

Why These Words? The three concept vocabulary words from the text are related. With your group, determine what the words have in common. How do the concept vocabulary words deepen your understanding of the poem?

Practice

⬛ **Notebook** Write a paragraph in which you describe an imaginary battle scene. Use all three of the concept vocabulary words. Be sure to use context clues that hint at each word's meaning.

Word Study

Anglo-Saxon Word Origins The three concept vocabulary words have Anglo-Saxon word origins. This means that the words or parts of the words are ancient and have been in the language since the Old English period, which ended in A.D. 1066.

Use a dictionary to look up these words that also have Anglo-Saxon word origins: *loathsome, dreadful, plight*. Discuss what you discover with your group.

⬛ WORD NETWORK

Add words related to imagination from the text to your Word Network.

☰ STANDARDS

Reading Literature
Determine the meaning of words and phrases as they are used in a text, including figurative and connotative meanings; analyze the impact of a specific word choice on meaning and tone.

Language
Determine or clarify the meaning of unknown and multiple-meaning words and phrases based on *grade 6 reading and content*, choosing flexibly from a range of strategies.
  c. Consult reference materials, both print and digital, to find the pronunciation of a word or determine or clarify its precise meaning or its part of speech.

Analyze Craft and Structure

Sound Devices Most **sound devices** are groupings of words that share certain sounds. They are sometimes called "musical devices," because they highlight the musical qualities of language. Rhyme is a sound device with which you are probably familiar. There are other types of sound devices that may be less obvious than rhyme but are no less important.

- **Onomatopoeia** is the use of a word that sounds like what it means. *Hiss* and *buzz* are onomatopoeic words.

- **Alliteration** is the repetition of the same consonant sound at the beginnings of stressed syllables in words that are close together. Here, the repeated *f* sound is alliterative: *"the white foam flew"*

- **Consonance** is the repetition of final consonant sounds in stressed syllables with different vowel sounds. Here, the repeated *n* sound creates consonance: *"dawn goes down"*

Practice

CITE TEXTUAL EVIDENCE to support your answers.

Work on your own to complete the chart. Identify the repeated sound or sounds in the underlined groups of words in each passage from the poem. Then, state what sound device each passage presents. (Note that some passages have more than one sound device.) Share and discuss your responses with your group and answer the questions that follow.

PASSAGE	REPEATED SOUND(S)	TYPE(S) OF SOUND DEVICE(S)
The jaws that bite, <u>the claws that catch!</u> (line 6)		
The vorpal blade went <u>snicker-snack!</u> (line 18)		
<u>Come to my arms, my beamish boy!</u> (line 22)		
O frabjous day! <u>Callooh! Callay!</u> (line 23)		

⎙ Notebook

1. Lewis Carroll is famous for inventing words. Explain what real-life sounds each of these invented words suggests: (a) *whiffling,* (b) *burbled,* (c) *galumphing.*

2. How do you think Carroll's use of sound devices adds to the poem? For example, do the sound devices make the poem seem sillier, more imaginative, more lively, or something else? Explain your thinking.

JABBERWOCKY

Author's Style

Invented Language In "Jabberwocky," Lewis Carroll uses **invented language**, or words that he has made up, to entertain readers and to challenge their imaginations. For example, he invents words such as *brillig* and *vorpal*. He does not explain what these words are supposed to mean, and they cannot be found in a dictionary. Instead, readers use their imaginations to fill in their meanings.

As you read "Jabberwocky," look at the **syntax** of each sentence, or how all of the words are arranged. Notice that not all of the words are invented. Carroll mixes invented words with real words such as *and, the, did, were, my,* and *that.* The arrangement of these real words helps readers determine the parts of speech of the invented words. Readers can figure out whether each invented word is a noun, a verb, an adjective, or an adverb and then imagine what the word may mean.

Consider this passage from "Jabberwocky":

> . . . *the slithy toves/ Did gyre and gimble in the wabe. . . .* (lines 1–2)

Carroll invented the four underlined words. By looking at the arrangement of the real words, you can figure out the part of speech of each invented word. Then, you can infer, or guess, what each word might mean.

- *The* at the beginning of the clause shows that a noun will follow. *Toves* must be a plural noun.

- *Slithy* must be an adjective that describes the *toves. Slithy* looks like the real word *slither,* which means "move like a snake."

- *Did* shows that *gyre* and *gimble* must be verbs. *Gyre* sounds like the real word *gyrate,* which means "rotate" or "spin."

- *In* and *the* show that *wabe* must be a noun.

Bringing all of these ideas together, you can infer that a *tove* may be a snakelike creature that spins in circles. Imagine how that would look!

Read It

As a group, choose one stanza from "Jabberwocky." First, mark all of the invented language. Then, look at the real words that you know. Use the arrangement of the words to figure out the part of speech of each of the invented words. Finally, work together to infer a possible meaning for each invented word. Discuss what you imagine is happening.

Write It

📓 **Notebook** Use invented language to write a stanza about an imaginary animal. Invent your own nouns, verbs, adjectives, and adverbs. However, also use real words such as *the, a, he, she, it, were, did,* and *with.* Arrange all of the words in such a way that a reader can infer what the invented words may mean. When you have finished, trade stanzas with a group member, and try to decipher the meanings of each other's stanzas.

STANDARDS

Reading Literature
Determine the meaning of words and phrases as they are used in a text, including figurative and connotative meanings; analyze the impact of a specific word choice on meaning and tone.

Language
- Demonstrate command of the conventions of standard English grammar and usage when writing or speaking.
  e. Recognize variations from standard English in their own and others' writing and speaking, and identify and use strategies to improve expression in conventional language.
- Determine or clarify the meaning of unknown and multiple-meaning words and phrases based on *grade 6 reading and content,* choosing flexibly from a range of strategies.
  a. Use context as a clue to the meaning of a word or phrase.
- Demonstrate understanding of figurative language, word relationships, and nuances in word meanings.
  b. Use the relationship between particular words to better understand each of the words.

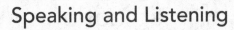

Speaking and Listening

Assignment

Work with your group to create and deliver an oral presentation based on the poem "Jabberwocky." Choose from the following options:

- Prepare and present a **dramatic poetry reading** of "Jabberwocky" in which you read aloud the poem with expression while acting it out so that your audience can picture and feel what is happening in the poem. Use costumes and props to enhance your performance.

- Create a **multimedia presentation** of "Jabberwocky" in which you illustrate the poem through graphics, images, artwork, music, and other multimedia displays.

Project Plan As a group, review the poem and determine what types of props, costumes, or multimedia to use in your presentation. Then, make a list of the tasks you will need to accomplish in order to complete your presentation, and assign tasks to each group member. For example, one group member could be responsible for multimedia research or costume and prop design.

TASK	GROUP MEMBER

Practice Decide which group members will be responsible for reading or narrating the different parts of the poem during your presentation. Practice delivering your presentation as a group. Use these guidelines to improve your presentation techniques:

- vary the volume, pitch, and tone of your voice to express emotion
- use appropriate pacing, speaking quickly when needed to convey excitement or suspense
- to keep listeners engaged, make eye contact with your audience regularly

Listen and Evaluate As you listen to other groups' presentations, jot down any questions you have and note interesting elements of each presentation. Wait until each group has finished their presentation before asking your questions or offering your comments.

✐ EVIDENCE LOG

Before moving on to a new selection, go to your Evidence Log, and record what you learned from "Jabberwocky."

☰ STANDARDS

Speaking and Listening
- Engage effectively in a range of collaborative discussions with diverse partners on *grade 6 topics, texts, and issues,* building on others' ideas and expressing their own clearly.
  a. Come to discussions prepared, having read or studied required material; explicitly draw on that preparation by referring to evidence on the topic, text, or issue to probe and reflect on ideas under discussion.
  b. Follow rules for collegial discussions, set specific goals and deadlines, and define individual roles as needed.

- Present claims and findings, sequencing ideas logically and using pertinent descriptions, facts, and details to accentuate main ideas or themes; use appropriate eye contact, adequate volume, and clear pronunciation.
- Include multimedia components and visual displays in presentations to clarify information.

About the Author

Esha Chhabra (b. 1991) is a journalist who has written for *the New York Times, the San Francisco Chronicle*, and *the Guardian*. Chhabra is a graduate of Georgetown University and studied global politics at the London School of Economics.

The Importance of Imagination

Concept Vocabulary

As you perform your first read of "The Importance of Imagination," you will encounter these words.

template	parameters	model

Context Clues If these words are unfamiliar to you, try using **context clues**—other words and phrases that appear near the unfamiliar words—to help you determine their meanings. There are various types of context clues that may help you as you read. Here are two examples of how to use context clues to determine meaning.

> **Definition:** The palace was **magnificent**, grand in its size ad beauty.
>
> **Contrast of Ideas:** The winners of the race **glided** across the finish line, while the remaining competitors **stumbled** behind them.

Apply your knowledge of context clues and other vocabulary strategies to determine the meanings of unfamiliar words you encounter during your first read.

First Read NONFICTION

Apply these strategies as you conduct your first read. You will have an opportunity to complete a close read after your first read.

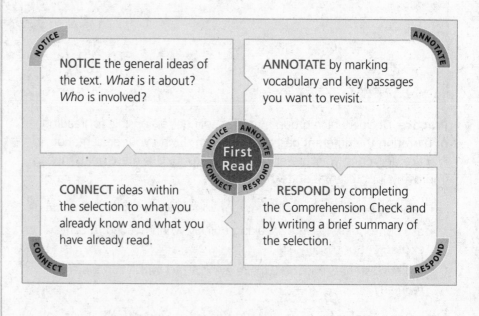

NOTICE the general ideas of the text. *What* is it about? *Who* is involved?

ANNOTATE by marking vocabulary and key passages you want to revisit.

CONNECT ideas within the selection to what you already know and what you have already read.

RESPOND by completing the Comprehension Check and by writing a brief summary of the selection.

First Read

☰ STANDARDS

Reading Informational Text
By the end of the year, read and comprehend literary nonfiction in the grades 6–8 text complexity band proficiently, with scaffolding as needed at the high end of the range.

Language
• Determine or clarify the meaning of unknown and multiple-meaning words and phrases based on *grade 6 reading and content,* choosing flexibly from a range of strategies.
  a. Use context as a clue to the meaning of a word or phrase.

The Importance of Imagination

Esha Chhabra

BACKGROUND

A curriculum vitae, or CV, is a short account of a person's background, skills, education, and work experience. In the United States, a CV is similar to a resume. Resumes are usually no longer than one page. Many employers require these documents for job applications and look at them carefully to decide who they should hire.

SCAN FOR MULTIMEDIA

1   While growing up, I'd never really considered how important it is to be imaginative. It's a childhood profession, you could say. It comes naturally. Then we hit an age when we're presented with a scantron[1] of bubble-in options, a **template** for a CV that we need to create, and Excel.[2] At that point, our learning has to fit into certain **parameters**: within that little bubble, within the one page limit, and within a tiny digital graph. So, what happens to our imagination?

2   It seems to fade.

3   Being Asian (as I am) doesn't help. The assumption that you're more apt for engineering or medicine is like a nagging tail. We have a so-called fondness for numbers apparently. If you're Asian, you must be good at math—of course.

4   Well, then I turned out to be an oddball. I developed an affinity for words and images instead. At the age of 12, my dream was to be a professional doodler, which could turn into a career as a cartoonist, if it went well. And my parents indulged me in that dream. Unlike others, who may have thought that was ridiculous,

NOTES

Mark context clues or indicate another strategy you used to help you determine meaning.

template (TEHM pliht) *n.*

MEANING:

parameters (puh RAM uh tuhrz) *n.*

MEANING:

---

1. **scantron** refers to a paper form used for multiple-choice tests.
2. **Excel** widely used computer program for creating spreadsheets and graphs.

they got me drawing books. When my mother saw me sitting idle, or falling asleep among a pile of school books, she'd suggest, "Why don't you draw for a bit?" Over a decade later, little has changed. She still chuckles at my drawings, tells me to draw more often, and has preserved that notebook.

5   As I grew older, as the reading list of books grew longer, the assignments tougher, and jobs took up any spare time as a student in college, that ability to just sit down and pour your imagination onto a blank canvas began to disappear. Rather, that creative side had to reinvent itself.

6   My high school history teacher once told me that history is not a timeline; it's a story. She threw out the linearity of history. She made what was dry and ancient, charming, engaging, and at times, even humorous. That was her imagination at work. And it helped me develop a love for the social sciences. Our imaginations can be quite contagious, I learned.

7   But can this love for the imaginative ever find a place in the real world? Certainly.

8   Imagination creates not just fairy tales and children's books but a new vision for the way we conduct our lives. Imaginations challenge the norm, push boundaries, and help us progress.

9   We need to encourage more creativity. Forget the CV for a bit.

10   If we encourage that brilliant math student to be imaginative as well, he could use those algorithms[3] to innovate. If we encourage the biology student to be imaginative as well, she could design a new sustainable fuel source for us. If we encourage that economics buff to be imaginative as well, he could build a new people-friendly business **model**. The tools are there. You just need to reorient them towards the unexpected. That's where creativity—at home, in the classroom, and in the workplace—is so essential.

11   That's why, last week I found myself, sitting with my mom late at night, rereading Shel Silverstein's poems for children. Turns out, they're just as good for adults, maybe even better. ≈

---

3. **algorithms** (AL guh rihth uhmz) *n.* steps for solving a problem, usually related to math.

Mark context clues or indicate another strategy you used to help you determine meaning.

model (MOD uhl) *n.*

MEANING:

Comprehension Check

Complete the following items after you finish your first read. Review and clarify details with your group.

1. According to the author, what happens to our imagination when we grow up?

2. What was the author's dream at age 12?

3. What did the author's history teacher say about history?

4. 📓 **Notebook** Write a summary of "The Importance of Imagination" to confirm your understanding of the text.

- -

RESEARCH

Research to Clarify Choose at least one unfamiliar detail from the text. Briefly research that detail. In what way does the information you learned deepen your understanding of the essay? Share your findings with your group.

Research to Explore Choose something that interested you from the text, and formulate a research question that you might use to learn more about it.

THE IMPORTANCE OF IMAGINATION

Close Read the Text

With your group, revisit sections of the text you marked during your first read. **Annotate** details that you notice. What **questions** do you have? What can you **conclude**?

Analyze the Text

> **CITE TEXTUAL EVIDENCE**
> to support your answers.

Complete the activities.

1. **Review and Clarify** With your group, reread paragraph 10 of the selection. Discuss with your group what the author means when she writes, "The tools are there. You just need to reorient them towards the unexpected"?

2. **Present and Discuss** Now, work with your group to share passages from the selection that you found especially important. Discuss what you noticed in the selection, what questions you asked, and what conclusions you reached.

3. **Essential Question:** *Where can imagination lead?* What has this essay taught you about imagination? Discuss with your group.

🔀 WORD NETWORK

Add words related to imagination from the text to your Word Network.

≔ STANDARDS

Reading Informational Text
• Cite textual evidence to support analysis of what the text says explicitly as well as inferences drawn from the text.
• Determine a central idea of a text and how it is conveyed through particular details; provide a summary of the text distinct from personal opinions or judgments.
• Analyze in detail how a key individual, event, or idea is introduced, illustrated, and elaborated in a text.

Language
Determine or clarify the meaning of unknown and multiple-meaning words and phrases based on *grade 6 reading and content,* choosing flexibly from a range of strategies.
b. Use common, grade-appropriate Greek or Latin affixes and roots as clues to the meaning of a word.

LANGUAGE DEVELOPMENT

Concept Vocabulary

template	parameters	model

Why These Words? The three concept vocabulary words from the text are related. With your group, determine what the words have in common. How do these word choices enhance the impact of the text?

Practice

📄 **Notebook** Confirm your understanding of these words from the text by using them in a paragraph. Be sure to include context clues that hint at each word's meaning.

Word Study

Greek Prefix: *para-* The Greek prefix *para-*, which means "beside" or "alongside," contributes to the meanings of many English words. For example, *parallel* lines are lines that run alongside each other. Use a dictionary to look up these words related to careers: *paralegal, paramedic, paramilitary.* Discuss with your group how the prefix *para-* contributes to the meaning of each word.

Analyze Craft and Structure

Author's Influences A **reflective essay,** such as "The Importance of Imagination," presents the author's thoughts, beliefs, and reflections on an idea or experience—in this case, the topic of imagination. The author's thoughts and beliefs about a topic are affected by the **author's influences**, or the factors that affect his or her writing. These influences may include historical factors, such as important or newsworthy events that happened during the author's lifetime. Authors are also influenced by cultural factors. Cultural factors may include:

- the places an author has lived
- the author's upbringing and education
- the way in which an author lives his or her life
- an author's personal experiences

An author's influences affect the issues he or she thinks are important. It is important to consider how an author's influences may have shaped the **central idea** about which he or she is writing. For example, an author may choose to focus on promoting environmental awareness because of a pollution problem in his or her own town.

As you read a reflective essay, use key details in the text to **make inferences,** or educated guesses, about the effect of the author's influences on the central ideas in his or her writing.

> **CITE TEXTUAL EVIDENCE**
> to support your answers.

Practice

Use this chart to identify three of the author's influences, and explain how each influence affects the central idea of the essay. Share your responses with your group.

AUTHOR'S INFLUENCES	EFFECT ON CENTRAL IDEA

THE IMPORTANCE OF
IMAGINATION

Conventions

Pronoun-Antecedent Agreement A **pronoun** is a word takes the place of one or more nouns or other pronouns. The word that the pronoun refers to is called the **antecedent**. Follow these rules for pronoun-antecedent agreement.

PRONOUN-ANTECEDENT AGREEMENT	
Agreement in Number: A pronoun and its antecedent must agree in number (singular or plural).	**Singular:** Creativity is important because it leads to innovation. **Plural:** My stepparents said that they would pay for my art classes.
Agreement in Person: A pronoun and its antecedent must agree in person. Use a first-person pronoun with a first-person antecedent. Use a third-person pronoun with a third-person antecedent.	**First-Person:** I asked whether Li would show me how to draw. **Third-Person:** The skydivers know that they had to check their parachutes.
Clear Antecedent: Every pronoun must have a clear antecedent. Problems may arise if a pronoun has more than one possible antecedent.	**Unclear:** Juan told Frank that he was going to win the prize. **Clear:** Juan told Frank that Frank was going to win the prize.

To find and fix errors in your writing related to pronoun use, follow these steps: First, identify each pronoun/antecedent pair that you used. Second, make sure the pronoun refers to a specific antecedent. Third, decide whether the antecedent is singular or plural. Fourth, determine whether the antecedent is in the first, second, or third person. Finally, choose the pronoun that agrees with the antecedent in number and in person.

Read It

Identify the pronoun/antecedent pair in each sentence. Mark whether they agree. If they do not agree, identify the type of agreement error.

1. Mr. Cano gave his permission to look for a new summer job.

2. After Olga finished doing homework, they took a walk alone.

3. Select the books you want, and put it in the box.

Write It

📓 **Notebook** Rewrite the following sentences so that they demonstrate correct pronoun-antecedent agreement.

1. When the author was young, their parents encouraged her to be as creative as possible.

2. Imagination and creativity are not just about drawing and painting. It is also about making progress and pushing boundaries.

■■ STANDARDS

Language
Demonstrate command of the conventions of standard English grammar and usage when writing or speaking.
  c. Recognize and correct inappropriate shifts in pronoun number and person.
  d. Recognize and correct vague pronouns.

Writing to Sources

Assignment

Work individually to write an explanatory essay on one of the following topics:

- [ ] a **comparison-and-contrast essay** in which you compare your childhood experience with imagination with that of the author
- [ ] a **cause-and-effect essay** in which you explain the ways in which the author's influences caused her to develop her current views on imagination

Gather Text Evidence First, review the essay and note details that are relevant to your topic. The types of details you choose will depend on which assignment you chose:

- If you chose a comparison-and-contrast essay, note your reaction to details from the essay: Did you identify with what the author said? Or, did you feel that you couldn't relate to her experience? You may react differently to different details.

- If you chose a cause-and-effect essay, identify details that reveal what influenced the author and her views on imagination. Then, make a clear connection between each detail and her perspective.

Use this chart to record your notes.

TEXT DETAIL	WHAT IT REVEALS ABOUT MY TOPIC

Write Your Essay As you draft your essay, be sure to organize your ideas clearly. Using transitional words and phrases can help you connect your ideas in a logical way. For example, in a comparison-and-contrast essay, transitions, such as *similarly* and *however*, can highlight similarities and differences. In a cause-and-effect essay, you might include transitions, such as *since* and *therefore*, to show causes and effects.

Share and Revise After you finish drafting your essay, exchange essays with a group member. Provide feedback to your classmate by noting places in which his or her ideas are unclear or disconnected as well as any points that need more supporting details and examples. Remember to be polite and offer helpful suggestions when giving others feedback.

☑ **EVIDENCE LOG**

Before moving on to a new selection, go to your Evidence Log, and record what you learned from "The Importance of Imagination."

▤ STANDARDS

Writing

- Write informative/explanatory texts to examine a topic and convey ideas, concepts, and information through the selection, organization, and analysis of relevant content.

  a. Introduce a topic; organize ideas, concepts, and information, using strategies such as definition, classification, comparison/contrast, and cause/effect; include formatting, graphics, and multimedia when useful to aiding comprehension.

  b. Develop the topic with relevant facts, definitions, concrete details, quotations, or other information and examples.

  c. Use appropriate transitions to clarify the relationships among ideas and concepts.

- With some guidance and support from peers and adults, develop and strengthen writing as needed by planning, revising, editing, rewriting, or trying a new approach, focusing on how well purpose and audience have been addressed.

SOURCES

• from ALICE'S ADVENTURES IN WONDERLAND

• JABBERWOCKY

• THE IMPORTANCE OF IMAGINATION

Perform a Fictional Narrative

Assignment

At the end of the except from *Alice's Adventures in Wonderland*, Alice can see Wonderland through a tiny door, but cannot figure out how to fit through it. Work with your group to write and perform a **fictional narrative** in which you tell a story about where Alice goes and what happens when she gets through the door. Use this story starter to begin your narrative:

When Alice finally gets through the tiny door…

In your performance, use costumes, props, and music to help the audience picture the characters, setting, and events in your narrative.

STANDARDS

Writing
Write narratives to develop real or imagined experiences or events using effective technique, relevant descriptive details, and well-structured event sequences.
  a. Engage and orient the reader by establishing a context and introducing a narrator and/or characters; organize an event sequence that unfolds naturally and logically.
  b. Use narrative techniques, such as dialogue, pacing, and description, to develop experiences, events, and/or characters.
  d. Use precise words and phrases, relevant descriptive details, and sensory language to convey experiences and events.

Plan With Your Group

Develop Your Ideas As a group, brainstorm for ideas about how to complete the story starter. As you discuss ideas with your group, allow all members to offer suggestions. You may develop a completely new story for Alice, or you may draw on parts of Lewis Carroll's story. For example, you may choose to use the setting of Wonderland, but change the characters Alice encounters and the adventures she has there. Alternatively, you could imagine a new setting for the adventures of Alice and the White Rabbit. Use the questions in the chart to guide you in this process. As you record your ideas, note words and phrases that will help you to vividly describe the setting, characters, and Alice's thoughts and feelings.

QUESTION	NOTES
How does Alice finally get through the door? What does she find when she gets there? Who does she meet?	
What happens to Alice? What adventure does she have? What challenges does she face?	
How does Alice feel? What does she want? How will she get home?	

Draft Your Narrative Once you have decided how to tell your story, use the notes from your chart to draft your fictional narrative Your written narrative will be the basis for your performance. Use narrative techniques, such as description and dialogue, to develop your characters' personalities. Include sensory details to paint an engaging picture of the setting.

Plan Your Performance Use your written narrative to plan your performance. Decide which group members will assume the roles of characters and which members will narrate the performance. Then, decide how to best use costumes, props, and music to make your narrative come to life.

Rehearse With Your Group

Practice With Your Group Practice delivering your performance with your group. Use your voice, expressions, and gestures to portray the characters and events in your narrative in an engaging way. Remember to make eye contact with your audience at appropriate intervals. Use the checklist to evaluate your first rehearsal of the performance. Then, use your evaluation and these instructions to guide your revision.

CONTENT	USE OF MEDIA	PRESENTATION TECHNIQUES
☐ The narrative responds to the prompt in a creative way.	☐ The performance includes costumes, props, and music that help the audience picture the setting and the characters.	☐ Speakers make eye contact with the audience at appropriate points in the performance.
☐ The narrative develops the characters using dialogue and description.		☐ Speakers adjust their voices and use gestures and expressions to portray characters and events in an engaging way.
☐ The narrative uses sensory details to create a vivid setting.		

Fine-Tune the Content Sometimes it is hard to describe a setting to an audience in a way that makes it seem real. If the way in which you picture the setting doesn't come through in your performance, add more sensory details to the narrated portion to ensure your audience can visualize the scene.

Brush Up on Your Presentation Techniques Performers should use voices that are expressive, and contribute to developing the characters' personalities or the setting and mood of the scene. Discuss how the characters should sound at different points in your performance. For example, when should Alice sound soft and sweet? When should she sound loud and angry? Also, consider the ways in which the narrators can adjust the tone of their voices to help convey details about the setting and mood. For example, if it the setting is a dark, threatening forest, the narrator may want to speak with a low, worried tone that conveys a sense of danger.

Present and Evaluate

Perform your group's narrative for the class. As you watch other groups perform, note differences in the ways in which you responded to the prompt. Evaluate how well other groups' presentations meet the checklist requirements.

⊞ STANDARDS

Speaking and Listening
• Engage effectively in a range of collaborative discussions with diverse partners on *grade 6 topics, texts, and issues,* building on others' ideas and expressing their own clearly.
  b. Follow rules for collegial discussions, set specific goals and deadlines, and define individual roles as needed.

• Present claims and findings, sequencing ideas logically and using pertinent descriptions, facts, and details to accentuate main ideas or themes; use appropriate eye contact, adequate volume, and clear pronunciation.
• Include multimedia components and visual displays in presentations to clarify information.

ESSENTIAL QUESTION:

Where can imagination lead?

Sometimes imaginary characters and their adventures in fantastical worlds can teach you about the real world and about yourself. In this section, you complete your study of imagination by exploring an additional selection related to the topic. You'll then share what you learn with classmates. To choose a text, follow these steps.

Look Back Think about the selections you have already studied. What more do you want to know about the topic of imagination?

Look Ahead Preview the texts by reading the descriptions. Which one seems most interesting and appealing to you?

Look Inside Take a few minutes to scan through the text you chose. Choose a different one if this text doesn't meet your needs.

Independent Learning Strategies

Throughout your life, in school, in your community, and in your career, you will need to rely on yourself to learn and work on your own. Review these strategies and the actions you can take to practice them during Independent Learning. Add ideas of your own for each category.

STRATEGY	ACTION PLAN
Create a schedule	• Understand your goals and deadlines. • Make a plan for what to do each day. •
Practice what you have learned	• Use first-read and close-read strategies to deepen your understanding. • After you read, evaluate the usefulness of the evidence to help you understand the topic. • Consider the quality and reliability of the source. •
Take notes	• Record important ideas and information. • Review your notes before preparing to share with a group. •

SCAN FOR
MULTIMEDIA

CONTENTS

Choose one selection. Selections are available online only.

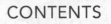

SCAN FOR
MULTIMEDIA

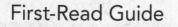

First-Read Guide

Use this page to record your first-read ideas.

🔧 **Tool Kit**
First-Read Guide and
Model Annotation

Selection Title: _____

NOTICE

NOTICE new information or ideas you learn about the unit topic as you first read this text.

ANNOTATE

ANNOTATE by marking vocabulary and key passages you want to revisit.

CONNECT

CONNECT ideas within the selection to other knowledge and the selections you have read.

RESPOND

RESPOND by writing a brief summary of the selection.

≡ **STANDARD**

Reading Read and comprehend complex literary and informational texts independently and proficiently.

Close-Read Guide

Use this page to record your close-read ideas.

Selection Title: _____

🔧 **Tool Kit**
Close-Read Guide and
Model Annotation

Close Read the Text

Revisit sections of the text you marked during your first read. Read these sections closely and **annotate** what you notice. Ask yourself **questions** about the text. What can you **conclude**? Write down your ideas.

Analyze the Text

Think about the author's choices of patterns, structure, techniques, and ideas included in the text. Select one, and record your thoughts about what this choice conveys.

QuickWrite

Pick a paragraph from the text that grabbed your interest. Explain the power of this passage.

_____
_____
_____
_____
_____
_____
_____
_____

☰ STANDARD

Reading Read and comprehend complex literary and informational texts independently and proficiently.

Share Your Independent Learning

Prepare to Share

Where can imagination lead?

Even when you read something independently, you can continue to grow by sharing what you have learned with others. Reflect on the text you explored independently, and write notes about its connection to the unit. In your notes, consider why this text belongs in this unit.

Learn From Your Classmates

Discuss It Share your ideas about the text you explored on your own. As you talk with your classmates, jot down ideas that you learn from them.

Reflect

Review your notes, and mark the most important insight you gained from these writing and discussion activities. Explain how these ideas add to your understanding of the topic of imagination.

Review Notes for a Fictional Narrative

At the beginning of this unit, you expressed an idea about the following question:

> **What might happen if a fictional character were to come into the real world?**

✎ EVIDENCE LOG

Review your Evidence Log and your QuickWrite from the beginning of the unit. Did you learn anything new?

NOTES

Identify at least three key situations or events that occurred because of either the author's or character's imagination.

1.

2.

3.

Identify an interesting character from one of the selections and note some his or her character traits:

_____

_____

Identify some sensory details that you might use to develop the real-world setting of your narrative:

_____

_____

Evaluate the Strength of Your Evidence Do you have enough details and examples, both from the texts and your own experience, to write a well-developed, engaging fictional narrative? If not, make a plan.

☐ Brainstorm for details to add ☐ Talk with my classmates

☐ Reread a selection ☐ Ask an expert

☐ Other: _____

☰ STANDARDS

Writing
Write narratives to develop real or imagined experiences or events using effective technique, relevant descriptive details, and well-structured event sequences.
   d. Use precise words and phrases, relevant descriptive details, and sensory language to convey experiences and events.

SOURCES

- WHOLE-CLASS SELECTIONS

- SMALL-GROUP SELECTIONS

- INDEPENDENT-LEARNING SELECTION

PART 1

Writing to Sources: Fictional Narrative

In this unit, you met a variety of fictional characters whose imaginations led them to unusual and fantastical places. You also considered the importance of imagination in real-life situations.

Assignment

Choose a character from one of the selections you read in this unit, and write a **short story** that explores the following question:

> What might happen if a fictional character were to come into the real world?

Use the following story starter to begin your narrative: *One day, _____ showed up on my doorstep, and. . . .*

As you draft, establish a vivid setting and a clear point of view. Use narrative techniques, descriptive details, and sensory language to develop your characters and their experiences. Logically organize the events in your narrative and connect them with transitions. Your narrative should end with a conclusion that resolves the conflicts, or struggles, your characters face in the story.

Reread the Assignment Review the assignment to be sure you fully understand it. You may use the story starter provided as the first sentence of your narrative. However, if your imagination is fired up and you would like to start your story in a different way, feel free to do so.

Review the Elements of a Fictional Narrative Before you begin writing, read the Fictional Narrative Rubric. Once you have completed your first draft, check it against the rubric. If one or more of the elements is missing or not as strong as it could be, revise your narrative to add or strengthen that component.

WORD NETWORK

As you write and revise your fictional narrative, use your Word Network to help vary your word choices.

STANDARDS

Writing
- Write narratives to develop real or imagined experiences or events using effective technique, relevant descriptive details, and well-structured event sequences.
- Produce clear and coherent writing in which the development, organization, and style are appropriate to task, purpose, and audience.
- Write routinely over extended time frames and shorter time frames for a range of discipline-specific tasks, purposes, and audiences.

Fictional Narrative Rubric

	Focus and Organization	Evidence and Elaboration	Language Conventions
4	The introduction is engaging and clearly establishes a setting and a point of view. Events in the narrative progress logically and are connected by effectively used transitions. The conclusion is memorable and resolves the conflicts the characters face over the course of the story.	The narrative effectively uses techniques, such as dialogue, pacing, and description, to develop characters, events, and experiences in memorable way. The narrative effectively uses descriptive details and sensory language to vividly portray the characters and develop the setting.	The narrative intentionally follows standard English conventions of usage and mechanics.
3	The introduction is mostly engaging and establishes a setting and a point of view. Events in the narrative progress logically and are connected by transitions. The conclusion resolves the conflicts the characters face over the course of the story.	The narrative uses techniques, such as dialogue, pacing, and description, to develop characters, events, and experiences. The narrative uses descriptive details and sensory language to portray the characters and develop the setting.	The narrative follows standard English conventions of usage and mechanics.
2	The introduction establishes a setting and a point of view. Events in the narrative sometimes progress logically and are occasionally connected by transitions. There is a conclusion, but it does not fully resolve the conflicts the characters face over the course of the story.	The narrative sometimes uses techniques, such as dialogue, pacing, and description, to develop characters, events, and experiences. The narrative occasionally uses descriptive details and sensory language, but some word choices are vague and imprecise.	The narrative sometimes follows standard English conventions of usage and mechanics, but also contains grammar and spelling errors.
1	The introduction does not establish a setting and a point of view, or there is no introduction. Events in the narrative do not progress logically and are not connected by transitions. The conclusion does not connect to the narrative, or there is no conclusion.	The narrative does not use techniques, such as dialogue, pacing, and description, to develop characters, events, and experiences. Word choices are vague, and the narrative does not use descriptive details and sensory language to portray characters or develop the setting.	The narrative does not follow standard English conventions of usage and mechanics, and contains many grammar and spelling errors.

PART 2
Speaking and Listening: Storytelling

Assignment
After completing the final draft of your short story, present it to the class orally during a class **storytelling** session.

:≣ STANDARDS
Speaking and Listening
• Present claims and findings, sequencing ideas logically and using pertinent descriptions, facts, and details to accentuate main ideas or themes; use appropriate eye contact, adequate volume, and clear pronunciation.
• Adapt speech to a variety of contexts and tasks, demonstrating command of formal English when indicated or appropriate.

Take the following steps to make your presentation during the storytelling session lively and engaging:

- Read your story with expression by changing your voice when reading different characters' parts and adjusting your tone to suit the events.
- As you speak, pronounce words clearly, and make eye contact with your audience regularly to keep listeners engaged.

Review the Rubric The criteria by which your presentation will be evaluated appear in the rubric below. Review these criteria before presenting to ensure that you are prepared.

	Content	Organization	Presentation Techniques
3	The introduction engages and orients listeners by establishing a clear point of view, and introducing the characters and the setting.	The speaker spends the right amount of time on each part of the story.	The speaker makes eye contact and speaks clearly with adequate volume.
	The setting, characters, and events are brought to life through the use of narrative techniques, descriptive details, and sensory language.	The story includes a smooth sequence of events that is easy for listeners to follow.	The speaker adjusts his or her voice to accurately reflect different characters and events.
	The conclusion resolves conflicts and provides listeners with a sense of resolution, or completion.		
2	The introduction establishes the characters and the setting.	The speaker mostly spends the right amount of time on each part of the story.	The speaker makes some eye contact and usually speaks clearly.
	The setting, characters, and events are developed through the use of some narrative techniques, descriptive details, and sensory language.	The story includes a sequence of events that listeners can mostly follow.	The speaker sometimes adjusts his or her voice to reflect different characters and events.
	The conclusion resolves conflicts in a vague way, but leaves listeners with questions.		
1	The introduction may vaguely establish the setting and the characters, or may be nonexistent.	The speaker spends too much time on some parts of the story and not enough time on others.	The speaker does not make eye contact and does not speak clearly.
	Narrative techniques, descriptive details, and sensory language are not used to develop the setting, characters, and events.	The sequence of events is unclear and listeners have difficulty following the story.	The speaker does not adjust his or her voice to reflect different characters and events.
	The conclusion does not relate to story events, or is nonexistent.		

Reflect on the Unit

Now that you've completed the unit, take a few moments to reflect on your learning.

Reflect on the Unit Goals

Look back at the goals at the beginning of the unit. Use a different colored pen to rate yourself again. Think about readings and activities that contributed the most to the growth of your understanding. Record your thoughts.

Reflect on the Learning Strategies

💬 Discuss It Write a reflection on whether you were able to improve your learning based on your Action Plans. Think about what worked, what didn't, and what you might do to keep working on these strategies. Record your ideas before a class discussion.

Reflect on the Text

Choose a selection that you found challenging, and explain what made it difficult.

Explain something that surprised you about a text in the unit.

Which activity taught you the most about imagination? What did you learn?

SCAN FOR
MULTIMEDIA

Exploration

The road to the unknown can be dangerous and challenging, but people continue to explore it.

Hang Son Doong

Discuss It Why might explorers want to discover unknown places?

Write your response before sharing your ideas.

SCAN FOR
MULTIMEDIA

UNIT 5

ESSENTIAL QUESTION:

What drives people to explore?

LAUNCH TEXT
ARGUMENT MODEL
What on Earth Is Left
to Explore?

🖥 WHOLE-CLASS LEARNING

ANCHOR TEXT: MEMOIR
from A Long
Way Home
Saroo Brierley

MEDIA: VIDEO
BBC Science Club: All
About Exploration
narrated by Dara Ó Briain

👥 SMALL-GROUP LEARNING

NEWS ARTICLE
Mission Twinpossible
TIME For Kids

EPIC RETELLING
from Tales From
the Odyssey
Mary Pope Osborne

COMPARE

BLOG
To the Top of
Everest
Samantha Larson

MEDIA: GRAPHIC NOVEL
from Lewis & Clark
Nick Bertozzi

👤 INDEPENDENT LEARNING

OPINION PIECE
Mars Can Wait.
Oceans Can't.
Amitai Etzioni

NONFICTION NARRATIVE
from Shipwreck at the
Bottom of the World
Jennifer Armstrong

HISTORICAL FICTION
from Sacajawea
Joseph Bruchac

EXPOSITORY NONFICTION
The Legacy of Arctic
Explorer Matthew
Henson
James Mills

INFORMATIVE ARTICLE
Should Polar Tourism
Be Allowed?
Emily Goldberg

PERFORMANCE TASK
WRITING FOCUS:
Write an Argument

PERFORMANCE TASK
SPEAKING AND LISTENING FOCUS:
Present an Advertisement

PERFORMANCE-BASED ASSESSMENT PREP
Review Evidence for an Argument

PERFORMANCE-BASED ASSESSMENT

Argument: Essay and Speech

PROMPT:

Should kids today be encouraged to become explorers?

Unit Goals

Throughout this unit, you will deepen your understanding of exploration by reading, writing, speaking, listening, and presenting. These goals will help you succeed on the Unit Performance-Based Assessment.

Rate how well you meet these goals right now. You will revisit your ratings later when you reflect on your growth during this unit.

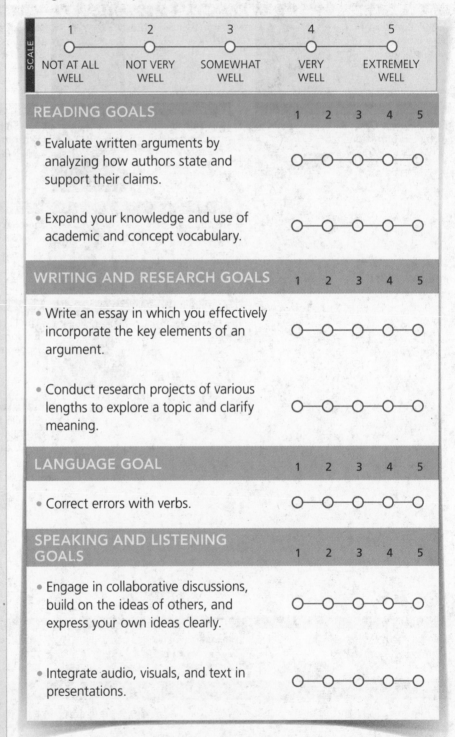

SCALE					
	1	2	3	4	5
	NOT AT ALL WELL	NOT VERY WELL	SOMEWHAT WELL	VERY WELL	EXTREMELY WELL

READING GOALS   1 2 3 4 5

- Evaluate written arguments by analyzing how authors state and support their claims.

- Expand your knowledge and use of academic and concept vocabulary.

WRITING AND RESEARCH GOALS   1 2 3 4 5

- Write an essay in which you effectively incorporate the key elements of an argument.

- Conduct research projects of various lengths to explore a topic and clarify meaning.

LANGUAGE GOAL   1 2 3 4 5

- Correct errors with verbs.

SPEAKING AND LISTENING GOALS   1 2 3 4 5

- Engage in collaborative discussions, build on the ideas of others, and express your own ideas clearly.

- Integrate audio, visuals, and text in presentations.

:: STANDARDS

Language
Acquire and use accurately grade-appropriate general academic and domain-specific words and phrases; gather vocabulary knowledge when considering a word or phrase important to comprehension or expression.

SCAN FOR MULTIMEDIA

Academic Vocabulary: Argument

Understanding and using academic terms can help you read, write, and speak with precision and clarity. Here are five academic words that will be useful in this unit as you analyze and write arguments.

Complete the chart.

1. Review each word, its root, and the mentor sentences.

2. Use the information and your own knowledge to predict the meaning of each word.

3. For each word, list at least two related words.

4. Refer to the dictionary or other resources if needed.

TIP

FOLLOW THROUGH
Study the words in this chart, and mark them or their forms wherever they appear in the unit.

WORD	MENTOR SENTENCES	PREDICT MEANING	RELATED WORDS
critical ROOT: **-crit-** "judge"	**1.** I don't think she liked the story because she had many *critical* comments. **2.** It is *critical* to follow the steps exactly, otherwise the experiment might fail.		critic; critically
assume ROOT: **-sum- / -sumpt-** "take up"	**1.** If you get the leash, the puppy will *assume* you're taking him for a walk. **2.** Jon won the election and will *assume* the role of mayor.		
compel ROOT: **-pel-** "drive"	**1.** His disregard of the rules may *compel* the group to dismiss him. **2.** In the movie, the bad guy tries to *compel* the hero to give up.		
valid ROOT: **-val-** "strong"	**1.** You need a *valid* password to log in to the network. **2.** If you want to convince me, you had better use *valid* reasons.		
coherent ROOT: **-her- / -hes-** "cling"; "stick"	**1.** Present your information in a clear, *coherent* order so it is easy to understand. **2.** Sam's speech was *coherent* because he used clear logic and evidence.		

This selection is an example of an **argument,** a type of writing in which an author states and defends a position on a topic. This is the type of writing you will develop in the Performance-Based Assessment at the end of the unit.

As you read, look at the way that the author builds a case. Mark the text to help you answer this question: What is the author's position, and what evidence supports it?

What on Earth Is Left to Explore?

NOTES

1   At the beginning of the 1800s, the United States was a young country. Most people lived in small towns clustered on the Atlantic coast. To the west lay an entire continent, full of mystery and promise.

2   Government leaders believed that exploration of the continent was important. Exploration would bring knowledge and resources. Urged on by President Thomas Jefferson, Congress funded a small expedition to explore the lands west of the Mississippi River. The Lewis and Clark expedition became one of the most famous exploratory journeys in history.

3   In the modern world, the idea of exploration has changed. Cars, trains, and airplanes have made the world seem much smaller. People seem to be everywhere. Thousands have climbed Mount Everest, the world's highest mountain. There are even people living in Antarctica, the world's coldest continent. In addition, the Internet allows people to visit faraway places through the screens of their computers. Given these changes, some people may ask whether exploration matters anymore. Is there anything left to explore? The answer is simple: Exploration matters as much today as it ever has.

4   Let's start with ocean exploration. It is true that much of Earth has been visited and charted. However, we should remember that people actually live on less than twenty percent of the planet. We inhabit the land, but Earth is mostly ocean. Vast stretches of the

SCAN FOR
MULTIMEDIA

oceans are hidden under miles of water. The little we do know about these secret places is fascinating. For example, almost a quarter of Earth is made up of a single mountain range. It just happens to be under the sea! Consider the other wonders we might find as we explore.

5   Ocean exploration might help us solve tough problems. For example, it might lead to new food sources for the planet's growing population. It may also help us find ways to slow damage to the environment. These types of problems threaten all of us, and we need solutions. They make the need for ocean exploration more important than ever.

6   Space exploration is another area of great importance. Human beings have always been interested in the skies. We are curious about the stars and planets and the possibility that they hold other intelligent life. Satisfying that curiosity is one good reason to explore space. Another reason is that by exploring beyond Earth, we will answer essential questions about the history of our solar system and of the universe itself. This will help us understand our own planet and ourselves better. Human exploration of space also has practical benefits. According to NASA (National Aeronautics and Space Administration), space exploration pushes us to "expand technology, create new industries, and help to foster a peaceful connection with other nations."

7   Lewis and Clark did not know what they would find as they set out on their journey. They only knew that they would have an adventure. In the end, their efforts added to the country's territory and to people's knowledge and understanding. The results of exploration may not always be that impressive, but that may not be the point. The need to explore and extend the boundaries of knowledge remains vital and should continue. ❧

WORD NETWORK FOR EXPLORATION

Vocabulary A Word Network is a collection of words related to a topic. As you read the selections in this unit, identify interesting words related to the idea of exploration and add them to your Word Network. For example, you might begin by adding words from the Launch Text, such as *expedition, wilderness,* and *curiosity.* Continue to add words as you complete this unit.

expedition

wilderness   EXPLORATION

curiosity

🛠 **Tool Kit**
Word Network Model

Summary

Write a summary of "What on Earth Is Left to Explore?" A **summary** is a concise, complete, and accurate overview of a text. It should not include a statement of your opinion or an analysis.

Launch Activity

Four-Corner Debate Consider this statement: **There is nothing left on Earth to explore.** Decide your position and check one of the boxes. Then, briefly note why you feel this way.

☐ Strongly Agree ☐ Agree ☐ Disagree ☐ Strongly Disagree

_____

- Each corner of the classroom represents one position on the question. Go to the corner of the room that represents your position. Briefly discuss reasons for your position with the others in your corner. Make a list of three strong reasons.

- Start off the debate by stating your position and one reason. Then, go around the room, presenting positions and reasons.

- If you change your mind as the debate continues, move to the corner that represents your new position. Then, explain why your thinking changed.

QuickWrite

Consider class discussions, the video, and the Launch Text as you think about the prompt. Record your first thoughts here.

PROMPT: **Should kids today be encouraged to become explorers?**

EVIDENCE LOG FOR EXPLORATION

Review your QuickWrite. Summarize your point of view in one sentence to record in your Evidence Log. Then, record evidence from "What on Earth Is Left to Explore?" that supports your point of view.

After each selection, you will continue to use your Evidence Log to record the evidence you gather and the connections you make. This graphic shows what your Evidence Log looks like.

🔧 **Tool Kit**
Evidence Log Model

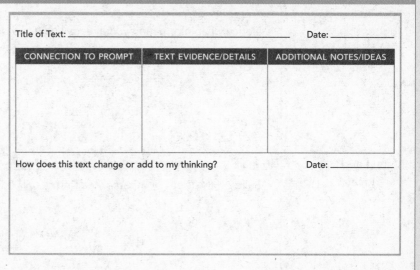

Title of Text: _____ Date: _____

CONNECTION TO PROMPT	TEXT EVIDENCE/DETAILS	ADDITIONAL NOTES/IDEAS

How does this text change or add to my thinking? Date: _____

ESSENTIAL QUESTION:

What drives people to explore?

Exploration may be physical, involving travel to unknown places. It may be mental, involving new ways of looking at a topic. In many cases, it requires both action and imagination. You will work with your whole class to learn more about exploration. The selections you will read present different ideas about explorers and exploration.

Whole-Class Learning Strategies

Throughout your life, in school, in your community, and in your career, you will continue to learn and work in large-group environments.

Review these strategies and the actions you can take to practice them as you work with your whole class. Add ideas of your own for each step. Get ready to use these strategies during Whole-Class Learning.

STRATEGY	ACTION PLAN
Listen actively	• Eliminate distractions. For example, put your cellphone away. • Keep your eyes on the speaker. •
Clarify by asking questions	• If you're confused, other people probably are, too. Ask a question to help your whole class. • If you see that you are guessing, ask a question instead. •
Monitor understanding	• Notice what information you already know and be ready to build on it. • Ask for help if you are struggling. •
Interact and share ideas	• Share your ideas and answer questions, even if you are unsure. • Build on the ideas of others by adding details or making a connection. •

SCAN FOR
MULTIMEDIA

CONTENTS

About the Author

Saroo Brierley (b. 1981) was born in a tiny village in India. At around the age of 5, he accidentally boarded a train alone and was whisked away from his family, hopelessly lost. He ended up at an orphanage in the West Bengal capital of Kolkata, formerly known as Calcutta. Brierley was eventually adopted by an Australian family and was raised in Tasmania. After twenty-five years of separation, Brierley finally succeeded in his quest to find his Indian family.

🔑 **Tool Kit**
First-Read Guide and Model Annotation

⊞ STANDARDS

Reading Informational Text
By the end of the year, read and comprehend literary nonfiction in the grades 6–8 text complexity band proficiently, with scaffolding as needed at the high end of the range.

from A Long Way Home

Concept Vocabulary

You will encounter the following words as you read the excerpt from *A Long Way Home*. Before reading, note how familiar you are with each word. Then, rank the words in order from most familiar (1) to least familiar (6).

WORD	YOUR RANKING
deliberate	
quest	
thorough	
obsessive	
intensity	
relentlessly	

After completing the first read, come back to the concept vocabulary and review your rankings. Mark changes to your original rankings as needed.

First Read NONFICTION

Apply these strategies as you conduct your first read. You will have an opportunity to complete the close-read notes after your first read.

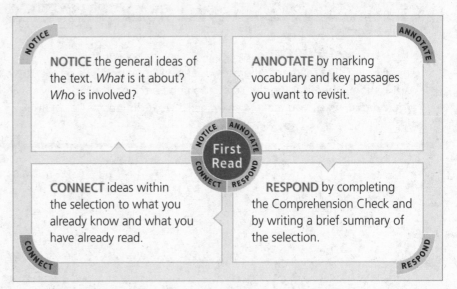

NOTICE the general ideas of the text. *What* is it about? *Who* is involved?

ANNOTATE by marking vocabulary and key passages you want to revisit.

CONNECT ideas within the selection to what you already know and what you have already read.

RESPOND by completing the Comprehension Check and by writing a brief summary of the selection.

First Read

from
A Long Way Home

Saroo Brierley

BACKGROUND

In his memoir *A Long Way Home*, Saroo Brierley shares his memories of searching for his hometown and his birth family. He describes the detailed method he used to locate them after decades of separation. At this point in the memoir, Brierley has recently graduated from college and moved in with his friend Byron.

SCAN FOR MULTIMEDIA

1 Alas, the new search didn't start out as an obsession.

2 If Byron wasn't home, I might spend a couple of hours musing over the various "B" towns[1] again. Or I might make a casual sweep down the east coast, to see what was there. I even checked out a Birampur in Uttar Pradesh, near Delhi, in the central north of India, but that was a ridiculously long way from Kolkata, and I couldn't have traveled that far in twelve or so hours. It turned out it doesn't even have a train station.

3 These occasional forays showed the folly of searching by town, particularly when I wasn't sure about the names. If I was going to do this, I needed to be strategic and methodical about it.

NOTES

---

1. **"B" Towns** Brierley remembers that the name of the train station near his hometown begins with a "B." This is the station at which he boarded a train and became lost.

4   I went over what I knew. I came from a place where Muslims and Hindus lived in close proximity and where Hindi was spoken. Those things were true of most of India. I recalled all those warm nights outside, under the stars, which at least suggested it wouldn't be in the colder regions of the far north. I hadn't lived by the sea, although I couldn't rule out that I'd lived near it. And I hadn't lived in the mountains. My hometown had a railway station—India was riddled with train lines, but they didn't run through every single village and town.

5   Then there was the opinion of the Indians at college that I looked like someone from the east, perhaps around West Bengal. I had my doubts: in the eastern part of the country, the region took in some of the Himalayas,[2] which wasn't right, and part of the Ganges Delta, which looked much too lush and fertile to be my home. But as these were people who had firsthand experience of India, it seemed silly to dismiss their hunch.

6   I also thought I could remember enough landmark features to recognize my hometown if I came across it, or to at least narrow the field. I clearly recalled the bridge over the river where we played as kids and the nearby dam wall that restricted the river's flow below it. I knew how to get from the train station to our house, and I knew the layout of the station.

7   The other station I thought I remembered quite well was the "B" one, where I'd boarded the train. Although I'd been there quite a few times with my brothers, they'd never let me leave it, so I knew nothing of the town outside the station—all I'd ever seen beyond the exit was a sort of small ring road for horse carts and cars, and a road beyond it that led into the town. But still, there were a couple of distinguishing features. I remembered the station building and that it only had a couple of tracks, over the other side of which was a big water tank on a tower. There was also a pedestrian overpass across the tracks. And just before the train pulled into town from the direction of my home, it crossed a small gorge.

8   So I had some vague thoughts on likely regions, and some ways of identifying "Ginestlay"[3] and the "B" place if I found them. Now I needed a better search method. I realized that the names of places had been a distraction, or were at least not the right place to start. Instead, I thought about the end of the journey. I knew that train lines linked the "B" place with Kolkata. Logic dictated, then, that if I followed all the train lines out of Kolkata, I would eventually find my starting point. And from there, my hometown was itself up the line, not far away. I might even come upon my

---

2. **Himalayas** (hihm uh LAY uhz) tallest mountain range in the world.
3. **"Ginestlay"** Brierley remembered this as the name of his hometown, but no one he asked had heard of it and he could not find it on a map.

home first, depending on how the lines linked up. This was an intimidating prospect—there were many, many train lines from the national hub of Kolkata's Howrah Station, and my train might have zigzagged across any of the lines of the spider's web. It was unlikely to be a simple, straight route.

9 Still, even with the possibility of some winding, irregular paths out of Howrah, there was also a limit to how far I could have been transported in the time frame. I'd spent, I thought, a long time on the train—somewhere between twelve and fifteen hours. If I made some calculations, I could narrow the search field, ruling out places too far away.

10 Why hadn't I thought of the search with this clarity before? Maybe I had been too overwhelmed by the scale of the problem to think straight, too consumed by what I didn't know to focus on what I did. But as it dawned on me that I could turn this into a painstaking, **deliberate** task that simply required dedication, something clicked inside. If all it took were time and patience to find home, with the aid of Google Earth's[4] god's-eye view, then I would do it. Seeing it almost as much an intellectual challenge as an emotional **quest**, I threw myself into solving it.

11 First, I worked on the search zone. How fast could India's diesel trains travel, and would that have changed much since the eighties? I thought my Indian friends from college might be able to help, especially Amreen, whose father would likely have a more educated guess, so I got in touch with them. The general consensus was around seventy or eighty kilometers an hour. That seemed like a good start. Figuring I had been trapped on the train for around twelve to fifteen hours, overnight, I calculated how many kilometers I might have traveled in that time, which I put at around a thousand, or approximately 620 miles.

12 So the place I was looking for was a thousand kilometers along a train line out of Howrah Station. On Google Earth you can draw lines on the map at precise distances, so I made a circular boundary line of a thousand kilometers around Kolkata and saved it for my searches. That meant that as well as West Bengal, my search field included the states of Jharkhand, Chhattisgarh, and nearly half of the central state of Madhya Pradesh to the west, Orissa to the south, Bihar and a third of Uttar Pradesh to the north, and most of the northeastern spur of India, which encircles Bangladesh. (I knew I wasn't from Bangladesh, as I'd have spoken Bengali, not Hindi. This was confirmed when I discovered

---

4. **Google Earth** computer program that displays satellite images of the world.

that a rail connection between the two countries had only been established a few years ago.)

13   It was a staggering amount of territory, covering some 962,300 square kilometers, over a quarter of India's huge landmass. Within its bounds lived 345 million people. I tried to keep my emotions out of the exercise, but I couldn't help but wonder: Is it possible to find my four family members among these 345 million? Even though my calculations were reliant on guesswork and were therefore very rough, and even though that still presented me with a huge field within which to search, it felt like I was narrowing things down. Rather than randomly throwing the haystack around to find the needle,[5] I could concentrate on picking through a manageable portion and set it aside if it proved empty.

Image from Google Earth.

14   The train lines within the search zone wouldn't all simply stretch out to the edge in a straight radius, of course—there would be a lot of twists, turns, and junctions, as they wound around and traveled much more than a thousand kilometers before they

---

5. **haystack . . . needle** the saying "finding a needle in a haystack" means looking for something almost impossible to find.

reached the boundary edge. So I planned to work outward from Kolkata, the only point of the journey I was certain about.

15   The first time I zoomed in on Howrah Station, looking at the rows of ridged gray platform roofs and all the tracks spilling out of it like the fraying end of a rope, I was amazed and shocked that I'd once trod barefoot along these walkways. I had to open my eyes wide to make sure what I was looking at was real. I was about to embark on a high-tech version of what I'd done in my first week there, twenty years ago, randomly taking trains out to see if they went back home.

16   I took a deep breath, chose a train line, and started scrolling along it.

17 Immediately, it became clear that progress would be slow. Even with broadband, my laptop had to render the image, which took time. It started a little pixelated, then resolved into an aerial photograph. I was looking for landmarks I recognized and paid particular attention to the stations, as they were the places I remembered most vividly.

18   When I first zoomed out to see how far I'd gone along the track, I was amazed at how little progress the hours of scrolling and studying had brought me. But rather than being frustrated and impatient, I found I had enormous confidence that I would find what I was looking for as long as I was **thorough**. That gave me a great sense of calm as I resumed my search. In fact, it quickly became compelling, and I returned to it several nights a week. Before I turned in each night, I'd mark how far I'd gone on a track and save the search, then resume from that point at the next opportunity.

19   I would come across goods yards, overpasses and underpasses, bridges over rivers and junctions. Sometimes I skipped along a bit but then nervously went back to repeat a section, reminding myself that if I wasn't methodical, I could never be sure I'd looked everywhere. I didn't jump ahead to look for stations in case I missed a small one—I followed the tracks so I could check out anything that came along. And if I found myself reaching the edge of the boundary I'd devised, I'd go back along the train line to a previous junction and then head off in another direction.

20   I remember one night early on, following a line north, I came to a river crossing not far outside a town. I caught my breath as I zoomed in closer. The dam wall was decaying, but maybe the area had since been reconstructed? I quickly dragged the cursor to roll the image along. Did the countryside look right? It was quite green, but there were a lot of farms on the outskirts of my town. I watched as the town unpixelated before my eyes. It was quite small. Too small, surely. But with a child's perspective . . .

NOTES

CLOSE READ
ANNOTATE: A **simile** compares two unlike things using the word *like* or *as*. Mark the simile in paragraph 15.

QUESTION: Why might the author have used a simile to describe what he was viewing on his computer screen?

CONCLUDE: How does the simile help the reader to better understand the challenges the author is facing?

thorough (THUR oh) *adj.* including everything possible; careful and complete

And there was a high pedestrian overpass across the tracks near the station! But what were the large blank areas dotted around the town? Three lakes, four or five even, within the tiny village's bounds—and it was suddenly obvious that this wasn't the place. You didn't clear whole neighborhoods to put in lakes. And of course, many, many stations were likely to have overpasses, and many towns would be situated near life-giving rivers, which the tracks would have to cross. How many times would I wonder if all the landmarks aligned, only to be left with tired, sore eyes and the realization that I was mistaken again?

21   Weeks and then months passed with my spending hours at a time every couple of nights on the laptop. Byron made sure I spent other nights out in the real world so I didn't become an Internet recluse. I covered the countryside of West Bengal and Jharkhand in these early stages without finding anything familiar, but at least it meant that much of the immediate vicinity of Kolkata could be ruled out. Despite the hunch of my Indian friends, I'd come from farther away.

22   Several months later, I was lucky enough to meet someone with whom I started a new relationship, which made the search less of a priority for a while. Lisa and I met in 2010 through a friend of Byron's and mine. We became friends on Facebook, and then I asked her for her phone number. We hit it off immediately; Lisa's background is in business management and she is smart, pretty, and can hold a great conversation. However, we had an unsettled start together, with a couple of breakups and reunions, which meant there was a similar inconsistency in the periods I spent looking on the Internet, before we finally settled into the lasting relationship we have today.

23   I didn't know how a girlfriend would take to the time-consuming quest of her partner staring at maps on a laptop. But Lisa understood the personal and growing importance of the search, and was patient and supportive. She was as amazed as anyone about my past, and wanted me to find the answers I was looking for. We moved into a small flat[6] together in 2010. I thought of the nights I spent there on the laptop as being a pastime, like playing computer games. But Lisa says that even then, with our relationship in full swing, I was **obsessive**. Looking back, I can see that this was true.

24   After all the years of my story being in my thoughts and dreams, I felt I was closing in on the reality. I decided this time I wasn't going to listen to anybody who said, "It might be time to move on," or "It's just not possible to find your hometown in

obsessive (uhb SEHS ihv) *adj.* tending to think or worry so much about something that you cannot think about anything else

---

6. **flat** *n.* apartment.

all of India like this." Lisa never said those things, and with her support, I became even more determined to succeed.

25   I didn't tell many people what I was doing anyway. And I decided not to tell my parents. I was worried they might misunderstand my intentions. I didn't want them to think that the **intensity** of my search revealed an unhappiness with the life they'd given me or the way they'd raised me. I also didn't want them to think that I was wasting time. So even as it took up more and more of my life, I kept it mostly to myself. I finished work with Dad at five p.m., and by five-thirty I would be back at the laptop, slowly advancing along train tracks and studying the towns they led to. This went on for months—it had been over a year since I started. But I reasoned that even if it took years . . . or decades . . . it was possible to eventually sift completely through a haystack. The needle would have to show up if I persisted.

26   Slowly, over several more months, I eliminated whole areas of India. I traced all the connections within the northeastern states without finding anything familiar, and I was confident that I could rule out Orissa, too. Determined to be thorough, no matter how long it took, I started following lines farther out than my original thousand-kilometer zone. South beyond Orissa, I eliminated Andhra Pradesh, five hundred kilometers farther down the east coast. Jharkhand and Bihar didn't offer up anything promising, either, and as I wound up in Uttar Pradesh, I thought I'd keep going to cover most of the state. In fact, the states eventually replaced my zone boundary as a way of marking my progress. Ruling out areas state by state provided a series of goals that spurred me on.

27   Unless I had something pressing to do for work, or some other unbreakable commitment, I was on the laptop seven nights a week. I went out with Lisa sometimes, of course, but the moment we got home I was back on the computer. Sometimes I caught her looking at me strangely, as though she thought I might have gone a bit crazy. She'd say, "You're at it again!" but I would reply, "I have to . . . I'm really sorry!" I think Lisa knew she simply had to let me exhaust myself of the interest. I became distant during that time, and although Lisa would have been within her rights to feel alone in this still-new relationship, we worked through it. Perhaps to some extent sharing something so fundamental to me strengthened our connection—and that came through when we sometimes talked about what it all meant. It wasn't always easy for me to articulate,[7] especially as I was trying to keep a lid on my expectations, trying to convince myself it was a fascinating exercise, not a deeply meaningful personal quest. Talking to Lisa

---

7. **articulate** (ahr TIHK yuh layt) *v.* express clearly using words.

intensity (ihn TEHN suh tee) *n.* great focus or concentration; strong commitment

CLOSE READ

ANNOTATE: In paragraph 27, mark details that show how often Brierley is searching for his hometown at this point.

QUESTION: What do these details reveal about how his search is progressing?

CONCLUDE: How do these details help the reader to better understand Brierley's state of mind?

sometimes revealed the underlying importance of the search to me: that I was looking for my home to provide closure and to understand my past and perhaps myself better as a result, in the hope that I might somehow reconnect with my Indian family so they would know what had happened to me. Lisa understood all this and didn't resent it, even if there were times when she wanted to ban me from staring at the screen for my own sake. Once in a while she would simply come over and shut my laptop and place it on the floor because I was becoming so obsessive about my search.

28   At times Lisa admitted her own greatest fear: that I would find what I thought I was looking for, go back to India, and somehow be wrong or fail to find my family there. Would I return to Hobart[8] and simply start again, obsessively searching online? I couldn't answer her questions any more than I could allay her fears. I couldn't allow myself to think about failure.

29   If anything, I became more intense about my search as 2010 drew to a close, and the speed of our newly acquired broadband connection made it quicker to refresh the images and zoom in and out. But I still had to take it slowly—if I rushed, I'd leave myself open to wondering later if I'd missed anything and then going back in an endless cycle. And I had to try not to bend my memories to fit what I was looking at.

30   By early 2011, I was concentrating more on areas within India's center, in Chhattisgarh and Madhya Pradesh. I spent months poring over them, **relentlessly**, methodically.

31   Of course, there were times when I doubted the wisdom, and even the sanity, of what I was doing. Night after night, with the day's last reserves of energy and willpower, I sat staring at railway lines, searching for places my five-year-old mind might recognize. It was a repetitive, forensic[9] exercise, and sometimes it started to feel claustrophobic, as if I were trapped and looking out at the world through a small window, unable to break free of my course in a mind-twisting echo of my childhood ordeal.

32   And then one night in March around one in the morning, in just such a mood, spent with frustration, I took a wild dive into the haystack, and it changed everything.

33   As always, on March 31, 2011, I had come home from work, grabbed my laptop, opened Google Earth, and settled in for a session on the sofa, stopping only briefly for dinner when Lisa got home. I was examining the central west at this time, so I picked up there, "traveling" a train line near my former search zone

relentlessly (rih LEHNT lihs lee) *adv.* without stopping; with determination

---

8. **Hobart** capital of Tasmania, an island state of Australia, where Brierley lives.
9. **forensic** (fuh REHN sihk) *adj.* careful and detailed, similar to the scientific methods used to solve a crime.

boundary. Even with quicker broadband, it was still slow going. I continued for what seemed like ages, looking at a few stations, but as usual, when I zoomed out, I found I'd only covered a tiny area. I thought that the countryside looked a bit green for my dusty old town, but I knew by now that India's landscape changed appearance regularly as you moved across it.

34   After a few hours, I had followed a line to a junction. I took a break, checking Facebook for a while before rubbing my eyes, stretching my back, and returning to my task.

35   Before zooming in, I idly flicked the map along to get a quick picture of where the westerly line out of the junction headed, and watched hills, forests, and river sweep by, a seemingly endless terrain of reasonably similar features. I was distracted by a large river that fed into what looked like a massive, deep blue lake called Nal Damayanti Sagar, which was surrounded by some lush country and had mountains to its north. For a while, I enjoyed this little exploration, indulgently unrelated to my search, like a recreational hike of grand proportions. It was getting late, after all, and I'd turn in soon.

36   There didn't seem to be any train lines in this part of the country, which might have been why it was relaxing to look at. But once I'd noticed that, I found myself almost subconsciously looking for one. There were villages and towns dotted around here and there, and I wondered how the people traveled without rail—perhaps they didn't move around much? And farther west, still no tracks! Then as the countryside flattened out into farmland, I finally came across a little blue symbol denoting a train station. I was so attuned to looking for them, I was somehow relieved to find this one, and I checked out the tiny wayside station, just a few buildings to the side of a reasonably major train line with several tracks. Out of habit, I started tracing the route as it wound southwest. I quickly came across another station, a bit bigger, again with a platform on only one side of the tracks, but some areas of the township on either side. That explained the overpass, and was that . . . was that a water tower just nearby?

37   Holding my breath, I zoomed in for a closer look. Sure enough, it was a municipal water tank just across from the platform, and not far from a large pedestrian overpass spanning the railway line. I scrolled over to the town side and saw something incredible—a horseshoe-shaped road around a square immediately outside the station. Could it be—perhaps it was the ring road I used to be able to see from the platform! Was it possible? I closed my

> Could it be—perhaps it was the ring road I used to be able to see from the platform! Was it possible?

CLOSE READ

ANNOTATE: In paragraph 37, mark the words the author emphasizes with italics.

QUESTION: Why does the author choose to emphasize these words?

CONCLUDE: How does this emphasis help the reader understand Brierley's thoughts and emotions?

eyes and went back twenty four years in time to when I would walk to the station's exit and see the ring road with an island in the middle. I thought to myself, *This is unique; I haven't seen this before.* I zoomed out, discovering that the train line skimmed the northwestern edge of a really large town. I clicked on the blue train station symbol to reveal its name . . . Burhanpur. My heart nearly stopped. *Burhanpur!*

38   I didn't recognize the town itself, but then I'd never been in it—I'd never left the platform. I zoomed back in and re-examined the ring road, the water tower, the overpass, and they were all positioned where I remembered them. That meant that not far away, just up the line, I should find my hometown, "Ginestlay."

39   Almost afraid to do so, I dragged the cursor to pull the image north along the train line. When I saw that the track crossed a gorge just on the edge of the built-up area, I was flooded with adrenaline—I remembered in a flash that the train I took with my brothers traveled on a small bridge over a gorge like that before pulling into the station. I pushed on more urgently, east then northeast, in just moments zooming over seventy kilometers

of green farms, forested hills, and small rivers. Then I passed across some dry, flat land, broken up by a patchwork of irrigated farmland and the occasional small village, before I hit a bridge over a substantial river. Ahead I was able to see the town's outskirts. The river's flow was significantly reduced below the bridge by dam walls on either side. If this was the right place, this was the river I used to play in, and there should be a bigger concrete dam wall to my right a little farther from the bridge . . .

40   There it was!

41   I sat staring at the screen for what seemed like an eternity. What I was looking at matched the picture in my head exactly. I couldn't think straight; I was frozen with excitement, terrified to go on.

42   Finally, after a couple of minutes, I forced myself to take the next step, slowly, nervously. I tried to calm myself so I didn't jump to any rash conclusions. If I really was looking at "Ginestlay" for the first time in twenty-four years, then I should be able to follow the path I remembered from the river back to the train station, only a short way up ahead. I began to drag the cursor again, slowly rolling the map to trace the course of the path, which wound gently alongside a tributary stream, left and right, around a field, under a street overpass and then . . . the station. I clicked on the blue symbol and the name came up on the screen: Khandwa Railway Station.

43   The name meant nothing to me.

44   My stomach knotted. How could this be?

45   Things had looked so right all the way from Burhanpur, which had to be the "B" town I had tried to remember. But if the bridge and the river were correct, where was "Ginestlay"? I tried not to despair. I had spent a lot of time in and around our local train station as a boy, so I checked off what I remembered—the three platforms, the covered pedestrian overpass that connected them, an underpass road beneath the tracks at the northern end. But it wasn't so much the existence of these reasonably common features but their position in relation to each other that would identify the specific place that I was looking for. It all checked out. I also remembered a huge fountain in a park near the underpass, and I went looking. Sure enough, it was a little indistinct, but I thought I detected its familiar circular shape in a central clearing, surrounded by trees.

46   From here, I knew the route to where my home should be. This was why I'd gone over and over it in my head since I was a little boy: so that I would never forget it.

47   Now, as a man, I followed the road up from the fountain and along the route of the underpass, and then the streets and alleys I had walked as a child—the way I used to imagine myself walking

NOTES

CLOSE READ

ANNOTATE: In paragraph 41, mark the words that show Brierley's reaction to the image on his screen.

QUESTION: Why might Brierley react with these feelings?

CONCLUDE: How does the description of his reaction add suspense to Brierley's narrative?

when I lay in bed at night, in the safe comfort of my house in Hobart, trying to project myself back to my village home to let my mother know I was okay. Before I realized I'd gone far enough, I was looking down at the neighborhood I knew as a boy.

48   Still, nothing like "Ginestlay" came up on the map. It was the strangest feeling, and one that I became familiar with over the next year or so—part of me was certain, but still another part of me doubted. I was sure this was the right place, but for all this time I'd also been sure of the name "Ginestlay." Khandwa rang no bells whatsoever. Maybe "Ginestlay" was a part of Khandwa? A suburb? That seemed possible. I looked through the maze of alleys where my family lived, and although the image wasn't as clear as what I would get when I looked at where I lived in Hobart, I was sure I could see the little rectangular roof of my childhood home. Of course, I'd never seen the place from above, but the building was the right shape and in precisely the correct location. I hovered over the streets for a while, astonished, trying to take it all in. Finally I couldn't contain my excitement any longer.

49   I called out to Lisa, "I've found my hometown! You've gotta come and see this!" It was only then that I realized the time. I'd been at the computer for over seven hours nonstop, except for dinner.

50   Lisa poked her head around the corner, yawning, in her nightie. It took her a moment to wake up properly, but even half-asleep she could see my excitement. "Are you sure?" she asked.

51   "This is it, this is it!" I replied.

52   In that moment, I was convinced. "This is my hometown!"

53   It had taken eight months of intense searching, and it was nearly five years since I'd first downloaded Google Earth.

54   Lisa grinned and hugged me tightly. "That's so great! You did it, Saroo!" ❧

Comprehension Check

Complete the following items after you finish your first read.

1. What is the goal of Saroo Brierley's search?

2. What is the main resource Brierley uses to conduct his search?

3. According to the author, what is Lisa's greatest fear?

4. What is "Ginestlay"? Does Brierley ever find it?

5. 📓 **Notebook** Write a summary of the memoir to show your understanding.

- -

RESEARCH

Research to Clarify Choose at least one unfamiliar detail from the text. Briefly research that detail. In what way does the information you learned shed light on an aspect of the text?

Research to Explore Choose something that interests you from the text, and formulate a research question.

from A LONG WAY HOME

Close Read the Text

1. This model, from paragraph 13, shows two sample annotations, along with questions and conclusions. Close read the passage, and find another detail to annotate. Then, write a question and conclusion.

Close Read
ANNOTATE · QUESTION · CONCLUDE

ANNOTATE: The author has included numbers and statistics in this passage.

QUESTION: What information is provided by these details?

CONCLUDE: The data reveal how difficult Brierley's search will be.

It was a staggering amount of territory, covering some 962,300 square kilometers…. Within its bounds lived 345 million people. I tried to keep my emotions out of the exercise, but I couldn't help but wonder: Is it possible to find four family members among these 345 million?

ANNOTATE: The author asks himself a question.

QUESTION: What purpose does this question serve?

CONCLUDE: This question creates suspense and reveals Brierley's doubt.

2. For more practice, go back into the text and complete the close read sections.

3. Revisit a section of the text you found important during your first read. Read this section closely and **annotate** what you notice. Ask yourself **questions** such as "Why did the author make this choice?" What can you **conclude**?

🔧 Tool Kit
Close-Read Guide and Model Annotation

Analyze the Text

CITE TEXTUAL EVIDENCE to support your answers.

📓 **Notebook** Respond to these questions.

1. (a) **Connect** How does Brierley emphasize the importance of his search method and process throughout the excerpt?
   (b) **Infer** What do those text details suggest about Brierley's personality?

2. **Interpret** Review paragraph 29. What does Brierley mean when he says "And I had to try not to bend my memories to fit what I was looking at"?

3. **Essential Question:** *What drives people to explore?* What has this text revealed about what drives people to explore?

Analyze Craft and Structure

Central Ideas: Autobiographical Writing An **autobiography** is a true account of events and experiences written by the person who directly experienced them. A **memoir** is a type of autobiography that focuses on a specific period in the author's life or an experience that holds particular significance for the author.

Autobiographical writing relates an author's thoughts, feelings, and reflections on the events and experiences he or she describes. Autobiographies and memoirs can communicate a variety of insights including:

- what the author learned from the event or experience
- what the author values and his or her goals in life
- how the author feels about other people in his or her life
- how the author relates to his or her environment and the world
- how the author responds to the **conflicts,** or struggles, with which he or she is faced

These insights help to develop the author's **central ideas,** or main points. To determine an author's central ideas in a text, analyze and connect details that reveal the author's reflections and insights.

Practice

CITE TEXTUAL EVIDENCE to support your answers.

Notebook Review the excerpt from *A Long Way Home.* Use the chart to identify the author's central ideas in each passage. Then, answer the questions that follow.

PARAGRAPH(S)	DETAILS THAT REVEAL REFLECTIONS AND INSIGHTS	CENTRAL IDEA OF PASSAGE
10		
17–18		
31		

1. Review your completed chart. What inference can you make about the central idea of the text as a whole, based on the central ideas you identified for each passage?

2. (a) Review paragraphs 48–51. What conflicting feelings does Brierley express in this passage? (b) How does the method and process of Brierley's search create inner conflict?

3. What comparisons does Brierley make between his childhood journey and his quest to find his hometown as an adult?

4. (a) What role do Brierley's childhood memories play in his search? (b) What do they reveal about Brierley's goals?

Concept Vocabulary

deliberate	thorough	intensity
quest	obsessive	relentlessly

Why These Words? The concept vocabulary words relate to the idea of searching or exploring. Saroo Brierley uses these words as he describes his search for his hometown in India. For example, Brierley discusses how his search must be *deliberate*, or carefully planned, if he has any chance of succeeding.

1. How does the concept vocabulary sharpen the reader's understanding the author's experiences while on his mission?

2. What other words in the selection connect to this concept?

Practice

📓 **Notebook** Demonstrate your understanding of the concept vocabulary words by writing a paragraph in which you describe an imaginary quest. For example, you may write about a quest to find a mythical creature or a hidden treasure. Include three concept vocabulary words, other than *quest*, in your paragraph.

Word Study

Latin Suffix: -ive The Latin suffix *-ive* means "pertaining to," "tending to," or "serving to do." Words that contain this suffix are usually adjectives. In *A Long Way Home*, Brierley describes his behavior and attitude as *obsessive* because he tended to think about his search so much that he neglected his personal relationships.

1. Find another word in paragraph 23 that contains the Latin suffix *-ive*, and write a brief definition of it.

2. Explain how the suffix *-ive* contributes to the meanings of the following words: *active, inclusive, possessive.*

☰ STANDARDS

Reading Informational Texts
Analyze in detail how a key individual, event, or idea is introduced, illustrated, and elaborated in a text.

Language
Determine or clarify the meaning of unknown and multiple-meaning words and phrases based on *grade 6 reading and content*, choosing flexibly from a range of strategies.
  b. Use common, grade-appropriate Greek or Latin affixes and roots as clues to the meaning of a word.

Author's Style

Word Choice and Mood Saroo Brierley's memoir contains rich descriptive details. In his narrative he introduces people, events, and ideas and then provides additional details to further illustrate and elaborate. The depth of description enables readers to fully engage in Brierley's journey, along with him. Here are some descriptive examples from *The Long Way Home*:

- **Description of Actions:** *I traced all the connections within the northeastern states without finding anything familiar, and I was confident that I could rule out Orissa, too.*
- **Description of Places:** *I zoomed back in and re-examined the ring road, the water tower, the overpass, and they were all positioned where I remembered them.*
- **Description of Emotions:** *Finally, after a couple of minutes, I forced myself to take the next step, slowly, nervously. I tried to calm myself so I didn't jump to any rash conclusions.*

Writers' word choices also help to create **mood,** or atmosphere. Mood can be described using adjectives such as *gloomy, upbeat, eerie,* and *lighthearted*. Sometimes the mood of a narrative shifts to match the main character's experiences and observations; sometimes the mood of a story stays the same throughout.

Practice

Complete the chart by marking descriptive words in the passages provided from the memoir. Then, in the column to the right, describe the mood of the passage.

PASSAGE FROM TEXT	MOOD OF PASSAGE
I recalled all those warm nights outside, under the stars, which at least suggested it wouldn't be in the colder regions of the far north. I hadn't lived by the sea, although I couldn't rule out that I'd lived near it. And I hadn't lived in the mountains. My hometown had a railway station—India was riddled with train lines, but they didn't run through every single village and town. (paragraph 4)	
If anything, I became more intense about my search as 2010 drew to a close, and the speed of our newly acquired broadband connection made it quicker to refresh the images and zoom in and out. But I still had to take it slowly—if I rushed, I'd leave myself open to wondering later if I'd missed anything and then going back in an endless cycle. (paragraph 29)	
I thought to myself, *This is unique; I haven't seen this before.* I zoomed out, discovering that the train line skimmed the northwestern edge of a really large town. I clicked on the blue train station symbol to reveal its name . . . Burhanpur. My heart nearly stopped. *Burhanpur!* (paragraph 37)	

from A LONG WAY HOME

Writing to Sources

In an **argument**, an author makes a claim in which he or she states an opinion on a topic or an issue. Then, the author tries to persuade readers to adopt this opinion by providing reasons and supporting evidence for it.

Assignment

When we think of explorers, we often think of pioneers who travel to new and unknown places. Write an **argument** in which you state a claim in response to the following question:

Is Saroo Brierley an explorer? Why, or why not?

Consider Brierley's search and how he conducted his search, as well as what you think an explorer should try to accomplish.

- Begin your argument by clearly stating whether or not you think Brierley is an explorer—this is your claim.

- Support your claim by providing logical reasons and evidence from the text.

- Organize your reasons and evidence clearly, and use transition words and phrases to clarify and connect your ideas.

- Include a strong conclusion that restates your claim in a new way and provides an additional idea or insight.

Vocabulary Connection You may want to use some concept vocabulary words and descriptive details in your writing.

deliberate	thorough	intensity
quest	obsessive	relentlessly

- -

Reflect on Your Writing

After you have written your argument, answer the following questions.

1. What do you think was the most challenging part of the assignment?

2. How would you revise your argument to improve it?

3. Why These Words? The words you choose make a difference in your writing. Which words did you choose to help you convey precise ideas?

STANDARDS

Writing
Write arguments to support claims with clear reasons and relevant evidence.
  a. Introduce claim(s) and organize the reasons and evidence clearly.
  b. Support claim(s) with clear reasons and relevant evidence, using credible sources and demonstrating an understanding of the topic or text.
  c. Use words, phrases, and clauses to clarify the relationships among claim(s) and reasons.
  e. Provide a concluding statement or section that follows from the argument presented.

Speaking and Listening

An annotated map is a type of map that includes descriptions and explanations of map locations. Annotated maps enable viewers to quickly and easily find information.

Assignment

As a class, create an **annotated map** in which you trace the route Brierley follows on March 31, 2011, when he finally finds his childhood home.

1. **Prepare for the Activity** Work individually to review the excerpt, and take notes on the specific locations Brierley describes in paragraphs 33–54. Use print or online resources to locate a map of India to familiarize yourself with the locations he discusses.

2. **Find the Locations** As a class, use your notes to mark the locations from the March 31st search on a map of India, print or digital, that your teacher provides.

3. **Paraphrase Descriptions** Once you have identified the locations on the map, take turns with classmates to **paraphrase,** or restate Brierley's descriptions of the area. Include details about what he remembers as well as what he sees as he approaches and zooms in on his hometown.

4. **Annotate the Map** Annotate the map with the paraphrased descriptions. When you **annotate**, you add notes that give additional information or explain something. If you are using a print map, use sticky notes or notecards with pins to add your annotations. If you are using a digital map, create text boxes and enter your paraphrases there.

5. **Discuss** Once your map is complete, discuss the map as a class. Use these questions as a guide for your discussion:

   - How does the map help you to visualize Brierley's search?
   - How does seeing a map of India enable you to grasp the enormous scope of his search?
   - How did the process of annotating the map deepen your understanding of the excerpt?

About the Narrator

The Irish comedian **Dara Ó Briain** (b. 1972) is a self-described "geek." He attended University College, Dublin, and studied math and theoretical physics. Ó Briain is best known, however, for his comedy and for his hosting of many popular television shows, including the British version of *The Apprentice: You're Fired* and *Mock the Week*.

BBC Science Club: All About Exploration

Media Vocabulary

The following words or concepts will be useful to you as you analyze, discuss, and write about animated videos.

cut-out animation: technique that uses flat characters, backgrounds, and props cut from materials such as paper, cardboard, and fabric	Cut-out animation involves moving cut-out objects in small steps to imitate natural movement while taking a picture at each step.
object animation: form that involves the movement of non-drawn objects, such as a book or a pen	• The objects used in this type of animation are generally not designed to look like a recognizable human or animal character. • Animated objects are not made of flexible materials, such as clay or wax.
real-time animation: style in which animated events or objects are reproduced so that they appear to be occurring or moving at the same speed they would in real life	• Interactive video games commonly use real-time animation to mimic the pace of natural movements. • Animated movies also use real-time animation to give viewers the impression of real life.

First Review MEDIA: VIDEO

Apply these strategies as you watch the video. As you watch, note the time codes of sections so that you can easily revisit them.

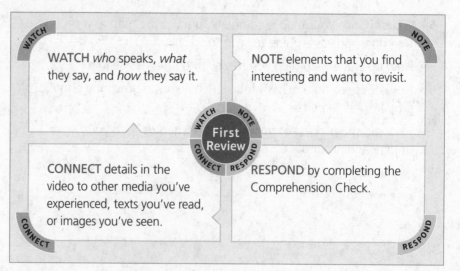

WATCH who speaks, what they say, and how they say it.

NOTE elements that you find interesting and want to revisit.

CONNECT details in the video to other media you've experienced, texts you've read, or images you've seen.

RESPOND by completing the Comprehension Check.

First Review

WATCH NOTE CONNECT RESPOND

STANDARDS

Reading Informational Text
By the end of the year, read and comprehend literary nonfiction in the grades 6–8 text complexity band proficiently, with scaffolding as needed at the high end of the range.

Language
Acquire and use accurately grade-appropriate general academic and domain-specific words and phrases; gather vocabulary knowledge when considering a word or phrase important to comprehension or expression.

BBC Science Club:
All About Exploration

BACKGROUND

In the video, the narrator mentions the pioneering scientist Dr. Robert Goddard, who invented liquid-fueled rockets in the early 20th century. Goddard devoted his life to researching and developing rockets, laying the groundwork for space exploration. An insightful physicist and inventor, Goddard envisioned the possibility of space flight, and his contributions were essential to making space travel a reality. The Goddard Space Flight Center in Maryland, a major NASA research laboratory, was established in his memory.

SCAN FOR
MULTIMEDIA

NOTES

Comprehension Check

Complete the following items after you finish your first review.

1. How did ancient Greeks navigate?

2. Why didn't Columbus know he wasn't in India?

3. What was the problem with the early balloons used for air travel?

4. Why didn't the *New York Times* initially believe that it was possible to go to the moon?

MEDIA VOCABULARY

Use these words as you discuss and write about the video.

cut-out animation
object animation
real-time animation

Close Review

Watch the video or parts of it again. Write any new observations that seem important. What questions do you have? What can you conclude?

Analyze the Media

CITE TEXTUAL EVIDENCE
to support your answers.

📓 **Notebook** Respond to these questions.

1. (a) Draw Conclusions What conclusions can you draw about the ways in which exploration has been influenced by advancements in navigation? **(b) Make a Judgment** Do you think that navigational advancements or technological advancements were more important to expanding our ability to explore? Explain.

2. Interpret At the beginning of the video, the narrator says that people need "effective means and methods" to explore. What does he mean by this statement?

3. Evaluate How effective is the use of animation in conveying information about exploration?

4. Essential Question: *What drives people to explore?* What have you learned about what drives people to explore from watching the video?

📰 **STANDARDS**
Reading Informational Texts
Cite textual evidence to support analysis of what the text says explicitly as well as inferences drawn from the text.

Research

The video "All About Exploration" provides a humorous but factual look at the history of exploration.

Assignment

Perform research to identify an explorer whose accomplishments could be added to the "All About Exploration" video. Then, create a **storyboard** in which you provide information about the explorer and his or her exploration activities.

Research and Plan Begin by performing research on an explorer from history. Once you have identified the explorer, consult various sources and take careful notes about his or her mission, the dates of the mission, and the success of the mission. Strive to find facts, explanations, quotations, or other interesting information that will bring your explorer to life.

Draft a Storyboard Once your research is completed, use a storyboard template like this one to present your ideas. Draw or find images that depict key events of the exploration. Style the images to match the style in "All About Exploration." Then, add captions to images in which you indicate the voiceover narration that would accompany the images. Challenge yourself to create a humorous tone as in the original video.

STORYBOARD

Present Once you are happy with your storyboard, share it with your classmates. If you are comfortable using digital tools, consider animating your images and recording the voiceover narration. If you prefer, simply present your storyboard on an overhead projector and read the voiceover narration as classmates listen.

📝 EVIDENCE LOG

Before moving on to a new selection, go to your Evidence Log and record what you learned from the video.

📊 STANDARDS

Writing
• Write informative/explanatory texts to examine a topic and convey ideas, concepts, and information through the selection, organization, and analysis of relevant content.
　b. Develop the topic with relevant facts, definitions, concrete details, quotations, or other information and examples.

• Conduct short research projects to answer a question, drawing on several sources and refocusing the inquiry when appropriate.

Speaking and Listening
Include multimedia components and visual displays in presentations to clarify information.

WRITING TO SOURCES

• *from* A LONG WAY HOME

• BBC SCIENCE CLUB: ALL ABOUT EXPLORATION

Write an Argument

You have read an excerpt from a memoir and watched a video that discuss different aspects of exploration. In *A Long Way Home*, the author describes how he used Google Earth to search for his childhood home in India. In "BBC Science Club: All About Exploration" viewers learn about the history of exploration.

Assignment

Use your knowledge of both the memoir and the video to take and defend a position on the topic of exploration. Write a brief **argumentative essay** in which you state and support your position on this question:

> Can anyone be an explorer?

Include examples and details from the memoir and the video, as well as your own observations to support your reasoning.

Elements of an Argument

An **argumentative essay** is a short work in which a writer presents a position and supports it with reasons and evidence. The purpose is to persuade readers to think a certain way about the topic. An effective argumentative essay contains these elements:

- a claim, or statement of a position
- clear, convincing reasons that relate to the claim
- evidence, or facts and examples that support the claim
- a clear organization, including an introduction, a body, and a conclusion
- transitional words and phrases that make the relationships among claims and reasons clear
- a concluding statement or section that follows from the ideas presented earlier in the essay
- a formal style that takes the subject and reader seriously
- error-free grammar, including accurate use of verbs

Model Argument For a model of a well-crafted argument, see the Launch Text, "What on Earth Is Left to Explore?"

Challenge yourself to find all of the elements of an effective argument in the text. You will have an opportunity to review these elements as you prepare to write your own argument.

LAUNCH TEXT

What on Earth Is Left to Explore?

ACADEMIC VOCABULARY

As you craft your argument, consider using some of the academic vocabulary you learned in the beginning of the unit.

critical
assume
compel
valid
coherent

▤ STANDARDS

Writing
• Write arguments to support claims with clear reasons and relevant evidence.
• Draw evidence from literary or informational texts to support analysis, reflection, and research.
  b. Apply *grade 6 Reading standards* to literary nonfiction.
• Write routinely over extended time frames and shorter time frames for a range of discipline-specific tasks, purposes, and audiences.

Prewriting / Planning

Write a Working Claim A working claim is a statement of your main idea that will help you get started with your writing. It allows you to try out your ideas and evidence. Depending on how your essay develops, you may wind up keeping your working claim or you may change it completely. Write a working claim here.

Working Claim: _____

_____

Consider Other Opinions Considering how other people feel or think about a topic can strengthen your argument. Think about questions readers might have about your position, or opinions that might differ from yours. Plan to answer those questions or address those opinions in your essay. Use these sentence starters to pull your ideas together.

A different opinion is _____

The reason someone might think this is because _____

The reason this idea is not convincing is _____

Collect Evidence The most important evidence you will use comes from the memoir and video. However, you may want to support your position with other types of details, as well. Consider using these types of evidence:

- **facts:** statements that can be proved true
- **statistics:** facts presented in the form of numbers
- **anecdotes:** brief stories that can be used as examples
- **quotations from authorities:** statements from experts
- **examples:** specific people, situations, or events that support a general idea

Using a variety of evidence can make your argument stronger. In the Launch Text, the writer includes a variety of examples to support the point that "people seem to be everywhere."

> *Thousands have climbed Mount Everest, the world's highest mountain. There are even people living in Antarctica, the world's coldest continent. In addition, the Internet allows people to visit faraway places through the screens of their computers.*
> —from "What on Earth Is Left to Explore?"

Connect Across Texts As you write your essay, you will use evidence from both the video and the memoir to support your ideas. Include that evidence in different ways. For example, use **exact quotations** if the exact words are important. Otherwise, **paraphrase**, or restate ideas in your own words.

✒ EVIDENCE LOG

Review your Evidence Log and identify key details you may want to cite in your argument.

▤ STANDARDS

Writing
Write arguments to support claims with clear reasons and relevant evidence.
    a. Introduce claim(s) and organize the reasons and evidence clearly.
    b. Support claim(s) with clear reasons and relevant evidence, using credible sources and demonstrating an understanding of the topic or text.

Drafting

Organize Ideas Argumentative essays include three sections: an **introduction,** a **body,** and a **conclusion.** Each section should build on the one that came before it, and every point should support your main claim. Look at the guidelines for each section given in the chart. Then, add notes about the ideas and evidence you will include in each part of your essay. This outline will help you plan a logical order for your ideas and evidence.

SECTION	GUIDELINES	PLAN FOR EACH SECTION
Introduction Present the topic and claim.	• Engage readers with interesting information. • Clearly state the claim.	
Body Give supporting reasons and evidence.	• Use one paragraph for each reason. • Include a topic sentence, or main idea, in each paragraph. • Use strong evidence.	
Conclusion Sum up the argument.	• Restate the claim in different words. • End with a strong, statement.	

STANDARDS
Writing
Write arguments to support claims with clear reasons and relevant evidence.
e. Provide a concluding statement or section that follows from the argument presented.

Write a First Draft Use your outline to write your first draft. Be sure to write an introduction that will grab the reader's attention. Then, present your supporting reasons in a logical order. Provide a strong conclusion that ends your argument with a clear statement.

LANGUAGE DEVELOPMENT

Word Choice for Style and Tone

In an argument, your writing style should be formal. Your **tone,** or attitude, should be serious. These two qualities help make your ideas believable, which strengthens your argument. To create and maintain the right style and tone, pay careful attention to your word choice throughout your essay.

Read It

These sentences from the beginning, middle, and end of the Launch Text are both formal and serious.

Passage 1 (beginning): *To the west lay an entire continent, full of mystery and promise.*

Passage 2 (middle): *Vast stretches of the oceans are hidden under miles of water.*

Passage 3 (end): *The need to explore and extend the boundaries of knowledge remains vital and should continue.*

Write It

As you draft your essay, avoid using slang, people's first names, and contractions. In addition, apply the following strategies to choose words that create the formal style and serious tone you need:

- **Choose accurate words.** Informal or exaggerated expressions may be fun, but they may not say exactly what you mean. In an argument, avoid exaggeration. Choose accuracy over excitement.

  Original Sentence: The number of tourists has <u>gone through the roof</u>.
  Revised Sentence: The number of tourists has <u>increased</u>.

- **Avoid absolute words.** Words such as *all, always, never,* and *only* may lead to statements that are too broad. Replace them with words you can defend.

  Original Sentence: Climbing Mount Everest is not as special because <u>everyone</u> has done it.
  Revised Sentence: Climbing Mount Everest is not as special because <u>many people</u> have done it.

- **Use reasonable words.** Charged words can capture readers' interest, but make sure you focus more on facts. Always avoid name-calling.

  Original Sentence: Exploring a cave without proper equipment is <u>stupid</u>.
  Revised Sentence: Exploring a cave without proper equipment is <u>risky</u>.

STANDARDS

Writing
- Write arguments to support claims with clear reasons and relevant evidence.
  d. Establish and maintain a formal style.

Language
Use knowledge of language and its conventions when writing, speaking, reading, or listening.
  b. Maintain consistency in style and tone.

Revising

Evaluating Your Draft

Use the following checklist to evaluate the effectiveness of your first draft. Then, use your evaluation and the instruction on this page to guide your revision.

FOCUS AND ORGANIZATION	EVIDENCE AND ELABORATION	CONVENTIONS
☐ Introduces a clear claim.	☐ Provides clear reasons and strong evidence that supports them.	☐ Observes the conventions of standard English grammar.
☐ Provides a conclusion that follows from the argument.	☐ Uses words, phrases, and clauses that clarify the relationships among ideas.	
☐ Establishes a logical organization and develops a clear progression.	☐ Establishes and maintains a formal style and serious tone.	

⊹ WORD NETWORK

Include words from your Word Network in your narrative.

Revising for Focus and Organization

Show Connections Reread your argument. Revise your sentences to clarify the relationships between the claim you make and the evidence you provide. Use transition words such as *because, in fact,* or *therefore* to show the connections among ideas.

Revising for Evidence and Elaboration

Check Your Evidence Make sure that you have stated your ideas with authority and supported them with relevant evidence from the texts. Also consider *how* you have presented evidence. Make sure you have chosen the approach that gives readers information in the most effective way.

- **Summarize,** or briefly restate ideas, to give readers information quickly.
- **Paraphrase,** or restate ideas in your own words, when you wish to help readers understand a complicated idea.
- **Quote** a writer's or a speaker's exact words when they are especially interesting or powerful.

Make sure to clearly introduce each piece of evidence you use. Explain why it is important and how it connects to your ideas.

≡ STANDARDS

Writing
Write arguments to support claims with clear reasons and relevant evidence.
a. Introduce claim(s) and organize the reasons and evidence clearly.
b. Support claims with clear reasons and relevant evidence, using credible sources and demonstrating an understanding of the topic or text.
c. Use words, phrases, and clauses to clarify the relationships among claim(s) and reasons.

Exchange essays with a classmate. Use the checklist to evaluate your classmate's essay and provide supportive feedback.

1. Is the claim clear?

☐ yes ☐ no If no, explain what confused you.

2. Is the organization logical?

☐ yes ☐ no If no, explain what was confusing about the organization.

3. Does the conclusion logically wrap up the essay?

☐ yes ☐ no If no, point out what is missing.

4. What is the strongest part of your classmate's essay?

_____

_____

Editing and Proofreading

Edit for Conventions Reread your draft for accuracy and consistency. Correct errors in grammar and word usage. Make sure you have used words that accurately reflect your meaning. Avoid using any words that you are uncertain about. Check a dictionary, glossary, or other reference to make sure you have used every word correctly.

Proofread for Accuracy Read your draft carefully, looking for errors in spelling and punctuation. Make sure that you have not confused words that sound the same. For example, ships *sail* across the *sea*, they don't *sale* across the *see*.

Publishing and Presenting

Use technology to create a slide show to accompany your essay. Find images that support the claims you make, and add explanations of the images to your essay. Record a presentation of the slide show with audio of your essay and post it online to a school or class website. Share your presentation with your classmates and offer polite feedback in the comments section of the website.

Reflecting

Think about what you learned by writing your argument. What could you do differently to make writing an argument simpler or easier?

STANDARDS

Writing
• With some guidance and support from peers and adults, develop and strengthen writing as needed by planning, revising, editing, rewriting, or trying a new approach.
• Use technology, including the Internet, to produce and publish writing as well as to interact and collaborate with others; demonstrate sufficient command of keyboarding skills to type a minimum of three pages in a single sitting.

Language
• Demonstrate command of the conventions of standard English grammar and usage when writing or speaking.

e. Recognize variations from standard English in their own and others' writing and speaking, and identify and use strategies to improve expression in conventional language.

ESSENTIAL QUESTION:

What drives people to explore?

Explorers of faraway places, the ocean depths, and outer space must adapt to and survive in new and extremely challenging conditions. In this section, you will read about some of those conditions. You will work in a group to examine the concept of exploration.

Small-Group Learning Strategies

Throughout your life, in school, in your community, and in your career, you will continue to learn and work with others.

Review these strategies and the actions you can take to practice them as you work in teams. Add ideas of your own for each step. Use these strategies during Small-Group Learning.

STRATEGY	ACTION PLAN
Prepare	• Complete your assignments so that you are prepared for group work. • Organize your thinking so you can contribute to your group's discussion. •
Participate fully	• Make eye contact to signal that you are listening and taking in what is being said. • Use text evidence when making a point. •
Support others	• Build on ideas from others in your group. • Invite others who have not yet spoken to join the discussion. •
Clarify	• Paraphrase the ideas of others to ensure that your understanding is correct. • Ask follow-up questions. •

CONTENTS

PERFORMANCE TASK

SPEAKING AND LISTENING FOCUS

Present an Advertisement

The Small-Group readings feature explorers, both real and imaginary, who face different challenges and make different discoveries as they travel to new places. After reading, your group will create and present an advertisement in which you try to persuade readers to participate in an upcoming expedition to a new frontier.

COMPARE

Working as a Team

1. Take a Position In your group, discuss the following question:

> Would you rather explore an ancient civilization in the middle of a desert or an island in the middle of the ocean?

As you take turns sharing your positions, be sure to provide reasons for your choices. After all group members have shared, come to a consensus, or agreement, as to the pros and cons of each option.

2. List Your Rules As a group, decide on the rules that you will follow as you work together. Samples are provided; add two more of your own. You may add or revise rules based on your experience together.

- Everyone should participate in group discussions.
- People should not interrupt.

- _____

  _____

- _____

  _____

3. Apply the Rules Practice working as a group. Share what you have learned about exploration. Make sure each person in the group contributes. Take notes and be prepared to share with the class one thing that you heard from another member of your group.

4. Name Your Group Choose a name that reflects the unit topic.

Our group's name: _____

5. Create a Communication Plan Decide how you want to communicate with one another. For example, you might use online collaboration tools, email, or instant messaging.

Our group's decision: _____

_____

Making a Schedule

First, find out the due dates for the Small-Group activities. Then, preview the texts and activities with your group and make a schedule for completing the tasks.

SELECTION	ACTIVITIES	DUE DATE
Mission Twinpossible		
from Tales From the Odyssey		
To the Top of Everest		
from Lewis & Clark		

Working on Group Projects

As your group works together, you'll find it more effective if each person has a specific role. Different projects require different roles. Before beginning a project, discuss the necessary roles and choose one for each group member. Here are some possible roles; add your own ideas.

Project Manager: monitors the schedule and keeps everyone on task

Researcher: organizes research activities

Recorder: takes notes during group meetings

_____

_____

_____

_____

_____

About the Source
TIME For Kids is a weekly classroom news magazine for kids. Real-world topics are explored both in the magazine and on the website. Science, technology, and social issues are discussed in a way that is easy for young readers to understand. Many *TIME For Kids* articles are actually written by kid reporters and deal with subjects that kids enjoy, such as sports, travel, and entertainment.

Mission Twinpossible

Technical Vocabulary

As you perform your first read, you will encounter these words.

program manager	sample group	endurance test

Infer Meaning Technical terms are often made up of two familiar words that combine to have a specialized meaning. If a technical term is unfamiliar to you, try using your knowledge of the individual words to make an **inference,** or an educated guess, about the term's meaning.

> **Unfamiliar Term:** *genetic makeup*
>
> **Familiar Individual Words:** *genetic* and *makeup*
>
> **Inferred Meaning:** *Genetic* relates to genes, the parts of your DNA that you inherit from your parents and that determine your personal traits. *Makeup* is the way something is made, or put together. Using your knowledge of these words, you can make an inference that *genetic makeup* means "the way in which a person's inherited traits come together."

Make inferences and use other vocabulary strategies to determine the meanings of unfamiliar words and technical terms you encounter during your first read.

First Read NONFICTION

Apply these strategies as you conduct your first read. You will have an opportunity to complete a close read after your first read.

▤ STANDARDS

Reading Informational Text
By the end of the year, read and comprehend literary nonfiction in the grades 6–8 text complexity band proficiently, with scaffolding as needed at the high end of the range.

Language
• Determine or clarify the meaning of unknown and multiple-meaning words and phrases based on *grade 6 reading and content,* choosing flexibly from a range of strategies.
• Demonstrate understanding of figurative language, word relationships, and nuances in word meanings.
  b. Use the relationship between particular words to better understand each of the words.
• Acquire and use accurately grade-appropriate general academic and domain-specific words and phrases; gather vocabulary knowledge when considering a word or phrase important to comprehension or expression.

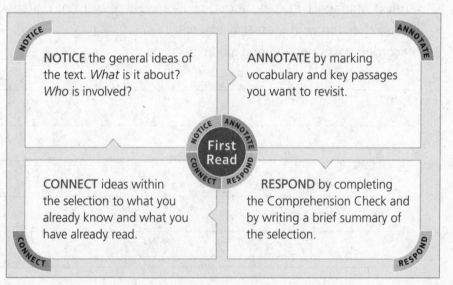

NOTICE the general ideas of the text. *What* is it about? *Who* is involved?

ANNOTATE by marking vocabulary and key passages you want to revisit.

First Read

CONNECT ideas within the selection to what you already know and what you have already read.

RESPOND by completing the Comprehension Check and by writing a brief summary of the selection.

Mission Twinpossible

BACKGROUND

So far, human participation in space exploration has been limited to missions close to Earth. Astronaut crews have been living and working in the International Space Station in Earth's orbit since 2000. The farthest a person has gone is to the moon, but the next step may be landing on Mars, Earth's nearest planet.

SCAN FOR
MULTIMEDIA

1   When Scott Kelly calls home from the International Space Station (ISS) sometime this year, whoever answers the phone might simply hang up on him. The call will be welcome, but the connection can be bad. That can happen when you're placing your call from 229 miles above the Earth. "When someone answers, I have to say, 'It's the space station! Don't hang up!'" says Scott.

2   But his brother, Mark, knows the crackle of an extraterrestrial[1] signal in his ear. Mark is a former astronaut who has been to space four times. Mark is also known for being married to former congresswoman Gabrielle Giffords, who was hurt in an assassination attempt in 2011.

3   Mark and Scott, 50, are identical twins. They have the same genetic makeup. Though they have served a combined seven missions, the brothers have never gone to space together.

NOTES

---

1. **extraterrestrial** (ehks truh tuh REHS tree uhl) *adj.* not from Earth.

program manager (PROH gram man ih juhr) *n.*

MEANING:

sample group (SAM puhl groop) *n.*

MEANING:

endurance test (ehn DUR uhns tehst) *n.*

MEANING:

A Year in Space

4 In March,[2] Scott will leave his family in Houston, Texas, for a one-year stay aboard the ISS. It will set a single-mission record for a US astronaut. Scott will share his marathon mission with Russian cosmonaut Mikhail Kornienko. A rotating cast of 13 other crew members will join them for shorter visits.

5 The US has long dreamed of sending astronauts to Mars. The biggest problem with reaching this goal is, simply, the human body. We are designed for Earth. In space, bones get brittle, eyeballs lose their shape, hearts beat less efficiently, and balance goes awry. "There's quite a bit of data [on human health] for six months in orbit," says space-station **program manager** Mike Suffredini. "Do things change at one year?"

6 NASA needs subjects to test the long-term effects of space. In a perfect experiment, every subject would have a control subject on Earth with the exact same genes. This would help scientists separate the changes that come from being in space from those that are a result of growing the same year older on Earth. In the Kelly brothers—and only the Kelly brothers—NASA has that two-person **sample group**.

Star Twins

7 Scott's days on the ISS will be packed with science experiments, exercise, and monitoring and fixing the station's systems. The station is stocked with movies and books, and the crew can surf the Internet.

8 On this flight, Scott and Kornienko will be very closely monitored with medical and psychological tests. Mark will undergo similar study on the ground. Scientists hope that comparing the data will shed light on the impact of spending a long time in space.

9 Scott's upcoming mission may be equal parts science experiment, **endurance test**, and human drama. To the Kelly brothers, it is just the latest mile in a journey they've shared for half a century. &

---

2. **March** This article was written in 2015.

Comprehension Check

Complete the following items after you finish your first read. Review and clarify details with your group.

1. According to the selection, what is the biggest problem with reaching the goal of sending astronauts to Mars?

2. What happens to the human body in space?

3. How long will Scott Kelly stay at the International Space Station?

4. What will Mark Kelly do while his brother is on the International Space Station?

5. 🖹 **Notebook** Write a summary of the news article.

- -

RESEARCH

Research to Clarify Choose at least one unfamiliar detail from the text. Briefly research that detail. In what way does the information you learned shed light on an aspect of the article?

Research to Explore Choose something that interests you from the article, and formulate a research question.

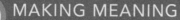

MISSION TWINPOSSIBLE

TIP

GROUP DISCUSSION

If you disagree with a classmate, it is okay to voice your disagreement, as long as you do so respectfully. Wait for your classmate to finish speaking, and then politely explain why your opinion differs. Some of the best discussions emerge from differing opinions!

 WORD NETWORK

Add words related to exploration from the text to your Word Network.

≔ STANDARDS

Language
• Determine or clarify the meaning of unknown and multiple-meaning words and phrases based on *grade 6 reading and content,* choosing flexibly from a range of strategies.
  b. Use common, grade-appropriate Greek or Latin affixes and roots as clues to the meaning of a word.
  c. Consult reference materials, both print and digital, to find the pronunciation of a word or determine or clarify its precise meaning or its part of speech.
• Acquire and use accurately grade-appropriate general academic and domain-specific words and phrases; gather vocabulary knowledge when considering a word or phrase important to comprehension or expression.

Close Read the Text

With your group, revisit sections of the text you marked during your first read. **Annotate** details that you notice. What **questions** do you have? What can you **conclude**?

- -

Analyze the Text

CITE TEXTUAL EVIDENCE to support your answers.

📑 **Notebook** Complete the activities.

1. **Review and Clarify** Reread paragraph 6 of the article. Use a dictionary of scientific terms to determine the meaning of the term *control subject*. Why might having a control subject be important when conducting a science experiment? Discuss with your group.

2. **Present and Discuss** Now, work with your group to share the passages from the text that you found especially important. Discuss what you noticed in the article, what questions you asked, and what conclusions you reached.

3. **Essential Question:** *What drives people to explore?* What has this article taught you about why people are driven to explore?

LANGUAGE DEVELOPMENT

Technical Vocabulary

program manager	sample group	endurance test

Why These Words? Many fields of study have specialized vocabularies. Although you may recognize some of the individual words, they combine to form technical terms that have specific meanings. Use a dictionary of scientific terms to determine the precise meaning of each of these technical terms. How does understanding each term's precise meaning deepen your understanding of the text?

Word Study

Latin Root: *-dur-* The word *endurance* is part of the technical vocabulary term *endurance test*. The Latin root *-dur-* in *endurance* means "hard," "to hold out," or "to last."

Explain how the root *-dur-* contributes to the meaning of the technical vocabulary term *endurance test*. Then, find the definition of each of the following words, and explain how the root *-dur-* contributes to the its meaning: *durable, duress, duration.*

Analyze Craft and Structure

Central Idea: Make Inferences The **central idea** is the most important point in a text. Sometimes, the central idea is stated directly, but more often it is implied, or suggested. When a central idea is implied, the reader must make inferences to identify it. An **inference** is a logical conclusion that you develop about information that is not directly stated. To make inferences about a central idea, combine your prior knowledge, or what you already know, with the key details that the author provides. Remember that the details in a text are not equal. The key details are the ones that support or tell more about the central idea. Follow these guidelines to distinguish key details from unimportant ones:

- Key details often reveal the topic or subject of the text.
- Key details are sometimes repeated throughout the text in different ways or in different words.
- Key details are related to other details in the text.
- Together, key details support the central idea.

As you make inferences to determine the central idea of a text, ask yourself questions about the details the author included, such as *Why did the author include this detail?*, *Does this detail help readers understand the central idea?*, and *How does this detail support the central idea?*

STANDARDS

Reading Informational Text

• Cite textual evidence to support analysis of what the text says explicitly as well as inferences drawn from the text.

• Determine a central idea of a text and how it is conveyed through particular details; provide a summary of the text distinct from personal opinions or judgments.

• Analyze in detail how a key individual, event, or idea is introduced, illustrated, and elaborated in a text.

• Analyze how a particular sentence, paragraph, chapter, or section fits into the overall structure of a text and contributes to the development of the ideas.

Practice

CITE TEXTUAL EVIDENCE to support your answers.

With your group, reread the paragraphs from the selection that are identified in the chart. Use the key details in each paragraph to make inferences about the central idea of the paragraph. Then, combine your inferences to infer the central idea of the news article as a whole.

PARAGRAPH	INFERENCES ABOUT CENTRAL IDEA
Paragraph 5	
Paragraph 7	
Paragraph 8	
Central Idea of "Mission Twinpossible":	

MISSION TWINPOSSIBLE

Conventions

Prepositions and Prepositional Phrases A **preposition** relates a noun or a pronoun that follows it to another word in the sentence. In the sentence *The book is on the table,* the preposition *on* relates the noun *table* to another word in the sentence, *book.*

A **prepositional phrase** begins with a preposition and ends with a noun or pronoun—called the **object of the preposition**. In the prepositional phrase *on the table,* the preposition is *on,* and the object of the preposition is *table.* This chart shows a number of commonly used prepositions.

COMMONLY USED PREPOSITIONS			
above	below	in	over
across	beneath	into	through
after	between	near	to
against	by	of	toward
along	down	on	under
at	during	onto	until
before	for	out	up
behind	from	outside	with

Read It

📓 **Notebook** In the selection, find a prepositional phrase that contains each of these prepositions. Then, determine the object of each preposition.

1. above   **3.** at   **5.** from

2. with   **4.** for   **6.** to

Write It

Write a short paragraph in which you explain whether you would like to go on a yearlong space mission. In your paragraph, correctly use at least three of the commonly used prepositions. Then, exchange paragraphs with a member of your group. Identify each prepositional phrase in your classmate's paragraph.

⊞ STANDARDS

Language
Demonstrate command of the conventions of standard English grammar and usage when writing or speaking.

Research

Assignment

Work with your group to write a **how-to guide.** Choose from the following options:

☐ **Option 1:** The article mentions the negative effects that the lack of gravity in space has on the human body. Conduct research to learn more about how astronauts minimize these negative effects while they are traveling in space. Write a how-to guide for keeping fit in space.

☐ **Option 2:** Astronauts must go through years of training and preparation before traveling to space. Conduct research to find out more about the training and preparation required to become an astronaut. Write a how-to guide for people who want to become astronauts.

Conduct Research As you conduct your research, keep in mind that your purpose is to explain a specific process. In order to create a clear explanation, identify the following:

- important steps
- the order in which the steps should be completed
- any materials required to complete the task—for example, exercise equipment

Take care to include only essential information about staying fit in space or becoming an astronaut. Unnecessary information will distract readers and make the steps of the process you are explaining difficult to follow.

Organize Your Information A clear organizational format is an important part of any successful how-to essay. Make sure you explain and order the steps in the process clearly and precisely. Use transitional words, such as *first, next, after, then,* and *finally,* to keep the order clear. Use visuals, such as illustrations and diagrams, to help your readers understand information that might be complicated or confusing.

Cite Your Sources Include a **works-cited list**, also called a **bibliography**, at the end of your guide. This list should include bibliographic information for all the sources that you used to write your guide. Ask your teacher what citation style you should use when creating your list of sources. Failure to properly credit your sources can be considered **plagiarism** because you are using the ideas, words, or work of someone else as if it is your own.

✐ EVIDENCE LOG

Before moving on to a new selection, go to your Evidence Log and record what you learned from "Mission Twinpossible."

≔ STANDARDS

Writing

- Write informative/explanatory texts to examine a topic and convey ideas, concepts, and information through the selection, organization, and analysis of relevant content.
  a. Introduce a topic; organize ideas, concepts, and information, using strategies such as definition, classification, comparison/contrast, and cause/effect; include formatting, graphics, and multimedia when useful to aiding comprehension.
  b. Develop the topic with relevant facts, definitions, concrete details, quotations, or other information and examples.
  c. Use appropriate transitions to clarify the relationships among ideas and concepts.

- Conduct short research projects to answer a question, drawing on several sources and refocusing the inquiry when appropriate.

- Gather relevant information from multiple print and digital sources; assess the credibility of each source; and quote or paraphrase the data and conclusions of others while avoiding plagiarism and providing basic bibliographic information for sources.

from TALES FROM THE ODYSSEY

Comparing Texts

In this section, you will read and compare two works about adventure and challenges. First, you will complete the first-read and close-read activities for the excerpt from *Tales From the Odyssey*.

TO THE TOP OF EVEREST

About the Author

Mary Pope Osborne (b. 1949) has lived an adventurous life. Her father was in the military, and her family moved seven times before Osborne was fifteen. As a young adult, she explored sixteen Asian countries with friends. Osborne began to write in her thirties. Today, she is best known for her series *The Magic Tree House*. "There is no career better suited to my eccentricities, strengths, and passions than that of a children's book author," Osborne says.

from Tales From the Odyssey

Concept Vocabulary

As you perform your first read, you will encounter these words.

invaded	violent	offended	wrath

Context Clues If these words are unfamiliar to you, try using **context clues**—other words and phrases that appear in nearby text—to help you determine their meanings. There are various types of context clues that may help you as you read.

Synonyms: Tourism depends on visitors who participate in **leisure** and entertainment activities.

Contrast of Ideas: Once a **sullen** girl, Elena had grown into a bright, cheerful young woman.

Apply your knowledge of context clues and other vocabulary strategies to determine the meanings of unfamiliar words you encounter during your first read.

First Read FICTION

Apply these strategies as you conduct your first read. You will have an opportunity to complete a close read after your first read.

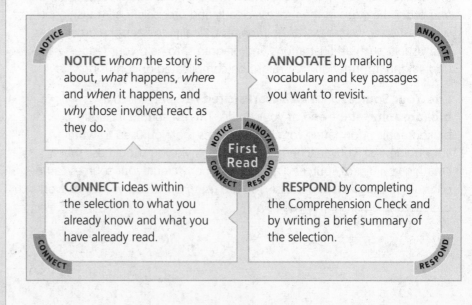

NOTICE *whom* the story is about, *what* happens, *where* and *when* it happens, and *why* those involved react as they do.

ANNOTATE by marking vocabulary and key passages you want to revisit.

CONNECT ideas within the selection to what you already know and what you have already read.

RESPOND by completing the Comprehension Check and by writing a brief summary of the selection.

First Read

NOTICE · ANNOTATE · CONNECT · RESPOND

☰ STANDARDS

Reading Literature
By the end of the year, read and comprehend literature, including stories, dramas, and poems, in the grades 6–8 text complexity band proficiently, with scaffolding as needed at the high end of the range.

Language
Determine or clarify the meaning of unknown and multiple-meaning words and phrases based on *grade 6 reading and content,* choosing flexibly from a range of strategies.
  a. Use context as a clue to the meaning of a word or phrase.

from
TALES
From the
ODYSSEY

Mary Pope Osborne

BACKGROUND

In *Tales From the Odyssey*, Mary Pope Osborne adapts the famous Greek epic by Homer called the *Odyssey*. Homer's prequel to the *Odyssey* was called the *Iliad*, which tells the story of the Trojan War, a ten year war between the Greeks and the people of Troy. In the *Odyssey*, Homer tells the story of Odysseus, a Greek king and war hero, and the long, dangerous journey he and his men make on their way home from the Trojan War. The excerpt from Osborne's retelling starts at the beginning of the their ten year journey.

SCAN FOR
MULTIMEDIA

The Odyssey Begins

1   Soon after the Greek ships left Troy, the skies began to blacken. Lightning zig-zagged above the foamy sea. Thunder shook the heavens.

2   Mighty winds stirred the water. The waves grew higher and higher, until they were rolling over the bows of the ships.

3   "The gods are punishing us!" the Greek warriors shouted. "We shall all drown!"

4   As his men frantically fought the storm, Odysseus felt bewildered. Why was Zeus, god of the skies, hurling his thunderbolts at them? Why was Poseidon, lord of the seas, sending great waves over the waters?

5   Odysseus turned to his men. "What has happened to anger the gods?" he shouted. "Tell me!"

NOTES

Mark context clues or indicate another strategy you used that helped you determine meaning.

invaded (ihn VAYD ihd) *v.*

MEANING:

violent (VY uh luhnt) *adj.*

MEANING:

offended (uh FEHND ihd) *v.*

MEANING:

wrath (rath) *n.*

MEANING:

6   "Before we left Troy,[1] Greek warriors **invaded** Athena's[2] temple!" said one of his men. "They were **violent** and disrespectful."

7   Odysseus was stunned. The Greeks had **offended** the goddess who had helped them to victory! And now her anger might drown them all.

8   The wind grew stronger. It whipped the sails of the Greek ships and slashed them to rags. "Lift your oars!" Odysseus shouted to his men. "Row! Row to shore!"

9   The Greeks struggled valiantly against the mighty wind and waves. Fighting for their lives, they finally rowed their battered ships to a strange shore. There they found shelter in a rocky cave.

10   The storm raged for two more days and nights. Then, on the third day, a fair wind blew, the sun came out, and the wine-dark sea was calm at last.

11   "Now we can continue on our way," Odysseus said to his men. "Athena is no longer angry." In the rosy dawn, he ordered them to raise their tattered sails and set off again for Ithaca.[3]

12   But, alas, the **wrath** of Athena had not been fully spent. Hardly had Odysseus reached the open sea than another gale began to blow.

13   For many days, Odysseus and his men fought the wind and the waves, refusing to surrender to the storm. Finally, on the tenth day, there was sudden calm.

14   Odysseus ordered his fleet to sail into the cove of a leafy green island. There he hoped to find food and drink for his hungry, weary men.

15   The Greeks dropped anchor. Then they dragged themselves ashore. They drank cool, fresh water from a spring and collapsed onto the sand.

16   As Odysseus rested, he ordered three of his men to explore the island and look for provisions.

18   When the three had not returned by late afternoon, Odysseus grew angry. Why did they tarry? he wondered.

18   Odysseus set out in search of the men. He moved through the brush and brambles, calling their names.

19   He had not gone far when he came upon a group of peaceful islanders. They greeted him with warm, friendly smiles. And they offered him their food—lovely bright flowers.

---

1. **Troy** site of the Trojan War in the Greek oral and literary tradition.
2. **Athena's** In Greek mythology, Athena is the daughter of Zeus and the goddess of wisdom and victory in war.
3. **Ithaca** Greek island that is Odysseus's home.

20   Odysseus was famished. But just as he was about to eat the
flowers, he caught sight of his missing men. The three were lying
on the ground with dreamy smiles on their faces.

21   Odysseus called each man by name, but none of them
answered. They did not even look at him.

22   "What have you done to them?" he asked the islanders.

23   "We have given them our flowers to eat," an islander answered.
"This is our greatest gift. The gods would be angry if we did not
offer to feed our guests."

24   "What sort of flowers are these?" Odysseus asked.

25   "They come from the lotus tree," the islander said. "They have
the magical power of forgetfulness. They make a man forget
the past."

26   "Forget his memories of home?" asked Odysseus. "And his
memories of his family and friends?"

NOTES

27   The lotus-eaters only smiled. They again offered Odysseus their sweet, lovely flowers. But he roughly brushed them away. He pulled his three men to their feet and commanded them all to return to their ships at once.

28   The men began to weep. They begged to be left behind so they could stay on the island and eat lotus flowers forever.

29   Odysseus angrily herded the men back to the ships. As they drew near the shore, the three tried to escape. Odysseus called for help.

30   "Tie their hands and feet!" he shouted to his crew. "Make haste! Before others eat the magic flowers and forget their homes, too!"

31   The three flailing men were hauled aboard and tied to rowing benches. Then Odysseus ordered the twelve ships to push off from shore.

32   Once more, the Greeks set sail for Ithaca, sweeping the gray sea with their long oars. As they rowed past dark islands with jagged rocks and shadowy coves, Odysseus felt troubled and anxious. What other strange wonders lurked on these dark, unknown shores?

The Mysterious Shore

33   Soon the Greek ships came upon a hilly island, thick with trees. No humans seemed to live there. Hundreds of wild goats could be heard bleating from the island's gloomy thickets.

34   Odysseus ordered his men to drop anchor in the shelter of a mist-covered bay. By the time the Greeks had lowered their sails, night had fallen. The moon was hidden by clouds. In the pitch dark, the men lay down on the sandy shore and slept.

35   When daylight came, the men woke to see woodland nymphs,[4] the daughters of Zeus, driving wild goats down from the hills. The hungry Greeks eagerly grabbed their bows and spears and slew more than a hundred goats.

36   All day, the Greeks lingered on the island, feasting on roasted meat and drinking sweet wine. As the sun went down, they stared at a mysterious shore across the water. Smoke rose from fires on the side of a mountain. The murmur of deep voices and the bleating of sheep wafted through the twilight.

37   *Who lives there? Who stokes those fires?* Odysseus wondered silently. *Are they friendly or lawless men?*

38   Darkness fell, and the Greeks slept once more on the sand. When he was wakened by the rosy dawn, Odysseus stared again

---

4. **woodland nymphs** female spirits of the natural world and nurses to the Greek gods.

at the mysterious shore in the distance. Though he was yearning to set sail for Ithaca, a strange curiosity had taken hold of him.

39   Odysseus woke his men. "I must know who lives on that far shore," he said. "With a single ship, I will lead an expedition to find out whether they are savages or civilized humans. Then we will continue our journey home."

40   Odysseus chose his bravest men to go with him. They untied a ship from their fleet and pushed off from the island.

41   Soon the Greeks were swinging their long oars into the calm face of the sea, rowing toward the mysterious shore. When they drew close, they dropped anchor beneath a tall, rocky cliff.

42   Odysseus filled a goatskin with the best wine he had on board, made from the sweetest grapes. "This will be our gift to repay the hospitality of anyone who welcomes us into his home," he said.

43   He ordered some of this men to remain with the ship, then led the rest up the side of the cliff. On a ledge high above the water, they discovered a large, shady clearing. On the other side of the clearing, creeping vines hung over the mouth of a cave. The Greeks pushed past the vines and stepped inside.

44   The cave was filled with young goats and lambs. Pots of cheese and pails of goat's milk were everywhere. But there was no sign of a shepherd.

45   "Hurry!" said one of Odysseus's men. "Let us grab provisions and leave!"

46   "Yes! We should drive the lambs down to our ship before their master returns!" said another.

47   "No," said Odysseus. "We will wait awhile. . . . I am curious to see who lives here."

48   The Greeks made a fire and gave an offering to the gods. Then they greedily took their fill of milk and cheese. Finally, in the late afternoon, they heard whistling and bleating.

49   "Ah, the shepherd returns," Odysseus said. "Let us step forward and meet this man."

50   But when they peered out of the cave, the Greeks gasped with horror—for the shepherd was no a man at all. He was a monster. ❧

Comprehension Check

Complete the following items after you finish your first read. Review and clarify details with your group.

1. At the beginning of the epic retelling, why are the gods punishing Odysseus and his men?

2. What do the islanders give Odysseus' men at the first place they stop?

3. At the second place Odysseus and his men stop, what do they find in the cave?

4. 🗒 **Notebook** Confirm your understanding of the excerpt from *Tales From the Odyssey* by writing a brief summary.

- -

RESEARCH

Research to Clarify Choose at least one unfamiliar detail from the text. Briefly research that detail. In what way does the information you learned shed light on an aspect of the retelling?

Research to Explore Choose something that interests you from the text, and formulate a research question that you might use to find out more about it.

Close Read the Text

With your group, revisit sections of the text you marked during your first read. **Annotate** details that you notice. What **questions** do you have? What can you **conclude**?

ANNOTATE · QUESTION · **Close Read** · CONCLUDE

from TALES FROM THE ODYSSEY

Analyze the Text

CITE TEXTUAL EVIDENCE to support your answers.

Complete the activities.

1. **Review and Clarify** If events in a story are the opposite of what you expect, the effect is called **situational irony**. Reread paragraphs 33–50 of the epic retelling. Why is the ending ironic? What effect does the situational irony have on you as a reader?

2. **Present and Discuss** Now, work with your group to share passages from the excerpt that you found especially interesting. Discuss what you noticed in the text, what questions you asked, and what conclusions you reached.

3. *Essential Question: What drives people to explore?* What has this retelling taught you about what drives people to explore?

LANGUAGE DEVELOPMENT

Concept Vocabulary

invaded	violent	offended	wrath

Why These Words? The concept vocabulary words from the text are related. With your group, determine what the words have in common. How does the author's word choice help develop the characters and settings in the myth?

Practice

📓 **Notebook** With your group, write a brief paragraph predicting what will happen to Odysseus and his men after they meet the monster mentioned at the end of the selection. Use all four concept vocabulary words in your paragraph.

Word Study

Latin Root: -vad-   In the epic retelling, the gods are angry because the Greek warriors invaded Athena's temple. The word *invaded* is formed from the Latin prefix *in-*, which means "in" or "into," and the Latin root *-vad-*, which means "go." Write a sentence or two in which you explain how knowing the meaning of the root *-vad-* helps you understand the meaning of *invaded*. Then, use a dictionary to find the definitions of the words *evade* and *pervade*. Discuss with your group how these words are related to the word *invaded*.

🔲 **WORD NETWORK**

Add words related to exploration from the text to your Word Network.

📋 **STANDARDS**

Reading Literature
Determine the meaning of words and phrases as they are used in a text, including figurative and connotative meanings; analyze the impact of a specific word choice on meaning and tone.
Language
Determine or clarify the meaning of unknown and multiple-meaning words and phrases based on *grade 6 reading and content,* choosing flexibly from a range of strategies.
   b. Use common, grade-appropriate Greek or Latin affixes and roots as clues to the meaning of a word.
   c. Consult reference materials, both print and digital, to find the pronunciation of a word or determine or clarify its precise meaning or its part of speech.

from TALES FROM THE ODYSSEY

Analyze Craft and Structure

Universal Theme Stories of Odysseus have been around, in some form, for thousands of years. One reason they have lasted so long is that people still connect with their messages and with their portrayals of human nature. In other words, their themes are universal. A **universal theme** is a message or insight about life that is expressed in the literature and art of all cultures and time periods. Examples include the importance of courage, the power of love, and the danger of greed.

The ancient version of the *Odyssey* is an **epic**—a long poem about heroes. Even though the version you read was adapted for our times, the universal themes remain. To find universal themes in the epic retelling, focus on the main character, analyze the problems he faces, and notice how he responds or changes as a result.

Practice

CITE TEXTUAL EVIDENCE to support your answers.

📓 **Notebook** Work together to examine how this universal theme is expressed in the epic retelling: *We are all tested by life's challenges.* Complete the activity and answer the questions.

1. Use the chart to identify details from the text that show specific types of challenges Odysseus faces.

CHALLENGES FROM OTHERS	CHALLENGES FROM HIMSELF
Which people and gods create problems for Odysseus?	What feelings or thoughts does Odysseus struggle with?

2. **(a)** In what ways do the characters' personalities make their problems worse? **(b)** In what ways do their personalities make them better?

3. **(a)** How does Odysseus overcome problems with others? **(b)** How does Odysseus overcome problems that arise from his own thoughts or feelings? Explain.

4. What might the ways in which Odysseus responds to problems suggest about how people can or should deal with challenges? Explain.

📑 STANDARDS

Reading Literature
• Determine a theme or central idea of a text and how it is conveyed through particular details; provide a summary of the text distinct from personal opinions or judgments.
• Analyze how a particular sentence. chapter, scene, or stanza fits into the overall structure of a text and contributes to the development of the theme, setting, or plot.

Conventions

Participial and Gerund Phrases A **participle** is a verb form that acts as an adjective. The **present participle** of a verb ends in *-ing*: *relaxing music*. The **past participle** of a regular verb ends in *-ed*: *a relaxed position*. For irregular verbs, you must memorize the past participle form: *broken promises*.

A **participial phrase** combines a present or past participle with other words; the entire phrase acts as an adjective:

> *Relaxing on the patio*, Jo fell asleep. **(The participial phrase modifies *Jo*.)**

> *The small ship, beaten by the winds, couldn't manage to reach the shore.* (The participial phrase modifies **ship**.)

A **gerund** is a verb form that also ends in *-ing* but is used as a noun: *I like relaxing*.

A **gerund phrase** combines a gerund with other words; the entire phrase acts as a noun:

> *Relaxing in your spare time is important.* **(The gerund phrase is the subject of the sentence.)**

> *The sailors tried anchoring the ship.* **(The gerund phrase is the object of the verb *tried*.)**

Read It

Identify and label all the participles, gerunds, participial phrases, and gerund phrases in each of these sentences from the excerpt from *Tales From the Odyssey*.

1. Fighting for their lives, they finally rowed their battered ships to a strange shore.

2. The murmur of deep voices and the bleating of sheep wafted through the twilight.

3. The three flailing men were hauled aboard and tied to rowing benches.

Write It

⊟ **Notebook** Think of a fictional adventure at sea that you could write as a story. Then, write the first paragraph of that story. Include at least one participial phrase and at least one gerund phrase.

⎙ EVIDENCE LOG

Before moving on to a new selection, go to your Evidence Log and record what you have learned from the excerpt from *Tales from the Odyssey*.

⊞ STANDARDS

Language
Demonstrate command of the conventions of standard English grammar and usage when writing or speaking.

from TALES FROM THE
ODYSSEY

Comparing Texts

You will now complete the first-read and close-read activities for "To the Top of Everest." Then, you will compare the blog with the excerpt from *Tales From the Odyssey*.

TO THE TOP OF EVEREST

About the Author

In 2007, American **Samantha Larson** (b. 1988) became the youngest person to climb the "Seven Summits"—the highest mountains on each of the seven continents. Larson climbed her first, Mount Kilimanjaro in Africa, at the age of 12. She finished her quest when she successfully reached the top of Mount Everest at age 18. Larson calls Everest "much harder, longer, and higher" than the other peaks. "It was one big challenge," she recalls, but adds, "Deep down, I thought I would make it."

⋮☰ STANDARDS

Reading Informational Text
By the end of the year, read and comprehend literary nonfiction in the grades 6–8 text complexity band proficiently, with scaffolding as needed at the high end of the range.

Language
Determine or clarify the meaning of unknown and multiple-meaning words and phrases based on *grade 6 reading and content,* choosing flexibly from a range of strategies.

To the Top of Everest

Concept Vocabulary

As you perform your first read, you will encounter these words.

| expedition | trek | journeys | destination |

Context Clues If these words are unfamiliar to you, try using **context clues** other words and phrases that appear in nearby text—to help you determine their meanings. There are various types of context clues that may help you as you read.

> **Definition: Cygnets**, or young swans, tend to be larger than ducklings or chicks of the same age.
>
> **Elaborating Details:** As the **acrobat**, performed the crowd cheered at every leap, flip, and somersault

Apply your knowledge of context clues and other vocabulary strategies to determine the meanings of unfamiliar words you encounter during your first read.

First Read NONFICTION

Apply these strategies as you conduct your first read. You will have an opportunity to complete a close read after your first read.

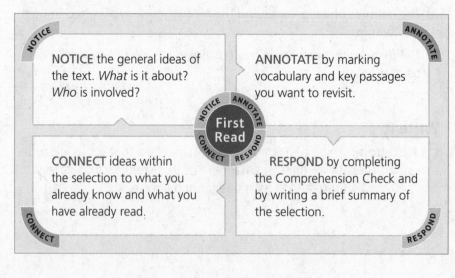

NOTICE the general ideas of the text. *What* is it about? *Who* is involved?

ANNOTATE by marking vocabulary and key passages you want to revisit.

First Read

CONNECT ideas within the selection to what you already know and what you have already read.

RESPOND by completing the Comprehension Check and by writing a brief summary of the selection.

To the Top of Everest

Samantha Larson

BACKGROUND

Mount Everest is the highest mountain in the world, rising approximately 29,000 feet above sea level. It is part of the Asian mountain range called the Himalayas, and is located on the border between Nepal and Tibet. Tibetans refer to the mountain as Chomolunga, or "Mother Goddess of the Earth." In 1953, Sir Edmund Hillary of New Zealand and Sherpa Tenzing Norgay of Nepal became the first people to reach Mount Everest's summit. Sherpas are an ethnic group that is native to the highest regions in Nepal and are known for their abilities in mountaineering. Sherpas are still valued today for their key role in successful attempts to climb Mount Everest.

SCAN FOR
MULTIMEDIA

NOTES

Friday, March 30, 2007
Here we go ⟶ Kathmandu!

1 Today is the day! Our bags are (nearly) packed and we're (just about) ready to go. I've got eleven hours to run around doing last minute errands before our plane takes off.

2 I arrived back in Long Beach from New York last Saturday, where I've been since our return from Cho Oyu. When I wasn't training by running, swimming at the pool, taking dance classes, or rock climbing, I was taking oboe lessons, French, and photography classes. Hopefully I'll be able to take some great pictures on this **expedition**!

Mark context clues or indicate another strategy you used that helped you determine meaning.

expedition (ehks puh DIHSH uhn) *n.*

MEANING:

3 It has been a very exciting week in all our general trip preparation mayhem, filled with lots of gear sorting and FedEx package arrivals. But now my dad and I are pretty much all set to go.

4 See you in Kathmandu!

trek (trehk) *n.*

MEANING:

journeys (JUR neez) *n.*

MEANING:

destination (dehs tuh NAY shuhn) *n.*

MEANING:

Monday, April 2, 2007
Kathmandu

5 After nearly 24 hours of travel we finally arrived in Kathmandu yesterday afternoon. Doug, my dad, and I met up with the rest of the team (Victor, James, and Wim) at our hotel in Kathmandu. We had a group meeting where we went over the route we are going to take to base camp, and then we picked up some odds and ends at one of the dozens of local climbing stores.

6 The team is flying to Lukla to begin the **trek** to base camp early tomorrow morning.

Wednesday, April 4, 2007
Namche Bazaar

7 Yesterday after a very scenic flight and a heart-stopping landing on a small airstrip perched on the side of a mountain, we arrived in Lukla to begin the trek to base camp. Lukla was filled with excitement as porters organized their loads and trekkers began their **journeys**. From Lukla, we hiked for about 4 hours through the beautiful Nepalese countryside, passing through several villages until we reached the village of Monjo, where we stayed the night in the Monjo Guesthouse. I think my dad and I got the big sleep that we needed to catch up on our jetlag; around 4 in the afternoon, we decided to take a "nap" that lasted until 7 the next morning!

Thursday, April 12, 2007
Base Camp

8 We made it to base camp yesterday afternoon. Today we are going to practice crossing the ladders over the Khumbu Icefall. We are well and safe.

9 En route here we visited Lama Gesa and he blessed our journey. It was an amazing experience!

10 I am going to try and connect my laptop and charge it with my solar charger—we will see if that works.

11 More to follow. . . .

Monday, April 16, 2007
Rest Day

12 Yesterday we got an early start for our first time through the icefall. We left around 6:30 in the morning, with the idea that we would turn around 11—we did not necessarily have a **destination** in mind, it was more for acclimatization[1] and to get an idea of

---

1. **acclimatization** (uh kly muh tuh ZAY shuhn) *n.* process of allowing the body to adjust to the climate, especially at high altitude.

what the icefall was like. However, at 11 we were about half an hour from the top of the icefall, so we decided to just continue to the top.

13 It was quite fun climbing up the icefall. The ladders that we had to cross over crevasses[2] were especially exciting. I was pretty tired by the time we got back to base camp, but today was a rest day (our first), so I've had plenty of time to recover.

14 Tomorrow we are going up to camp one to spend the night. Camp one is about an hour further than we went yesterday. The next day we will go up to tag camp two and then come back down to base camp.

Thursday, April 19, 2007
Puja

15 The day before yesterday we all made it up to camp one to spend the night. This time we were able to get through the Khumbu Icefall an hour quicker than the last. We had a pretty good night at camp one; my dad and I both had a bit of a headache at first, but we were both able to eat and sleep well.

16 Camp one is at the start of the Western Cwm.[3] Yesterday, from camp one we continued up the Cwm to camp two. The Cwm is infamous for being very uncomfortably hot, but yesterday it was actually really nice. It was very beautiful, and we could see the summit of Everest, which we haven't been able to see since before we got to base camp. After we tagged camp two we came all the way back down to base camp. It was a long day, and we all returned pretty tired. However, it was nice to be back in base camp, and after dinner we watched *Mission Impossible III* on Ben's laptop (from the London Business School team). Unfortunately the power ran out about halfway through, but I have been asked to charge up my laptop so we can finish tonight.

17 Today was the Puja, which is a ceremony that the Sherpas organize. A Lama comes up and performs many chants to ask the mountain gods for permission to climb the mountain, and to ask for protection. I had my ice ax and my crampons[4] blessed in the ceremony. As part of the ceremony, they also put out long lines of prayer flags coming out from the stupa where the ceremony was performed. Afterwards, they passed out lots of yummy treats.

---

2. **crevasses** (kruh VAS ihz) *n.* deep cracks in ice or a glacier.
3. **Western Cwm**   broad valley at the base of Mount Everest.
4. **crampons** (KRAM puhnz) *n.* metal plates with spikes that are attached to boots to provide greater traction.

18 While we were up at camp one, the shower tent was set up here at base camp. It's just a little bucket of water with a hose attached to it, but definitely 15 minutes of heaven.

Saturday, April 28, 2007
Base Camp

19 We are back at base camp! We came down from camp two yesterday, and arrived just in time for lunch. We were delayed a bit in the morning because we were radioed from base camp that there was a break in the icefall, and we didn't want to leave until we knew that the "ice doctors" had fixed up the route. As we came down, we found that the break was in a flat area known as the "football field" that we had previously designated as a "safe" area to take a little rest. And the whole shelf just collapsed!

20 Now that we have spent a night at camp three, we are done with the acclimatization process. We are going to take a few days for rest and recovery, and then we just wait for good weather to make a summit bid. We plan to go back down to Pengboche tomorrow so we can really get a good rest at lower altitude before our summit attempt.

21 Here is what we have been up to these past few days:

4/23/07

22 Yesterday we all made it up to camp one for the night. We were joined by Tori from the London Business School team, because she wasn't feeling 100% when her team went up the day before.

23 Today we all came up to camp two. It was very hot coming up the Cwm this time, and we all had heavy packs because we had to bring up what we had left at camp one the last time we stayed there. It certainly made it a lot harder work!

4/24/07

24 Despite the fact that I caused us to get a later start than planned this morning (I had a particularly hard time getting out of my warm sleeping bag into the cold air) we accomplished our goal for the day. We went up the very first pitch of the Lhotse Face, and are now back at camp two for the evening.

4/26/07

25 Yesterday we went about halfway up the Lhotse Face to camp three to spend the night. This was a new record for my dad and me, as our highest night ever! Camp three is at about 23,500 feet, and our previous highest night was at camp two on Cho Oyu, at 23,000 feet. We arrived at camp three around noon, and then had a lot of time to kill in our tents, as it wasn't really safe to go more than five feet outside the tent without putting on crampons and clipping into the fixed ropes. Thankfully, I had not yet reached a hypoxic[5] level where I couldn't enjoy my book.

26 Coming up the Lhotse Face was a bit windy, and some parts were pretty icy. It gets fairly steep, so I was glad to have my ascender, which slides up the rope, but not back down, so you can use it as a handhold to pull yourself up.

Sunday, May 6, 2007
Back from Holiday

27 We're back at base camp from our little holiday down the mountain.

28 Now that we are back in base camp, we are just waiting till we can go for our summit attempt. The ropes are not yet fixed to the summit. Once the ropes are fixed, we hope there will soon be a good weather window.

Friday, May 11, 2007
Base Camp

29 We're still at base camp. Hopefully we'll be able to go up soon though.

---

5. **hypoxic** (hy POK sihk) *adj.* having too little oxygen.

30   We've tried to hold on to our fitness these past few days by doing some sort of activity each day. We've been ice climbing in a really neat cave near base camp, and we've also been on hikes up Pumori to Pumori base camp, and then up to camp one. Pumori is a 7145-meter mountain near Everest.

Saturday, May 12, 2007
Still at Base Camp

31   It looks like we're going to be able to go up soon for our summit attempt. Fingers crossed!

32   We've gotten our oxygen masks and tested them out. I was able to get my oxygen saturation back up to 100% this morning! After I turned off the oxygen, I only had a few seconds of being at pseudo sea level before it went back down, though.

33   We're all getting a little restless hanging around base camp.

Monday, May 14, 2007
Camp 2

34   We finally started our summit push yesterday, making our way from base camp to camp two. We don't have Internet access up here, but we were able to relay this information to our correspondents in New York via satellite phone. We're taking a rest day today, and plan to press on tomorrow. If all goes well, we should summit on the 17th.

Thursday, May 17, 2007
Summit!

35   We made it to the top! Now all we have to do is get back down . . .

Wednesday, May 23, 2007
Back Home!

36   We've been in a big rush getting back home, and I haven't been able to update for a while, as I have not had Internet access. We woke up this morning at 16,000 feet in a village called Lobuche, and this evening my dad and I arrived back at sea level in Long Beach! The rest of the team are celebrating in Kathmandu—my dad and I skipped out on the celebration to make it back in time for my brother Ted's college graduation in New York.

37   The day after we summited, we came down from the South Col (camp four) to camp two. I was very tired at that point, but glad that we had all made it back safely lower on the mountain. It was amazing how after being to almost 30,000 feet, 20,000-foot camp two felt like it was nearly at sea level!

38   The day after that, we came back down to base camp, where we received lots of warm hugs and congratulations.

39 We only had one night back at base camp, as the next day (the 20th), we packed up our bags and headed down the valley. Base camp had a strange, empty feeling—it was sad to leave my little tent that had been my home for the past 2 months! My dad, Doug, Wim, and I were hoping to get a helicopter out of Lobuche on the 21st to save a little time, but Victor and James decided to walk down to the Lukla airstrip to fly out to Kathmandu on the 23rd. However, even though we awoke on the 21st to a beautiful, clear day in Lobuche, apparently there were clouds lower down the valley, so the helicopter couldn't fly in until the 23rd either. It was kind of hard waiting those two days in Lobuche. We were just an hour away from a hot shower and a big meal, if only those clouds would clear!

40 Once the helicopter landed in Kathmandu, I was greeted by a mob of journalists and cameramen. I was so surprised! After nearly 20 hours of travel, my dad and I landed at LAX[6] and were greeted by my family, and some more news people. Now we only have a few hours before we jump back on a plane to go to New York! I am very excited to see my mom and brother though.

41 Thank you everyone for all of your wonderful comments and your support!!! ❧

6. **LAX** *n.* Los Angeles International Airport.

Comprehension Check

Complete the following items after you finish your first read. Review and clarify details with your group.

1. Who blessed Larson's journey before she began?

2. What is a Puja?

3. How high is camp three?

4. On what day did Larson reach the top of Mount Everest?

5. 🖥 **Notebook** Confirm your understanding of the blog posts by writing a brief summary.

- -

RESEARCH

Research to Clarify Choose at least one unfamiliar detail from the text. Briefly research that detail. In what way does the information you learned shed light on an aspect of the blog posts?

Research to Explore Choose something that interests you from the text, and formulate a research question that you might use to find out more about it.

Close Read the Text

With your group, revisit sections of the text you marked during your first read. **Annotate** details that you notice. What **questions** do you have? What can you **conclude**?

TO THE TOP OF EVEREST

Analyze the Text

> **CITE TEXTUAL EVIDENCE**
> to support your answers.

Complete the activities.

1. **Review and Clarify** With your group, review paragraphs 35–41. Discuss with your group the reasons for the six-day gap between blog posts. Consider reasons Larson gives, and speculate about others.

2. **Present and Discuss** Now, work with your group to share passages from the blog that you found especially important. Discuss what you noticed in the selection, what questions you asked, and what conclusions you reached.

3. **Essential Question: *What drives people to explore?*** What has this blog taught you about what drives people to explore?

TIP

GROUP DISCUSSION
In a group discussion, listening is just as important as speaking. When others are speaking, be sure to give them your full attention.

LANGUAGE DEVELOPMENT

Concept Vocabulary

expedition	trek	journeys	destination

Why These Words? The concept vocabulary words from the blog are related. With your group, determine what the words have in common. Add another word that fits the concept.

Practice

📓 **Notebook** Confirm your understanding of the concept vocabulary words by using each one in a sentence. Include context clues that hint at each word's meaning.

Word Study

Latin Root: *-ped-* The Latin root *-ped-* in *expedition* means "foot." Use this information to answer these questions.

1. Which of these words containing *-ped-* have a meaning connected to feet? Use a dictionary to check your answers.
   - a. pediatrician
   - c. pedal
   - b. pedestal
   - d. peddler

2. What other words related to "feet" are formed from the root *-ped-*? Use a dictionary to check your answers.

⊞ WORD NETWORK

Add words related to exploration from the text to your Word Network.

▤ STANDARDS

Language
Determine or clarify the meaning of unknown and multiple-meaning words and phrases based on *grade 6 reading and content*, choosing flexibly from a range of strategies.
  b. Use common, grade-appropriate Greek or Latin affixes and roots as clues to the meaning of a word.
  c. Consult reference materials, both print and digital, to find the pronunciation of a word or determine or clarify its precise meaning or its part of speech.
  d. Verify the preliminary determination of the meaning of a word or phrase.

TO THE TOP OF EVEREST

Analyze Craft and Structure

Central Idea A **central idea** is an important point that is supported by other details and examples in the text. Certain types of informal writing, such as blogs, friendly letters, or diary entries, are not necessarily written with one central idea in mind. Authors are simply writing about their daily life experiences. However, by grouping together particular details and determining what is repeated or emphasized, you can identify a central idea.

The blog entries you read offer numerous details about Samantha Larson's trip to and ascent of Mount Everest. Some of the details revolve around preparation and training, others around the physical effort required to climb the world's highest mountain, and still others about the emotions—from excitement to boredom—that Larson experiences during her trip. The central idea of this blog is an overarching statement that can tie together these diverse collections of details.

Practice

CITE TEXTUAL EVIDENCE
to support your answers.

📓 **Notebook** Work together to complete the activity and answer the questions.

1. Identify details from the blog entries that fit into the categories listed in the chart. Then, work together to state a central idea that ties these details together.

TYPES OF DETAILS	EXAMPLES FROM BLOG
preparation and training	
effort required to climb Everest	
thoughts and feelings	
Central Idea:	

2. **(a)** What were some of the difficulties that Larson experienced on her trip to and up Mount Everest? **(b)** Did these difficulties seem hard for her to overcome? Explain.

3. Which type of detail does Larson emphasize in her blog? Why do you think that is?

4. Do you think Larson possesses the qualities of an explorer? Why, or why not?

STANDARDS

Reading Informational Text
• Determine a central idea of a text and how it is conveyed through particular details; provide a summary of the text distinct from personal opinions or judgments.
• Analyze in detail how a key individual, event, or idea is introduced, illustrated and elaborated in a text.

Conventions

Subject Complements Writers use subject complements to provide more information about their subjects. A **subject complement** is a noun, a pronoun, or an adjective that appears after a linking verb, such as *be, become, remain, look, seem,* or *feel.*

There are two kinds of subject complements. A **predicate nominative** is a noun or pronoun that renames or identifies the subject. A **predicate adjective** is an adjective that describes the subject.

PREDICATE NOUN OR PRONOUN	PREDICATE ADJECTIVE
I am *she.*	That popcorn looks *delicious.*
Cindy *will become* a doctor.	You have seemed *cheery* all week.
He *remains* a fool.	My legs felt *exhausted.*

Read It

Identify the subject complement(s) in each of these sentences from "To the Top of Everest." Label each one as a predicate noun or a predicate adjective.

1. We are well and safe.

2. I was pretty tired by the time we got back to base camp, but today was a rest day. . . .

3. It has been a very exciting week. . . .

Write It

Complete each sentence with a subject complement. Use either a predicate adjective or a predicate noun, as indicated in parentheses.

1. People who travel to remote regions are _____.
   (predicate adjective)

2. Climbing the peak of Mount Everest could be a great
   _____. (predicate noun)

STANDARDS

Language
Demonstrate command of the conventions of standard English grammar and usage when writing or speaking.

To the Top of Everest **473**

from TALES FROM THE ODYSSEY

TO THE TOP OF EVEREST

Writing to Compare

Both the excerpt from Mary Pope Osborne's *Tales From the Odyssey* and Samantha Larson's blog suggest that exploration and adventure offer both risks and rewards. Deepen your understanding of the two texts and the nature of exploration by comparing and writing about them.

Assignment

Write a **comparison-and-contrast essay** in which you discuss how these two selections present the risks and rewards of exploration and adventure. Consider the risks and dangers the Greek warriors face in the *Odyssey*. Explain the rewards they experience or expect. Also, discuss the risks and dangers Larson faces as she climbs Mount Everest. Consider the rewards she experiences or hopes to receive. At the end of your essay, express your opinion about which selection better shows the risks and rewards of exploration.

Planning and Prewriting

Analyze the Texts Work with your group to discuss the tale and blog entries. Identify specific events and details related to risk or danger. Then, identify other details or events related to rewards. Make sure to consider different types of risks and rewards. For example, risks might involve physical, emotional, or mental dangers. In the same way, rewards can be material—involving money or comfort, for example—or emotional. Capture your observations and notes in the chart.

	from TALES FROM THE ODYSSEY	TO THE TOP OF EVEREST
Risks and Dangers		
Rewards		

📝 **Notebook** Respond to these questions.

1. In the two selections, why are characters or people in risky situations? Was it their choice or was it their fate?

2. Do the reasons characters or people are in risky situations affect how their feelings and actions? Explain.

☷ STANDARDS

Reading Literature
Compare and contrast texts in different forms or genres in terms of their approaches to similar themes and topics.
Writing
• Write informative/explanatory texts to examine a topic and convey ideas, concepts, and information through the selection, organization, and analysis of relevant content.
  b. Develop the topic with relevant facts, definitions, concrete details, quotations, or other information and examples.
• Draw evidence from literary or informational texts to support analysis, reflection, and research.
  a. Apply *grade 6 reading standards* to literature.

Drafting

Write a Main Idea Write two or three sentences that sum up your ideas. State how the two selections show risks and rewards in ways that are the same and different. Use compare and contrast key words such as those underlined in the frames.

Sentence Frames: <u>Both</u> the excerpt from *Tales From the Odyssey* and Larson's blog posts show _____

_____

<u>However,</u> the stories from the *Odyssey* show _____

_____

<u>In contrast,</u> the blog entries _____

_____

Organize Ideas Consider using one of these two ways to organize your essay.

Block Organization	Point-by-Point Organization
I. *Tales From the Odyssey*	**I. Risks Characters/People Face**
A. risks characters face	A. *Tales From the Odyssey*
B. reasons they face the risks	B. To the Top of Everest
C. rewards they receive	**II. Risks**
II. To the Top of Everest	A. *Tales from the Odyssey*
A. risks people face	B. To the Top of Everest
B. reasons they face the risks	**III. Rewards They Receive**
C. rewards they receive	A. *Tales from the Odyssey*
	B. To the Top of Everest

Use Transitions When you write a comparison-and-contrast essay, you will need to shift from one topic to another. Use transition words and phrases, such as the ones shown here, to make shifts in your ideas clear.

COMPARISON	CONTRAST
and, also, additionally, likewise, in the same way, both, similarly	*but, however, on the other hand, in a different way, in contrast, although*

Review, Revise, and Edit

Reread your draft, and ask yourself these questions:

- Have I used words that say exactly what I mean?
- Did I leave out any details that I want to include?
- Does the order of my ideas make sense?

Swap drafts with group members and give feedback on one another's work. Discuss the changes your peers recommend and make the ones you feel are important. Fix any spelling or grammar errors you find.

✒ EVIDENCE LOG

Before moving on to a new selection, go to your Evidence Log and record what you learned from "To the Top of Everest."

≣ STANDARDS

Writing
- Write informative/explanatory texts to examine a topic and convey ideas, concepts, and information through the selection, organization, and analysis of relevant content.
  a. Introduce a topic; organize ideas, concepts, and information, using strategies such as definition, classification, comparison/contrast, and cause/effect; include formatting, graphics, and multimedia when useful to aiding comprehension.
  c. Use appropriate transitions to clarify the relationships among ideas and concepts.

About the Author

Nick Bertozzi (b.1970) was introduced to comics by his father before he could read. As an adult, he developed his own mini-comic while working in the marketing department at DC Comics. Besides being an illustrator and an author of graphic novels, Bertozzi is also a computer programmer and an educator who has taught his craft at several prestigious art schools.

from Lewis & Clark

Media Vocabulary

The following words or concepts will be useful to you as you analyze, discuss, and write about graphic novels.

penciler: artist who sketches the basic layout for each panel	• A penciler shows the figures, expressions, objects, and backgrounds in each panel. • The amount of detail in the drawings varies from penciler to penciler.
inker: artist who goes over the penciled art in ink	• An inker uses pen and brush with ink to create an image that will print well. • The amount of detail left for the inker to fill in depends on how much detail was done by the penciler.
letterer: artist who letters the dialogue and captions	• A letterer fills in the speech ballons and may also place them in the panel. • Different weights, shapes, and sizes of letters can convey different emotions and meanings.

First Review MEDIA: GRAPHIC NOVEL

Apply these strategies as you conduct your first review. You will have an opportunity to complete a close review after your first review.

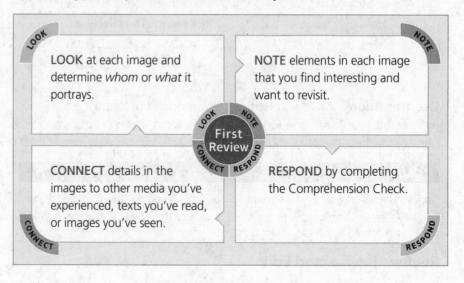

LOOK at each image and determine *whom* or *what* it portrays.

NOTE elements in each image that you find interesting and want to revisit.

CONNECT details in the images to other media you've experienced, texts you've read, or images you've seen.

RESPOND by completing the Comprehension Check.

BACKGROUND

The Lewis and Clark expedition (1804–1806) was a major exploration of the northwestern United States that allowed the government to later claim the area. The band of explorers and their co-leaders, Captain Meriwether Lewis and Lieutenant William Clark, were known as the Corps of Discovery.

SCAN FOR
MULTIMEDIA

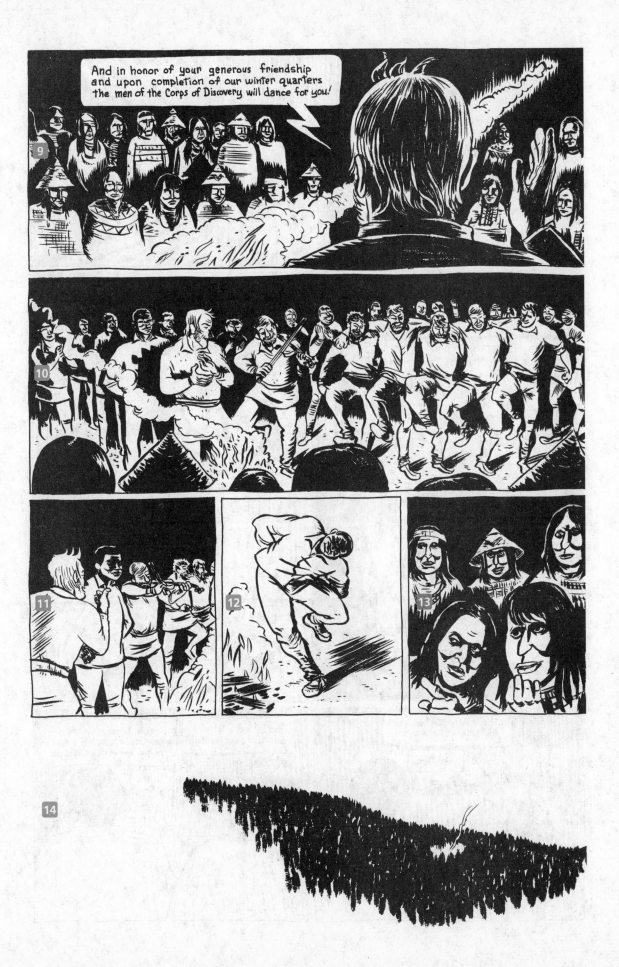

Comprehension Check

Complete the following items after you finish your first review. Review and clarify details with your group.

1. What are the men building?

2. Why doesn't Captain Lewis help with the construction of the building?

3. Who or what are the Clatsop?

4. Why does Ordway say, "It's no wonder you're all such a scrawny bunch"?

MEDIA VOCABULARY

Use these words as you discuss and write about the graphic novel.

penciler
inker
letterer

🔗 **WORD NETWORK**

Add words related to exploration from the text to your Word Network.

Close Review

Revisit the graphic novel and your first-review notes. Write down any new observations that seem important. What **questions** do you have? What can you **conclude**?

Analyze the Media

CITE TEXTUAL EVIDENCE to support your answers.

Complete the activities.

1. **Present and Discuss** Choose the section of the graphic novel you found most interesting or powerful. Discuss what you noticed, what questions you asked, and what conclusions you reached.

2. **Review and Synthesize** With your group, review the illustrations in the selection. How do the illustrations add to your understanding of what it was like to be a member of the Lewis and Clark expedition? What do they tell you that the words do not?

3. **Essential Question:** *What drives people to explore?* What has this graphic novel taught you about exploration? Discuss with your group.

Research

A timeline is a way of displaying events in the order in which they actually occurred over time.

from LEWIS & CLARK

> ## Assignment
>
> As a group, conduct research to learn more about the Lewis and Clark expedition, including the events and people presented in the graphic novel. Then, create and present an **annotated timeline** of important events in the expedition. You may present your timeline digitally, as a poster, or through another method of visual display.

Conduct Research Work with your group to find credible print and digital sources of information about the Lewis and Clark expedition. As you research, note the specific dates and locations of important events as well as the source from which you obtained the information. Pick five or six key events to highlight in your timeline. Then, find images to accompany at least three events; for example, you might use a map to accompany the arrival of the expedition in a new location, or an illustration of Lewis or Clark to highlight an event in which the explorer played an important role.

Organize Your Timeline First, arrange the events you will include in your timeline in **chronological order**, or the order in which the events actually happened. The first event on your timeline should have the earliest date, and the last should have the latest date.

Create Your Annotations To annotate your timeline, use the information and images from your research to create a brief explanatory note for each event. In each note, write a sentence or two in which you summarize what happened and why it was important. If you are including an image in an annotation, you should provide a short caption in which you describe the image and explain how it connects to the event it illustrates.

Assemble and Present Once you have finished your annotations, assemble your timeline to display in your presentation. Assign group members to explain the information about each event during the presentation.

✐ EVIDENCE LOG

Before moving on to a new selection, go to your Evidence Log, and record what you learned from the graphic novel *Lewis & Clark*.

▤ STANDARDS

Reading Informational Text
• Integrate information presented in different media or formats as well as in words to develop a coherent understanding of a topic or issue.

Writing
• Conduct short research projects to answer a question, drawing on several sources and refocusing the inquiry when appropriate.
• Gather relevant information from multiple print and digital sources; assess the credibility of each source; and quote or paraphrase the data and conclusions of others while avoiding plagiarism and providing basic bibliographic information for sources.

Speaking and Listening
• Interpret information presented in diverse media and formats and explain how it contributes to a topic, text, or issue under study.
• Include multimedia components and visual displays in presentations to clarify information.

Present an Advertisement

Assignment

You have read about expeditions to remote places. Now, write and present an argument in the form of an **advertisement** that answers this question:

Why should we explore new frontiers?

You may imagine and advertise an upcoming expedition on Earth, in space, or to an imagined location. It can take place in the past, the present, or the future.

Plan With Your Group

Analyze the Text As a group, review the selections in this section and analyze the ways in which the selections would make exploration seem exciting to potential tourists. Record your notes in the chart shown. Then, when the chart is complete, decide what kind of expedition to advertise, as well as the location, time, and purpose of the expedition.

TITLE	NOTES
Mission Twinpossible	
from Tales From the Odyssey	
To the Top of Everest	
from Lewis & Clark	

Discuss Advertising Elements With your group, discuss what you know about advertising. How do advertisers convince customers to buy their products? Then, decide whether to make your advertisement a poster or a digital graphic.

Gather Evidence and Media Examples Scan the selections to record specific examples that would add interest and strengthen your argument for participating in the imagined expedition. Brainstorm for types of media that would make the advertisement more enticing. Consider photographs, illustrations, music, charts, graphs, and video clips. Allow each group member to make suggestions.

Create a Draft As a group, design and create your advertisement. Assign roles to each member—for instance, finding media, organizing examples, writing text, and advertisement design. Also, decide which group member or members will be presenting the advertisement to the class.

Rehearse With Your Group

Practice With Your Group Practice presenting your ad to the class. Use this checklist to evaluate the effectiveness of your group's first run-through. Then, use your evaluation and these instructions to guide your revision.

CONTENT	USE OF MEDIA	PRESENTATION TECHNIQUES
☐ The ad presents a convincing argument for joining the expedition. ☐ The ad maintains consistency in style and tone.	☐ Media components are relevant and well chosen. ☐ Media components add to the excitement of the expedition.	☐ Speakers make eye contact and speak clearly with adequate volume. ☐ Speakers sound enthusiastic and persuasive.

Fine-Tune the Content Reread your advertisement. If it is not convincing, find places where you can strengthen your argument. If necessary, review your notes and add evidence to support your claim. Use engaging, precise language to draw attention to exciting adventures that await potential explorers. Consider listing the benefits of joining the expedition someplace in your advertisement.

Improve Your Use of Media Review your media components. Do your visuals provide enough relevant evidence to convince thrill-seekers to join your expedition? If not, carefully choose vivid photographs or graphics to provide a dramatic illustration of the claim you make in your argument.

Present and Evaluate

When you present your advertisement, be sure to pronounce words clearly and maintain appropriate eye contact. As your classmates deliver their group presentations, consider whether they have been successful in convincing you to participate in their expeditions. Listen attentively and evaluate their content, use of media, and presentation skills.

≡ STANDARDS

Speaking and Listening
• Delineate a speaker's argument and specific claims, distinguishing claims that are supported by reasons and evidence from claims that are not.
• Present claims and findings, sequencing ideas logically and using pertinent descriptions, facts, and details to accentuate main ideas or themes; use appropriate eye contact, adequate volume, and clear pronunciation.
• Include multimedia components and visual displays in presentations to clarify information.
Language
Maintain consistency in style and tone.

ESSENTIAL QUESTION:

What drives people to explore?

What challenges do explorers face in unfamiliar environments? In this section, you will complete your study of exploration by studying an additional selection related to the topic. You'll then share what you learn with classmates. To choose a text, follow these steps.

Look Back Think about the selections you have already studied. What more do you want to know about the topic of exploration?

Look Ahead Preview the texts by reading the descriptions. Which one seems most interesting and appealing to you?

Look Inside Take a few minutes to scan through the text you chose. Make another selection if this text doesn't meet your needs.

Independent Learning Strategies

Throughout your life, in school, in your community, and in your career, you will need to rely on yourself to learn and work on your own. Review these strategies and the actions you can take to practice them during Independent Learning. Add ideas of your own for each category.

STRATEGY	ACTION PLAN
Create a schedule	• Understand your goals and deadlines. • Make a plan for what to do each day. •
Practice what you have learned	• Use first-read and close-read strategies to deepen your understanding. • After you read, evaluate the usefulness of the evidence to help you understand the topic. • Consider the quality and reliability of the source. •
Take notes	• Record important ideas and information. • Review your notes before preparing to share with a group. •

SCAN FOR
MULTIMEDIA

Choose one selection. Selections are available online only.

CONTENTS

PERFORMANCE-BASED ASSESSMENT PREP

Review Evidence for an Argument

Complete your Evidence Log for the unit by evaluating what you have learned and synthesizing the information you have recorded.

SCAN FOR MULTIMEDIA

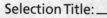
First-Read Guide

Use this page to record your first-read ideas.

Selection Title: _____

 **Tool Kit**
First-Read Guide and
Model Annotation

NOTICE new information or ideas you learn about the unit topic as you first read this text.

ANNOTATE by marking vocabulary and key passages you want to revisit.

CONNECT ideas within the selection to other knowledge and the selections you have read.

RESPOND by writing a brief summary of the selection.

::: STANDARD

Reading Read and comprehend complex literary and informational texts independently and proficiently.

Close-Read Guide

Use this page to record your first-read ideas.

Selection Title: _____

Close Read the Text

Revisit sections of the text you marked during your first read. Read these sections closely and **annotate** what you notice. Ask yourself **questions** about the text. What can you **conclude**? Write down your ideas.

Analyze the Text

Think about the author's choices of patterns, structure, techniques, and ideas included in the text. Select one, and record your thoughts about what this choice conveys.

QuickWrite

Pick a paragraph from the text that grabbed your interest. Explain the power of this passage.

_____

_____

_____

_____

_____

_____

_____

_____

▤ STANDARD

Reading Read and comprehend complex literary and informational texts independently and proficiently.

Share Your Independent Learning

Prepare to Share

What drives people to explore?

Even when you read something independently, your understanding continues to grow when you share what you have learned with others. Reflect on the text you explored independently, and write notes about its connection to the unit. In your notes, consider why this text belongs in this unit.

Learn From Your Classmates

💬 **Discuss It** Share your ideas about the text you explored on your own. As you talk with your classmates, jot down ideas that you learn from them.

Reflect

Review your notes, and mark the most important insight you gained from these writing and discussion activities. Explain how this idea adds to your understanding of the topic of exploration.

⊟ STANDARDS

Speaking and Listening
Engage effectively in a range of collaborative discussions with diverse partners on *grade 6 topics, texts, and issues,* building on others' ideas and expressing their own clearly.

Review Evidence for an Argument

At the beginning of this unit you took a position on the following question:

> ## Should kids today be encouraged to become explorers?

✎ EVIDENCE LOG

Review your Evidence Log and your QuickWrite from the beginning of the unit. Has your position changed?

☐ YES	☐ NO
Identify at least three pieces of evidence that convinced you to change your mind.	Identify at least three pieces of evidence that reinforced your initial position.
1.	1.
2.	2.
3.	3.

State your claim now: _____

_____

_____

Identify a possible counterclaim, or opposing position: _____

_____

_____

Evaluate the Strength of Your Evidence Consider your argument. Do you have enough evidence to support your claim? Do you have enough evidence to disprove possible counterclaims? If not, make a plan.

☐ Do more research ☐ Talk with my classmates

☐ Reread a selection ☐ Ask an expert

☐ Other: _____

⋮≡ STANDARDS

Writing
Write arguments to support claims with clear reasons and relevant evidence.
  b. Support claim(s) with clear reasons and relevant evidence, using credible sources and demonstrating an understanding of the topic or text.

SOURCES

- WHOLE-CLASS SELECTIONS
- SMALL-GROUP SELECTIONS
- INDEPENDENT-LEARNING SELECTION

PART 1
Writing to Sources: Argument

In this unit, you read about a variety of explorers and considered different perspectives on important issues related to exploration.

Assignment

Write an **argument** in which you state and defend a claim in response to the following question:

> Should kids today be encouraged to become explorers?

First, state your claim, and then develop a coherent argument to support that claim. Organize your argument logically, and support your claim with valid evidence from credible sources. Use precise words to clarify the relationships among the reasons and the claim. Include a conclusion that follows from your argument. Strive to maintain a formal tone throughout your writing.

Reread the Assignment Review the assignment to be sure you fully understand it. The task may reference some of the academic words presented at the beginning of the unit. Be sure you understand each of the words given below in order to complete the assignment correctly. Also, consider using the academic vocabulary words in your argument. These words may help you to clarify your claims with precise word choices.

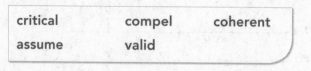

critical	compel	coherent
assume	valid	

⊹ WORD NETWORK

As you write and revise your argument, use your Word Network to help vary your word choices.

⠿ STANDARDS

Writing
• Write arguments to support claims with clear reasons and relevant evidence.
• Write routinely over extended time frames and shorter time frames for a range of discipline-specific tasks, purposes, and audiences.

Language
Use knowledge of language and its conventions when writing, speaking, reading, or listening.
  b. Maintain consistency in style and tone.

Review the Elements of Effective Argument Before you begin writing, read the Argument Rubric. Once you have completed your first draft, check it against the rubric. If one or more of the elements is missing or not as strong as it could be, revise your essay to add or strengthen that element.

Argument Rubric

	Focus and Organization	Evidence and Elaboration	Conventions
4	The introduction is engaging and states the claim in a compelling way. The claim is supported by clear reasons and relevant evidence. Words, phrases, and clauses are used to clarify the relationships among the claim and reasons. The conclusion clearly follows from the argument.	Sources are credible and support the claim. The tone of the argument is formal and objective. Words are carefully chosen and suited to purpose and audience.	The argument correctly uses standard English conventions of usage and mechanics.
3	The introduction is mostly engaging and states the claim. The claim is mostly supported by clear reasons and relevant evidence. Words, phrases, and clauses are mostly used to clarify the relationships among the claim and reasons. The conclusion mostly follows from the argument.	Sources are mostly credible and mostly support the claim. The tone of the argument is mostly formal and objective. Words are mostly suited to purpose and audience.	The argument mostly demonstrates accuracy in standard English conventions of usage and mechanics.
2	The introduction somewhat states the claim. The claim is supported by some reasons and evidence. Words, phrase, and clauses are occasionally used to clarify relationships among the claim and reasons. The conclusion somewhat follows from the argument.	Sources are somewhat credible and somewhat support the claim. The tone of the argument is occasionally formal and objective. Words are somewhat suited to purpose and audience.	The argument demonstrates some accuracy in standard English conventions of usage and mechanics.
1	The introduction does not clearly state the claim. The claim is not supported by reasons and evidence. Words, phrase, and clauses are not used to clarify relationships among the claim and reasons. The conclusion does not follow from the argument.	Sources are not credible nor do they support the claim. The tone is informal. Words are not suited to purpose or audience.	The argument contains mistakes in standard English conventions of usage and mechanics.

PART 2

Speaking and Listening: Speech

Assignment

After completing the final draft of your argument, use it as the foundation for a brief **speech.**

Do not simply read your argument aloud. Take the following steps to make your presentation lively and engaging.

- Review your argument and annotate the most important reasons and evidence. Refer to the annotations to guide your presentation.
- Keep your audience in mind, and adapt the wording of your speech as needed to appeal to them.
- Use appropriate eye contact. Make sure to pronounce words clearly and speak loudly enough for people to hear you. Vary your volume and your talking speed to emphasize key points.

Review the Rubric Before you deliver your presentation, check your plans against this rubric. If one or more of the elements is missing or not as strong as it could be, revise your presentation.

STANDARDS

Speaking and Listening
• Present claims and findings, sequencing ideas logically and using pertinent descriptions, facts, and details to accentuate main ideas or themes; use appropriate eye contact, adequate volume, and clear pronunciation.
• Adapt speech to a variety of contexts and tasks, demonstrating command of formal English when indicated or appropriate.

	Content	Organization	Presentation Techniques
3	The introduction is engaging and establishes the claim in a compelling way. The presentation includes strong, clear reasons and relevant evidence to support the claim. The conclusion clearly follows from the argument.	Ideas progress logically, with clear transitions so that the argument is easy to follow. Important ideas are given emphasis and are well supported.	The speaker maintains effective eye contact and speaks clearly with adequate volume.
2	The introduction establishes the claim. The presentation includes some clear reasons and relevant evidence to support the claim. The conclusion somewhat follows from the argument.	Ideas progress logically with some transitions between ideas.that the argument is easy to follow. Important ideas are sometimes emphasized and are supported.	The speaker sometimes maintains effective eye contact and speaks somewhat clearly and with adequate volume.
1	The introduction does not clearly establish the claim. The presentation does not include reasons or evidence to support the claim. The conclusion does not follow from the argument.	Ideas do not progress logically. Important ideas are not emphasized and may lack support.	The speaker does not maintain effective eye contact or speak clearly with adequate volume.

Reflect on the Unit

Now that you've completed the unit, take a few moments to reflect on your learning.

Reflect on the Unit Goals

Look back at the goals at the beginning of the unit. Use a different-colored pen to rate yourself again. Then, think about the readings and activities that contributed the most to the growth of your understanding. Record your thoughts.

Reflect on the Learning Strategies

◯ Discuss It Write a reflection on whether you were able to improve your learning based on your Action Plans. Think about what worked, what didn't, and what you might do to keep working on these strategies. Record your ideas before participating in a class discussion.

Reflect on the Text

Choose a selection that you found challenging, and explain what made it difficult.

Explain something that surprised you about a text in the unit.

Which activity taught you the most about exploration? What did you learn?

RESOURCES

TABLE OF CONTENTS

Marking the Text: Strategies and Tips for Annotation

When you close read a text, you read for comprehension and then reread to unlock layers of meaning and to analyze a writer's style and techniques. Marking a text as you read it enables you to participate more fully in the close-reading process.

Following are some strategies for text mark-ups, along with samples of how the strategies can be applied. These mark-ups are suggestions; you and your teacher may want to use other mark-up strategies.

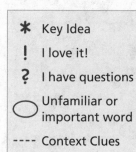

* Key Idea

! I love it!

? I have questions

◯ Unfamiliar or important word

---- Context Clues

Suggested Mark-Up Notations

WHAT I NOTICE	HOW TO MARK UP	QUESTIONS TO ASK
Key Ideas and Details	• Highlight key ideas or claims. • Underline supporting details or evidence.	• What does the text say? What does it leave unsaid? • What inferences do you need to make? • What details lead you to make your inferences?
Word Choice	• Circle unfamiliar words. • Put a dotted line under context clues, if any exist. • Put an exclamation point beside especially rich or poetic passages.	• What inferences about word meaning can you make? • What tone and mood are created by word choice? • What alternate word choices might the author have made?
Text Structure	• Highlight passages that show key details supporting the main idea. • Use arrows to indicate how sentences and paragraphs work together to build ideas. • Use a right-facing arrow to indicate foreshadowing. • Use a left-facing arrow to indicate flashback.	• Is the text logically structured? • What emotional impact do the structural choices create?
Author's Craft	• Circle or highlight instances of repetition, either of words, phrases, consonants, or vowel sounds. • Mark rhythmic beats in poetry using checkmarks and slashes. • Underline instances of symbolism or figurative language.	• Does the author's style enrich or detract from the reading experience? • What levels of meaning are created by the author's techniques?

CLOSE READING

First Read
NOTICE ANNOTATE
CONNECT RESPOND

* Key Idea
! I love it!
? I have questions
◯ Unfamiliar or important word
---- Context Clues

In a first read, work to get a sense of the main idea of a text. Look for key details and ideas that help you understand what the author conveys to you. Mark passages which prompt a strong response from you.

Here is how one reader marked up this text.

NOTES

MODEL

INFORMATIONAL TEXT

from Classifying the Stars

Cecilia H. Payne

1   Sunlight and starlight are composed of waves of various lengths, which the eye, even aided by a telescope, is unable to separate. We must use more than a telescope. In order to sort out the component colors, the light must be dispersed by a prism, or split up by some other means. For instance, sunbeams passing through rain drops are transformed into the myriad-tinted rainbow. The familiar rainbow spanning the sky is Nature's most glorious demonstration that light is composed of many colors.

2   The very beginning of our knowledge of the nature of a star dates back to 1672, when Isaac Newton gave to the world the results of his experiments on passing sunlight through a prism. To describe the beautiful band of rainbow tints, produced when sunlight was dispersed by his three-cornered piece of glass, he took from the Latin the word *spectrum*, meaning an appearance. The rainbow is the spectrum of the Sun. . . .

3   In 1814, more than a century after Newton, the spectrum of the Sun was obtained in such purity that an amazing detail was seen and studied by the German optician, Fraunhofer. He saw that the multiple spectral tints, ranging from delicate violet to deep red, were crossed by hundreds of fine dark lines. In other words, there were narrow gaps in the spectrum where certain shades were wholly blotted out. We must remember that the word spectrum is applied not only to sunlight, but also to the light of any glowing substance when its rays are sorted out by a prism or a grating.

First-Read Guide

Use this page to record your first-read ideas.

You may want to use a guide like this to organize your thoughts after you read. Here is how a reader completed a First-Read Guide.

Selection Title: _____Classifying the Stars_____

NOTICE new information or ideas you learned about the unit topic as you first read this text.

Light = different waves of colors. (Spectrum)

Newton - the first person to observe these waves using a prism.

Faunhofer saw gaps in the spectrum.

ANNOTATE by marking vocabulary and key passages you want to revisit.

Vocabulary
    myriad
    grating
    component colors

Different light types = different lengths

Isaac Newton also worked theories of gravity.

Multiple spectral tints? "colors of various appearance"

Key Passage:
Paragraph 3 shows that Fraunhofer discovered more about the nature of light spectrums: he saw the spaces in between the tints.

CONNECT ideas within the selection to other knowledge and the selections you have read.

I remember learning about prisms in science class.

Double rainbows! My favorite. How are they made?

RESPOND by writing a brief summary of the selection.

Science allows us to see things not visible to the naked eye. What we see as sunlight is really a spectrum of colors. By using tools, such as prisms, we can see the components of sunlight and other light. They appear as single colors or as multiple colors separated by gaps of no color. White light contains a rainbow of colors.

CLOSE READING

ANNOTATE · QUESTION · **Close Read** · CONCLUDE

* Key Idea
! I love it!
? I have questions
◯ Unfamiliar or important word
---- Context Clues

In a close read, go back into the text to study it in greater detail. Take the time to analyze not only the author's ideas but the way that those ideas are conveyed. Consider the genre of the text, the author's word choice, the writer's unique style, and the message of the text.

Here is how one reader close read this text.

MODEL

INFORMATIONAL TEXT

NOTES

TOOL KIT: CLOSE READING

from Classifying the Stars
Cecilia H. Payne

explanation of sunlight and starlight

*
1 Sunlight and starlight are composed of waves of various lengths, which the eye, even aided by a telescope, is unable to separate.

What is light and where do the colors come from?

? We must use more than a telescope. In order to sort out the component colors, the light must be dispersed by a prism, or split up by some other means. For instance, sunbeams passing through rain drops are transformed into the ⟨myriad⟩-tinted rainbow. The familiar rainbow spanning the sky is Nature's most **!** glorious demonstration that light is composed of many colors.

This paragraph is about Newton and the prism.

*
2 The very beginning of our knowledge of the nature of a star dates back to 1672, when Isaac Newton gave to the world the results of his experiments on passing sunlight through a prism.

What discoveries helped us understand light?

To describe the beautiful band of rainbow tints, produced when sunlight was dispersed by his three-cornered piece of glass, he took from the Latin the word *spectrum*, meaning an appearance. The rainbow is the ⟨spectrum⟩ of the Sun. . . .

*
3 In 1814, more than a century after Newton, the spectrum of the Sun was obtained in such purity that an amazing detail was seen and studied by the German optician, Fraunhofer. He saw that

Fraunhofer and gaps in spectrum

the multiple spectral tints, ranging from delicate violet to deep red, were crossed by hundreds of fine dark lines. In other words, there were narrow gaps in the spectrum where certain shades were wholly blotted out. We must remember that the word spectrum is applied not only to sunlight, but also to the light of any glowing substance when its rays are sorted out by a prism or a ⟨grating⟩.

Close-Read Guide

Use this page to record your close-read ideas.

You can use the Close-Read Guide to help you dig deeper into the text. Here is how a reader completed a Close-Read Guide.

Selection Title: _Classifying the Stars_

Close Read the Text

Revisit sections of the text you marked during your first read. Read these sections closely and **annotate** what you notice. Ask yourself **questions** about the text. What can you **conclude?** Write down your ideas.

Paragraph 3: Light is composed of waves of various lengths. Prisms let us see different colors in light. This is called the spectrum. Fraunhofer proved that there are gaps in the spectrum, where certain shades are blotted out.

More than one researcher studied this and each built off the ideas that were already discovered.

Analyze the Text

Think about the author's choices of patterns, structure, techniques, and ideas included in the text. Select one, and record your thoughts about what this choice conveys.

The author showed the development of human knowledge of the spectrum chronologically. Helped me see how ideas were built upon earlier understandings. Used dates and "more than a century after Newton" to show time.

QuickWrite

Pick a paragraph from the text that grabbed your interest. Explain the power of this passage.

The first paragraph grabbed my attention, specifically the sentence "The familiar rainbow spanning the sky is Nature's most glorious demonstration that light is composed of many colors." The paragraph began as a straightforward scientific explanation. When I read the word "glorious," I had to stop and deeply consider what was being said. It is a word loaded with personal feelings. With that one word, the author let the reader know what was important to her.

WRITING

Argument

When you think of the word *argument,* you might think of a disagreement between two people, but the word has another meaning, too. An argument is a logical way of presenting a belief, conclusion, or stance. A good argument is supported with reasoning and evidence.

Argument writing can be used for many purposes, such as changing a reader's opinion or bringing about an action or a response from a reader.

Elements of an Argumentative Text

An **argument** sets forth a belief or stand on an issue. A well-written argument may convince the reader, change the reader's mind, or motivate the reader to take a certain action.

An effective argument contains these elements:

- a precise claim
- consideration of alternate claims, or opposing positions, and a discussion of their strengths and weaknesses
- logical organization that makes clear connections among claim, reasons, and evidence
- valid reasoning and evidence
- a concluding statement or section that follows from and supports the argument
- formal and objective language and tone
- error-free grammar, including accurate use of transitions

Celebrities Should Try to Be Better Role Models

A lot of Celebrities are singers or actors or actresses or athletes. Kids spend tons of time watching Celebrities on TV. They listen to their songs. They read about them. They watch them play and perform. No matter weather the Celebrities are good people or bad people. Kids still spend time watching them. The kids will try to imitate what they do. Some of them have parents or brothers and sisters who are famous also.

Celebrities don't seem to watch out what they do and how they live. Some say, *"Why do I care? It's none of you're business"!* Well, that's true. But it's bad on them if they do all kinds of stupid things. Because this is bad for the kids who look up to them.

Sometimes celebrity's say they wish they are not role models. *"I'm just an actor!" "I'm just a singer"!* they say. But the choice is not really up to them. If their on TV all the time, then kids' will look up to them, no matter what. It's stupid when Celebrities mess up and then nothing bad happens to them. That gives kids a bad lesson. Kids will think that you can do stupid things and be fine. That is not being a good role model.

Some Celebrities give money to charity. That's a good way to be a good role model. But sometimes it seems like Celebrities are just totally messed up. It's hard always being in the spotlight. That can drive Celebrities kind of crazy. Then they act out.

It is a good idea to support charities when you are rich and famous. You can do a lot of good. For a lot of people. Some Celebrities give out cars or houses or free scholarships. You can even give away your dresses and people can have an auction to see who will pay the most money for them. This can help for example the Humane Society. Or whatever charity or cause the celebrity wants to support.

Celebrities are fun to watch and follow, even when they mess up. I think they don't realize that when they do bad things, they give teens wrong ideas about how to live. They should try to keep that under control. So many teens look up to them and copy them, no matter what.

The claim is not clearly stated in the introduction or elsewhere.

Some of the ideas in the essay do not relate to the stated position or focus on the issue.

The word choice in the essay is not effective and lends it an informal tone.

The progression of ideas is not logical or well-controlled.

Errors in spelling, capitalization, punctuation, grammar, usage, and sentence boundaries are frequent. The fluency of the writing and effectiveness of the essay are affected by these errors.

The conclusion does not clearly restate the claim.

MODEL

ARGUMENT: SCORE 2

Celebrities Should Try to Be Better Role Models

Most kids spend tons of time watching celebrities on TV, listening to their songs, and reading about them. No matter how celebrities behave—whether they do good things or bad—they are role models for kids. They often do really dumb things, and that is not good considering they are role models.

Sometimes celebrity's say they wish they were not role models. "*I'm just an actor!*" or, "*I'm just a singer!*" they say. But the choice is not really up to them. If they are on TV all the time, then kids' will look up to them. No matter what. It's really bad when celebrities mess up and then nothing bad happens to them. That gives kids a false lesson because in reality there are bad things when you mess up. That's why celebrities should think more about what they are doing and what lessons they are giving to kids.

Some celebrities might say, "*Why do I care? Why should I be bothered?*" Well, they don't have to. But it's bad on them if they do all kinds of stupid things and don't think about how this affects the kids who look up to them. Plus, they get tons of money, much more even than inventors or scientists or other important people. Being a good role model should be part of what they have to do to get so much money.

When you are famous it is a good idea to support charities. Some celebrities give out cars, or houses, or free scholarships. They even sometimes give away their dresses and people have an auction to see who will pay the most money for them. This can help for example the Humane Society, or whatever charity or cause the celebrity wants to support.

Sometimes it seems like celebrities are more messed up than anyone else. That's in their personal lives. Imagine if people wanted to take pictures of you wherever you went, and you could never get away. That can drive celebrities kind of crazy, and then they act out.

Celebrities can do good things and they can do bad things. They don't realize that when they do bad things, they give teens wrong ideas about how to live. So many teens look up to them and copy them, no matter what. They should make an effort to be better role models.

The introduction does not state the argument claim clearly enough.

Errors in spelling, grammar, and sentence boundaries decrease the effectiveness of the essay.

The word choice in the essay contributes to an informal tone.

The writer does not make use of transitions and sentence connections.

Some of the ideas in the essay do not relate to the stated position or focus on the issue.

The essay has a clear conclusion.

ARGUMENT: SCORE 3

Celebrities Should Try to Be Better Role Models

Kids look up to the celebrities they see on TV and want to be like them.
Parents may not *want* celebrities to be role models for their children,
but they are anyway. Therefore, celebrities should think about what
they say and do and live lives that are worth copying. Celebrities
should think about how they act because they are role models.

"I'm just an actor!" or, *"I'm just a singer!"* celebrities sometimes say.
"Their parents and teachers are the ones who should be the role models!"
But it would be foolish to misjudge the impact that celebrities have
on youth. Kids spend hours every day digitally hanging with their
favorite stars. Children learn by imitation, so, for better or worse,
celebrities are role models. That's why celebrities should start
modeling good decision-making and good citizenship.

With all that they are given by society, celebrities owe a lot back to
their communities and the world. Celebrities get a lot of attention,
time, and money. Often they get all that for doing not very much:
acting, singing, or playing a sport. It's true; some of them work
very hard. But even if they work very hard, do they deserve to be
in the news all the time and earn 100 or even 1000 times more than
equally hard-working teachers, scientists, or nurses? I don't think so.
After receiving all that, it seems only fair that celebrities take on the
important job of being good role models for the young people who
look up to them.

Celebrities can serve as good role models is by giving back. Quite a
few use their fame and fortune to do just that. They give scholarships,
or even build and run schools; they help veterans; they visit hospitals;
they support important causes such as conservation, and women's
rights. They donate not just money but their time and talents too. This
is a great way to be a role model.

Celebrities should recognize that as role models, they have a
responsibility to try to make good decisions and be honest. Celebrities
should step up so they can be a force for good in people's lives and in
the world.

The writer's word choice is good but could be better.

The introduction mostly states the claim.

The ideas relate to the stated position and focus on the issue.

The sentences are varied and well controlled and enhance the effectiveness of the essay.

The progression of ideas is logical, but there could be better transitions and sentence connections to show how ideas are related.

The conclusion mostly follows from the claim.

WRITING

ARGUMENT: SCORE 4

Celebrities Should Try to Be Better Role Models

Like it or not, kids look up to the celebrities they see on TV and want to be like them. Parents may not *want* celebrities to be role models for their children, but the fact is that they are. With such an oversized influence on young people, celebrities have a responsibility to think about what they say and do and to live lives that are worth emulating. In short, they should make an effort to be better role models.

The writer has chosen words that contribute to the clarity of the essay.

The writer clearly states the claim of the argument in the introduction.

Sometimes celebrities say they don't want to be role models. "I'm just an actor!" or "I'm just a singer!" they protest. "Their parents and teachers are the ones who should be guiding them and showing them the right way to live!" That is all very well, but it would be foolish to underestimate the impact that celebrities have on children. Kids spend hours every day digitally hanging out with their favorite stars. Children learn by imitation, so for better or worse, celebrities act as role models.

The essay is engaging and varied.

Celebrities are given a lot of attention, time, and money. They get all that for doing very little: acting, singing, or playing a sport very well. It's true some of them work very hard. But even if they work hard, do they deserve to be in the news all the time and earn 100 or even 1,000 times more than equally hardworking teachers, scientists, or nurses? I don't think so.

There are no errors to distract the reader from the fluency of the writing and effectiveness of the essay.

With all that they are given, celebrities owe a lot to their communities and the world. One way they can serve as good role models is by giving back, and quite a few celebrities use their fame and fortune to do just that. They give scholarships or even build and run schools; they help veterans; they entertain kids who are sick; they support important causes such as conservation and women's rights. They donate not just money but their time and talents too.

The writer uses transitions and sentence connections to show how ideas are related.

Celebrities don't have to be perfect. They are people too and make mistakes. But they should recognize that as role models for youth, they have a responsibility to try to make good decisions and be honest about their struggles. Celebrities should step up so they can be a force for good in people's lives.

The writer clearly restates the claim and the most powerful idea presented in the essay.

Argument Rubric

	Focus and Organization	Evidence and Elaboration	Conventions
4	The introduction is engaging and states the claim in a compelling way. The claim is supported by clear reasons and relevant evidence. Reasons and evidence are logically organized so that the argument is easy to follow. The conclusion clearly restates the claim and the most powerful idea.	Sources are effectively credible and accurate. The argument demonstrates an understanding of the thesis by providing strong examples. The tone of the argument is formal and objective.	The argument intentionally uses standard English conventions of usage and mechanics. The argument effectively uses words, phrases, and clauses to clarify the relationships among claim(s) and reasons.
3	The introduction is mostly engaging and states the claim. The claim is mostly supported by logical reasons and evidence. Reasons and evidence are organized so that the argument is mostly easy to follow. The conclusion mostly restates the claim.	Sources are mostly credible and accurate. The argument mostly demonstrates an understanding of the thesis by providing adequate examples. The tone of the argument is mostly formal and objective.	The argument mostly demonstrates accuracy in standard English conventions of usage and mechanics. The argument mostly uses words, phrases, and clauses to clarify the relationships among claim(s) and reasons.
2	The introduction somewhat states the claim. The claim is supported by some reasons and evidence. Reasons and evidence are organized somewhat logically with a few transitions to orient readers. The conclusion somewhat relates to the claim.	Some sources are relevant. The argument somewhat demonstrates an understanding of the thesis by providing some examples. The tone of the argument is occasionally formal and objective.	The argument demonstrates some accuracy in standard English conventions of usage and mechanics. The argument somewhat uses words, phrases, and clauses to clarify the relationships among claim(s) and reasons.
1	The claim is not clearly stated. The claim is not supported by reasons and evidence. Reasons and evidence are disorganized and the argument is difficult to follow. The conclusion does not include relevant information.	There is little or no reliable, relevant evidence The argument does not demonstrate an understanding of the thesis and does not provide examples. The tone of the argument is informal.	The argument contains mistakes in standard English conventions of usage and mechanics. The argument does not use words, phrases, and clauses to clarify the relationships among claim(s) and reasons.

WRITING

Informative/Explanatory Texts

Informative and explanatory writing should rely on facts to inform or explain. Informative writing serves several purposes: to increase readers' knowledge of a subject, to help readers better understand a procedure or process, or to provide readers with an enhanced comprehension of a concept. It should also feature a clear introduction, body, and conclusion.

Informative/explanatory texts present facts, details, data, and other kinds of evidence to give information about a topic. Readers turn to informative and explanatory texts when they wish to learn about a specific idea, concept, or subject area, or if they want to learn how to do something.

An effective informative/explanatory text contains these elements:

- a topic sentence or thesis statement that introduces the concept or subject
- relevant facts, examples, and details that expand upon a topic
- definitions, quotations, and/or graphics that support the information given
- headings (if desired) to separate sections of the essay
- a structure that presents information in a direct, clear manner
- clear transitions that link sections of the essay
- precise words and technical vocabulary where appropriate
- formal and objective language and tone
- a conclusion that supports the information given and provides fresh insights

Kids, School, and Exercise: Problems and Solutions

In the past, children ran around and even did hard physical labor. Today most kid's just sit most of the time. They don't know the old Outdoor Games. Like tether ball. and they don't have hard chores to do. Like milking the cows. But children should be Physically Active quite a bit every day. That doesn't happen very much any more. Not as much as it should anyway.

Even at home when kid's have a chance to run around, they choose to sit and play video games, for example. Some schools understand that it's a problem when students don't get enough exercise. Even though they have had to cut Physical Education classes. Some also had to make recess shorter.

But lots of schools are working hard to find ways to get kid's moving around again. Like they used to long ago.

Schools use volunteers to teach kid's old-fashioned games. Old-fashioned games are an awesome way to get kid's moving around like crazy people.

Some schools have before school activities. Such as games in the gym. Other schools have after school activities. Such as bike riding or outdoor games. They can't count on kid's to be active. Not even on their own or at home. So they do the activities all together. Kids enjoy doing stuff with their friends. So that works out really well.

If you don't exercise you get overweight. You can end up with high blood pressure and too much colesterol. Of course its also a problem if you eat too much junk food all the time. But not getting enough exercise is part of the problem too. That's why schools need to try to be part of the solution.

A break during class to move around helps. Good teachers know how to use exercise during classes. There are all kinds of ways to move in the classroom that don't mean you have to change your clothes. Classes don't have to be just about math and science.

Schools are doing what they can to get kids moving, doing exercise, being active. Getting enough exercise also helps kid's do better in school. Being active also helps kids get strong.

There are extensive errors in spelling, capitalization, punctuation, grammar, usage, and sentence boundaries.

Many of the ideas in the essay do not focus on the topic.

The word choice shows the writer's lack of awareness of the essay's purpose and tone.

The essay's sentences are not purposeful, varied, or well-controlled. The writer's sentences decrease the effectiveness of the essay.

The essay is not well organized. Its structure does not support its purpose or respond well to the demands of the prompt.

The essay is not particularly thoughtful or engaging.

MODEL

INFORMATIVE: SCORE 2

Kids, School, and Exercise: Problems and Solutions

In the past, children ran around a lot and did chores and other physical work. Today most kid's sit by a TV or computer screen or play with their phones. But children should be active for at least 60 minutes a day. Sadly, most don't get nearly that much exercise. And that's a big problem.

Some schools understand that it's a problem when students don't get enough exercise. Even though they have had to cut Physical Education classes due to budget cuts. Some also had to make recess shorter because there isn't enough time in the schedule. But they are working hard to find creative ways that don't cost too much or take up too much time to get kid's moving. Because there's only so much money in the budget, and only so much time in the day, and preparing to take tests takes lots of time.

Schools can use parent volunteers to teach kid's old-fashioned games such as kick-the-can, hopscotch, foursquare, tetherball, or jump rope. Kid's nowadays often don't know these games! Old-fashioned games are a great way to get kid's moving. Some schools have before school activities, such as games in the gym. Other schools have after school activities, such as bike riding or outdoor games. They can't count on kid's to be active on their own or at home.

A break during class can help students concentrate when they go back to work. There are all kinds of ways to move in the classroom. And you don't have to change your clothes or anything. Wiggling, stretching, and playing a short active game are all good ideas. Good teachers know how to squeeze in time during academic classes like math and language arts.

Not getting enough exercise is linked to many problems. For example, unhealthy wait, and high blood pressure and colesterol. When students don't' get enough exercise, they end up overweight.

Physical activity also helps kid's do better in school. Kids who exercise have better attendance rates. They have increased attention span. They act out less. They have less stress and learn more. Being active also helps muscles and bones. It increases strength and stamina.

Schools today are doing what they can to find a solution by being creative and making time for physical activity before, during, and after school. They understand that it is a problem when kid's don't get enough exercise.

Not all the ideas in the essay focus on the topic.

The writer uses some transitions and sentence connections.

Some of the ideas in the essay are reasonably well developed. Some details and examples add substance to the essay.

Some ideas are well developed. Some examples and details are well chosen and specific and add substance to the essay.

Some details are specific and well chosen.

There are errors in spelling, punctuation, grammar, usage, and sentence boundaries that decrease the effectiveness of the essay.

The essay is not well organized. Its organizing structure does not support its purpose well or respond well to the demands of the prompt.

INFORMATIVE: SCORE 3

Kids, School, and Exercise: Problems and Solutions

A 2008 report said school-age children should be physically active for at least 60 minutes a day. Sadly, most children don't get nearly that much exercise. Lots of schools have cut Physical Education classes because of money and time pressures. And there's less recess than there used to be. Even at home when kids have a chance to run around, many choose screen time instead. No wonder so many of us are turning into chubby couch potatoes!

Not getting exercise is linked to many problems, for example unhealthy weight, and high blood pressure and cholesterol. Studies show physical activity also helps students do better in school: it means better attendance rates, increased attention span, fewer behavioral problems, less stress, and more learning. Being active helps develop strong muscles and bones. It increases strength and stamina.

Many schools around the country get that there are problems when students are inactive. They are working hard to find creative solutions that don't cost too much or take up precious time in the school schedule.

Some schools are using parent volunteers to teach kids active games such as kick-the-can, hopscotch, foursquare, tetherball, or jump rope. These games are more likely to get kids moving than just sitting gossiping with your friends or staring at your phone. Some schools have before school activities such as run-around games in the gym. Other schools have after school activities such as bike riding or outdoor games. They can't count on kids to be active on their own.

There are all kinds of fun and healthy ways to move in the classroom, without changing clothes. An active break during class can help students concentrate when they go back to work. Creative teachers know how to squeeze in active time even during academic classes. Wiggling, stretching, and playing a short active game are all good ideas.

Schools today understand that it is a problem when kids don't get enough exercise. They are doing what they can to find a solution by being creative and making time for physical activity before, during, and after school.

The essay is fairly thoughtful and engaging.

Almost all the ideas focus on the topic.

The ideas in the essay are well developed, with well-chosen and specific details and examples.

The writer uses transitions and connections, such as *"Not getting exercise is linked…"* *"Many schools …"* *"Some schools…"* *"Other schools…"*

Ideas in the essay are mostly well developed.

Words are chosen carefully and contribute to the clarity of the essay.

TOOL KIT: WRITING

WRITING

INFORMATIVE: SCORE 4

Kids, School, and Exercise: Problems and Solutions

In 2008, the U.S. Department of Health and Human Services published a report stating that all school-age children need to be physically active for at least 60 minutes a day. Sadly, most children don't get nearly the recommended amount of exercise. Due to budget cuts and time pressure, many schools have cut Physical Education classes. Even recess is being squeezed to make room for more tests and test preparation.

The writer explains the problem and its causes.

Lack of exercise can lead to many problems, such as unhealthy weight, high blood pressure, and high cholesterol. Physical activity helps develop strong muscles and bones, and it increases strength and stamina. Studies show physical activity leads to better attendance rates, increased attention span, fewer behavioral problems, less stress, and more learning. When kids don't get enough physical activity, a lot is at stake!

The writer clearly lays out the effects of the problem.

Many schools around the country are stepping up to find innovative solutions—even when they don't have time or money to spare. Some have started before-school activities such as active games in the gym. Others have after-school activities such as bike riding or outdoor games. Just a few extra minutes a day can make a big difference!

The writer turns to the solution. The essay's organizing structure supports its purpose and responds to the demands of the prompt.

Some schools try to make the most of recess by using parent volunteers to teach kids active games such as kick-the-can, hopscotch, foursquare, tetherball, or jump rope. Volunteers can also organize races or tournaments—anything to get the kids going! At the end of recess, everyone should be a little bit out of breath.

The writer includes specific examples and well-chosen details.

Creative educators squeeze in active time even during academic classes. It could be a quick "brain break" to stretch in the middle of class, imaginary jump rope, or a game of rock-paper-scissors with legs instead of fingers. There are all kinds of imaginative ways to move in the classroom, without moving furniture or changing clothes. And research shows that an active break during class can help students focus when they go back to work.

The progression of ideas is logical and well controlled.

Details and examples add substance to the essay.

Schools today understand the problems that can arise when kids don't have enough physical activity in their lives. They are meeting the challenge by finding opportunities for exercise before, during, and after school. After all, if students do well on tests but end up unhealthy and unhappy, what is the point?

The essay is thoughtful and engaging.

Informative Rubric

	Focus and Organization	Evidence and Elaboration	Conventions
4	The introduction is engaging and sets forth the topic in a compelling way. The ideas progress logically. A variety of transitions are included to show the relationship among ideas. The conclusion follows from the rest of the essay.	The topic is developed with relevant facts, definitions, details, quotations, and examples. The tone of the essay is formal. The vocabulary is precise and relevant to the topic, audience, and purpose.	The essay uses standard English conventions of usage and mechanics.
3	The introduction is somewhat engaging and sets forth the topic in a way that grabs readers' attention. The ideas progress somewhat logically. Some transitions are included to show the relationship among ideas. The conclusion mostly follows from the rest of the essay.	The topic is developed with some relevant facts, definitions, details, quotations, and other examples. The tone of the essay is mostly formal. The vocabulary is generally appropriate for the topic, audience, and purpose.	The essay demonstrates general accuracy in standard English conventions of usage and mechanics.
2	The introduction sets forth the topic. More than one idea is presented. A few transitions are included that show the relationship among ideas. The conclusion does not completely follow from the rest of the essay.	The topic is developed with a few relevant facts, definitions, details, quotations, or other examples. The tone of the essay is occasionally formal. The vocabulary is somewhat appropriate for the topic, audience, and purpose.	The essay demonstrates some accuracy in standard English conventions of usage and mechanics.
1	The topic is not clearly stated. Ideas do not follow a logical progression. Transitions are not included. The conclusion does not follow from the rest of the essay.	The topic is not developed with reliable or relevant evidence. The tone is informal. The vocabulary is limited or ineffective.	The essay contains mistakes in standard English conventions of usage and mechanics.

TOOL KIT: WRITING

WRITING

Narrative

Narrative writing conveys an experience, either real or imaginary, and uses time order to provide structure. Usually its purpose is to entertain, but it can also instruct, persuade, or inform. Whenever writers tell a story, they are using narrative writing. Most types of narrative writing share certain elements, such as characters, setting, a sequence of events, and, often, a theme.

Elements of a Narrative Text

A **narrative** is any type of writing that tells a story, whether it is fiction, nonfiction, poetry, or drama.

An effective nonfiction narrative contains these elements:

- an engaging beginning in which characters and setting are established
- characters who participate in the story events
- a well-structured, logical sequence of events
- details that show time and place
- effective story elements such as dialogue, description, and reflection
- a narrator who relates the events from a particular point of view
- use of language that brings the characters and setting to life

An effective fictional narrative usually contains these elements:

- an engaging beginning in which characters, setting, or a main conflict is introduced
- a main character and supporting characters who participate in the story events
- a narrator who relates the events of the plot from a particular point of view
- details that show time and place
- narrative techniques such as dialogue, description, and suspense
- use of language that vividly brings to life characters and events

NARRATIVE: SCORE 1

Mind Scissors

There's a bike race. Right away people start losing. But me and Thad were winning. Thad is the kid who always wins is who is also popular. I don't like Thad. I pumped pumping hard at my pedals, I knew the end was coming. I looked ahead and all I could see was Thad, and the woods.

I pedaled harder and then I was up to Thad. That was swinging at me, I swerved, I kept looking at him, I was worried!

That's stick had untied my shoelace and it was wrapped around my pedal! But I didn't know it yet.

We were out of the woods. I still wanted to win, I pedaled even faster. than my pedals stopped!

I saw with my mind the shoelace was caught in my pedal. No worries, I have the superpower of mind scissors. That's when my mind looked down and I used my mind scissors. I used the mind scissors to cut the shoelace my right foot was free.

That's how I became a superhero. I save people with my mind scissors now.

The story's beginning is not clear or engaging.

The narrative does not include sensory language and precise words to convey experiences and to develop characters.

Events do not progress logically. The ideas seem disconnected, and the sentences do not include transitions.

The narrative contains mistakes in standard English conventions of usage and mechanics.

The conclusion does not connect to the narrative.

TOOL KIT: WRITING

WRITING

NARRATIVE: SCORE 2

Mind-Scissors

When I was a baby I wound up with a tiny pair of scissors in my head. What the doctors couldn't have predicted is the uncanny ability they would give me. This past summer that was when I discovered what I could do with my mind-scissors.

Every summer there's a bike race. The kid who always wins is Thad who is popular.

The race starts. Right away racers start losing. After a long time pumping hard at my pedals, I knew the end was coming. I looked ahead and all I could see was Thad, and the woods.

I pedaled harder than ever. I was up to Thad. I turned my head to look at him. He was swinging a stick at me, I swerved, I kept looking at him, boy was I worried.

We were now out of the woods. Still hopeful I could win, I pedaled even faster. Suddenly, my pedals stopped!

Oh no! Thad's stick had untied my shoelace and it was wrapped around my pedal!

I was going to crash my bike. That's when my mind looked down. That's when I knew I could use my mind-scissors. I used the mind scissors to cut the shoelace my right foot was free.

That's how I won the race.

The story's beginning introduces the main character.

Events in the narrative progress somewhat logically, and the writer use some transition words.

The writer uses some description in the narrative.

The narrative demonstrates some accuracy in standard English conventions of usage and mechanics.

The words vary between vague and precise. The writer uses some sensory language.

The conclusion is weak and adds very little to the narrative.

Mind-Scissors

When I was a baby I wound up with a tiny pair of scissors in my head. Lots of people live with pieces of metal in their heads. We just have to be careful. What the doctors couldn't have predicted is the uncanny ability they would give me.

> The story's beginning is engaging and clearly introduces the main character and situation.

Every summer there's a bike race that ends at the lake. The kid who always wins is Thad Thomas the Third, who is popular. This past summer that was about to change. It's also when I discovered what I could do with my mind-scissors.

> Events in the narrative progress logically, and the writer uses transition words frequently.

The race starts. Right away racers start falling behind. After what seemed an eternity pumping hard at my pedals, I knew the end had to be in sight. I looked ahead and all I could see was Thad, and the opening to the woods—the last leg of the race.

I felt like steam was coming off my legs. I could see Thad's helmet. I turned my head to flash him a look. Only, Thad was the one who was gloating! And then I saw it—he was holding a stick he had pulled off a low-hanging branch.

> The writer uses precise words and some sensory language to convey the experiences in the narrative and to describe the characters and scenes.

He jabbed it toward me. I swerved out of the way. I kept pedaling, shifting my eyes to the right, to see what he was going to do.

But I waited too long. Then Thad made a slashing motion. Then he tossed the stick aside, yelled, "Yes!" and zoomed forward.

> The writer uses some description and dialogue to add interest to the narrative and develop experiences and events.

What happened? I felt nothing. We were now out of the woods and into the clearing before the finish line. Still hopeful I could win, I pedaled even faster. Suddenly, there was a jerk. My pedals had stopped!

I looked down. Oh no! My shoelace was wrapped around my pedal! Thad's stick had untied it!

> The narrative demonstrates accuracy in standard English conventions of usage and mechanics.

I looked for a place to crash. That's when my head started tingling. I looked down at the shoelace. I concentrated really hard. I could see the scissors in my mind, floating just beside the pedal. Snip! The shoelace broke and my foot was free.

Thad was too busy listening to his fans cheer him on as I rode past him. Thanks to the mind-scissors, I won.

> The conclusion follows from the rest of the narrative.

TOOL KIT: WRITING

WRITING

MODEL

NARRATIVE: SCORE 4

Mind-Scissors

As long as I wear my bike helmet, they say I'll be okay. Lots of people live with pieces of metal in their heads. We just have to be careful. When I was a baby I wound up with a tiny pair of scissors in mine. What the doctors couldn't have predicted is the uncanny ability they would give me.

Every summer there's a bike race that ends at the lake. The kid who always wins is Thad Thomas the Third, who is popular, but if you ask me, it's because he knows how to sweet-talk everyone. This past summer that was about to change. It's also when I discovered what I could do with my mind-scissors.

The race starts. Right away, racers start falling behind. After what seemed an eternity pumping hard at my pedals, I knew the end had to be in sight. I looked ahead and all I could see was Thad and the opening to the woods—the last leg of the race.

I put my stamina to the test—pedaling harder than ever, I felt like steam was coming off my legs. Thad's red helmet came into view. As I could sense I was going to overtake him any second, I turned my head to flash him a look. Only, to my befuddlement, Thad was the one who was gloating! And then I saw it—he was holding a stick he had pulled off a low-hanging branch.

He jabbed it toward me. I swerved out of the way. Was he trying to poke me with it? I kept pedaling, shifting my eyes to the right, to see what he was going to do.

But I waited too long. Thad made a slashing motion. Then he tossed the stick aside, yelled, "Yes!" and zoomed forward.

What happened? I felt nothing. We were now out of the woods and into the clearing before the finish line. Still hopeful I could win, I pedaled even faster. Suddenly, there was a jerk. My pedals had stopped!

I looked down. Oh no! My shoelace was wrapped around my pedal! Thad's stick had untied the shoelace!

I coasted as I looked for a place to crash. That's when my head started tingling. I got this funny notion to try something. I looked down. I had the tangled shoelace in my sights. I concentrated really hard. I could see the scissors in my mind, floating just beside the pedal. Snip! The shoelace broke and my right foot was free.

Thad was busy motioning his fans to cheer him on as I made my greatest effort to pedal back up to speed. Guess who made it to the finish line first?

The story's beginning is engaging and introduces the main character and situation in a way that appeals to a reader.

The writer uses techniques such as dialogue and description to add interest to the narrative and to develop the characters and events.

Events in the narrative progress in logical order and are linked by clear transitions.

Writer uses vivid description and sensory language to convey the experiences in the narrative and to help the reader imagine the characters and scenes.

The writer uses standard English conventions of usage and mechanics.

Writer's conclusion follows from the events in the narrative.

Narrative Rubric

	Focus and Organization	Development of Ideas/ Elaboration	Conventions
4	The introduction is engaging and introduces the characters and situation in a way that appeals to readers. Events in the narrative progress in logical order and are linked by clear transitions. The conclusion effectively follows from and reflects on the narrated experiences or events.	The narrative effectively includes techniques such as dialogue and description to add interest and to develop the characters and events. The narrative effectively includes precise words and phrases, relevant descriptive details, and sensory language to convey experiences and events. The narrative effectively establishes voice through word choice, sentence structure, and tone.	The narrative intentionally uses standard English conventions of usage and mechanics. The narrative effectively varies sentence patterns for meaning, reader interest, and style.
3	The introduction is somewhat engaging and clearly introduces the characters and situation. Events in the narrative progress logically and are often linked by transition words. The conclusion mostly follows from and reflects on the narrated experiences or events.	The narrative mostly includes dialogue and description to add interest and develop experiences and events. The narrative mostly includes precise words and sensory language to convey experiences and events. The narrative mostly establishes voice through word choice, sentence structure, and tone.	The narrative mostly demonstrates accuracy in standard English conventions of usage and mechanics. The narrative mostly varies sentence patterns for meaning, reader interest, and style.
2	The introduction occasionally introduces characters. Events in the narrative progress somewhat logically and are sometimes linked by transition words. The conclusion adds very little to the narrated experiences or events.	The narrative includes some dialogue and descriptions. The words in the narrative vary between vague and precise, and some sensory language is included. The narrative occasionally establishes voice through word choice, sentence structure, and tone.	The narrative demonstrates some accuracy in standard English conventions of usage and mechanics. The narrative occasionally varies sentence patterns for meaning, reader interest, and style.
1	The introduction does not introduce characters and an experience or there is no clear introduction. The events in the narrative do not progress logically. The ideas seem disconnected and the sentences are not linked by transitions. The conclusion does not connect to the narrative or there is no conclusion.	Dialogue and descriptions are not included in the narrative. The narrative does not incorporate sensory language or precise words to convey experiences and to develop characters. The narrative does not establish voice through word choice, sentence structure, and tone.	The narrative contains mistakes in standard English conventions of usage and mechanics. The narrative does not vary sentence patterns for meaning, reader interest, and style.

Conducting Research

You can conduct research to gain more knowledge about a topic. Sources such as articles, books, interviews, or the Internet have the facts and explanations that you need. Not all of the information that you find, however, will be useful—or reliable. Strong research skills will help you find accurate information about your topic.

Narrowing or Broadening a Topic

The first step in any research is finding your topic. Choose a topic that is narrow enough to cover completely. If you can name your topic in just one or two words, it is probably too broad. Topics such as mythology, hip hop music, or Italy are too broad to cover in a single report. Narrow a broad topic into smaller subcategories.

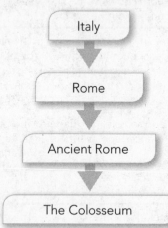

Italy

Rome

Ancient Rome

The Colosseum

When you begin to research, pay attention to the amount of information available. If there is way too much information on your topic, you may need to narrow your topic further.

You might also need to broaden a topic if there is not enough information for your purpose. A topic is too narrow when it can be thoroughly presented in less space than the required size of your assignment. It might also be too narrow if you can find little or no information in library and media sources. Broaden your topic by including other related ideas.

Generating Research Questions

Use research questions to focus your research. Specific questions can help you avoid wasting time. For example, instead of simply hunting for information about Peter Pan, you might ask, "What inspired J. M. Barrie to write the story of Peter Pan?" or "How have different artists shown Peter Pan?"

A research question may also lead you to find your topic sentence. The question can also help you focus your research plan. Write your question down and keep it in mind while you hunt for facts. Your question can prevent you from gathering unnecessary details. As you learn more about your topic, you can always rewrite your original question.

Consulting Print and Digital Sources

An effective research project combines information from multiple sources. It is important not to rely too heavily on a single source. The creativity and originality of your research depends on how you combine ideas from many places. Plan to include a variety of these resources:

- **Primary and Secondary Sources:** Use both primary sources (firsthand or original accounts, such as interview transcripts and newspaper articles) and secondary sources (accounts that are not created at the time of an event, such as encyclopedia entries).

- **Print and Digital Resources:** The Internet allows fast access to data, but print resources are often edited more carefully. Plan to include both print and digital resources in order to guarantee that your work is accurate.

- **Media Resources:** You can find valuable information in media resources such as documentaries, television programs, podcasts, and museum exhibitions.

- **Original Research:** Depending on your topic, you may wish to conduct original research to include among your sources. For example, you might interview experts or eyewitnesses or conduct a survey of people in your community.

Evaluating Sources It is important to evaluate the credibility and accuracy of any information you find. Ask yourself questions such as these to evaluate other sources:

- **Authority:** Is the author well known? What are the author's credentials? Does the source include references to other reliable sources? Does the author's tone win your confidence? Why or why not?

- **Bias:** Does the author have any obvious biases? What is the author's purpose for writing? Who is the target audience?

- **Currency:** When was the work created? Has it been revised? Is there more current information available?

Using Online Encyclopedias

Online encyclopedias are often written by anonymous contributors who are not required to fact-check information. These sites can be very useful as a launching point for research, but should not be considered accurate. Look for footnotes, endnotes, or hyperlinks that support facts with reliable sources that have been carefully checked by editors.

Using Search Terms

Finding information on the Internet is easy, but it can be a challenge to find facts that are useful and trustworthy. If you type a word or phrase into a search engine, you will probably get hundreds—or thousands—of results. However, those results are not guaranteed to be relevant or accurate.

These strategies can help you find information from the Internet:

- Create a list of topic keywords before you begin using a search engine. Use a thesaurus to expand your list.

- Enter six to eight keywords.

- Choose unique nouns. Most search engines ignore articles and prepositions. Verbs may lead to sources that are not useful. Use modifiers, such as adjectives, when necessary to specify a category. For example, you might enter "ancient Rome" instead of "Rome."

- Use quotation marks to focus a search. Place a phrase in quotation marks to find pages that include exactly that phrase. Add several phrases in quotation marks to narrow your results.

- Spell carefully. Many search engines correct spelling automatically, but they cannot catch every spelling error.

- Scan search results before you click them. The first result isn't always the most useful. Read the text and notice the domain before make a choice.

- Consult more than one search engine.

Evaluating Internet Domains

Not everything you read on the Internet is true, so you have to evaluate sources carefully. The last three letters of an Internet URL identify the site's domain, which can help you evaluate the information of the site.

- **.gov**—Government sites are sponsored by a branch of the United States federal government and are considered reliable.

- **.edu**—Information from an educational research center or department is likely to be carefully checked, but may include student pages that are not edited or monitored.

- **.org**—Organizations are nonprofit groups and usually maintain a high level of credibility but may still reflect strong biases.

- **.com** and **.net**—Commercial sites exist to make a profit. Information might be biased to show a product or service in a good light.

Taking Notes

Use different strategies to take notes:

- Use index cards to create notecards and source cards. On each source card, record information about each source you use—author, title, publisher, date of publication, and relevant page numbers. On each notecard, record information to use in your writing. Use quotation marks when you copy exact words, and indicate the page number(s) on which the information appears.

- Photocopy articles and copyright pages. Then, highlight relevant information. Remember to include the Web addresses of printouts from online sources.

- Print articles from the Internet or copy them directly into a "notes" folder.

You will use these notes to help you write original text.

Source Card

```
                              [A]
Papp, Joseph,
and Elizabeth Kirkland

Shakespeare Alive!

Bantam Books, 1988

```

Notecard

```
Only the upper classes could read.

Most of the common people in
Shakespeare's time could not read.
Source Card: A, p. 5.
```

Quote Accurately Responsible research begins with the first note you take. Be sure to quote and paraphrase your sources accurately so you can identify these sources later. In your notes, circle all quotations and paraphrases to distinguish them from your own comments. When photocopying from a source, include the copyright information. Include the Web addresses of printouts from online sources.

Reviewing Research Findings

You will need to review your findings to be sure that you have collected enough accurate and appropriate information.

Considering Audience and Purpose

Always keep your audience in mind as you gather information. Different audiences may have very different needs. For example, if you are writing a report for your class about a topic you have studied together, you will not need to provide background information in your writing. However, if you are writing about the topic for a national student magazine, you cannot assume that all of your readers have the same information. You will need to provide background facts from reliable sources to help inform those readers about your subject. When thinking about your research and your audience, ask yourself:

- Who am I writing for?
- Have I collected enough information to explain my topic to this audience?
- Do I need to conduct more research to explain my topic clearly?
- Are there details in my research that I can leave out because they are already familiar to my audience?

Your purpose for writing will also affect your research review. If you are researching to satisfy your own curiosity, you can stop researching when you feel you understand the answer completely. If you are writing a research report that will be graded, you need to think about your assignment. When thinking about whether or not you have enough information, ask yourself:

- What is my purpose for writing?
- Will the information I have gathered be enough to achieve my purpose?
- If I need more information, where might I find it?

Synthesizing Sources

Effective research writing is more than just a list of facts and details. Good research synthesizes—gathers, orders, and interprets—those elements. These strategies will help you synthesize effectively:

- Review your notes. Look for connections and patterns among the details you have collected.
- Organize notes or notecards to help you plan how you will combine details.
- Pay close attention to details that emphasize the same main idea.
- Also look for details that challenge each other. For many topics, there is no single correct opinion. You might decide to conduct additional research to help you decide which side of the issue has more support.

Types of Evidence

When reviewing your research, also think about the kinds of evidence you have collected. The strongest writing combines a variety of evidence. This chart describes three of the most common types of evidence.

TYPE OF EVIDENCE	DESCRIPTION	EXAMPLE
Statistical evidence includes facts and other numerical data used to support a claim or explain a topic.	Statistical evidence are facts about a topic, such as historical dates, descriptions about size and number, and poll results.	Jane Goodall began to study chimpanzees when she was 26 years old.
Testimonial evidence includes any ideas or opinions presented by others. Testimonies might be from experts or people with special knowledge about a topic.	Firsthand testimonies present ideas from eyewitnesses to events or subjects being discussed.	Goodall's view of chimps has changed: "When I first started at Gombe, I thought the chimps were nicer than we are. But time has revealed that they are not. They can be just as awful."
	Secondary testimonies include commentaries on events by people who were not directly involved.	Science writer David Quammen points out that Goodall "set a new standard, a very high standard, for behavioral study of apes in the wild."
Anecdotal evidence presents one person's view of the world, often by describing specific events or incidents.	An anecdote is a story about something that happened. Personal stories can be part of effective research, but they should not be the only kind of evidence presented. Anecdotes are particularly useful for proving that broad generalizations are not accurate.	It is not fair to say that it is impossible for dogs to use tools. One researcher reports the story of a dog that learned to use a large bone as a back scratcher.

► RESEARCH

Incorporating Research Into Writing

Avoiding Plagiarism

Whether you are presenting a formal research paper or an opinion paper on a current event, you must be careful to give credit for any ideas or opinions that are not your own. Presenting someone else's ideas, research, or opinion as your own—even if you have phrased it in different words—is *plagiarism*, the equivalent of academic stealing, or fraud.

Do not use the ideas or research of others in place of your own. Read from several sources to draw your own conclusions and form your own opinions. Incorporate the ideas and research of others to support your points. Credit the source of the following types of support:

- Statistics
- Direct quotations
- Indirectly quoted statements of opinions
- Conclusions presented by an expert
- Facts available in only one or two sources

When you are drafting and revising, circle any words or ideas that are not your own. Follow the instructions on pages R32 and R33 to correctly cite those passages.

Reviewing for Plagiarism Take time to review your writing for accidental plagiarism. Read what you have written and take note of any ideas that do not have your personal writing voice. Compare those passages with your resource materials. You might have copied them without remembering the exact source. Add a correct citation to give credit to the original author. If you cannot find the questionable phrase in your notes, think about revising your word choices. You want to be sure that your final writing reflects your own thinking and not someone else's work.

Quoting and Paraphrasing

When including ideas from research into your writing, you will decide to quote directly or paraphrase.

Direct Quotation Use the author's exact words when they are interesting or persuasive. You might decide to include direct quotations in these situations:

- to share a strong statement
- to reference a historically significant passage
- to show that an expert agrees with your position
- to present an argument to which you will respond

Include complete quotations, without deleting or changing words. If you need to leave out words for space or clarity, use ellipsis points to show where you removed words. Enclose direct quotations in quotation marks.

Paraphrase A paraphrase restates an author's ideas in your own words. Be careful to paraphrase accurately. Beware of making sweeping generalizations in a paraphrase that were not made by the original author. You may use some words from the original source, but a good paraphrase does more than simply rearrange an author's phrases, or replace a few words with synonyms.

Original Text	"Some teens doing homework while listening to music and juggling tweets and texts may actually work better that way, according to an intriguing new study performed by two high-school seniors."
	Sumathi Reddy, "Teen Researchers Defend Media Multitasking"
Patchwork Plagiarism phrases from the original are rearranged, but they too closely follow the original text.	An intriguing new study conducted by two high-school seniors suggests that teens work better when they are listening to music and juggling texts and tweets.
Good Paraphrase	Two high-school students studied homework habits. They concluded that some people do better work while multitasking, such as studying and listening to music or checking text messages at the same time.

Maintaining the Flow of Ideas

Effective research writing is much more that just a list of facts. Maintain the flow of ideas by connecting research information to your own ideas. Instead of simply stating a piece of evidence, use transitions to connect information you found from outside resources and your own thinking. The transitions in the box on the page can be used to introduce, compare, contrast, and clarify.

Choosing an effective organizational strategy for your writing will help you create a logical flow of ideas. Once you have chosen a clear organization, add research in appropriate places to provide evidence and support.

Useful Transitions

When providing examples:

for example   for instance   to illustrate   in [name of resource], [author]

When comparing and contrasting ideas or information:

in the same way   similarly   however   on the other hand

When clarifying ideas or opinions:

in other words   that is   to explain   to put it another way

RESEARCH

ORGANIZATIONAL STRUCTURE	USES
Chronological order presents information in the sequence in which it happens.	historical topics; science experiments; analysis of narratives
Part-to-whole order examines how several categories affect a larger subject.	analysis of social issues; historical topics
Order of importance presents information in order of increasing or decreasing importance.	persuasive arguments; supporting a bold or challenging thesis
Comparison-and-contrast organization presents similarities and differences.	addressing two or more subjects

Formats for Citing Sources

When you cite a source, you acknowledge where you found your information and you give your readers the details necessary for locating the source themselves. Within the body of a paper, you provide a short citation, a footnote number linked to a footnote, or an endnote number linked to an endnote reference. These brief references show the page numbers on which you found the information. Prepare a reference list at the end of a research report to provide full bibliographic information on your sources. These are two common types of reference lists:

- A bibliography provides a listing of all the resources you consulted during your research.
- A works-cited list indicates the works your have referenced in your writing.

The chart on the next page shows the Modern Language Association format for crediting sources. This is the most common format for papers written in the content areas in middle school and high school. Unless instructed otherwise by your teacher, use this format for crediting sources.

Focus on Citations When you revise your writing, check that you cite the sources for quotations, factual information, and ideas that are not your own. Most word-processing programs have features that allow you to create footnotes and endnotes.

Identifying Missing Citations These strategies can help you find facts and details that should be cited in your writing:

- Look for facts that are not general knowledge. If a fact was unique to one source, it needs a citation.
- Read your report aloud. Listen for words and phrases that do not sound like your writing style. You might have picked them up from a source. If so, use you notes to find the source, place the words in quotation marks, and give credit.
- Review your notes. Look for ideas that you used in your writing but did not cite.

MLA (8th Edition) Style for Listing Sources

Book with one author	Pyles, Thomas. *The Origins and Development of the English Language.* 2nd ed., Harcourt Brace Jovanovich, 1971. [Indicate the edition or version number when relevant.]
Book with two authors	Pyles, Thomas, and John Algeo. *The Origins and Development of the English Language.* 5th ed., Cengage Learning, 2004.
Book with three or more authors	Donald, Robert B., et al. *Writing Clear Essays.* Prentice Hall, 1983.
Book with an editor	Truth, Sojourner. *Narrative of Sojourner Truth.* Edited by Margaret Washington, Vintage Books, 1993.
Introduction to a work in a published edition	Washington, Margaret. Introduction. *Narrative of Sojourner Truth,* by Sojourner Truth, edited by Washington, Vintage Books, 1993, pp. v–xi.
Single work in an anthology	Hawthorne, Nathaniel. "Young Goodman Brown." *Literature: An Introduction to Reading and Writing,* edited by Edgar V. Roberts and Henry E. Jacobs, 5th ed., Prentice Hall, 1998, pp. 376–385. [Indicate pages for the entire selection.]
Signed article from an encyclopedia	Askeland, Donald R. "Welding." *World Book Encyclopedia,* vol. 21, World Book, 1991, p. 58.
Signed article in a weekly magazine	Wallace, Charles. "A Vodacious Deal." *Time,* 14 Feb. 2000, p. 63.
Signed article in a monthly magazine	Gustaitis, Joseph. "The Sticky History of Chewing Gum." *American History,* Oct. 1998, pp. 30–38.
Newspaper article	Thurow, Roger. "South Africans Who Fought for Sanctions Now Scrap for Investors." *Wall Street Journal,* 11 Feb. 2000, pp. A1+. [For a multipage article that does not appear on consecutive pages, write only the first page number on which it appears, followed by the plus sign.]
Unsigned editorial or story	"Selective Silence." Editorial. *Wall Street Journal,* 11 Feb. 2000, p. A14. [If the editorial or story is signed, begin with the author's name.]
Signed pamphlet or brochure	[Treat the pamphlet as though it were a book.]
Work from a library subscription service	Ertman, Earl L. "Nefertiti's Eyes." *Archaeology,* Mar.–Apr. 2008, pp. 28–32. *Kids Search,* EBSCO, New York Public Library. Accessed 7 Jan. 2017. [Indicating the date you accessed the information is optional but recommended.]
Filmstrips, slide programs, videocassettes, DVDs, and other audiovisual media	*The Diary of Anne Frank.* 1959. Directed by George Stevens, performances by Millie Perkins, Shelley Winters, Joseph Schildkraut, Lou Jacobi, and Richard Beymer, Twentieth Century Fox, 2004. [Indicating the original release date after the title is optional but recommended.]
CD-ROM (with multiple publishers)	Simms, James, editor. *Romeo and Juliet.* By William Shakespeare, Attica Cybernetics / BBC Education / Harper, 1995.
Radio or television program transcript	"Washington's Crossing of the Delaware." *Weekend Edition Sunday,* National Public Radio, 23 Dec. 2013. Transcript.
Web page	"Fun Facts About Gum." ICGA, 2005–2017, www.gumassociation.org/index.cfm/facts-figures/fun-facts-about-gum. Accessed 19 Feb. 2017. [Indicating the date you accessed the information is optional but recommended.]
Personal interview	Smith, Jane. Personal interview, 10 Feb. 2017.

All examples follow the style given in the MLA Handbook, 8th edition, published in 2016.

MODEL

Evidence Log

Unit Title: __Discovery__

Perfomance-Based Assessment Prompt:
Do all discoveries benefit humanity?

My initial thoughts:
Yes - all knowledge moves us forward.

As you read multiple texts about a topic, your thinking may change. Use an Evidence Log like this one to record your thoughts, to track details you might use in later writing or discussion, and to make further connections.

Here is a sample to show how one reader's ideas deepened as she read two texts.

Title of Text: __Classifying the Stars__   Date: __Sept. 17__

CONNECTION TO THE PROMPT	TEXT EVIDENCE/DETAILS	ADDITIONAL NOTES/IDEAS
Newton shared his discoveries and then other scientists built on his discoveries.	Paragraph 2: "Isaac Newton gave to the world the results of his experiments on passing sunlight through a prism." Paragraph 3: "In 1814 . . . the German optician, Fraunhofer . . . saw that the multiple spectral tints . . . were crossed by hundreds of fine dark lines."	It's not always clear how a discovery might benefit humanity in the future.

How does this text change or add to my thinking? This confirms what I think.   Date: __Sept. 20__

Title of Text: __Cell Phone Mania__   Date: __Sept. 21__

CONNECTION TO THE PROMPT	TEXT EVIDENCE/DETAILS	ADDITIONAL NOTES/IDEAS
Cell phones have made some forms of communication easier, but people don't talk to each other as much as they did in the past.	Paragraph 7: "Over 80% of young adults state that texting is their primary method of communicating with friends. This contrasts with older adults who state that they prefer a phone call."	Is it good that we don't talk to each other as much? Look for article about social media to learn more about this question.

How does this text change or add to my thinking?   Date: __Sept. 25__
Maybe there are some downsides to discoveries. I still think that knowledge moves us forward, but sometimes there are negative effects.

Word Network

A word network is a collection of words related to a topic. As you read the selections in a unit, identify interesting theme-related words and build your vocabulary by adding them to your Word Network.

Use your Word Network as a resource for your discussions and writings. Here is an example:

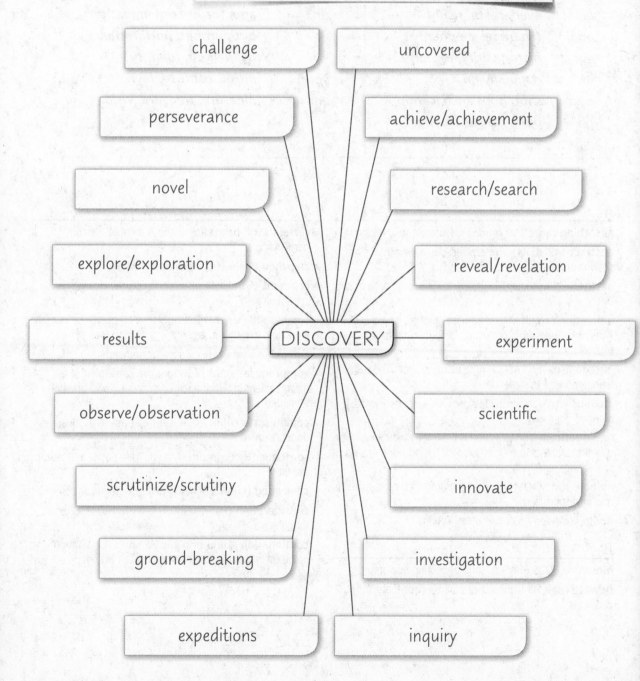

ACADEMIC / CONCEPT VOCABULARY

Academic vocabulary appears in **blue type**.

Pronunciation Key

Symbol	Sample Words	Symbol	Sample Words
a	*at*, *catapult*, *Alabama*	oo	*boot*, *soup*, *crucial*
ah	*father*, *charms*, *argue*	ow	*now*, *stout*, *flounder*
ai	*care*, *various*, *hair*	oy	*boy*, *toil*, *oyster*
aw	*law*, *maraud*, *caution*	s	*say*, *nice*, *press*
awr	*pour*, *organism*, *forewarn*	sh	*she*, *abolition*, *motion*
ay	*ape*, *sails*, *implication*	u	*full*, *put*, *book*
ee	*even*, *teeth*, *really*	uh	*ago*, *focus*, *contemplation*
eh	*ten*, *repel*, *elephant*	ur	*bird*, *urgent*, *perforation*
ehr	*merry*, *verify*, *terribly*	y	*by*, *delight*, *identify*
ih	*it*, *pin*, *hymn*	yoo	*music*, *confuse*, *few*
o	*shot*, *hopscotch*, *condo*	zh	*pleasure*, *treasure*, *vision*
oh	*own*, *parole*, *rowboat*		

A

absorbing (ab ZAWR bihng) *v.* learning; fully taking in

abstract (AB strakt) *adj.* expressed in a way that is not specific or realistic

aesthetic (ehs THEHT ihk) *adj.* having to do with beauty or art

animation (an uh MAY shuhn) *n.* process of making films or cartoons from drawings, computer graphics, or photos

antagonism (an TAG uh nihz uhm) *n.* hostility; state of being opposed to someone

anxiously (ANGK shuhs lee) *adv.* in a worried, uneasy manner; nervously

apologetically (uh pol uh JEHT ihk lee) *adv.* in a way that shows someone is sorry for having done or said something; regretfully

assume (uh SOOM) *v.* take for granted; take on, as a role or responsibility

audio (AW dee oh) *n.* recorded sound

B

blossom (BLOS uhm) *n.* state of bearing flowers

beware (bee WAIR) *v.* act carefully in case there is danger

C

certain (SUR tuhn) *adj.* without a doubt; reliable; particular

clenched (klehncht) *adj.* gripped tightly

coherent (koh HIHR uhnt) *adj.* logical; clearly communicated

community (kuh MYOO nuh tee) *n.* people or animals who exist together in a place

compel (kuhm PEHL) *v.* force; command

compromise (KOM pruh myz) *n.* settlement of a disagreement in which each side gives up part of what it wanted

compulsory (kuhm PUHL suhr ee) *adj.* that must be done; required

consequently (kon suh KWEHNT lee) *adv.* as a result; therefore

consumed (kuhn SOOMD) *adj.* absorbed; occupied

consideration (kuhn sihd uh RAY shuhn) *n.* careful thought

continuation (kuhn tihn yoo AY shuhn) *n.* state of going on without interruption; unbroken action

contribute (kuhn TRIHB yoot) *v.* give or provide along with others

convince (kuhn VIHNS) *v.* persuade

critical (KRIHT uh kuhl) *adj.* disapproving or having a negative opinion about; very important

cultivate (KUHL tuh vayt) *v.* prepare the soil for planting crops

curiosity (kyoo ree OS uh tee) *n.* eager desire to know

cut-out animation (KUHT owt) (an uh MAY shuhn) *n.* technique that uses flat characters, backgrounds, and props cut from materials such as paper, cardboard, and fabric

D

declare (dih KLAIR) *v.* make a statement; announce

deliberate (dih LIHB uhr iht) *adj.* carefully thought over in advance; planned

desperate (DEHS puhr iht) *adj.* suffering extreme need or frustration; with little hope

destination (dehs tuh NAY shuhn) *n.* place where someone or something is going

devouring (dih VOW rihng) *v.* taking in greedily

dialogue (DY uh log) *n.* spoken conversation between or among characters

digesting (dih JEH stihng) *v.* thinking over; mentally taking in

disgusted (dihs GUHS tihd) *adj.* feeling a strong dislike; annoyed

distraught (dihs TRAWT) *adj.* very troubled and unhappy

distressed (dih STREHST) *adj.* troubled; upset

domesticated (duh MEHS tuh kay tihd) *adj.* changed from a wild state to a tame state

dominate (DOM uh nayt) *v.* rule or control

E

elaborate (ih LAB uh rayt) *v.* explain by adding more details

enactment (ehn AKT muhnt) *n.* state of being made into law

encapsulation (ehn kap suh LAY shuhn) *n.* choice of important scenes to display in each panel

endurance test (ehn DUR uhns) (tehst) *n.* test to measure the ability of a person to deal with physical activity

entitled (ehn TY tuhld) *v.* had certain rights given to; earned certain rights

exclude (ehk SKLOOD) *v.* shut out; keep from entering, happening, or being

expedition (ehks puh DIHSH uhn) *n.* journey or trip made for a special purpose

F

feathery (FEH<u>TH</u> uhr ee) *adj.* light and airy, like the touch of a feather

foe (foh) *n.* enemy

G

gradually (GRAJ oo uhl ee) *adv.* in a way that is little by little

H

host (hohst) *n.* someone who introduces and talks to the guests on a television or radio program

humming (HUHM ihng) *v.* singing with closed lips and without words

I

ignorance (IHG nuhr uhns) *n.* state of lacking knowledge, learning, or information

illustrate (IHL uh strayt) *v.* provide pictures, diagrams or maps that explain or decorate; provide an example that demonstrates an idea

images or graphics (IHM uh jihz) (GRAF ihks) *n.* representations of a person or thing

impetuous (ihm PEHCH yoo uhs) *adj.* acting suddenly with little thought

inker (IHNGK uhr) *n.* artist who goes over the penciled art in ink

insincerity (ihn sihn SEHR uh tee) *n.* lack of honesty; untruthfulness

inspire (ihn SPYR) *v.* influence; stimulate creative effort

intensity (ihn TEHN suh tee) *n.* great focus or concentration; strong commitment

interview (IHN tuhr vyoo) *n.* recorded conversation in which someone is asked questions about his or her life, experiences, or opinions

invaded (ihn VAYD ihd) *v.* attacked; entered with force

irritable (IHR uh tuh buhl) *adj.* easily annoyed or angered

J

journeys (JUR neez) *n.* trips from one place to another

L

lamented (luh MEHN tihd) *v.* said in a way that showed sadness or sorrow

letterer (LEHT uhr uhr) *n.* artist who letters the dialogue and captions

light and shadow (lyt) (SHAD oh) drawing techniques that add depth to an image

loftily (LAWF tih lee) *adv.* in a superior manner

loneliness (LOHN lee nihs) *n.* feeling of being alone or isolated from others

M

malicious (muh LIHSH uhs) *adj.* having or showing bad intentions

memorize (MEHM uh ryz) *v.* learn well enough to later recall; learn by heart

microchips (MY kroh chihps) *n.* small pieces of computer technology that have integrated circuits

milled (mihld) *v.* moved about in a confused way

misapprehension (mihs ap ree HEHN shuhn) *n.* incorrect understanding; wrong idea

miserable (MIHZ uhr uh buhl) *adj.* extremely unhappy or uncomfortable

model (MOD uhl) *n.* set of ideas to be followed as a plan or an example

mournfully (MAWRN fuh lee) *adv.* in a way that expresses grief or sadness

N

narrator (NA ray tuhr) *n.* person who tells a story

nonchalantly (non shuh LONT lee) *adv.* done in an unconcerned way

nostalgic (nuhs TAL jihk) *adj.* longing for the past

notable (NOHT uh buhl) *adj.* worthy of notice; remarkable; important

novelty (NOV uhl tee) *n.* something new, fresh, or unusual

O

object animation (OB jehkt) (an uh MAY shuhn) *n.* form that involves the movement of non-drawn objects, such as a book or a pen

objective (uhb JEHK tihv) *n.* aim or goal

obsessive (uhb SEHS ihv) *adj.* tending to think or worry so much about something that you cannot think about anything else

obstacle (OB stuh kuhl) *n.* something that stands in the way or stops progress

offended (uh FEHND ihd) *v.* hurt the feelings of someone; affected in an unpleasant way

P

panel (PAN uhl) *n.* individual frame of a comic, depicting a single moment

parameters (puh RAM uh tuhrz) *n.* boundaries; characteristics

pathetically (puh THEHT ihk lee) *adv.* in a way that causes someone to feel pity

patiently (PAY shuhnt lee) *adv.* bearing annoyance, hardship, or pain calmly and without complaint or anger

peeped (peept) *v.* looked through a small hole or crack; looked without being noticed

penciler (PEHN suhl uhr) *n.* artist who sketches the basic layout for each panel

perspective (puhr SPEHK tihv) *n.* point of view; ability to see how ideas relate to one another

pessimistic (pehs uh MIHS tihk) *adj.* expecting the worst; focused on the bad aspects of a situation

pixels (PIHK suhlz) *n.* smallest elements of an image that can be individually processed in a video display system

podcast (POD kast) *n.* digital audio or video file or recording, usually part of a series, that can be downloaded from the Internet

presume (prih ZOOM) *v.* take for granted; assume something to be the case

process (PROS ehs) *v.* gain an understanding of

program manager (PROH gram) (MAN ih juhr) *n.* person who is in charge of a project

purist (PYOOR ihst) *n.* someone who is strict about following traditional ways

Q

quest (kwehst) *n.* long search undertaken in order to find or realize something

quivering (KWIHV uhr ihng) *n.* trembling; shivering

R

real-time animation (REEL tym) (an uh MAY shuhn) *n.* style in which animated events or objects are reproduced so that they appear to be occurring or moving at the same speed they would in real life

recognize (REHK uhg nyz) *v.* identify something from memory or description; acknowledge as worthy of appreciation; honor

reflect (rih FLEHKT) *v.* think carefully

refugee (rehf yoo JEE) *n.* person who flees to another country to escape danger, as in time of war

relentlessly (rih LEHNT lihs lee) *adv.* without stopping; with determination

respected (rih SPEHK tihd) *adj.* honored; treated with esteem

S

sample group (SAM puhl) (groop) *n.* group of people that are taken from a larger group and studied

shushes (SHUHSH ihz) *v.* tells or signals someone to be quiet

shyly (SHY lee) *adv.* in a shy manner; in a bashful way

silently (SY luhnt lee) *adv.* without noise

skittered (SKIHT uhrd) *v.* moved lightly or quickly

slain (slayn) *v.* killed

sorrowfully (SAWR oh fuhl ee) *adv.* done with sadness

speculate (SPEHK yuh layt) *v.* guess, using information that is uncertain or incomplete

speech balloon (speech) *(buh LOON) n.* display of what a character is speaking or thinking

squish (skwihsh) *n.* spongy, cushioned feeling when walking on a flexible surface

stage directions (stayj) (duh REHK shuhnz) important information that is provided by the playwright about the setting, characters, and action

stubborn (STUB uhrn) *adj.* refusing to give in, obey, or accept

sufficient (suh FIHSH uhnt) *adj.* as much as needed

surmise (suhr MYZ) *v.* guess, using only intuition or imagination

suspiciously (suh SPIHSH uhs lee) *adv.* based on a lack of trust or belief; disbelievingly; cautiously

T

template (TEHM pliht) *n.* pattern or shape to be used as an example

tenseness (TEHNS nihs) *n.* tightness in the muscles of the body

thorough (THUR oh) *adj.* including everything possible; careful and complete

thoughtfully (THAWT fuhl lee) *adv.* showing careful consideration or attention

threateningly (THREHT uhn ihng lee) *adv.* in a frightening or alarming way

timidly (TIHM ihd lee) *adv.* in a shy or fearful way; cautiously

transform (trans FAWRM) *v.* convert or change

trek (trehk) *n.* difficult, slow, or long journey

trigonometry (trihg uh NOM uh tree) *n.* field of math that deals with the relationships between the sides and angles of triangles

twirl (twurl) *v.* turn around and around quickly

twist (twihst) *v.* wind or spin around one another

V

valid (VAL ihd) *adj.* acceptable; based on and supported by facts

vanished (VAN ihsht) *v.* disappeared

various (VAIR ee uhs) *adj.* different from one another

violent (VY uh luhnt) *adj.* using strong, rough force that causes injury

voiceover (VOYS oh vuhr) *n.* voice commenting on the action or narrating a film off-camera

W

wild (wyld) *adj.* living in nature without human control; not tame

wondered (WUHN duhrd) *v.* thought about; questioned

wrath (rath) *n.* intense anger

VOCABULARIO ACADÉMICO / VOCABULARIO DE CONCEPTOS

El vocabulario académico está en **letra azul**.

A

absorbing / asimilando v. aprendiendo; adquiriendo conocimientos por completo

abstract / abstracto adj. expresado de manera no específica ni realista

aesthetic / estético adj. relacionado con la belleza o el arte

animation / animación s. proceso de crear películas o caricaturas a partir de dibujos, gráficas de computadora o fotos

antagonism / antagonismo s. hostilidad; estado de oponerse a una persona

anxiously / ansiosamente adv. de manera estresada y nerviosa

apologetically / arrepentido adv. de una manera que muestra sentimiento de pesar por haber hecho o dicho algo

assume / suponer v. dar por hecho; conjeturar; sostener

assumption / suposición s. consideración de algo como cierto

audio / audio s. sonido grabado

B

beamish / radiante adj. resplandeciente; que siente optimismo y alegría

blossom / flor s. brote de las plantas del que se formará el fruto

beware / cuidarse de v. actuar con cuidado por si hay peligro

C

caption / leyenda s. título o explicación breve

certain / incuestionable adj. que no presenta dudas; fiable

character design / diseño del personaje s. proceso de desarrollar el papel y la personalidad de un personaje mediante ilustraciones y gráficos

clenched / contraído v. apretado; constreñido

coherent / coherente adj. que se comunica con claridad y lógica

community / comunidad s. las personas o los animales que viven en un lugar determinado

compel / obligar v. forzar; ordenar

compromise / mutuo acuerdo s. acuerdo alcanzado por partes distintas o enfrentadas en el que cada parte cede en algo

compulsory / obligatorio adj. que se debe hacer; exigido

consequently / por consiguiente adv. en consecuencia; por lo tanto

consumed / abstraído adj. absorto en, ocupado con

consideration / consideración s. pensar sobre algo y analizarlo con atención

continuation / continuación s. acción de seguir sin interrupción; acción que no se detiene

contribute / contribuir v. dar o aportar junto con otras personas

convince / convencer v. persuadir

critical / crítico crucial adj. que suele estar en contra de hechos e ideas / muy importante

cultivate / cultivar v. preparar la tierra para plantar cultivos

curiosity / curiosidad s. anhelo de saber algo

cut-out animation / animación con recortes s. técnica que utiliza figuras planas, fondos y objetos recortados de materiales tales como papel, cartón y tela

D

declare / declarar v. decir algo públicamente; anunciar

deliberate / meditado adj. pensado de antemano; que se ha reflexionado qué hacer atenta y detenidamente

desperate / desesperado adj. que sufre necesidad o frustración extrema y con poca esperanza

destination / destino s. lugar al que se dirige alguien o algo

devouring / devorando v. consumiendo de manera voraz

dialogue / diálogo s. conversación oral entre dos o más personajes

digesting / digiriendo v. pensando con concentración para entender algo bien

disgusted / indignado adj. con un fuerte sentimiento de desaprobación; molesto

distraught / desconsolado adj. muy preocupado y triste

distressed / consternado adj. apenado; molesto

domesticated / domesticado adj. que cambió de un estado salvaje a uno manso

dominate / dominar v. dirigir o controlar

E

elaborate / profundizar v. explicar incluyendo muchos detalles

enactment / promulgación s. acto de publicar oficialmente una ley

encapsulation / encapsulación s. selección de las escenas importantes que van a aparecer en cada viñeta

endurance test / prueba de resistencia s. prueba que mide la capacidad física de una persona

entitled / tener derecho v. disfrutar de algún derecho, ya sea otorgado o logrado

exclude / excluir *v.* dejar fuera; impedir que entre, que ocurra o que esté

expedition / expedición *s.* excursión o viaje que tiene un propósito determinado

F

feathery / ligero *adj.* que no pesa mucho y es vaporoso, como una pluma de ave

foe / rival *s.* enemigo

G

gradually / gradualmente *adv.* que ocurre poco a poco

H

host / presentador *s.* persona que presenta y habla con los invitados en un programa de televisión o de radio

humming / tatareo *s.* acción de cantar con los labios cerrados y sin palabras

I

ignorance / ignorancia *s.* falta de conocimiento, educación o información

illustrate / ilustrar *v.* hacer dibujos, diagramas o mapas para explicar o decorar una historia; proveer un ejemplo que demuestre una idea

images or graphics / imágenes o gráficas *s.* representaciones de una persona o cosa

impetuous / impulsivo *adj.* que actúa repentinamente y con poca reflexión

inker / entintador *s.* artista que repasa con tinta un dibujo hecho a lápiz

insincerity / insinceridad *s.* falta de honestidad; falsedad

inspire / inspirar *v.* influenciar; animar al esfuerzo creativo

intensity / intensidad *s.* cualidad de concentrarse o comprometerse del todo

interview / entrevista *s.* conversación grabada en la cual se hacen preguntas a una persona sobre su vida, sus experiencias o sus opiniones

invaded / invadió *v.* atacó; entró por la fuerza

irritable / irritable *adj.* que se enoja o indigna fácilmente

J

journeys / travesías *s.* viajes de un lugar a otro

L

lamented / lamentó *v.* expresó pena o tristeza

letterer / rotulista *s.* artista que escribe los textos de los diálogos y las leyendas

light and shadow / luces y sombras *s.* técnica de dibujo mediante la cual se le da profundidad a una imagen

loftily / altivamente *adv.* con aire de superioridad

loneliness / soledad *s.* sentimiento de aislamiento y de abandono

M

malicious / malicioso *adj.* que tiene o demuestra malas intenciones

memorize / memorizar *v.* aprender algo de manera que pueda recordarse perfectamente luego

microchips / microchips *s.* pequeñas piezas utilizadas en la informática y que tienen circuitos integrados

milled / vagó *v.* se movió desplazándose sin orden ni dirección

misapprehension / malentendido *s.* confusión

miserable / miserable *adj.* profundamente infeliz e incómodo

model / modelo *s.* conjunto de ideas que se deben seguir como plan de acción o ejemplo

mournfully / tristemente *adv.* de una manera que manifiesta pena y desconsuelo

N

narrator / narrador *s.* persona que cuenta una historia

nonchalantly / con aire despreocupado *adv.* hecho de manera indiferente

nostalgic / nostálgico *adj.* que extraña el pasado

notable / notable *adj.* digno de atención; destacado; señalado

novelty / novedad *s.* algo nuevo, fresco o inusual

O

object animation / animación de objetos *s.* técnica que utiliza los movimientos de objetos que no han sido dibujados, como un libro o una pluma

objective / objetivo *s.* finalidad o meta

obsessive / obsesivo *adj.* que se preocupa tanto por algo que no puede pensar en otra cosa

obstacle / obstáculo *s.* algo que se cruza en nuestro camino o nos impide progresar

offended / ofendió *v.* hirió los sentimientos de alguien; afectó de manera desagradable

P

panel / viñeta *s.* cada uno de los recuadros de un cómic, mostrando un momento individual

parameters / parámetros *s.* límites; características

pathetically / patéticamente *adv.* de manera que provoca pena a una persona

patiently / pacientemente *adv.* que aguanta dificultades o dolor de manera voluntaria y calmada

peeped / miró furtivamente *v.* miró por un pequeño agujero o a través de una grieta; miró sin que nadie se diera cuenta

penciler / dibujante *s.* artista que bosqueja las viñetas en una página

perspective / perspectiva *s.* efecto de la distancia en la apariencia de un objeto

pessimistic / pesimista *adj.* que espera que pase lo peor, que se fija en los inconvenientes

pixels / píxels *s.* elementos más pequeños de los que se compone una imagen y que pueden controlarse individualmente en un sistema de video

podcast / podcast *s.* archivo digital o de audio o de video, que forma normalmente parte de una serie y se puede descargar de Internet

presume / presumir *v.* suponer que algo es cierto; asumir

process / procesar *v.* lograr el entendimiento de información

program manager / director de programas *s.* persona que está a cargo de un proyecto

pungent / acre *adj* que tiene un olor fuerte y áspero

purist / purista *s.* alguien que hace las cosas de manera estrictamente tradicional

Q

quest / búsqueda *s.* acción de ir en busca de algo, expedición larga

quivering / temblando *s.* estremecimiento o temblor

R

real-time animation / animación en tiempo real *s.* técnica que consiste en simular que eventos u objetos animados ocurran o se muevan a la misma velocidad que en la vida real

recognize / reconocer *v.* identificar algo a través de la memoria o mediante una descripción

reflect / reflexionar *v.* pensar detenidamente

refugee / refugiado *s.* persona que huye de su país natal, por ejemplo durante un período de guerra

relentlessly / implacablemente *adv.* sin detenerse; con determinación

remember / recordar *v.* evocar o traer a la memoria; no olvidarse

respected / respetado *adj.* venerado; tratado con aprecio

S

sample group / grupo de muestra *s.* grupo de personas provenientes de un grupo más grande que son sometidas a un estudio

sensation / sensación *s.* sentimiento de emoción e interés

shushes / hace callar *v.* manda o señala a alguien que guarde silencio

shyly / tímidamente *adv.* de manera tímida; de manera vergonzosa

silently / silenciosamente *adv.* de manera silenciosa; sin ruido

skittered / se escabulió *v.* se movió sutil y rápidamente

slain / asesinado *v.* ha matado

solid drawing / dibujo sólido *s.* técnica para hacer que una imagen parezca tridimensional

sorrowfully / tristemente *adv.* hecho con pena

speculate / especular *v.* pensar sobre algo y formar una idea sin tener información definitiva

speech balloon / globo de diálogo *s.* espacio donde se escribe lo que el personaje dice o piensa

squish / blandura *s.* sensación suave y esponjosa que se tiene al caminar en una superficie flexible y mullida

stage directions / acotaciones *s.* información importante que provee el dramaturgo sobre el escenario, los personajes y la acción

stubborn / terco *adj.* que se niega a ceder, obedecer o aceptar algo

surmise / conjeturar *v.* adivinar; pensar algo sin tener datos definitivos en que basarse

sufficient / suficiente *adj.* bastante para cubrir lo necesario

suspiciously / sospechosamente *adv.* con recelo, que causa desconfianza

T

template / patrón *s.* plantilla o forma fija que se usa como ejemplo

tenseness / tensión *s.* tirantez de los músculos del cuerpo

thorough / riguroso *adj.* meticuloso; completo; incluyendo cada detalle posible

thoughtfully / atentamente *adv.* de manera considerada y atenta

threateningly / amenazadoramente *adv.* de manera que da miedo o alarmante

timidly / tímidamente *adv.* con timidez o de manera temerosa

transform / transformar *v.* convertir o cambiar

trek / caminata *s.* excursión larga o difícil

trigonometry / trigonometría *s.* campo de las matemáticas que trata de las relaciones entre los lados y ángulos de los triángulos

twirl / dar vueltas *v.* girar sobre sí mismo rápidamente

twist / girar *v.* enrollarse o dar vueltas alrededor de sí mismo

V

valid / válido *adj.* aceptable; que se basa o respalda con hechos

vanished / desapareció *v.* se esfumó, dejó de estar a la vista

various / variados *adj.* diferentes los unos de los otros

violent / violento *adj.* con fuerza y brusquedad que causa daño

voiceover / voz en off *s.* voz que comenta sobre la acción o narra una película detrás de la cámara

W

wild / salvaje *adj.* que vive en la naturaleza sin control humano

wondered / se preguntó *v.* pensó; reflexionó

wrath / furia *s.* rabia intensa

LITERARY TERMS HANDBOOK

ALLEGORY An *allegory* is a story or tale with two or more levels of meaning—a literal level and one or more symbolic levels. The events, setting, and characters in an allegory are symbols for ideas and qualities.

ALLITERATION *Alliteration* is the repetition of initial consonant sounds. Writers use alliteration to draw attention to certain words or ideas, to imitate sounds, and to create musical effects.

ANALOGY An *analogy* makes a comparison between two or more things that are similar in some ways but otherwise unalike.

ANECDOTE An *anecdote* is a brief story about an interesting, amusing, or strange event. Writers tell anecdotes to entertain or to make a point.

ARGUMENT An *argument* is a logical way of presenting a belief, conclusion, or stance. A good argument is supported with reasoning and evidence.

ASSONANCE *Assonance* is the repetition of similar vowel sounds in stressed syllables that end with different consonants, as in seal and meet.

AUTHOR'S INFLUENCES An *author's influences* are things that affect his or her writing. These include *historical factors*, such as world events that took place during the author's lifetime, and *cultural factors*, such as the author's upbringing, education, lifestyle, and personal experiences.

AUTHOR'S PURPOSE An *author's purpose* is his or her main reason for writing. Texts are written to inform, to persuade, to entertain, to describe, and to express the author's point of view. In many cases, an author has more than one purpose, or reason, for writing.

AUTHOR'S STYLE *Style* is an author's typical way of writing. Many factors determine an author's style, including diction; tone; use of characteristic elements such as figurative language, dialect, rhyme, meter, or rhythmic devices; typical grammatical structures and patterns; typical sentence length; and typical methods of organization.

AUTOBIOGRAPHY An *autobiography* is the story of the writer's own life, told by the writer. Autobiographical writing may tell about the person's whole life or only a part of it.

Because autobiographies are about real people and events, they are a form of nonfiction. Most autobiographies are written in the first person.

BIBLIOGRAPHY A list of sources used at the end of an essay is a *bibliography*. Also called a *works-cited list*, a bibliography can have different citation styles, such as MLA. Failure to properly cite sources is considered

plagiarism because you are using someone else's work without giving proper credit.

BIOGRAPHY A *biography* is a form of nonfiction in which a writer tells the life story of another person. Most biographies are written about famous or admirable people. Although biographies are nonfiction, the most effective ones share the qualities of good narrative writing.

CENTRAL IDEA Sometimes a writer will state the *central idea* of a text *directly,* but other times the central idea is implied. An *implied* central idea is identified by *making an inference*.

CHARACTER A *character* is a person or an animal that takes part in the action of a literary work. The main, or *major,* character is the most important character in a story, poem, or play. A *minor* character is one who takes part in the action but is not the focus of attention.

CHARACTERIZATION *Characterization* is the act of creating and developing a character. Authors use two major methods of characterization—*direct* and *indirect.* When using *direct* characterization, a writer states the *character's traits,* or characteristics.

When describing a character *indirectly,* a writer depends on the reader to draw conclusions about the character's traits. Sometimes the writer tells what other participants in the story say and think about the character.

CHARACTER TRAITS *Character traits* are the qualities, attitudes, and values that a character has or displays— for example, dependability, intelligence, selfishness, or stubbornness.

CHRONOLOGICAL ORDER In a nonfiction narrative, the writer often sequences events in *chronological order*, so that one event proceeds to the next in the order in which they actually happened, from first to last.

CLAIM A *claim* is an statement in a text that can be called into question. Claims can be facts or *opinions*.

CLIMAX The *climax,* also called the turning point, is the high point in the action of the plot. It is the moment of greatest tension, when the outcome of the plot hangs in the balance.

COMPARISON-AND-CONTRAST ESSAY A *comparison-and-contrast essay* analyzes the similarities and differences between two texts. Comparison-and-contrast essays can be written using different methods of organization. Using *block organization*, one subject is discussed completely, then the other subject is discussed. *Point-by-point* organization discusses one point at a time of both subjects before moving on to the next.

CONFLICT A *conflict* is a struggle between opposing forces. Conflict is one of the most important elements of stories, novels, and plays because it causes the action. There are two kinds of conflict: external and internal. An **external conflict** is one in which a character struggles against some outside force, such as another person. Another kind of external conflict may occur between a character and some force in nature.

An **internal conflict** takes place within the mind of a character. The character struggles to make a decision, take an action, or overcome a feeling.

CONSONANCE *Consonance* is the repetition of final consonant sounds in stressed syllables with different vowel sounds, as in sit and cat.

CONNOTATIONS The **connotation** of a word is the set of ideas associated with it in addition to its explicit meaning. The connotation of a word can be personal, based on individual experiences. More often, cultural connotations—those recognizable by most people in a group—determine a writer's word choices.

DEBATE A **debate** is a formal discussion in which opposing sides of a question are argued.

DENOTATION The **denotation** of a word is its dictionary meaning, independent of other associations that the word may have. The denotation of the word *lake,* for example, is "an inland body of water." "Vacation spot" and "place where the fishing is good" are connotations of the word *lake.*

DESCRIPTION A **description** is a portrait, in words, of a person, place, or object. Descriptive writing uses images that appeal to the five senses—sight, hearing, touch, taste, and smell.

DIALOGUE A **dialogue** is a conversation between characters. In poems, novels, and short stories, dialogue is usually set off by quotation marks to indicate a speaker's exact words.

In a play, dialogue follows the names of the characters, and no quotation marks are used.

DRAMA A **drama** is a story written to be performed by actors. Although a drama is meant to be performed, one can also read the **script**, or written version, and imagine the action. The **script** of a drama is made up of dialogue and stage directions. The **dialogue** is the words spoken by the actors. The **stage directions,** usually printed in italics, tell how the actors should look, move, and speak. They also describe the setting, sound effects, and lighting.

Dramas are often divided into parts called **acts.**

The acts are often divided into smaller parts called **scenes.**

DRAMATIC READING A **dramatic reading** is an oral presentation that includes powerful dramatic expression, gestures, and body language to help express feelings and ideas.

EDITORIAL An editorial is a type of argument in which the writer presents a viewpoint on an issue.

ELEMENTS In organizing an essay, a writer needs to put together various **elements** to explain ideas in a logical way.

ENJAMBMENT An **enjambment**, or run-on line, is the continuation of a sentence between lines of poetry without end punctuation. It is the opposite of an **end-stopped line**.

ESSAY An **essay** is a short nonfiction work about a particular subject. Most essays have a single major focus and a clear introduction, body, and conclusion.

There are many types of essays. An **informal essay** uses casual, conversational language. A **historical essay** gives facts, explanations, and insights about historical events. An **explanatory essay** is a short piece of nonfiction in which the author explains, defines, or interprets ideas, events, or processes. A **reflective essay** is a brief prose work in which an author presents his or her thoughts or feelings—or reflections—about an experience or an idea. An **expository essay** explains an idea by breaking it down. A **narrative essay** tells a story about a real-life experience. A **how-to essay** explains a process. A **persuasive essay** offers an opinion and supports it.

EVIDENCE Effective arguments and persuasive essays use **evidence** to support claims. Facts, statistics, anecdotes, examples, and quotations from authorities are forms of evidence used by writers.

EXPOSITION In the plot of a story or a drama, the **exposition,** or introduction, is the part of the work that introduces the characters, setting, and basic situation.

EXPOSITORY WRITING *Expository writing* is writing that explains or informs.

FANTASY A **fantasy** is highly imaginative writing that contains elements not found in real life. Examples of fantasy include stories that involve supernatural elements, stories that resemble fairy tales, stories that deal with imaginary places and creatures, and science-fiction stories.

FICTION *Fiction* is prose writing that tells about imaginary characters and events. Short stories and novels are works of fiction. In **historical fiction**, real events, places, or people are adapted into a fictional story. Other writers rely on imagination alone.

FIGURATIVE LANGUAGE *Figurative language* is writing or speech that is not meant to be taken literally. The many types of figurative language are known as **figures of speech.** Common figures of speech include metaphor, personification, and simile. Writers use figurative language to state ideas in vivid and imaginative ways.

FLASHBACK A *flashback* is a scene within a story that interrupts the sequence of events to relate events that occurred in the past.

FREE VERSE *Free verse* is poetry not written in a regular, rhythmical pattern, or meter. The poet is free to write lines of any length or with any number of stresses, or beats. Free verse is therefore less constraining than *metrical verse,* in which every line must have a certain length and a certain number of stresses.

GENRE A *genre* is a division or type of literature. Literature is commonly divided into three major genres: poetry, prose, and drama. Each major genre is, in turn, divided into lesser genres, as follows:

1. *Poetry:* lyric poetry, concrete poetry, dramatic poetry, narrative poetry, epic poetry
2. *Prose:* fiction (novels and short stories) and nonfiction (biography, autobiography, letters, essays, and reports)
3. *Drama:* serious drama and tragedy, comic drama, melodrama, and farce

IDIOMS *Idioms* are expressions that have different meanings from the literal meanings

IMAGERY *Imagery* is the use of vivid word pictures writers use to appeal to one or more of the five senses. Writers use images to describe how their subjects look, sound, feel, taste, and smell. Poets often paint images, or word pictures, that appeal to your senses. These pictures help you experience the poem fully.

INFER To *infer* is to make an educated guess about *implied* information in a text.

INFERENCE An *inference* is a logical assumption made about information in a text that is not directly stated. *Prior knowledge* and *key details* are used to make inferences about *implied* ideas.

IRONY *Irony* is a contradiction between what happens and what is expected. The three main types of irony are *situational irony, verbal irony,* and *dramatic irony.*

MEDIA ACCOUNTS *Media accounts* are reports, explanations, opinions, or descriptions written for television, radio, newspapers, and magazines. While some media accounts report only facts, others include the writer's thoughts and reflections.

MEMOIR A *memoir* is a type of autobiography that focuses on a particularly meaningful period or series of events in the author's life. A memoir is typically written from the *first-person point of view* in which the author, or narrator, takes part in the story's events. The author will refer to himself or herself using the pronoun *I.*

METAPHOR A *metaphor* is a figure of speech in which something is described as though it were something else. A metaphor, like a simile, works by pointing out a similarity between two unlike things.

MYTH A *myth* is a fictional tale that describes the actions of heroes or gods.

MYTHOLOGY *Mythology* is the system of myths belonging to a culture.

NARRATION *Narration* is writing that tells a story. The act of telling a story is also called narration. Each piece is a *narrative.* A story told in fiction, nonfiction, poetry, or even in drama is called a narrative.

NARRATIVE A *narrative* is a story. A narrative can be either fiction or nonfiction. Novels and short stories are types of **fictional narratives**. Biographies and autobiographies are **nonfiction narratives**. Poems that tell stories are also narratives.

NARRATOR A *narrator* is a speaker or a character who tells a story. The narrator's perspective is the way he or she sees things. A *third-person narrator* is one who stands outside the action and speaks about it. A *first-person narrator* is one who tells a story and participates in its action.

NONFICTION *Nonfiction* is prose writing that presents and explains ideas or that tells about real people, places, objects, or events. Autobiographies, biographies, essays, reports, letters, memos, and newspaper articles are all types of nonfiction.

NOVEL A *novel* is a long work of fiction. Novels contain such elements as characters, plot, conflict, and setting. The writer of novels, or novelist, develops these elements. In addition to its main plot, a novel may contain one or more subplots, or independent, related stories. A novel may also have several themes.

ONOMATOPOEIA *Onomatopoeia* is the use of words that imitate sounds. *Crash, buzz, screech, hiss, neigh, jingle,* and *cluck* are examples of onomatopoeia. *Chickadee, towhee,* and *whippoorwill* are onomatopoeic names of birds.

Onomatopoeia can help put the reader in the activity of a poem.

OPINION An *opinion* is a belief that cannot be proven as fact and appeals to reader's emotions.

ORGANIZED STRUCTURE The body of an essay presents ideas in an *organized structure*, such as comparison-and-contrast or cause-effect. The writer should provide *support* for the ideas in the form of evidence, examples, or quotations.

OUTLINE An *outline* lists the main ideas of an essay or presentation and helps to organize ideas in a logical sequence. A typical outline structure is:

I. Thesis Statement

II. Body of Presentation

  A. First Idea

B. Second Idea

C. Third Idea

III. Conclusion: Importance of Ideas

OXYMORON An *oxymoron* (pl. *oxymora*) is a figure of speech that links two opposite or contradictory words, to point out an idea or situation that seems contradictory or inconsistent but on closer inspection turns out to be somehow true.

PACING Writers use *pacing* to slow down or speed up the action in a scene. Action is slowed down by adding more description and longer sentences. Action speeds up by using shorter sentences. Pacing helps you draw attention to an important idea or build suspense.

PERSONIFICATION *Personification* is a type of figurative language in which a nonhuman subject is given human characteristics.

PERSUASION *Persuasion* is used in writing or speech and attempts to convince the reader or listener to adopt a particular opinion or course of action. Newspaper editorials, letters to the editor, political campaign speeches, and advertisements use persuasion.

PERSUASIVE TECHNIQUES *Persuasive techniques* are used to strengthen an argument. *Repetition*, or repeating a word or phrase so that it makes an impact, is one persuasive technique. *Appeals to authority* show that a higher power supports an idea. *Appeals to emotion* influence readers by using words that create positive or negative feelings. *Appeals to reason* use logical arguments backed by facts.

PLAYWRIGHT A *playwright* is a person who writes plays. William Shakespeare is regarded as the greatest playwright in English literature.

PLOT *Plot* is the sequence of events in which each event results from a previous one and causes the next. In most novels, dramas, short stories, and narrative poems, the plot involves both characters and a central conflict. The plot usually begins with an *exposition* that introduces the setting, the characters, and the basic situation. This is followed by the *inciting incident,* which introduces the central conflict. Events then increase the tension of the conflict with *rising action* until it reaches a high point of interest or suspense, the *climax.* The climax is followed by the *falling action,* or end, of the central conflict. Any events that occur during the *falling action* make up the *resolution,* or *denouement.*

Some plots do not have all of these parts. Some stories begin with the inciting incident and end with the resolution.

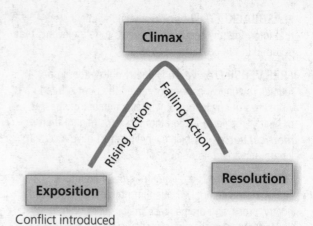

Conflict introduced

POETRY *Poetry* is one of the three major types of literature, the others being prose and drama. Most poems make use of highly concise, musical, and emotionally charged language. Many also make use of imagery, figurative language, and sound devices such as rhythm, rhyme, repetition, and onomatopoeia. Major types of poetry include lyric poetry, narrative poetry, and concrete poetry.

POINT OF VIEW *Point of view* is the perspective, or vantage point, from which a story is told. The storyteller is either a narrator outside the story or a character in the story. *First-person point of view* describes a story told by a character who uses the first-person pronoun "I."

The two kinds of *third-person point of view,* limited and omniscient, are called "third person" because the narrator uses third-person pronouns such as "he" and "she" to refer to the characters. There is no "I" telling the story.

In stories told from the *omniscient third-person point of view,* the narrator knows and tells about what each character feels and thinks.

In stories told from the *limited third-person point of view,* the narrator relates the inner thoughts and feelings of only one character, and everything is viewed from this character's perspective.

PROSE *Prose* is the ordinary form of written language. Most writing that is not poetry, drama, or song is considered prose. Prose is one of the major genres of literature and occurs in two forms—fiction and nonfiction.

PROTAGONIST The *protagonist* is the main character in a literary work. Often, the protagonist is a person, but sometimes it can be an animal.

REPETITION *Repetition* is the use, more than once, of any element of language—a sound, word, phrase, clause, or sentence. Repetition is used in both prose and poetry.

RESOLUTION The *resolution* is the outcome of the conflict in a plot.

RHYTHM *Rhythm* is the pattern of stressed and unstressed syllables in spoken or written language.

SCENE A *scene* is a section of uninterrupted action in the act of a drama.

SCIENCE FICTION *Science fiction* combines elements of fiction and fantasy with scientific fact. Many science-fiction stories are set in the future.

SENSORY LANGUAGE *Sensory language* is writing or speech that appeals to one or more of the five senses.

SETTING The *setting* of a literary work is the time and place of the action. The setting includes all the details of a place and time—the year, the time of day, even the weather. The place may be a specific country, state, region, community, neighborhood, building, institution, or home. Details such as dialects, clothing, customs, and modes of transportation are often used to establish setting. In most stories, the setting serves as a backdrop—a context in which the characters interact. Setting can also help create a feeling, or atmosphere.

SHORT STORY A *short story* is a brief work of fiction. Like a novel, a short story presents a sequence of events, or plot. The plot usually deals with a central conflict faced by a main character, or protagonist. The events in a short story usually communicate a message about life or human nature. This message, or central idea, is the story's theme.

SIMILE A *simile* is a figure of speech that uses *like* or *as* to make a direct comparison between two unlike ideas. Everyday speech often contains similes, such as "pale as a ghost," "good as gold," "spread like wildfire," and "clever as a fox."

SOUND DEVICES Poets use *sound devices* to create musical effects, reinforce meaning, develop tone, and emphasize the sound relationships among words. Sound devices include *repetition, onomatopoeia, alliteration, consonance,* and *assonance.*

SPEAKER The *speaker* is the imaginary voice a poet uses when writing a poem. The speaker is the character who tells the poem. This character, or voice, often is not identified by name. There can be important differences between the poet and the poem's speaker.

STAGE DIRECTIONS *Stage directions* are notes included in a drama to describe how the work is to be performed or staged. Stage directions are usually printed in italics and enclosed within parentheses or brackets. Some stage directions describe the movements, costumes, emotional states, and ways of speaking of the characters.

STAGING *Staging* includes the setting, lighting, costumes, special effects, music, dance, and so on that go into putting on a stage performance of a drama.

STANZA A *stanza* is a group of lines of poetry that are usually similar in length and pattern and are separated by spaces. A stanza is like a paragraph of poetry—it states and develops a single main idea.

SYMBOL A *symbol* is anything that stands for or represents something else. Symbols are common in everyday life. A dove with an olive branch in its beak is a symbol of peace. A blindfolded woman holding a balanced scale is a symbol of justice. A crown is a symbol of a king's status and authority.

SYMBOLISM *Symbolism* is the use of symbols. Symbolism plays an important role in many different types of literature. It can highlight certain elements the author wishes to emphasize and also add levels of meaning.

SYNTAX The organization of words into sentences is *syntax*. Poets often play with syntax to highlight ideas.

TECHNICAL LANGUAGE *Technical language* is words or language specific to a particular topic, process, or industry.

THEME The *theme* is a central idea, concern, or purpose in a literary work. A theme can usually be expressed as a generalization, or a general statement, about human beings or about life. The theme of a work is not a summary of its plot. The theme is the writer's central idea.

Although a theme may be stated directly in the text, it is more often presented indirectly. When the theme is stated indirectly, or implied, the reader must figure out what the theme is by looking carefully at what the work reveals about people or about life.

THESIS A *thesis* is a sentence that states the controlling idea of an essay.

TONE The *tone* of a literary work is the writer's attitude toward his or her audience and subject. The tone can often be described by a single adjective, such as *formal* or *informal, serious* or *playful, bitter,* or *ironic.* Factors that contribute to the tone are word choice, sentence structure, line length, rhyme, rhythm, and repetition.

TOPIC SENTENCE Each paragraph of an essay should have a *topic sentence* that states the main idea of the paragraph. The paragraph also has facts and examples to support the main idea.

UNIVERSAL THEME A *universal theme* is a message about life that is expressed regularly in many different cultures and time periods. Folk tales, epics, and romances often address universal themes such as the importance of courage, the power of love, or the danger of greed.

VERSE *Verse* is a form of literature also called poetry. *Free verse* is not written in a regular, rhythmical pattern, or meter. The poet is free to write lines of any length or with any number of stresses, or beats. Free verse is therefore less constraining than *metrical verse,* in which every line must have a certain length and a certain number of stresses.

VOICE *Voice* describes a writer's distinct style. A writer's voice can be influenced by *word choice,* the writer's choice and use of specific words; *sentence structure,* or the way the writer constructs a sentence; and *tone,* or the writer's attitude toward the subject.

MANUAL DE TÉRMINOS LITERARIOS

ALLEGORY / ALEGORÍA Una *alegoría* es una historia o un cuento con dos o más niveles de significado (un nivel literal y uno o más niveles simbólicos). Los eventos, escenarios y personajes de una alegoría son símbolos de ideas y cualidades.

ALLITERATION / ALITERACIÓN Una *aliteración* es la repetición de sonidos consonánticos iniciales. Los escritores usan la aliteración para dirigir la atención de los lectores hacia ciertas palabras o ideas, imitar sonidos o crear efectos musicales.

ANALOGY / ANALOGÍA Una *analogía* establece una comparación entre dos o más cosas que presentan similitudes, pero son distintas en todo lo demás.

ANECDOTE / ANÉCDOTA Una *anécdota* es un cuento corto sobre un evento extraño, interesante o divertido. Los escritores cuentan anécdotas para entretener o explicar algo importante.

ARGUMENT / ARGUMENTO Un *argumento* es una manera lógica de expresar una opinión, una conclusión o una postura. Un buen argumento contiene razonamientos y pruebas.

ASSONANCE / ASONANCIA Una *asonancia* es la repetición de sonidos vocálicos similares a partir de la última sílaba acentuada, como en *foca* y *nota*.

AUTHOR'S INFLUENCES / INFLUENCIAS DEL AUTOR Las *influencias del autor* son cosas que influyen en su escritura. Algunas de estas influencias incluyen *factores históricos*, como los sucesos mundiales en la vida del autor, y *factores culturales*, como la niñez, educación, estilo de vida y experiencias personales del autor.

AUTHOR'S PURPOSE / PROPÓSITO DEL AUTOR El *propósito del autor* es la razón principal por la que este autor o autora escribe. Los textos se escriben para informar, persuadir, entretener, describir y expresar el punto de vista del autor. En muchos casos, un autor tiene varios propósitos o razones por los que escribir.

AUTHOR'S STYLE / ESTILO DEL AUTOR El *estilo* es la forma de escribir típica de un autor. Hay muchos factores que determinan el estilo del autor: la dicción, el tono, el uso de elementos característicos como el lenguaje figurativo, el dialecto, la rima, la métrica o los distintos recursos rítmicos; las estructuras y patrones gramaticales típicos, el tamaño típico de la frase; y los métodos típicos de organización textual.

AUTOBIOGRAPHY / AUTOBIOGRAFÍA Una *autobiografía* es la historia de la vida del propio autor. Los textos autobiográficos pueden hablar de la vida completa del autor o solo de una parte.

Como las autobiografías tratan sobre gente y acontecimientos reales, se les considera no ficción. La mayoría de las autobiografías están escritas en primera persona.

BIBLIOGRAPHY / BIBLIOGRAFÍA Se conoce como *bibliografía* a la lista que se incluye al final de un ensayo con las fuentes que se utilizaron. También llamada *lista de obras citadas*, para su elaboración se sigue una guía de estilo como, por ejemplo, la de MLA. No citar las fuentes se considera *plagio* porque se usa el trabajo de otra persona sin reconocerle el mérito al autor.

BIOGRAPHY / BIOGRAFÍA Una *biografía* es un tipo de texto de no ficción donde el escritor explica la historia de la vida de otra persona. La mayoría de las biografías son sobre gente famosa y admirable. Aunque las biografías se consideran libros de no ficción, las de mayor calidad suelen compartir cualidades con los textos narrativos.

CENTRAL IDEA / IDEA CENTRAL En ocasiones el escritor expone la *idea central* de un texto *directamente*, pero en otros casos la idea central está *implícita*. Una idea central implícita se identifica al *hacer una inferencia*.

CHARACTER / PERSONAJE Un *personaje* es una persona o un animal que participa en la acción de una obra literaria. El personaje *principal* o protagonista es el más importante de una historia, poema u obra teatral. El personaje *secundario* participa también en la acción pero no es el centro de atención.

CHARACTERIZATION / CARACTERIZACIÓN *Caracterización* es la acción de crear y desarrollar un personaje. Los autores utilizan dos métodos principales de caracterización: *directa* e *indirecta.*

Cuando se utiliza la caracterización *directa*, el escritor describe los *rasgos del personaje* o sus características.

En cambio, cuando se describe a un personaje *indirectamente*, el escritor depende del lector para que se puedan extraer conclusiones sobre los rasgos del personaje. A veces el escritor cuenta lo que otros personajes que participan en la historia dicen o piensan sobre el personaje en cuestión.

CHARACTER TRAITS / RASGOS DEL PERSONAJE Los *rasgos del personaje* son cualidades, actitudes y valores que un personaje tiene o manifiesta, por ejemplo la fiabilidad, inteligencia, egoísmo o terquedad.

CHRONOLOGICAL ORDER / ORDEN CRONOLÓGICO En una narrativa de no ficción, el escritor suele ordenar los sucesos en *orden cronológico*, es decir, los sucesos se describen en el orden que tuvieron lugar, del primero al último.

CLAIM / AFIRMACIÓN Una *afirmación* es una declaración que puede cuestionarse. Las afirmaciones pueden ser hechos u *opiniones*.

CLIMAX / CLÍMAX El *clímax,* también llamado momento culminante, es el punto más elevado de acción de una trama. Es el momento de mayor tensión, es decir, cuando el desenlace de la trama pende de un hilo.

COMPARISON-AND-CONTRAST ESSAY / ENSAYO DE COMPARACIÓN Y CONTRASTE Un *ensayo de comparación y contraste* analiza las semejanzas y diferencias entre dos textos. Los ensayos de comparación y contraste pueden tener distintos métodos de organización. En una *organización de método de bloques*, se trata primero uno de los asuntos y después el otro. En una *organización de punto por punto* se trata un aspecto de cada asunto antes de pasar al siguiente aspecto.

CONFLICT / CONFLICT Un *conflicto* es una lucha entre fuerzas opuestas. El conflicto es uno de los elementos más importantes de los cuentos, novelas y obras de teatro porque provoca la acción. Hay dos tipos de conflictos: externos e internos.

Un *conflicto externo* se da cuando un personaje lucha contra una fuerza ajena a él, como por ejemplo otra persona. Otro tipo de conflicto externo puede ocurrir entre un personaje y una fuerza de la naturaleza.

Un *conflicto interno* tiene lugar en la mente de un personaje. El personaje lucha por tomar una decisión, llevar a cabo una acción o frenar un sentimiento.

CONNOTATION / CONNOTACIÓN La *connotación* de una palabra es el conjunto de ideas que se asocian con esta más allá de su significado explícito. La connotación de una palabra puede ser personal, basada en una experiencia individual. Con frecuencia son las connotaciones culturales, aquellas que son reconocibles por la mayoría de las personas de un grupo, las que determinan la elección de un autor.

CONSONANCE / CONSONANCIA La *consonancia* es la repetición desde de la última sílaba acentuada de las mismas vocales y consonantes. Por ejemplo: *zapato* y *gato*.

DEBATE / DEBATE Un *debate* es una discusión formal en la que se argumentan puntos de vista opuestos sobre un mismo asunto.

DENOTATION / DENOTACIÓN La *denotación* de una palabra es su significado del diccionario, independientemente de otras asociaciones que se le puedan otorgar. La denotación de la palabra *lago* sería "una masa de agua que se acumula en un terreno". "Un lugar de vacaciones" o "un lugar adonde se puede ir de pesca" son connotaciones de la palabra *lago*.

DESCRIPTION / DESCRIPCIÓN Una *descripción* es un retrato en palabras de una persona, lugar u objeto. Los textos descriptivos usan imágenes que se relacionan con los cinco sentidos: vista, oído, tacto, gusto y olfato.

DIALOGUE / DIÁLOGO Un *diálogo* es una conversación entre personajes. En los poemas, novelas y cuentos en inglés, los diálogos se indican normalmente entre comillas para señalar que estas son las palabras exactas que dice un personaje.

En una obra de teatro, los diálogos se colocan detrás de los nombres de los personajes y no se utilizan comillas.

DRAMA / DRAMA Un *drama* es una historia escrita para ser representada por actores. Aunque está destinada a ser representada, también se puede, únicamente, leer el guión o texto e imaginar la acción. El *guión* está compuesto de diálogos y acotaciones. Los *diálogos* son las palabras que dicen los personajes. Las *acotaciones* aparecen normalmente en cursiva e indican qué apariencia deben tener los personajes, y cómo deben moverse o hablar. También describen la escenografía, los efectos de sonido y la iluminación.

Los dramas suelen estar divididos en distintas partes denominadas *actos*.

Los actos aparecen a menudo divididos en partes más pequeñas denominadas *escenas*.

DRAMATIC READING / LECTURA DRAMATIZADA Una *lectura dramatizada* es una presentación oral que incluye gran expresividad dramática, gestos y lenguaje corporal para transmitir sentimientos e ideas.

EDITORIAL / EDITORIAL Un *editorial* es un tipo de argumento en el que el escritor presenta un punto de vista sobre un asunto.

ELEMENTS / ELEMENTOS Al organizar un ensayo, el escritor debe reunir diversos *elementos* para explicar las ideas de una manera lógica.

ENJAMBMENT / ENCABALGAMIENTO En un *encabalgamiento*, o verso encabalgado, la oración continúa de un verso al siguiente. Es lo opuesto a un *verso no encabalgado*.

ESSAY / ENSAYO Un *ensayo* es un texto de no ficción corto sobre un tema particular. La mayoría de los ensayos se concentran en un único aspeco fundamental y tienen una introducción clara, un desarrollo y una conclusión.

Hay muchos tipos de ensayos. Un *ensayo informal* emplea lenguaje coloquial y conversacional. Un *ensayo histórico* nos presenta hechos, explicaciones y conocimientos sobre acontecimientos históricos. Un *ensayo explicativo* aclara, define e interpreta ideas, acontecimientos o procesos. En un *ensayo reflexivo* el autor presenta sus pensamientos y sentimientos o reflexiones sobre una experiencia o idea. Un *ensayo expositivo* expone una idea desglosándola. Un *ensayo narrativo* cuenta una historia sobre una experiencia real. Un *ensayo de proceso* explica cómo hacer algo. Un *ensayo argumentativo* ofrece una opinión y la argumenta.

EVIDENCE / EVIDENCIA Los argumentos efectivos y los ensayos persuasivos utilizan *evidencia* para respaldar sus afirmaciones. Los datos, estadísticas, anécdotas, ejemplos y citas de fuentes fiables son algunas de las evidencias que emplean los escritores.

EXPOSITION / PLANTEAMIENTO En el argumento de una historia o drama, el *planteamiento* o introducción es la parte de la obra que presenta a los personajes, el escenario y la situación más básica.

EXPOSITORY WRITING / TEXTO EXPOSITIVO Un *texto expositivo* es un texto que explica e informa.

FANTASY / LITERATURA FANTÁSTICA La *literatura fantástica* son textos con elementos muy imaginativos que no pueden encontrarse en la vida real. Algunos ejemplos de literatura fantástica incluyen historias que contienen elementos supernaturales, historias que recuerdan a los cuentos de hadas, historias que tratan de lugares y criaturas imaginarias e historias de ciencia ficción.

FICTION / FICCIÓN La *ficción* son obras en prosa que hablan de sucesos y personajes imaginarios. Los relatos y las novelas son obras de ficción. En la *ficción histórica* se incluyen eventos, lugares o personas reales en la obra de ficción. Otros escritores se sirven únicamente de la imaginación.

FIGURATIVE LANGUAGE / LENGUAJE FIGURADO El *lenguaje figurado* es un texto o diálogo que no se debe interpretar literalmente. Los numerosos tipos de lenguaje figurado son conocidos como *figuras retóricas.* Algunas de las más comunes son las metáforas, las personificaciones y los símiles. Los escritores utilizan el lenguaje figurado para expresar ideas de una manera imaginativa y vívida.

FLASHBACK / ESCENA RETROSPECTIVA Una *escena retrospectiva* es una escena dentro de una historia que interrumpe la secuencia temporal de los acontecimientos para contar un acontecimiento que ocurrió en algún momento del pasado.

FREE VERSE / VERSO LIBRE El *verso libre* es poesía que no está escrita en un patrón rítmico ni métrico corriente. El poeta es libre de escribir versos del tamaño que prefiera con un número libre de acentos. Por consiguiente, el verso libre es menos limitador que el *verso métrico*, en el que cada verso debe contener acentos y un número concreto de sílabas.

GENRE / GÉNERO Un *género* es una clase o tipo de literatura. La literatura se divide normalmente en tres géneros principales: poesía, prosa y drama. Cada uno de estos géneros está, a su vez, dividido en otros géneros más pequeños:

1 *Poesía:* poesía lírica, poesía concreta, poesía dramática, poesía narrativa, poesía épica

2 *Prosa:* ficción (novelas y cuentos) y no ficción (biografías, autobiografías, cartas, ensayos y reportajes)

3 *Drama:* drama serio y tragedia, comedia, melodrama y farsa

IDIOMS / MODISMOS Los *modismos* son expresiones idiomáticas que tienen un significado diferente a su significado literal.

IMAGERY / IMAGINERÍA La *imaginería* es el uso que le da el escritor al lenguaje para crear descripciones visuales vívidas que se relacionan con uno o varios de los cinco sentidos. Los escritores utilizan imágenes para describir qué apariencia tienen, cómo suenan, sienten, saben y huelen los personajes u objetos descritos. Los poetas suelen dibujar imágenes o hacer una descripción visual que se vincule con los sentidos. Estas descripciones visuales nos ayudan a experimentar el poema en su totalidad.

INFER / INFERIR *Inferir* es hacer una deducción lógica acerca de la información que está *implícita* en un texto.

INFERENCE /INFERENCIA Una *inferencia* es una suposición lógica que se hace acerca de la información que no se detalla directamente en un texto. Se usan el *conocimiento previo* y los *detalles clave* para hacer inferencias sobre las ideas *implícitas*.

IRONY / IRONÍA Una *ironía* es una contradicción entre lo que ocurre realmente y lo que se espera que pase. Los tres tipos principales de ironía son: *ironía situacional*, *ironía verbal* e *ironía dramática.*

MEDIA ACCOUNTS / REPORTAJES PERIODÍSTICOS Los *reportajes periodísticos* son relatos, explicaciones, opiniones o descripciones escritas para televisión, radio, periódicos o revistas. Si bien algunos reportajes periodísticos solo relatan hechos, otros incluyen también las opiniones y reflexiones del autor.

MEMOIR / MEMORIAS Unas *memorias* es un tipo de autobiografía que se concentra en un período particular y significativo, o en una serie de acontecimientos de la vida del autor. Las memorias se suelen escribir en *primera persona* dado que el autor o narrador participa en los acontecimientos de la historia. El autor se refiere a sí mismo con el pronombre "yo" y la conjugación en primera persona del singular.

METAPHOR / METÁFORA Una *metáfora* es una figura retórica que se utiliza para identificar una cosa con algo distinto. Una metáfora, al igual que un símil, se obtiene identificando las similitudes que comparten dos cosas distintas.

MYTH / MITO Un *mito* es un relato de no ficción que describe las acciones de héroes o dioses.

MYTHOLOGY / MITOLOGÍA La *mitología* es el sistema de mitos de una cultura determinada.

NARRATION / NARRACIÓN Una *narración* es un texto que cuenta una historia. También se denomina narración a la acción de contar una historia. Cada una de estas creaciones son *textos narrativos*. Una historia contada en ficción, no ficción, poesía o incluso en drama es conocida como narración.

NARRATIVE / TEXTO NARRATIVO Un *texto narrativo* es una historia. Un texto narrativo puede ser de ficción y de no ficción. Las novelas y los cuentos son tipos de *textos narrativos de ficción*. Las biografías y las autobiografías son *textos narrativos de no ficción*. Los poemas que cuentan una historia pueden ser también textos narrativos.

NARRATOR / NARRADOR Un *narrador* es la persona o personaje que cuenta una historia. El punto de vista del narrador es la manera en la que él o ella ve las cosas. Un *narrador en tercera persona* es aquel que solo habla de la acción sin implicarse en ella. Un *narrador en primera persona* es aquel que cuenta una historia y toma parte en su acción.

NONFICTION / NO FICCIÓN Una *no ficción* es un texto en prosa que presenta y explica ideas, o que habla sobre gente, lugares, objetos o acontecimientos reales. Las autobiografías, biografías, ensayos, reportajes, cartas, memorandos y artículos periodísticos son todos diferentes tipos de no ficción.

NOVEL / NOVELA Una *novela* es una obra larga de ficción. Las novelas contienen elementos tales como los personajes, la trama, el conflicto y los escenarios. Los escritores de novelas o novelistas desarrollan estos elementos. Aparte de tu trama principal, una novela puede contener una o varias subtramas, o narraciones independientes o relacionadas con la trama principal. Una novela puede contener también diversos temas.

ONOMATOPOEIA / ONOMATOPEYA Una *onomatopeya* es el uso de palabras que imitan sonidos. *Cataplam, zzzzzz, zas, din don, glu glu glu, achís* y *crag* son ejemplos de onomatopeyas. El *cuco*, la *urraca* y el *pitirre* son nombres onomatopéyicos de aves.

La onomatopeya puede ayudar al lector a sumergirse en la descripción de un poema.

OPINION / OPINIÓN Una *opinión* es una creencia que no se puede corroborar y que apela a las emociones del lector.

ORGANIZED STRUCTURE / ESTRUCTURA ORGANIZATIVA En el cuerpo de un ensayo se presentan las ideas mediante una *estructura organizativa*, como comparación y contraste o causa y efecto. El escritor debe *respaldar* las ideas mediante el uso de evidencia, ejemplos o citas.

OUTLINE / BOSQUEJO Un *bosquejo* es una lista de las ideas principales de un ensayo o presentación y ayuda a organizar las ideas en una secuencia lógica. La estructura típica de los bosquejos es la siguiente:

I. Planteamiento

II. Cuerpo de la presentación

  A. Primera idea

  B. Segunda idea

  C. Tercera idea

III. Conclusión: importancia de las ideas

OXYMORON / OXÍMORON Un *oxímoron* (pl. *oxímoron*) es una figura retórica que vincula dos palabras contrarias u opuestas con el fin de indicar que una idea o situación, que parece contradictoria o incoherente a simple vista, encierra algo de verdad cuando la analizamos detenidamente.

PACING / RITMO LITERARIO Los escritores usan el *ritmo literario* para hacer más lenta o más rápida la acción en una escena. La acción se hace más lenta al agregar descripciones y usar oraciones más largas. La acción se acelera al usar oraciones más cortas. El ritmo literario destaca una idea importante o crea suspenso.

PERSONIFICATION / PERSONIFICACIÓN La *personificación* es una figura retórica con la que se atribuyen características humanas a un animal o una cosa.

PERSUASION / PERSUASIÓN La *persuasión* se utiliza cuando escribimos o hablamos para convencer a nuestro lector o interlocutor de que debe adoptar una opinión concreta o tomar un rumbo en sus decisiones. Los editoriales periodísticos, las cartas al editor, los discursos de las campañas políticas y los anuncios utilizan la persuasión.

TÉCNICAS PERSUASIVAS Las *técnicas persuasivas* se utilizan para reforzar un argumento. La *repetición*, es decir, repetir una palabra o frase para que tenga más efecto, es una técnica persuasiva. Las *apelaciones a la autoridad* indican que alguien poderoso respalda una idea. Las *apelaciones a las emociones* influencian a los lectores mediante el uso de palabras que crean sentimientos positivos o negativos. Las *apelaciones a la razón* utilizan argumentos lógicos respaldados por hechos.

PLAYWRIGHT / DRAMATURGO Un *dramaturgo* es una persona que escribe obras de teatro. A William Shakespeare se le considera el mejor dramaturgo de la literatura inglesa.

PLOT / TRAMA La *trama* es la secuencia de acontecimientos en la cual cada uno de estos acontecimientos es el resultado de otro acontecimiento anterior y la causa de uno nuevo que lo sigue. En la mayoría de novelas, dramas, relatos y poemas narrativos, la trama contiene personajes y un conflicto central. La trama suele comenzar con un *planteamiento* o introducción que presenta los escenarios, los personajes y la situación básica. Los sucesos aumentan la tensión del conflicto mediante la *acción ascendente* hasta que alcanza el punto más elevado de interés o suspenso, el *clímax.* El clímax va seguido de una *acción descendente* del conflicto central. Todos los acontecimientos que ocurren durante la *acción descendente*, o final, forman el *desenlace*.

Algunas tramas no tienen todas estas partes. Algunas historias comienzan con la acción ascendente y acaban con un desenlace.

Presentación del conflicto

POETRY / POESÍA La *poesía* es uno de los tres géneros más importantes de la literatura junto con la prosa y el drama. La mayoría de los poemas utilizan lenguaje muy conciso, musical y cargado de emoción. Muchos también emplean imágenes, lenguaje figurado y recursos sonoros como la rima, el ritmo, la repetición y la onomatopeya. Los tipos de poesía más importante son la poesía lírica, la poesía narrativa y la poesía concreta.

POINT OF VIEW / PUNTO DE VISTA El *punto de vista* es la perspectiva, el punto de observación, desde el que se cuenta una historia. Puede tratarse de un narrador situado fuera de la historia o un personaje dentro de ella. El *punto de vista en primera persona* corresponde a un personaje que utiliza la primera persona "yo" o la conjugación de los verbos en primera persona del singular.

Los dos tipos de *punto de vista en tercera persona*, parcial y omnisciente, son conocidos como "tercera persona" porque el narrador utiliza los pronombres de tercera persona como "él" y "ella" y la conjugación de los verbos en tercera persona para referirse a los personajes. Por el contrario, no se utiliza el pronombre "yo".

En las historias contadas desde el *punto de vista en tercera persona omnisciente*, el narrador sabe y cuenta todo lo que sienten y piensan los personajes.

En las historia contadas desde el *punto de vista en tercera persona limitado*, el narrador relata los pensamientos y sentimientos de solo un personaje, y se cuenta todo desde la perspectiva de este personaje.

PROSE / PROSA La *prosa* es la forma más corriente del lenguaje escrito. La mayoría de los textos escritos que no se consideran poesía, drama ni canción son textos en prosa. La prosa es uno de los géneros más importantes de la literatura y puede ser de ficción o de no ficción.

PROTAGONIST / PROTAGONISTA El *protagonista* es el personaje principal de una obra literaria. Aunque suele ser una persona, a veces puede tratarse también de un animal.

REPETITION / REPETICIÓN La *repetición* se da cuando se utiliza más de una vez cualquier elemento del lenguaje (un sonido, una palabra, una expresión, un sintagma o una oración). La repetición se emplea tanto en prosa como en poesía.

RESOLUTION / DESENLACE El *desenlace* es la resolución del conflicto en una trama.

RHYTHM / RITMO El *ritmo* es el patrón de sílabas acentuadas y átonas en el lenguaje hablado o escrito.

SCENE / ESCENA Una *escena* es una sección de acción ininterrumpida dentro de alguno de los actos de un drama.

SCIENCE FICTION / CIENCIA FICCIÓN La *ciencia ficción* combina elementos de ficción y fantásticos con hechos científicos. Muchas historias de cienca ficción están situadas en el futuro.

SENSORY LANGUAGE / LENGUAJE SENSORIAL El *lenguaje sensorial* es texto o diálogo que tiene relación con uno o varios de los cinco sentidos.

SETTING / ESCENARIO El *escenario* de una obra literaria es el tiempo y lugar en los que ocurre la acción. El escenario incluye todos los detalles sobre el tiempo y el lugar: el año, el momento del día o incluso el tiempo atmosférico. El lugar puede ser un país concreto, un estado, una región, una comunidad, un barrio, un edificio, una institución o el propio hogar. Los detalles como los dialectos, ropa, costumbres y medios de trasporte se emplean con frecuencia para componer el escenario. En la mayoría de historias, los escenarios sirven de telón de fondo, es decir, de contexto en el que los personajes interactúan. El escenario también puede contribuir a crear una cierta sensación o un ambiente.

SHORT STORY / CUENTO Un *cuento* es una obra corta de ficción. Al igual que sucede en una novela, los cuentos presentan una secuencia de acontecimientos o trama. La trama suele contener un conflico central al que se enfrenta un personaje principal o protagonista. Los acontecimientos en un cuento normalmente comunican un mensaje sobre la vida o la naturaleza humana. Este mensaje o idea central es el tema de la historia.

SIMILE / SÍMIL Un *símil* es una figura retórica que utiliza *como* o *igual que* para establecer una comparación entre dos ideas distintas. Las conversaciones que mantenemos a diario también contienen símiles como, por ejemplo, "pálido como un muerto", "se expande igual que un incendio" y "listo como un zorro".

SOUND DEVICES / RECURSOS SONOROS Los poetas usan *recursos sonoros* para crear efectos musicales, enfatizar el mensaje, desarrollar el tono y resaltar la relación sonora entre las palabras. Algunos de los recursos sonoros son: *repetición, onomatopeya, aliteración, consonancia* y *asonancia.*

SPEAKER / YO POÉTICO El *yo poético* es la voz imaginaria que emplea un poeta cuando escribe un poema. El yo poético es el personaje que dice el poema. Este personaje o voz no suele identificarse con un nombre. Hay notables diferencias entre el poeta y el yo poético.

STAGE DIRECTIONS / ACOTACIONES Las *acotaciones* son notas que se pueden encontrar en un texto dramático en las que se describe como se debe interpretar o escenificar la obra. Las acotaciones suelen aparecer en cursiva y encerradas entre paréntesis o corchetes. Algunas acotaciones describen los movimientos, el vestuario, los estados de ánimo y el modo en el que deben hablar los personajes.

STAGING / ESCENOGRAFÍA La *escenografía* engloba la ambientación, iluminación, vestuario, efectos especiales, música y baile que deben aparecer en el escenario donde se representa un drama.

STANZA / ESTROFA Una *estrofa* es un grupo de versos de un poema que suelen tener el mismo tamaño y patrón, y están separadas por espacios entre ellas. Una estrofa es como un párrafo en poesía: presenta y desarrolla una única idea principal.

SYMBOL / SÍMBOLO Un *símbolo* es algo que simboliza o representa una cosa diferente. Los símbolos son muy comunes en nuestra vida diaria. Una paloma con una rama de olivo en el pico es un símbolo de la paz. Una mujer con los ojos vendados sujetando una balanza es un símbolo de la justicia. Una corona es un símbolo del poder y la autoridad de un rey.

SYMBOLISM / SIMBOLISMO El *simbolismo* es el uso de los símbolos. El simbolismo juega un papel importante en muchos tipos de literatura. Puede ayudar a destacar algunos elementos que el autor quiere subrayar y añadir otros niveles de significado.

SYNTAX / SINTAXIS El orden de las palabras en una oración es la *sintaxis*. Los poetas suelen jugar con la sintaxis para resaltar las ideas.

TECHNICAL LANGUAGE / LENGUAJE TÉCNICO El *lenguaje técnico* son las palabras o terminología que se usa para hablar de un tema, proceso o industria en particular.

THEME / TEMA El *tema* es la idea central, asunto o propósito de una obra literaria. Un tema se expresa comúnmente como una generalización o declaración general sobre los seres humanos o la vida. El tema de una obra no es el resumen de su trama. El tema es la idea central del escritor.

Aunque el tema puede ser expuesto directamente en el texto, a menudo se suele presentar indirectamente. Cuando se expone el tema indirecta o implícitamente, el lector podrá deducirlo observando lo que se muestra en la obra sobre la vida y las personas.

THESIS / TESIS La *tesis* es una oración que expresa la idea principal de un ensayo.

TONE / TONO El *tono* de una obra literaria es la actitud del escritor hacia sus lectores o aquello sobre lo que escribe. El tono puede ser descrito con un único adjetivo como, por ejemplo, *formal* o *informal, serio* o *jocoso, amargo* o *irónico.* Los factores que contribuyen a crear el tono son la elección de las palabras, la estructura de la oración, el tamaño de un verso, la rima, el ritmo y la repetición.

TOPIC SENTENCE / ORACIÓN TEMÁTICA Cada uno de los párrafos de un ensayo debe tener una *oración temática* que expresa la idea principal del párrafo. El párrafo debe también tener datos y ejemplos que respalden la idea principal.

UNIVERSAL THEME / TEMA UNIVERSAL Un *tema universal* es un mensaje sobre la vida que se expresa habitualmente en muchas culturas y períodos históricos diferentes. Los cuentos populares, epopeyas y romances suelen abordar temas universales como la importancia de la valentía, el poder del amor o el peligro de la avaricia.

VERSE / VERSO El *verso* es un tipo de literatura también conocida como poesía. El *verso libre* no sigue un patrón regular y rítmico, es decir, no sigue la métrica. El poeta es libre para escribir versos de distintas extensiones o con diferente cantidad de acentos. Por lo tanto, el verso libre es menos restrictivo que el *verso métrico*, en el cual los versos deben tener una extensión determinada y un número particular de acentos.

VOICE / VOZ La voz describe el estilo particular del escritor. La voz del escritor se ve influenciada por la *elección de palabras*, es decir, la preferencia y uso que el escritor hace de ciertas palabras; la *estructura de las oraciones* o manera en la que el escritor construye las oraciones; y el *tono* o actitud del escritor hacia aquello sobre lo que escribe.

GRAMMAR HANDBOOK

PARTS OF SPEECH

Every English word, depending on its meaning and its use in a sentence, can be identified as one of the eight parts of speech. These are nouns, pronouns, verbs, adjectives, adverbs, prepositions, conjunctions, and interjections. Understanding the parts of speech will help you learn the rules of English grammar and usage.

Nouns A **noun** names a person, place, or thing. A **common noun** names any one of a class of persons, places, or things. A **proper noun** names a specific person, place, or thing.

Common Noun	Proper Noun
writer, country, novel	Charles Dickens, Great Britain, *Hard Times*

Pronouns A **pronoun** is a word that stands for one or more nouns. The word to which a pronoun refers (whose place it takes) is the **antecedent** of the pronoun.

A **personal pronoun** refers to the person speaking (first person); the person spoken to (second person); or the person, place, or thing spoken about (third person).

	Singular	Plural
First Person	I, me, my, mine	we, us, our, ours
Second Person	you, your, yours	you, your, yours
Third Person	he, him, his, she, her, hers, it, its	they, them, their, theirs

A **reflexive pronoun** reflects the action of a verb back on its subject. It indicates that the person or thing performing the action also is receiving the action.

I keep *myself* fit by taking a walk every day.

An **intensive pronoun** adds emphasis to a noun or pronoun.

It took the work of the president *himself* to pass the law.

A **demonstrative** pronoun points out a specific person(s), place(s), or thing(s).

this, that, these, those

A **relative pronoun** begins a subordinate clause and connects it to another idea in the sentence.

that, which, who, whom, whose

An **interrogative pronoun** begins a question.

what, which, who, whom, whose

An **indefinite pronoun** refers to a person, place, or thing that may or may not be specifically named.

all, another, any, both, each, everyone, few, most, none, no one, somebody

Verbs A **verb** expresses action or the existence of a state or condition.

An **action verb** tells what action someone or something is performing.

gather, read, work, jump, imagine, analyze, conclude

A **linking verb** connects the subject with another word that identifies or describes the subject. The most common linking verb is *be*.

appear, be, become, feel, look, remain, seem, smell, sound, stay, taste

A **helping verb,** or **auxiliary verb,** is added to a main verb to make a verb phrase.

be, do, have, should, can, could, may, might, must, will, would

Adjectives An **adjective** modifies a noun or pronoun by describing it or giving it a more specific meaning. An adjective answers the questions:

What kind?	*purple* hat, *happy* face, *loud* sound
Which one?	*this* bowl
How many?	*three* cars
How much?	*enough* food

The articles *the, a,* and *an* are adjectives.

A **proper adjective** is an adjective derived from a proper noun.

French, Shakespearean

Adverbs An **adverb** modifies a verb, an adjective, or another adverb by telling *where, when, how,* or *to what extent.*

will answer *soon, extremely* sad, calls *more* often

Prepositions A **preposition** relates a noun or pronoun that appears with it to another word in the sentence.

Dad made a meal *for* us. We talked *till* dusk. Bo missed school *because of* his illness.

Conjunctions A **conjunction** connects words or groups of words. A **coordinating conjunction** joins words or groups of words of equal rank.

bread *and* cheese, brief *but* powerful

Correlative conjunctions are used in pairs to connect words or groups of words of equal importance.

both Luis *and* Rosa, *neither* you *nor* I

Subordinating conjunctions indicate the connection between two ideas by placing one below the other in rank or importance. A subordinating conjunction introduces a subordinate, or dependent, clause.

> We will miss her *if* she leaves. Hank shrieked *when* he slipped on the ice.

Interjections An **interjection** expresses feeling or emotion. It is not related to other words in the sentence.

> ah, hey, ouch, well, yippee

PHRASES AND CLAUSES

Phrases A **phrase** is a group of words that does not have both a subject and a verb and that functions as one part of speech. A phrase expresses an idea but cannot stand alone.

Prepositional Phrases A **prepositional phrase** is a group of words that begins with a preposition and ends with a noun or pronoun that is the **object of the preposition.**

> before dawn   as a result of the rain

An **adjective phrase** is a prepositional phrase that modifies a noun or pronoun.

> Eliza appreciates the beauty **of a well-crafted poem.**

An **adverb phrase** is a prepositional phrase that modifies a verb, an adjective, or an adverb.

> She reads Spenser's sonnets **with great pleasure.**

Appositive Phrases An **appositive** is a noun or pronoun placed next to another noun or pronoun to add information about it. An **appositive phrase** consists of an appositive and its modifiers.

> Mr. Roth, **my music teacher,** is sick.

Verbal Phrases A **verbal** is a verb form that functions as a different part of speech (not as a verb) in a sentence. **Participles, gerunds,** and **infinitives** are verbals.

A **verbal phrase** includes a verbal and any modifiers or complements it may have. Verbal phrases may function as nouns, as adjectives, or as adverbs.

A **participle** is a verb form that can act as an adjective. Present participles end in *-ing;* past participles of regular verbs end in *-ed.*

A **participial phrase** consists of a participle and its modifiers or complements. The entire phrase acts as an adjective.

> Jenna's backpack, **loaded with equipment,** was heavy.
> **Barking incessantly,** the dogs chased the squirrels out of sight.

A **gerund** is a verb form that ends in *-ing* and is used as a noun.

A **gerund phrase** consists of a gerund with any modifiers or complements, all acting together as a noun.

> **Taking photographs of wildlife** is her main hobby. [acts as subject]
> We always enjoy **listening to live music.** [acts as object]

An **infinitive** is a verb form, usually preceded by *to,* that can act as a noun, an adjective, or an adverb.

An **infinitive phrase** consists of an infinitive and its modifiers or complements, and sometimes its subject, all acting together as a single part of speech.

> She tries **to get out into the wilderness often.** [acts as a noun; direct object of *tries*]
> The Tigers are the team **to beat.** [acts as an adjective; describes *team*]
> I drove twenty miles **to witness the event.** [acts as an adverb; tells why I drove]

Clauses A **clause** is a group of words with its own subject and verb.

Independent Clauses An independent clause can stand by itself as a complete sentence.

> George Orwell wrote with extraordinary insight.

Subordinate Clauses A subordinate clause cannot stand by itself as a complete sentence. Subordinate clauses always appear connected in some way with one or more independent clauses.

> George Orwell, **who wrote with extraordinary insight,** produced many politically relevant works.

An **adjective clause** is a subordinate clause that acts as an adjective. It modifies a noun or a pronoun by telling *what kind* or *which one.* Also called relative clauses, adjective clauses usually begin with a **relative pronoun:** *who, which, that, whom,* or *whose.*

> "The Lamb" is the poem **that I memorized for class.**

An **adverb clause** is a subordinate clause that, like an adverb, modifies a verb, an adjective, or an adverb. An adverb clause tells *where, when, in what way, to what extent, under what condition,* or *why.*

The students will read another poetry collection **if their schedule allows.**

When I recited the poem, Mr. Lopez was impressed.

A **noun clause** is a subordinate clause that acts as a noun.

William Blake survived on **whatever he made as an engraver.**

SENTENCE STRUCTURE

Subject and Predicate A **sentence** is a group of words that expresses a complete thought. A sentence has two main parts: a *subject* and a *predicate*.

A **fragment** is a group of words that does not express a complete thought. It lacks an independent clause.

The **subject** tells *whom* or *what* the sentence is about. The **predicate** tells what the subject of the sentence does or is.

A subject or a predicate can consist of a single word or of many words. All the words in the subject make up the **complete subject.** All the words in the predicate make up the **complete predicate.**

Complete Subject	Complete Predicate
Both of those girls	have already read *Macbeth*.

The **simple subject** is the essential noun, pronoun, or group of words acting as a noun that cannot be left out of the complete subject. The **simple predicate** is the essential verb or verb phrase that cannot be left out of the complete predicate.

Both of those girls | **have** already **read** *Macbeth*.
[Simple subject: *Both;* simple predicate: *have read*]

A **compound subject** is two or more subjects that have the same verb and are joined by a conjunction.

Neither the horse nor the driver looked tired.

A **compound predicate** is two or more verbs that have the same subject and are joined by a conjunction.

She **sneezed and coughed** throughout the trip.

Complements A **complement** is a word or word group that completes the meaning of the subject or verb in a sentence. There are four kinds of complements: *direct objects, indirect objects, objective complements,* and *subject complements.*

A **direct object** is a noun, a pronoun, or a group of words acting as a noun that receives the action of a transitive verb.

We watched the **liftoff**.

She drove **Zach** to the launch site.

An **indirect object** is a noun or pronoun that appears with a direct object and names the person or thing to which or for which something is done.

He sold the **family** a mirror. [The direct object is *mirror.*]

An **objective complement** is an adjective or noun that appears with a direct object and describes or renames it.

The decision made her **unhappy**.
[The direct object is *her.*]

Many consider Shakespeare the greatest **playwright.** [The direct object is *Shakespeare.*]

A **subject complement** follows a linking verb and tells something about the subject. There are two kinds: *predicate nominatives* and *predicate adjectives.*

A **predicate nominative** is a noun or pronoun that follows a linking verb and identifies or renames the subject.

"A Modest Proposal" is a **pamphlet.**

A **predicate adjective** is an adjective that follows a linking verb and describes the subject of the sentence.

"A Modest Proposal" is **satirical.**

Classifying Sentences by Structure

Sentences can be classified according to the kind and number of clauses they contain. The four basic sentence structures are *simple, compound, complex,* and *compound-complex.*

A **simple sentence** consists of one independent clause.

Terrence enjoys modern British literature.

A **compound sentence** consists of two or more independent clauses. The clauses are joined by a conjunction or a semicolon.

Terrence enjoys modern British literature, but his brother prefers the classics.

A **complex sentence** consists of one independent clause and one or more subordinate clauses.

Terrence, who reads voraciously, enjoys modern British literature.

A **compound-complex sentence** consists of two or more independent clauses and one or more subordinate clauses.

Terrence, who reads voraciously, enjoys modern British literature, but his brother prefers the classics.

Classifying Sentences by Function

Sentences can be classified according to their function or purpose. The four types are *declarative, interrogative, imperative,* and *exclamatory.*

A **declarative sentence** states an idea and ends with a period.

An **interrogative sentence** asks a question and ends with a question mark.

An **imperative sentence** gives an order or a direction and ends with either a period or an exclamation mark.

An **exclamatory sentence** conveys a strong emotion and ends with an exclamation mark.

PARAGRAPH STRUCTURE

An effective paragraph is organized around one **main idea,** which is often stated in a **topic sentence.** The other sentences support the main idea. To give the paragraph **unity,** make sure the connection between each sentence and the main idea is clear.

Unnecessary Shift in Person

Do not change needlessly from one grammatical person to another. Keep the person consistent in your sentences.

> **Max** went to the bakery, but **you** can't buy mints there. [shift from third person to second person]

> **Max** went to the bakery, but **he** can't buy mints there. [consistent]

Unnecessary Shift in Voice

Do not change needlessly from active voice to passive voice in your use of verbs.

> Elena and I **searched** the trail for evidence, but no clues **were found.** [shift from active voice to passive voice]

> Elena and I **searched** the trail for evidence, but we **found** no clues. [consistent]

AGREEMENT

Subject and Verb Agreement

A singular subject must have a singular verb. A plural subject must have a plural verb.

> **Dr. Boone uses** a telescope to view the night sky.
> The **students use** a telescope to view the night sky.

A verb always agrees with its subject, not its object.

> *Incorrect:* The best part of the show were the jugglers.
> *Correct:* The best part of the show was the jugglers.

A phrase or clause that comes between a subject and verb does not affect subject-verb agreement.

> His **theory**, as well as his claims, **lacks** support.

Two subjects joined by *and* usually take a plural verb.

> The **dog** and the **cat are** healthy.

Two singular subjects joined by *or* or *nor* take a singular verb.

> The **dog** or the **cat is** hiding.

Two plural subjects joined by *or* or *nor* take a plural verb.

> The **dogs** or the **cats are** coming home with us.

When a singular and a plural subject are joined by *or* or *nor,* the verb agrees with the closer subject.

> Either the **dogs** or the **cat is** behind the door.
> Either the **cat** or the **dogs are** behind the door.

Pronoun and Antecedent Agreement

Pronouns must agree with their antecedents in number and gender. Use singular pronouns with singular antecedents and plural pronouns with plural antecedents.

> **Doris Lessing** uses **her** writing to challenge ideas about women's roles.
> **Writers** often use **their** skills to promote social change.

Use a singular pronoun when the antecedent is a singular indefinite pronoun such as *anybody, each, either, everybody, neither, no one, one,* or *someone.*

> Judge **each** of the articles on **its** merits.

Use a plural pronoun when the antecedent is a plural indefinite pronoun such as *both, few, many,* or *several.*

> **Both** of the articles have **their** flaws.

The indefinite pronouns *all, any, more, most, none,* and *some* can be singular or plural depending on the number of the word to which they refer.

> **Most** of the *books* are in **their** proper places.
> **Most** of the *book* has been torn from **its** binding.

Principal Parts of Regular and Irregular Verbs

A verb has four principal parts:

Present	Present Participle	Past	Past Participle
learn	learning	learned	learned
discuss	discussing	discussed	discussed
stand	standing	stood	stood
begin	beginning	began	begun

Regular verbs such as *learn* and *discuss* form the past and past participle by adding *-ed* to the present form. **Irregular verbs** such as *stand* and *begin* form the past and past participle in other ways. If you are in doubt about the principal parts of an irregular verb, check a dictionary.

The Tenses of Verbs

The different tenses of verbs indicate the time an action or condition occurs.

The **present tense** expresses an action that happens regularly or states a current condition or general truth.

> Tourists **flock** to the site yearly.

Daily exercise **is** good for your heallth.

The **past tense** expresses a completed action or a condition that is no longer true.

> The squirrel **dropped** the nut and **ran** up the tree.
> I **was** very tired last night by 9:00.

The **future tense** indicates an action that will happen in the future or a condition that will be true.

> The Glazers **will visit** us tomorrow.
> They **will be** glad to arrive from their long journey.

The **present perfect tense** expresses an action that happened at an indefinite time in the past or an action that began in the past and continues into the present.

> Someone **has cleaned** the trash from the park.
> The puppy **has been** under the bed all day.

The **past perfect tense** shows an action that was completed before another action in the past.

> Gerard **had revised** his essay before he turned it in.

The **future perfect tense** indicates an action that will have been completed before another action takes place.

> Mimi **will have painted** the kitchen by the time we finish the shutters.

Degrees of Comparison

Adjectives and adverbs take different forms to show the three degrees of comparison: the *positive*, the *comparative*, and the *superlative*.

Positive	Comparative	Superlative
fast	faster	fastest
crafty	craftier	craftiest
abruptly	more abruptly	most abruptly
badly	worse	worst

Using Comparative and Superlative Adjectives and Adverbs

Use comparative adjectives and adverbs to compare two things. Use superlative adjectives and adverbs to compare three or more things.

> This season's weather was **drier** than last year's.
> This season has been one of the **driest** on record.
> Jake practices **more often** than Jamal.
> Of everyone in the band, Jake practices **most often.**

Pronoun Case

The **case** of a pronoun is the form it takes to show its function in a sentence. There are three pronoun cases: *nominative*, *objective*, and *possessive*.

Nominative	Objective	Possessive
I, you, he, she, it, we, you, they	me, you, him, her, it, us, you, them	my, your, yours, his, her, hers, its, our, ours, their, theirs

Use the **nominative case** when a pronoun functions as a *subject* or as a *predicate nominative*.

> **They** are going to the movies. [subject]

The biggest movie fan is **she.** [predicate nominative]

Use the **objective case** for a pronoun acting as a *direct object*, an *indirect object*, or the *object of a preposition*.

> The ending of the play surprised **me**. [direct object]
> Mary gave **us** two tickets to the play. [indirect object]
> The audience cheered for **him.** [object of preposition]

Use the **possessive case** to show ownership.

> The red suitcase is **hers.**

Diction The words you choose contribute to the overall effectiveness of your writing. **Diction** refers to word choice and to the clearness and correctness of those words. You can improve one aspect of your diction by choosing carefully between commonly confused words, such as the pairs listed below.

accept, except

Accept is a verb that means "to receive" or "to agree to." *Except* is a preposition that means "other than" or "leaving out."

> Please **accept** my offer to buy you lunch this weekend.

> He is busy every day **except** the weekends.

affect, effect

Affect is normally a verb meaning "to influence" or "to bring about a change in." *Effect* is usually a noun meaning "result."

> The distractions outside **affect** Steven's ability to concentrate.

> The teacher's remedies had a positive **effect** on Steven's ability to concentrate.

among, between

Among is usually used with three or more items, and it emphasizes collective relationships or indicates distribution. *Between* is generally used with only two items, but it can be used with more than two if the emphasis is on individual (one-to-one) relationships within the group.

> I had to choose a snack **among** the various vegetables.

> He handed out the booklets **among** the conference participants.

> Our school is **between** a park and an old barn.

> The tournament included matches **between** France, Spain, Mexico, and the United States.

amount, number

Amount refers to overall quantity and is mainly used with mass nouns (those that can't be counted). *Number* refers to individual items that can be counted.

> The **amount** of attention that great writers have paid to Shakespeare is remarkable.

> A **number** of important English writers have been fascinated by the legend of King Arthur.

assure, ensure, insure

Assure means "to convince [someone of something]; to guarantee." *Ensure* means "to make certain [that something happens]." *Insure* means "to arrange for payment in case of loss."

> The attorney **assured** us we'd win the case.

> The rules **ensure** that no one gets treated unfairly.

> Many professional musicians **insure** their valuable instruments.

bad, badly

Use the adjective *bad* before a noun or after linking verbs such as *feel, look,* and *seem.* Use *badly* whenever an adverb is required.

> The situation may seem **bad**, but it will improve over time.

> Though our team played **badly** today, we will focus on practicing for the next match.

beside, besides

Beside means "at the side of" or "close to." *Besides* means "in addition to."

> The stapler sits **beside** the pencil sharpener in our classroom.

> **Besides** being very clean, the classroom is also very organized.

can, may

The helping verb *can* generally refers to the ability to do something. The helping verb *may* generally refers to permission to do something.

> I **can** run one mile in six minutes.

> **May** we have a race during recess?

complement, compliment

The verb *complement* means "to enhance"; the verb *compliment* means "to praise."

> Online exercises **complement** the textbook lessons.

> Ms. Lewis **complimented** our team on our excellent debate.

compose, comprise

Compose means "to make up; constitute." *Comprise* means "to include or contain." Remember that the whole comprises its parts or is composed of its parts, and the parts compose the whole.

> The assignment **comprises** three different tasks.

> The assignment is **composed** of three different tasks.

> Three different tasks **compose** the assignment.

different from, different than

Different from is generally preferred over *different than*, but *different than* can be used before a clause. Always use *different from* before a noun or pronoun.

> Your point of view is so **different from** mine.

> His idea was so **different from** [or **different than**] what we had expected.

farther, further

Use *farther* to refer to distance. Use *further* to mean "to a greater degree or extent" or "additional."

> Chiang has traveled **farther** than anybody else in the class.

> If I want **further** details about his travels, I can read his blog.

fewer, less

Use *fewer* for things that can be counted. Use *less* for amounts or quantities that cannot be counted. *Fewer* must be followed by a plural noun.

> **Fewer** students drive to school since the weather improved.
>
> There is **less** noise outside in the mornings.

good, well

Use the adjective *good* before a noun or after a linking verb. Use *well* whenever an adverb is required, such as when modifying a verb.

> I feel **good** after sleeping for eight hours.
>
> I did **well** on my test, and my soccer team played **well** in that afternoon's game. It was a **good** day!

its, it's

The word *its* with no apostrophe is a possessive pronoun. The word *it's* is a contraction of "it is."

> Angelica will try to fix the computer and **its** keyboard.
>
> **It's** a difficult job, but she can do it.

lay, lie

Lay is a transitive verb meaning "to set or put something down." Its principal parts are *lay, laying, laid, laid. Lie* is an intransitive verb meaning "to recline" or "to exist in a certain place." Its principal parts are *lie, lying, lay, lain.*

> Please **lay** that box down and help me with the sofa.
>
> When we are done moving, I am going to **lie** down.
>
> My hometown **lies** sixty miles north of here.

like, as

Like is a preposition that usually means "similar to" and precedes a noun or pronoun. The conjunction *as* means "in the way that" and usually precedes a clause.

> **Like** the other students, I was prepared for a quiz.
>
> **As** I said yesterday, we expect to finish before noon.

Use **such as,** not **like,** before a series of examples.

> Foods **such as** apples, nuts, and pretzels make good snacks.

of, have

Do not use *of* in place of *have* after auxiliary verbs such as *would, could, should, may, might,* or *must.* The contraction of *have* is formed by adding *-ve* after these verbs.

> I **would have** stayed after school today, but I had to help cook at home.
>
> Mom **must've** called while I was still in the gym.

principal, principle

Principal can be an adjective meaning "main; most important." It can also be a noun meaning "chief officer of a school." *Principle* is a noun meaning "moral rule" or "fundamental truth."

> His strange behavior was the **principal** reason for our concern.
>
> Democratic **principles** form the basis of our country's laws.

raise, rise

Raise is a transitive verb that usually takes a direct object. *Rise* is intransitive and never takes a direct object.

> Iliana and Josef **raise** the flag every morning.
>
> They **rise** from their seats and volunteer immediately whenever help is needed.

than, then

The conjunction *than* is used to connect the two parts of a comparison. The adverb *then* usually refers to time.

> My backpack is heavier **than** hers.
>
> I will finish my homework and **then** meet my friends at the park.

that, which, who

Use the relative pronoun *that* to refer to things or people. Use *which* only for things and *who* only for people.

That introduces a restrictive phrase or clause, that is, one that is essential to the meaning of the sentence. *Which* introduces a nonrestrictive phrase or clause—one that adds information but could be deleted from the sentence—and is preceded by a comma.

> Ben ran to the park **that** just reopened.
>
> The park, **which** just reopened, has many attractions.
>
> The man **who** built the park loves to see people smiling.

when, where, why

Do not use *when, where,* or *why* directly after a linking verb, such as *is.* Reword the sentence.

> *Incorrect:* The morning is when he left for the beach.
>
> *Correct:* He left for the beach in the morning.

who, whom

In formal writing, use *who* only as a subject in clauses and sentences. Use *whom* only as the object of a verb or of a preposition.

> **Who** paid for the tickets?
>
> **Whom** should I pay for the tickets?
>
> I can't recall to **whom** I gave the money for the tickets.

your, you're

Your is a possessive pronoun expressing ownership. *You're* is the contraction of "you are."

> Have you finished writing **your** informative essay?
>
> **You're** supposed to turn it in tomorrow. If **you're** late, **your** grade will be affected.

Capitalization

First Words

Capitalize the first word of a sentence.

Stories about knights and their deeds interest me.

Capitalize the first word of direct speech.

Sharon asked, "Do you like stories about knights?"

Capitalize the first word of a quotation that is a complete sentence.

Einstein said, "Anyone who has never made a mistake has never tried anything new."

Proper Nouns and Proper Adjectives

Capitalize all proper nouns, including geographical names, historical events and periods, and names of organizations.

Thames River	John Keats	the Renaissance
United Nations	World War II	Sierra Nevada

Capitalize all proper adjectives.

Shakespearean play	British invaision
American citizen	Latin American literature

Academic Course Names

Capitalize course names only if they are language courses, are followed by a number, or are preceded by a proper noun or adjective.

Spanish	Honors Chemistry	History 101
geology	algebra	social studies

Titles

Capitalize personal titles when followed by the person's name.

Ms. Hughes   Dr. Perez   King George

Capitalize titles showing family relationships when they are followed by a specific person's name, unless they are preceded by a possessive noun or pronoun.

Uncle Oscar   Mangan's sister   his aunt Tessa

Capitalize the first word and all other key words in the titles of books, stories, songs, and other works of art.

Frankenstein   "Shooting an Elephant"

Punctuation

End Marks

Use a **period** to end a declarative sentence or an imperative sentence.

We are studying the structure of sonnets.
Read the biography of Mary Shelley.

Use periods with initials and abbreviations.

D. H. Lawrence	Mrs. Browning
Mt. Everest	Maple St.

Use a **question mark** to end an interrogative sentence.

What is Macbeth's fatal flaw?

Use an **exclamation mark** after an exclamatory sentence or a forceful imperative sentence.

That's a beautiful painting!   Let me go now!

Commas

Use a **comma** before a coordinating conjunction to separate two independent clauses in a compound sentence.

The game was very close, but we were victorious.

Use commas to separate three or more words, phrases, or clauses in a series.

William Blake was a writer, artist, and printer.

Use commas to separate coordinate adjectives.

It was a witty, amusing novel.

Use a comma after an introductory word, phrase, or clause.

When the novelist finished his book, he celebrated with his family.

Use commas to set off nonessential expressions.

Old English, of course, requires translation.

Use commas with places and dates.

Coventry, England   September 1, 1939

Semicolons

Use a **semicolon** to join closely related independent clauses that are not already joined by a conjunction.

Tanya likes to write poetry; Heather prefers prose.

Use semicolons to avoid confusion when items in a series contain commas.

They traveled to London, England; Madrid, Spain; and Rome, Italy.

Colons

Use a **colon** before a list of items following an independent clause.

Notable Victorian poets include the following: Tennyson, Arnold, Housman, and Hopkins.

Use a colon to introduce information that summarizes or explains the independent clause before it.

She just wanted to do one thing: rest.

Malcolm loves volunteering: He reads to sick children every Saturday afternoon.

Quotation Marks

Use **quotation marks** to enclose a direct quotation.

"Short stories," Ms. Hildebrand said, "should have rich, well-developed characters."

An **indirect quotation** does not require quotation marks.

Ms. Hildebrand said that short stories should have well-developed characters.

Use quotation marks around the titles of short written works, episodes in a series, songs, and works mentioned as parts of collections.

"The Lagoon"   "Boswell Meets Johnson"

Italics

Italicize the titles of long written works, movies, television and radio shows, lengthy works of music, paintings, and sculptures.

Howards End   *60 Minutes*   *Guernica*

For handwritten material, you can use underlining instead of italics.

<u>The Princess Bride</u>   <u>Mona Lisa</u>

Dashes

Use **dashes** to indicate an abrupt change of thought, a dramatic interrupting idea, or a summary statement.

I read the entire first act of *Macbeth*—you won't believe what happens next.

The director—what's her name again?—attended the movie premiere.

Hyphens

Use a **hyphen** with certain numbers, after certain prefixes, with two or more words used as one word, and with a compound modifier that comes before a noun.

seventy-two

self-esteem

president-elect

five-year contract

Parentheses

Use **parentheses** to set off asides and explanations when the material is not essential or when it consists of one or more sentences. When the sentence in parentheses interrupts the larger sentence, it does not have a capital letter or a period.

He listened intently (it was too dark to see who was speaking) to try to identify the voices.

When a sentence in parentheses falls between two other complete sentences, it should start with a capital letter and end with a period.

The quarterback threw three touchdown passes. (We knew he could do it.) Our team won the game by two points.

Apostrophes

Add an **apostrophe** and an *s* to show the possessive case of most singular nouns and of plural nouns that do not end in *-s* or *-es*.

Blake's poems   the mice's whiskers

Names ending in *s* form their possessives in the same way, except for classical and biblical names, which add only an apostrophe to form the possessive.

Dickens's   Hercules'

Add an apostrophe to show the possessive case of plural nouns ending in *-s* and *-es*.

the girls' songs   the Ortizes' car

Use an apostrophe in a contraction to indicate the position of the missing letter or letters.

She's never read a Coleridge poem she didn't like.

Brackets

Use **brackets** to enclose clarifying information inserted within a quotation.

Columbus's journal entry from October 21, 1492, begins as follows: "At 10 o'clock, we arrived at a cape of the island [San Salvador], and anchored, the other vessels in company."

Ellipses

Use three ellipsis points, also known as an **ellipsis,** to indicate where you have omitted words from quoted material.

Wollestonecraft wrote, "The education of women has of late been more attended to than formerly; yet they are still . . . ridiculed or pitied. . . ."

In the example above, the four dots at the end of the sentence are the three ellipsis points plus the period from the original sentence.

Use an ellipsis to indicate a pause or interruption in speech.

"When he told me the news," said the coach, "I was . . . I was shocked . . . completely shocked."

Spelling

Spelling Rules

Learning the rules of English spelling will help you make **generalizations** about how to spell words.

Word Parts

The three word parts that can combine to form a word are roots, prefixes, and suffixes. Many of these word parts come from the Greek, Latin, and Anglo-Saxon languages.

The **root word** carries a word's basic meaning.

Root and Origin	Meaning	Examples
-leg- (-log-) [Gr.]	to say, speak	*legal, logic*
-pon- (-pos-) [L.]	to put, place	*postpone, deposit*

A **prefix** is one or more syllables added to the beginning of a word that alter the meaning of the root.

Prefix and Origin	Meaning	Example
anti- [Gr.]	against	*antipathy*
inter- [L.]	between	*international*
mis- [A.S.]	wrong	*misplace*

A **suffix** is a letter or group of letters added to the end of a root word that changes the word's meaning or part of speech.

Suffix and Origin	Meaning and Example	Part of Speech
-ful [A.S.]	full of: *scornful*	adjective
-ity [L.]	state of being: *adversity*	noun
-ize (-ise) [Gr.]	to make: *idolize*	verb
-ly [A.S.]	in a manner: *calmly*	adverb

Rules for Adding Suffixes to Root Words

When adding a suffix to a root word ending in *y* preceded by a consonant, change *y* to *i* unless the suffix begins with *i*.

  ply + -able = pliable   happy + -ness = happiness
  defy + -ing = defying   cry + -ing = crying

For a root word ending in *e*, drop the *e* when adding a suffix beginning with a vowel.

  drive + -ing = driving   move + -able = movable
  SOME EXCEPTIONS: traceable, seeing, dyeing

For root words ending with a consonant + vowel + consonant in a stressed syllable, double the final consonant when adding a suffix that begins with a vowel.

  mud + -y = muddy   submit + -ed = submitted
  SOME EXCEPTIONS: mixing, fixed

Rules for Adding Prefixes to Root Words

When a prefix is added to a root word, the spelling of the root remains the same.

  un- + certain = uncertain   mis- + spell = misspell

With some prefixes, the spelling of the prefix changes when joined to the root to make the pronunciation easier.

  in- + mortal = immortal   ad- + vert = avert

Orthographic Patterns

Certain letter combinations in English make certain sounds. For instance, *ph* sounds like *f*, *eigh* usually makes a long *a* sound, and the *k* before an *n* is often silent.

  pharmacy   n**eigh**bor   **k**nowledge

Understanding **orthographic patterns** such as these can help you improve your spelling.

Forming Plurals

The plural form of most nouns is formed by adding -*s* to the singular.

  computer**s**   gadget**s**   Washington**s**

For words ending in *s*, *ss*, *x*, *z*, *sh*, or *ch*, add -*es*.

  circus**es**   tax**es**   wish**es**   bench**es**

For words ending in *y* or *o* preceded by a vowel, add -*s*.

  key**s**   patio**s**

For words ending in *y* preceded by a consonant, change the *y* to an *i* and add -*es*.

  cit**ies**   enem**ies**   troph**ies**

For most words ending in *o* preceded by a consonant, add -*es*.

  echo**es**   tomato**es**

Some words form the plural in irregular ways.

  women   oxen   children   teeth   deer

Foreign Words Used in English

Some words used in English are actually foreign words that have been adopted. Learning to spell these words requires memorization. When in doubt, check a dictionary.

  sushi   enchilada   au pair   fiancé
  laissez faire   croissant

INDEX OF SKILLS

Boldface numbers indicate pages where terms are defined.

INDEX OF SKILLS

Vocabulary

Writing

INDEX OF AUTHORS AND TITLES

The following authors and titles appear in the print and online versions of *my*Perspectives.

INDEX: INDEX OF AUTHORS AND TITLES

ADDITIONAL SELECTIONS: AUTHOR AND TITLE INDEX

The following authors and titles appear in the Online Literature Library.

INDEX: INDEX OF AUTHORS AND TITLES

ACKNOWLEDGMENTS AND CREDITS

ACKNOWLEDGMENTS

The following selections appear in this grade level (Grade 6) of *my*Perspectives. Some selections appear online only.

3D Systems. *Dog Receives Prosthetic Legs Made by 3D Printer*, courtesy of 3D Systems, Inc.

BBC News Online. "Michaela DePrince: The War Orphan Who Became a Ballerina" from BBC, October 15, 2012. Used with permission; "The Girl Who Gets Gifts From Birds" from BBC, February 25, 2015. Used with permission.

BBC Worldwide Americas, Inc. *The Secret Life of the Dog*-BBC ©Two BBC Worldwide Learning; Animation of the history of exploration ©BBC Worldwide Learning.

Bloomsbury Publishing Plc. "Eleven" from *Woman Hollering Creek* by Sandra Cisneros. Copyright ©Sandra Cisneros. Used with permission of Bloomsbury Publishing.

Bolinda Publishing. Excerpted from *A Long Way Home* by Saroo Brierley with Larry Buttrose. Copyright ©2013 Saroo Brierley. Used with permission of Bolinda Publishing.

Candlewick Press and Amnesty International. "Prince Francis" from *Free? Stories about Human Rights*, edited by Roddy Doyle. Copyright ©2009 by Amnesty International. Published by Candlewick Press.

Charles Scribner's Sons. *The Wind in the Willows* by Kenneth Grahame (1908).

Chhabra, Esha. "The Importance of Imagination" by Esha Chhabra, from *The Importance of Imagination*, http://www.dailygood.org/story/207/the-importance-of-imagination/. Used with permission of the author.

Chronicle Books. "Oranges" from *New and Selected Poems* ©1995 by Gary Soto. Used with permission Chronicle Books LLC, San Francisco. Visit ChronicleBooks.com.

Column Five Media. "The Age of Exploration: Life on the Open Seas" ©2015, A&E Television Networks, LLC. All Rights Reserved.

Creative Book Services. Audio of text for "Lewis and Clark" courtesy of the author, Nick Bertozzi.

Deboodt, Ryan. *Hang Son Doong Largest Cave* ©Ryan Deboodt

DePrince, Michaela. "Michaela DePrince: Ballet Dancer" courtesy of Michaela DePrince.

Discovery Communications, LLC. "Dolphins Talk Like Humans" by Jennifer Viegas, posted on the Discovery News website on September 6, 2011. Courtesy of Discovery Communications, LLC.

Disney-Hyperion Books. *Tales of the Odyssey* by Mary Pope Osborne. Text copyright ©2002 by Mary Pope Osborne. Used by permission of Disney-Hyperion Books.

ESPN Magazine, LLC. "Best of the Spelling Bee" ©ESPN.

Etienne, Stefan. "Teens and Technology Share a Future" by Stefan Etienne, from *Huffington Post*, March 6, 2014. Copyright ©2014. Used with permission of the author.

Hanging Loose Press. "Sonnet, Without Salmon" reprinted from *What I've Stolen, What I've Earned* ©2014 by Sherman Alexie, by permission of Hanging Loose Press.

HarperCollins Publishers. *Tales of the Odyssey* by Mary Pope Osborne. Text copyright ©2002 by Mary Pope Osborne. Used by permission of HarperCollins Publishers.

Henry Holt & Company. From *Lewis & Clark* ©2011 by Nick Bertozzi. Reprinted by permission of First Second, an imprint of Roaring Book Press, a division of Holtzbrinck Publishing Holdings limited Partnership. All rights reserved.

Hogan, Linda E. "Predators" by Linda E. Hogan, from *9 Poems*. Used with permission of the author.

Houghton Mifflin Harcourt Publishing Co. *Hachiko: The True Story of a Loyal Dog* by Pamela S. Turner. Text copyright ©2004 by Pamela S. Turner. Reprinted by permission of Houghton Miffilin Harcourt Publishing Company. All rights reserved; "All Watched Over by Machines of Loving Grace" from *The Pill Versus the Springhill Mine Disaster* by Richard Brautigan. Copyright ©1968 by Richard Brautigan. Reproduced by permission of Houghton Mifflin Harcourt Publishing Company. All rights reserved; Excerpt from *Sacajawea: The Story of Bird Woman and the Lewis and Clark Expedition* by Joseph Bruchac. Copyright ©2000 by Joseph Bruchac. Reprinted by permission of Houghton Mifflin Harcourt Publishing Company. All rights reserved.

IBM Corporation. "The Internet of Things" ©IBM External Submissions.

J. Boylston & Company, LLC. From *My Life with the Chimpanzees* by Jane Goodall. Used with permission of J. Boylston & Company Publishers.

K-MB CREATIVE NETWORK NY, Inc. "Michaela DePrince: Ballet Dancer" ©K-MB Creative Network NY.

Khan, Leena. "The Black Hole of Technology" by Leena Khan, from *Huffington Post*, January 20, 2015. Used with permission of the author.

Larson, Samantha. "To the Top of Everest" by Samantha Larson. Used with permission of the author.

Loesch, Cailin. "Is Our Gain Also Our Loss?" by Cailin Loesch, from *Huffington Post*, November 14, 2014. Used with permission of the author.

MacMillan. *White Fang* by Jack London (1906).

Mountaineers Books. "The Legend of Artic Explorer Matthew Henson" ©2014. Reprinted with permission from *The Adventure Gap: Changing the Face of the Outdoors* by James Edward Mills, Mountaineers Books, Seattle.

National Geographic Creative. "People of the Horse: Special Bond" by National Geographic ©National Geographic Creative.

New York Public Radio. NPR "Bored...and Brilliant?": A Production of WNYC Studios.

NPR (National Public Radio). ©2012 National Public Radio, Inc. News report titled "Pet Therapy: How Animals And Humans Heal Each Other" by Julie Rovner was originally published on NPR.org on March 5, 2012, and is used with the permission of NPR. Any unauthorized duplication is strictly prohibited.

PARS International Corporation. "Mars Can Wait. Oceans Can't" from CNN.com, August 17, 2012 ©2012 Turner Broadcast Systems, Inc. All rights reserved. Used by permission and protected by the Copyright Laws of the United States. The printing, copying, redistribution, or retransmission of this Content without express written permission is prohibited.

Penguin Books, Ltd. (UK). "Monday, March 30, 1992," "Sunday, April 12, 1992," "Tuesday, April 14, 1992," "Saturday,

of Viking Books, an imprint of Penguin Publishing Group, a division of Penguin Random House LLC.

The Times Online. "Congo the Chimpanzee" from *The Times*, September 25, 2005. Copyright ©2005 News Syndication.

Time-Life Syndication. "Mission Twinpossible" ©2005 Time Inc. All rights reserved. Reprinted/Translated from *Time for Kids* and published with permission of Time Inc. Reproduction in any manner in any language in whole or in part without written permission is prohibited.

United Nations Publications. Declaration of the Rights of the Child, ©United Nations. Reprinted with the permission of the United Nations.

University of Pennsylvania Press. "Our Wreath of Rosebuds," from *Changing Is Not Vanishing: A Collection of American Indian Poetry to 1930* by Corinne, edited by Robert Dale Parker. Copyright ©2011. Reprinted with permission of the University of Pennsylvania Press.

Villanueva, Alma Luz. "I Was a Skinny Tomboy Kid" by Alma Luz Villanueva. Used with permission of the author.

Wall Street Journal. "Teen Researchers Defend Media Multitasking" republished with permission of Dow Jones, Inc, from *Wall Street Journal*, October 13, 2014; permission conveyed through Copyright Clearance Center, Inc.

Wesleyan University Press. Wright, James. "A Blessing" from *Above the River* ©1990 by James Wright. Reprinted with permission of Wesleyan University Press, www.wesleyan.edu/wespress.

William Morris Endeavor. "another way," "believing," "brooklyn rain," "gifted," "sometimes," "uncle robert" and "wishes" from *Brown Girl Dreaming* by Jacqueline Woodson, copyright ©2014 by Jacqueline Woodson. Used by permission William Morris Endeavor Entertainment, LLC.

William Morris Endeavor Entertainment, LLC. "The Fun They Had" from I*saac Asimov: The Complete Stories of Vol. 1* by Isaac Asimov. Copyright ©1951 by Isaac Asimov. Used with permission of William Morris Endeavor Entertainment, LLC.

WNET. "Jabberwocky" from *Through the Looking Glass* by Lewis Carroll ©WNET.

Wylie Agency. "The Shah of Blah" from *Haroun and The Sea of Stories* by Salman Rushdie. Copyright ©1990 by Salman Rushdie, used by permission of The Wylie Agency LLC.

YGS Group. "7-Year-Old Girl Gets New Hand From 3-D Printer" ©The Associated Press, Reprinted with permission of the YGS Group.

ACKNOWLEDGMENTS AND CREDITS

Credits